SO YOU WANT TO BE A JEWELRY DESIGNER
Merging Your Voice With Form

By Warren Feld

SO YOU WANT TO BE A JEWELRY DESIGNER
Merging Your Voice With Form

By Warren Feld

**A Book About How To
Develop A Fluency In Jewelry Design,
Taking You Beyond Craft,**

**And How To Create Jewelry
Which Draws People's Attention**

That is my hope

Warren Feld Jewelry Publisher
www.warrenfeldjewelry.com
2022

SO YOU WANT TO BE A JEWELRY DESIGNER:
Merging Your Voice With Form

by Warren Feld

Published by
Warren Feld Jewelry
718 Thompson Ln, Ste 123
Nashville, TN 37204
www.warrenfeldjewelry.com

COPYRIGHT © 2022, Warren Feld

All rights reserved. This book or parts thereof may not be reproduced in any form, stored in any retrieval system, or transmitted in any form by any means—electronic, mechanical, photocopy, recording, or otherwise—without prior written permission of the publisher, except as provided by United States of America copyright law and fair use. For permission requests, contact: Warren Feld, warren@warrenfeldjewelry.com, 615-479-3776.

Cover by Warren Feld

ISBN: 979-8-9857221-5-4

Disclaimers: This book and its content provided herein are simply for educational purposes. For those aspects of jewelry making and design which require legal or accounting advice, the information provided here is not a substitute for that advice. Every effort has been made to ensure that the content provided in this book is accurate and helpful for my readers. No liability is assumed for losses or damages due to the information provided. You are responsible for your own choices, actions and results.

Library of Congress Control Number: 2022903106

Table of Contents

Acknowledgements, p. 7
An Introduction, p. 11

Section 1-JEWELRY BEYOND CRAFT, p. 19
1. Jewelry Beyond Craft, p. 21

Section 2-GETTING STARTED, p. 27
2a. Becoming the Bead Artist and Jewelry Designer, p. 29
2b. 5 Questions Every Jewelry Designer Should Have An Answer For, p. 39
2c. Channeling Excitement, p. 51
2d. Developing Your Passion, p. 65
2e. Cultivating Practice, p. 79

Section 3-WHAT IS JEWELRY, p. 97
3. What Is Jewelry, Really?, p. 99

Section 4-MATERIALS, TECHNIQUES AND TECHNOLOGIES, p. 113
4a. Materials - Knowing What To Know, p. 115
4b. Techniques and Technologies - Knowing What To Do, p. 143
4c. Mixed Media, Mixed Techniques, p. 175

Section 5-RULES OF COMPOSITION, CONSTRUCTION, AND MANIPULATION, p. 179
5a. Composition - Playing With Blocks Called Design Elements, p. 181
5b. The Jewelry Designer's Approach To Color, p. 197
5c. Point Line Plane Shape Form Theme, p. 231
5d. Jewelry Design Principles: Composing, Constructing, Manipulating, p. 253
5e. How To Design An Ugly Necklace -- The Ultimate Challenge, p. 289
5f. Architectural Basics, p. 309
5g. Architectural Basics - Anatomy of a Necklace, p. 335
5h. Architectural Basics – Sizing, p. 343

Section 6-DESIGN MANAGEMENT, p. 349
6a. The Proficient Designer: The Path To Resonance, p. 351
6b. Jewelry Design: A Managed Process, p. 377
6c. Designing With Components, p. 387

Section 7-INTRODUCING YOUR DESIGNS PUBLICLY, p. 407

7a. Shared Understandings and Desires, p. 409
7b. Backward-Design Is Forwards Thinking, p. 437

Section 8-DEVELOPING THOSE INTUITIVE SKILLS WITHIN, p. 445
8a. Creativity Isn't Found, It's Developed, p. 447
8b. Inspiration and Aspiration, p. 459
8c. Your Passion For Design, p. 467

Section 9-JEWELRY IN CONTEXT, p. 483
9a. Contemporary Jewelry Is Not A Look - It's A Way Of Thinking, p. 485
9b. Contemporizing Traditional Jewelry, p. 499
9c Fashion Style Taste Art Design, p. 513
9d. Designing With The Brain In Mind: Perception, Cognition, Sexuality, p. 523
9e. Self-Care, p. 535

Section 10-TEACHING DISCIPLINARY LITERACY, p. 543
10. Teaching Disciplinary Literacy In Jewelry Design, p. 545

Final Words of Advice, p. 579
Thank You, p. 581
About Warren Feld, p. 583
Other Articles and Tutorials, p. 587

ACKNOWLEDGEMENTS

For Jayden Alfre Jones
Jewelry Designer
Life Partner

The Journey

I was burnt out in my job as Director of a non-profit, health care organization when I met Jayden at a local bar. I was so bored in my job. Bored with the people I worked with. Bored with the tasks. Bored with the goals. I felt so disconnected from the field of health care. I wanted to stop the world and jump off. But into what, I had no idea.

I so much yearned for some creative spark. Some creative excitement. Something that challenged me, was artistic, was fun. And someone to do these things with. And, in 1987, I met Jayden. Jayden epitomizes creativity.

Soon after we met, Jayden moved to Nashville. But she was having difficulty finding a job. There was a recession going on at the time. At one point, I asked her what she could do, and she said that she could make jewelry. I thought we could build a business around that.

And so we did. Land of Odds was born.

Initially the business was oriented around Jayden's design work. She made all kinds of jewelry from beads to wire to silver fabrication to lampwork. And at first, I had little interest in actually making or designing jewelry. But gradually, very gradually, I began learning the various techniques and the different kinds of materials and components. We took in a lot of repairs. I found it intellectually challenging to figure out why something broke – construction, technique, something about the wearing. I began to formalize some ideas and hypotheses into rules and principles.

Around 1998, Jayden and I wanted to offer jewelry making classes in our shop. But we did not want to repeat and replicate the types of classes already offered at other craft and bead shops in town. We did not want to do the Step-by-Step paint-by-number approach to jewelry making. We wanted to integrate architectural considerations with those of art. While we recognize that all jewelry making has some aspect of craft to it, we wanted to inspire our students to go beyond this. *Jewelry beyond craft.*

Over the next couple of years, with the help and guidance from many local artisans and craft teachers, we developed an educational curriculum embedded within what is called the *Design Perspective*. That is, our classes would teach students how to manage both beauty and functionality, and how to make the necessary tradeoffs between these within their finished pieces. Our classes would guide students in developing a literacy and fluency in jewelry design.

Eventually Jayden retired and our business began to revolve around my own designs and my developing understanding of the Design Perspective. After 35+ years in the business, I came away with some strong beliefs about what jewelry designers should be taught and how they should be taught. I've encapsulated all this within this text *So You Want To Be A Jewelry Designer* and its companion book *Conquering The Creative Marketplace*.

Thank You

In 2016, I took some time off to do Teach For America. I highly recommend this experience. It is very difficult, very challenging and very rewarding. Part of the training was taking two intensive graduate courses in education at Lipscomb University. The focus was on literacy and comprehension and how to teach these.

I had been struggling for some unifying concepts bridging the different disparate things I had learned and applied in the different kinds of jewelry making I was doing. Was there a common theme relevant to all types of jewelry making and design? Could jewelry design rightly be considered a discipline all its own? Was there a body of knowledge and practices which could form the core of a professional identity unique to jewelry design?

My Lipscomb professors – Ally Hauptman and Julie Simone – provided, what for me, were the missing pieces to my puzzle. We talked at length about *disciplinary literacy* and *shared understandings* and *backward design*. We worked diligently on delineating *essential questions*. We put into effect *rubrics* of levels of understanding and levels of performance. And things began to click for me. Ally and Julie were instrumental in my ability to write this book.

Ronnie Steinberg – a student, a customer and a friend -- assisted me in some editing. She was a great sounding board for ideas and the integration of ideas in this book.

My students over the years lived up to my high expectations about design. This is the simplest way I can put it. Presenting information and teaching technique according to my principles resulted in better work, more inquisitiveness, and a comfort with greater challenges. This is what I hoped to get. This is what I got. This motivated me – a lot!

Cynthia Rutledge is a master bead weaving artist. I had the unique opportunity and privilege to interview her weekly over the course of one year in 2004. A group of my advanced students in Nashville were interested in what makes a bead weaving artist. How did they get started? What influenced their passion? How did they come up with some of the technical aspects of their designs? Who influenced them? Cynthia was very sensitive and aware of the kinds of techniques she brought to bear to give her pieces structure and shape. In comparing some of her work to other master bead weavers, the comparisons were revealing. My advanced group and I could see, based on Cynthia's detailed analytic explanations, how some technical strategies achieved better or worse shape, or had better or worse movement, drape and flow. These interviews began to focus my search for a *disciplinary literacy* in jewelry design, though, at the time, I did not have this label for it.

BOOK 1: So You Want To Be A Jewelry Designer

Becoming a Jewelry Designer is exciting. With each piece, you are challenged with this profound question: *Why does some jewelry draw people's attention, and others do not?* Yes there are some craft and art aspects to jewelry making. But when jewelry designers turn to how-to books or art theory texts, however, these do not uncover the necessary answers. They do not show you how to make trade-offs between beauty and function. Nor how to introduce your pieces publicly. You get insufficient practical guidance about knowing when your piece is finished and successful. In short, you do not learn about *design*. You do not learn the essentials about how to go beyond basic mechanics, anticipate the wearer's understandings and desires, or gain management control over the process. *So You Want To Be A Jewelry Designer* reinterprets how to apply techniques and modify art theories from the Jewelry Designer's perspective. This very detailed book reveals how to become literate and fluent in jewelry design.

The major topics covered include,

1. Jewelry Beyond Craft: Gaining A Disciplinary Literacy and Fluency in Design
2. Getting Started
3. What Is Jewelry, Really?
4. Materials, Techniques and Technologies
5. Selecting Design Elements, Like Color, and Applying Rules of Composition, Construction and Manipulation
6. Design Management
7. Introducing Your Designs Publicly
8. Developing Those Intuitive Skills Within: Creativity, Inspiration and Aspiration, Passion
9. Jewelry In Context
10. Teaching Disciplinary Literacy In Jewelry Design

BOOK 2: Conquering The Creative Marketplace

Many people learn beadwork and jewelry-making in order to sell the pieces they make. Based both on the creation and development of my own jewelry design business, as well as teaching countless students over the past 35+ years about business and craft, I want to address what should be some of your key concerns and uncertainties. I want to share with you the kinds of things (specifically, *a business mindset* and confidence) it takes to start your own jewelry business, run it, anticipate risks and rewards, and lead it to a level of success you feel is right for you. I want to help you plan your road map.

I will explore answers to such questions as: How does someone get started marketing and selling their pieces? What business fundamentals need to be brought to the fore? How do you measure risk and return on investment? How does the creative person develop and maintain a passion for business? To what extent should business decisions affect artistic choices? What similar traits to successful jewelry designers do those in business share? How do you protect your intellectual property?

Useful for the hobbyist who wants to sell a few pieces, as well as the designer who wants a self-supporting business, the major topics covered include,

1. Integrating Business With Design
2. Getting Started
3. Financial Management
4. Product Development, Creating Your Line, and Pricing
5. Marketing, Promotion, Branding
6. Selling
7. Professional Responsibilities and Strategic Planning
8. Professional Responsibilities and Gallery / Boutique Representation
9. Professional Responsibilities and Creating Your Necessary Written Documents

An Introduction

	Guiding Questions: *(1) How does jewelry design take you beyond art or craft?* *(2) What does it mean to be fluent and literate in design?* *(3) What are the implications for defining jewelry as an "object" versus as an "intent"?* *(4) Must jewelry be judged only as worn?* *(5) Why does some jewelry draw your attention, and others do not?* *(6) How do you judge a piece as finished and successful?* *(7) Why is disciplinary literacy in design important for introducing your works publicly, as well as selling your works in the creative marketplace?*
"Blue Waterfall", FELD, 2015	

| **Key Words:**
think like a jewelry designer
disciplinary literacy
fluency
flexibility
originality | *jewelry as object*
jewelry as intent
jewelry is art only as it is worn
boundary between jewelry and person | *the Design Perspective*
art
craft
developmental learning
good design |

Find Out How To
Think, Speak, and Work
As A Jewelry Designer

<u>**An Introduction**</u>

You *make* jewelry. That is what you *do*.

But when you *think* jewelry and *speak* jewelry and *work* jewelry, this is what you *become*.

Yes, jewelry making has aspects of craft to it. But it is so much more. It is art. It is architecture. It is communicative and interactive. It is reflective of the jewelry designer's hand. And it defines or reaffirms the self- and social-identities of everyone who wears it, views it, buys it, exhibits it, collects it, talks about it.

To go beyond craft as a jewelry designer, you need to become literate in this discipline called jewelry design. As a person literate in jewelry design, you become your authentic, creative self, someone who is fluent, flexible and original. You gain the skills necessary to design jewelry whether the situation is familiar or not. You are a jewelry designer.

The literate jewelry designer grasps the differences between *jewelry as object* and *jewelry as intent*. That is, you recognize how a piece of jewelry needs to be orchestrated from many angles. How jewelry making involves more than following a set of steps. How jewelry, without design, is just sculpture. How jewelry is a very communicative, public and interactive work of art and design. How jewelry focuses attention. How true design enhances the dignity of the person wearing it. And how the success of a jewelry designer, and associated practice or business, comes down to what's happening at the boundary between the jewelry and the body – that is, *jewelry is art only as it is worn*.

I Am A Jewelry Designer

I am a Jewelry Designer.

I have been designing jewelry and teaching classes for over 30 years now.

What excites me is finding answers to such questions as:

- What does it mean to be fluent and literate in design?
- What are the implications for defining jewelry as an "object" versus as an "intent"?
- Why does some jewelry draw your attention, and others do not?
- How does jewelry design take you beyond art or craft?
- How do you judge a piece as finished and successful?
- Why is disciplinary literacy in design important for introducing your works publicly, as well as selling your works in the creative marketplace?

My ideas have developed and evolved over time. These are ideas about jewelry, its design, and the necessary tradeoffs between appeal and functionality. These are ideas which express the *why* and the *how* jewelry design differs from art or craft. These are ideas which are embedded in and emerge from the special disciplinary and literacy requirements all jewelry designers need to learn so that they can *think and speak and work like designers*. These are ideas about how to introduce jewelry into the creative marketplace. These ideas center on *fluency, flexibility* and *originality*. And that's what you want to be as a jewelry designer: fluent, flexible and original.

I teach classes in jewelry design and applications.

I want my students to learn the mechanics of various techniques. This is obvious. But I want them to go beyond the basic mechanics. I want them to be able to have a great degree of management control over the interplay of aesthetic elements. I also want them to have a great degree of insight, strategy and "smartness" in how things get constructed architecturally. Last, I want them, and this is important, to understand and recognize and incorporate into their designs how and why people *desire* things – why they want to wear things and why they want to buy things and why they want to tell all their friends about the things they are wearing and buying.

Literacy involves all these things: craft, art, design, context. Teaching a disciplinary literacy specific to jewelry design is a lot like teaching literacy in reading and writing. We want our students to comprehend. We want them to be able to be self-directed in organizing and implementing their basic tasks. We want them to be able to function in unfamiliar situations and respond when problems arise. We want them to develop an originality in their work – originality in the sense that they can differentiate themselves from other jewelry designers. We want them to anticipate the shared understandings their various audiences have about whether a piece is *inhabitable* – that is, finished and successful *for them*. We want them to think like designers. And, we want a high level of automaticity in all this. The basic jewelry design curriculum does not accomplish this. There is an absence of strategy and strategic thinking.

Hence this book and guide for anyone who wants to become a successful jewelry designer. This book is for someone who wants to develop that strategic kind of thinking and speaking and doing which underly their discipline we call Jewelry Design.

I Own A Bead Store

I own a bead store.

In the 1990s, my partner and I decided we wanted to set up a training program, but something different than what already existed. It was obvious to us that what already existed wasn't working.

It came down to this: our bead store customers and our jewelry making students were not challenging us. They were not pushing us to seek out new materials. They were not demanding that we more critically evaluate the quality, usefulness, and long term staying power of various stringing materials and jewelry findings options. They were not wondering why some things broke or didn't come together well. They were not encouraging us to explore the craft, improve upon it, search for more variations on existing methods and more ideas about new methods, and see where we could take it.

The typical customer, at that time, would learn one technique, apply it to one pattern, and do this pattern over and over again, perhaps only varying the colors. They would make at least 10 or 12 of the exact same pieces, again, typically only varying in color choices, and carry them around in zip lock plastic bags secured in their purses. They rarely deviated from using the same materials, the same clasps, the same jewelry findings. They never asked questions about what else they could do. They never varied their techniques. They never challenged themselves. They never questioned why things broke, or didn't come together well, or why people liked or didn't like the pieces they were making.

Students wanted us to tell them, step-by-step, how to do it. They didn't want to think about it. They just wanted to make something quickly, that looked good on them, matched what they were wearing, and could be worn home. Uninterested in whether there were better stringing materials for the project. Or a more clever way to construct the clasp assembly. Or better choices of colors, patterns, textures or materials. Or things they could do to make the piece move better, drape better and be more comfortable to wear. Or even take the time to consider the appropriateness of the technique or the appropriateness of the piece itself, given where and when and how the piece was intended to be worn.

We began to see that this was not a customer or student problem. It was not any personal characteristics. Or motivations. Or experiences. Or skill level. This was a problem about what they learned and how they were taught and their level of expectations about what to assume and what to anticipate. They weren't learning or getting taught that disciplinary way of asking questions, solving problems and day-to-day thinking unique to jewelry designers. They were not learning how to become literate in design. Their expectations about what was good, acceptable, finished, successful – you get the idea – were low. Bead and jewelry magazines, video tutorials, craft and bead stores, jewelry design programs set these low bars and reinforced them. As a result, they convinced their readers and students and practitioners to understand jewelry merely as an object to be worn, *not inhabited*. And not part of any kind of public interaction or dialog.

Jewelry design, at the time we began in business, was considered more a hobby or an avocation than an occupation or a profession. There was the assumption that no special knowledge was required. You were either creative or you were not. And all it took to make a piece of jewelry was to reduce a project to a series of steps where jewelry making was basically paint-by-numbers.

Art and Design concepts were dumbed down for jewelry makers, rather than elaborated and reinforced. It was assumed that everyone universally used the same criteria for judging a piece as finished and successful. As a consequence, there was a lot of standardization in jewelry designs, materials and construction. Too much sameness. Not enough variation and originality. Too much focus on fashion and product consumption. Too much diminishing of individuality and the reflection of the artist's hand in design. And with all this standardization, an increasing risk that the jewelry artist was no longer a necessary and critical part of jewelry making and its design.

Around this time, the art world seemed to want to make a big push to encompass jewelry, as well. Jewelry was defined as a subset of painting or sculpture. And this lent an air of professionalization to the field. Jewelry making here became a beauty contest. But jewelry design was divorced from the materials it was made from, the constructive choices necessary for it to function, and the person who was to wear it.

Before designing jewelry, I had been a painter. For several years when I began designing jewelry, I approached jewelry projects as if I were painting them. This was very frustrating. I couldn't get the color effects I wanted to achieve. Or the sense of line and shape and dimension. To compensate for my repeated feelings of failure, I actually pulled out my acrylic paints and canvas and painted my creations as I had visualized them in my mind. I could paint jewelry well. But, stuck as I was in this painter-as-designer-rut, I could not satisfactorily translate my vision into a satisfying piece of jewelry.

It finally began to dawn on me the things which needed to be learned and needed to be taught. I needed to approach jewelry from the jewelry's standpoint. I needed to understand the components and beads used in jewelry on their own terms – *how they asserted themselves* within each of my projects. Beads and related components were not paints. I needed to understand what happened to all these components over time. I needed to understand how the placement of each component, as well as clusters of components, affected people within the situations they found themselves. I needed to understand much more about light and shadow and reflection and refraction. I needed more insight into how things moved, draped and flowed, all the while keeping their shape. Starting with a merely mechanical view of making jewelry wasn't cutting it. Nor was starting with an artistic view of the aesthetics of jewelry. We needed to incorporate aspects of design, as well.

My partner and I began organizing our evolving ideas and values about the designing of jewelry into something we called *The Design Perspective*. These ideas and values form a sort of **Design Manifesto**. They are principles at the core of any jewelry design discipline. These principles take the designer beyond craft. They integrate art with function and context. These principles were, and continue to be, as follows, and it is my hope, as you read through the book, that these become yours, as well.

The Design Manifesto

First (and foremost):
Jewelry is art only as it is worn.

Second:
Jewelry should reflect the artist's intent Creativity is not merely Doing. It's Thinking, as well.

Third:
Jewelry is something affected by, and in return, affects the contexts within which it is introduced. The purpose of jewelry design is to communicate a designer's idea in a way which others understand and will come to desire. Jewelry is not designed in a vacuum; rather, it results from the interaction of the artist and his or her various audiences, and is communicative at its core.

Fourth:
Jewelry design should be seen as a constructive process involving the balancing act of maintaining both shape (structure) as well as good movement, drape and flow (support);

jewelry should be seen as more architectural than craft or art alone.

Fifth:
Design choices are best made and strategically managed at the boundary between jewelry and person, where the artist can best determine when enough is enough, and the piece is most resonant.

Sixth:
Jewelry must succeed aesthetically, functionally, and contextually, and, as such, jewelry design choices must reflect the full scope of all this, if jewelry is to be judged as finished, successful and, most importantly, resonant.

Seventh:
Everyone has a level of creativity within them, and they can learn and be taught how to be better and more literate jewelry designers.

Eighth:
Students need to learn a deeper understanding about why some pieces of jewelry attract your attention, and others do not. Successful teaching of jewelry design requires strategies leading students to be more literate in how they select, combine and arrange design elements, and to be fluent, flexible and original in how they manipulate, construct, and reveal their compositions.

Ninth:
Successful jewelry designing can only be learned within an agreed upon disciplinary literacy. That is, jewelry design requires its own specialized vocabulary, grammar and way of thinking things through and solving problems in order to prepare the designer to be fluent, flexible and original.

Tenth (and final):
Disciplinary literacy should be learned developmentally. You start at the beginning, learn a core set of skills and how they are inter-related and inter-dependent. Then you add in a second set of integrated and inter-dependent skills. Next and third set, and so forth, increasing the sophistication of skills in a developmental and integrative sense. The caveat, if you have been making jewelry for a while, it is particularly helpful to go back and relearn things in an organized, developmental approach, which can be very revealing, even to the experienced designer, about how your design choices impact your pieces and your success.

Our curriculum emerged from our understandings about disciplinary literacy in jewelry design and our attempts to implement what we learned from it. This curriculum evolved into this book.

Here you will begin to understand

- The challenges jewelry designers face
- How to channel your excitement
- How to develop your passion
- How to cultivate your practice
- How to understand what jewelry means and how jewelry is used by various audiences
- The variety of materials, techniques and technologies you might want to explore and incorporate into what you do
- The creative process, and the things involved in translating inspirations into aspirations into designs
- What it means to develop a passion for design
- The role desire plays in how people come to recognize and understand whether a piece is finished and successful, and how values are set and imposed on any piece of jewelry
- Principles of composition, construction and manipulation, and the intricacies and dependencies of various design elements, such as color, point, line, plane, shape, forms, themes, among others
- Creating and using components
- The architectural bases of jewelry design
- What the ideas underlying "good design" are, as well as those associated with "good contemporary design"
- How design concepts are applied in real life
- The psychological, cognitive and sexuality underpinnings of jewelry design
- Your professional responsibilities as a jewelry designer
- Entering the creative marketplace and threading the business needle
- Self-care
- In fact, the book covers the full range of things you need to learn (or teach others) in order become fluent, flexible and original in jewelry design

Sadly, the field of jewelry design has little academic scholarship relative to the ideas which must support it. This is mostly because jewelry design is not thought of as a discipline apart from art or craft. And this is a disservice to we designers.

Most description and analysis focus on the accomplishments of various successful designers. These texts detail their biographies, their use of artistic elements and techniques, and their influence over styles and fashions. This information is important, but insufficient to support jewelry design as a profession all its own, relevant for today and tomorrow, and inclusive of all of us who call ourselves jewelry designers.

This book covers the bases of those critical professional, think-like-a-designer skills designers need to develop and become proficient in.

Also, check out my website (http://www.warrenfeldjewelry.com/) (www.warrenfeldjewelry.com).

Enroll in my jewelry design and business of craft Video Tutorials (https://so-you-want-to-be-a-jewelry-designer.teachable.com/p/home) online. Begin with my ORIENTATION TO BEADS & JEWELRY FINDINGS COURSE (https://so-you-want-to-be-a-jewelry-designer.teachable.com/p/orientation-to-beads-jewelry-findings/?preview=logged_out).

Follow my articles on Medium.com.
https://warren-29626.medium.com/

Subscribe to my Learn To Bead blog (https://blog.landofodds.com/) (https://blog.landofodds.com).

Visit Land of Odds online (https://www.landofodds.com/) (https://www.landofodds.com)for all your jewelry making supplies.

Check out my Jewelry Making and Beadwork Kits (http://www.warrenfeldjewelry.com/wfjkits.htm).

Add your name to my email list (https://mailchi.mp/4032bd33748d/so-you-want-to-be-a-jewelry-designer).

My ARTIST STATEMENT (http://www.warrenfeldjewelry.com/wfjartiststatement.html)

My TEACHING STATEMENT (http://www.warrenfeldjewelry.com/pdf/TEACHING STATEMENT.pdf).

My DESIGN PHILOSOPHY (http://www.warrenfeldjewelry.com/wfjdesignapproach.htm).

My PROFESSIONAL PROFILE (http://www.warrenfeldjewelry.com/pdf/PROFESSIONAL PROFILE-Creative.pdf).

My PORTFOLIO (http://www.warrenfeldjewelry.com/pdf/PORTFOLIO.pdf).

SECTION 1:

JEWELRY BEYOND CRAFT

1. JEWELRY BEYOND CRAFT: GAINING A DISCIPLINARY LITERACY AND FLUENCY IN DESIGN

"Canyon Sunrise", FELD, 2008

Guiding Questions:
(1) What knowledge, skills and understandings must the jewelry designer have in order to be fluent in design?
(2) How do you optimize both aesthetics and functionality within each piece of jewelry?
(3) How do you learn to be fluent in design?
(4) How do you best apply your fluency in design within the creative marketplace?
(5) How do shared understandings and desires come into play within the jewelry design process?
(6) How does the designer achieve a coherency and consistency within their work?

Key Words:
occupation	inspiration	shared understandings
profession	aspiration	coherency
aesthetic requirements	decoding	consistency
functional requirements	composition	management
contextual requirements	construction	fluency
making trade-offs	manipulation	disciplinary literacy
	expressing intent	knowing when piece is
	creative marketplace	finished and successful

Abstract:

Long thought merely a craft, or, sometimes alternatively, a subset of art, painting and sculpture, we have begun to recognize that Jewelry Design is something more. Jewelry making encapsulates the designer's anticipation, not only of aesthetic requirements, but also those of function and context, as well. Creating jewelry means understanding how to make strategic design choices at the boundary between jewelry and person. Translating inspirations and aspirations into designs and finished products requires an intuitive, integrative sensitivity to shared understandings brought to the design situation by the designer and all the audiences ultimately invested in the product. The better designer is able to bring a high level of coherence and consistency to the process of managing all this – shared understandings, knowledge and skills, evaluative review, and reflection and adjustment. This is called 'fluency' in design. For the jewelry designer, there is a defined set of concepts and principles which revolve around this disciplinary literacy – the professional way of thinking through design, production, communication, marketing, selling and critique – and how to be proficient at this. This is what this book is all about.

DISCIPLINARY LITERACY AND FLUENCY IN DESIGN

Jeremy thought that the only thing he wanted to do in life was design jewelry. He loved it. So it was not a question of "if" or "when" or "how". But he told me it was always important not to get tricked by fashion. It was mandatory not to seek the trendy object. Not to turn away from that odd thing. And to pay very close attention to the details of how jewelry designers think, act, speak and reflect.

I thought about his advice a lot over the years of my own career as a jewelry designer. The disciplined designer needs to be attuned to the discipline way of seeing the world, understanding it, responding to it, and asserting that creative spark within it. Yes, I believe jewelry designers have a special way of thinking through selecting design elements, composing, constructing, and manipulating objects. Different than crafters. Different than artists. Different than other disciplines and their core ways of defining things and thinking things through.

Yet jewelry design does not yet exist as an established discipline. It is claimed by art. It is claimed by craft. It is claimed by design. And each of these more established disciplines offer conflicting advice about what is expected of the designer. How should she think? How should she organize her tasks? How should she tap into her creative self? How should she select materials, techniques and technologies? How should she assert her creativity and introduce her ideas and objects to others? How much does she need to know about how and why people wear and inhabit jewelry? What impact should she strive to have on others or the more general culture and society as a whole?

In this book, I try to formulate a disciplinary literacy unique and special and legitimate for jewelry designers. Such literacy encompasses a basic vocabulary about materials, techniques, color and other design elements and rules of composition. It also includes the kinds of thinking routines and strategies jewelry designers need to know in order to be fluent, flexible and original. It includes what the jewelry designer needs to know and do when introducing their pieces publicly, either to have others wear, buy or collect their pieces.

These routines and strategies are at the heart of the designer's knowledges, skills and understandings related to creativity, elaboration, embellishment, reflection, critique and metacognition. This disciplinary literacy in design is very similar to how sounds are made into music. This literacy is very similar to how words are made into literature. There is an underlying vocabulary and grammar to jewelry design, from decoding to comprehension to fluency. The jewelry designer is dependent upon this disciplinary literacy to the extent that she or he is able to move from inspiration to aspiration to implementation and management towards finish and success.

At the heart of this disciplinary literacy are the tools and strategies designers use to think through and make choices which optimize aesthetics and functionality within a specific context. Again, these literacy tools and strategies enable the designer to create something out of nothing, to translate inspiration into aspiration, and to influence content and meaning in context.

There are four sets of tools, routines and strategies which designers employ to determine how to create, what to create, how to know a piece is finished and how to know a piece is successful.

These are,

(1) Decoding

(2) Composing, Constructing and Manipulating

(3) Expressing Intent and Content

(4) Expressing Intent and Content within a Context

You don't become a jewelry designer to **be** something.

You become a jewelry designer to **do** something.

The question becomes: How do you learn to do that *something*?

How do you learn to be fluent, flexible and original in design? And develop an automaticity? And self-direction? And an ability to maneuver within new or unfamiliar situations? And a comfort when introducing your pieces in public?

We call this '*literacy*'. For the jewelry designer, *literacy* means developing the abilities to *think like a designer*. These include,

- *Reading* a piece of jewelry. Here you the designer are able to break down and *decode* a piece of jewelry into its essential graphical and design elements. This aspect of fluency and literacy is very *descriptive*.

- *Writing* a piece of jewelry. Here you the designer are able to identify, create or change the *arrangement of these design elements* within a *composition*. Fluency and literacy are very *analytical*.

- *Expressing* a piece of jewelry. Here you the designer use the design elements and principles underlying any arrangement to convey *content and meaning*. Fluency and literacy are very *interpretive*.

- *Expressing* a piece of jewelry *in context*. Here you the designer are able to anticipate, reflect upon and incorporate into your own thinking the understandings and reactions of various client groups to the piece, the degree they desire and value the piece, and whether they see the piece as finished and successful. The jewelry is introduced publicly, whether for someone to admire or wear or buy or collect. The designer comfortably moves back and forth between the objective and subjective, and the universal and the specific. The designer analyzes contextual variables, particularly the shared understandings as these relate to desire, and in line with that, thus determining value and worth. Fluency and literacy are very *judgmental*.

Everyone knows that anyone can put beads and other pieces together on a string and make a necklace. But can anyone make a necklace that draws attention? That evokes some kind of emotional response? That resonates with someone where they say, not merely "I like that", but, more importantly, say "I want to wear that!" or "I want to buy that!"? Which wears well, drapes well, moves well as the person wearing it moves? Which is durable, supportive and keeps its silhouette and shape? Which doesn't feel underdone or over done? Which is appropriate for a given context, situation, culture or society?

True, anyone can put beads on a string. But that does not make them artists or designers. From artists and designers, we expect jewelry which is something more. More than parts. More than an assemblage of colors, shapes, lines, points and other design elements. More than simple arrangements of lights and darks, rounds and squares, longs and shorts, negative and positive spaces. We expect to see the artist's hand. We expect the jewelry to be impactful for the wearer. We expect both wearer and viewer, and seller and buyer, and exhibitor and collector, to share expectations for what makes the jewelry finished and successful.

Jewelry design is an occupation in the process of professionalization. Regrettably, this betwixt and between status means, when the designer seeks answers to questions like *what goes together well?*, or *what would happen if?*, or *what would things be like if I had made different choices?*, the designer still has to rely on contradictory advice and answers. Should s/he follow the Craft Approach? Or rely on Art Tradition? Or take cues from the Design Perspective? Each larger paradigm, so to speak, would take the designer in different directions. This can be confusing. Frustrating. Unsettling.

As a whole, the jewelry design profession has become strong in identifying things which go together well. There are color schemes, and proven ideas about shapes, and balance, and distribution, and proportions. But when we try to factor in the individualistic characteristics associated with the designer and his or her intent, things get muddied. And when we try to anticipate the subjective reactions of all our audiences, as we introduce our creative products into the creative marketplace, things get more muddied still. What should govern our judgments about success and failure, right and wrong? What should guide us? What can we look to for helping us answer the *What would happen if* or *What would things be like if* questions?

ESSENTIAL QUESTIONS ABOUT JEWELRY DESIGN WORTH ANSWERING

As you work your way through the chapters in this book, it is important to recognize and understand the larger social and professional contexts within which jewelry design is but a part, and your place in it. Towards this end, I have formulated some essential questions every designer needs to have answers for and have deeper understandings about. Another way to look at this is that *answers* to these questions become your *evidence* for determining whether you are on the right track for becoming fluent in jewelry design.

(1) Why are there disciplinary conflicts between art and craft, and between art and design?

(2) How do you resolve tensions between aesthetics and functionality within an object like jewelry?

(3) What is jewelry, and what is it for?

(4) Is jewelry necessary?

(5) What does it mean to be *successful* as a jewelry artist working today?

(6) What does it mean to *think like a jewelry designer*? How does this differ from *thinking like an artist* or *thinking like a craftsperson*?

(7) How does the jewelry designer know when a piece is *finished* and *successful*?

(8) How do you place a value on a piece of jewelry?

(9) How do you introduce your jewelry into a public setting, either to wear or to collect or to buy?

(10) Why does some jewelry draw your attention, and others do not?

(11) What does it mean to be a *contemporary* jewelry designer?

Let's get started discussing these questions. Let's explore the scope of their answers, and the kinds of things you need to learn and development within yourself as a jewelry designer.

SECTION 2:

GETTING STARTED

GETTING STARTED
2a. BECOMING THE BEAD ARTIST AND JEWELRY DESIGNER:
The Ongoing Tensions Between Inspiration and Form

"Japanese Fragrance Garden Bracelet", piece and inspiration, FELD, 2018

Guiding Questions:
(1) How do you merge your voice and intent with the jewelry forms you want to create?
(2) What does it mean, not merely to make jewelry, but to design it?
(3) How do you know when you emerge as a successful jewelry designer?
(4) Is jewelry design an avocation, an occupation, or a profession?
(5) Do you chase the 'idea' or the 'material'?

Key Words: *inspiration* *form* *voice* *the idea or the material*	*design elements* *appeal* *durable* *satisfying* *purpose*	*to design jewelry* *occupation* *profession* *fluency, flexibility, originality*

Abstract:

As a jewelry designer, you have a purpose. Your purpose is to figure out, untangle and solve, with each new piece of jewelry you make, how both you, as well as the wearer, will understand your inspirations and the design elements and forms you chose to express them, and why this piece of jewelry is right for them. Not as easy as it might first appear. There are no pre-set formulas here. There are artistic principles of composition, yes, but how you implement them is still up to you. Moreover, your pieces have to wear well, drape well, and connect with the desires of people who will want to wear or buy them. Jewelry design involves an ongoing effort, on many levels, to merge voice and inspiration with form. Often challenging, but very rewarding.

Also, See My Video Tutorial: ORIENTATION TO BEADS & JEWELRY FINDINGS (https://so-you-want-to-be-a-jewelry-designer.teachable.com/p/orientation-to-beads-jewelry-findings) *https://so-you-want-to-be-a-jewelry-designer.teachable.com/p/orientation-to-beads-jewelry-findings*

BECOMING THE BEAD ARTIST AND JEWELRY DESIGNER:
The Ongoing Tensions Between Inspiration and Form

As a jewelry designer, you have a purpose. Your purpose is to figure out, untangle and solve, with each new piece of jewelry you make, how both you, as well as the wearer or buyer, will understand your inspirations and the design elements and forms you chose to express them, and why this particular piece of jewelry is right for them. Not as easy as it might first appear. There are no pre-set formulas here. There are artistic principles of composition, yes, but how you implement them is still up to you. Moreover, your pieces have to wear well, drape well, and connect with the desires of people who will want to wear or buy them.

You will want the piece to be beautiful and appealing. So you will be applying a lot of art theories about color, perspective, composition and the like. You will quickly discover that much about color use and the use of lines and planes and shapes and so forth in art is very subjective. People see things differently. They may bring with them some biases to the situation. Many of the physical materials you will use may not reflect or refract the color and other artistic effects more easily achieved with paints.

You want the piece to be durable. So you will be applying a lot of theories and practices of architects and engineers and mechanical physicists. You will need to intuitively and intrinsically understand what about your choices leads to the jewelry keeping its shape, and what about your choices allows the jewelry to move, drape and flow. You also will be attentive to issues of physical mechanics, particularly how jewelry responds to forces of stress, strain and movement. This may mean making tradeoffs between beauty and function, appeal and durability, desire and acceptance.

You want the piece to be satisfying and accepted by various viewing, wearing, buying and collecting audiences. So you will have to have some understanding of the role jewelry plays in different people's lives. Jewelry is more than some object to them; jewelry is something they inhabit -- reflective of soul, culture, status, aspiration. You will recognize that people ascribe the qualities of the jewelry to the qualities of the person wearing it. You will bring to the forefront ideas underlying psychology and anthropology and sociology, and even party planning, while designing your jewelry or introducing it publicly. You may find the necessity to compromise part of your vision for something socially acceptable, or in some degree of conformance with a client's taste or style.

What Paths To Follow When Becoming A Designer

Sometimes becoming a designer begins by touching some beads. Or running a strand of pearls through your hand. Or the sight of something perfectly worn around the wrist, or upon the breast, or up near the neck. Or trying to accessorize an outfit. Or finding something for a special occasion.

Jewelry designers are extraordinarily blessed to do what they love for a living. For many, they have turned a hobby into an avocation into a lifestyle.

But it's not like a regular job. There are many intangibles. Such as, what exactly is *creativity* and *creative thinking*? What are all the things that have to come together to recognize that creative spark when it hits you in your heart, gut or head? How do you translate that into something real, with beauty, with function, and with purpose? How do you mesh your views of and desires for aesthetics and functionality with those of your many audiences – wearer, viewer, buyer, seller, collector, exhibiter, teacher and student?

What exactly does it mean to design jewelry, and how do you know it is the right path for you? This is a tough question. You may love jewelry, but not know how to make it. You may get off on creative problem solving or be a color addict but not know what specific techniques and skills you need to learn, in what organized way, with what direction, leading you towards becoming that better jewelry designer. You may wonder what it means and what it takes to be successful as a designer. You may feel the motivation, but not know what the jewelry designer really has to do each day.

You may be taking classes and getting some training, but how do you know when you have arrived? How do you know when you have emerged as a successful professional jewelry designer? And what are your responsibilities and obligations, once you get there?

THERE IS SO MUCH TO KNOW

There is so much to know, and so many types of choices to make. Which clasp? Which stringing material? Which technique? Which beads, findings and components? Which strategy of construction? Which silhouette? What aesthetic you want to achieve? How you want to achieve it? Drape, movement, context, durability? How to organize and manage the design process?

And this is the essence of this book – a way to learn all the kinds of things you need to bring to bear, in order to create a wonderful and functional piece of jewelry. Whether you are just beginning your beading or jewelry making avocation, or have been beading and making jewelry awhile – time spent with the material in these segments will be very useful. You'll learn the critical skills and ideas. You'll learn how these inter-relate. And you'll learn how to make better choices.

We want to gauge how the designer grows within the craft, and takes on the challenges during their professional lives. This involves an ongoing effort to merge voice and inspiration with form. Often this effort is challenging. Sometimes paralyzing. Always fulfilling and rewarding.

Jewelry design is a *conversation*. The conversation is ongoing, perhaps never-ending. The conversation is partly internal and partly external. The conversation is partly a reflection about process, refinement, questioning, translating feelings into form, impressions into arrangements, life influences into choice. It touches on desire. It reflects value and values. Aesthetics matter. Architecture and function matters. People matter. Context and situation matter.

Jewelry focuses attention. Inward for the artist. Outward for the wearer and viewer. In many directions socially and culturally and situationally. Jewelry is a voice which must be expressed and heard, and hopefully, responded to.

At first that voice might not find that exact fit with its audience. There is some back and forth in expression, as the jewelry is designed, refined, redesigned, and re-introduced publicly. But jewelry, and its design, have great power. They have the power to synthesize a great many voices and expectations into something exciting and resonant.

JEWELRY DESIGN:
An Occupation In Search Of Professionalization

Jewelry design is an activity which occupies your time.

How the world understands what you do when you occupy that time, however, is in a state of flux and confusion, and which often can be puzzling or disorienting for the jewelry artist, as well.

Is what you are doing merely a *hobby* or an *avocation*? Is it something anyone can do, anytime they want, without much preparation and learning?

Is what you do an *occupation*? Does it require learning specialized technical skills? Is it something that involves your interaction with others? Is it something you are paid to do?

Or is what you do a *profession*? Is there a specialized body of knowledge, perspectives and values, not just mechanical skills, to learn and apply? Do you provide a service to the public? Do you need to learn and acquire certain insights which enable you to serve the needs of others?

Are you part of another occupation or profession, or do you have your own? Is jewelry design merely a craft, where you make things by following sets of steps?

Is jewelry design an art, where your personal inspirations and artistic sense is employed to create things of aesthetic beauty for others to admire, as if they were sculptures? Is the jewelry you create to be judged as something separate and apart from the person wearing it?

Or is jewelry design its own thing. Is it a design activity where you learn specialized knowledge, skills and understandings in how to integrate aesthetics and functionality, and where your success can only be judged at the boundary between jewelry and person – that is, only as the jewelry is introduced publicly and is worn?

The line of demarcation between occupation and profession is thin, often blurred, but for the jewelry designer, this distinction is very important. It feeds into our sense of self and self-esteem. It guides us in the choices we make to become better and better at our craft, art and trade. It influences how we introduce our jewelry to the public, and how we influence the public to view, wear, exhibit, purchase or collect the things we make.

What Does It Mean To Become A Professional?

At the heart of this question is whether we are paid and rewarded either solely for the number of jewelry pieces which we make, or rather for the skill, knowledge and intent underlying our jewelry designs.

If the former, we do not need much training. Entry into the activity of jewelry design would be very open, with a low bar. Our responsibility would be to turn out pieces of jewelry. We would not encumber ourselves too much with art theory or design theory. We would not concern ourselves, in any great depth, and certainly not struggle with jewelry's psycho-socio-cultural impacts.

If the latter, we would need a lot of specialized training and experience. Entry into the activity of jewelry design would be more controlled, most likely staged from *novice* to *master*. Our responsibility would be to translate our inspirations into aspirations into designs. It would also be to influence others viewing our work to be inspired to think about and reflect and emote those things which have excited the designer, as represented by the jewelry itself. And it would also be to enable others to find personal, and even social and cultural, success and satisfaction when wearing or purchasing this piece of jewelry.

To become a professional jewelry designer is to learn, apply and experience a way of *thinking like a designer*. *Fluent* in terms about materials, techniques and technologies. *Flexible* in the applications of techniques and the organizing of design elements into compositions which excite people. Able to develop workable design strategies in unfamiliar or difficult situations. *Communicative* about intent, desire, purpose, no matter the context or situation within which the designer and their various audiences find themselves. *Original* in how concepts are introduced, organized and manipulated, and in how the designer differentiates themselves from other designers.

The designs of artisans who make jewelry reflect and refract cultural norms, as well as such things as societal expectations, historical explanations and justifications, and those psychological precepts which individuals apply to make sense of themselves and for themselves within a larger setting. As such, the jewelry designer has a major responsibility, both to the individual client, as well as to the larger social setting or society, to foster that the ability for the client to fulfill that hierarchy of needs, and to foster the coherency and rationality of the community-at-large and his or her fit within it.

All this can happen in a very small, narrow way, or a very large and profound way. In either case, the professional roles of the jewelry designer remain the same. Successfully learning how to play these roles – *fluency, flexibility, communication, originality* – becomes the basis for how the jewelry designer is judged and the extent of his or her recognition and success.

Why People Like To Bead and Make Jewelry

Most people, when they get started beading or making jewelry, don't have this overwhelming urge to become star jewelry designers. On the contrary, fame and fortune as a designer are some of the furthest things from their minds. Most people look to jewelry making and beading to fulfill other needs.

Over the years I've seen many people pick up beading and jewelry making as a hobby. They are drawn to these for many reasons, but most often, to make fashionable jewelry at a much lower cost than they would find for the same pieces in a Department store, or to repair jewelry pieces they especially love. When you start with the parts, and the labor is all your own, it is considerably less expensive than the retail prices you would find in a store for the same pieces.

Some people want to make jewelry for themselves. Others want to make handmade gifts. Giving someone something of great value, that reflects a personal expression of creativity, and a labor of love – you can't beat it. And everyone loves jewelry.

When people get into beading and jewelry making, they discover it's fun. Even addictive. They tap into their inner-creative-self. They see challenges, and find ways to meet them. They take classes. They buy books and magazines. They join beading groups and bead societies and jewelry making collaboratives. They have beading and jewelry making parties with their friends. They scour web-sites on-line looking for images of and patterns for jewelry. They comb the web and the various beading, jewelry-making and craft magazines, looking for sources and resources. They join on-line jewelry and bead boards, on-line forums, on-line web-rings, on-line ezines, groups, and on-line blogs. They take shopping trips to malls and boutiques and like little good Agatha Christies and Sherlock Holmes, they spy, looking for fashions, fashion trends, and fashionistas. They attend traveling bead shows. And every town they visit, they schedule some free time to check out the local bead stores and boutiques.

As people get more into beading and jewelry making, some discover that these avocations are not only sources of artistic self-expression, but also have many meditative qualities. They are relaxing. They take your mind off the here and now, and transport you to a very calming place.

Still, for others, beading and jewelry making become a way to earn some extra income. They might be to supplement what you're making now. They might be ways to generate some extra dollars after you retire. They might be the start of your own business as a designer of jewelry. They might be a sense of independence and self-reliance. Having someone pay you for something you made is often the hook that gets people addicted to beadwork and jewelry making.

Most people, however, are content just to *make* jewelry. There are no professional Design paths to pursue. They may realize that they are out there somewhere, but don't particularly care. Or sometimes they are unfamiliar with or can't see all the possibilities. Perhaps they get stuck. No mentor, no book, no magazine, no project to entice them or spark an interest in something more than what they are doing now. But it suffices. Beading and jewelry making relaxes them, gives them a creative outlet, things to enjoy, other like-minded people to be with.

For those fewer people, however, who get a whiff of what it means to *design* jewelry, and jewelry which resonates, well, what a trip they are in for.

Do You Chase *The Idea* or *The Material*?

It is important up front to ask yourself, as a jewelry artist, what is more important to you: *the piece of jewelry itself,* or *the reason why it was made*? The material object? Or the idea?

The *idea* is about cause and effect. How the inspiration resulted in choices about colors, materials and techniques. How the artist's intent is revealed through choices about composition, arrangements and manipulation of design elements. How the jewelry relates to the person and to the body? How the artist anticipates how others will understand whether a piece is finished and successful, and whether the piece incorporates these shared understandings into the choices made about design.

As solely a *material object*, the jewelry so designed shies away from resonance. It becomes something to be judged apart from the wearer. It too often gets co-opted by global forces tending towards standardization and same-old-same-old designs. The designer's mastery is barely referenced or attended to. The designers voice is reduced to noise. The very real fear is that, with globalization and standardization, the designer's voice will no longer be needed.

Jewelry as idea fosters communication and connection between the artist and his or her various audiences. It bridges thinking. It bridges emotion. It bridges social, cultural and/or situational ties. It goes beyond simple adornment and ornamentation. It becomes interactive, and emerges from a co-dependency between artist and audience, reflective and indicative of both.

Analyzing reasons, finding connections, and conceptualizing forms, components and arrangements are the primary functions of jewelry designer survival.

Otherwise, why make jewelry? Why make something so permanent to reflect your inner motivations, efforts, even struggles, to translate inspiration into this object? Why make something wearable, especially when each piece is usually not worn all the time? Why make something that might have such an intimate relationship with the body and mind? Why make something that can have real consequences for the wearer as the jewelry is worn in social, cultural or specific situational settings?

The Challenging Moments

Developing yourself as a jewelry designer has several challenging moments. Learning.

Recognizing. Getting Inspired. Creating. Organizing. Constructing. Managing. Presenting. Marketing. Selling. You want to maintain high expectations and goals for yourself, and see these all these challenging moments through.

Some challenging moments include the following:

1. Learning your craft and continually growing and developing within your profession

2. Recognizing how jewelry *design* goes beyond basic mechanics and aesthetics, thus, differs from *craft* and differs from *art*, and then learning and working accordingly.

3. Getting Inspired

4. Translating Inspiration into a design

5. Implementing that design both artistically and architecturally by finding that balance between beauty (*must look good*) and functionality (*must wear well*)

6. Organizing your work space and all your stuff

7. Managing a design process

8. Introducing your pieces publicly, and anticipating how others (wearer, viewer, seller, marketer, exhibitor, collector, teacher, student, for example) will desire your pieces, as well as judge your pieces as finished (*parsimonious*) and successful (*resonant*)

9. Infusing your pieces with a sense of yourself, your values, your aesthetics, your *originality*

10. Developing a *fluency* and *flexibility* when working with new materials, new techniques and technologies, and new design expectations, including well-established ideas about fix-it strategies when confronted with unfamiliar situations

11. Differentiating your jewelry and yourself from other jewelry designers

12. If selling your pieces, then linking up to and connecting with those who will market and buy your pieces

Some Bottom-Line Advice For The Newly Emerging Jewelry Designer

Always keep working and working hard. Set up a routine, and do at least one thing every day.

Find a comfortable place to work in your home or apartment. Develop strategies for organizing your projects, your supplies and your tools, and for keeping things generally organized over time. But don't overdue the organizing thing. A little chaos can be OK, and even, sometimes, trigger new ideas.

Give yourself permission to play, experiment, go down many paths. Everything you work on doesn't have to meet the criterion of perfection, be cool, or become the next Rembrandt. A key part of the learning process is trial and error, hypothesis, test, and conclusion. This helps you develop fix-it strategies so that you can overcome unfamiliar or problematic situations, enhancing your skills as a designer.

Don't let self-doubt and any sense of impending failure take over you, and paralyze you. Designer's block, while it may happen occasionally, should be temporary. Jewelry projects usually evolve, and involve some give and take, change and rearrangement. Often the time to complete a project can be lengthy, and you have to maintain your interest and inspiration over this extended time period.

Don't get stuck in a rut. Try new materials. Try new colors. Try new designs. Try new styles. Try to add variation, new arrangements, smart embellishments. Learn new techniques and technologies.

Over the next few sections, I am going to expand on what it means to know jewelry design as a professional endeavor, how to channel your excitement, develop your passion, and cultivate your practice.

GETTING STARTED
2b. BECOMING THE BEAD ARTIST AND JEWELRY DESIGNER:
5 Essential Questions For Which Every Jewelry Designer Should Have An Answer

	Guiding Questions: *(1) Is jewelry making craft, art or design?* *(2) How do you think creatively?* *(3) How do you leverage strengths and weaknesses in materials and techniques?* *(4) How do you evoke emotions and resonance?* *(5) How do you know your piece is finished and successful?*
"Etruscan Vestment", FELD, 2008	

Key Words: essential craft vs art vs design harmony variety	create Designer's Tool Box materials techniques skill	fluency empowerment emotional response resonance parsimony

Abstract:

People have different motivations and ambitions when making jewelry. These can be as simple as an avocation or hobby, or more involved as a business or career. Jewelry making is an investment in time and materials. It requires, not only strong creativity skills, but also persistence and perseverance to take a project from inspiration to aspiration to implementation. A lot of the success in this pursuit comes down to an ability to make and follow through on many artistic and design decisions. Developing this ability – a fluency, flexibility and originality in design -- means that the designer has become empowered to answer these 5 essential questions: (1) Is jewelry making a craft, an art or design? (2) How do you think creatively? (3) How do you leverage the strengths of various materials and techniques, and minimize weaknesses? (4) How do the choices you make in any one jewelry design evoke emotions and resonate? and, (5) How do you know your piece is finished and successful?

5 Essential Questions Every Jewelry Designer Should Have An Answer For

Interested in trying your hand at jewelry design? Before you begin, consider the following 5 questions I pose for you...

1. *Is what you do Art, Craft or Design?*
2. *How do you decide what you want to create?*
3. *What materials (or techniques) work well together, and which do not?*
4. *What things do you do so that your finished piece evokes an emotional response?*
5. *How do you know when your piece is done?*

People have different motivations and ambitions when making jewelry. These can be as simple as an avocation or hobby, or more involved as a business or career. Jewelry making is an investment in time and materials. It requires, not only strong creativity skills, but also persistence and perseverance to take a project from inspiration to aspiration to implementation. It means understanding that jewelry can only be judged as finished and successful as the piece is worn. Jewelry design is more than the application of a set of techniques; it is a mind-set, as well. It is a way of thinking like a designer.

A lot of the achievement and accomplishment in this pursuit of jewelry design comes down to an ability to make and follow through on many artistic and design decisions. Some have to do with managing a process, which can take an extended period of time. It also comes down to being fluent, flexible and original in your thinking through design. The greater your disciplinary literacy, the more empowered and confident you become in your design work.

Susan is one example of what happens when uncertainty -- that paralysis or deer-in-the-headlights feeling that we so often face -- sets in. Susan felt very unsure of herself. And unsure of her jewelry. Would people like it? Was the color mix appropriate? Was the construction secure? Was the price smart and fair? She allowed all this uncertainty to affect her design work – she had difficulty finishing pieces she was working on, starting new projects, and getting her work out there.

Like many of my jewelry design and beadwork students, Susan needed to be fluent as a designer. With fluency comes empowerment, confidence and success.

Fluency and Empowerment

The *fluent* jewelry designer is able to think like a designer. The jewelry designer is more than a craftsperson and more than an artist. The jewelry designer must learn a specialized language, and specialized way of balancing the needs for appeal with the needs for functionality. The jewelry designer must intimately recognize and understand the roles jewelry plays for individuals as well as the society as a whole. The designer must learn how art, architecture, physical mechanics, engineering, sociology, psychology, context, even party planning, all must come together and get expressed at the point where jewelry meets the boundary of the person, that is, as the jewelry is worn.

And to gain that fluency, the designer must commit to learning a lot of vocabulary, ideas and terms, and how these imply content and meaning through expression. The designer will need to be very aware of personal thoughts and thinking as these get reflected in all the choices made in design. The designer will have to be good at anticipating the understandings and judgements of many different audiences, including the wearer, viewer, seller, exhibitor, client, and collector.

With fluency comes empowerment. The *empowered* designer has a confidence that whatever needs to be done, or whatever must come next, the designer can get through it. *Empowerment* is about making and managing choices. These choices could be as simple as whether to finish a piece or not. Or whether to begin a second piece. The designer will make choices about how to draw someone's attention to the piece, or present the piece to a larger audience. She or he may decide to submit the piece to a magazine or contest. She or he may want to sell the piece and market it. The designer will make choices about how a piece might be worn, or who might wear it, or when it might be worn, in what context.

And for all these choices, the jewelry designer might need to overcome a sense of fear, boredom, or resistance. The designer might need to overcome anxiety, a sense of giving up, having designer's block, feeling unchallenged, and even laziness.

In order to make better artistic and design choices, the Fluent and Empowered Jewelry Designer should have answers to these 5 critical questions:

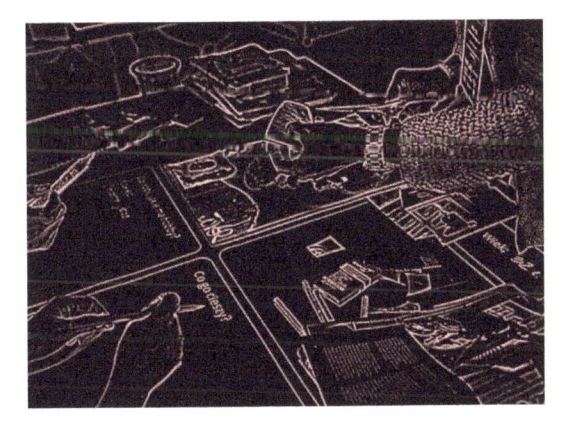

Question 1: Should BEADWORK and JEWELRY MAKING be considered ART or CRAFT or DESIGN?

The jewelry designer confronts a world which is unsure whether jewelry is *"craft"* or *"art"* or its own special thing I'll call *"design"*. This can get very confusing and unsettling. Each approach has its own separate ideas about how the designer should think, speak, work, and how he or she should be judged.

CRAFT: When defined as *"craft,"* jewelry is seen as something that anyone can do – no special powers are needed to be a jewelry designer. Design is seen as a step-by-step process, almost like paint-by-number. Designers color within the lines. The craft piece or project has functional value but limited aesthetic value. As *"craft"*, there is somewhat of a pejorative meaning — it's looked down upon, thought of as something less than art.

If following the Craft Approach, the designer would learn a lot of techniques and applications in a step-by-step fashion. The designer, based on their professional socialization into Craft, would assume that:

a) The outlines and the goals of any piece or project can be specified in a clear, defined way.

b) Anyone can do these techniques.

c) There is no specialized knowledge that a designer needs to know beyond how to do these step-by-step techniques and applications.

d) If a particular designer has a strong sense of design, this is something innate and cannot be learned or taught.

e) There is little need to vary or adapt these techniques and applications.

f) The primary goal is functionality.

g) There are no consequences if you have followed the steps correctly.

As *"craft"*, we still recognize the interplay of the artist's hand with the piece and the storytelling underlying it. We honor the technical prowess. People love to bring art into their personal worlds, and the craftsperson offers them functional objects which have some artistic sensibilities.

ART: When defined as *"art"*, jewelry is seen as something which transcends itself and its design. It is not something that anyone can do without special insights and training. The goal of any project would be harmony with a little variety, and some satisfaction and approval.

"Jewelry as art" evokes an emotional response. Functionality should play no role at all, or, if an object has some functional purpose, then its functional reason-for-being should

merely be supplemental. For example, the strap on a necklace is comparable to the frame around a painting, or the pedestal for a sculpture. They supplement the art. They are not included with nor judged as part of the art work.

If following the Art Tradition, the jewelry designer would learn a lot of art theories and rules about the manipulation of design elements, such as color, movement, perspective, within the piece. Then, the designer would keep rehearsing these until their application becomes very intuitive. The jewelry designer, based on their professional socialization into Art, would assume that:

   a) Whether the piece outlines are clear from the beginning, or emergent or process-like, what is most important is that art theories and rules be applied at each little increment along the way.

   b) The jewelry designer as artist must learn some specialized knowledge – art theories and rules – in order to be successful.

   c) The outcomes would be judged on visual and art criteria alone, as if they were paintings or sculptures on display.

   d) While everyone has within them the creative abilities to design jewelry as an artist, for most people, this must be learned.

   e) The primary goals are beauty and appeal. Beauty and appeal are typically judged in terms of harmony and variety.

   f) If you have not applied the theories and rules optimally, the piece would be judged as incomplete and unsuccessful.

What is nice about the Art Tradition is that the goal is Beauty. Beauty is achieved through smart choices and decisions. The designer as artist is not encumbered by having to follow specific steps or patterns. Nor is the designer encumbered by the structural and functional properties of all the pieces or elements she or he uses – only their beauty. The designer does not have to compromise Beauty for Functionality.

DESIGN: When defined as *"design"*, you begin to focus more on construction and functionality issues. You often find yourself making tradeoffs between appeal and functionality. You incorporate situational relevance into your designs. You anticipate what the client (and the various audiences of the client) understands as something which is finished and successful. You see "choice" as more multidimensional and contingent. You define success only in reference to the jewelry as it is worn.

If following the Design Perspective, the designer would have to learn a lot of things. These would include things in art, architecture, engineering, social science, psychology, behavioral science, and anthropology. The designer would develop those professional skills and insights, what we might call *disciplinary literacy*, so that she or he could bring a lot of disparate ideas and applications to the fore, depending on what the situation warranted.

The designer, based on their professional socialization into Design, would assume that:

a) Whether the piece or project outlines are clear or emergent, what is most important is the ability to bring a wide range of design principles and applications to the situation.

b) The designer must learn a lot of specialized knowledge, some related to art, and some related to several other disciplines, such as architecture and social science.

c) The outcomes must find the best fit between considerations about appeal with concerns about functionality. Functionality is not an add-on. It is an equal, competing partner with beauty and appeal.

d) The designer does not design in a vacuum. She or he must anticipate the shared understandings among self, client and the various audiences of the client about what evidence might be used to judge the piece as finished and successful. These anticipations about shared understandings and evidence must be incorporated into the design process and how it is managed.

e) Anyone can learn to be a designer, but fluency and literacy in the profession involves the development of skills and insights over a period of time.

f) The primary goal is to find the best fit between appeal and functionality within a given context or situation.

g) The consequences for not finding that best fit is some level of client dissatisfaction.

The Design Perspective is very relevant for the education and training of designers. Here, the designer is seen as a multi-functional professional. The designer must bring a lot of very different kinds of skills and abilities to bear, when constructing a piece or developing a project. The professional has to be able to manage artistic design, functionality, and the interaction of the piece with the client as well as that client's environment. This approach also believes that *Design* should be appreciated as its own discipline – not a subset of sculpture or painting. And that a piece as designed can only be understood *as it is worn*.

However you define your work as ART or CRAFT or DESIGN will determine what skills you learn, how you apply them, and how you introduce your pieces to a wider audience. The Craft Approach ignores the need to learn a specialized knowledge and approach. The Art Tradition focuses solely on the artistic merits of the piece, and assumes the client will have a more passive relationship to it, as if the client were standing in front of the piece on display in a museum. The Design Perspective focuses on how to anticipate shared understandings and desires and incorporate these into how best to a make tradeoffs between appeal and functionality.

[One approach is not necessarily better than another. Just different, with different implications. The bias in this book is to define jewelry as DESIGN, with its own disciplinary-specific, specialized knowledge and skills base, where jewelry is judged as art only at the point it is worn, and where jewelry-making is seen as a communicative process.]

QUESTION 2: How do you decide what you want to create? What kinds of things do you do to translate your passions and inspirations into jewelry? What is your creative process?

Applying yourself creatively can be fun at times, but scary at other times. It is work. You are creating something out of nothing. There is an element of risk. You might not like what you end up doing. Your friends might not like it. Nor your family. You might not finish it. Or you might do it wrong. It may seem easier to go with someone else's project.

Applying creativity means developing abilities to generate options and alternatives, and narrowing these down to specific choices. It means developing an ease and comfort generating fix-it strategies when approaching unknown situations or problematic ones. It means figuring out how to translate inspiration into design in a way that inspires others and taps into their desires. It means differentiating yourself from other jewelry designers as a measure of your originality.

Creative people…

Set no boundaries and set no rules. They go with the flow. They don't conform to expectations.

Play. They pretend they are kids again.

Experiment. They take the time to do a lot of What Ifs and Variations On A Theme and Trial and Error.

Keep good records. They make good notes and sketches of what seems to work, and what seems to not work.

Evaluate. They learn from their successes and mistakes.

As jewelry designers gain more and more creative experiences, they begin to assemble what I call a *Designer's Tool Box*. In this virtual box are a set of thinking routines, strategies and fix-it strategies which have worked well in the past, are very workable in and of themselves, and are highly adaptive when used in unfamiliar situations. Every jewelry designer should develop their own Designer Tool Box. This vastly contributes to success in creative thinking and application.

QUESTION 3: What kinds of MATERIALS work well together, and which ones do not? This applies to TECHNIQUES as well. What kinds of TECHNIQUES (or combinations of techniques) work well when, and which ones do not?

A successful jewelry design has a character of its own as well as some kind of evocative essence. Let's call this a tone. The choice of materials, including beads, clasps, and stringing materials, and the choice of techniques, including stringing, weaving, wire working, glassworks, metalworks, clayworks, cements that tone into place. Techniques link the designer's intent with the client's expectations. The successful designer has a depth of knowledge about materials, their attributes, their strengths, their weaknesses, and is able to leverage the good and minimize the bad within any design. The same can be said of techniques.

The choice of materials and the choice of techniques set the tone and chances of success for your piece. Materials and techniques establish the character and personality of your designs. They contribute to understandings whether the piece is finished and successful.

However, there are no perfect materials (or techniques) for every jewelry project. Selecting materials (or techniques) is about making smart, strategic choices. This means relating your choices to your design and marketing goals. It also frequently means having to make tradeoffs and judgment calls between aesthetics and functionality. Last, materials (or techniques) may have different relationships with the designer, wearer or viewer depending on how they are intended to be used, and the situational or cultural contexts.

For some designs, the incorporation of mixed media or mixed techniques can have a synergistic effect – increasing (or decreasing) the appeal and/or functionality of the piece, better than any one media or technique alone. It can feel more playful and experimental and fun to mix media or techniques. But there may be adverse effects, as well. Each media or technique will have its own structural and support requirements. Each will enable the control of light and shadow, space and mass, dimension and movement in different ways. Each will react differently to various physical forces impacting the piece when worn or the project when used. So it becomes difficult for the designer to successfully utilize any one medium or technique, as well as much more difficult to coordinate and integrate more than one media or technique.

There are many implications of choice. There are light/shadow issues, pattern, texture, rhythm, dimensionality, proportions, placement and color issues. There are mechanics, shapes, forms, durability, drape, flow and movement issues. There are positive and negative space issues. There are issues related to your clients (and their various audiences).

It is important to know what happens to all these materials over time. It is important to know how each technique enhances or impedes architectural requirements, such as allowing the piece to move and drape, to respond to stresses and strains, or to assist the piece in maintaining a shape. Each material and technique has strengths and weaknesses, pros and cons, and contingencies affecting their utilization. The designer needs to leverage the strengths and minimize the weaknesses.

All of these choices:
... affect the look
... affect the drape
... affect the feel
... affect the durability
... affect both the wearer's and viewer's responses
... relate to the context

Question 4: Beyond applying basic techniques and selecting quality materials, how does the Jewelry Designer evoke an emotional and resonant response to their jewelry? What skill-sets do Designers need in order to think through powerful designs?

An artistic and well-designed piece of jewelry should **evoke an emotional response**. In fact, ideally, it should go beyond this a bit, and have what we call ***"resonance"***. The difference between an *emotional response* and *resonance* is reflected in the difference between someone saying, "That's beautiful," from saying "I need to wear that piece," or, "I need to buy that piece."

Quite simply: If no emotional response, and preferably, resonance, is evoked, then the jewelry is poorly designed. Evoking an emotional and resonant response takes the successful selection and arrangement of materials, the successful application of techniques as well as the successful management of skills.

Unfortunately, beaders and jewelry makers too often focus on materials or techniques and not often enough on skills. It is important to draw distinctions here.

Materials and techniques are necessary but not sufficient to get you there. You need skills.

The classic analogy comparing materials, techniques and skills references cutting bread with a knife. Material: bread and knife. Technique: How to hold the knife relative to the bread in order to cut it. Skill: The force applied so that the bread gets cut successfully.

Skills are the kinds of things the jewelry designer applies which enhance his or her capacity to control for bad workmanship and know when the piece is finished. Skills, not techniques, are what empower the designer to evoke emotional and resonant responses to their work.

These skills include:

- *Judgment*
- *Presentation*
- *Care and dexterity*
- *Knowing when "enough is enough"*
- *Understanding how art theory applies to the "bead" and to "jewelry when worn"*
- *Understanding the architectural underpinnings of each technique, that is, how design choices minimize stresses and strains, and how these choices enhance, or impede, what you are trying to do*
- *Taking risks*
- *Anticipating the desires, values, and shared understandings all client audiences of the designer have about when a piece should be considered finished and successful*
- *Recognizing that jewelry is art only as it is worn*

QUESTION #5: When is enough enough? How does the jewelry artist know when the piece is done? Overdone? Or underdone? What is the evidence? How do you edit? What fix-it strategies do you come up with and employ?

In the bead and jewelry arenas, you see piece after piece that is either over-embellished or under-done. Things may get too repetitive with the elements and materials. Or the pieces don't feel that they are quite there yet.

For every piece of jewelry there will be that point of *parsimony* when *enough is enough*. We want to find that point where experiencing the "whole" is more satisfying than experiencing any of the parts. That point of parsimony is where, if we added (or subtracted) one more thing, we would detract from the whole of our design.

Knowing that point of parsimony is also related to anticipating how and when others will judge the piece as finished and successful. And what to do about it when judged unfinished or unsuccessful.

There is no one best way -- only your way

The ***fluent and empowered jewelry designer*** will have answers to these 5 essential questions, though not every designer will have the same answers, nor is there one best answer.

Yet it is unacceptable to avoid answering any of these 5 questions, for fear you might not like the answer.

The fluent and empowered jewelry designer will have learned the skills for making good choices. He or she will recognize that jewelry design is a process of management and communication. The fluent and empowered designer manages how choices are made. These choices include making judgments about selecting and combining materials, both physical and aesthetic, and techniques, both alone or in tandem, into wearable art forms and adornment, expressive of the desires of self and others. The artist's hand will be very visible in their work.

This is jewelry making and design.

This is at the core of how jewelry designers think like jewelry designers.

This is the substantive basis which informs how the designer introduces jewelry publicly.

And this is what this book is all about: Developing your disciplinary literacy in jewelry design. That means, learning to be fluent, flexible and original in design, and how to think and communicate like a designer.

GETTING STARTED
2c. CHANNELING YOUR EXCITEMENT

Jayden Alfre Jones at work

Guiding Questions:
(1) Why do you want to become a jewelry designer?
(2) How do you channel your excitement?
(3) How do you manage and overcome doubt and self-doubt?
(4) What is your Getting Started story?
(5) How do you bring some aspects of originality to your pieces?

Key Words: ambition / motivation support group types of creatives purpose	doubt and self-doubt originality differentiation personalization jewelry designer channel excitement	Getting Started story aspirations valuing support group

Abstract:

Why do you want to become (or are already on the way to becoming) a jewelry designer? What drives you? How do you channel your excitement? Is it something to do with what type of person you are? How you view the world? How you want to fill your time? It turns out there are many types of people who become jewelry designers. Although they may have different aspirations and ambitions underlying their excitement about jewelry design, they find common ground and a common way of thinking about making and designing jewelry. But because jewelry design has not yet become a full-fledged, recognizable discipline all its own, it sometimes becomes difficult to get clarity on how to channel your excitement into an avocation or career. Your support group is often made up of a polyglot of crafters and artists, some who do not fully understand jewelry making and design. Advice can be diffuse. Clients have difficulty evaluating the value of your work, frequently expressing misunderstandings about what is good. This can lead to self-doubt, which better designers learn to manage and overcome.

GETTING STARTED:
CHANNELING YOUR EXCITEMENT
What drives you to pursue your passion for jewelry?

"Why Are You A Jewelry Artist?"
As if you had a choice...

It often is difficult for others to understand why you consider yourself a jewelry artist. How did this come to be? How did you get started? Were you always artistic? Is your family crafty? How did you learn these things? Why jewelry? Why do you get so excited about all this? Do you want to make a living out of it? Can you really sell things?

They don't really feel these things like you do. They don't feel this pulsing heart, this urge to create, and this passion to make jewelry. When you get started making jewelry, it's hard to stop. It becomes ingrained in you. What may have begun as a hobby evolves into something you cannot live without. Applying your creative self becomes habit, almost addicting, often relaxing and self-affirming ... and painful to do without.

As a jewelry artist, you have a purpose in life. It is something you do because you must do it. It is what helps you function in life. You make new amazing pieces, share these, and make some more new amazing pieces. You have those little conversations with yourself about the various choices you are making, when designing a piece of jewelry, and this can be therapeutic, informative, reaffirming. And, you are ever in search of developing those insightful, smart strategies for merging voice with form, aesthetics with function, your intent with the desires of others.

Jewelry designers are extraordinarily blessed to do what they love for a living. For many, they have turned a hobby into an avocation into a lifestyle.

But it's not like a regular job. There are many intangibles. Such as, what exactly is *creativity*, and how do you apply it? What are all the things which have to come together to recognize that creative spark when it hits you in your heart, gut or head, and how to translate that into something real, with beauty, with function, and with purpose? How do you mesh your view of aesthetics and functionality with those of your many audiences – wearer, viewer, buyer, seller, exhibiter, collector, teacher and student?

What exactly does it mean to design jewelry, and how do you know it is the right path for you? This is a tough question. You may love jewelry, but not know how to make it. You may get off on creative problem solving or be a color addict but not know what specific techniques and skills you need to learn, in what organized way, with what direction, leading you towards becoming that better jewelry designer. You may feel the motivation, but not know what the jewelry designer really has to do each day.

You may be taking classes and getting some training, but how do you know when you have arrived? How do you know when you have emerged as a successful professional jewelry designer? How do you know you have mastered the necessary disciplinary literacy – fluency, flexibility, originality? And what are your responsibilities and obligations, once you get there?

Surviving and thriving as a jewelry designer requires an understanding of the way things work and how you will fit into all this – making, presenting, selling, reflecting and critiquing.

Not Just One Type Of Person

There is not just one type of person who becomes a jewelry designer. There are many, many types of people who find jewelry design a common passion. They may have different ambitions. They may prefer to use different techniques and materials. They may have different expectations for financial success. They may have different compulsions for creating jewelry. But the excitement is there for each of them.

We can differentiate people who become jewelry designers by their aspirations ([1] Neuendorf, 2016) – why they became jewelry designers. Some jewelry designers fit one type of aspiration; others, more than one. But the contour of their lives brings them to similar places within jewelry and its design. How do your motivations and ambitions compare?

There are 5 basic types of Creatives which can be defined by their aspirations:

- o Social Interactants
- o Compulsive Creators
- o Lifestyle of Freedom Seekers
- o Financial Success Achievers
- o People Who Find Themselves Making Jewelry Through Happenstance and Chance

Social Interactants

This type of Creative often seeks out other creatives and forms a social network. Social Interactants may be makers. They may be sellers or exhibitors or collectors. But their excitement comes, in part, by looking for ways to interact and meet and share close-knit social ties. Part of the reason is to learn new ideas. Another part is to get feedback and critique. The social group and network will offer support, advice, career and business opportunities and direction. These are people you can lean on when times get tough. There might even be some shared glamour and celebrity, depending on the artists and their group.

Social Interactants typically seek recognition for their efforts and their works. The success of any piece of jewelry depends on the judgements of the various audiences which interact with it. Social interactants allocate a good deal of their time anticipating how others will understand and react to any piece of jewelry. They spend time seeking out opportunities to display their works publicly.

Compulsive Creators

There is this innate, compulsive, don't-fight-it desire that some jewelry designers have for creating jewelry. This is the Compulsive Creator. Applying creative thinking is at the core of their excitement. Composing, constructing and manipulating design elements is intrinsically rewarding. There is a strong, profound commitment to jewelry design, and this directed energy is often associated with productivity and success.

Compulsive Creators love what they do. It allows them to think creatively. They allocate a lot of their time towards achieving a high level of quality and sophistication.

Lifestyle of Freedom Seekers

These Freedom Seeker designers like to set their own pace, establish their own routines, work when the spirit moves them. A regular 9 to 5 job is not for them. They like to make their own rules and be self-directed. Any financial insecurity and uncertainty that comes with this is worth the price to pay for a lifestyle of freedom.

Excitement equals freedom and the strategies for incorporating whatever comes. These designers believe that this freedom allows them to experience the world around them in a greater depth and to a greater degree. In turn, they have more understandings for how to find and then turn inspirations into finished jewelry designs.

Financial Success Achievers

Financially Successful jewelry designers can do quite well for themselves, but it takes a lot of drive, organization and business and marketing sense. Jewelry design can be a lucrative career with such determination, gaining visibility, and a little bit of being in the right place at the right time. Accumulating money or wealth is a big part of the excitement.

Some designers seek to make jewelry design a self-supporting career. However, many designers primarily look for money to supplement their income or retirement. Some look to make enough money to pay for their supplies.

Sometimes, designers make jewelry to seek wealth, rather than income. They accumulate many pieces of jewelry and many unusual supplies and components to achieve wealth as success.

Financial Success Achievers typically try to create a business around their jewelry.

Happenstance and Chance

Not everyone who becomes a jewelry designer aspired to be one. Sometimes people fall into it. They need a piece of jewelry to match an outfit and decide to make something themselves, then get hooked. They watch someone make jewelry, then get intrigued. They try to repair a broken piece of jewelry by themselves. They accompany a friend to a jewelry making class, then want to try it out. Their excitement evolves over time.

A Myriad of Aspirations and Ambitions

Aspirations and ambitions vary. No matter what your personal aspirations and ambitions are, there is no one best way or right way. It becomes a matter of the designer finding that balance of design, self, and other-life which works for them, and drives their passion.

Jewelry designers are motivated to become designers for many different reasons. But motivations are only a start at channeling one's excitement. These aspirations and motivations make up only a small part of what it truly takes to be a successful designer. Designers need to develop skills and techniques, creative thinking, design process management, and disciplinary literacy, to continue on their pathway to success.

BECOMING THE BEAD ARTIST AND JEWELRY DESIGNER:
Your *Getting Started* Story

When did you first realize you had a passion for designing jewelry?

[While you are thinking about this, now is a good time to get out your pen and paper and jot down some thoughts.]

Everyone has a "*Getting Started*" story. This is a story you tell over and over again. In it, you express your wonderment and passion. You talk about your excitement, your aspirations, your motivations and how you decided to channel them. You go over the steps you went through to discover what it is that drives you to create. You recall who influenced you, when and why. You remember different pathways and crossroads, where you decided to pursue your interests in one direction or another. You reflect on your expectations before you got started, and how these evolved or changed as you began to make and design jewelry.

Sometimes your story begins by touching some beads. Or running a strand of pearls through your hand. Or the sight of something perfectly worn around the wrist, upon the breast, or up near the neck. Othertimes, it may begin by taking a class, or deciding to make a special pair of earrings to match a particular outfit. Or thinking you want to make a piece of jewelry you saw someone wearing on TV or in a photospread in some magazine.

Your *Getting Started* story is a measure of what you have discovered, and what you need to discover still. It is a foil against which to measure your successes, and some not-so-successful things. It represents your insight and foresight when making both personal development and jewelry design choices.

And, it is very important to be cognizant and aware of how your *Getting Started* story follows you throughout your career in your marketing and exhibiting. It becomes part of your business name, your brochures, your advertising. It becomes part of your description, your elevator pitch, your tag line. It underlies how you talk about yourself and your jewelry.

It becomes one of the major ways other people get to know you, get interested in you, and want to wear or display things made by you. You will always need to have a *Getting Started* story, and you will always come to rely on this story to further your literacy development in design, as well as your creative and business ambitions.

Better designers are very *metacognitive* of what they do. That is, they are very aware of all the choices they've made, and their implications and consequences. This means reflection. It means evaluation. It means critiquing.

Writing your Getting Started story is a necessary, early first step towards developing your metacognitive abilities as a designer. So, even at this very beginning of your jewelry making path, take some notes. Keep a journal. Be aware of what is driving you.

Doubt / Self-doubt

For the novice, all that excitement at the beginning, when thinking about making jewelry and making some pieces, sometimes collides with a wall of developing self-doubt. *It's not easy to quiet a doubt.*

The jewelry artist organizes their life around an inspiration. There is some fuzziness here. That inspiration has some elements of ideas, but not necessarily crystal clear ones. That inspiration has some elements of emotions – it makes you feel something – but not necessarily something you can put into words or images or fully explain. You then need to translate this fuzzy inspiration into materials, into techniques, into color, into arrangements, into a coherent whole.

You start to make something, but realize you don't know how to do it. But you want to do it, and do it now. However, to pick up the needed skills, you realize you can't learn things all at once. You can't do everything you want to do all at once. That initial excitement often hits a wall. Things take time to learn. There are a lot of trial and error moments, with a lot of errors. Pieces break. Combining colors and other design elements feels very awkward. Picking the right clasps and rings and connectors and stringing materials is fraught with implications. Silhouettes are confusing. You might get the right shape for your piece, but it is difficult to get the right movement, drape and flow, without compromising that shape.

To add to this stress and strain, you need to show your jewelry off. You might want someone to like it. To want it. To need it. To desire it. To buy it. To wear it. To wear it more than once. To wear it often. To exhibit it. To collect it. To show and talk about it with others. And how will all these other people recognize your creative spark, and your abilities to translate that spark into a wonderful, beautiful, functional piece of jewelry, appropriate for the wearer and appropriate for the situation?

Frequently, because of all this, the artist experiences some sense of doubt and self-doubt. Some paralysis. Can't get started. Can't finish something. Wondering why they became a jewelry designer in the first place.

Doubt holds you back from seizing your opportunities.

It makes getting started or finishing things harder than they need to be.

It adds uncertainty.

It makes you question yourself.

It blocks your excitement, perhaps diminishing it.

While sometimes doubt and self-doubt can be useful in forcing you to think about and question your choices, it mostly holds you back.

Having doubt and self-doubt is common among all artistic types. What becomes important is how to manage and overcome it, hence, my idea of *Channeling Your Excitement*, so that doubts do not get in the way of your creative process and disciplinary development, but rather, inform them.

There are 8 major ways in which jewelry designers get caught beginning to fall into that abyss we call self-doubt:

1) *What If I'm Not Creative Enough or Original Enough or Cannot Learn or Master or Don't Know a Particular Technique?*

2) *What If No One Likes What I Make?*

3) *What If No One Takes Me Seriously As An Artist And Designer?*

4) *I Overthink Things and Am A Bit of a Perfectionist.*

5) *How Can I Stay Inspired?*

6) *Won't People Steal My Work?*

7) *Being Over Confident or Under Confident*

8) *Role Confusion*

1. What If I'm Not Creative Enough or Original Enough or Cannot Learn or Master or Don't Know a Particular Technique?

Everyone has some creativity baked into their being. It is a matter of developing your way of thinking and doing so that you can apply it. This takes time.

So does originality. The word *originality* can be very off-putting, but it does not have to be.

At first, originality will mean that you will try different ways of personalizing projects. There are always things you can do to bring some aspects of originality to your pieces. This might be the choice of colors, or using a special clasp, or rearranging some elements in your composition.

Again, as with creativity, the ability to be more and more original will evolve over time. It is helpful to think of originality, not necessarily as coming up with something completely new, but rather as *differentiation* – how you differentiate yourself from other jewelry designers.

For almost everyone, you don't begin your design career at the height of your levels of creativity and originality. Yes, if you look around you, other people are more creative and original than you or have more skills than you. Don't let these observations be a barrier to your own development as a jewelry designer. You get there through persistence and hard work. You handle your inner critic. You may not be there, yet – the key word here is *yet*. But you will be.

2. *What If No One Likes What I Make?*

We all have fears about how our creativity and originality are going to be evaluated and judged. We project our self-doubts to the doubts we think we see and feel from others. What if no one wants to wear my pieces, or buy my works?

We can't let these outsider reactions dictate our lives and creative selves. A key part of successful jewelry design is learning how to introduce what we do publicly. At the least, it is the core nature of the things we create that they are to be worn on the body. Jewelry is a very public thing.

Turn negative comments into positive ideas, motivators, insights, explorations. Allow yourself some give and take, some needs to step back awhile, some needs to tweak. Jewelry design and jewelry making are iterative processes. They in no way are linear. Your outcomes and their success are more evolutionary, than guaranteed.

Distressing about what others may think of your work can be very damaging to your self-esteem. It can amplify your worries. Don't go there.

Don't become your worst critic.

3. *What If No One Takes Me Seriously As An Artist And Designer?*

Jewelry design is an occupation in search of a profession. You will find that a lot of people won't recognize your passion and commitment. They may think anyone can design jewelry. They may think of jewelry making as a craft or some subset of art, not as something unique and important in and of itself. They may wonder how you can make a living at this.

The bottom line: if you don't take yourself seriously as a jewelry designer, no one else will.

People will take you seriously as they see all the steps you are taking to master your craft and develop yourself as a professional.

4. I Over Think Things And Am A Bit Of A Perfectionist

Some designers let a sense that their work is not as good as imagined get in the way. They never finish anything. They let doubt eat away at them.

Perfectionism is the enemy of the good. It's great to be meticulous, but emotionally, we get wrecked when anything goes astray, or any little thing is missing, or you don't have that exact color or part you originally wanted.

Go ahead and plan. Planning is good. It's insightful. It can be strategic. But also be sure to be adaptable and realistic. Each piece is a stepping stone to something that will come next.

The better jewelry designer develops a *Designer's Toolbox* – a collection of fix-it strategies to deal with the unfamiliar or the problematic.

Overthinking can be very detrimental. You can't keep changing your mind, trying out every option, thinking that somewhere, someplace there exists a better option. Make a choice and get on with it. You can tweak things later.

Yes, attention to detail is important. But so is the value of your time. You do not want to waste too much time on trivial details.

Be aware when you begin over-analyzing things. Stop, take a breath, make a decision, and move on.

5. How Can I Stay Inspired?

Designing a piece of jewelry takes time, sometimes a long time. That initial inspirational spark might feel like it's a dying ember.

Don't let that happen.

Translate that inspiration into images, colors, words, sample designs, and surround your work space with these.

Talk about your inspiration in detail with family and friends.

6. Won't People Steal My Work?

Many jewelry designers fear that if they show their work publicly, people will steal their ideas. So they stop designing.

Yet jewelry design is a very communicative process which requires introducing your work publicly. If you are not doing this, then you are creating simple sculptures, not jewelry.

Yes, other people may copy your work. See this source of doubt as an excuse. It is a self-imposed, but unnecessary, barrier we might impose to prevent us from experiencing that excitement as a jewelry designer. Other people will never be able to copy your design prowess – how you translate inspiration into a finished piece. That is unique and special to you. It is why the general public responds positively to you and your work.

7. *Over Confidence can blind you to the things you need to be doing and learning, and Under Confidence can hinder your development as a designer.*

Too often, we allow *under confidence* to deter us from the jewelry design and making tasks at hand. We always question our lack of ability and technical prowess for accomplishing the necessary tasks at hand. It is important, however, to believe in yourself. To believe that you can work things out when confronted with unfamiliar or problematic situations. It is important to develop your skills for thinking like a designer. Fluency. Flexibility. Originality. There is a vocabulary to learn. Techniques to learn. Strategies to learn. These develop over time with practice and experience. You need to believe in your abilities to develop as a designer over time.

With *over confidence* comes a naivete. You close off the wisdom to listen to what others have to say or offer. You stunt your development as an artist. You overlook important factors about materials and techniques to the detriment of your final designs and products. You close yourself off to doubt and self-doubt, which is unfortunate. Doubt and self-doubt are tools for asking questions and questioning things. These help you grow and develop as an artist and designer. These influence your ability to make good, professional choices in your career.

8. *Role Confusion*

Jewelry artists play many roles and wear different hats. Each has its own set of opportunities, requirements, and pressures that the artist must cope with. It's a *balancing act* extraordinaire.

First, people who make jewelry wear different hats: Artist and Designer, Manufacturer, Distributor, Retailer, and Exhibitor.

Second, people who make jewelry have different needs: Artistic Excellence, Recognition, Monetary Gain, or Financial Stability.

Third, the artist needs to please and satisfy themselves, as well as other various clients.

Fourth, the artist constructs pieces which need to function in different settings: Situational, Cultural, Sociological, Psychological.

Last, the artist must negotiate a betwixt and between situation – a rite of passage – as they relinquish control over the piece and its underlying inspirations to the wearer and the viewer, who have their own needs, desires and expectations.

This gets confusing. It affects how you pick materials and supplies. Which techniques you use. What marketing strategies you employ. How you value and price things. And the list goes on.

It is important to be aware (*metacognitive*) of what role(s) you play when, and why. Given the role, it is important to understand the types of choices you need to make, when constructing a piece of jewelry. It is critical to understand the tradeoffs you will invariably end up making, and their consequences for the aesthetic, emotional and functional success of your pieces.

Some Advice

While doubt and self-doubt can hinder our development as jewelry designers, some degree of these may be helpful, as well.

To develop yourself as a jewelry designer, and to continue to grow and expand in your profession, you must have a balanced amount of both doubt and self-doubt. Uncertainty leads to questioning. A search for knowledge. Some acceptance of trial and error and experimentation. A yearning for more reliable information and feedback.

Jewelry design uses a great deal of emotion as a Way of Knowing. Emotions cloud or distort how we perceive things. They may lead to more doubt and worry and lack of confidence. But they also enhance our excitement when translating inspirations into designs.

- *Don't let your inner doubts spin out of control. Be aware and suppress them.*
- *Be real with yourself and your abilities.*
- *Keep a journal. Detail what your doubts are and the things you are doing to overcome them.*
- *Create a developmental plan for yourself. Identify the knowledge, skills and understandings you want to develop and grow into.*
- *Remember what happened in the past the last time doubt got in your way. Remember what you did to overcome this doubt. Remember that probably nothing negative actually happened.*
- *Talk to people. These can be friends, relatives and colleagues. Don't keep doubts unto yourself.*
- *Don't compare yourself to others. This is a trap. Self-reflect and self-evaluate you on your own terms.*
- *Worrying about what others think? The truth is that people don't really care that much about what you do or not do.*
- *Don't beat yourself up.*

- *Get re-inspired. This might mean surrounding yourself with images and photos of things. It might mean a walk in nature. It might me letting someone else's excitement flow over to you.*
- *Take breaks.*
- *See setbacks as temporary.*
- *Celebrate small steps.*
- *Keep developing your skills.*
- *Set goals for yourself.*

Surviving As A Jewelry Designer

Designers focus their attention inward, looking, listening, sensing and searching themselves at length, only later to redirect their findings outward, creating jewelry to be displayed publicly or worn by others or sold. Doing this well often requires having several coping strategies.

Designers have to bridge the gap between inspiration and execution. This requires a lot of thought, understanding and skill.

Having both right- (*creative*) and left- (*administrative*) brain skills is a good place to be.

Don't let the craft substitute for your personal identity. It's always great to get compliments on what you make. This bolsters your self-esteem. *But you should have good self-esteem based on who you are as a person, not on the pieces of jewelry you make.* Self-esteem should come from within you, not external to you. Related to all this is that you do not want to take negative comments about your work personally. Evaluate and use the feedback objectively.

Take risks. Play. Experiment. Don't be afraid to try new colors, new arrangements, new techniques, or place yourself in new settings with new people. Don't be afraid to fail. Don't get stuck in a rut making the same things over and over again. You may find yourself not growing as an artist and as a person.

As best as you can, avoid comparing yourself to others.

Learn to recognize when enough is enough. You can't be all things to all people for all designs for all situations for all contingencies. You need to set some limits and boundaries for yourself so you don't get too frustrated or burnt out or broke. You will never have enough parts or enough time or enough creative energy or enough money to make everything people ask you to make.

Successful artists are able to define what *success* means to them. They don't get caught up with what other people might define as *success*.

Successful artists typically dedicate a specific time and place for creating. They develop a routine. They don't work all hours of the day, or in a disorganized environment.

Create a consistent, coherent body of design work. Encapsulate this in a PORTFOLIO, Artist Resume, and Artist Statement.

Keep some kind of journal documenting your thoughts, design ideas, problems and solutions. This can be something very formal, or something loosely organized.

Usually, if you want to make a living at jewelry design, you'll need a multi-method, multi-venue approach.

Merging Your Voice and Inspiration With Form

Jewelry design is an ongoing process of finding how to merge your artistic voice and inspiration with form. As you become more fluent and comfortable with all the vocabulary and materials and techniques, you take on more and more challenges.

Jewelry design is a conversation. It is a quiet conversation between what you come to feel and understand as inspiration, and what logical options you might bring to bear on translating that inspiration into a design. It is a conversation between you the designer and someone else as the wearer. It might also be a conversation between you the maker with someone else as the viewer, buyer, seller, exhibiter or collector.

The conversation is never done. It is a dialog. It is a back-and-forth process of refining, questioning and translating your feelings, impressions, ideas, influences into a visual grammar, forms and arrangements, and content, intent and meanings. Everything comes into play, and everything matters.

Some of the conversation is inward, and some of the conversation is very interactional. Part of the conversation focuses on generating a lot of possibilities. Another part concentrates on narrowing down those possibilities. During all this iteration, your artistic voice gets closer and closer to merging with that final jewelry form.

As your fluency in jewelry design grows, you find that all this conversation and all divergence and convergence of ideas and feelings and choices, gets reflected and sensed within your jewelry designs. This is how you develop and channel your excitement and passion.

This is how your jewelry begins to resonate.

FOOT NOTES

(1) Henri Neuendorf (https://news.artnet.com/about/henri-neuendorf-205), *A Young*

Artist's Brief Guide to Art World Ambition, Art World, November 18, 2016
 As referenced in: https://news.artnet.com/art-world/4-motivations-that-make-artists-successful-752957

[2] Drew Kimble, ***Five Fears That Can Destroy An Artist***, Skinny Artist
As referenced in: https://skinnyartist.com/5-fears-that-can-destroy-an-artist/

GETTING STARTED
2d. DEVELOPING YOUR PASSION

Workshop at Be Dazzled Beads

Guiding Questions:
(1) How should I learn and develop my jewelry designing skills?
(2) Where can I learn jewelry making skills? How will I know if I have mastered these?
(3) What are the different types of beading and jewelry making?
(4) What type of tasks do beaders and jewelry makers do?
(5) What types of tools do I need to get started?

Key Words:	*types of beading / jewelry making*	*learning objectives*
passion		*skill levels*
skills	*jewelry making tasks*	*self-esteem*
learning opportunities	*jewelry making tools*	*making choices*
how do you learn?		*support system*

Abstract:
Design is about knowledge, skill and understanding. Knowledge requires time and preciseness. Skill requires care and attention. Understanding requires empathy and insight. While you may be passionate about making jewelry, you are not born with the knowledge, skill and understandings necessary for jewelry design. These must be learned and developed over time. It is through this process of investment in self that the designer's passions emerge and expand. It is important to know the kinds of things you need to learn, and how you need to guide your education.

GETTING STARTED:
DEVELOPING YOUR PASSION
Passions Aren't Found, They Are Developed!

Design is about knowledge, skill and understanding. Knowledge requires time and preciseness. Skill requires care and attention. Understanding requires empathy and insight.

You are not born with the knowledge, skill and understandings necessary for jewelry design. These must be learned and developed over time. Anyone and everyone can learn these. Everyone has a creative capacity within them. There are many different ways to express things creatively. But one has to learn to express their thoughts and feelings creatively, step by step, developmentally over a period of time. It is through this process of investment in self that the designer's passions emerge and expand.

It is important not to give up too easily, if designing and making jewelry seems too difficult at first. Difficulty does not equate to a lack of passion. It does not equate to a lack of ability. It does not equate to a lack of creativity. Many things will be difficult, particularly at first.

Nor does any waxing and waning of motivation imply that jewelry design is not for you. It's natural that jewelry design does not provide an endless, infinite, always-there motivation. This does not mean you have lost your passion for it.

Passions must be cultivated. As do technical abilities and creative thinking. These all must be developed.

HOW DO YOU LEARN?

Many people who begin to bead and make jewelry want to rush to the finish line. They want to learn everything at once. They buy beads and parts indiscriminately. They try to use stringing and other materials insufficient to meet their design goals. They fail to anticipate how to finish off the clasp assembly. Their choices of colors often less than appealing. They don't have the right tools. They purchase every book they can find. They take classes and view video tutorials on anything that interests them or catches their eye, no matter what the skill levels involved. They want to create those perfect, elaborate pieces Now. Not later. Now.

Beading and jewelry making are not things to rush into, however. These are not things to learn haphazardly. Not everything is something you can easily pick up without having someone else show you.

This is a hobby and avocation and even a career which requires you to know a lot of things. You need to know a lot about materials. You need to know a lot about quality issues underlying these materials, and what happens to these materials over time. You need to be mechanical and comfortable using tools to construct things. You need to learn many basic techniques. You need to understand physical mechanics and what happens to all these materials and pieces, when jewelry is worn. You need to be familiar with art theories and design theories and their applications. You must be aware of some architectural basics and physical mechanics which inform you how things keep their shape and how things move, drape and flow. You need to understand people, their psychology, the dynamics of the groups they find themselves in, and their cultural rules which get them through the day.

There is so much to learn, that you can't learn it all at once. And there is so much to bring to bear, when making a piece of jewelry, that it is difficult to access all this information, if you haven't learned how everything is interrelated and interdependent.

Where can you learn jewelry making skills?...

Local craft or bead store	Self-taught, crafting at home
Community college	On-the-job training
University (art, fiber arts, metalsmithing, fashion)	Certifications
	Art institutes
Jewelry design program	Art grants
Fashion schools	How-to books
Bead and Jewelry Making Magazines	Video tutorials
Social media groups	Networking with other craft artists

It's important to learn in an *organized, developmental* way. You want to be always asking how things are interrelated. What depends on what? You want to pose what-if questions so that you can train yourself to anticipate the implications and consequences of making one choice over another. What happens If? What happens When? What enhances? What impedes? What synergizes? What can be leveraged, and toward what objective? You want to reflect on your outcomes.

Towards this end, you learn a core set of integrated and inter-dependent skills. Then learn another set of integrated and inter-dependent skills, perhaps at a slightly higher skill level, and how these link back to the core. Then learn yet another set of skills, again, increasing the skill level, how they link back to the first set, and then link back to the core. And so forth. Only in this way will you begin to know if you are learning the right way, and learning the right things.

There Are Many Ways To Learn

People apply different learning styles, when developing their beading and jewelry-making knowledge, skills and understandings. Each has pros and cons. Different people come to learn with different strategies or combinations of strategies. What is your preferred learning style? These learning styles and strategies include:

(1) *Rote Memory*

(2) *Analogously*

(3) *Contradictions*

(4) *Assimilation*

(5) *Constructing Meanings*

Most people learn by **Rote Memory**. They follow a set of steps, and they end up with something. They memorize all the steps. In this approach, all the choices have been made for them. So they never get a chance to learn the implications of their choices. Why one bead over another? Why one stringing material over another? How would you use the same technique in a different situation? You pick up a lot of techniques, but not necessarily many skills.

Other people learn **Analogously**. They have experiences with other crafts, such as sewing or knitting or woodworking or other craft, and they draw analogies. Such and Such is similar to Whatnot, so I do Whatnot the same way I do Such and Such. This can work to a point. However, beading and jewelry making can often be much more involved with composition, construction and manipulation, requiring making many more types of choices, than in other crafts. And there are still the issues of understanding the quality of the pieces you use, and what happens to them, both when jewelry is worn, as well as when jewelry is worn over time.

Yet another way people learn is through **Contradictions**. They see cheap jewelry and expensive jewelry, and analyze the differences. They see jewelry people are happy with, and jewelry people are not happy with, and analyze the differences. They see fashion jewelry looked down upon by artists, and art jewelry looked down upon by fashionistas, and they analyze the differences.

Assimilation is a learning approach that combines *Analogous Learning* and L*earning Through Contradictions*. People pursue more than one craft, keeping one foot in one arena, and another foot in the other. They teach themselves by analogy and contradiction. This assumes that multiple media and multiple techniques mix, and mix easily. Often, however, this is not true. Philosophies of design and technique differ. That means, the thinking about how a media and technique assert needs for shape and drape will have a different basis, not necessarily compatible. Usually one medium (or technique) has to predominate for any one project to be successful. So assimilative learning can lead to confusion and poor products, trying to meet the special concerns and structures of each craft simultaneously. It is challenging to mix media and/or techniques. Often the fundamentals of each particular craft need to be learned and understood in and of themselves.

The last approach to learning a craft is called **Constructing Meanings**. In this approach, you learn groups of things, and how to apply an active or thematic label to that grouping. For example, you might learn about beading threads, such as Nymo, C-Lon and FireLine, applying each one separately to accomplish the same project. In this way you begin to learn to evaluate each one's strengths and weaknesses, especially in terms of Managing Thread Tension or allowing movement, drape and flow. You might learn about crystal beads, Czech glass beads, and lampwork beads, and then again, concurrently and in comparison, learn the pros and cons of each, in terms of achieving good color blending strategies. You might learn peyote stitch and Ndebele stitch, and how to combine them within the same project.

In reality, you learn a little in each of these different learning styles and strategies. The Constructing Meanings approach, what is often referred to as the Art & Design Perspective, usually is associated with more successful and satisfying learning. This approach provides you with the tools for making sense of a whole lot of information – all the information you need to bring to bear to make a successful piece of jewelry, one that is both aesthetically pleasing and optimally functioning.

The Types of Things You Need To Learn

There is so much to know, and so many types of choices to make. Which clasp? Which stringing material? Which technique? Which beads? Which strategy of construction? What aesthetic you want to achieve? How you want to achieve it? Drape, movement, context, durability.

Types of Beading and Jewelry Making

> Stringing, Assembling
> Bead Weaving, Bead Working
> Wire Working, Wire Wrapping, Wire Weaving
> Silversmithing, Metal Work, Cold Connections, Fabrication
> Casting
> Fiber Arts, Knitting, Crochet, Micro-Macrame, Bead Embroidery, Kumihimo, Knotting, Braiding
> CAD (Computer Aided Design)
> Enameling
> Lampworking and Glass Blowing
> Stamping, Engraving
> Polymer Clay, Precious Metal Clay, Sculpting
> Lapidary
> Woodwork, Carving

Lots to know. One mistake most people make is that they learn everything randomly. Some things on their own. Some from books. Some from friends. In no special order. Without any plan.

And because there are so many things that you need to bring to bear, when creating a piece of jewelry, that it is difficult to see how everything links up. How everything is inter-related and mutually dependent. And how to make the best, most strategic and most satisfying series of inter-related choices.

Types of Tasks Jewelry Makers and Beaders Do

> Adjust, reshape, resize, create and attach clasp assemblies
> Cutting stones, setting stones, determining value and authenticity of stones
> CAD (Computer Aided Design), 3-D Printing
> Fabrication, stamping, engraving, casting, soldering, cold connections, shape metal wire and sheet, annealing
> Model and mold building, sculpting

> Manage thread tension, create self-supporting shapes, manage movement, drape and flow
> String, weave, netting, embellish, embroider, knit, crochet, braid, knot, wrap, assemble
> Understand jewelry-making as a process, from beginning to end
> Select color, proportion, volume, shape, forms, size, silhouettes, themes
> Place and Arrange design elements and components
> Read patterns, figures, graphs
> Select materials and techniques
> Determine measurements
> Assess stress, strain, strength, suppleness, stability and synergy
> Understand and access the creative marketplace, introduce their pieces publicly

And this is the essence of this book – a way to learn all the kinds of things you need to bring to bear, in order to create a wonderful and functional piece of jewelry. When you are just beginning your beading or jewelry making avocation, or have been beading and making jewelry awhile – time spent with the material in these segments will be very useful. You'll learn the critical skills and ideas. You'll learn how these inter-relate and are mutually interdependent. And you'll learn how to make better choices – fluent, flexible and original.

In the class curriculum I teach, students are guided to learn the following objectives:

> A. Technical Mechanics
>   1. Managing tension, whether using thread, cord, string or wire
>   2. Holding your piece to work it
>   3. Reading simple patterns, figures, graphs
>   4. Selecting appropriate materials
>   5. Identifying areas of potential weakness, and strategies for dealing with these
>   6. Determining measurements, including width and length of a piece, especially in relationship to bead and other component sizes
>   7. Extending your piece, such as adding thread or wire
>   8. Finishing off your piece and adding the clasp assembly
>
> B. Understanding Craft Basis of Technique or Stitch
>   1. Starting the technique or stitch
>   2. Implementing the basic technique or stitch
>   3. Finishing off the basic technique or stitch

> 4. Learning variations on the technique or stitch
> 5. Embellishing the Stitch, including fringe, edge, bail, strap, connectors
>
> C. Understanding Art & Design Basis of Technique or Stitch
> 1. Learning implications when choosing different sizes/shapes of beads or other components, or using different stringing materials
> 2. Understanding relationship of the technique or stitch in comparison to other techniques or stitches
> 3. Understanding how bead asserts its need for color
> 4. Creating your own design with this technique or stitch, in reference to design elements and jewelry design principles of composition
> 5. Creating shapes, components and forms with this technique or stitch, and establishing themes
> 6. Building in structural supports, and other support elements, into the design
>
> D. Becoming a Bead Weaving or Jewelry Making Designer
> 1. Developing a personal style
> 2. Valuing or pricing your work
> 3. Teaching others the technique or stitch
> 4. Promoting yourself and your work
> 5. Advocating for jewelry as "Art" and as "Design"

Progress in our education program is conceptualized in this *Learning Rubric* we use, and might provide you with a way to steer your learning process:

BE DAZZLED BEADS: EDUCATIONAL RUBRIC:
Learning How To Think Like A Jewelry Designer

Learning Stage	Jewelry Defined As...	I know I've mastered this level when...
PREPARATION	[Not yet defined]	I have assembled basic supplies and tools, and set up a workspace
BEGINNER (Decoding)	*Object* – defined apart from the maker, wearer and viewer, and apart from any inspiration or aspiration	I am familiar with the range of materials, beads, jewelry findings, components, stringing materials, tools and types of techniques used in jewelry making, and all associated quality issues and issues of choice. I can identify and list the basic design elements present in any piece of jewelry. I can explain which design elements are independent – that is, can function on their own, and which are dependent – that is, require the presence of other design elements I have mastered the mechanics of the major techniques in the jewelry making/design interest area(s) I have chosen
INTERMEDIATE (Comprehending)	*Content / Expression* – conveys and expresses meaning; reflects ideas about how inspiration is to be translated into a design; inspires someone to respond emotionally	I can select and arrange design elements into a pleasing composition. I can anticipate both aesthetic and architectural requirements of my piece as it is to be worn. I am comfortable self-directing my design process. I know 1 – 2 variations in techniques I use. I am beginning to develop

		"Fix-It" strategies when approaching new or difficult situations.
ADVANCED *(Fluent, Flexible, Original)*	*Action / Intent / Communicative Interaction* – conveying content in context; design choices understood as emerging from interaction between artist and various client audiences; jewelry reflects artist's intent	I have well-developed tool box of "Fix-It" strategies for dealing with unknown situations, with a high degree of automaticity in their use. I understand how the steps in the mechanics of every technique I use allow the piece to maintain its shape (structure), and how other steps allow the piece to maintain good movement, drape and flow (support). My jewelry reflects both parsimony in the choices of elements, and resonance in its expressive qualities for the wider audiences; I understand how this differs from traditional art concepts of "harmony" and 'variety" I can anticipate shared understandings as these are used to judge my piece as finished and successful; I understand how wider audiences affect the coherence – decoherence- contagion impacts of my designs I am very metacognitive of all the composition, construction, and manipulation choices I have made, and constantly reflective of the effects and implications of these choices

INTER-RELATING AND INTEGRAT-ING ALL LEVELS (*Disciplinary Literacy*) How we begin to build and expand our definitions of jewelry and design	**JEWERLY DESIGN DISCUSSION SEMINARS**		
	1. Good Design 2. Contemporary Design 3. Composition 4. Manipulation 5. Resonance 6. Beads and Color 7. Points, Lines, Planes, Shapes, Forms, Themes 8. Architectural Basics 9. Contemporizing Traditional Jewelry 10. Mixed Media / Mixed Techniques 11. Designing An Ugly Necklace	12. Backwards Design 13. What Is Jewelry? 14. Is Jewelry Making Teachable, or Merely Intuitive? 15. Can I Survive As A Jewelry Artist? 16. Creativity Isn't Found, It Is Developed 17. Jewelry Design Management 18. 5 Questions Every Jewelry Designer Should Answer	19. The Multiple Responsibilities of Being a Professional Jewelry Artist 20. Your Work Space 21. Design Theater 22. Overcoming Designer's Block 23. Fashion, Style, Taste or Art? 24. Threading the Business Needle 25. Using Components 26. Perception, Cognition 27. Sexuality and Jewelry

On My Own, Through Books and Video Tutorials, Or Through Classes?

   I always tell people it is easier to start by having someone show you what to do, either with a friend, or in a class, than trying to teach yourself out of a book or video tutorial. Books and videos are good at teaching you basic mechanics. But they are poor in teaching you the artistry and design skills you will need as a jewelry artist and designer. After working with a person, then go back to the books and online tutorials. You'll get more out of them this way.

   Particularly important to learn, and what you pick up best from another human being, include:

- *how to hold the piece while working it*
- *how to manage when you need to have firmer tension, and when you need to relax your tension, as you hold the piece*
- *what about the technique allows your project to maintain its shape, and what about the technique allows your project to move, drape and flow*
- *how to attach a clasp assembly or otherwise finish off your project*

- what materials are most suited to the project, and which are not
- whether this, or another technique, is best suited to the project goals
- how to prepare your materials, if necessary, before you use them
- which tools you should be using, and how to hold them and use them
- how to size things
- how to read instructions, diagrams, and figures
*- how to anticipate what your potential customer or client would want
  from any piece of jewelry*

Try to learn things in a developmental order. Start with beginner projects, graduate to advanced beginner and intermediate, then finally, to advanced. Take your time. Don't rush to the finish line. You will learn more and be a better designer for it.

Try to learn things by groupings or categories. Vary things. You might start by doing the same project using three different stringing materials. You might try doing the same project using different types of clasps. You might create a compositional arrangement, and then play by rearranging or by changing out certain components or colors for others. Comparative learning is a very strong teacher.

Types of Tools Needed To Get Started

Scissors	Ruler	Work Surface or Pad
Chain nose pliers (inside of jaws smooth)	Crimping pliers	Bead board
	Hammers and mallets	Round nose pliers
Flat Nose Pliers	Steel block plate	Ring, Jump Ring, and
Side Cutters	Doming block, anvil	bracelet mandrels
Flush Cutters	Sizing cones	Needles, wax
Tweezers and Awl	Hand held torch and fire-proof work surface	Jeweler's saw and blades
Assorted sizes of hard wire, cable wire, bead cord and bead thread, elastic string	Bead stoppers / clamps	Good lighting
	Color wheel	Comfortable seating

Reading Patterns and Instructions

Infuriating! That's how many people, beginners and advanced alike, feel when they try to understand patterns and instructions.

Know up-front that most diagrams and figures are poorly drawn, and most instructions are poorly written. The instructors who write these often leave out critical steps – especially for new beaders and jewelry makers who are unfamiliar with many of the things these instructors assume that you know. Most often, they leave out critical information showing you the pathway, and how to negotiate that pathway, from where you are to where you are going next. It's obvious to the instructor. But not so obvious to you.

In patterns, this *"where-am-I, where-am-I-going-next"* information is frequently unclear or omitted. You did Step 1 OK. You understand what Step 2 is about. But you don't know how to get from Step 1 to Step 2.

Othertimes, the patterns are overly complex, often, in the editorial interest of reducing the number of printed pages. Instead of showing a separate pattern or diagram for each step, the editors frequently try to show you three, four, five or more steps in the same diagram. So you have a bird's nest of lines, and a spider-web's road map – and you're nowhere.

I tell people, that you need to re-write the instructions and re-draw the patterns or diagrams in a way you personally understand. This is very helpful.

Self Esteem – Making Choices

Crafts enhance people's self esteem. This is good.

You make a piece of jewelry. People like it, and express this to you.

However, sometimes people let the craft substitute for their personal identities. Friends and family praise the jewelry, thus praise the jewelry maker. It's nice to have your ego stroked. But you need to remember that there is more to you than the pieces you have made.

And you don't want to put yourself into a tightly bounded box, where you shy away from risks. You don't want to find yourself making the same piece over and over again, afraid to try something else, should someone not like it. You also don't want to find yourself making kit after kit after kit, without any personalizing of someone else's creativity, or better yet, without venturing off to create your own patterns and ideas.

The primary source of "self-esteem" should come from within you. Not external to you. When someone says they don't like your design, or they don't like your choice of colors, they are not saying they don't like you. They like you, or they wouldn't express an honest opinion about your work.

The true Artist and Designer come from this inner place. They are able to bring their integral sense of self-esteem, a part of their very being, to the fore, when designing and constructing a piece of jewelry as art.

Their choices are informed by a sense of self. And that sense of self is self-validated within each piece of jewelry they create. No matter what anyone else thinks – good, bad or indifferent.

Selling vs. Keeping: Saying Good-Bye

It is so difficult to part with pieces you have made. There is a natural attraction. You have poured time, money, and effort towards completing them. You put off other things you could have done, in order to finish them.

I remember submitting an entry to a Swarovski Create Your Own Style contest. First, all I had to send was a picture and a write-up. This was exciting – the anticipation of winning, connecting on some level to Swarovski – like connecting to a celebrity.

And I waited and waited to hear from them. And I did. One day an email popped up on my computer, indicating that I had made the semi-finals. The next step was to send in the actual piece.

My initial elation soon deteriorated into a type of grief. I had spent over 150 hours and over $1500.00 creating this piece. I did not want to let it go. Once sent, Swarovski kept them. I knew I wouldn't get it back.

Although I could have wrapped and packaged my piece in a part of a day, it took me a week. I'd wrap and unwrap. Put it in one display box, then decide that wasn't good enough. Another display box, and didn't like how it sat in the box. Some reconfiguring the positioning, and then I had to close the box. Wanted to see it one more time, then closed the lid again.

I put the display box into the shipping box, but couldn't seal it up. I left the shipping box open and sitting on a table in my studio. Had to see the piece several more times.

Then, I didn't like the way the display box sat in the shipping box. Changed shipping boxes. Tried setting the display box several different ways.

Finally closed the shipping box. Labeled it clearly. Printed the shipping label. Felt I needed more documentation and insurance, should the box get lost.

Took a deep breath. Drove the box to the UPS office. Dropped it off.

And felt like I had lost my best friend. I was scared. Empty. Totally disconnected from the excitement of getting selected as a semi-finalist by Swarovski.

Finding Compatriots: You Need A Support System

While you bead and make jewelry alone a good part of the time, it's no fun to always bead and make jewelry alone. It's good to become part of a support network – even build your own.

Some people form informal beading or jewelry making groups, and hold meetings once or twice a week at their homes. Others join more formal local bead societies and clubs and collaborations. People take classes and workshops. They find like-minded people in social networks and forums and message groups online, and share images and stories with them.

You will also find compatriots by attending bead and jewelry shows. Some are local. Some are geared to a national audience, like a convention.

There are national societies and guilds for jewelry and beading, which you can join. You can find these listed online.

You learn a lot from compatriots. Everyone does things just a little differently. Everyone's interests take you places you never thought of before.

FOOTNOTES

[1] Olga Khazan, *Find Your Passion' Is Awful Advice*, The Atlantic, 7/12/18
As referenced in:
https://www.theatlantic.com/science/archive/2018/07/find-your-passion-is-terrible-advice/564932/ 7/12/18

GETTING STARTED
2e. CULTIVATING YOUR PRACTICE

"Crystal Excitement", FELD, 2004

Guiding Questions:
(1) What does success as a designer mean to you?
(2) How do you explain what you do as a jewelry designer to others unfamiliar with the profession?
(3) What does "good organization' mean?
(4) What happens when I introduce my work publicly?
(5) How do I build criticality and legitimacy into my practice?
(6) How do I find balance between creativity and production, and between jewelry making and all the other parts of my life?
(7) What are the different career paths which can utilize my jewelry design skills?

Key Words:		
success	*criticality*	*career paths*
finish	*legitimacy*	*multi-venue approach*
organization	*balance between creativity and production*	*creative marketplace*
your practice	*coherency*	*influencers*
introduce work publicly	*work space*	*collaboration*
product development	*bookkeeping / accounting*	*client base*
product distribution	*marketing and selling*	*self-care*
product promotion	*inventory*	*managing attention*
	innovation vs. standardization	*push-pull*
		visibility

Abstract:
It can be difficult to define the scope of jewelry design. There's your inspiration and intent. The availability and your current knowledge about materials and techniques. There are the perceptions and desires of your various audiences. What you do as an artist and designer may involve several different kinds of tasks. Your Practice, and how you define and live it depends on gaining some clarity in terms of (1) Having a definition of what success as a designer means to you, (2) Developing a production (and marketing) routine,

(3) Creating a consistent and coherent body of work, (4) Being very organized, (5) If selling or exhibiting, taking a multi-venue approach, (6) Developing a Criticality where you are reflecting, evaluating, validating, legitimizing, being very metacognitive, (7) Self-Care and finding balance in your life.

GETTING STARTED:
CULTIVATING YOUR PRACTICE
Building that relevance into your work

What Is Your Practice?

What do you (or will you) say to people who ask you what you do for a living? When you say, "Jewelry Designer", you probably get a "That's nice" or "Oh, you make jewelry," and perhaps a far-away look. Most people can't imagine exactly what you do. Their images and experiences with jewelry and what it can look like, the materials available to use, the techniques applied are somewhat limited. Not everyone knows you can craft jewelry by hand, not just by machine.

It can be difficult to define the scope of jewelry design. There's your inspiration and intent. The availability and knowledge about materials and techniques. There are the perceptions and desires of your various audiences. What you do as an artist and designer may involve several different kinds of tasks. Your process may be conventional or unconventional. And it's not just the "What do you do" aspect of the question, but the concurrently implied "Can you make a living at this" aspect of the question, as well. It's almost as if they are about to say, "What do you really do?"

The response you want to come up with is your personal understanding and recognition about your passion for design, and all the things that drive this passion. Your excitement in telling your story will become infectious, and, while they still might not comprehend everything you do or the how and why you do it, they will certainly see that you are a jewelry designer, one who is intent on achieving some level of success within the profession.

Your Practice, and how you define and live and succeed in it depends on gaining some clarity in terms of[1]...,

    (1) Having a definition of what *Success* as a designer means to you

    (2) Developing a production (and marketing) *Routine*

    (3) Creating a *Consistent and Coherent body of work*

    (4) Being very *Organized*

    (5) If selling or exhibiting, taking a *Multi-Venue Approach*

    (6) Developing a *Criticality* where you are reflecting, evaluating, validating, legitimizing, being very metacognitive

    (7) *Self-Care* and finding balance in your life

(1) Defining Success

Not every designer is going to define success in the same way. In fact, there will be dramatic differences. Some people may want to focus on applying their creative skills. They search for artistic excellence. Others may want to make money. They want monetary gain and, perhaps, financial stability. Still others may want to be a part of a social network of other creative types. They might want a support network, seek collaboration, or find recognition.

Some people want to do this full time, and others part time. Some want to earn enough money to pay for their habit; others want to make money to supplement their income; still others want to make enough money to be self-supporting.

Success is all about you. What do you want? How much effort and organization will it take to match your ambition and goals? How much time and money do you want to invest in your education and development? Are you aiming to be a crafter, an artist, or a designer?

Success depends on many factors. But key to all, and foremost, is that you brainstorm with yourself, be brutally honest, and list the goals you prefer and want to achieve. Prioritize these. More successful designers find some balance among creativity, business, and recognition. But your ambitions may be different, and just as legitimate in finding success.

Know that achieving any level or definition of success will take time and effort, often sacrifices. The jewelry designer should set expectations and work strategies accordingly.

(2) The Day-To-Day Routine

While everyone has their own process and their own flow, more successful designers establish some kind of work routine. They allocate a specific work space within which to create. They keep their inventory of parts and finished pieces very organized. And, key here, they set up a schedule for (a) researching ideas and inspirations, (b) working in a production mode, (c) presenting or marketing their work to others, (d) reflecting on their practice.

Periodically, evaluate your process. Are there things you can do to improve your efficiency or effectiveness? Can you better manage your productivity? Do you want to emphasize jewelry which are *one-offs*, or do you want to make many copies of the same piece? Do you work better at a certain time of day, or day of the week? Have you programmed in *breaks*? Is there a comfortable balance between work time and break time? Would it be helpful to take the last 15 minutes of your day to set up for tomorrow?

Plot out your weekly schedule on a calendar or spreadsheet. Set some objectives about how many pieces you want to finish per week or per month. If interruptions, say from friends or family, get too annoying, make them aware of your schedule and ask them to help you protect your creative time and space.

It is important to note here that there is a fundamental tension between *productivity* and *creativity*. The former tries to put you in a box. The latter tries to keep you from getting stuck in a box. This can be frustrating.

Yet artists and designers, overall, who are able to provide some structure to their creative time tend to be more successful in their practice. These artists and designers set a routine and schedule for both *making jewelry time* as well as *thinking about designing time*. They also structure in time for introducing their ideas publicly as well as reflecting on the efficiency and effectiveness of everything they do – tangible and otherwise.

(3) Creating A Consistent and Coherent Body Of Work

Jewelry designers are free to create whatever they want. And usually, novices would be wise to try out a lot of different techniques, and use a lot of different materials, and create a lot of different designs. Think of this as play and experimentation. It's how you learn to be a designer.

But as you develop more as a designer, it makes more sense to set some limits and begin to define a personal style, coherency and brand identity.

Your style reflects what you are passionate about. It may focus on a particular technique, material or design. Or it may focus on integrating and combining several things. But with all the things you do, there is some coherence to it. It becomes more associated and identified with you and you become more recognized with it. The consistency ties you to your work.

This doesn't limit variation and creativity in your work. It primarily means that wearers and buyers and collectors of your jewelry can sense the artist's hand, that is you, reflected by the pieces you create.

Coherency has several dimensions to it. The designer achieves a level of coherency in how the majority of these dimensions *(listed below), not necessarily all dimensions*, are reflected in any one piece. Thus, the designer still has a lot of room for variation in their work and style.

These *dimensions of coherency* about which designers may be selective include,

- The choice of materials
- The choice of techniques
- How pieces are presented, displayed, organized, situated with other pieces
- How pieces and collections are named
- Packaging
- Color palettes

- The use of forms and themes
- Personalization, differentiation and originality
- The use of negative vs. positive space
- The use of point, line, plane and shape
- Arrangements, placements, distributions of design elements within the piece
- Control over light, shadow, bright, dull
- The marriage and resulting tradeoffs between aesthetics and functionality
- Silhouettes
- Quality in materials, quality in craftsmanship, quality in finish, quality in presentation
- The degree the piece reflects your business name and emotionally connects to your brand identity

(4) Organization

Good organization involves

(a) Inventory *(how you organize, track and replenish it)*

(b) Work space *(how you create productive areas for work, business and creative reflection)*

(c) Bookkeeping and accounting *(how you manage your finances)*

(d) Business logistics, such as researching venues, getting to venues, tracking your pieces, shipping, product development and distribution, marketing, web-presence and social media management *(how you manage the other business aspects of what you do)*

Good organization will help you avoid a lot of frustration and disarray. Learn to use spreadsheets and apps. These will save you a lot of time and minimize a lot of grief and worry. You'll have more time to create, and need less time to keep things organized and up-to-date.

Think of and treat your inventory of materials, and all that it takes to achieve a satisfactory level of quality in your pieces, as *investments*, rather than *costs*. It gets more productive to reflect on *What Is Your Return On Investment (ROI)?*, rather than on *What Does This Cost?* This will go a long way in clarifying for you what is important, and what is less so, and how to prioritize things in the face of limits on time and other resources.

Your workspace might be a part of a room, it might be an entire room in your home, or even a complete studio space outside your home.

Divide your "work space" into three distinct areas: where you create, where you handle all the business things, and where you relax, think and reflect.

As you develop your work and related spaces, you should try to anticipate what it will take to scale each of these up, as you get more established as a jewelry designer. Are your spreadsheets and computer apps robust enough to grow with your developing career and business, as well?

**(5) A Multi-Venue Approach
Towards The Creative Marketplace**

Successful jewelry designers are able to get the visibility and legitimacy they want and deserve. They know what to expect when exposing their work publicly within the creative marketplace.

They are good at communicating their ideas and their value, when approaching art and craft show vendors, stores and boutiques, galleries, and buyers and collectors, or applying for art grants or doing demonstrations. They are able to get articles written about them in blogs, newspapers, magazines and jewelry editorials. And, very importantly, they use a multi-venue approach (*diversification*) when introducing their jewelry into the marketplace. At a minimum, this multi-venue approach will include both an on-line strategy and a bricks-and-mortar strategy.

Legitimacy as an artist requires massive exposure, most often in diverse locations and venues. It is unusual for a single venue or location, whether you are looking for exhibitions or for sales, to be sufficient for a designer to achieve that needed legitimacy and become successful. You will need to have your jewelry pieces in many venues.

There are many online directories and other resources to help you find the wide variety of venues useful to the further development of your jewelry design career.

What To Expect When Exposing Your Work Publicly

No jewelry designer works in a vacuum, and no piece of jewelry is complete until it has been shared with an audience.

No wearer or purchaser of jewelry is going to see the piece as merely an object of adornment. They will interact with the piece in a much more intimate way, and very much so influenced by the jewelry creator and all the choices made in the design.

Part of the jewelry designer's development as a professional involves an ability to anticipate and understand how various audiences express desire and how various audiences judge a piece of jewelry to be finished and successful. Jewelry is here to amaze and intrigue. It is here to entice someone to wear it, purchase it, show it around. It is here to share the inspiration and prowess of the designer with those who see, feel, touch and inhabit it.

The more successful designer takes the time to explore how an audience is engaged with the piece. The designer learns insights in how any piece of jewelry evokes emotions and resonates with others. The designer is very sensitive to the experience people have at the point of purchase or gifting. Finish and presentation are very important. Acquiring jewelry is special and unique a process. Jewelry is not something we must have to meet some innate need; rather, it is something we desire because it stirs something in us.

Approaching Stores and Galleries

Although some jewelry designers may feel uneasy mixing art with business, for most it is a necessity. Yet, you do not have to sacrifice *wonder* for *reality*. Most designers sell their pieces, so recognizing the things about coordinating art with business become very important.

Typically small stores and boutiques, websites and online sales platforms, and galleries will sell your jewelry, either outright, or on consignment. Their goal is to turn a profit, and they are at greater risk than the artist. That means their interests, in most cases, take precedence over those of the artist. It is the venue that displays, promotes, prices, trains employees to talk about your jewelry to customers, and keeps the pieces clean. Available selling-space is always limited. When your jewelry takes up space in these venues, it is an opportunity cost to the business – they lose the opportunity to carry someone else's work which might be more appropriate to the setting, or might sell better.

There are different types of stores, websites and galleries. Each satisfies a different market niche for jewelry. Each has a different level of understanding about what jewelry really is, and all the choices the jewelry designer has made to design and create each piece.

When approaching stores or galleries to display and sell your pieces, it is critical that the artist understand how these venues function, who their audiences are, and what the attendant risks to them are, should they decide to exhibit and/or sell your pieces.

The first step is to be your authentic, passionate self. Your jewelry will not speak for itself. So, in spite of any feelings of vulnerability you might have when approaching stores and galleries, you will need to talk about yourself and your jewelry. You do not want to feel "salesy" when speaking with business or gallery owners and representatives. You do not want to feel pushy. Or desperate. But you want them to get to *Yes*.

You speak to them on their terms. They want to know the real you. What excites you. The history behind the design choices you make. Your understanding of yourself as an artist, and your understanding of your virtual client, her desires, wants and motivations. How do you connect to your audience through your jewelry?

> *o Who are your best customers likely to be?*
> *o How would you describe them: demographics, shopping behaviors, wants and desires?*
> *o Why are they attracted to your work?*
> *o How and where do they find out about you and your work?*
> *o What is your Getting Started story?*
> *o How would you go about persuading someone to buy a piece of jewelry you made – what's in it for them? How does it connect with them emotionally? How would it make their lives better?*

Do some research ahead of time. The internet has a wealth of information you can pull up. Before you meet with them, get an understanding of the types of jewelry artists and their materials they carry in their venues. These venues are always on the lookout for new talent. They are most likely to say *Yes* to a jewelry designer whose style and materials fit in, but do not duplicate, what they already are showing.

Also research who their customer base is. They are most likely to say *Yes* to a jewelry designer whose audience either mirrors their existing customer base, or incrementally adds to and expands it at the margin. They most likely will not want to spend resources (and thus add risk) by going after a completely new and different customer base.

Push vs. Pull. One more thing. You can either *push* your way in, or use *pull* to get in. For most of us, particularly when we are getting started, have only *push* at our disposal. We might cold call, or set up a formal interview, or initiate a conversation with someone at a gallery opening or art show.

But *pull* always works better. Here we leverage something or someone to get to the right place or person at the right time. An established designer or academic might set up an appointment for you with one of their contacts, for example. You might be wearing one of your pieces and someone comes up to admire it. You might work out an arrangement with an influencer online.

Influencers

In today's world, there is a manic competition for attention (what colloquially is called *eyeballs*). Then, also, a frenetic effort to retain and manipulate that attention. Attention creates value. Often, it is difficult for the individual jewelry artist to get a leg up in this world without some significant help. Again, as mentioned above, if you can use *pull*, you'll go farther, faster than if you have to rely on *push*.

Influencers are one of the backbones of internet culture and one way to use *pull*. Their business model centers on ways to shape everything we do in our lives from how we shop to how we learn to how we dress. Influencers are part micro-celebrity and part entrepreneur. They are opinion leaders and have been able to garner a large audience. They have proven themselves to be able to exploit how people distribute their time and attention.

Influencers typically work on a quid-pro-quo basis. In exchange for some products you give them, they promote them. Sometimes a fee may be involved. They take photos, they wear your jewelry, they interact with audiences, they get your message out on different platforms, they sponsor content.

The Value of Collaboration

It can be so easy for any jewelry designer to get so wrapped up in creating things that they isolate themselves. But this is not the ideal situation.

At a minimum, it is very helpful, and very healthy, to have a support group. People you can talk to and talk things out with. People who can give you good feedback.

It is also very invigorating to collaborate on a project with someone else – *A2A, that is, artist to artist*. You can get an infusion of new ideas, sensibilities and strategies. You can get challenged. You become more self-aware of your own styles and preferences. You come up with new ideas about coordinating your own authentic, creative self with that of someone else.

Maintaining A Client Base

Much of any jewelry designer's success comes down to maintaining a high level of *visibility*. Regularly keeping in touch with your client base is extremely important here.

Keep good documentation about who bought your pieces, when, why, for how much, and their address, email, phone numbers.

Maintain a web presence, either as a unique website, and/or a presence on social media platforms.

Create a mailing/emailing list, and use it frequently.

Have business cards handy at all times.

Do promotions to expand your mailing/emailing lists. Call to actions are very effective, such as offering a *'discount coupon good for the next 7 days'*. Or directing them to see your new pieces online by clicking a link.

Keep them up-to-date about where your pieces may be found, and what you are working on now.

(6) Criticality

Criticality is something you want to build into your Practice. It is not something to avoid or minimize.

Criticality is about making choices. It is about separating and confronting and going beyond your piece in order to build in that relevance jewelry needs as it gets exposed to the public.

Criticality helps you close the distance between the jewelry you create and the person it has been created for.

Criticality aids you in revealing the implications and consequences of all your choices. About materials. About techniques. About colors and patterns and textures and forms. Each form of jewelry requires endless and constant adjustments, and you should be very critically aware of what, why and how.

Criticality is necessary for you to continue to grow and develop as a professional jewelry designer.

Criticality is not a put-down of the artist. Rather it is a way of reflecting, evaluating and being very metacognitive of all the choices made in design and construction, and a lot of what-if envisioning and analysis of possible alternative choices. It is an exploratory thing. It adds understanding and comprehension.

Criticality assists in creating a dialog between artist and all the various audiences with whom the artist interacts. Towards that end, it is helpful to actively bring others into that criticality discussion, where we now have the prospects of many voices merging into a form. It can be difficult to be objective about your own work. And you may not be aware of how the quality of your work stacks up with others, and where it needs to be.

Legitimacy

Your legitimacy as a jewelry designer, your reputation, your visibility, your opportunities, to some degree, flow from this process of criticality. Legitimacy comes from both local and more general validation. Validation results from these processes of critical observation and analysis of your work and of how you conduct yourself within your practice.

Your various audiences that view your work critically, in turn, bring your work in contact with the external world. They look for a high level of coherence within the design and its execution. They describe it critically as to its qualifications for matching desire, establishing appeal, having personal or general value and meaning. For successful jewelry designers, this contagion continues, diffuses, and grows.

Legitimacy engenders a deeper level of confidence among artist, wearer and viewer. The relationships are stimulated, enriched, given more and more value. Jewelry is more than a simple object; it is a catalyst for interaction, for relationships, for engagement, for emotion. Legitimacy results in trust and validation.

With globalization and rapid technological changes, the jewelry designer is confronted with additional burdens, making the effort to achieve legitimacy ever more difficult. That is because these larger forces bring about more and more standardization of jewelry. They rapidly bring fashions and styles to the fore, only to scrap them, in the seemingly blink of an eye, for the next hot thing. They channel images of jewelry pieces around and around the world taking on a sameness, and lowering people's expectations to what jewelry could be about.

If the products around the world are essentially the same, then the only thing the customer will care about is price. They won't care who made it. They won't care about quality.

Innovation begins to disappear. With its disappearance, the role of the jewelry designer diminishes. The jewelry designer becomes more a technician with no professional identity or concerns. The jewelry simply becomes the sum of its parts – the market value of the beads, metals and other components. There are few, if any, pathways to legitimacy.

That's not what we want. And that makes it ever more important that jewelry designers see themselves as professionals, and develop their disciplinary literacy – fluency, flexibility and originality in design. Aspects of design which cannot be globalized. Or standardized. Or accomplished without the work, knowledge, skills, understandings and insights of a professional jewelry designer.

(7) Finding Balance – Self Care

Making jewelry and living a creative life can wear and tear on both your physical, as well as mental, health. It's important that you have a plan of self-care and balance that you have thought about and structured ahead of time.

Take breaks. Play. Experiment. Take walks. Don't isolate yourself. Develop a support system.

Exercise. Take good care of your hands, finger nails, wrists, arms, neck, back and eyes. If you need to read with glasses, then you need to make jewelry with glasses. There are lots of different tools specific to different situations – use them all. Elastic wrist bands, thumb-support gloves, elbow bands do great to preserve your fingers, wrists and elbows. There are lots of ergonomic tools and chairs and lighting. With a lot of metalsmithing and lampworking, you'll need goggles, perhaps special lenses to filter out the glare of torch flames. Make these your friends.

There will be creative aspects to what you do, and administrative aspects to what you do. Find some balance between your right brain and your left brain.

Spend a lot of time feeding your creative well with ideas, inspirations, motivations and a deep appreciation for what artists do well.

Take some time to explore new materials, techniques and technologies.

There will be slow times and seasonal ups and downs. Plan ahead of time how you will occupy yourself during slow periods.

There will be times you will have designer's block. You will be stuck, usually a difficulty getting started, or if your piece is getting developed over a long period of time, some difficulty staying motivated. Develop strategies you can refer to on how to stay motivated, and on how to stop yourself from sabotaging your progress. It is important to know what you can and cannot control.

Train yourself with a mindset for rejection. Not everyone will like what you do. Not everyone will want to wear or buy the pieces you've invested your heart and soul in. That's not your problem. It's their problem. Don't make it yours.

Get involved with your profession.

Finding A Job Which Utilizes Your Jewelry Making Experience

There are actually many career pathways for people who have backgrounds in jewelry making and bead working. Besides the obvious pathways of making jewelry to sell, or teaching jewelry making, there are still many job and career opportunities for you.

You may have to do a little more leg work, and a little more tree-shaking. Don't assume, however, when the linear pathway is blocked, that all pathways are blocked. They are not.

Finding jobs and pathways
utilizing your skills as a jewelry designer...

Jewelry maker	Custom designer
Illustrator	Engraver
Fashion designer	Sales
Stylist	Merchandising
Metalsmith	Website design
Teacher	Data analyst
Lapidary	Grants writer/reviewer
Gemologist	Program director
Jewelry repair	Video instructor or host
Wood worker	Jewelry assessor
Fiber artist	Display and Packaging
Lampworking and glass blowing	Influencer
Physical and Occupational Therapist	Writer
Counseling	Business Developer

Some types of jobs/careers which might use your talents....

There are a lot of private companies, nonprofit agencies, government agencies, and foundations and philanthropic agencies that work with disadvantaged groups, and need people to provide technical assistance to these groups. These groups might be inner city. They might be rural. They might be overseas.

Very often, projects these businesses and organizations work on have a craft-angle to them. They may need people to teach crafts, to teach people to transfer their craft skills into marketable skills, or to assist people in applying for loans to start up businesses, usually small loans and usually things associated with selling crafts.

Banks have found it profitable to make "micro-loans". These loans are very small amounts, and usually given to women in developing countries, to help them leverage their skills — often craft skills — to make a business out of them. Banks need personnel to
- Develop loan forms, documentation and procedures
- Find opportunities for making these loans
- Working with people to teach them how to apply for these loans
- Working with people to teach them how to be more accountable with loan moneys
- Working with people to teach them how to translate their craft skills into marketable skills (called *transfer of technology*). Often this means helping them find resources to get materials, make choices about materials and what would be most cost-effective, and how to market their products
- Working with people to find markets for, and otherwise promote, their products
- Helping people form cooperatives so that they can buy materials more cheaply, and sell and market their products cooperatively

Government and International Agencies need people to....
- Determine where — what communities, what demographics — they can most likely leverage local talents to better people's lives. Crafts, particularly beading and jewelry making, provide very useful talents around which to leverage
- Evaluate local technologies — and these include all craft technologies — in terms of readiness and/or capability for cost-effective technology transfer
- Do some community organizing to make local people aware of governmental assistance (or other assistance), and to help them complete applications for this assistance
- Evaluate these kinds of programs to determine success, and make recommendations about how to increase these successes
- Document craft technologies, particularly among native, tribal, or isolated groups that are in danger of becoming extinct
- Similarly, to create ways to preserve craft technologies which are in danger of becoming extinct, or which became extinct a long time ago, and which be restored. A good example is how South Korea restored the art of celadon pottery making, or China's work at preserving Yixing Tea Pot making.

Military Agencies do similar things as governmental ones, except from a slightly different perspective. They want to know, in an anthropological sense, how people value different local technologies — including craft technologies –, and which ones can military and related civilian advisors assist the locals with, to improve their economy and security.

Philanthropic Foundations have many missions. One mission is to improve and secure the health, welfare, and social economy of particular areas or population groups. Crafts are one way of accomplishing this, particularly if working with disadvantaged populations or areas.
Crafts are things people do all the time, that are attractive as products (and services if you are teaching), improve the quality of life, and form the roots of good businesses — especially start-ups.

Another mission of Philanthropic organizations is to pre-test different strategies for social and economic development. Again crafts, and beads especially, can form the basis of many strategies for business development, empowerment of minorities and women, assistance for the elderly, technology transfer, and the like.

Philanthropic organizations need people who can…
- Develop grants, rules and applications
- Find community organizations to apply for these grants
- Evaluate the success of grants
- Work with academics and consultant experts to generate experimental ideas to be tested through grants
- Work with local, state and national government agencies to find cost-sharing ways of testing out these "ideas"
- In similar way, find and negotiate public-private partnerships towards this end

Information technology and website development companies, with Google a prime example, are in the business of translating reality into tables of data that can easily be accessed and assessed. These types of companies need people who can
- Translate craft terms and activities into categories for which data can be consistently collected, organized, stored and analyzed
- Work with museums and galleries which buy, own, exhibit, store or display crafts, to develop ways to collect and categorize routine data on these collections and their importance to different types of people and groups
- Sell the use of these craft-specific databases to companies or individuals that will use them
- Work with craft magazines, museums, schools, galleries and the like to help standardize some of the terminologies and valuations associated with various crafts, to make it easier to collect and sort data about them
- Assist craft artists in development of websites
- Assist craft artists in marketing their websites, especially through social media sites
- Develop blogs
- Develop advertising and marketing materials
- Develop packaging and branding materials

- o   Digitize images of craft items

Museums, Galleries and Libraries employ craft artists to…
- o   Catalog and digitize collections
- o   Document quality of items
- o   Restore aged or otherwise damaged pieces
- o   Write brochures and promotional materials
- o   Organize exhibits
- o   Raise funds for exhibits
- o   Advocate for funds among government agencies and philanthropic groups
- o   Organize a "crafts" section where none has existed before
- o   Promote fine crafts
- o   Organize a craft show to raise money and/or awareness

Many museums, galleries and libraries have tons of things in storage that have only loosely been documented, and need much more documentation and organization.

Non-Profit Groups employ all kinds of people with all kinds of backgrounds. They always need help with many fund-raising or program-targeting things. Your craft knowledge can play a very useful role here.

For example, take your local breast cancer society. Think of all the kinds of craft-type things you can make, and for which they can sell, to raise money. You could organize a craft brain trust among your friends, and turn out item after item with breast cancer awareness themes and colors. Or you could scour the internet for breast cancer awareness craft items, and make them work for you. And you could repeat this success for many other local nonprofit groups.

One of my friends went to the Atlanta Gift Show, and identified vendors that had products that could easily be adapted for breast cancer awareness. She worked out with each one what the minimum orders would be, how much lead time would be needed between placing an order and receiving the merchandise, and price. Then she went to local breast cancer groups and presented them with the options. She added 15% to the prices as her commission. These organizations fund raise all the time, and are in major need of new things to sell and promote. My friend had to lay out very little money — basically the cost of a trip to Atlanta, some phone calls and paperwork — and generated a very lucrative business for herself.

I remember spending some time in Sloan Kettering Memorial Hospital in New York City. This hospital specializes in cancer treatment. I was observing patient activities. One of these activities involved volunteers pushing a cart around with various craft activities for patients to do.

Most of the patients in the rooms in the Ward I was on could barely move their bodies, arms and hands. They were very medicated, and had many needles and IV's stuck into them during their stay. All the craft projects on these carts required considerable manual dexterity — knitting, beading with seed beads, crocheting. The volunteers would cheerily come into the room, announce themselves, and ask if the patient wanted any of these fun crafts to do. The patients would shake their heads No, and grunt. The patients could barely move. And the volunteers left the room, unconcerned.

I took a trip to FAO Schwartz — the toy store — and came back with sets of interlocking building blocks. The blocks were made from different colors of plastic. They were different shapes. A patient could easily hold one or two pieces in their hands without requiring much manual dexterity. The pieces fit together easily by interlocking two pieces, where a slot had been cut out in each. These were a big hit on the Ward. They allowed creativity, without much manual dexterity. The pieces were large enough, that the patient could manipulate them with their hands, and not worry about losing any, if they dropped to the floor.

In **hospitals and health care settings**, I've helped create programs to assist occupational therapists with improving manual dexterity with the elderly, therapists with improving attention spans with children, conducting memory agility tests with patients, and many more programs, utilizing crafts materials and technics.

There are plenty of social and community problems to solve, many different kinds of businesses and organizations responsible for solving these problems, and many solutions which require crafts — materials or technologies which are workable, do-able, saleable, and implementable. There most likely won't be advertised positions for these kinds of things. But you would be surprised how easy it can be to create your own job opportunities and ones which utilize your craft experiences and knowledge.

When Approaching These Potential Employers and Consultants, Be Sure To...

1. Be able to clearly define how your craft knowledge/experience can help your prospective employer solve some of her/his (NOT YOUR) problematic situations.
2. Research prospective employers, their websites and marketing materials. Identify the key words and buzz words in their materials. Be sure to include these in your written and oral presentations to them.
3. Approach the prospective employer by phone or in person first. Then follow-up with a resume and cover letter. Don't assume that, because you can make the intellectual link between job and solution, that the employer will see this link when reading a resume. You'll probably have to educate the employer a bit. This really doesn't take much effort.
4. Cite examples of what kinds of things you can do. If you can identify other programs or individuals with success stories, do so.
5. If you make your "job search" also a "mission to educate people about crafts", you'll be surprised how much energy and excitement you bring to the job interview situation.

Now that you have gotten started in your jewelry designing career, you will need to think about what jewelry really is, and you will need to learn in-depth about materials and techniques.

FOOTNOTES

(1) Horejs, Jason. "5 Strategies Successful Artists Follow to Thrive in Their Careers," RedDotBlog, 2/21/19.
As referenced in:
https://reddotblog.com/5-strategies-successful-artists-follow-to-thrive-in-their-careers/

SECTION 3:

WHAT IS JEWELRY

3. WHAT IS JEWELRY, *Really*?

"Tibetan Dreams", Feld, 2010

Guiding Questions:
(1) What is it about jewelry that people see and value enough to want to buy it and wear it?
(2) What are the expressive qualities, roles and powers of jewelry?
(3) What are the problems different conceptions or definitions of jewelry present, and what kinds of responses or solutions can jewelry designers come up with?
(4) How does jewelry convey meaning?
(5) What role(s) does jewelry play in people's lives?
(6) Is jewelry more an object or an action / interaction?
(7) How does jewelry arbitrate how people interrelate, interact, and communicate?
(8) How does jewelry assist people in not feeling alone?

Key Words:	*forms*	*sensation*
jewelry	*materials*	*functionality*
object	*design elements*	*aesthetics*
content / meaning	*inspirations*	*value / desire*
action / intent	*techniques*	*order / chaos*
dialectic	*arrangements / composition*	*shared understandings*
communication	*public presentations*	*psychological self*
	exhibitions	

Abstract:

We create and wear jewelry because we do not want to feel alone. But "not wanting to feel alone" can mean different things to different people. People want to feel a connection, and jewelry is an important tool or signifier for them. The jewelry designer must have insight here. The designer needs to understand what jewelry really is in order to make the kinds of successful choices about forms, materials, design elements, inspirations, techniques, arrangements, public presentations and exhibitions and the like. Why do people touch it, wear it, buy it, display it, share it, collect it? There are different frameworks, that is different types of evidence or lenses, from which the designer might draw such understanding, including the sensation of jewelry as OBJECT, CONTENT, INTENT or DIALECTIC. All these lenses share one thing in common – communication. Although jewelry can be described in the absence of communicative interaction, the designer can never begin to truly understand what jewelry really is without some knowledge about its creation and without somehow referencing the designer, the wearer, the viewer and the context.

WHAT IS JEWELRY, Really?

Simply put, we create and wear jewelry because *we do not want to feel alone.*

But *"not wanting to feel alone"* can mean different things to different people. People want to feel a connection, and jewelry is an important tool or signifier for them. The jewelry designer, in order to make the best choices and the most strategic choices throughout the process of designing a piece of jewelry, requires some detail and clarity here. What does it mean to say that we create and wear jewelry *so we do not want to feel alone*?

We might want to reaffirm that we are similar (or different) than someone else or some other group or culture. We might want to signal some connection (or disconnection or mal-connection) with a higher power or mystical source or sense of well-being or with some idea, concept or meaning. We might want to express an intent or feeling or emotion.

We might want to differentiate what it means to be yourself relative to something else, whether animate or inanimate, functional or artistic, part of a dialectic conversation with self or other. We might want to signal or differentiate status, intelligence, awareness, and resolution. We might want to separate ourselves from that which is sacred and that which is profane.

Whatever the situation, jewelry becomes something more than simple decoration or adornment. It becomes more than an object which is worn merely because this is something that we do. It becomes more than a functional object used to hold things together. It is communicative. It is connective. It is intentional. And concurrently, it must be functional and appealing and be seen as the result of an artist's application of technique and technology.

The word *jewelry* derives from the Latin *"jocale"* meaning plaything. It is traditionally defined as a personal adornment or decoration. It is usually assumed to be constructed from durable items, though exceptions are often made for the use of real flowers. It is usually made up of materials that have some perceived value. It can be used to adorn nearly every part of the body.

Prehistoric Necklaces 40000 B.C

One of the earliest evidences of jewelry was that of a Neanderthal man some 115,000 years ago. What was it – and we really need to think about this and think this through – which made him craft the piece of jewelry and want to wear it? Mere decoration? Did it represent some kind of status? Or religious belief? Or position or role? Or sexuality and sensuality? Or was it symbolic of something else? Was this a simplified form or representation of something else?

Did this Neanderthal have concerns about craft and technique? Did the making of it require some special or innovative technology? Did the cost of materials come into play? Was this an expression of art? Self? Power? A show of intelligence and prowess? A confirmation of shared beliefs, experiences and values? Was it something he made himself, or was it something given to him as a gift or token of recognition?

Picture yourself there at this very moment. What happened at the point this Neanderthal man put this piece of jewelry on? Did this reduce or increase social and cultural barriers between himself and others? Did this define a new way of expression or a new way of defining the self? Did this impact or change any kind of outcome? Did this represent a divergence between craft and art? Was this piece of jewelry something that had to be worn all the time? Were the purposes and experiences of this Neanderthal man similar to why and how we design and adorn ourselves with jewelry today?

We know that this Neanderthal man was not the last person to wear a piece of jewelry. Jewelry continued in importance over time. Jewelry mattered. It was an object we touched. And it was an object we allowed to touch our bodies. The object had form. The form encapsulated meaning. We allowed others to view the jewelry as we wore it, and when we did not.

Making and wearing jewelry became very widespread about 5,000 years ago, especially in India and Mesopotamia, but worldwide as well. While some cultures banned jewelry or limited its forms and uses (*see medieval Japan or ancient Rome, for example*), they could not maintain these restrictions over time. People want to support the making of jewelry, the wearing of it, the exhibiting of it in public, and the accumulating of it. People want to touch it. Display it. Comment about it. Talk about it with others. Collect it, trade it, buy it, sell it.

As jewelry designers, we need to understand the why's ... Why make jewelry at all? Why develop different techniques and use different materials and come up with different arrangements? Why do people want to wear jewelry and buy jewelry? How does jewelry fulfill the passions of the designer and the desires of people who want to buy it and wear it?

We observe that jewelry is everywhere, worn by all types of people, on various parts of the body, in many different kinds of situations. Jewelry must possess a kind of inherent value for the artist, the wearer, the viewer, the buyer, the collector, and the society as a whole.

So we have to continue to wonder, Why is jewelry so coveted universally? Why is it important? How is understanding *'What Jewelry Is Really'* necessary for making the kinds of successful choices about forms, materials, design elements, inspirations, techniques, arrangements, public presentations and exhibitions and the like?

Let us review the range of definitions and justifications for jewelry before fine-tuning any ideas and conclusions. Each understanding leads us in different directions when filling in the blanks of this constructive phrasing:

Jewelry means to me .... therefore,
these are the types of choices I need to make as a designer
to know my pieces are finished and successful,
including things like ....

These different definitional frameworks about jewelry are things characterized by sensations the jewelry evokes in designer, wearer and viewer. These frameworks, or sources of evidence, influence how the designer thinks about and organizes the jewelry making work to be done.

These frameworks for defining what jewelry really is include,

SENSATION OF JEWELRY AS *OBJECT*:
1. **ROUTINE: Merely something that we do with little or no reflection**
2. **MATERIAL: Objects that we use as materials characterized or sorted by design elements, such as color, pattern, texture, volume, weight, reflective and refractive properties**
3. **ARRANGEMENT AND FORMS: Materials are sorted by various Principles of Composition into arrangements and forms, expressing things like rhythm, focus, and juxtaposition of lines and planes**
4. **TECHNIQUE: Steps or routines we use to assemble and construct**
5. **FUNCTIONALITY: Things which have a useful purpose and practicality**

SENSATION OF JEWELRY AS *CONTENT*:

6. **MEANING:** Things to which we assign meaning(s), especially where such meaning(s) transcends materials, functions and techniques
7. **VALUE:** Things to which we assign monetary and economic value, particularly materials

SENSATION OF JEWELRY AS *INTENT*:

8. **ORDER OUT OF CHAOS:** A sense-making attempt to control and order the world
9. **SELF-IDENTITY:** An agent of personality

SENSATION OF JEWELRY AS *DIALECTIC*:

10. **INTERACTION AND SHARED UNDERSTANDINGS:** A way to create, confirm and retain connections through intent, interaction, desire, and shared understanding

Yet, no matter what the framework or source of evidence we use to try to make sense about what jewelry really is, all these lenses share one thing in common – jewelry is more than ornament and decoration; it is *sensation* and *communication,* as well. Although we can *describe* jewelry in the absence of knowledge about its creation, we cannot begin to *understand* what jewelry really is without somehow referencing the artist, the wearer, the viewer and the context.

Let's review in more detail each type of *Sensation of Jewelry*, what it is, what it's design implications are.

"Tibetan Dreams", detail, FELD, 2010

SENSATION OF JEWELRY AS *OBJECT*

Too often, ideas about communication and meaning and intent get too messy and complicated. We seek a simpler framework within which to understand what jewelry is all about. We try to fit the idea of jewelry into the confines of a box we call "object".

As an object, it is decoration. Sculptural adornment. Jewelry succeeds as "object" to the extent that everyone everywhere universally agrees to what it is, how it is made, what it is made from, why it was made, and in what ways it is used. This universality in defining and evaluating jewelry helps us not to feel alone.

OBJECT: Jewelry As Something That We Do. Wearing jewelry might simply be something that we do. We put on earrings. We slip a ring onto a finger. We clasp a necklace around our neck or a bracelet around our wrist. It is habit. Routine. Not something to stop and ask why. A necklace is a necklace. An earring is an earring. We mechanically interact with decorative objects we call jewelry.

OBJECT: Jewelry As A Material. Sometimes we want to get a little more specific and describe what this object or 'box' is made of. It is some kind of material. Jewelry encompasses all types of stones and metals, in various shades and colors, and light-impacting properties, which the artist has taken tools to them to shape and sharpen. Sometimes we want to further delineate the character of materials within and around this box. We refer to this as selecting various design elements such as color, pattern, texture.

OBJECT: Jewelry As Arrangements and Forms. Sometimes we want to even further elaborate on our placement of materials within our pieces (thus, objects) in terms of Principles of Composition. These Principles refer to arrangements and organized forms to create movement, rhythm, focal point, balance, distribution. We apply this framework in a static way. Jewelry is reduced to an object, somehow apart from its creator and disconnected from any wearer or viewer.

OBJECT: Jewelry As The Application of Technique(s). We can also understand jewelry as object in a more dynamic sense. It is something which is created by the application of one or more techniques. The techniques are applications of ideas often corralled into routines. The object is seen to evolve from a starting point to a finishing point. As object, it is reduced to a series of organized steps. These steps are disconnected from insight, inspiration, aspiration or desire. There is no human governance or interference.

OBJECT: Jewelry As Function and Practicality. In a similar dynamic way, the object may be seen to have function. It may hold up something, or keep something closed. It may, in a decorative sense, embellish a piece of clothing or secure a hair style. It may assist in the movement of something else. It is not understood to have any meaning beyond its function. As it coordinates the requirements of form to the requirements of function, it plays a supportive, practical role, not a substantive role. As such, it is unimportant. It might allow the wearer to change position of the necklace on the neck. It might better enable the piece to move with the body. But it should not demand much insight or reflection by creator, wearer, or viewer.

"Tibetan Dreams", detail, FELD, 2010

SENSATION OF JEWELRY AS *CONTENT*

However, as we get closer to defining the object as one that is sensed and experienced and which evokes an emotional response, it becomes more difficult to maintain that the object does not reflect meaning, does not result from some kind of thought process and intent, and does not communicate quite a lot about the designer, the wearer, the viewer and the situation. Jewelry when worn and which succeeds becomes a sort of identifier or locator, which can inform the wearer and the viewer about particular qualities or content, such as where you belong, or what you are about, or what your needs are. So we sense jewelry not so much as an object universally understood, but something with more nuance, interest, meaning, and value, with an element of subjective references.

Jewelry without content, after all, can skew to the superficial, boring, monotonous, and unsatisfying. Without meaning and value, jewelry has little to offer.

These shared recognitions and valuing of meanings helps us not to feel alone.

CONTENT: Jewelry As Meaning. Jewelry when worn signals, signifies or symbolizes something else. It is a type of recognizable short-hand. It is a powerful language of definition and expression. By representing meaning, it takes responsibility for instigating shared understandings, such as membership in a group or delineating the good from the bad. It might summarize difficult to express concepts or emotions, such as God, love, loyalty, fidelity. It might be a stand-in marker for status, power, wealth, connection and commitment. It might visually represent the completion or fulfillment of a rite of passage – puberty, adulthood, marriage, birthing, and death.

Sometimes, the sensation of jewelry as meaning derives from energy and powers we believe can transfer from the meaning of the materials the jewelry is made of to ourselves. These might be good luck, or good fortune, or good health, or good love, or good faith or protection from harm. Various gemstones, metals and other materials are seen to have mystical, magical and supernatural qualities that, when touching the body, allow us to incorporate these powers with our own.

CONTENT: Jewelry As Value. When we refer to meaning as having power, sacredness, respect, significance, we are beginning to assign a *value* to it. A sensation of value may emerge from how rare the item is – its material rarity or the rarity of how it was constructed or where it came from or who made it or who was allowed to wear it. It may emerge from how bright it is or the noteworthy arrangement of its elements. Its value may emerge from how pliable or workable the material is. Its value might be set from how tradable it is for other materials, objects, access or activities.

By assigning value, we determine things like importance, uniqueness, appeal, status, need, want, and demand. We establish control over how and how often a piece of jewelry will change hands. We establish some regulation over how individuals in a group, culture or society interact and transact with one another.

"Tibetan Dreams", detail, FELD, 2010

SENSATION OF JEWELRY AS *INTENT*

Someone has to infuse the object with all this content, and this proactive act leads us to the idea of *intent*. Often this imposition of meaning begins with the jewelry artist. Jewelry becomes a means of self-expression. The artist, in effect, tells the world who the artist is, and what the artist wants to happen next.

The artist might be subdued or bold, colorful or monochromatic, simple or complex, extravagant or economical, logical or romantic, deliberate or spontaneous. The artist might be direct or indirect in how meanings get communicated. It is important, in order to understand the meaning of an object, to begin by delineating the artist's inspiration, aspiration and intent.

The jewelry artist begins with nothing and creates something. The unknown, the unknowable, the nothingness is made more accessible.

The artist fills in a negative space with points, lines, planes, shapes, forms and themes. Color, pattern and texture are added. Things get organized and arranged.

Though often unstated, it becomes obvious that of all the possible choices the artist could have made in design, that some choices were ignored and excluded, while others were not. Some negative space is left so. Some positive space has direction, motion, weightiness. Somethings are abstract; other things realistic. These and related choices have implications and consequences.

The question becomes, what influences that artist's selections? Successful jewelry reveals the artist's hand.

Our senses and perceptions of the coherence in the artist's inspiration and intent, as reflected in our interpretations of that artist's jewelry, helps us not to feel alone. We may see coherence as a subjective thing or a universally understood thing. It doesn't matter which. If we believe we can make sense of things because they have a purpose, if the jewelry feels and seems coherent in some way again because we sense it is purposeful and intentional, we feel safe, and that we have reduced the risks in life. We do not feel so left alone.

INTENT: Jewelry As Creating Order Out Of Chaos. Partly, what the artist does is attempt to order the world. The artist looks for clues within him- or herself (inspiration and intent). The artist formulates concepts and a plan for translating inspiration and intent into a design. The artist determines whether to take into account the expectations of others (shared understandings) about what would be judged as finished and successful.

Jewelry is an object created out of chaos and which has an order to it. The order has content, meaning and value. It has purpose and coherency based on color and texture and arrangement. Mass placed within space.

Jewelry as an organized, ordered, coherent object – something out of nothingness -- reflects the hypotheses the artist comes up with about how to translate inspiration into aspiration, and do this in such a way that the derived jewelry is judged positively. The artist anticipates how others might experience and sense the object on an emotional level.

It reflects the shared understandings among artist, wearer and viewer about emotions, desires, inherent tensions and yearnings and how these play out in everyday life.

The artist makes the ordered chaos more coherent, and this coherence becomes contagious through the artist's choices about creative production and design. The artist lets this contagion spread. To the extent that others share the artist's ideas about coherence, the more likely the work will be judged finished and successful. And no one – not the artist, not the wearer, not the viewer, not the buyer, not the collector – will feel alone.

The process of bringing order to chaos continues with the wearer. The wearer introduces the piece of jewelry into a larger context. We have more contagion – what we might call viral. The jewelry as worn causes more, ever-expanding tension and efforts at balance and resolution. There is an effort to figure out the original artist intent and ideas about coherence as reflected in design.

Unsuccessful efforts at design, where the artist's intent becomes obscured, reverse the process, and the object – our piece of jewelry – then brings about *de*coherence. Decoherence may come in the forms of bad feedback, inappropriate feedback, less than satisfying feedback, or no feedback at all.

Decoherence means the wearer may not get that sense of self s/he seeks. S/he may feel less motivated to wear the piece. S/he may store the piece or give the piece away. As this decoherence filters down to the level of the artist, any necessary support in design may be lost. There will be fewer clients, fewer opportunities to display the works publicly, and fewer sales. The artist's motivation may diminish.

INTENT: Jewelry As An Agent of Personality. People wear jewelry because they like it. It becomes an extension of themselves. It is sensed as self-confirming, self-identifying and self-reconfirming. Liking a piece of jewelry gets equated with liking oneself, or as a strategy for getting others to express their like for you. Jewelry makes us feel more like ourselves. We might use jewelry to help us feel emotionally independent, or we might come to rely on jewelry for emotional support and feedback – that positive comment about the jewelry we are wearing --, leading us down the path to emotional dependency.

Jewelry may have personal significance, linking one to their past, or one to their family, or one to their group. It may be a way to integrate history with the present. It is a tool to help us satisfy our need to affiliate.

Jewelry may help us differentiate ourselves from others. It may assist us in standing out from the crowds. Conversely, we may use it to blend into those multitudes, as well.

Jewelry fulfills our needs. If we look at Maslow's Hierarchy of Needs, after meeting our basic physiological needs such as for food and water, and our safety needs, such as for shelter, we can turn to jewelry to meet our additional social needs for love and belonging and self-esteem. Designing and creating jewelry can form an additional basis for our needs for self-actualization.

We may derive our personality and sense of soul and spirit from the qualities we assign the jewelry we wear. We do not merely wear jewelry as some object; more specifically, we *inhabit* jewelry. If ruby jewelry symbolizes passion, we may feel passion when wearing it. We may use jewelry as an expressive display of who we feel we are and want to be seen as in order to attract mates and sexual partners. We use jewelry in a narcissistic way to influence the alignment of the interests and desires among artist, weaver, viewer, buyer, collector, exhibiter, and seller.

In similar ways, we may derive our sense of belief, devotion and faith to a higher power or spiritual being or God from wearing jewelry. It may help us feel more connected to that religious, spiritual something within ourselves. It may remind us to stay on our religious path.

As an agent of our psychological selves, jewelry is used to resolve those core conflicts – Who are we? Why do we exist? How should we relate to other people around us? Jewelry orients us in coming to grips with our *self-perceived* place within critical contradictions around us. Trust and mistrust. Living and dying. Good and evil. Pleasure and pain. Permission and denial. Love and hate. Experience and expectation. Traditional and contemporary. Rational and reasonable.

"Tibetan Dreams", FELD, 2010

SENSATION OF JEWELRY AS *DIALECTIC*

DIALECTIC: Jewelry As Interaction and Shared Understandings. Jewelry is a two-way street. It is a way to create, confirm and retain connections. At its very core, it is interactive and communicative. It is more an *action* than an *object*. Jewelry can start a conversation. Jewelry encapsulates a very public, ongoing matrix of choices and interactions among artist, wearer and viewer, with the purpose of getting responses. It is a dialectic.

The optimum position to view jewelry is on a person's body, where and when its dialectical power is greatest. Again, it is very public, yet concurrently, very intimate. We exhibit jewelry. It forces reaction, response and reciprocity. Jewelry helps us *negotiate, in relatively non-threatening ways,* those critical tensions and contradictions in life, not merely define them.

It very publicly forces us to reveal our values, delineate tensions and contradictions which might result, and resolve all those betwixt and between qualities which occur as the artist, wearer, viewer, marketer, seller, exhibitor and collector try to make sense of it all. Conversely, jewelry, as worn, may signal that any negotiation would be futile, but this is a dialectic, communicative act, as well.

Jewelry expresses or implies things, the relevance of which emerges through interactions. There is an exchange of meaning. There is some reciprocity between the artist expressing an inspiration with the desire for a reaction, and the wearer evaluating the success of the piece and impacting the artist, in return. We have those coherence-contagion-decoherence behavioral patterns discussed above.

Jewelry is persuasive. It allows for the negotiation of influence and power in subtle, often soft-pedalled ways. It helps smooth the way for support or control. Compliance or challenge. Wealth and success or poverty and failure. High or low status. Social recognition. An expression of who you know, and who might know you. Jewelry is a tool for managing the dynamics between any two people.

Jewelry is emotional and feeling, with attempts by the artist to direct these, and with opportunities for others to experience these. It is not that we react emotionally to the beauty of an object. It is not mechanical or fleeting. It is more of a dialectic. The jewelry is an expression of an artist's inspiration and intent. We react emotionally to what we sense as that expression as it resonates from the object itself. This resonance ebbs and flows, waxes and wanes, over time as the object is worn in many different situations.

Jewelry draws attention. It becomes a virtual contract between artist and wearer. The artist agrees to design something that will call attention to the wearer and that wearer's preferred sense of self. The wearer agrees to wear something that reaffirms the artist's insights for all to witness and experience and draw support.

Jewelry may cue the rules for sexual and sensual interactions. Nurturing and desire. Necklaces draw attention to the breasts. Earrings to the ear and neck. Rings to the hands. Jewelry, such as a wedding band, may confirm a relationship, and signal permission for various forms of touching that otherwise would not be appropriate. The silhouettes and placements of jewelry on the body indicate where it may be appropriate for the viewer to place his gaze, and where it would not.

We don't feel alone because we have opportunities to have a dialectic experience – a dialogue between self and artist, self and others, self and self – all catalyzed by the piece of jewelry, and our sensation of all the choices that had to be made in order for it to exist, in order for it to feel coherent, in order for it for fulfill desire, and in order for all of this to somehow feel contagious and resonant. We don't feel alone because the jewelry taps into something inside us that makes us want to wear it, buy it and share it.

Jewelry Ages In Place With Us[2]

Jewelry comforts us as we age in place. The bracelet we got for graduation still worn on an occasion when we are 65. The ring he bought her when she was in her 20's still worn on the day she passed away.
With jewelry, we will never feel alone as we grow older. As our body changes in pallor and texture. As we gain weight or lose weight. As we change our styles of clothing or hair or activity.

This constellation of material objects, distributed across the human body, reflects transformation, movement, growth, and behavior. These reflect the life we live, and how we lived it. These are stories of how we performed our lives over time. They reveal an otherwise unseen perspective on life as the body ages, and we live through time. They show that not all lived lives have been ad libbed.

The jewelry will also show its age over time. Changes in color, perhaps fading, perhaps becoming duller or spotty. A clasp may have been replaced. The piece may have been restrung. It may have been shortened or lengthened. It may have been worn a lot. Or lost for a while. Or given away. Its associative or symbolic value may have changed.

Jewelry is life performed. Both are observable. Both indicative of our place – our aura – in the world around us as time goes on. Both an experience – often changing – of a point of view from the hand that crafted the piece in the first place, and the desires of the person who wore the piece over time. We possess it and wear it so it reminds us that we are not alone.

**Knowing What Jewelry Really Is
Translates Into Artistic and Design Choices**

Knowing what jewelry really is better connects the artist to the various audiences the artist seeks to reach. It results in better outcomes. More exhibits. More sales. More collections. Better self-esteem. Better representation of self in various contexts and situations.

Jewelry asks the designer, the wearer, the viewer, and the buyer to participate in its existence. In a somewhat subtle way, by allowing communication, dialog, evaluation, and emotion, jewelry allows each one not to feel alone. It allows each one to express intent, establish a sense of self, and introduce these intents and self-expressions into a larger social context.

Jewelry judged as finished and successful results from these shared understandings and desires among designer, viewer and wearer, and how these influence their subsequent choices. These choices extend to materials and arrangements. They extend to how the artist determines what is to be achieved, and how the work is talked about and presented to others. These anticipate the reactions of others, beliefs about saleability, assumptions about possible inclusions in exhibitions, knowing what is appealing or collectible.

The designer is always omnipresent in the jewelry s/he creates. The designer, through the jewelry, and how it is worn on the body, to some extent, arbitrates how other sets of relationships interact, transfer feelings, ideas and emotions, reduce ambiguity, influence one another, and make sense of the world around them.

These sets of relationships, through which jewelry serves as a conduit, include:
artist and wearer
wearer and viewer
artist and self
artist and buyer
seller and buyer
artist and seller
seller and client
artist and exhibiter
artist and collector
exhibiter and collector
wearer/buyer and their network of social relationships

In the abstract, jewelry is a simple object. We make it. We wear it. We sell it. We buy it. We exhibit it. We collect it. But in reality, jewelry channels all the artist's and wearer's and viewer's and buyer's energy – the creative sparks, the tensions, the worries, the aspirations, the representations, the assessments of risks and rewards, the anticipations of influence and affect. Jewelry becomes the touchstone for all these relationships. It is transformational. It is a manifestation of their internal worlds. An essence resonant in context. A comforting togetherness, inclusion, reaffirmation.

The better jewelry designer is one who anticipates these shared understandings about what makes a piece of jewelry finished and successful, and can incorporate these understandings within the jewelry design process s/he undertakes. Knowing what jewelry really is forms a critical aspect of what sets jewelry design as a discipline apart from that of art or craft. Knowing what jewelry really is and how it helps us not feel alone forms the basis of the professional identity and disciplinary literacy of the jewelry designer.

FOOTNOTES

[1] Grosz, Stephen, The Examined Life: How We Lose and Find Ourselves, NY: W.W.Norton & Company, 2014.

[2] Pravu Mazumdar, *Jewellery as Performance: on Gisbert Stach's Experiments with Jewellery and Life*, Klimt02, 11/22/2019
　　As referenced in:
　　https://klimt02.net/forum/articles/jewellery-performance-gisbert-stach-pravu-mazumdar?utm_source=phplist1288&utm_medium=email&utm_content=HTML&utm_campaign=Both+art+and+advertisement+propose+what+could+count+as+modern+versions+of+the+ornament+says+Pravu+Mazumdar+and+much+more+at+Klimt02+Newsletter+495

SECTION 4:

MATERIALS, TECHNIQUES AND TECHNOLOGIES

MATERIALS, TECHNIQUES AND TECHNOLOGIES
4a. MATERIALS: *Knowing What To Know*

Beads, Clasps, Stringing Materials, Wire

Guiding Questions:
(1) How do materials establish the character and personality of jewelry? How should they be selected, combined and arranged?
(2) What criteria should you use when selecting materials appropriate to your design and marketing goals?
(3) What types of materials are there?
(4) How do materials differ in terms of their properties?
(5) How does the designer maximize the strengths and minimize the weaknesses – that is, leverage – the materials?
(6) How does the designer establish the relationship between visual quality and structural stability?
(7) How does the designer establish the relationship between visual quality and support or jointedness?
(8) How does the choice of material influence the choice of technique?
(9) How do materials reflect the time, era, and sociocultural context and historical value of the piece?

Key Words:		
materials	properties	technique
select / combine /arrange	leveraging	support / jointedness
criteria	visual quality	structure / shape
quantity / quality	structural stability	value
budget	the canvas	stringing / aesthetic / functional
non-materialistic qualities	sensations	mechanical / physical / chemical
	symbolism	cost / durability

Abstract:
Materials establish the character and personality of jewelry. They contribute to

understandings whether the piece is finished and successful. However, there are no perfect materials for every project. Selecting materials is about making smart, strategic choices. This means relating your materials choices to your design and marketing goals. It also frequently means having to make tradeoffs and judgment calls between aesthetics and functionality. There are three types of materials – Stringing, Aesthetic, and Functional. Each material has three types of properties – Mechanical, Physical and Chemical. Materials differ in quality and value. They differ in the associational and emotional connections which they evoke. They differ in their functional efficiency and effectiveness to lend pieces an ability to retain a shape, while at the same time, an ability to move, drape and flow. They differ in cost and durability. Last, materials may have different relationships with the designer, wearer or viewer depending on how they are intended to be used, and the situational or cultural contexts.

MATERIALS: *Knowing What To Know*
The materials I use are alive

The world of jewelry design and the materials used can be complex, especially for jewelry designers just starting out in their careers. The novice, but also the more experienced designer, as well, often run up against some terms and properties of materials they have not dealt with before. Materials affect the appeal of the piece. They affect its structural integrity. They affect the cost. They affect how people view, sense, desire and understand the piece, its coherence, its relationship to the designer, and its value.

If you wanted to gain an understanding of materials, You Would Be Very Aware Of...

You would be very aware of *where they came from, how they were described, sold and marketed.* You would be very aware of the beads and jewelry findings and stringing materials and tools, their qualities, when they were useful and when they were not, and what happened to them when they age. You would be very aware of what country the material was made or found in, how the material was manufactured, synthesized or gotten at, if it was modified or changed in any way, and how it came to market. You would be very aware if the product was sold at different levels of quality, even if this was not differentiated on the product's label. It would also be important to be very aware how any of these aspects of the material have changed over time, or might change over time in the future.

You would be very aware that *there was no such thing as the perfect material.* There are only better materials, given your situation and goals. There is no perfect bead for every situation. No perfect clasp. No perfect stringing material. Every choice you make as a jewelry designer will require some tradeoffs and judgment calls. The more you understand the quality of the materials in the pieces you are working with are made of, and the clearer you are about your design goals, and if you are selling things, your marketing goals, as well, the more prepared you will be to make these kinds of choices.

You would be very aware that *materials have different values and life spans, and this must relate to your project goals*. The choices you make for fashion jewelry will rely on very different critieria than the choices you make for investment quality pieces. You would not want to use metalized plastic beads, for example, in a piece you call an *heirloom* bracelet. Metalized plastic beads are a metal shell around a milky white plastic bead. The shell will chip easily. On the other hand, when doing *fashion jewelry*, these very inexpensive beads, and which have a short life-span, would be perfect. Not only are they cheap, but because they are cheap, there are lots and lots more styles and shapes and textures.

If your goal is to create more investment quality pieces, then you would not want to buy lampwork beads which have not been appropriately annealed (that is, if not cooled down correctly, they will fracture and break easily). You would buy appropriately annealed ones, but which are considerably more expensive. This may affect the look of your pieces. For an inexpensive, fashion oriented piece, your necklace made up entirely of lampwork beads which have *not* been appropriately annealed might be very affordable. It would have that great handmade, artisan look. It might sell for only $60.00. If the necklace was made up of all quality lampwork beads, -- it would have the exact same look and style as its inexpensive cousin, but it might have to retail for $600-800.00. Usually, with more investment quality lampwork beads, you might just use one, or perhaps three of these considerably more expensive lampwork beads, and have a lot of cord showing, or a lot of filler beads, to keep the piece affordable. This would be a very different design look and style.

Again, for an investment quality piece, you would want to use crystal beads manufactured in Austria or the Czech Republic, and not ones manufactured elsewhere. And you would not let yourself be fooled when the front of the package says "Austrian Crystal" when the back says "Made In China". Crystal beads made in China are not as bright, there are more production issues and flaws in the beads, and the holes are often drilled off-center when compared to their "Made In Austria" counterparts. But crystal beads more appropriate for that investment quality piece might be overkill for a fashion piece where you want to add a pop of brightness without a lot of additional cost. Often the cheaper cousins have some interesting colors or shapes not available in the more expensive lines.

You would want to be very aware of *the different treatments of beads and metals*. Some things are radiated, heated, reconstituted, partly synthesized, lacquered, coated or dyed. Sometimes this is a good thing and these treatments enhance the quality of materials in appearance and durability. Othertimes this is a bad thing, negatively affecting the quality or look and sensibility of the materials.

You would be very aware that *many of the materials you use are described in ways that do not provide you with sufficient information to make a choice*. Take the material *gold-filled*. The definition of *gold-filled* is that the material is a *measurable layer of real gold fused to brass, sometimes copper*. But the legal definition does not tell you how thick the gold has to be over the brass for the material to be called gold-filled. So in the market, some gold-filled has very little gold and will lose its gold very quickly, and other gold-filled has a thicker layer and will keep its gold, its shine, its shape for decades.

Or sterling silver. Sterling silver is supposed to be 92.5% silver (marked .925). The alloy, that is the remaining 7.5%, is supposed to contain, by law, a lot of copper. However, many manufacturers substitute some nickel for the copper to keep the cost down. The addition of nickel in the alloy makes the sterling silver less expensive, yes, but it also makes it more brittle. It is the difference between being able to open and close the loop on an ear wire, off of which to hang the dangle, many, many times or only two or three times before the wire loop breaks.

Lots of sterling silver items get marked .925. And in jewelry making, many of the pieces we use are so small, there is no .925 stamp on them. Besides a change of what is in the alloy affecting the usefulness and value, many other things happen in the marketplace, as well. Many sterling silver items have been cast. What frequently happens is that some of the silver is lost in the casting process, so it is no longer at 92.5%. Manufacturers are supposed to make note of this, but many just stamp .925 on these items. Some shops label items as sterling silver, but in reality, are selling you pieces that are nickel. And some places will sell you something silver plated, but attach a sterling silver .925 tag to it and which is marked .925 on it off the clasp. The tag is sterling; the jewelry is not. I've seen some major craft stores, many chain stores in the malls, and some major jewelry stores sell metalized plastic jewelry and jewelry components and label it *.925*.

Flexible, nylon coated cable wires are one of the primary types of stringing materials. The measure of cable wire strength is called *tensile strength*. This has to do with what the wires are made of, what the nylon sheathing is made of, and how thick that nylon sheathing is. What makes the wire strong is the nylon sheathing's ability to maintain the twist in the wire. As soon as the integrity of the nylon sheathing is violated, the wire untwists and immediately breaks. You will not see *tensile strength* referenced on the labels of these products. The information which is referenced (number of strands, wire thickness) gives you some information needed to make a choice, but insufficient information to make an actual choice. Even when they list the number of strands, this doesn't give you enough factual information to depend on. One brand's high-end, 7-strand is stronger and more supple than that same brand's 49-strand middle range product. This same brand's middle range 49-strand product is stronger and more supple than another brand's high end 49-strand product.

You would also be very aware that *you cannot assume that there is consistency and uniformity for any given product*. There are many production issues that arise in the manufacture of glass beads, for example. Some beads are perfect. Some have flaws. These flaws might include some flat surfaces when everything should be rounded. The color not going all the way through. Holes drilled off-centered. Bead sizes and hole sizes inconsistent from bead to bead. Some bead holes that are especially sharp. Some beads which have coated coloration which is poorly applied and chips off quickly. In clothing, these beads with flaws would be labeled *irregulars*, but they are not so labeled in beads. Some companies specialize in selling you perfect manufactured glass beads; other companies specialize in selling you the irregulars. They don't advertise that fact. Either quality looks the same when you buy it; they just don't hold up the same in close examination or from wear.

You would be aware that *fabricated and stamped metal pieces are more durable than cast metal pieces, but a lot more expensive, and with a smaller palette of designs for the artist.* You would be aware that the measure of *pound strength* on any label is the weakest piece of information to grab onto. The law only defines how pound strength should be measured. Since most products are manufactured abroad, little care is taken to guarantee the validity of this information.

You would be aware that *materials which are dyed may be a different color from batch to batch*. The color of the material is affected by the barometric pressure outside the manufacturing facility the day they are dyed. The factory cannot control for this.

You would be aware that *there are a lot of things to know about the materials used in jewelry design*.

It Is All About Choices

Materials play a significant role in jewelry design. You need to relate and justify the choices you make about selecting and using materials to your design goals (and, if selling your pieces, to your marketing goals, as well). Sometimes your choices are preformulated and planned; othertimes, these choices are spontaneous and emerge within your process of design. But these are all choices to be made, with inevitable impacts and consequences.

It is through the characteristics and qualities of the materials that the designer comes to keenly and fully appreciate values, intents, desires, and understandings associated with any design.

It is also through the most effective presentation specific to the materials that the designer experiences the piece to its best advantage and potential. The effectiveness results from the designer's ability to maximize the strengths of each material, while minimizing its weaknesses. This is called *leveraging*.

It is a useful exercise, as well, to attempt to simplify and edit the materials and reflect upon whether the piece feels more satisfying and successful, or less so. One key goal of any designer is to reach a point of *parsimony* where enough is enough.

Appreciation of materials, their selection, use and arrangement lead the designer to see, feel, think and listen to the visual poetry laid out before them. Jewelry is more than functional adornment. It resonates. Materials and their juxtapositions contribute to this. This appreciation allows the artist to share inspiration and intent with other audiences, the wearer and viewer included. The materials influence the artist in discovery, expression, invention, re-invention, and originality. They become part of the human experience in jewelry design.

For example, you might be in a situation having decide whether to purchase an $80.00 strand of 6mm round garnet beads, or a $28.00 strand of these same beads.

In that $80.00 strand, all the beads actually measure 6mm. They are all perfectly round. The holes are drilled well, and drilled through the center. There are no chips at the hole. There is good coloration, and the coloration from bead to bead is very consistent.

In that $28.00 strand, none of the beads measure 6mm. They are a bit smaller, perhaps 5.5mm, but slightly inconsistent from bead to bead along the strand. Sizes are approximate, not exact. Several beads on the strand are not perfectly round. Some have flat surfaces on them. There are many chips at the hole, suggesting that they are not drilled well. Some are drilled off-center. The coloration is good from afar, but a close exam reveals that some beads are less desirable than others.

This situation doesn't present an easy choice, however. If you are making fashion jewelry, the less expensive strand might be the best choice. Fashion jewelry is not worn for a long time. It is not an investment. It is a look. These beads are less expensive. In this context, the flaws, in this case, may not be so much as a *flaw*, as more a *variation*. The variations might enhance the fashion piece, adding a sense of fun, surprise and funkiness. The poorly drilled holes might mean that these beads will crack and break from wear, but given that fashion jewelry is not worn for a long time, this is a non-issue.

If you are making a more investment quality piece, the more expensive garnet beads might be the better choice. They have more value, resulting from the higher quality. The consistency in quality results in a more classic, timeless look. These beads will last a long time. Here, the inconsistencies in the less expensive strand of beads definitely would be viewed as *flaws*, not *variations*.

Types of Materials

One of the most fundamental and practical aspects of jewelry design is the importance of the materials. The choices jewelry designers make when selecting materials influence the form, content and movement of their pieces. Every material brings something special to the creative process and the finished jewelry pieces. The material influences, not only the designer, but the wearer and viewer themselves, how they perceive it, the values they place on it, and the extent they desire it.

The types of materials jewelry designers might choose are only limited by the imagination of the designer, and that designer's budget. I have compiled a short listing of the more prevalent materials used in jewelry design.

I distinguish among three types of materials which are:
  1. ***Stringing Materials** –*

which are used to form the canvas of our jewelry,

...from those materials called
  2. ***Aesthetic Materials** –*

which form the primary visual vocabulary and expressiveness of the
  piece, but also may contribute some functionality,

...from those materials called

3. Functional Materials –

which solely or primarily have practical value, but only sometimes, most likely inadvertently, add to the aesthetic expression of the piece.

1. STRINGING MATERIALS *(The Canvas)*

The canvas is the part of the piece of jewelry onto which things are placed. The canvas is usually some kind of stringing material, and the things placed on it typically are beads and charms. The canvas supports the piece, its shaping and its silhouette. It may or may not be visible in the piece. But the canvas can be anything, including thread, cable wire, hard wire, bead cord, leather, waxed cotton, fabric and ribbon, wire mesh, sheet metal, beadwoven foundation, chains, and the like. It can be like a string, or it can be like a flat sheet.

The designer selects the canvas or stringing material based on a vision of the structure of the piece, including both its supportive requirements as well as its appearance-related qualities. The particular selection will also impact the durability of the structure. Sometimes the selection of canvas takes on a symbolic meaning, such as using hemp in friendship bracelets or antiwar jewelry, or using leather in biker jewelry.

Types of stringing materials or canvas include:

   a. **Beading thread**
   b. **Cable thread**
   c. **Bead cord, hemp, knotting cord**
   d. **Cable wires**
   e. **Stretchy Cords**
   f. **Thicker cords**
   g. **Hard wire**
   h. **Chain**
   i. **Ribbon, Fabric**
   j. **A soft or pliable flat surface**
   k. **Fused glass**
   l. **Metal sheet**
   m. **Bead woven foundation**

(a) Beading thread:

Typically shaped like a typewriter ribbon, made from bonded nylon. It is something we wax before using it. Materials are strung onto thread using a beading needle. The thread is attached to the clasp assembly by tying knots. Glue should never be applied to these knots. If the beading thread is twisted, rather than bonded, it will break very easily.

Structure: Piece is very supple and moves, drapes and flows very easily. Provides little resistance to the weight of materials placed on it

Durability: Very durable when waxed, unless the holes of beads are very sharp

(b) Cable thread:

This is a material where threads are braided together and encased in a nylon sheathing. The strength of cable thread comes from the ability of the nylon sheathing to maintain the twist in the encased threads. As soon as the nylon sheathing is violated, the threads immediately untwist and break. Used similarly as beading thread, but cable thread is round, not flat. You use a needle. Waxing is optional, but strongly suggested. Unlike beading thread, you only need to pass through each bead once. You tie knots to the clasp assembly. Glue should never be applied to these knots. Cable thread sold in bead stores is non-biodegradable. That sold in fishing stores or fishing departments is biodegradable.

Structure: Piece is very supple and moves, drapes and flows easily, but not as easily as with beading thread.

Durability: Very durable, but the nylon sheathing can be compromised easily from body oils, perfume oils, and cosmetics. Waxing will protect the nylon sheathing.

(c) Bead cord, hemp, knotting cord:

This is a material where threads or fibers are braided or twisted together so that they look pretty. This cord is used when you want the stringing material to show, such as putting knots between beads, or where you have a cluster of beads, then the cord showing, another cluster of beads, the cord showing, and so forth. You use this material to macramé, knot, braid, knit, and crochet. You usually do not wax this material. That would make it look ugly. The primary purpose is to make your piece look attractive when the stringing material is to show.

Bead cord may be nylon or silk. You use silk with real pearls, but I suggest using the nylon with other materials. You will need a needle, usually a collapsible eye or big eye needle. You tie knots to secure the cord to a clasp assembly. You minimize the use of glue applied to knots, but you usually need to apply glue to the final knot. You want to minimize movement of beads and pendants on any bead cord. Movement means two things: (a) movement up and down the cord because of slack, and (b) movement rotating around the cord because of lack of resistance. Bead cords fray easily and the holes of beads are sharp, looking similar to a broken soda bottle.

Structure: Piece is a little stiffer than with bead thread or cable thread, but still feels supple. Will drape well, but respond imperfectly to the movement of the body.

Durability: Silk naturally deteriorates in 3-5 years; nylon does not.
Bead cord made from other natural materials will also deteriorate
over a relatively short period of time.
The movement and rotation of beads will begin to fray the cord.

(d) Cable Wires:

This flexible stringing material consists of wires braided together and encased in nylon. The strength comes from the ability of the nylon sheathing to keep the twist in the wires. If the nylon sheathing is compromised in any way, the wires will immediately untwist and the cable will break at that point. The wire is stiff enough to be its own needle. You use crimp beads to secure the cable wire to a clasp assembly because it is more difficult to tie a secure knot with the cable wire. A crushed crimp adds a more pleasing appearance than tying a knot, but it adds risk. A crushed crimp is like razor blade, always trying to saw right through the cable when the jewelry is worn.

Structure: Piece will be stiff, and never take the shape of the body.
Piece will typically rotate in the opposite direction from the
movement of the body or arm it rests on.

Durability: Very durable. The nylon sheathing can be compromised
easily from body oils, perfume oils, and cosmetics. Usually crimp
beads are used to secure the clasp, and these increase the risk the
cable will break at the crimp, when compared to the durability of
tying a knot. Remember: one crimp on each end is more than
sufficient.

(e) Stretchy Cords, like elastic string, gossamer floss, elastic cord:

These materials are not particularly durable and lose their elasticity over time. People like these because they hate clasps, and you don't use clasps with these. You stretch the cord by pulling on it several times before using it, to minimize memory loss. You secure these by tying knots (preferably surgeon's knot), and putting glue (any glue except superglue) on the knots. Be sure to coat the bottom of the knot, as well as the top of the knot. Elastic cord is fabric covered around an elastic thong or floss.

Structure: Piece will stretch and return back to its original shape and size.

Durability: Material deteriorates and loses both its integrity as well as its memory over time, especially if left exposed to the air, or worn frequently. This can break down within one or two years, when left exposed to air and sunlight. The round elastic string is the most durable among the stretchy cords. The floss is the least durable.

(f) Thicker cords like leather, waxed cotton, ultra suede lace, rubber thong, and rat tail (satin cord):

These cords are stiff enough to be their own needle. You usually need special jewelry findings, such as crimp ends, end caps, or cones with larger interior openings, to prepare the ends of the thicker cord, so that you can attach a clasp assembly. Some are glued on; some crimped. An alternative is to wire-wrap the ends to create loops from which to attach the clasp.

Structure: Similar to bead cord, but little stiffer.

Durability: Some cords, like leather, dry out over time and crack. Other cords, like waxed cotton and ultra suede, last a very long time. The rat tail tends to shred.

(g) Hard Wire:

Hard wire is not a stringing wire, per se. You can use it to make a chain or bead-chain. You can use it to make shapes, like clasps and ear wires. You can bundle it so that it might be stiff enough to retain the shape of a bracelet or cuff. You can create caged or bezel settings for stones. You can weave it or knit it to create patterns and textures. You create loops and rings to attach hard wire to a clasp assembly. Hard wire can be plated or enameled over steel, aluminum, copper or brass. Hard wire can be raw from the original material like sterling silver, gold filled, nickel, brass and copper.

Structure: Wire stiffness comes as dead soft, half hard and hard. You determine, given how much manipulation of the wire you plan on doing, how stiff you want the wire to be when you begin your project, so that it will hold and retain its shape. Each time you manipulate the wire, it becomes stiffer and stiffer and stiffer, until it becomes brittle and breaks.

Durability: Very durable. Wire 18 gauge or thicker has little risk of losing its shape, distorting, breaking, opening up or pulling apart. As you get thinner, the risk increases dramatically. Dead soft wire requires a lot more manipulation until it can hold its shape, than half hard or hard hard wire.

(h) Chain:

Wire is bent into links of various shapes and sizes, and these are interlinked together into a chain. Sometimes the links are soldered closed. Usually they are not. You can string things onto the chain. You can use the chain as part of the clasp assembly, often to make the size adjustable. You can use the chain as a design element throughout your piece. Chains can be made of raw metal, such as sterling silver. They can be plated metal, such as plated over brass or plated over steel or plated over aluminum. They can be plastic. Some of the types of underlying metals will break easily; others will not.

Structure: Thinner chains will be less able to keep their shape.

Durability: Chains can be very durable, particularly ones that have soldered links, wider links, and/or links created from thicker gauge wires.

(i) Ribbon, fabric:

These wider cords are sometimes used as a stringing material. They are secured at each end with ribbon or bar clamps, which then form either side of your clasp assembly.

Structure: Usually, these don't by themselves support a shape.

Durability: More aesthetic than functional

(j) A soft or pliable surface, such as Lacy's Stiff Stuff, Stiff Felt, Ultra suede sheet, Paper, Card Board, Poster Board, Rolled Out Polymer or Metal Clay, Brass Cuff Blank:

The canvas or stringing material does not have to be a narrow cord. It can be a wide, flat surface, off of which to bead, glue, stitch, embroider, carve, or sculpt. This type of canvas needs to have some amount of stiffness to hold a shape, but not too much that the jewelry made with it feels uncomfortable, or does not move naturally with the person.

Structure: If you were creating a pendant, you might want your canvas to be a little stiffer than if you were creating a bracelet.

Durability: Average durability

(k) Fused Glass:

Sometimes the flat canvas is a piece of glass. Other pieces of glass are fused onto this, using a kiln, in order to create a pattern or image.

Structure: Rigid shape.

Durability: Same as any other piece of glass.

(l) Metal Sheet:

Sometimes we fabricate a piece of jewelry, either using soldering, stamping, texturing, molding, casting, 3-D printing, or cold connections. Part of the sheet becomes our canvas or stringing material. With metal, we can flatten, dome, otherwise shape, stamp and texture.

Structure: These are very reliable materials for creating and maintaining shapes.

Durability: Soldered and stamped pieces are much more durable than molded or cast ones. 3-D printed materials would be used with casting. Cold connections could be used with any technique.

(m) Bead (or other material) Woven Foundation:

Sometimes we can weave a foundation out of beads (or other materials), giving us a flat surface off of which we can build things, apply things, or extend things.

Structure: The foundation can vary in stiffness. The foundation can vary in the volume and position of positive and negative spaces. This allows great flexibility in controlling for shape and the maintenance of shape.

Durability: This type of foundation usually increases the durability of the piece as a whole.

2. AESTHETIC MATERIALS

The canvas either passes through various aesthetic materials, or these are applied to the canvas or attached off the canvas in some way. These aesthetic materials are used for the yoke, the clasp assembly, the frame, the focal point, the center piece, the strap, and the bail.

Aesthetic Materials are expressive. They are part of the visual vocabulary and grammar of the jewelry. While some play functional roles, as well, they are usually selected for their expressive powers. Some materials evoke sensory or symbolic responses, as well. A touch, a feel, a color sense, sometimes a smell, which extends beyond its factual elements.

Any type of material can be selected to use as an aesthetic material. It can be something very specific, or a found object, or some kind of combobulation of things.

Aesthetic Materials we see often include,

- Glass, Fused glass, lampwork glass, blown glass
- Metals and Plated Metals
- Fibers
- Natural (gemstones, wood, bone, horn, shell, feathers)
- Synthetic (plastic)
- Polymer and Precious Metal Clay
- Ceramic, Porcelain, Clay, Raku
- Paper, lacquered paper
- Oxidizers, Patinas, Paints, Fabric Dyes and Paints, Stains, Metal Paints and Rouges
- Platings, Coatings
- Enameling

These aesthetic materials can be selected for their qualities of

(a) *Appeal*
(b) *Functionality*
(c) *Sensations or symbolism extending beyond the physical and decorative bases underlying these materials*

Aesthetic Materials:
(a) Appeal

The idea of appeal is a broad concept. It is sometimes universal. But often subjective.

There are many variables underlying the ideas of appeal and beauty. These include things like,

- Clarity, translucence, opacity
- Hardness, brittleness, softness, suppleness
- Malleability
- Luminescence, brightness, reflectiveness, refraction
- Color, color combinations, intensity, value
- Weight, lightness, heaviness, volume, density
- Movement and dimension
- Perceived value, worth, rarity
- Familiarity
- Cut, faceting, smoothness, carving, sculpting
- Shapes
- Direction, pointer, focal points, markings, striations, inclusions

Aesthetic Materials:
(b) Functionality

Some materials function better than others in certain situations. For example, sterling silver is very malleable, nickel is more brittle. Bending, shaping, coiling, weaving sterling silver requires much less effort, and with this, can lead to more artistic and design success, than using nickel or other wire material that is stiffer and harder than sterling.

Another example: Using needle and thread as your stringing material is very time consuming. It is awkward using needle and thread. You have to wax it. You want to pass through each bead a minimum of three times. Using a cable wire, instead, lets you go much faster. The cable wire is a self needle. You don't wax it. You only have to go through each bead once. If you are selling your pieces, it is virtually impossible to get your labor out of a needle and thread project. You almost have to use a cable wire, if you don't want to commit yourself to a life of slave labor.

Aesthetic Materials:
(c) Sensations and Symbolism

Materials have sensory and symbolic powers which extend beyond the materials themselves. Obviously, this can be very subjective. It might have psychological roots, sociological roots and/or cultural roots.

Things may feel warm, cold, soft, rough, oily, weighty. Things may represent romance, power, membership, religiosity, status.

Vanderbilt University's colors are gold and black, so using those colors in the Nashville, TN area might evoke a different emotional response than when used elsewhere. And there's that very-difficult-to-design-with University of Tennessee orange, again, in the Nashville area will evoke a very different response than elsewhere.

Materials like amber and bone and crystal are things people like to touch, not just look at. The sensation extends beyond the visual grammar.

3. FUNCTIONAL MATERIALS

These materials are used in practical terms. They help things hold together. They help pieces stay in place. They help make pieces adjustable in size. They help polish, finish things off, assist materials through stages in their processing and development. They may be used to prevent or retard a change in color, such as a lacquer finish or rhodium plating over sterling to prevent tarnishing. They help capture a form or shape. They are not a part of the visual and expressive vocabulary and grammar of the piece. Nor are they any kind of canvas.

Functional Materials which are more prominent include,

- Adhesives
- Solders
- Pickling, Flux
- Molding compounds
- Bead release
- Fixatives (like Krylon, lacquering, special platings, waxes, other things which create a protective barrier over something else).

It is especially important to know a lot about adhesives. Many people reach for a tube of Superglue or Gorilla glue for everything. Superglue and Gorilla glue have few uses in jewelry design. Superglue dries like glass, so the bond is like a piece of glass. When the jewelry moves, the bond shatters like glass, and the bond looks like a broken piece of glass. All jewelry moves when worn, so not a good choice. Gorilla glue expands when it dries and discolors with age.

Another glue many people reach for is hot glue. This glue melts at body temperature, so not a wise choice for necklaces, bracelets, earrings and pendants. It also discolors with age.

The best glue to use is jeweler's glue. Two brands are E6000 and Beacon 527. Basically the same glue, but the former is thick and the latter is runny. These glues take 10 minutes to set, so you can move things around for 10 minutes. At about 20 minutes, the consistency is like rubber cement and you can use your finger or a tweezers to take off any excess glue. Both glues take 24 hours to dry hard. They dry clear and remain clear over time. The bond does not expand. The bond is like rubber and acts as a shock absorber as the jewelry moves.

If using fabric, particularly silk (ribbon, bead cord, thread), you want to use a cement, rather than a glue. Glues work by forming a collar around an object, then tighten up as the water or other solvent evaporates. Cements work by adhering to each individual fiber. Many bead stringing materials as well as fabric are made up of tiny, compressed microfibers. Glue on fabric, as opposed to cement, will lose its grip, so to speak. With silk, I suggest either G-S Hypo Fabric Cement, or any fabric glue. Fabric glues and cements are tacky and stick to the individual micro-fibers in fabric.

Before using a glue, you want to know the characteristics of the bond, once dried.

These include things like,

- hardness, stiffness, ability to respond to stresses and strains without breaking or cracking
- whether dries clear, or yellows
- whether yellows with age
- whether it expands or not when it dries
- what materials it is most useful for
- whether you have to prepare the material's surface before using
- how long it takes to fully set
- how easy it is to wipe away and remove any excess glue
- whether where-ever you purchase the particular brand of glue, such as at a craft store or discount store or bead store, that this brand of glue is the same quality product
- how long the glue will last in its container before hardening or drying out

PROPERTIES OF MATERIALS

Besides the importance of knowing the *types of materials*, it is also important to know the *properties of materials*.

*The **Properties of Materials** include:*
(a) Mechanical properties,
(b) Physical properties, and
(c) Chemical properties.

(a) Mechanical Properties
Mechanical properties describe how a material reacts to an applied force.

These include,
- **_Strength:_** It's ability not to break under stress or strain
- **_Hardness:_** How easily it can be scratched, faceted, carved, sculpted, cut, sand blasted
- **_Elasticity:_** The ability to regain its shape after a stress has been applied to it
- **_Plasticity and Malleability:_** How much force it takes to make a material permanently deform without breaking
- **_Stiffness and Brittleness:_** At some point, these materials will be so brittle, they will not bend, and will just break in response to force. Wire materials, for example, get stiffer and more brittle, the more they are worked, such as from twisting, pulling, hammering, coiling and the like. Crystal is much more brittle than glass, so it more likely to break from movement or other force.
- **_Fatigue:_** When the material fails, after repeated wear and use
- **_Impact Strength:_** how much a material can withstand an impact
- **_Abrasion Resistance:_** When two materials rub against each other, what is the resistance before one or both break
- **Creep:** the slow movement of a material over time

(b) Physical Properties

Physical properties describe the inherent nature of the material. Some more important ones related to materials used in jewelry include:
- **_Density:_** mass and volume
- **_Porosity:_** the quality of being full of tiny holes; these might hold in something, like a perfume oil, or that something might easily leach out through washing or sweating, like a dye or lead. Or something might easily be let in such as air, cosmetics, chemicals in someone's sweat
- **_Water absorption, permeability and solubility_**
- **_Softening and Compression:_** how material holds up under different conditions
- **_Resistance to Heat and Fire_**
- **_Resistance to Cold_**
- **_Resistance to a number of cycles of sharp temperature variations without failing_**
- **_Changing form from solid to liquid to gas_**

(c) Chemical Properties

Chemical properties refer to how well the material holds up when exposed to chemicals. These chemicals may be in the air. They may be present in cosmetics, perfumes or hair sprays. They may be present in a person's sweat.

These include,
- **_Corrosion_**
- **_Melting, Dissolving, Removing_**

- *Etching*
- *Colorizing, Oxidizing, Patinas*
- *Platings*
- *Bonding, Adherring*
- *Biodegrading*

We have looked at types of materials and their properties. Now we need to understand how materials help establish the viability, finish and success of jewelry. Here our materials selection process begins to incorporate some *value judgments*.

Materials Help Establish
The Viability, Finish and Success of The Jewelry

Jewelry has character and personality. It is communicative. It is interactive. It evokes emotions and resonates. Within each piece is displayed intent, content, meaning, expression, and contextual relevance.

People intuitively or consciously recognize when it is finished, that is, when the addition or subtraction of any one design element would make the piece seem less satisfying or desirable.

Jewelry is judged as successful, to the extent it can maintain its shape while concurrently feeling comfortable, and moving, draping and flowing with the person, as the person wears the jewelry and moves with it on.

Every piece of jewelry has its artistic and individual character due to the many facets from which it is constructed. Stringing, Aesthetic and Functional Materials are three of these facets. Mechanical, Physical and Chemical Properties add some additional facets. These among other additional material choices determine both what can be made, as well as the character of what is made.

Material selection in jewelry design is not only about choosing the most attractive, or most obvious, or most affordable, or most durable materials available. Designers also choose materials for their sensual sensations, like warmth, their formal appearance, like classical, their functional practicality, like a clamp, or their geo-locality, like using materials found locally.

The material selection process is complex. It is influenced by many preconditions, choices made, and considerations to accommodate. Too often, however, designers focus mainly on the visual aspects of the materials, and not enough on other factors. In order to make well-considered and smart choices about materials, jewelry designers need a lot more information. They need information about the entirety of the material, as created or constructed, as visually impactful, as functionally helpful, as perceptually and cognitively understood and as symbolically relevant for designer, wearer and viewer.

Selecting Materials Is A Complicated Process

MATERIAL *(type and property)*	
TYPE - stringing - aesthetic - functional	**PROPERTY** - mechanical - physical - chemical

JEWELRY MAKING

- production process
- assembly, fabrication, construction
- finishing
- accommodating temporal issues
- cost

EXPERIENCE

- sensorial
- perception
- association and symbolism
- emotion and resonance

CONTEXT

- of use
- physical
- historical and geographic
- socio-cultural and psychological

PERSPECTIVE
- **artist** - **wearer** - **viewer** - **seller, buyer, exhibiter, collector, student, teacher**

***Stringing, Aesthetic, and sometimes, Functional Materials,
coupled with their various Mechanical, Physical and Chemical properties,
help to:***

> *(1) Establish a relationship between visual quality and structural stability (physical properties, shape, silhouette)*
> *(2) Establish a relationship between visual quality and support or jointedness (movement, drape and flow)*
> *(3) Influence the selection of the appropriate technique*
> *(4) Provide character and visual appeal*
> *(5) Reflect the time, era, and socio-cultural context and historical value of the piece*
> *(6) Mix aesthetic elements with functional ones*
> *(7) Highlight a theme or concept expressed in the design*
> *(8) Link the piece to a particular geography or location*
> *(9) Link the piece to its appropriate placement on the body*
> *(10) Determine the budget for the piece*
> *(11) Establish the relationship between quantity and quality, that is, how many similar pieces can be made*
> *(12) Best combine the materialistic qualities with the non-materialistic qualities of the project*

(1) Establish a relationship between visual quality and structural stability (physical properties, shape, silhouette)

Jewelry making materials signify *structural significance*. This may relate to the physical properties of the materials, such as hardness, brittleness, softness, pliability, porousness, and this list can go on and on. This may relate to the shapes of the materials, and the placement and interaction of the shapes within the piece, or the final silhouette. The same may be said for size, weight and volume. This may relate to the stability of the material or its color or finish over time.

The choices and arrangement of materials within a piece of jewelry determines its structure. Structure means shape and material integrity. Shape in jewelry may refer to the silhouette of the piece as a whole, or to individual shapes which occupy one or more sections of our finished piece of jewelry. It may refer to the positioning of positive and negative areas within the piece. When we refer to structure and shape and material, we imply structural integrity, and the degree we are able to maintain any shape, color or finish while the jewelry is worn over some period of time.

Example 1: We may create a bracelet using Austrian crystal beads strung on a beading thread. We achieve a high visual quality, at least initially. But these beads will cut through the threads when the bracelet is worn, thus ending with a very low structural stability.

Example 2: Sometimes a clam-shell bead tip is used to finish off each end of bead cord, when that is the stringing material. The bead cord, at its end, is tied into a knot, which sits inside the clam-shell, the cord coming out a hole in the bottom of the clam shell. We do not want the knot to work itself loose and slip through the hole. So we glue it. If we use a jeweler's glue, like E6000 or Beacon 527, these glues dry like rubber. With these glues, the knot can actually contort and work itself through the hole. If we use a glue like Superglue or G-S Hypo Cement, the knot will remain stiff and not be able to slip through the hole. However, the stiff knot reduces what is called support. It reduces the piece's jointedness, or ability to respond to stress and strain, thus an ability to best move, drape and flow. An alternative to glue is to thread an 11/0 seed bead, passing through the bead twice, before bringing the cord through the hole. This is secure. No glue is used as all. Full support is preserved.

Example 3: How long a metal plated finish lasts depends partly on the metal underneath it, and if it bonds to that metal. Metal plating bonds well to brass, so it lasts a long time before it fades away. Metal plating does not bond at all to aluminum, so it quickly chips off.

(2) Establish a relationship between visual quality and support or jointedness (movement, drape and flow)

Jewelry making materials enhance or impede support or *jointedness*. The selection and placement of materials, their density, weight, shape, and the like may enable the jewelry to take the shape of the body and move with the body, or not.

Things strung on beading thread will always take the shape of the body and move with the body; things strung on cable wire will not. But the designer has at their disposal several jewelry design tricks in construction which will make the cable wire function closer to needle and thread.

Example 1: A bracelet made up of very large beads, that when encircling the wrist, creates a very stiff circle, with much strain and stress on each bead, on the stringing material and on the clasp assembly. If the designer reworks the piece, to include small round spacer beads between each very large bead, the designer, in effect, has added what is called a rotator support system. Each very large bead can freely respond to stresses and *strain which result from adjusting to the body and its movement by rotating and pivoting around the spacer bead.*

Example 2: People usually pick a clasp after they have designed their piece. They look for something that will make do, perhaps easier to get on and off, and hopefully have some match to the piece. A clasp, however, should be understood as more than a clasp. It should be understood as a clasp assembly, which is a type of support system. The clasp assembly includes the clasp and everything else it takes to attach the beadwork to the clasp, like rings, loops, rivets, and the like. S-clasps are very attractive and a S-clasp design can always be found that feels an organic extension of the jewelry. An S-clasp needs a soldered ring off of each arm, and, if stringing on cable wire, a loop in the wire where it connects to the soldered ring. The crimp is never pushed all the way up to the clasp or ring. Each ring or loop is a support system or "joint", so our S-clasp needs 4 support systems in this case, to function correctly. With 4 supports on the S-clasp in a necklace, the clasp will always remain on the back of the neck, no matter how the person moves. Without 4 supports, it will not, and the necklace will keep turning around.

(3) Influence the selection of the appropriate technique

The designer must coordinate the selection of Stringing, Aesthetic and Functional Materials, and their inherent Mechanical, Physical and Chemical properties, so that they work in harmony with a particular technique used to assemble, weave, or otherwise secure them together in a finished piece of jewelry.

Conversely, the technique might dictate which materials will work best, and which will not. Bead weaving works with thread or cable thread, but not as easily with elastic string or cable wire.

There was a time when the materials used in any one piece were restricted to a few. Today any material can be used, as well as any combination of materials, without losing any appeal or value or desire.

Examples: A Czech glass bead with a hole size of .8mm would not slip a leather cord with a diameter of 1.5mm. It would be very difficult to create a loomed piece with beads of widely varying sizes. If mixing metals (say, silver, gold and brass) in a fabricated and soldered bracelet, care must be taken in the soldering strategy because each metal melts at a different temperature. You could not begin a wire weaving project using hard (thus, not bendable) hard-wire. We may select cable wire for our canvas. This would not be a suitable stringing material if the technique we wanted to apply was bead weaving.

(4) Provide character and visual appeal

The surface of a material has many characteristics which the jewelry designer leverages within the finished piece. Light might reflect off this surface, such as with opaque glass or shiny metal. Light might be brought into and below the surface before reflected back, such as with many gemstones and opalescent glass. Light might refract through the piece at different angles, even creating a prism effect.

The surface might be a solid color. It might be a mix of colors. It might be matte. It may have inclusions or markings. It may have fired on coloration effects. There may be tonal differences. There may be pattern or textural differences. It may have movement. It may have depth.

Example: It is often difficult to mix gemstone beads with glass beads. However, if you use glass beads which have a translucent quality to them, this glass mimics the relationship of light reflecting back to the eye with that of the gemstones. The finished piece will feel harmonious.

(5) Reflect the time, era, and socio-cultural context and historical value of the piece

Jewelry and its design and materials used can be iconic.

Jewelry can relate the symbolic value of the piece to certain historical themes and ideas, or to specific functions.

Jewelry can be used to preserve, conserve or restore certain cultural or historical values. The material(s) selected may glorify these. Their availability may be closely tied to the time and place. Their use within a piece may be socially subscribed.

Our understanding of how jewelry relates to these contexts can be used to document how jewelry and its design has evolved and spread.

Name an historical period, and you can visualize many of the materials used and the design sense. Roman. Victorian. Prehistoric. Modern.

Name a socio-cultural context. Religious. Wedding. Military. American Southwest. Tribal. College. Any rite of passage.

Example 1: Pearl knotted jewelry is very strongly associated with silk bead cord, pearl clasps, and bead tips. It is also very associated with Victorian jewelry. It would be difficult to substitute other materials and pieces, such as a different kind of clasp, or not knotting between beads, without the piece losing its appeal.

Example 2: A rosary is made as a bead chain, with a certain number of beads, often a certain size and material of bead, with a Y-shaped connector at its center. The rosary assists the wearer in prayer and religiosity. It's specific design and use of materials differentiates Catholicism from other religions.

(6) Mix aesthetic elements with functional ones

Jewelry is art only as it is worn. Its aesthetic elements must tightly coordinate with its functional ones, if the piece is to maintain its shape and silhouette, and move with the person, without distorting, feeling uncomfortable or breaking. Thus, its quality and durability are dependent upon how the designer successfully maneuvers the tradeoffs required between function and appeal. A good part of this success stems from how materials are selected, combined and arranged.

Jewelry and its design preserve the aesthetic qualities, without disrupting and losing focus of the practical ones.

Example: The clasp assembly on a piece of jewelry can be very organic, feeling an integral part of the piece. Or it can be very disruptive and annoying, as if it were a last choice and consideration, and the designer found a clasp that would make do. For an S-clasp to function appropriately, it needs at least one soldered ring off of the arm on each side of the clasp. While enhancing function, this will, at the same time, force the clasp assembly to take up more space and volume in the piece. This too might end up detracting from the overall appeal of the piece.

(7) Highlight a theme or concept expressed in the design

Materials may be selected, combined and arranged into forms and themes so that they represent larger meanings and concepts. Often this comes down to color, shape, placement, and arrangement. The materials bring out the theme or concept in the design.

Example: You create a piece of jewelry with a blue color scheme, using 4 shades of blue. If the piece is to be worn, say, going clubbing in the evening, you might select 4 shades of blue (metallic blue iris, montana blue, blue quartz, cornflower) which vary in intensity. That means, varying how bright or dull they are by selecting more (or less) vivid and saturated tones. The piece will be sensed as more sensual or powerful or energetic or impactful.

If the piece is to be worn, say, at work during the day, you might select 4 shades of blue (cobalt, sapphire, light sapphire, ultralight sapphire) which vary in value. That means, varying how light or dark they are by selecting tones that are basically the same color, but some have more (or less) black, grey or white underlying tones than others. The piece will be sensed as appealing but non-threatening.

(8) Link the piece to a particular geography or location

Materials may be strongly associated with a particular geography or location. Lapis is strongly associated with Afghanistan. Paint Rock with Tennessee.

Example: A necklace by a Tennessee designer made entirely with lampwork beads made by Tennessee artisans.

(9) Link the piece to its appropriate placement on the body

Jewelry can only be judged successful at the boundary between jewelry and the body. It must be able to conform to the body's shape. It must be able to comfortably move, drape and flow as the person moves and shifts positions.

Materials selection might begin with what materials would be most appropriate for a given type of jewelry. Or it might begin with what materials would be most appropriate for a certain body shape or size or placement.

Example 1: Very heavy beads used in earrings can make them uncomfortable. Creating a 4" earring dangle on a 4" head pin is not quite as a good a strategy as making a 4" earring dangle chain using eye pins. Think about what happens to the former vs. the latter when the wearer bends her head, then returns to the upright position.

Example 2: The wearer is very buxom. A necklace with a large and substantial centerpiece might look funny if it appears to rest on the breast as a book on a shelf.

(10) Determine the budget for the piece

The total expenditure incurred while designing a piece of jewelry might be, to a large extent, determined by the materials used. A designer often selects the material type based on a budget for the project. *[Techniques can also have a big impact on the cost, particularly when accounting for the time it takes to design and construct a piece of jewelry.]*

Example: A necklace made entirely of lapis lazuli beads might retail for $150.00. A similar necklace made entirely of lapis color glass beads might retail for $25.00. Both would look similar and take the same time to make.

(11) Establish the relationship between quantity and quality, that is, how many similar pieces can be made

The choice of materials affects the quality of the elements. Within a given project budget, and within a particular design goal, the quality of the materials may limit the number of similar pieces to be made, or the complexity or elaborateness of the design of any one piece.

Example: A stretchy bracelet made with lava beads might retail for $15.00. The materials – elastic string, lava beads, glue – are readily available and inexpensive. The designer could easily make 50 of these to sell, and stay within a reasonable budget. Change the materials to cable wire, crimp bead, horseshoe wire protector, crimp cover, black onyx beads, toggle clasp, and the investment in parts is considerably more. We have more *materials and more expensive materials. This bracelet might have to retail for $45.00. Staying within the same budget framework, the designer would only be able to make 16 of these.*

(12) Best combine the materialistic qualities with the non-materialistic qualities of the project

Every material has two over-arching qualities. The obvious is its physical properties and physicality. Let's call this *materialistic*. It is something that is measurable. In the realm of the mystic, it is ordinary or profane.

But the material also has qualities that extend beyond this. They can be sensory. They can be symbolic. They can be psychological. They can be contextual. Let's call this *non-materialistic*. It is something that is non-measurable. In the realm of the mystic, it is extraordinary and sacred.

Both properties must be considered when designing a piece of jewelry. They have equal importance, when selecting, placing and arranging materials and design elements within a piece.

Example: Take a Chakra bracelet strung on cable wire with a clasp. The beads used are gemstones. Each gemstone has spiritual and healing properties. Each gemstone has a coloration, and each different coloration, too, is associated with certain spiritual and healing properties. Moreover, every individual has their own unique needs for which set of gemstones and which assortment of colorations are best and most appropriate. This can get even more complicated in that each situation and context may have its own requirements. The person may end up needing several Chakra bracelets for different occasions. The designer could have used glass or acrylic beads, instead, which have less non-materialistic value, and might be less durable over time. The designer could have strung the beads on elastic string without using a clasp, again, less non-materialistic value and durable.

LESSONS LEARNED

Selecting materials involves a complicated set of choices, some tangible, some intangible, some personal, some in anticipation of the perceptions of others.

Some lessons learned...

1. *You can use any material you want when designing jewelry*
2. *Material selection is a complicated decision making process*
3. *No material is perfect for every project*

4. *Don't assume you know what you know*
5. *Be skeptical. Always ask questions.*
6. *Select materials on both their aesthetic as well as functional properties*
7. *Don't sacrifice functionality for aesthetics*
8. *Anticipate what might happen to your materials over time as the jewelry is worn*
9. *Anticipate how your various audiences will respond to your selections of materials*
10. *Understand all the ins and outs of how your material got to market*
11. *Work within a budget*
12. *Match the quality of material to your design (and marketing) goals*

FOOTNOTES

(1) WASTIELS, Lisa and WOUTERS, Ine. Material Considerations in Architectural Design: A Study of the Aspects Identified by Architects for Selecting Materials. July, 2008.
As referenced in:
http://shura.shu.ac.uk/511/1/fulltext.pdf

MATERIALS, TECHNIQUES AND TECHNOLOGIES
4b. TECHNIQUES AND TECHNOLOGIES:
Knowing What To Do

Bead Stringing, Bead Weaving, Wire Working, Metalsmithing (starting top left clockwise)

Guiding Questions:
(1) How do techniques construct the relationship among parts so as to preserve shape while simultaneously allowing movement, drape and flow?
(2) How is technique used to express and enhance the artist's intent?
(3) What does it mean to say each technique has a philosophy?
(4) What is the relationship of technique to light, texture and ornamentation?
(5) How does technology enable the artist to expand technical prowess? To what extent should jewelry designers respond to technology?
(6) What is the difference between technique and skill?
(7) What are the different types of techniques used in jewelry making?

Key Words:		
technique	*philosophy of technique*	*composition*
skill	*light and shadow*	*artist's intent*
technology	*texture*	*space / mass*
preserve shape (structure)	*ornamentation*	*jewelry forms*
allow movement, drape,	*embellishment*	*intent*
flow (support)	*positive and negative*	*content*
managing tension	*space*	*expression*
clasp assembly	*tactile / visual*	*architectural basics*
parsimony	*types of jewelry making*	*stress / strain /*
resonance	*techniques*	*vulnerability*

Check out my online video tutorials (https://so-you-want-to-be-a-jewelry-designer.teachable.com/) which cover many useful jewelry making techniques.
https://so-you-want-to-be-a-jewelry-designer.teachable.com/

Abstract:
Jewelry Making Techniques bring materials together within a composition. Techniques construct the interrelationship among parts so that they preserve a shape, yet still allow the piece of jewelry to move with the person as the jewelry is worn. And Techniques manipulate the essence of the whole of the piece so as to convey the designer's intent and match it to the desires of wearer, viewer, buyer, seller, exhibitor, collector, student and teacher. Technique is more than mechanics. It is a philosophy. Thoughts transformed into choices. Part of this philosophy is understanding the role of technique to interrelate Space and Mass. Space and Mass are the raw materials of jewelry forms. Technique reduces the contrast between them in a controlled way and with significance for designer and client. Techniques have special relationships to light, texture and ornamentation. Technology enables us to expand our technical prowess with new materials, processes, styles and forms.

TECHNIQUES AND TECHNOLOGIES:
Knowing What To Do
Technique is Knowledge, Value, Creation

Jewelry Making Techniques are more than mechanics.

Techniques are ways to implement ideas. To transform thoughts and feelings into choices.

Techniques are knowledge, value and creation.

Jewelry Making Techniques bring materials together within a composition. Techniques construct the interrelationship among parts so that they preserve a shape, yet still allow the piece of jewelry to move with the person as the jewelry is worn. And Techniques manipulate the essence of the whole of the piece so as to convey the artist's intent and match it to the desires of wearer, viewer, buyer, seller, exhibitor, collector, student and teacher.

There are many different kinds of jewelry making techniques, as well as strategies and variations for implementing them. In fact, the jewelry designer has no proscriptions, no prescriptions, no expectations, no limits on how she or he decides to compose, construct and manipulate materials and structures and supports. It can be a technique that is learned. It can be one approximated. It can be totally new, emergent and spontaneous. It can be socially acceptable or not. The designer can pull, tug, roll, press, cut, carve, sculpt, emboss, embellish, embroider, sew, knit, weave, stamp, coil, bend, fold, twist, heat, cool, assemble, combine, dissolve, destruct, cast, wrap, solder, glue, wind, blow, or hammer.

In reality, it is impossible to discuss meaningfully the technique apart from the ideas, abilities and experiences of each jewelry designer, particularly in reference to knowing when a piece should be considered finished and successful. There will be some variations in how any designer applies a technique. This is called *skill*. One might pull harder or hammer harder than another. One might allow some more ease or looseness than another. One might use easy solder where another might choose hard solder. One might prefer a thinner thickness or gauge of stringing material, and another a thicker one. One might leverage the structural properties of one material, while another might choose other materials with different properties towards the same end. One might apply the technique, following Step XYZ before Step ABC, and another, apply the technique in reverse, altering the steps to be XYA and ABZ.

But our primary focus here is on technique apart from skill. This lets us see why some designers are masterful at technique, while others are not.

While there are a lot of different methods and applications designers can choose from, all too often, however, when selecting techniques, jewelry designers fail themselves (and their clients). They disappoint. They do not understand how to select techniques. They do not fully understand the basic mechanics. They do not fully understand the expressive powers of techniques.

Because of this, they are unaware of the responsibilities, as artist and designer, which come with selecting and applying techniques. In turn, designers make inadequate choices. They might choose the simple, the handy, the already learned. They might choose what they see other designers using. They might choose what they see in magazines and books and videos which get spelled out in Step1-Step2-Step3 fashion.

But often they are naïve in their choices. They lack an understanding of each technique and its philosophy. They do not understand that there are lot of things more to any technique beyond its simple mechanics. Techniques are not step-by-step. They are more a process rather than a routine. They are a collection of knowledge, skill, understanding, choices, decisions, tradeoffs, intents with implication and consequence. Techniques anticipate shared understandings and desires between artist and audience about finish and success. Because of all this, techniques are very dependent on the artisan's fluency in design.

Moreover, jewelry designers often do not recognize that each and every technique can and should be varied, experimented and played with. They do not understand that techniques do not work or accommodate every situation. That is, jewelry designing is not a "Have-Technique-Will-Travel" type of professional endeavor. Techniques need to be selected and adapted to the problems or contexts at hand.

They do not understand that there is more to techniques than securing an arrangement of elements. They do not understand that techniques must find some balance or tradeoffs between maintaining shape(s) and managing support(s), that is movement, drape and flow.

They do not understand how their choice of technique, and the decisions they make about how to apply it, influence the response of others to jewelry materials and forms they create. Technique, compounded by skill, can be very determinative of outcome.

SPACE AND MASS AND A PHILOSOPHY OF TECHNIQUE

Space and *Mass* are the raw materials of jewelry form. Space is void. Mass is something. Some jewelry depends more on the expression of Space; others more on the expression of Mass. Whatever the designer's goals and intents, Technique permits a reduction of the contrast between space and mass. Towards this end, Technique communicates the significance of a mass within a space by controlling it.

Publicly demonstrating this control communicates intent, meaning and expressiveness.

The jewelry artist begins by confronting a void. There is space, but there is nothing in it. *Space.*

Into this space or void, the artist introduces mass. This may begin with a point or a line or a plane or a specific shape or color or texture or pattern. More mass is added. *Mass.*

The designer sets boundaries, places and distributes things, brings things together, determines the scale, signifies directions and dimensions. The designer begins to co-relate the mass to the space around, within, or through it. *Mass on Space.*

The designer regulates the relationship and relative importance of the surface of the mass to the entirety of the mass itself. Sometimes the mass (or its surface) is expected to be static. Sometimes it is expected to move. Occasionally ornamentation is added. In the context of jewelry, some of this mass should be able to hold a shape; other of this mass should be able to move, drape and flow when worn. *Mass on Mass.*

Technique makes something out of nothingness. It is designed. It is constructed. The act of implementing a technique – that is, revealing a pattern of choice behaviors -- is communicative. It has intent. *Mass, Space, Intent.*

Eventually, the designer applies Technique to this mass, and in so doing, creates composition. Things are assembled. They are pulled together. The mass suddenly has order. It has organization. It is communicative. It interacts with the desires others place on it. It evokes an emotional response. It references a context or situation in which it is to be worn. *Mass, Space, Intent, Content.*

Thus, things placed within the space are pulled together, juxtaposed, connected, inter-related in some way. We call this *composition*. Composition might mean how the jewelry designer:

- Treats the surface
- Emphasizes dimension
- Joins units
- Impresses into things, onto things or through things
- Pulls or Stretches or Twists things
- Covers, embellishes, frames or exposes things

- Asserts or changes the scale
- Determines sizes, shapes and volumes
- Arranges, Places, Distributes things
- Relates positive to negative space
- Creates a rhythm, form or theme
- Expects things to move or be static
- Anticipates who might wear it, how it might be worn, and where it might be worn

A piece of jewelry becomes a wholly finite environment within what otherwise would have been nothingness. But filling this space with form is not enough. It is not the end of the designer's role and responsibility.

With order, organization and communication come significance, meaning, implication, connectedness and consequence for everyone around it. Expression occurs. An explanation or story emerges.

The designer must give this mass-in-space a quality other than emptiness. It must have content, meaning, purpose. The designer must allow this mass-in-space to be enjoyed. Again, expressed. Much of this comes down to materials and techniques. *Mass, Space, Intent, Content, Public Exhibition.*

That means the designer must impose upon this space some personal **Philosophy of Technique**—hopefully employing artistic and design knowledge, skill and understanding. This philosophy is how this designer thinks-like-a-designer. It becomes a key part of the designer's fluency, adaptability, and originality as a professional. It is how the designer touches things and brings things together.

This is a philosophy of selection, implementation and management of mass-in-space which:

- Balances, equalizes, meditates
- Restricts
- Releases
- Senses and newly senses
- Becomes a standpoint, a flashpoint, or a jumping off point
- Sees new possibilities, forecasts, anticipates or expects
- Creates and re-creates feelings
- Plays with tolerances, stresses and strains
- Makes things parsimonious where enough is enough

- Results in things which are understood as finished, successful and resonant

The mass has form and arrangement within space. It begins to convey sensation and feelings and content and meaning. But the designer still has not completed the job. *Jewelry cannot be fully experienced in anticipation.* It must be worn. It must be inhabited. It must communicate, interact, connect. Any philosophy of technique must account for all of this. *Mass, Space, Intent, Content, Public Exhibition, Dialectic.*

The elemental parts and their pleasing arrangement into a whole must allow it to be enjoyed by others. Be influenced by it. Persuaded. A desire to touch it. See it. Wear it. Buy it. Display it. Show it to others. Others, on some level, must accept the designer's Philosophy of Technique, that is, the designer's definition with intent for manipulating mass within space, in order to:

- Recognize how to look at it and react to it
- Understand how to wear it
- Be inspired as the artist was inspired
- Feel the balance, harmony, variety, cacophony, continuity, interdependence among spaces and masses
- Anticipate the effects of movement, drape and flow
- Get a sense of psycho-socio-cultural release
- Get a sense of psycho-socio-cultural restriction
- Know when the piece is finished and successful
- Judge the piece in terms of value and worth
- Assess the risk within some context of wearing or purchasing it
- Assess the risk within some context of sharing it with others

Designers over time gain fluency in their philosophies of several techniques. Such fluency is recognized and comes to the fore when Techniques serve the desires, understandings and values of both designer and client. Techniques and the philosophies (ways of thinking) which underly them must fully communicate the particular intent, concepts and experiences expressed by the jewelry designer. They must anticipate, as well, the particular shared understandings and desires others have about whether the piece will be judged finished and successful.

Designer and client have a special relationship which comes to light within the composed, constructed and manipulated piece of jewelry as it is introduced and expressed publicly.

Through Technique. Through Skill. And a Philosophy.

TECHNIQUES INVOLVE RELATIONSHIPS

Techniques, and the relative skill in applying them, are used to resolve the relational tensions underlying the craftmanship, artistry and design of any piece of jewelry. How these relationships are implemented and managed affect how the finished jewelry will be perceived sensorially, sensually, and symbolically. These will affect how the wearer/viewer recognizes the artist's intent. These will affect how the wearer/viewer sees their desires reflected within the piece, thus the value and worth of the piece to them.

In design terms, this is called **Expression**. *Expression in design* is the communication of quality and meaning. The designer expresses quality and meaning through the selection, implementation and application of technique. We sometimes refer to this as *skill*. A technique will have a function. It will have a set of mechanics and processes. It will have purpose. There will be variations in how the mechanics and processes will be put into effect. Sometimes it will require a stiffening up; othertimes a loosening up. A pressing or pulling harder or softer. A curving or straightening. A transformation from 2 dimensions to 3 dimensions. Repositioning. Altering texture.

The technique, its function and application will further get interpreted and transformed, that is, expressed, into wearable art. Similar to how sounds are made into music. And how words are made into literature. There is an underlying vocabulary and grammar to jewelry design, from decoding to comprehension to fluency.

Some aspects of expression are universal, but perhaps most are very subjective, reflective of the interpretations and intents (*philosophies*) of the artist, the wearer/viewer, and the general culture. Because of this, each and every expression of design through technique will have to resolve some underlying tensions.

Of special concern are these tensions and relationships:

1. *Aesthetic (beauty) vs. Architectural (function)*
2. *Should Parts Be Considered Center Stage or Supplemental*
3. *Special Relationship to Light and Shadow*
4. *Special Relationship to Texture*
5. *Special Relationship to Color and Ornamentation*

1. Aesthetic vs. Architectural

Jewelry Design all too often is viewed apart from the human body, as if we were creating sculptures, rather than wearable art. Yet its successful creation and implementation is not independent of the body, but moreso dependent upon it. It must feel good, move with the body, minimize the stresses and strains on the components and materials. And look good at the same time.

This sets up a tension in the relationship between the Aesthetic and the Architectural. The problems of jewelry design extend beyond the organizing of space and mass(es) within it. The designer must plan for and create a harmonious and expressive relationship between object and body and between object and person as the object is worn. This often means compromising. Trading off some of the aesthetics for more functionality.

A large amount of the appeal is based on the ability of the jewelry's construction to maintain its shape and silhouette, as well as the various shapes of its component parts, forms or themes. As the wearer moves, this becomes a tremendous challenge.

Similarly a large amount of the architectural integrity relates to how well the piece and its individual parts can move, shift, adjust in response to the forces of movement, drape and flow, without distorting any shape or silhouette, and without breaking or breakage.

Example of the Garden Urn

This 3-dimensional pendant – The Garden Urn – was created by the bead artist Cynthia Rutledge. It is constructed using a bead weaving technique called Even Count Tubular Peyote. As we move from bottom to top of the piece, first the rows are increased in width (vessel is made wider), and then near the top, decreased (vessel is made narrower). Here are some technique-related tradeoffs between aesthetics and functionality.

 "The Garden Urn", Cynthia Rutledge Aesthetic and Architectural Goals: 1. Piece holds its shape 2. No gap where making decrease 3. Bead pattern has natural flow from pre-decrease to post-decrease stitching	 *Decrease Option #1: Reduce subsequent row width by 1 bead, by stitching over the ditch* *Complete decrease in 3 row passes* *Result:* *1. Piece will not hold its shape without additional armature* *2. Slight gap* *3. Preserves peyote pattern, with some extra tension at point of decrease* *Response:* *a. Stuff with armature like cotton* *b. Embellish over gaps and where peyote pattern is disrupted*	 *Decrease Option #2: Reduce subsequent row width by 1 bead, by stitching into the ditch* *Complete decrease in 3 row passes* *Result:* *1. Piece holds it shape very tightly* *2. Slight gap* *3. Beads bunch up a bit at point of decrease* *Response:* *a. Embellish over gaps and where peyote pattern is disrupted*	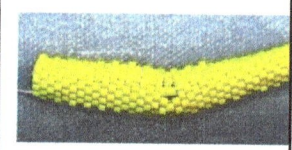 *Decrease Option #3: Reduce subsequent row width by 1 bead, by gradually stitching over the ditch* *Complete decrease in 5 row passes* *Result:* *1. Piece will not hold its shape without additional armature, but better than Option #1* *2. Slight gap, though smaller than other options* *3. The 2-beads-as-one placement visually disrupts peyote pattern, but no extra tension at point of decrease* *Response:*

			a. Stuff with armature like cotton (but won't need as much as Option #1) b. Embellish over gaps and where peyote pattern is disrupted
	Decrease Pattern: *First Row: Stitch over a down-bead* *Second Row: Add one bead over the ditch and between 2 up-beads* *Third Row: Peyote across the row, and pull tight.*	*Decrease Pattern:* *First Row: Stitch through the down-bead* *Second Row: Add one bead over the ditch and between 2 up-beads* *Third Row: Peyote across the row, and pull tight.*	*Decrease Pattern:* *First Row: Stitch over a down-bead* *Second Row: Add 2 beads over the ditch, and between 2 up-beads* *Third Row: Stitch through the 2-beads as one* *Fourth Row: Peyote across the row, again treating the 2-down-beads as one, and placing only 1 up-bead above them.* *Fifth Row:* *Peyote across the row, and pull tight.*

Before you choose and implement any technique…
STOP
ASK YOURSELF:
What about this technique and the steps involved in implementing this technique will help my piece maintain its **shape (structure)**?

Before you choose and implement any technique…
STOP
ASK YOURSELF:
What about this technique and the steps involved in implementing this technique will help my piece **move, drape and low (support)**?

2. **Should Parts Be Considered Core Center Stage or Supplemental**

The question becomes how the various parts or segments of the jewelry should relate to one another. We might have a strap, a yoke, a centerpiece or focal point, a bail, and a clasp assembly. There may be additional embellishment or fringing. The tension here becomes whether the jewelry as a whole should be judged critically as an expression of art and design, or only the centerpiece or focal point should be so judged.

With the latter, the non-center/focus parts of the jewelry are seen merely as supplemental. This is similar to how a frame functions for painting or a pedestal for a sculpture.

With the former, each segment or component part cannot exist or be expressive apart from any other. The piece must be judged as a whole. The whole must be more resonant or evocative than the sum of its parts.

Here we begin to question what exactly technique is. Is it only that set of mechanics and processes applied to only a section of the whole piece of jewelry? Or is it how the designer makes choices about construction and manipulation from getting from one end of the piece of jewelry to the other? Another way of saying this is: Should we judge the technique from the *art approach* or the *design perspective*?

Of primary importance: How the technique is implemented and managed in order to bring materials together within a composition. From the perspective of disciplinary literacy, there is no other choice than to consider all parts of the anatomy of a piece of jewelry important and never supplemental.

3. Special Relationship To Light And Shadow

Light and shadow are both critical design elements to be manipulated as a part of the jewelry designer's active decision making process. Yet, light and shadow affect the experience of any piece of jewelry in ways which are outside that designer's scope and control, as well. After all, jewelry is not typically made to hang in one place in a museum, with controlled lighting and positioning.

Light and shadow are necessary for the expression of the artist's intent and inspiration in jewelry. Because light and shadow move, change character, and come and go with their source, light and shadow have the power to give that mass of component parts a living quality. This effect is compounded (or foiled) as the wearer moves, changes position, travels from room to room or inside to outside.

The designer cannot control all this, but should be able to predict a lot of this behavior, and make appropriate design choices accordingly.

The designer can channel light through the selection of materials and their reflective, absorptive and refractive properties. The designer can play with color, pattern and texture. The designer can be strategic about the placement of positive and negative spaces. The designer can arrange or embellish surfaces in anticipation of all this. The designer can diffuse light or transform or distort colors. The designer can add movement or dimensionality to enliven their forms. The designer can even use light or shadow to hide things which might negatively affect the overall aesthetic.

The designer can conceptualize and visualize the piece as having a front side, a left side, a right side and a back side. The designer can think about the piece twisting and swinging and otherwise shifting positions. And plan for this.

The points, lines, planes and shapes incorporated into any piece of jewelry become receptacles of light and shadow which can change in character or form as time progresses, people move and contexts change. An important part in the success of jewelry designs is played by the quality and intensity of light (and shadow) within context.

4. Special Relationship to Texture

Jewelry is experienced both tactilely and visually.

Sometimes these complement each other; othertimes, they compete or conflict. Texture plays a major role here. On the one hand, it expresses something about the quality of the materials used. On the other, it gives a particular quality to light and shadow, and their interplay with the piece as worn.

Designers often select materials partly based on their tactile textures. They might also alter these textures to expand on the variety of expressive qualities that might be offered. The stone might be used as is. It might be smoothed and polished. It might be roughed up, sand-blasted, carved or chiseled. The material might end up expressing something about the natural state or about refinement and sophistication. Visually, the designer makes many choices about how to employ the materials. They may emphasize verticality over horizontality. Projecting over receding. Slow or fast rhythm. Opacity may be altered. They may overlap. The designer produces differing visual expressions based on patterns and how lighting of the surface conveys the sensory experience of these patterns.

A single texture, whether the goal is tactile or visual, is rarely employed alone in jewelry design. The actual variety of materials and treatments produces a complex of textures that must be composed and harmonized and resonant into the jewelry's expressive and consistent whole.

5. Special Relationship to Color and Ornament

Color is a characteristic of all jewelry making materials. It is a constant feature of any piece of jewelry. Materials might be selected for their color and visual appeal. Techniques might be selected for their ability to enhance or play with color and its visual appeal.

Yet, on the other hand, some jewelry making materials and techniques might be selected primarily for their structural properties – that is, their ability to be used to create, maintain, and retain shape or silhouette. They might be used as mere armature or to create that armature. Other jewelry making materials and techniques might be selected primarily for their support properties – that is, their ability to enhance movement, drape and flow.

The colors of these more function-specific materials or the effects resulting from how these more function-specific techniques manipulated them may not be suited to the expressive goals of the designer. Because of the nature of jewelry making techniques and components, there also may be an unintended or unwanted absence of color, such as gaps of light between beads.

Thus, as a result of these kinds of things, materials with more suitable expressive colors, either as is or as manipulated, are added to or extended from the surface as *embellishment* and *ornamentation*. Sometimes these materials are dyes or coatings or fired-on chemicals. Sometimes these materials are more substantive materials like glass, gemstone, wood or shell.

These ornamental materials may cover parts of the surface or hide the entire surface of the piece. They may disguise it. They may be used to alter how color is perceived and experienced. They may completely change the experience. But without technique, and a philosophy of technique, these ornamental options may make it impossible to achieve the sensory, visual or structural powers the ornamentation is meant to provide.

The tension arises when the designer makes choices whether the ornamentation is to be used to enhance the expressiveness of the piece as originally designed (*applied ornamentation*), or, whether the ornamentation is to be used to create a completely different meaning, decorative motif, or symbolic expression, regardless of appropriateness to that original design (*mimetic ornamentation*).

Applied ornamentation enhances the designer's power and control to assert intent and inspiration within the jewelry. Often applied ornamentation makes some reference to the underlying structures behind it. But the designer needs to be careful that this doesn't turn into merely *applied decoration*. As *ornament*, whatever is done is <u>integral to the piece</u>. As *decoration*, it is not.

Mimetic ornamentation is often used to make a piece more familiar, more accepting, more reassuring to various audiences. It might be used to disguise something. It might have symbolic value. Here, too, the designer needs to be careful that this doesn't turn into merely applied decoration.

A third consideration is whether the ornamentation is critical to the jewelry's functioning or materials (*inherent ornamentation*). It is important that it be organic to the piece. That is, it should derive directly from and be a function of the nature of the jewelry and the materials used. It may allow size adjustment. Its placement may reinforce to overcome vulnerabilities. It may redistribute stresses and strains. It may aid in movement. It may assist in maintaining a shape. It may rationalize color, texture and/or pattern within and throughout the piece.

SURVEY OF JEWELRY MAKING TECHNIQUES

There are many, many different types of techniques used in jewelry making. Each encompasses basic mechanics. Each is implemented within a procedure or process. Each is a form of expression.

These techniques or forms of expression differ from each other in terms of the choices the designer makes about how mass should get related to space for creating composition. They differ in how structure (*shape*) is created and preserved, and in how support (*movement, drape and flow*) is built in, achieved and maintained. They differ in how pattern and texture is created or added. These techniques differ, apart from the materials used, in how people interact with them, aesthetically, functionally, sensorially and sensually.

These techniques are not mutually exclusive, and are often combined. It is up to the designer to select the technique or techniques to be used, maximizing the strengths and minimizing the weaknesses of each (*leveraging*). Usually, the designer, when combining techniques, will want one technique to predominate. The designer does not want the underlying philosophies of two or more techniques to conflict, compete, or not coordinate.

Stringing, Bead Weaving

Bead Stringing | *Bead Weaving*

Beads and other components are *assembled* together into a composition and silhouette. The stringing materials range from the very narrow, like beading thread, cable thread and cable wire, to thicker, like bead cord, leather, waxed cotton, ribbon, satin cord, and braided leather. The stringing materials are often hidden, and typically play a supplemental role to the beads and other components within any composition.

Philosophy of Technique: Objects are placed and assembled together within a space in relationship to the direction and linearity of some type of stringing material or canvas. There is great attention to the use of points and lines, usually within a singular plane. Shapes are basic, often only in reference to a silhouette. Minimal attention is paid to dimensionality.

A piece is made stable by the rigidity of the stringing material or canvas. The stringing material or canvas is able to withstand tension and compression.

Often, designers place too much reliance on the clasp assembly to provide support (*movement, drape and flow*), instead of embedding support elements (*rings, loops, unglued-knots, hinges, springs, coils, rivets, rotators*) throughout the piece. In a similar way, often designers place too much reliance on the placement of objects on the canvas (*that is, stringing material*) for maintaining structure (*shape*), instead of other elements that could be used to maintain shape, while mitigating against stress and strain.

Each stringing and bead weaving technique and its procedures and processes for implementation rely on part of the implementation's steps to maintain a shape, and on part of the implementation's steps to allow for movement, drape and flow. The particular technique used to assemble the beads (*and related components*) sets the tone in pattern, shape, form and texture. Some stringing and bead weaving techniques are great at maintaining shapes. Other techniques are good at allowing for movement. The better techniques are good at accommodating both structure and support.

Knotting, Braiding, Knitting, Crocheting

| Knotting | Kumihimo |

The *stringing materials take center stage and somehow are intertwined*, either in combination with other elements, or alone. The composition may or may not include beads and other components. Occasionally glue is used, but its use should be minimized.

Philosophy of Technique: Within a space, the artist places and intertwines various types of stringing materials. The artist varies tightness and looseness, placement and distribution of sizes, volumes and mass to achieve the dual goals of structure and support.

A piece is made stable by the rigidity of the intertwining (*knotting, chaining, braiding*) of the stringing material or canvas. The intertwined stringing material or canvas is able to withstand tension and compression.

Each strategy for knotting or braiding attempts to simultaneously achieve structure and support. The technique might vary the placement of fixed points with the use of chaining to create lines, forms and planes within the composition. Considerable attention is paid to the positioning of positive and negative spaces.

There is a lot of attention to the use of line. These techniques allow for incorporation of various strategies for achieving a sense of dimensionality. The shapes may be allowed to stretch or contract, allowing easy response to issues resulting from stress or strain. Texture is a major emphasis.

Embroidery, Embellishment, Fringing

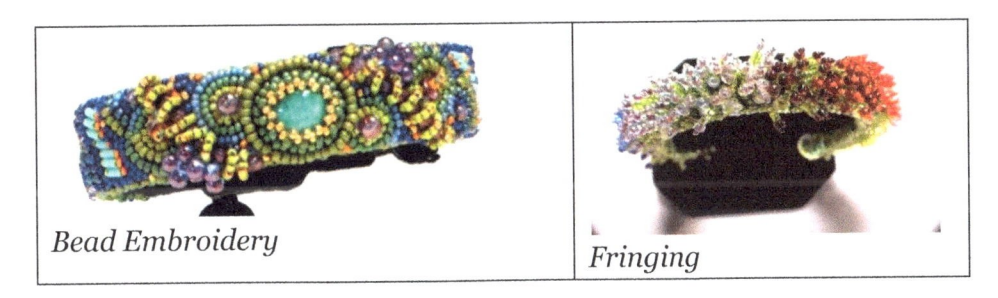

Bead Embroidery

Fringing

Elements are *attached to the surface of the canvas*. This surface is often referred to as the *foundation* or *base*. These elements may be glued or sewn or woven on. The canvas typically plays a diminished or supplemental role, though this is not a requirement.

Philosophy of Technique: The space available has been defined by a particular canvas. This might be a string. This might be a flat surface. Elements are placed on and secured to this surface; the mechanics here relate to structural goals. The pliability, manipulability, and/or maneuverability of the canvas relate to support goals.

A piece is made stable by the rigidity of the stringing material or canvas. The stringing material or canvas is able to withstand tension and compression.

The embellishment may be used to create a particular image, or pattern, or texture. Often it is used to add a sense of dimensionality and/or movement to a piece. It invites people to want to touch the composition because it adds a very sensual quality to a piece beyond the characteristics of the materials or colors used.

Stamping, Engraving, Etching

Stamped Piece

Elements are *embedded on or worked into the surface of the canvas*. The canvas may be comprised of any material, but most often metal or wood or clay.

Philosophy of Technique: The space available has been defined by a particular canvas. This is typically a flat surface of some kind, but not limited to any one material. Structural, as well as support, goals depend on the physical, functional and chemical properties of the canvas. Sometimes these properties are altered through the application of the techniques. Texture and pattern are major focuses.

A piece is made stable by the rigidity and material strength of the canvas coupled with that canvas's ability to maintain its integrity after it has been physically or chemically altered. The resulting canvas is able to withstand tension and compression.

Wire Working, Wire Wrapping, Wire Weaving

Wire Wrapping | *Wire Weaving*

Hard Wire is *manipulated into forms* which hold their shape, serve as structural supports, or create pleasing patterns and textures.

Philosophy of Technique: The designer places wires into a space. The wires may be bent to form lines, planes, shapes and forms. The wires may be interwoven, bundled together, coiled, or otherwise anchored or tied together to create a canvas and form the basic foundation of a piece of jewelry.

During the process of applying a wire technique and creating a piece of jewelry, the physical properties – in most cases, the stiffness -- of the wire must be changed. The designer takes wire, applies a technique to it, and continues to apply the technique until the wire is stiff enough to hold a shape. Each time you manipulate wire, it gets harder and harder and harder. If you manipulate it too much, it will become brittle and break. The wire can be pulled, coiled, bent, twisted, or hammered.

A piece is made stable by the stiffness or hardness of the canvas and its material strength, where it is stiff enough to hold a shape, but not so stiff as to become brittle and break. The resulting canvas is able to withstand tension and compression.

Considerable attention must be paid to strategies of support, that is, how things get joined and jointed. That is, whatever the piece of jewelry, it must be able to move freely, and withstand all sources of stress or strain.

For example, hard wire would not be used as a stringing material. If you put beads on the hard wire to create a bracelet or necklace, the wire would distort in shape when the piece is worn, but not return to its original shape. In this case, you would have to create several segments or components using the wire, and then make some kind of chain to create that jointedness and support. Picture a rosary which is a bead chain made of wire.

Metalsmithing, Fabrication, Cold Connections

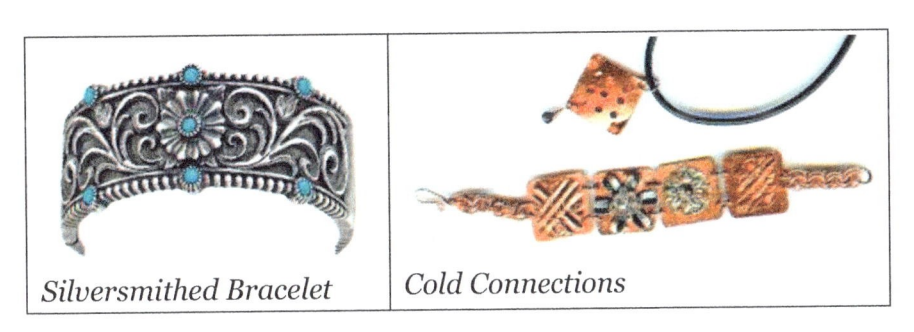

Silversmithed Bracelet | *Cold Connections*

Here metal is *shaped and formed* into a broad, *layered* canvas or a series of canvases we call components. Layers of sheet, wire and granules, or a series of components may be combined in some way, either to create a more complex composition, increase a sense of dimensionality or movement, or allow for jointedness, connectivity and support. The designer might use heat and solder – *fabrication*. Or the designer might use rivets, hinges, loops, rings, rotators – *cold connections*. The layers or the series of components may be textured or not.

Philosophy of Technique: Into a space, the designer places pieces of metal. These pieces of metal may sit side-by-side, on top of each other, overlap, sit perpendicular or at an angle. The components are attached together, using heat and solder, glue, or cold connections. Each layered canvas or component is a composition unto itself.

Canvases and components are rigid shapes and are constructed to withstand stress and strain. When constructing a piece of jewelry, typically the designer interconnects various components in a way which allows movement, drape and flow.

Interconnected components may be thematic or tell a story.

A piece is made stable by the rigidity and material strength of the canvas after it has been successfully altered through shaping, heat, soldered connection, glue or cold connection. The resulting canvas is able to withstand tension and compression, up until the point it bends or dents. Usually, if that happens, the piece can be unbent or undented. Considerable attention must be paid to strategies of support, that is, how things get joined and jointed.

Casting, Modeling, Molding, Carving, Shaping

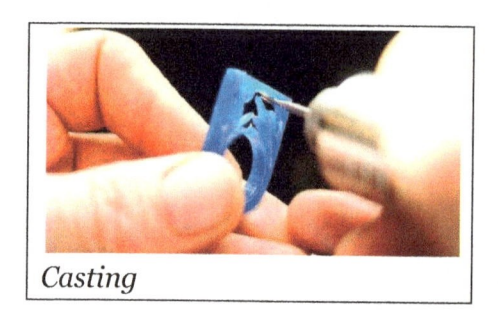

Casting

Here a *material is reconfigured and altered* into some kind of shape or form. The material may be rigid, like wood or stone. It may be malleable like clay or casting material. The material, once altered, may or may not be subject to additional actions to change its physical, functional or chemical properties, such as the application of heat or cold or a chemical bath.

Philosophy of Technique: The material is positioned within a space. As it is manipulated, it most likely will alter its relationship to that space. It will be able to play many roles from point to line to plane, and from shape to form to theme. The designer must be critically aware of how the technique will alter this relationship between space and mass, and light and shadow, and how these in turn, will affect form and composition.

A piece is made stable by the rigidity of the canvas after it has been shaped. Cast pieces have difficulty responding to strong forces. The resulting canvas is able to withstand tension and compression only to that point before it crumbles and breaks.

Structure and support considerations can either be built into the resulting component, or components may be treated in similar ways as in metalsmithing.

Lampworking, Wound Glass, Encasing

Lampwork Bead by Jayden Alfre Jones

Rods and stringers of glass are *heated by a torch and wound* around a steel rod called a mandrel. Sometimes shards of glass, sometimes with abstract patterns, sometimes representative of realistic images, are laid on the hot glass, and covered (encased) by a transparent glass wound over them. The result is a bead or pendant or a small sculpture.

Philosophy of Technique: The material slowly enters and occupies a defined space. The artist plays with different types of glass, glass colors and transparencies, rods of glass, pieces of glass, ground up glass, and metallic foils. Things are placed and layered and spiraled. Surfaces can be altered by tools. Once begun, the artist must take the technique to completion. Thus, the artist's ideas, focus, and intent are very concentrated and intense. Glass as a material requires the manipulation of the interpenetration of mass with space.

A piece is made stable by the properties of the glass. The resulting canvas is able to withstand tension and compression to the extent the properties of the glass will allow.

Glass Blowing

Glass Blown Bead

Air is forced through a steel straw. At the end of this straw is a blob of molten glass. The *air forces the glass to hollow out.* As this happens, the artist rolls it, hammers it, textures it, domes it, dimples it, otherwise shapes it until it is a finished piece. The artist may roll the glass over other pieces of glass, to melt them into the piece. As the glass cools, the result might be a bead or a pendant or a small sculpture.

Philosophy of Technique: The material expands within a space. This space may be very narrow and defined, or very expansive, perhaps ill-defined. The resulting object has surface and interior and exterior spaces. The qualities of the surface create a play between mass and space, and their interpenetration.

A piece is made stable by the properties of the glass. The resulting canvas is able to withstand tension and compression to the extent the properties of the glass walls will allow.

Computer Aided Design (CAD), 3-D Printing

3-D Printed

    Here the artist uses *computers to aid in the creation, modification, analysis, or optimization of a design.* The output is typically in the form of electronic files or technical drawings for 3-D printing, machining or other manufacturing operation. 3-D printing takes a CAD model and builds it, material layer by layer in an additive manufacturing fashion. Frequently, the 3-D printed object is a casting mold, rather than the finished piece.

    Philosophy of Technique: CAD can place points, lines and curves within a 2-dimensional space, or curves, surfaces and solids within a 3-dimensional space. CAD can simulate motion and its impact on any object. It can take into account other parameters and constraints. The final technical output must convey more than information about shape. It must convey information about the extents to which various materials may be used in the design, their dimensions and tolerances. It must convey information about the pros and cons of processes the artist might use in the design.

    One pay-off for the artist is that the computer can detail many more ways, and many more unexpected ways, to relate mass to space than typically thought of without it.

HOW TO LEARN TECHNIQUE

    A good design, poorly executed, is not worth all that much.

    So, how do we learn techniques is ways which help us develop ourselves as designers and be fluent in how we select, implement and apply them?

    We need to be very aware of what influences us in our:

    o Selection of Technique
    o Implementation of Technique
    o Application of Technique

Selection: *Anticipating What Will Happen If And When*

We begin to develop our fluency in technique at the point of *selection*. To select a technique is to anticipate what will happen to the piece of jewelry after it is designed, constructed and worn. This involves all our senses from thought to touch to sight.

When we *touch* a piece constructed using a particular technique, how will it feel? Will it curve or bend? Will it curve or bend in the direction we need it to? Will it drape nicely on the body? Move easily with the body? Feel comfortable when worn? Will it hold its shape? Its intended silhouette?

When we *see* a piece constructed using a particular technique, what will be the resulting pattern and texture? What will be the interplay of light and shadow? Will it look good from all sides when sitting on an easel? Will it look good from all sides when someone is wearing it? When that person is moving? Will all color issues be resolved? Will there be an acceptable balance between positive and negative spaces? Will there be an acceptable distribution of sizes, colors, shapes and volumes?

We play a *What-If game*. What-If we used a variation on the technique? What-If we used another technique? What-If we combined techniques or sequenced them or staggered them? What-if we settled for a little less beauty to achieve better movement, drape and flow?

We might do some *research*. Has the technique been used by another artist or in another project you were attracted to? Was it used successfully? Did it work well in terms of structure and support? Did it contribute to (or at least not detract from) the visual appearance of the piece?

We might do some *pre-testing*. Will the technique hold up to our expectations? Will it still work with some variation? Will it work under differing circumstances?

We are honest with ourselves about our *biases*. Will we pick something only because we have done it before? Or we are very familiar with it? Or it is the easiest or path of least resistance?

Implementation: *Basic Mechanics and Processes*

We want to learn the basic mechanics of each technique in a way which highlights their philosophies – that is, how we think them through. We think about managing:

- *Structure and Support*
- *How To Hold The Piece To Work It*
- *How To Distribute Stresses and Points of Vulnerability*
- *How To Create A Clasp Assembly*
- *How To Finish Off The Piece*

<u>**Structure and Support**</u>

To begin, we know that each and every technique has as part of its mechanics and processes some aspects which help us create and maintain structures (*shape*). And each and every technique has some aspects which help us create and maintain support (*movement, drape and flow*). We want to be able to break down any technique so that we can recognize what results in what.

> ### Right Angle Weave (RAW) Bead Weaving Stitch
>
> The RAW Stitch typically is a circle of 4 beads (a Right Angle Weave Unit) connected to another circle of 4 beads (a second RAW unit), with one bead shared. The thread path follows a "figure 8" pathway. As you add units, you will find yourself going up and around in one direction, then going down and around to add the next couple units, then up and around, and then down and around, and so forth, always following that figure 8.
>
> *Single RAW UNIT*
>
> *Two RAW units joined through a shared bead.*
>
> Right Angle Weave works a little like a coil spring mattress. When someone lies down on the mattress, you will want some of the coils to move together, and some to self-adjust semi-independently, if the mattress is to be comfortable and both support, as well as conform, to the body.
>
> **Structure.** In RAW, we create a RAW unit, usually consisting of 4 beads, and we connect this unit to the subsequent unit, through a shared bead. It is important that the beads within the single unit move as "one." That means, we need to get them as tightly abutted against each other as possible. When using bicone beads, for example, this is relatively easy. The bead shapes make them lock up tightly. But when using round beads, the beads do not lock up. In this case, it may be prudent to circle all 4 beads with our thread more than once, before proceeding to add the next RAW unit.
>
> **Support.** In our shared bead, however, we want a looser connection to the next RAW unit. We want our RAW units to move somewhat together, yet somewhat independently, in order to adequately adapt to the forces of movement as our bracelet is worn.

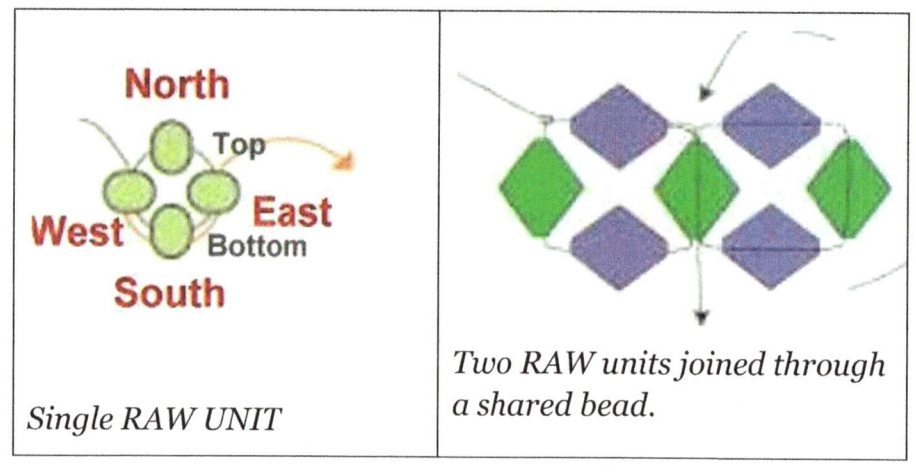

Petersburg Chain Bead Weaving Stitch

The St. Petersburg Chain stitch is a relatively simple stitch that generates a long, thin, flat length of beadwork. The result is very soft, feminine and airy.

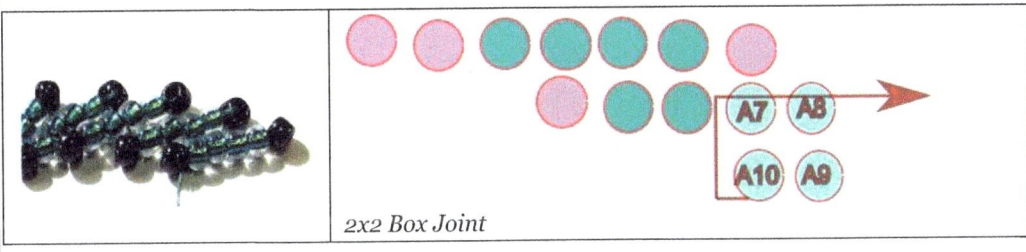

2x2 Box Joint

The crux of support or architectural structure in the Petersburg chain lies in a "2x2 box joint". The Petersburg chain stitch is a very, very loose stitch. This box joint creates the structural support for the strip of stitching to retain its shape, while adjusting to the forces of movement, drape and flow. Architecturally, however loose the stitching is for the rest of the Petersburg chain, we always want to tighten up our 4-bead box joint which connects each row.

Wire Woven Pendant Wrap

Wire weaving is a set of techniques, similar to basket weaving, where you wrap thin weave wires around thicker BASE or FRAME WIREs to create patterns and textures. You can then use these wire-woven strips to make all kinds of things, such as the framework to turn a cabochon or bead into a pendant, earring dangles, bracelets, bails, and the like.

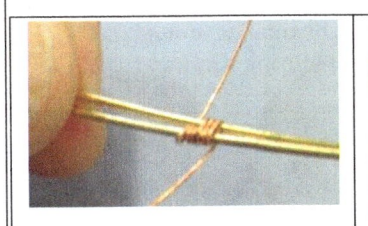

Thinner Weave Wire Coiling Around Thicker Base Wires

One Base Wire inserted through hole of the bead

Finished Pendant

Structure and Support. You begin with Base and Weave wires which are dead soft. They are very malleable. The Base wires stay dead soft and malleable, but the Weave wires harden as you coil them around the Base wires. Every time you manipulate wire, it gets harder and harder and harder. So the stiffness of the Weave wires allows the resulting woven canvas strip to maintain a shape and stay in place on the elongated teardrop bead. The softer Base wires allows you to wrap the weave around the bead. Running one Base wire through the hole of the bead and then creating a bail, thus hardening the Base wire at the top of the pendant, allows the pendant to be worn as jewelry without the teardrop bead slipping the wire woven canvas strip.

> **Bead Strung Bracelet**
>
> Bead stringing involves putting beads on some kind of stringing material, and securing them.
>
> *Arrow (top left) points to spacer bead (rotator support system).*
>
> **Structure.** The large beads, the stringing material (*canvas*), and the clasp assembly define the shape or silhouette of the piece. They determine the size and stability of the circle.
>
> **Support.** When using very large beads, however, that tight circle can put too much stress and strain on the piece, particularly when the wearer moves around. These beads can crack or break, as can the stringing material and clasp. The small spacer beads between each large bead are a type of support system called a *rotator support system*. As the bracelet is subject to outside forces resulting from movement, the larger beads can shift position by rotating around the spacer beads, thus rechanneling and absorbing those forces and minimizing stress and strain.

Holding The Piece To Work It

Next, the basic mechanics also includes strategies for *how to hold the piece while you work it*.

Picture yourself as an artist. An artist has an easel and something to use as a clamp to hold things in place.

A bead weaver would use their forefinger on one hand as an easel, pressing the developing bead work project against it, and then take their thumb on that same hand, and clamp down over the work to keep it in place.

A silversmith might use a steel bench block as an easel, and a vice as a clamp.

Someone doing braiding or knotting might use a clipboard as an easel and a bulldog clip as a clamp.

Your challenge is to hold the piece in such a way that you maximize your ability to implement a technique all the while maximizing the strengths of that technique and minimizing its weaknesses. This is called *leveraging*. You use whatever it is that is equivalent to the artist's easel and clamp in such a way that you can successfully leverage the technique for your purposes.

Holding your piece correctly also sends signals to your hands telling you when each individual step is completed, and when you are finished.

Distributed Stresses and Points of Vulnerability

In any piece of jewelry, it can be expected that the stress-bearing and strain-bearing strengths and weaknesses of each component will be unevenly distributed throughout the pieces. That is, there will be some areas or points in the piece of jewelry which will be more vulnerable to stresses and strains. This may cause the piece to break or lose its shape or otherwise disrupt its integrity.

The jewelry designer needs to be able to easily look at a piece or its sketch or design plan and identify all the points of vulnerability. After identifying these, the designer will need to figure out ways to compensate for these weaknesses in design.

Usually points of vulnerability occur in these places or situations:

- Where the clasp assembly is attached to the piece
- At the beginning and the end of the piece
- Along the edges
- Corners and inside corners
- Where components have very sharp holes or edges
- When using materials which degrade, deteriorate, bleed, rub off, distort, are too soft
- Where there is not an exact fit between two pieces or elements
- Where there is insufficient support or jointedness

These points of vulnerability may need reinforcement. More support or structural elements may need to be added. Things may need to be re-located or positioned within the design. They may need to be eliminated from the design.

Most often, places of vulnerability occur where the structures or supports in place take on the shapes of either *H, L, T,* or *U*. Think of these shapes as **hazards**. These shapes tend to split when confronted with external or internal forces. They tend to split because each leg is often confronted with different levels or directions of force. The legs are not braced. These hazardous shapes cry out for additional reinforcements or support or structural systems.

The Clasp Assembly

The *CLASP ASSEMBLY* usually consists of several parts. It includes everything it takes to attach the clasp to your work. Besides the Clasp itself, there are probably jump rings and connectors, crimp beads, clamps, cones, end caps or other jewelry findings.

Visually, the Clasp Assembly is part of the vernacular of the piece. Ideally, it should seem organically related to the piece or at least a logical inclusion.

Structurally, the Clasp Assembly should hold the piece together as the piece is worn. It may have some impact on maintaining the shape of the silhouette. It will have some impact on how well the jewelry maintains its position on the body, such as preventing a necklace from rotating around the upper torso.

Most importantly, the Clasp Assembly should be put together as a *support system*. It is the most important support system in any piece of jewelry. Support systems used in a necklace or bracelet are similar to the joints in your body. They aid in movement. They prevent any one piece from being adversely affected by the forces this movement brings to the piece. They keep the piece from being stiff. They make the piece look and feel better, when worn.

Ideally, the Clasp Assembly of any piece of jewelry should be designed first before the rest of the piece is designed, or designed currently with the rest of the piece. Too often, jewelry designers select the clasp after they have finished the rest of the piece. They do not seem to understand how the clasp assembly is an integral part of the implementation of any technique. In this case, not only does the clasp assembly look like it was the last choice, but it usually falls short of meeting its visual, structural and support roles.

Finishing Off The Piece

We always need to step back and reflect whether the piece as designed and implemented will be judged as finished and successful by each of the myriad audiences we hope to please. Will their judgments confirm or reject our philosophy of the particular technique(s) we used?

It is the challenge for the designer not to make the piece under-done or over-done. Each and every material and component part should be integral to the piece as a whole.

Application: *Achieving Expressiveness*

Expressiveness refers to the power of the piece of jewelry to fit with both the designer's as well as all other audience's expectations about desire, connectedness, power, value and worth. This is one and the same thing as measuring the extent to which both materials and techniques can be seen to have been leveraged, to maximize their strengths and minimize their weaknesses in the most parsimonious of ways.

A technique has been applied in the most expressive way at that point where the design elements and the materials selected have been composed, manipulated and constructed in the most optimum way. We can judge the degree of expressiveness by honing in on two concepts: *Parsimony* and *Resonance*.

Parsimony (maximum applied impact): *Parsimony* is when you know enough is enough. When the finished and successful piece is parsimonious, the relationship of all the Design Elements and their expressed attributes will be so strong, that to add or remove any one thing would diminish, not just the design, but rather the significance of the design. Parsimony is sometimes referred to in art and design as *Economy*, but the idea of economy is reserved for the visual effects. For jewelry designers, we want that economy or parsimony to apply to functional and situational effects, as well. The designer needs to be able to decide when enough is enough.

> ***Parsimony...***
> *- forces explanation; its forced-choice nature is most revealing about the artist's understandings and intentions*
>
> *- relies on evidence moreso than assumptions to get at criticality*
>
> *- focuses examination of the few elements that make a difference*

Resonance (coherency of applied impact): *Resonance* is some level of felt energy that is a little more than an emotional response. The difference between saying that piece of jewelry is *"beautiful"* vs. saying that piece of jewelry *"makes me want to wear it"*. Or that *"I want to touch it"*. Or *"My friends need to see this."* Or, *"I want to buy this."*

Resonance is something more than emotion. It is some kind of additional energy we see, feel and otherwise experience. Emotion is very reactive. Resonance is intuitive, involving, identifying. *Resonance* is an empathetic response where artist and audience realize a shared (or contradictory) understanding without losing sight of whose views and feelings belong to whom.

Resonance results from how the artist applies technique to control light, shadow, and their characteristics of warmth and cold, receding and approaching, bright and dull, light and dark. *Resonance* results from how the artist leverages the strengths of materials and techniques and minimizes their weaknesses. *Resonance* results from social, cultural and situational cues. *Resonance* results from how the artist takes us to the edge of universal, objective understandings, and pushes us every so slightly, but not too, too far, beyond that edge.

Jewelry which resonates...

- is communicative and authentic	- lets the materials and techniques speak
- shows the artist's hand as intention, not instinct	- anticipates shared understandings of many different audiences about design elements and principles, and some obvious inclusion, exclusion or intentional violation of them
- evokes both an emotional as well as energetic response from wearer and viewer	
- shows both degrees of control, as well as moments of the unexpected	- results from a design process that appears to have been more systemic (e.g., ingrained within an integrated process) than systematic (e.g., a step-by-step approach)
- makes something noteworthy from something ordinary	
- finds the whole greater than the sum of the parts	- both appeals and functions at the boundary where jewelry meets person

TECHNOLOGY AND JEWELRY DESIGN

The potential of technology merged with craft is infinite.

Technology includes things like,

- New methods, processes and materials
- New ways to implement ideas
- Ability to generate new styles
- Opportunity to create meaningful forms
- Unseen contributions to aesthetic structure and composition
- Less costly and/or more production-friendly methods for creating pieces, especially for projects which might not otherwise get implemented

New materials and composites are created and enter the marketplace every year.

New ways of extracting, shaping, finishing, stabilizing materials come on line each year.

Polymer, Metal and Crystal Clays allow the designer to sculpt things, then fire them, burning out the non-precious or non-valuable composite materials, and resulting in materials of precious or other valuable materials.

Computer Aided Design (CAD) and *3-D printing* provide the tools to jewelry designers to create things beyond their imaginations.

Electroforming enables the creation of lightweight pieces from various metals.

Lasers are used to weld, cut and decorate.

Laser-Sintering melts powdered metal, layer by layer, into a finished piece.

Jewelry makers and beaders frequently come up with new techniques, mechanics and processes for creating jewelry. Technology provides creatives with original ways of expression.

"Smart" elements are getting introduced into some designs, transforming your jewelry into a smart device. These might measure health and fitness; might change color and appearance to suit different environments or clothing; might warm or cool the body.

TO WHAT EXTENT SHOULD JEWELRY DESIGNERS RESPOND TO TECHNOLOGY?

Technology is a very powerful tool. Combined with craftmanship, it can create a new language of shape, object, and sensation. We have to be careful, however, that we use technology to support jewelry which is hand-made, and not supplant it.

The use of technology allows the designer to create new forms and materials that otherwise would not exist. Technology often translates into convenience and more rapid production. In today's globalized world, this might offer a competitive edge. Technology also enables more customization, and faster customization. Again, in a globalized world, this would offer a competitive advantage. Technology encourages us to look forward, rather than back, for our inspirations and insights.

Again, it is important to emphasize that we do not want all this technological efficiency to diminish the act of "creativity". We don't want to standardize everything and reduce everything into a set of how-to instructions. We want to expand our creative abilities. We want to increase the power of the designer to produce pieces reflective of the artist's hand. We want our jewelry to be as expressive as possible of the needs, wants and desires of our various clientele.

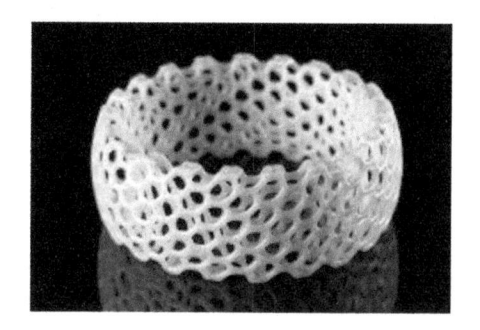

The impact of new jewelry-making technologies on our professional practice. Whether we use new technologies in our professional practice, or not, we cannot escape them. We must be up-to-date and aware of technological impacts on what we do and how we do it.

The impact of technology on work and jobs was the focus of an opinion piece in the New York Times by David H. Autor and David Dorn.

As jewelry designers, we are living through and with all the positives and negatives that arise through this technological change.

- How has technology affected what we do as designers?
- How has it affected what we do to survive and thrive as designers?
- Have we mechanized and computerized the jewelry design business into obsolescence?
- How have you had to organize your jewelry designer lives differently?

Given the rise of ...

- The internet,
- Ebay, Etsy and Amazon.com
- Blogs, Facebook, Twitter, Pinterest, Instagram
- New technologies and materials like precious metal clay, polymer clay, crystal clay, 3-D printing

- What has happened to your local bead stores? Jewelry stores? Boutiques? Galleries?
- What has happened to bead and jewelry making magazines?
- If you teach classes for pay, or sell kits and instructions, how do you compete against the literally millions of online tutorials, classes, instructions and kits offered for free?   How

does this affect what you teach or design to sell as kits?

- If you sell jewelry, how do you compete against the 60,000,000 other people who sell jewelry online? How does this affect your marketing, your pricing, your designs?
- If you make part of your living doing the arts and crafts show circuit, will there still be a need for this in the future?

FOOTNOTES

Autor, David H. and Dorn, David. "How Technology Wrecks the Middle Class", <u>New York Times</u>, August 24, 2013.
As referenced in:
https://opinionator.blogs.nytimes.com/2013/08/24/how-technology-wrecks-the-middle-class/

MATERIALS, TECHNIQUES AND TECHNOLOGIES
4c. MIXED MEDIA / MIXED TECHNIQUES

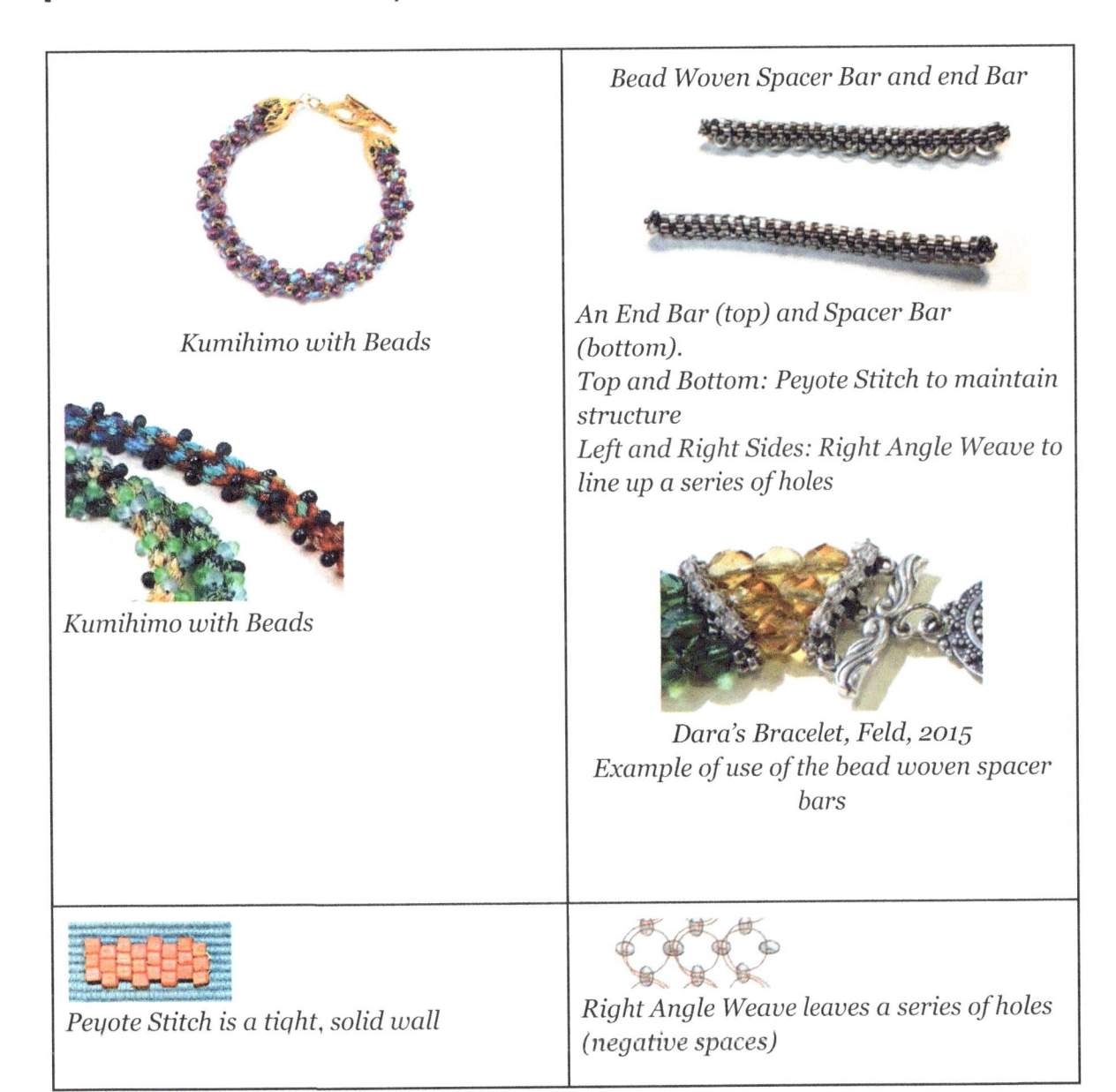

Kumihimo with Beads	*Bead Woven Spacer Bar and end Bar*
Kumihimo with Beads	*An End Bar (top) and Spacer Bar (bottom).* *Top and Bottom: Peyote Stitch to maintain structure* *Left and Right Sides: Right Angle Weave to line up a series of holes*
	Dara's Bracelet, Feld, 2015 *Example of use of the bead woven spacer bars*
Peyote Stitch is a tight, solid wall	*Right Angle Weave leaves a series of holes (negative spaces)*

> *Guiding Questions:*
> *(1) What kinds of things do you need to take into account when mixing materials or techniques?*
> *(2) What are the different types of mixed media /techniques projects?*

Key Words: *mixed media* *mixed techniques* *types of projects*	*synergistic effect* *leverage* *structure* *support*	*architectural basics* *collage* *found object*

Abstract:
For some jewelry designs, the incorporation of mixed media or mixed techniques can have a synergistic effect – increasing the appeal and/or functionality of the piece better than any one media or technique alone. It can feel more playful and experimental and fun to mix media or techniques. But there may be adverse effects, as well. Each media or technique will have its own structural and support requirements – that is, its own special characteristics and its own philosophy of technique. Each will react differently to various physical forces impacting the piece when worn. So it becomes more difficult for the designer to successfully coordinate and integrate more than one media or technique.

MIXED MEDIA / MIXED TECHNIQUES

It's my belief that you cannot combine two different media or two different techniques to make a piece of jewelry without letting one of them predominate over the other.

Whether combining fiber with beads or metal with beads or paint and sculpture with beads, or braiding with beads or metalwork with glasswork or glass beads with gemstone beads, it is difficult to have a successful, satisfying outcome, without letting one of the media or technique be dominant over the other.

Each media and technique has its own set of structural rules and requirements – that is, its own special characteristics and its own philosophy of technique. Each interacts with light and shadow very differently; that is, the materials and techniques associated with a particular media reflect, absorb and refract light differently. Each has different problems with and responses to physical mechanical forces impacting the piece internally and externally with different stresses and strains. Each requires different strategies for managing tradeoffs between aesthetics and functionality. Each triggers differing responses by wearers and viewers as to sensory, sensual and/or symbolic impressions.

These kinds of things make the viewer's experience and interaction with the media or technique and its resulting products different, from media to media and technique to technique.

So, you can have a "knitting" project that incorporates some beads, or a "beading" project that uses a knitting stitch and/or some yarn. In the former, knitting would predominate, with more focus on the fibers; in the latter, beading would predominate, with more focus on the beads. You can have a wire project which incorporates some beads, or a beading project which incorporates some wire elements.

But it is rare that you can look at a project, and say it concurrently meets the criteria for finish and success of both media – so, both a successful, satisfying knitting AND beading project, and both a successful wire AND beading project. It is difficult to preserve the integrity of either media if you force them to be co-equals.

It is difficult to mix materials within the same project. For example, it is difficult to mix glass and acrylic beads, or glass and gemstone beads…. Unless, you let one material become predominant over the other, or one technique become predominant over the other.

But all of this is very challenging, almost off-putting, to the jewelry designer who wants to combine media techniques and materials.

Types of Mixed Media / Mixed Technique Jewelry Projects

There are four distinct types of mixed media / mixed techniques projects.

Collage: Different materials or techniques are combined in an additive fashion. Often we create a foundation or base out of one material or technique, and embellish on top of it with another material or technique. It is very 2-dimensional.

Assemblage: This is a variant of the collage, where different materials or techniques are used to enhance the dimensionality or movement within a piece. The result is very 3-dimensional, sculptural and is very multiplicative.

Found Object: Various objects which are found and used by jewelry designers within their pieces because of their perceived artistic value.

Altered: An existing piece of jewelry will be reused and altered or modified physically, resulting in a different piece with a different sensibility. The original piece might be added to, cut up and re-arranged, materials changed, different techniques applied to reconstruct the piece.

How Can Two Things Come Together For Artistic Success?

For some jewelry designs, the incorporation of mixed media or mixed techniques can have a synergistic effect – increasing the appeal and/or functionality of the piece better than any one media or technique alone.

It can feel more playful and experimental and fun to mix media or techniques.

But there may be adverse effects, as well. Each media or technique will have its own structural and support requirements. Each will react differently to various physical forces impacting the piece when worn. So it becomes more difficult for the designer to successfully coordinate and integrate more than one media or technique.

Ask yourself,

How will you match tasks and/or materials?

How will you switch between them?

How will you adapt should one restrict or impede the flow of action?

How will you adapt should one alter or otherwise impede a shape or shapes within your piece?

What if it is easier to finish off the piece with one but not the other?

Typically, what works best overall is if you allow one media or technique to predominate. There its conformance to various art and design requirements will shine through without any sense of competition, incompleteness or discordance.

SECTION 5:

RULES OF COMPOSITION, CONSTRUCTION, AND MANIPULATION

RULES OF COMPOSITION, CONSTRUCTION, AND MANIPULATION
5a. JEWELRY DESIGN COMPOSITION: *PLAYING WITH BUILDING BLOCKS CALLED DESIGN ELEMENTS*

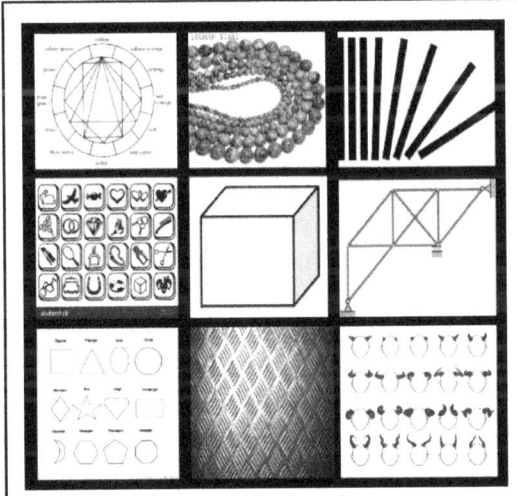

Design Elements, Image by FELD, 2020

Guiding Questions:
1. What are Design Elements? What do they do? Are they all alike?
2. Do design elements stand alone, or are they dependent on one another?
3. What does it mean to decode the design elements within a piece of jewelry?
4. How do you combine design elements in order to create an intended artistic expression?
5. How do you uncouple design elements if you are not achieving the intended results?
6. Are design elements universally understood, or are there subjective impressions involved?

Key Words: expression; jewelry making / design; design elements; dependent / independent; cluster	design thinking; disciplinary literacy /fluency; decoding; composition; construction; manipulation	graphic representation; expressive variations; attributes; universal / objective; subjective

Abstract:

Jewelry making is a constructive process of expression. The language of expression begins with the idea of Design Elements. Design Elements are the smallest, meaningful units of design. Design Elements function in a similar way as vowels and consonants in a language. They have form. They have meaning. They have expression. Some can stand alone, while others are dependent and must be clustered together. Better jewelry designers are aware of and can decode these expressive aspects of design elements and how they are included within any piece. This is one part of learning a disciplinary literacy in design. This literacy begins with a process of decoding and builds up to an intuitive fluency in design. This section focuses on this process of decoding.

JEWELRY DESIGN COMPOSITION:
PLAYING WITH BUILDING BLOCKS CALLED DESIGN ELEMENTS
Jewelry making is a constructive process of expression.

The language of expression begins with the idea of *Design Elements*. Design Elements are like building blocks and function a bit like the vowel and consonant letters of the alphabet. They have form. They have meaning. They can be assembled into different arrangements which extend their meaning and usefulness in expression. Recognizing the presence (or absence) of design elements and how they are assembled within different arrangements is called *decoding*.

There is an underlying poetry and logic to this process – a vocabulary and grammar, so to speak. Recognizing how this vocabulary and grammar is structured and applied, that is, decoding, then enables the jewelry designer to learn how to be *fluent in design*. Such recognition is critical in developing a coherent, consistent disciplinary literacy in jewelry design. Such disciplinary literacy is at the heart of a professional identity for jewelry design artisans.

This literacy structure in design has *four main components* to it:

1) **Vocabulary:** Design Elements As The Basis Of Composition
2) **Grammar:** Principles of Composition, Construction and Manipulation
3) **Strategy:** Project Management[1]
4) **Context/Culture:** Shared Understandings and Desires[2]

This chapter focuses on the first component – *Design Elements*.

It makes sense for the designer to begin with something like building blocks, which I call *Design Elements*. Design Elements, like building blocks, are tangible things. They can be visualized. They can be touched and moved around. They can be combined in different arrangements. They can be used to create many types of expressions. Design Elements include things like color, shape, texture, pattern, point, line, plane, movement, dimensionality, materials, use of space, and the like. Design Elements are the smallest, meaningful units of design.

Not every Design Element is alike. *Color* is different than *Shape* is different than *Texture*. *Movement* is different than *Balance* is different than *Dimensionality*. Learning about and understanding the differentiation among Design Elements becomes very important if the jewelry designer is to have sufficient power and insight over consistency, variation, coherence and unity in their designs. This power and insight is called *decoding*. Every jewelry designer needs to learn how to decode, if they are to be successful in design.

The first key differentiation has to do with independence and dependence. Some Design Elements are *syllabic* meaning they are independent and can stand alone. Others are non-syllabic, meaning they are dependent and cannot stand alone.

INDEPENDENT DESIGN ELEMENTS *(Color is an independent element)*	**DEPENDENT DESIGN ELEMENTS** *(Movement is a dependent element)*
Function like vowels in alphabet	*Function like consonants in alphabet*
Many expressive variations	*Limited expressive variations if used alone and not in combination*
Syllabic	*Non-syllabic*
Can stand alone and be expressive	*Do not often stand alone and more usually require an assist from an independent design element to extend their expression*
Expressions sensitive to placement or context	*Expressions consistent, somewhat insensitive to placement or context*

Another way to differentiate Design Elements is how to represent them visually. Design Elements have *graphic representations*. Graphic representations allow these elements to be recognized symbolically as a sort of short-hand.

Each Design Element also encompasses a range of acceptable meanings, which I call *expressive variations*. These expressive variations, while different among themselves, are still reflective of that Design Element. They have universal qualities in that people tend to *share understandings* about and have *preferences* and *desires* for what these expressive variations mean and how they are to be used.

Design Elements existing outside of any composition tend to be universally understood and objective, moreso than subjectively interpreted. Color Schemes, for example, are objective, agreed-upon combinations of colors seen as coherent and unifying. Thus, any color scheme is an expressive variation on the element of Color. This expressive variation of Color may be universally recognized outside the composition, but may be subjectively interpreted within it.

The universal, expressive variations associated with each Design Element are, in effect, *attributes* of that Design Element. These attributes have an objective quality to them in that there is general agreement among designer, viewer, wearer, buyer and seller as to what they express and how they might be used. There is an expectation that whatever role a person plays relative to the piece of jewelry, the Design Elements and their attributes will be decoded in a similar way.

At this stage in the jewelry design process, the focus is on a simple vocabulary. The vocabulary is made up of Design Elements and their expressive attributes. The vocabulary encapsulates a generally *shared understanding* of its meaning and how it is to be used. It is at the point of grammar, thus composition, construction and manipulation, that individual artists get to show their artistic hand in selecting and placing these elements into a finished piece of jewelry.

These Design Elements and their attributes can be arranged in different configurations I call **clusters**. Clusters may consist of independent Design Elements alone, dependent Design Elements alone, or a mix of both. For example, we may use an arrangement of glossy and matte *Color* beads to project *Dimensionality*. We may use different *Colors* of beads, rhythmically arranged, to project *Movement*.

Combinations of Design Elements into clusters can have different effects, from *synergy*, *antagonism*, *blending*, *bounding*, *freeing* and *inflection*.

Selecting Design Elements and clustering them does not occur in a vacuum. The designer selects and arranges Design Elements in anticipation of how these choices will be understood and desired by others in a *universal* or *objective* sense.

This is a process which I call "*Backward Design*".[3] The building blocks and their attributes are first selected in anticipation of these shared understandings. For instance, the designer might choose colors by anticipating how others will recognize the legitimacy and appeal of certain clusters of colors – color schemes.

If the viewer, wearer, buyer or seller of a piece of jewelry cannot understand and relate to its Design Elements and how they are clustered within the piece, they will not understand it. They will not appreciate it. They will not see it as a legitimate piece of artistic expression. It will not feel authentic. To others, if the piece lacks evidence of shared understandings, this will result in that jewelry (and by implication, the jewelry artisan) getting labeled, for example, as unsatisfying or boring or ugly or monotonous. Poor selection and utilization of Design Elements will mean people will not want to wear, buy it, or share it.

DESIGN ELEMENTS COMPRISE A VOCABULARY OF BASIC ARTISTIC EXPRESSION

Working with Design Elements is not much different than working with an alphabet.

An alphabet is made up of different letters. Each letter has different attributes – how it is graphically written, how it sounds, how it is used. Configurations of letters result in more sounds and more meanings and more ways to be used. Think of choosing a "t" and an "h", and combining them into "th" like in the word "they". We don't have a completely formed word yet, but we have the beginnings of a more meaningful unit than either letter standing alone.

A person working with an alphabet has to be able to decode the letters, sounds and meanings, as letters are used individually as well as in combination. As the speaker becomes better at decoding, she or he begins to build in understanding of implications for how any letter is used, again, individually or in combination. For instance, they might begin to recognize that when they combine "t" and "h" to get "th", they can also add an "e", but perhaps not a "z".

This is exactly what the jewelry designer does with Design Elements. The designer has to decode, that is, make sense of a series of elements and their attributes in light of our shared understandings about which Design Elements are appropriate, and how they should be legitimately expressed.

Let's examine a set of jewelry Design Elements in more detail and elaboration.

TABLE OF *INDEPENDENT* DESIGN ELEMENTS

DESIGN ELEMENT *Independent*	GRAPHIC REPRESENTATION	EXPRESSIVE VARIATIONS
Color		Schemes Hue and Saturation Simultaneity Effects Values and Intensity Temperature Receding or Projecting
Shape		Recognizable Focused Distinct Blended Abstract Filled or Empty Delimited, fixed, geometric Infinite, extending Distorted or overlapped Masculine or feminine Organic or mechanical Background, foreground, middle ground
Texture and Pattern		Regular, Predictable, Statistical Repeated or singular Random, Non-Statistical Feel or look Layered or Non-layered Smooth or Rough

Point, Line, Plane		2-Dimensional 3-Dimensional Conform or violate Connected or Unconnected Span and distance Actual or implied Thickness Silhouette Focused or unfocused Bounded or unbounded geometric or curved confined within plane; extends beyond plane
Material		Natural or Man-Made Soft or solid Heavy or light Single or mixed media Light refraction, reflection, absorption
Technique and Technology		Bead Weaving, Bead Stringing, Wire Working, Fiber, Clay, etc. With or without application of heat and/or pressure Fabricated or Machine Made Pattern or freeform

TABLE OF *DEPENDENT* DESIGN ELEMENTS

DESIGN ELEMENT *Dependent*	GRAPHIC REPRESENTATION	EXPRESSIVE VARIATIONS
Dimensionality		2-dimensional *(volume and mass; weight; density)* 3-dimensional *(relief, low relief, high relief)* Interior and Exterior Contours Frontal or in-the-round Open or closed forms Static or dynamic forms
Movement		Passive *(ex: use of color guides the eye)* Direction Linear or wave Physical *(ex: pieces, like fringe or spinners, actually move)* Stable or erratic Mechanical *(ex: structure of piece allows piece to drape and flow)*
Color Blending		Simultaneity effects Value and intensity Saturation and vibrance Distinct or blurred Dominant or recessive
Theme, Symbols		Surface or interpreted meaning(s) or inflected Power, position, protection, identification Clear or abstract referents Object as whole, or parts of object Repetition or not Individual, group, cultural, societal, universal

Beauty and Appeal		Sensually pleasing: visual, touch, auditory, taste, smell Objective or emotional Coherence, harmony and unity Fashion, style, timeliness, timelessness
Structure and Support		Stiff or flexible Flow and drape Linkage, connectivity Wearability Display Organization Articulation Autonomy vs. Temporariness Interactive with wearer, or not Fully, partially
Craftsmanship		Inspiration Skill and dexterity With tools, or not Design acumen Personality and preferences
Form, Segmentation, Components		Shape with Volume Whole or divided Organized or chaotic Perspective 2-dimensional or 3-dimensional Alignment Shading Positioning or spacing Simple or Complex
Balance and Distribution		Symmetrical *(By size, color, or shape)* Visual weight Visual size Asymmetrical *(By size, color, or shape)* Radial *(By size, color or shape)* Visual placement

		Random *(By size, color, or shape)* Stable or unstable Directed or undirected
Referents to specific idea or style		Vintage Revival Direct or implied Contemporary Literal or figurative Symbolic
Context, Situation, Culture		Economic, social, psychological, cultural, situational values Complicit artist, or not Derived meaning, or objective meaning
Negative and Positive Space		Figure or ground Form or no form Shading Perspective Depth Use of space around an object Interpenetration of space Illusion or reality Placement
Light and Shadow		Suggestive Gradient Perspective Shading Illumination Solid or Cast Dimensionality Moon

The Japanese Fragrance Garden Bracelet

"Japanese Fragrance Garden Bracelet", by Warren Feld, March 2018, photography by Warren Feld

For example, this is the kind of building blocks thinking I did when designing my Japanese Fragrance Garden Bracelet.

This bracelet has a rectangular foundation base which is a flat surface composed of 8 beads across and 65 beads long. The finishes of these beads in the base are either a luster finish or a dichroic finish. Off the base, I created flower stalks (fringes) that were 4-6 seed beads tall, and topped with a slightly larger and more brightly colored seed bead. The colors of the beads in the stalks vary from dark (near the base) to light (near the flower tip). Between each bed of flowers is a "moon bridge" – the kind you might expect when meandering through a Japanese garden.

See how I clustered independent and dependent Design Elements to achieve a particular expression.

What I Wanted To Achieve *'Japanese Fragrance Garden'*	*Design Elements I Thought About*
Movement with flower stalks where they would retain their verticality (thus not flop over) after the piece was worn.	**Technique:** Fringing technique **Technology:** Use of One-G beading thread which, unlike all other beading threads, has a springy quality to it. When the fringe is pulled out during wearing, the thread helps spring it back into place. Keeps fringe vertical rather than flattening. **Color:** To mimic how moving colors will be perceived, I varied color in flower stalks from dark at the bottom to medium to light at the top, just under the flower, and then used bright colors for the flowers topping off each stalk **Point, Line:** Easy for viewer to perceive and follow movement of points and lines, which are key elements in the piece
Dimensionality where the piece would not be seen as flat	**Point, Line:** Visually, the flower stalks lead the eye from the foundation base, up the stalks, and to the bright flower colors on top of the stalks. **Color:** I use a reflective foundation base of two types of bead finishes, (a) luster, and (b) dichroic. Both have a mirroring effect, making it difficult for the eye to see the "bottom", and at the same time reflecting the colors sitting above them.
Color Blending where as the eye moves up and down any flower stalk, or moves across the piece from end to end, everything feels coherent and unified	**Color:** I make a wide use of simultaneity effects, where the placement of one color affects the perception of the color next to it. This fools the brain into blending colors, which in reality, you cannot do easily with beads (as opposed to paints). **Shape/Points/Line/Pattern:** There is a consistent repetition of shapes, points and lines, and pattern, leading the viewer to be able to predict what should happen next along the bracelet, and again, fooling the brain into doing some color blending perceptual tricks of its own.

How Do You The Designer Learn A Vocabulary of Design?

Most designers probably started their jewelry making careers taking craft-oriented classes and following instructions in how-to books or online in how-to videos. They learned to repeat a set of steps and end up with something like what is pictured. The whole jewelry making approach, as craft, assumes that jewelry making is a natural process which anyone can do. Surround the budding artist with patterns, books and videos, and they will somehow become great jewelry designers.

Yet, although, in this craft approach, the artisans followed a set of steps over and over again, they really never actually learn how to make choices or evaluate implications or get any experience making judgement calls and tradeoffs when designing something that must look good and wear well at the same time. Jewelry making is not a natural skill that is learned automatically without thought, reflection and instruction. Jewelry designers need to be taught to design, and take advantage of those programs which do so. To become fluent in design, then, requires going beyond this approach of repeating steps.

Towards this end, I think it is much more useful to build an educational curriculum and program around the idea of *disciplinary literacy*. Designers need to learn how to explicitly and systematically think *design*. Designers need to be able to recognize the elements that make up a piece, how they were used, and how this leads to more or less success in evoking an expression or an emotional response.

Disciplinary Literacy, means, in part, that the designer is aware of the "*codes*" which were selected for a piece of jewelry. Thus, the designer is able to *segment* the piece and identify its Design Elements. The designer is also able to put Design Elements together and *blend* them or *cluster* them to achieve a desired expression. The better designer is very aware of all the codes, or Design Elements. The better designer is very aware of how the codes, or Design Elements, were selected, combined, blended, juxtaposed and expressed. And the designer is very aware of how and why clusters of Design Elements may sometimes get *bounded*; that is, may be unfortunately stuck within some indeterminant meaning or expression.

Towards this end, this means first learning how to *decode*. It means figuring out what universally accepted Design Elements should be used in a piece. It also means recognizing how these elements can vary, and how such variation can change the artistic or design expression of the piece.

Designers need to learn how Design Elements get clustered and constructed to convey certain expressions, and which cannot. To return to an analogous example used above, the Designer needs to recognize the "t" and recognize the "h" and feel comfortable in connecting "t" and "h" into "th". The Designer should be able to begin to recognize that "th" can be further linked to "e", but not "z".

At this stage, the designer is training to have some comfort recognizing and applying objective, shared understandings about what certain Design Elements mean, and the variations in how they might get expressed within a piece.

As the designer's education progresses, the student would gradually reduce their involvement with decoding, and increase the involvement with tasks involving *fluency*. This involves more in-depth learning about construction and manipulation. Here the designer learns how to define a personal style and approach, and implement it. The designer guides him/herself from creating the merely appealing, to the more resounding resonant.

So, to return to our alphabet analogy, the designer learns to form words, such as with our "t" and "h", and gather additional letters to form a word like "thesaurus". And the designer continues to learn how to use a word like "thesaurus" and further its meaning and expression in a phrase or sentence, such as "I do not like to use a thesaurus."

Lastly, fluency means that the designer has also learned to look for, anticipate and incorporate context clues. Design does not occur in a vacuum. It has implications which become realized in a context. That context might be historical, cultural or situational. To extend the analogy one more time, we would want to know under what "circumstances" the person did not like to use a thesaurus.

All this gets into the areas of grammar and process management, which I discuss in other chapters here in this book and published articles available online.[1,2]

FOOTNOTES

[1] Read my article *Jewelry Design: A Managed Process*, Klimt02.net Forum, https://klimt02.net/forum/articles/jewelry-design-managed-process-warren-feld

[2] I discuss a little about shared understandings in a yet unpublished article I wrote about Contemporary Design. From that article…
> "*Shared understandings* should be enduring, transferable, big ideas at the heart of what we think of as *contemporary jewelry*. These shared understandings are things which spark meaningful connections between designer and materials, designer and techniques, and designer and client. We need, however, to recognize that the idea of *understanding* is very multidimensional and complicated.
> Understanding is not one achievement, but more the result of several loosely organized choices. Understanding is revealed through performance and evidence. Jewelry designers must perform effectively with knowledge, insight, wisdom and skill to convince us – the world at large and the client in particular -- that they really understand what design, and with our case here, contemporary design, is all about. This involves a big interpersonal component where the artist introduces their jewelry to a wider audience and subjects it to psychological, social, cultural, and economic assessment.
> Understanding is more than knowledge. The designer may be able to articulate what needs to be done to achieve something labeled *contemporary*, but may not know

how to apply it.

Understanding is more than interpretation. The designer may be able to explain how a piece was constructed and conformed to ideas about *contemporary*, but this does not necessarily account for the significance of the results.

Understanding is more than applying principles of construction. It is more than simply organizing a set of Design Elements into an arrangement. The designer must match knowledge and interpretation about *contemporary* to the context. Application is a context-dependent skill.

Understanding is more than perspective. The designer works within a myriad of expectations and points of view about contemporary jewelry. The designer must dispassionately anticipate these various perspectives about contemporary design, and, bring some constructed point of view and knowledge of implications to bear within the design and design process.

We do not design in a vacuum. The designer must have the ability to empathize with individuals and grasp their individual and group cultures. If selling their jewelry, the designer must have the ability to empathize with small and larger markets, as well. Empathy is not sympathy. Empathy is where we can feel what others feel, and see what others see.

Last, understanding is self-knowledge, as well. The designer should have the self-knowledge, wisdom and insights to know how their own patterns of thought may inform, as well as prejudice, their understandings of contemporary design.

How the jewelry designer begins the process of creating a contemporary piece of jewelry is very revealing about the potential for success. The designer should always begin the process by articulating the essential shared understandings against which their work will be evaluated and judged. For now, let's refer to this as *Backwards Design*[4]. The designer starts with questions about assessment, and then allows this understanding to influence all other choices going forward."

---

[3] *Backwards Design*. I had taken two graduate education courses in Literacy and one in Planning that were very influential in my approach to disciplinary literacy. One of the big take-aways from **Understanding by Design** *by Grant Wiggins and Jay McTighe, 2nd Edition, Association for Supervision and Curriculum Development, 2005,* was the idea they introduced of *"backwards design"*. Their point is that you can better teach understanding if you anticipate the evidence others will use in their assessments of what you are trying to do. When coupled with ideas about teaching literacy and fluency *(see* **Literacy: Helping Students Construct Meaning** *by J. David Cooper, M. Robinson, J.A. Slansky and N. Kiger, 9th Edition, Cengage Learning, 2015)*, you can begin to introduce ideas about managing the design process in a coherent and alignable way.

RULES OF COMPOSITION, CONSTRUCTION, AND MANIPULATION
5b. THE JEWELRY DESIGNER'S APPROACH TO COLOR

Guiding Questions:
1. How does designing jewelry with color differ from an artist using color to paint?
2. How can the jewelry designer adapt basic color concepts in art to the special color requirements jewelry poses?
3. How does the bead (and other jewelry components) assert its need for color?
4. To what extent is the application of color universally understood vs. merely subjective?
5. What does it mean to clarify and intensify the color effects you want to achieve?
6. Is color something very specific and tangible or is it primarily more vague and a sensation?
7. How do we know our piece demonstrates a successful use of color?

Key Words:	universal vs. subjective	color balance
color	clarify and intensity	color proportions
sensation /	design element	simultaneous color
management	fluency	contrasts
design thinking	rhythm	colors within context
picking colors	movement	light values
value	dimensionality	combining colors
intensity	unity	blending / bridging
harmony	selection	after images
edginess	placement	color wheel
variety	distribution	color schemes
emotion	transition	color proportions
resonance	proportion	simultaneity effects
	composition	hue

Abstract
Color is the single most important Design Element, whether used alone, or in combination with other Design Elements. Yet jewelry creates a series of dilemmas for the colorist not always anticipated by what jewelry designers are taught in a typical art class. This chapter reviews the basic concepts in color theory and suggests how to adapt each of these to the special requirements of beads and jewelry. Special attention is paid to differentiating those aspects of color use we can consider as objective and universal from those which are more subjective. The fluent designer is one who can maneuver among universal understandings, sensations and subjective beliefs when selecting and implementing colors, color combinations and color blends. This involves managing the sensation of color balance (light values), the sensation of color proportions (color contrasts), and the sensation of simultaneous color contrasts (experiencing colors within a context) among designer, wearer and viewer.

Also See My Video Tutorial: [The Jewelry Designer's Approach To Color](https://so-you-want-to-be-a-jewelry-designer.teachable.com/p/the-jewelry-designer-s-approach-to-color) (https://so-you-want-to-be-a-jewelry-designer.teachable.com/p/the-jewelry-designer-s-approach-to-color) *(*[*https://so-you-want-to-be-a-jewelry-designer.teachable.com/p/the-jewelry-designer-s-approach-to-color*](https://so-you-want-to-be-a-jewelry-designer.teachable.com/p/the-jewelry-designer-s-approach-to-color)*)*

RETHINKING THE LEARNING OF "COLOR" IN JEWELRY DESIGN
You need to know how your materials assert their needs for color!

You cannot paint with beads and other jewelry components.

I am going to repeat this: *You cannot paint with beads and other jewelry components.*

When you take color class after color class rooted in art, they are teaching you how to paint. You can't do this with jewelry and beads.

As frustrating as this can be, you cannot ignore the fact that *Color* is the single most important Design Element. Colors, their selection, use and arrangement, are believed to have universal powers to get people to see things as harmonious and appealing. Color attracts attention.   A great use of color within an object, not only makes that object more coherent, it can be contagious, as well.   Using colors that do not work well together, or using too many colors or not enough colors, or using colors which look good on paper but distort in reality can put people off.

Designers can learn the artistic basics of Color concepts and theories. They can reference this visual language of color to influence how they go about making choices, including those about picking and using colors. However, jewelry artists who are fluent in design will be very aware of the limitations this artistic, painterly language imposes on them. They will have to learn how to decode, adjust and leverage their thinking to anticipate how the bead and other related and integrated materials assert their needs for color, and how to strategically compose, construct and manipulate them.

Jewelry, unlike painting or sculpture, has certain characteristics and requirements which rely on the management and control of color, its sensation and its variability with a slightly different emphasis than learned in a traditional art class. Jewelry is a 3-dimensional object, composed of a range of materials. Jewelry situates, moves and adjusts in relation to the human body and what that body is doing at the moment. To get the attention their jewelry deserves, jewelry artists must become fluent with color selection and application from their own disciplinary perspective. We must understand color in jewelry as the jewelry is worn, and worn in a particular context or situation.

Beads *[here I use 'beads' as a stand-in for all the component parts and stringing and canvas materials used in a piece of jewelry]* are curved or faceted or otherwise shaped, and the shape and texture and material and dimensionality affect the color, its variation and its placement and movement on the beads surface. They affect how light reflects and refracts, so depending on the angle at which you are standing, and how you are looking at the bead, you get some unexpected, unanticipated, sometimes unwanted colors in your piece of jewelry.

Additionally, you need to anticipate how the bead, when worn, can alter its color, depending on the source of light, the type and pace of movement of the wearer, and how the eye interacts with the bead at any point of time or positioning. There are many more color tensions that come from the interrelationships between positive and negative spaces. There are many gaps of light between each pair of beads, and you can't paint these in. The colors don't blend, don't merge, don't spill over, don't integrate. You can't create the millions of subtle color variations that you can with paint.

I'm not suggesting that beaders and jewelry makers be afraid of colors. Rather, they should embrace them. They should learn insights into understanding colors. They should be inspired by colors. They should express their artistic and creative selves through color. They should use color palettes to their fullest. They should recognize how their various audiences see and claim and interact with color.

It is most important that jewelry designers understand color, its use and application from their own disciplinary standpoint. In some sense, however, the approaches of most bead artists and jewelry designers too often remain somewhat painterly – too routed in the Art Model. The Art Model ignores things about functionality and context.   The Art Model does not anticipate all the additional management and control issues which arise with jewelry creation. The Art Model diminishes how the individuality of the designer, and the subjective responses of the wearer and viewer affect each other. In many respects, these are synergetic, mutually dependent and reciprocal. The Art Model understands the success of jewelry only as if the jewelry were sitting on an easel, not as it is worn.

As a result, color theories get oversimplified for the jewelry artist. "Value" is barely differentiated from "Intensity". Color selection focuses too much on *harmony* and *variety*, and too little on *resonance* and *edginess*. Color training too often steers jewelry designers towards a step-by-step, paint-by-number sort of approach to color selection and application. The co-dependent relationship between Color and other Design Elements is downplayed and glossed over. This is a major disservice.

So, I've tried to re-think how we could and should think about and learn *Color* for jewelry artists. Not easy. Art and Design Theory suggests that, in order for designers to make good choices about color, they need to break down color concepts and theories into learnable and digestible groups of skills. And then learn how the next set of skills builds upon the first.

Jewelry designers need to learn and rehearse what kinds of color choices they will be making as they create pieces of jewelry, and then be put in situations where they are forced to make these kinds of choices. We need to think of colors as *building blocks*, and the process of using colors, as one of *Creative Construction*. Creative Construction requires focusing on how color (and multiple colors) is (are) sensed, and sensed by various audiences which include the artist him- or herself, and the wearer and the viewer, and the exhibitor, collector, and the seller, if need be. Creative Construction also requires anticipating how color is sensed within those context(s) and situation(s) the jewelry will be worn.

So, that's where I'll begin with color: Delineating the types of choices that the jewelry designer needs to make, starting with choices about picking colors.

Picking Colors

As a design element, *color* is used to attract attention. It aids in grouping some objects and setting boundaries between others. It can emphasize and focus. It conveys meaning and value. Usually color enhances the aesthetics and appeal. Color can be used as an organizing tool and create segments, components, rhythms, movements, dimensions and hierarchical arrangements within your jewelry composition. Color can affect the figure/ground relationships of the composition.

There are many different kinds of choices involved, when using Color. Choices about colors based on our understanding of...

- o Personal strategies for picking colors or finding inspirations for colors
- o Color theories and concepts
- o How the bead (and related jewelry materials) asserts its (their) needs for color

- How color affects the viewers of color
- The process for designing jewelry with color
- The situation or context within which the jewelry is to be worn

Part of picking colors is very personal and subjective. And part of this is very strategic and must be managed. That is, part of picking colors is about anticipating more universal understandings about how various audiences will sense and pick colors.

How do you actually go about picking your colors, and then deciding on your final colors for your piece? What kinds of things influence you in choosing colors? What inspires you? Where do you look for inspiration? Do you have favorite colors and color combinations? Or colors and color combinations that you detest? How do you anticipate how others will view and evaluate the colors you pick?

Choosing Colors is an involved exercise. Most people avoid this kind of exercise, and settle for a set of colors that match. But, in design terms, Colors are used by the designer to clarify and intensify the effects she or he wants to achieve.

What does it mean to "clarify and intensify" the effects you might want to achieve?

For example, the artist may use color to clarify and/or intensify any of these kinds of things...

- Delineation of segments, forms, themes, areas
- Expressions of naturalism or abstraction
- Enhancing the sense of structure or physicality (forward/recede; emphasize mass or lines or surfaces or points)
- Playing with light (surprise, distort, challenge, contradict, provoke)
- Altering the natural relationship between the jewelry and the situation it is worn in (context, clothing, setting)

Color is the primary Design Element designers choose to express their intent, establish unity, create rhythm, set movement and dimensionality in place, enhance shape, make points, lines and planes come alive, and the like. Alas, too few people apply this kind of thinking and make this kind of effort when choosing colors.

For myself, I know that as I start to play with my design arrangements, I also begin to identify potential color issues. Designs are imperfect. Beads are imperfect. Colors are imperfect. With each issue, I try to figure out solutions – other things I can do with colors to make everything work. My choices begin with scientifically proven color theories – shared universals that virtually everyone has about picking colors.

In literacy terminology, this is called *decoding*. Then I begin to personalize my choices so that my results show more of my individuality as an artist. Some of these latter choices do not necessarily reflect shared universal understandings about color, its *sensation* and its use. In literacy terminology, my ability to move back and forth between the objective and subjective is called *fluency*.

Bead Choices

The bead – its very being – creates as series of dilemmas for the colorist. And each dilemma is only overcome through strategically making and managing choices about color and design.

Such dilemmas include things like...

- Beads are not the same as using paints
- Can't blend beads
- Boundary issues
- Issues associated with shapes, faceting, edges, crevices
- Jewelry reflects and refracts light, and this may change as the wearer moves, or lighting changes, or perspective and angle of vision changes, or materials or material mixes change
- Limits in the range of colors (and color tones) you can pick from
- Issues associated with the fact that jewelry as worn, takes many shapes/positions, as the person moves, and the color appearance may change or vary
- Beads are parts in whole compositions, and juxtaposition of 2 or more beads may change or vary the colors' appearance
- Jumping from bead to bead within the composition, means the viewer's mind has to fill in where there are gaps of color to give the illusion there is a continuance of color throughout the composition

Yet most people do not recognize or anticipate these kinds of dilemmas.

Emotions, Moods and Choices

The emotional and psychological effects of color are undeniable. These effects are usually felt through processes of color comparisons and contrasts. The better designer anticipates the goals of the wearer, and what emotions and moods the wearer wants to evoke in all that see the jewelry as worn. This might be appeal, beauty, trust, power, wealth, intelligence, and the list goes on.

Designing With Color – Many Choices

The jewelry designer must be strategic with color, which comes down to..
1. ***Selection***
2. ***Placement***
3. ***Distribution***
4. ***Transition***
5. ***Proportion***

Designers must be intentional, not only with the *selection* of colors, but in the *placement* of color within the piece, as well. The designer achieves balance and harmony, partly through the placement of colors. The designer determines how colors are *distributed* within the piece, and how colors *transition* from one color to the next. And the designer determines what *proportions* of each color are used, where in the piece, and how. These kinds of choices affect movement and rhythm, dimensionality, and resonance.

SUBJECTIVE or OBJECTIVE CHOICES?
Some Tools From Art Theory And Color Research

Many people are often skeptical that you can choose colors with any basis of objectivity and rationality. Choosing colors is intuitive, subjective, personal. You can't teach people to be better users of colors, because you're either born with a sense of color, or you are not.

People seem to have cultural or social expectations about the meanings of some colors. When Vanderbilt students see black and gold, they associate it with school colors. When others see black and gold, they associate it with something else. The same goes for University of Tennessee Orange, and so forth school to school.

THE JEWELRY DESIGNER'S APPROACH TO COLOR
Universal vs. Subjective

When you see GOLD and BLACK, what do you see?

If we are to be able to teach jewelry makers and beaders to be more scientific in their choices of colors, and be able to anticipate how their various audiences respond to colors, then we would need to have some objective rules, rules that refer universally to just about everyone. Rules that inform people what colors are best. What colors go together, which ones do not. Rules that show how to manipulate color and its expression in perfect and predictable ways.

But everything seems so subjective.

When people see colors on the vertical, they may respond very differently than when they see these same colors on the horizontal.

Look at flags of countries around the world. Many flag colors are red, white and blue.

If you look at France's flag, you have red/white/blue on the vertical.

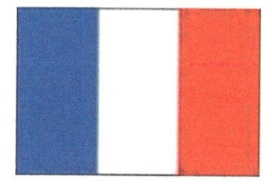

Russia's flag has red/white/blue on the horizontal.

You frequently find that people might like a color arrangement in a vertical organization, but feel very uncomfortable, or have much disdain for those same colors, when found in the horizontal.

COLOR TOOLS AND THEIR THEORETICAL BASIS
Sensation Management

Color research over the past 100 years or so suggests that there are many universals in how people perceive, understand and respond to colors. These universals provide the basis for several "***sensation-management-tools***" jewelry designers might use to help them manipulate various design elements and their arrangements within a jewelry composition. Some of the most useful color tools are those which designers use to control how to make one color relate to another. These have to do with creating and managing...

    A. **Sensations of Color Balance** *(Light Values)*

    B. **Sensations of Color Proportions** *(Color Contrast)*

    C. **Sensations of Simultaneous Color** *(Simultaneous Color Contrasts)*

As jewelry designers, *we need to know...*

- What these color TOOLS are, and with which we can play
- What the special demands beads (and all other materials) place on our use of these color TOOLS
- How we can *push* the limits of these color TOOLS to achieve harmony, variety and emotional responses
- How *Far We Can Push* the limits of these color TOOLS to achieve parsimony and resonance

Toward this end, we need to know a little bit about the art and color research and theories these tools are based upon. We need to understand some things about perception and cognition. That is, *we need to understand, as people interact with our jewelry, how the brain comes to see color, recognize color, and interpret color in context.*

Theory / Research Underlying These Color-Sensation Management Tools

My favorite book on the research into the theoretical bases of these kinds of color management tools is by Johannes Itten [2] called *The Elements of Color*. The most important theories about color universals for jewelry designers, as detailed in his book, include,

    (1)   ***After Images***

    (2)   ***Use of the Color Wheel***

(3)   ***Color Schemes***

(4)   ***Color Proportions***

(5)   ***Simultaneity Effects***

As a design element in and of itself, *Color* (and its attributes) are universally understood as if they were objective facts which comprise a visual vocabulary and grammar. It is important to understand how to employ universal understandings about color. This is a first step for any designer.

Universality, in and of itself, however, *is necessary but not sufficient* for understanding why some color use draws your attention, and others do not. Here aspects of subjective interpretations and reactions, given the context, have great influence. The fluent, successful jewelry designer should understand both those universal and subjective aspects of color. And this level of fluency become steps 2, 3, 4 and so forth for the designer.

The initial discussion below primarily concerns itself about color as a design element – that is, as something universal and objective. And then I slowly begin to incorporate the less universal aspects of color and the resulting control and management issues for the designer.

(1) After Images And The Sensation Of Color Balance

The first research had to do with **After Images**. If you stare at a particular color long enough, and close your eyes, you'll begin to see the color on the opposite side of the color wheel. So, if you stare at red, close your eyes, and you'll see green.

I know you want to do this, so stare away:

So our first color-sensation tools are based on **LIGHT VALUE**. Each color has its own energy signature. This seems to be universally perceived, and perceived in the same way.

Some colors have a positive energy signature; other colors have a negative energy signature. The brain wants to balance these out and harmonize them into some kind of zero-sum outcome. Everyone seems to see after images and see the same after images. It seems that the eye/brain wants somehow to neutralize the energy in color to achieve some balance or 0.0 point. *The brain always seeks a balanced energy in light and color.* The human eye is only "satisfied" when the complementary color is established.

[This is the basis underlying the various color schemes below.]

If red had an energy of +10 *(I'm making up this scale)*, and the eye/brain then convinced your psyche to see green, then I would suppose that green would have an energy of -10. Hence, we reach a 0.0 point (*+10 – 10 = 0*).

Again, the brain wants balance, harmony, beauty, non-threatening situations. The brain does *not* want edginess, tension, anxiety, fear, or ugliness. So, when you perceive red, your brain, in knee-jerk fashion, and in the absence of other information which might lead to a different interpretation of the situation, tries to compensate for the imbalance by also seeing green.

And we can continue to speculate that your eye/brain <u>does Not</u> want you the designer to overly clarify and intensify, should this result in a more resonant, perhaps edgy, composition. This takes you too far away from 0.0 energy, and starts to become threatening. It might excite you. It might revolt you. In either case you would react, feel, sense the power of color, but maybe not in a more perfectly balanced way the eye/brain would prefer.

But all jewelry designers need to know, and this is important, that their guiding star is "Resonance", and this usually means you want to take your pieces just a little beyond the harmony the brain seeks. Creating a little "edginess" in your jewelry can't hurt, and might better help in achieving that resonance and shared understanding about finish and success.

Yet, creating too much "edginess" might strike too forcefully at the heart of our prewired anxiety response, and our brain will not let us go there. Your eye/brain *does Not* want you to push yourself and your jewelry too far to the edge with color. This countervailing force might create tensions with your artistic and design intentions. Instead of resonance, your piece might generate feelings of boredom, confusion, dissatisfaction, even repulsiveness.

The eye/brain wants balance, harmony, monotony with just a little variety allowed. Red and green can seem so much fun at Christmas time. But if you put your red and green necklace on a copy machine, and took a photocopy of it, it would all look like one color of black. Red and green will always copy as the same color and shade of black. Harmonious, yes, but a bit boring and dull.

And that is how we perceive red and green together. And cognate them. We see red and green as the same. As the same color black. And if we assign red a +10 score, and green a -10 score, the eye/brain is happy to end up with a 0.0 score. This combination can be boring and monotonous. Combinations of red and green can feel unified and appear varied, yet somehow fail as choices in our jewelry designs.

And it is important to recognize, if your composition only uses red, that in reality, when something doesn't balance off the color red, in this case, the brain will create its own after image – some sensation of green -- to force that balance. The brain wants to feel safe and in harmony and balance. Everyone's brain seems to operate similarly so that this aspect of perceiving color is universally employed.

How far the jewelry designer should either accommodate or fight this universal tendency is up for debate. However, when initially picking colors to combine in a piece, we might try to achieve this 0.0 balance score (thus, a point of harmony and balance), and then, by clarifying and intensifying, deviate from it a little bit, but always with an eye on that 0.0 – what anyone's eye/brain is driving it to do. We want the eye/brain to feel satisfied and "safe", but as a designer, we also want to give the jewelry a punch, a wow, an edge. There are many color tricks and techniques that the designer can apply here.

(2) The Color Wheel: A Spectrum of Light Values
And The Sensation Of Color Balance

Science and Art Theory have provided us with tools to help us pick and combine colors. One tool is the Color Wheel. With almost every book about color, there is a Color Wheel. There are many color wheels and color selectors online. Some are more detailed than others. Some are easier to turn and manipulate. They all have different colors at the North, South, East and West points, but it is the same series of colors, ordered in the same way, color to color.

It is important to understand how to use the Color Wheel. This curtain of color provides the insights for selecting and arranging colors that might go together well. The color wheel helps us delineate what color choices we can make, and which combinations of colors might work the best together, to achieve a perceived harmony and balance.

The Color Wheel is a tool and a guide. It's not an absolute. Beads don't always conform to the colors on the wheel; nor do they reflect light and color in ways consistent with how these colors appear on the wheel.

Look at this color wheel:

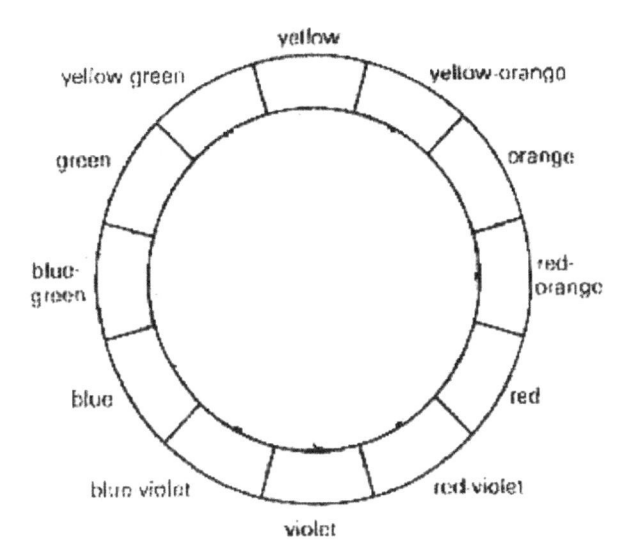

Get some color pencils, and color in all the colors around the wheel.

On the Color Wheel, there are 12 colors arranged into *three families of color*.

The **Primary Color** [3] family includes three colors: yellow, blue and red. These colors present the world as **Absolutes**. They are definitive, certain, and steady. They convey intelligence, security, and clarity.

The **Secondary Color** family includes those colors you can make by mixing any two primary colors. These three colors are: green, orange and violet. These colors present the world as **Contingencies**. They are situational, dependent on something, and questioning. They convey questioning, inquiry, risks assessed against benefits.

The **Tertiary Color** family includes six colors. Each of these colors is a mix of one of the primary colors and one of the secondary colors. These include: red-violet, yellow-orange, blue-green, blue-violet, yellow-green, red-orange. These colors show **Transitions**. These colors are useful for transitioning from one primary or secondary color to the next. They bridge, integrate, tie things together, stretch things out. They give a sense of before and after, lower then higher, inside and outside, betwixt and between. They convey ambiguity or a teetering on the fulcrum of a scale.

As you begin to pick colors, you will also want to manipulate them – make them lighter or darker, brighter or duller, more forward projecting or more receding, and the like. Expressions of color are referred to as *attributes*. Expressive attributes are the ways you use color as building blocks in design. So, here in the next sections of this chapter are some *important building block/color terms/attributes and vocabulary.*

(3) Color Schemes – Rules for Balancing Light Values
And The Sensation Of Color Balance

Color schemes are different, universally recognized and proven ways to use and combine colors, in order to achieve a pleasing or satisfying result.

Good color combinations based on color schemes have balanced, harmonious tonal values – their light energy levels balance out at the zero-zero (0.0) point. Better designers like to tweak these combinations a bit, in order to evoke an emotional and resonant response to their work.

Color Schemes, then, as represented in a Color Wheel, are based on harmonizing (e.g., zero-sum) combinations of colors. Color schemes – like the split complementary scheme of violet, yellow-green and

yellow-orange – are different combinations of colors the Light Values of which add up to zero, and achieve harmony.

You can place geometric shapes inside the Color Wheel, and rotate them, and where the corner-points hit the wheel, you have a good color combination. For example, if you place an equilateral triangle (all sides are equal length) within the circle, as in the diagram below, the corner-points touch Yellow, Red and Blue. If you rotate it two colors to the right, it touches Orange, Violet and Green.

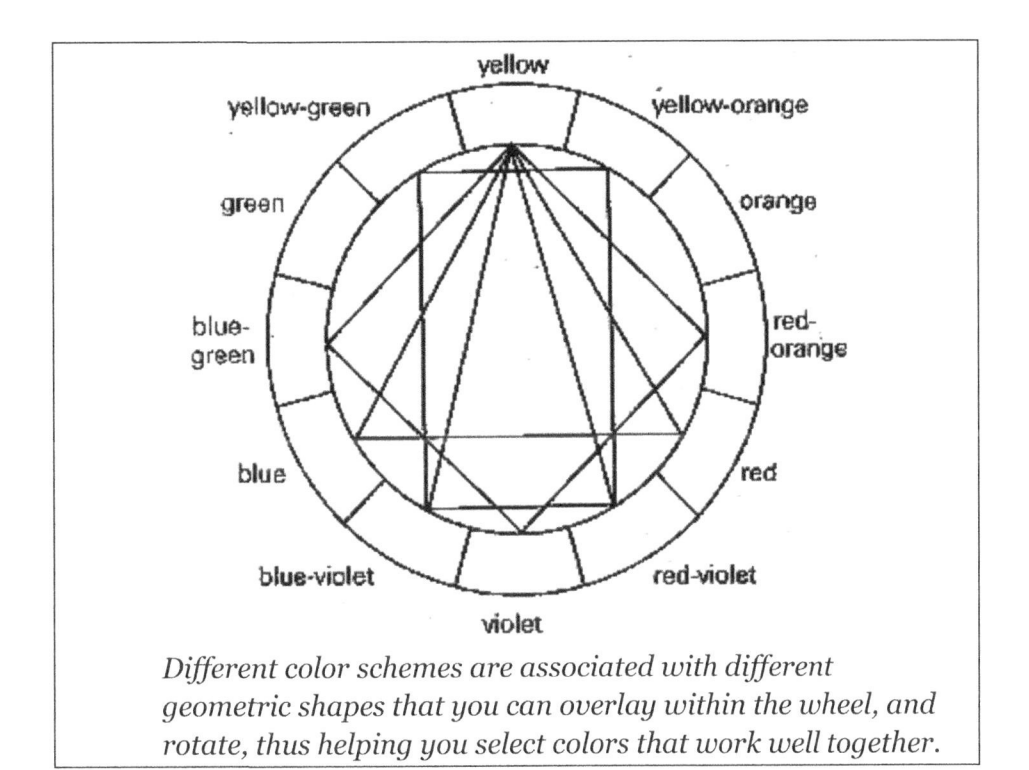

Different color schemes are associated with different geometric shapes that you can overlay within the wheel, and rotate, thus helping you select colors that work well together.

With color schemes, you always need to think about things like:
1. Whether one color should predominate, or all colors should be more or less equal
2. Whether there should always be a "splash of color", as interior designers like to say -- a "drama" color to achieve exciting, focal, look at me first effects
3. If symmetry works with or against your color choices
4. If you need to adjust intensity (brightness) or value (lightness) in each color, to get a better sense of satisfaction
5. If you need to adjust the proportions or distributional patterns or arrangements of each color used; that is, experiment with same colors, different placement or different sizes or different quantities or different shapes or mixes of shapes

Let's look at the three most popular, often-used Color Schemes – **Analogous**, **Complementary**, and **Split Complementary**.

Analogous

The analogous color scheme is where you pick any 3 hues which are adjacent to one another on the color wheel. For example, you might pick yellow-green, yellow, and yellow-orange. This scheme is a little trickier than it seems. It works best when no color predominates. Where the intensity of each color is similar. And the design is symmetrical. I also think this scheme works best when you have blocks of each color, rather than alternating each color. That is, BETTER: color 1, 1, 1, 1, 1, 2, 2, 2, 2, 3, 3, 3, 3 rather than

WORSE: color 1, 2, 3, 2, 1, 2, 3, 2, 1, 2, 3, 2, 1.

Complementary (*also known as "true complementary" or "dyadic"*)

The complementary color scheme is where you pick any 2 colors which are the direct opposite on the color wheel. For example, you might pick yellow and violet. To use this color scheme effectively, you would balance the contrast of the colors by value (lightness/darkness) and/or intensity (brightness/dullness). In this color scheme, one color has to predominate.

Split Complementary

This is the most popular color scheme. Here you choose three colors: a hue and the hues on either side of its complement. For example, you might choose yellow and blue-violet and red-violet *(thus, the two colors on either side of Violet – the complement)*. In this scheme, one color needs to predominate. This scheme works well with both symmetrical and asymmetrical designs. You can use an isosceles triangle *(has two sides with equal length)* within the Color Wheel to pick colors.

One thing I like to do with this scheme is arrange all my beads, then replace one color with one of the others, and vice versa. Let's say you had 20 blue-green (aqua), 10 orange, and 5 red beads, which you had laid out in a satisfactory arrangement. You could change it to 20 orange, 10 blue-green, and 5 red beads, and it would look just as good.

A lot of people have difficulty using the color *orange* in jewelry designs, but find it easy to use *blue-green*. Here's a nifty way to trick them into using *orange*, and liking it. Do the composition with *blue-green* dominant, then switch out all the *blue-green* for *orange*, and any *orange* you used for *blue-green*.

There are many other color schemes. Some examples:

Analogous Complementary: (3 analogous colors, and one complement of one of these 3). Example: blue-violet, violet, red-violet with yellow-green. I personally find any 4-color scheme the most difficult to use when designing jewelry.

Triadic: (3 tertiary hues equidistant on the color wheel.) Example: red-violet, yellow-orange, and blue-green. You can use an equilateral triangle within the color wheel to help you pick choices.

Tetradic: (Using 4 colors, a double complementary scheme). Example: Yellow-green, orange, red-violet, and blue. You can use a square or rectangle within the color wheel to help you pick choices. . Again, I personally find any 4-color scheme the most difficult to use when designing jewelry.

Hexadic: (Using 5 colors). Can use a pentagon within the color wheel to select your colors.

Monochromatic: (A single hue, though with different intensities, tints and shades)

Achromatic: (black and white and gray (without color))

Neutrals: (mixes of hues to get browns (or grays))

Clash: (combines a color hue with a color on either side of its complement).
Example: blue w/red-orange or orange-yellow

There are many books, as well as free on-line color scheme designer apps to check out and play with.

(4) Color Proportions
And the *Sensation of Color Contrasts*

Just because the Color Wheel suggests that the color choices will work well, doesn't mean that these will be successfully incorporated within your jewelry composition. It turns out that making color choices based on Light Values alone are less than perfect. Colors do not occur in a vacuum. They appear next to other colors. They appear within a situation or context. They reflect and refract light and shadow differently, depending on setting, lighting, and context.

That means, perceiving and recognizing one or more colors is important information to have, but not enough information for the brain to determine if the object is satisfying or not, or safe or not. People do not yet have enough information to make an absolute choice whether to wear or buy a piece of jewelry, at this point.

Color Contrasts. This brings us to the sensation of *Color Contrasts*. Color Contrasts relate to how **Colors appear together in different proportions.** These also affect and complicate the brain's processes of trying to harmonize them – that is, achieve a light value of zero.

213

Color Proportions. Another series of color research focused on the effects of *color proportions*. These scientifically derived proportions show the joint effect of 2 or more colors, if the brain is to score their sum as a value of 0.0. *(Again, I've made up this scoring, but you get the point about reaching equilibrium).* The brain would like to know, not only what color it is, but what proportion relative to other colors, we have before us.

As designers, to achieve a sense of harmony and balance, we are going to mimic what the brain does when seeing more than one color – we are going to vary the proportions so that, in combination, the sense of that perceptual and cognitive zero-sum game is still maintained.

And again, I'll make the point that not all compositions have to be perfectly harmonious.

Itten has a picture of the ideal and relative proportions of colors in harmony and balance.

Yellow to purple, 1:4 (This is read as "*1 in 4*", and means that *given 4 parts, 1 should be yellow and the remaining 3 should be purple.*)
Orange to blue, 1:3
Red to green, 1:2
Yellow to orange: 1:1.3

Choreographing Color Blending and Transitioning:
Playing With Color Proportions

ColorBlock Bracelet, Warren Feld, 2017
(playing with progressive proportions)

Every so often, you might want to create a rainbow, or some sequencing of colors, say from light to dark, where all the colors seem to emerge from the last, and bleed into the next. This is much more difficult with beads than with paints for all the usual reasons discussed above.

A *random* selection or placement of colors doesn't usually work as well as selecting and placing based on some more *mathematical formula*. *Alternating* or *graduating* colors doesn't always work as well, either. You must create a more complex, involved *patterning*. You must choreograph the layout of colors, so that, from a short distance, they look like they are blending, and gradually changing across the length of your piece.

Monet's Garden Bracelet, Kathleen Lynam, 2013
(using math formula)

One of the easier mathematical formulas to come up with as a way to choreograph things, is to play with color proportions. Go bead by bead or row by row, and begin with the ideal proportionate relationship between two colors. Gradually manipulate this down the piece by anticipating the next ideal proportionate relationship between the next two colors that need to follow.

In fact, any kind of statistical or mathematical formula underlying an arrangement will work better and be perceived as more satisfying than something random or intuitive, when managing color blending and transitions.

(5) Simultaneity Effects
And The Sensation Of Simultaneous Color Contrasts

It turns out there is even more to how the brain recognizes and tries to harmonize colors. Knowing (1) the color *(light value)* and (2) the relative proportions *(contrasts)* of color within the piece of jewelry is necessary, but still not enough for the brain to decide whether the piece of jewelry will be satisfying, wearable, buyable, finished and successful, or somewhat ugly, boring, dissatisfying or repulsive.

Some colors, when sitting on or near a particular color, are experienced differently, than when sitting on or near a different color. The line of research we are focusing on here deals with what are called **Simultaneity Effects**. *Colors can be affected by other colors around them (simultaneous color contrasts).* Colors in the presence of other colors get perceived differently, depending on the color combination.

Simultaneity Effects are a boon to the jewelry designer. They are great tools for such things as…

- Filling in the gaps of light between beads, and other managing the interface of negative and positive spaces
- Assisting in the blending of colors or the sense of movement of colors along a line or plane
- Assisting in establishing dimensionality in a piece that otherwise would appear flat
- Harmonizing 2 or more colors which don't quite match up on the color wheel
- Establishing frames, boundaries or silhouettes
- Re-directing the eye to another place, or creating sense of movement

For example, a White Square on a Black background looks bigger than a Black Square on a white background. White reaches out and overflows the boundary; black contracts.

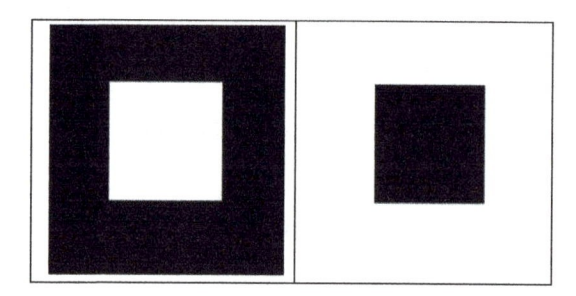

Gray always picks up some of the color characteristics of other colors around it.

Existence of these *simultaneity effects* is a great piece of information for the designer. There will be gaps of color and light between beads. Many bead colors are imperfect, particularly in combination. Playing with what I call "grays" *[thus, simultaneity effects]* gives the designer tools to overcome some of the color limitations associated with the bead.

Simultaneity effects trick the brain into filling in those gaps of light between beads. Simultaneity effects trick the brain into believing colors are more connected and blended and mutually-supportive than they would, if separately evaluated. Simultaneity effects trick the brain into seeing satisfying arrangements, rhythms, and dimensionality, where, without them, things would be unsatisfying instead.

A final example of simultaneity effects has to do with how people sense whether colors are warm or cool. In one composition, depending on the color mix, a particular color might be felt as "warm". In a second composition, with a different color mix, that same color might be felt as "cool".

Here the yellow square surrounded by white feels lighter, brighter and a different temperature than its counterpart. The red square surrounded by the black feels darker, duller, and a different temperature than its counterpart.

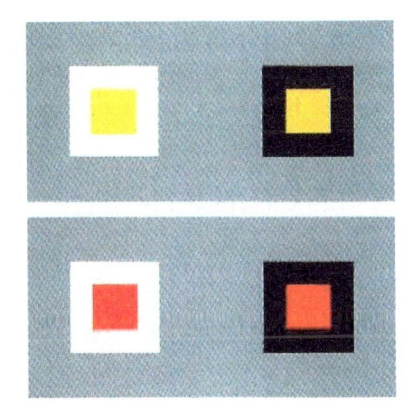

Again, simultaneity effects give tools to the jewelry designer for intensifying and clarifying the design, without disturbing the eye/brain pre-wired fear and anxiety responses. These allow you to "blend" and build "bridges" and create "transitions." You have a lot of tricks to use here which enable you to push the envelop with your designs. And still have your piece be judged as beautiful and appealing.

Simultaneity Effects are some of the easiest things the jewelry artist can control and manipulate, to fool the brain just a little bit. They let you bring in unexpected colors, and fool the brain into seeing color coordination and color blending. They let you convince the brain that the color proportions are correct when, in reality, they are not. They let you convince the brain to jump the cliff, which the gap between beads presents.

For the brain, gaps between beads – that is, areas with undefined colors, creates work for the brain, and is fraught with danger. The brain has to actually construct a color and meaning to fill in this gap. Without any clues or rules or assistance, it is more risky for the brain to *jump the cliff*, so to speak, and fill in the gaps with color, than it is for the brain to follow an easier pathway and simply define the jewelry as ugly or boring and reject it and move on. Similarly, simultaneity effects convince the brain to look around corners, go into crevices, explore and move around the whole piece from end to end.

It is at this point in the design process where the jewelry designer must be most fluent, creative and strategic in using color. *It is primarily and most often through establishing, and then managing, the sensation of simultaneous color contrasts where the designer begins to build that connection between audience and self, wearer and resonance, the wearing-of and the context, coherency and contagion.*

With Simultaneity Effects, colors begin to take on meanings and emotions. These can be as simple as sensations of warm and cold, close and far, approaching and fleeing, soft and harsh. Or they can be much more complex, even thematic and symbolic.

The Use of "GRAYS" (*simultaneity effects*) to tie things together – Blending, Bridging, Transitioning

With beads, the eye often needs to merge or coordinate colors, as it scans any piece. And then there are the gaps of light between beads. The eye needs help in spanning those gaps. The designer needs to build color "bridges" and "transitions", so that the eye doesn't fall off a cliff, so to speak, or have to make a leap of death from one bead, across the *gap*, all the way to the next.

One easy technique to use is to play with simultaneity effects. One such effect is where gray takes on the characteristics of the color(s) around it.

In beads, there are many colors that function as "grays" - gray, black diamond, alexandrite, Montana blue, prairie green, fuchsia, Colorado topaz – colors that have a lot of black or gray tones to them. Most color lined beads result in a gray effect (*where the glass encasing distorts the inside color*). Metallic finishes can result in a gray effect.

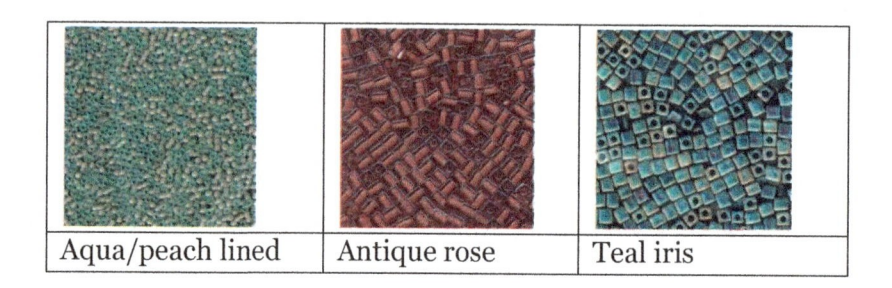

| Aqua/peach lined | Antique rose | Teal iris |

In one piece I made, for example, I used 11/0 peach lined aqua beads as a "gray" to tie in larger teal and antique rose beads together. While aqua is different than teal and the peach is different than the antique rose, in combination, the aqua/peach-lined beads acted like a *gray*. When close to the teal iris beads, the aqua took on the teal color; when close to the antique rose beads, the peach took on the antique rose color. Gray colors pull from one bead, and transition to the next in a very subtle way, that tricks the brain, but does not disturb it.

Also one note: Your jewelry, then, will appear differently on different colored backgrounds. It might be displayed on various easels or pads that are different colors. It might be an image on a TV or computer or phone screen, where the background is black. Or it might be an image in print where the background is white. Or you might have created a special background image for your jewelry. You might have strung your pieces on stringing materials or canvases of different colors, each color with a very different impact on the perception of color overall.

Expressive Attributes of Color and Color Contrasts:
Important Color Terms and Vocabulary

Each color on the wheel is called a **HUE**. Hues are pure colors – any color except black or white. And if you look again, there is no black or white on the Color Wheel.

BLACK is the absence of color. We consider black to be opaque. Usually, when people see black, they tend to see shadows. With black, designs tend to feel older, more antique'y, richer, more traditional and solid, and seem to have a patina around them.

WHITE is all the colors merged together. When all colors in "light" merge, you get White. When all the colors in paints or pigments are merged, you get a neutral gray-black or beige. With White, designs tend to feel sharper, brighter, more contemporary.

INTENSITY and VALUE. Better jewelry designers are those who master how to play with **INTENSITIES** and play with **VALUES**. This means they know and are comfortable with manipulating bright and dull (*intensity*), and light and dark (*value*). They know the subtle differences among red, pink and maroon, and how viewers react to these. They know how to punctuate – BAM! – with Yellow, and EASE - with purple, and CALM - with blue.

The contrasts between *Bright and Dull* or *Light and Dark* are not quite the same. *Bright and Dull* (*intensity*) have to do how powerful the color is when reflected into the eye and translated into neural impulses to the brain. Yellow-green, yellow, and red are the brightest colors because they trigger the most energetic neural responses. Low intensity is duller; high intensity is brighter.

Think of a Stop Sign. It could have just as easily been Red, Pink or Maroon. Red is the most intense – the brightest of the 3 – and hence the sign is Red. You can see red from the farthest distance away. Red is "Bright (*intensity*)", but not necessarily "Lighter (*values*)" than Pink or Maroon.

The contrasts between *Light and Dark* are called **VALUES**. A lower value is darker, though not necessarily duller (*intensity*). Pink has a higher value than maroon, because it is lighter. The amount of white, gray or black tones underlying the hue or pure color determines the value – that is, how light or dark a color is.

Unfortunately, in many texts and guides written by Bead Artists and Jewelry Designers, they combine the concepts of intensity and value into a single concept they refer to as "*Values*". Bead Artists and Colorists often write that the "secret" to using colors is to vary "values". When they refer to "values", they are actually combining these two color theory concepts – "values" and "intensities". Both are really different, so this combined meaning is a disservice to the bead artist and jewelry designer trying to learn to control color choices and color expression.

So, as you work with people to create jewelry for them, you make choices about, and then manipulate:

  - Colors
  - Balance and Harmony (distribution, placement, and proportions)
  - Intensities
  - Values
  - Simultaneity effects

INTENSITY AND VALUES EXERCISES

Values Exercise:

Use your Blue Pencil, as well as your White, Gray and Black Pencils, to color in the 2nd column. Start by coloring in all the squares with a medium shade of blue.
Using your white, gray and black pencils, now vary the darkness of the blue to approximate the darkness of the grays in the 1st column

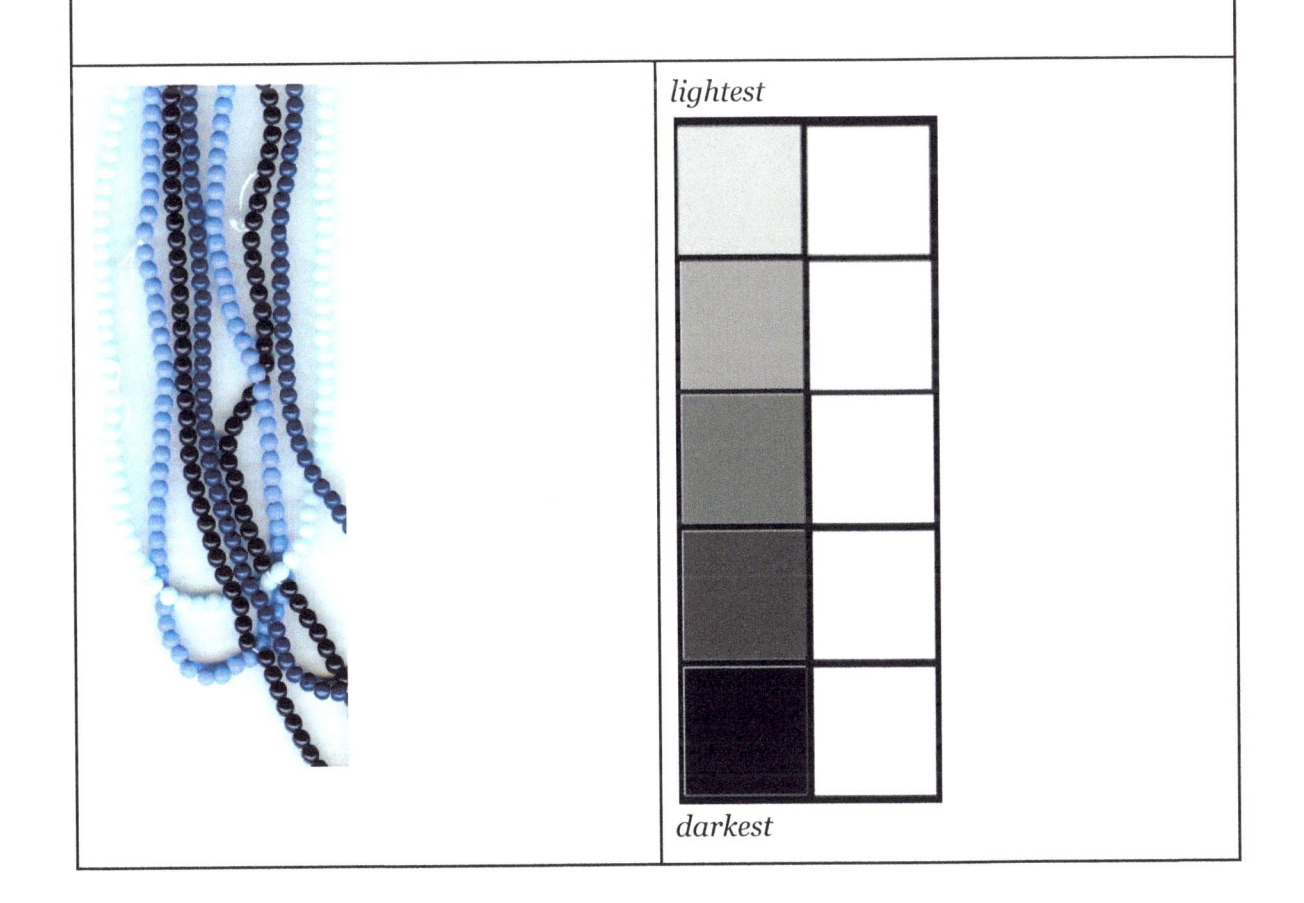

lightest

darkest

Intensity Exercise:
Use your color pencils – yellow, red, green, brown, blue. Color in each cell of the table, putting the brightest color on top as in the beads sample pictured. Put the dullest color on the bottom. Arrange the other colors in between from brightest to dullest, in that order.

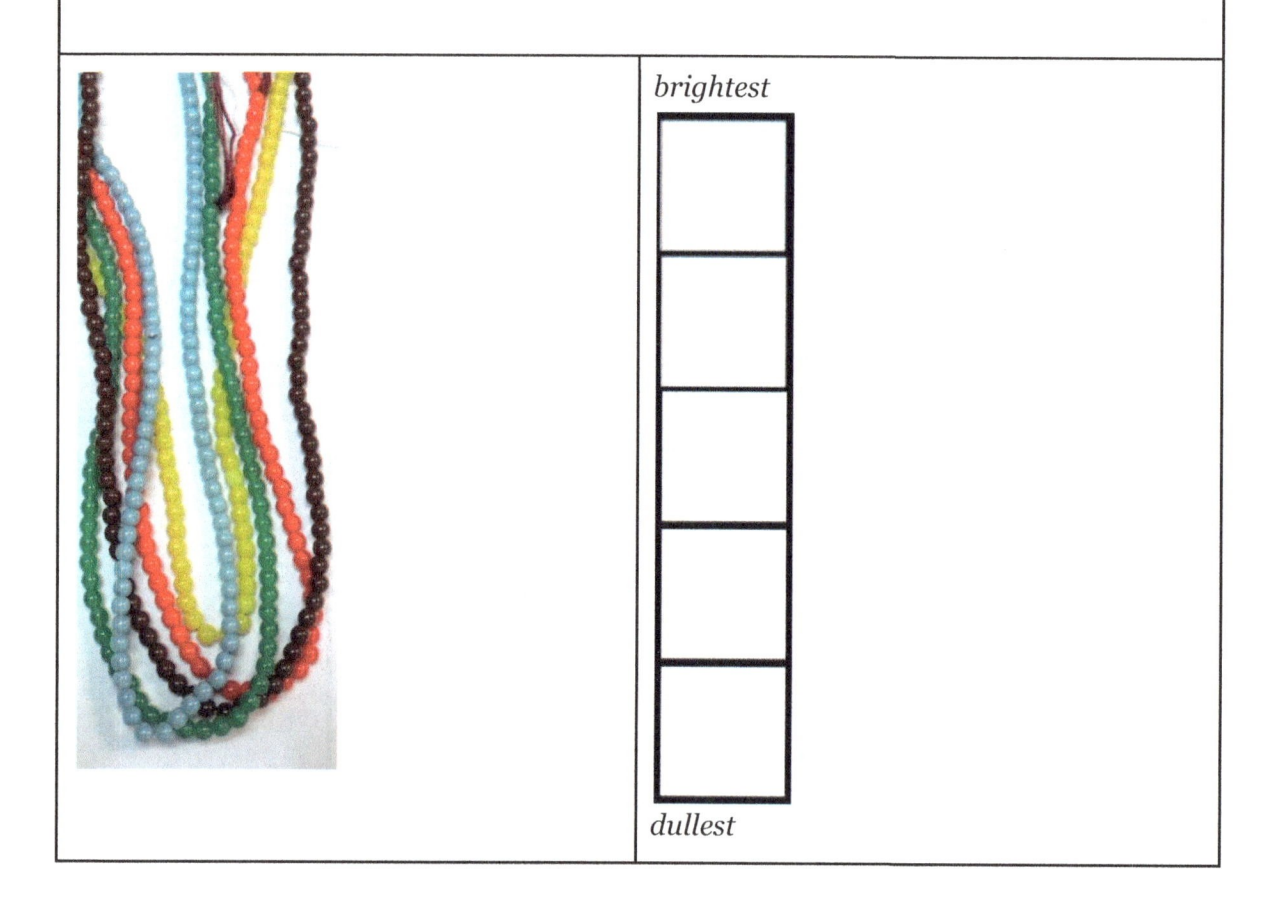

brightest

dullest

Let's say you wanted to design a necklace with blue tones.

If you were designing this necklace for someone to wear at work, it would probably be made up of several blue colors but which vary very little in *intensities*. To give it some interest, it might be a mix of light blue, blue, dark blue and very dark blue. Thus, the piece is pretty, but does not force any power or sexuality issues on the situation. It will minimize intensity. You might vary the values to give the piece variety and interest.

More appropriate for work setting

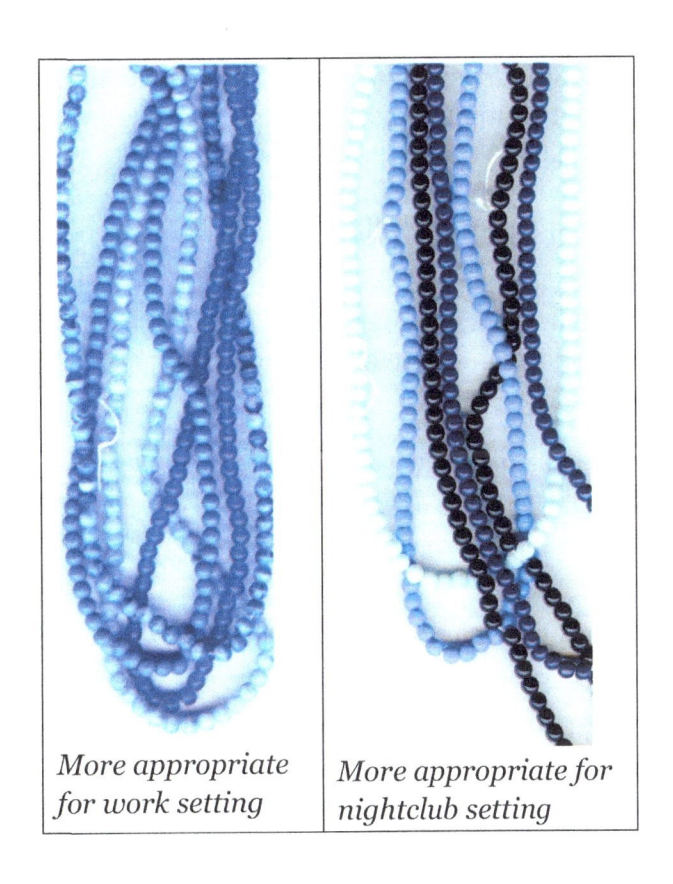

More appropriate for nightclub setting

If you were making this same necklace for someone to go out on the town one evening, you might use several blue colors which vary a lot in *intensity*. You might mix periwinkles and Montana blues and cobalt blues and blue quartzes. You want to make a power or sensual statement here, and the typical necklace someone would wear to work just won't do. You would concentrate on building in intensity much moreso than value.

Let's continue with some more important color building blocks or concepts.

HUE, TINT SHADE AND TONE

HUE
TINT
SHADE
TONE

223

TINT, **SHADE** and **TONE** are similar to values and intensities. They are another way of saying similar things about manipulating color Hues. **TINTS** are colors with white added to them. Pink is a tint of Red. **SHADES** are colors with black or gray added to them. Maroon is a shade of Red. And **TONES** define the relative darkness of a color. Violet is a dark tone and yellow is a light tone. Red and green have the same tonal value.

"Tones" are what copy machines pick up, and the depth of the black on a photocopy relates to the tonal value of the colors on the original paper you are copying. Red and green photocopy the same black color. They have the same tonal value.

TEMPERATURE. Colors also have Temperature.
Some colors are **WARM**. The addition of black tends to warm colors up. Warm colors are usually based in Red. Red-Orange is considered the warmest color. Warm colors tend to project forward.

COOL colors are usually based in Blue. Green-blue is the coldest color. Addition of white often cools colors. Cool colors tend to recede.

The perception of temperature in colors is universal. Whether a particular color is sensed as warm or cold can be very subjective. Also, given the other colors which surround them, however, typically what are warm colors may appear as cold, and vice versa. Again, There can be a lot of subjectivity entering the situation here about how different people sense color temperatures.

Juxtaposing colors creates **MOVEMENT** and **RHYTHM**. By creating patterns, you guide the brain/eye in its circuitous route around the piece, as it tries to make sense of it. Juxtaposing Warm with Cool colors increases the speed or sense of movement.

Some colors tend to **PROJECT FORWARD** and others tend to **RECEDE**. Yellow is an advancing color. Black recedes. You can play with this effect to trick the viewer into seeing a more **MULTI-DIMENSIONAL** piece of jewelry before her. By mixing different colors and different finishes, you can create a marvelous sense of dimensionality.

- Faceted, Glossy beads will tend to look closer and capture the foreground
- Smooth, Glossy beads will tend to capture the middle ground
- Matte, Dull, Frosted, or Muted beads will tend to fall into the background

To Reiterate Some of The Key Ideas and Understandings

The color research begins to open up ideas about how the brain processes color, and which of these processes might be seen as universal, and which more subjective.
The brain first perceives, then tries to understand the color as a color. It senses *Light Values*.

The brain perceives, then tries to understand the color relative to other colors around it. It senses *Color Contrasts*.

At the same time, the brain perceives and tries to understand the color within some context or situation, to gauge more meaning or emotional content. It interprets *Simultaneous Color Contrasts* within the boundaries of a context, situation, personal or group culture.

The END RESULT is simple:
Should we consider the jewelry to be finished and successful?
Should we like the jewelry or not like it?
Should it get and hold our attention, or not?
Should we approach it, or avoid it?
Should we get excited about it, or not?
Should we comment about it to others?

Should we touch it?
Should we buy it?
Should we wear it?

All this perceptual and cognitive and interpretive activity happens very quickly, but somewhat messy. Some of it follows universal precepts. Some of it is very subjective. Our brain is trying everything it can to make sense of the situation. It tries to zero-sum the light values. It has to take in information about a color's energy signature. It has to take in information about how much of one color there is in relation to other colors. It has to take in information about emotional and other meaningful content the juxtaposition of any group of colors within any context or situation represents.

With any piece of jewelry, the artist and designer is at the core of this all. It is the designer, in anticipation of how others perceive, recognize, interpret and desire colors in their lives, who establishes how color is used, and manages its expression within the piece. The jewelry designer is the manager. The designer is the controller. The designer is the influencer. The designer establishes and conveys intent and meaning. The designer anticipates shared understandings and desires.

DECODING COLOR AS A DESIGN ELEMENT

A composition in orange and blue.

Art and design theory informs us how to objectively use color. That means, there are universally accepted shared understandings, expectations and desires about what makes a piece of jewelry more satisfying (or more dissatisfying) in terms of choices about color.

So, when we refer to our lessons above about color use, and examine *the orange and blue necklace above*, we can recognize some problematic choices about color.

The first is about color proportions. The most satisfying proportionate relationship between orange and blue is 1:3. That means, for every 3 parts, one should be orange and two should be blue. In our illustrated composition, the relationship is more 1:2 or half orange and half blue. To make this piece more attractive and satisfying, we would need to reduce the amount of orange and increase the amount of blue.

The second is about color schemes. Here we have a 2-color, complimentary color scheme, with equal amounts of orange and blue. To make this piece more attractive and satisfying as a complimentary color scheme, we have learned that one of the two colors should predominate. Either we have to add more orange, or have to add more blue.

So, we have decoded our Color Design Element and we see that the proportions are less than optimal, and the color scheme chosen is less than optimal. To make the necklace more appealing, and in conformance with universally agreed upon understandings about good color use, we will need to increase the amount of blue and decrease the amount of orange, so that we get a 1:3 (orange to blue) proportionate outcome, and we allow one color to predominate.

Let's look at another example:

Composition in green, white and red.

First, white is not considered a color. We can ignore it.

Second, proportionately, there should be equal amounts of green to that of red. The relationship is 1:2, meaning for every 2 parts, 1 should be green and 1 should be red. Proportionately, in this piece, we are close to this proportionate relationship.

Third, we have, in effect, since we ignore white, a 2-color complimentary color scheme. We have learned that in this scheme, one color should predominate.

That means, in this composition, the current use of color will not and cannot work. It results in an unacceptable and unsatisfying use of color. Proportionately, both colors need to be equal. Color Scheme wise, one color needs to clearly predominate. We can't conform to both universally-accepted shared understandings about the use of green and red in a 2-color scheme.

DESIGNING JEWELRY WITH COLOR

Always remember that your choice of color(s) should be secondary to the choices you make about concept, theme, arrangement and organization. Color should be used to enhance your design thinking. *Color should not, however, be the design.*

When we study color from a design standpoint, we think of color as part of the jewelry's structure. That means, color is not merely a decorative effect or object. It is more like an integral building block component which has been organized or arranged within a larger composition. As a component, it is a *Design Element*.

Color is the most important Design Element. It is independent and syllabic. It can both stand alone, as well as easily be combined with other Design Elements. There are some universal aspects when color is objectively understood as an element of design.

As part of an arrangement, we begin to treat color in terms of Principles of Composition, Construction and Manipulation. Color takes on some subjectivity. Its effects become much more dependent on the artist's intent, the situation in which the jewelry is worn, and the shared understandings and desires of various client audiences.

Color is used to express meaning and enhance meaningful expressions. We use color to express elements of the materials used, like glass or gemstone. We use color to express or emphasize elements of the forms we are creating. We use color to enhance a sense of movement or dimension. We use color to express moods and emotions. We use color to influence others in sharing the artist's inspirations and aspirations.

As designers, we...

- Anticipate how the parts we use to make a piece of jewelry assert their needs for color
- Anticipate shared universal understandings among self, viewer, wearer, exhibitor and seller about color and its use
- Think through how colors relate to our inspirations and how they might impact our aspirations
- Pick colors
- Place and arrange colors
- Distribute the proportions of colors
- Play with and experiment with color values and color intensities
- Leverage the synergistic effects and what happens when two (or more) colors are placed next to one another
- Create focus, rhythm, balance, dimension and movement with color

- Create satisfying blending and transitioning strategies using color
- Anticipate how color and the play of color within our piece might be affected by contextual or situational variables
- Reflect on how our choices about color affect how the piece of jewelry is judged as finished and successful by our various client audiences
- Use color to promote the coherency of our pieces, and the speed and extent to which attention by others continues to spread

Fluent designers can decode color and its use intuitively and quickly, and apply color in more expressive ways to convey inspiration, show the designer's strategy and intent, and trigger an especially resonant, energetic response by wearers and viewers alike.

Don't get into a Color Rut

And a last piece of advice.

Don't get into a color rut.

Experiment with different colors.

Force yourself to use colors you usually do not use or avoid.

If it's too psychologically painful, make a game of it.

FOOTNOTES

[1] Pantone website https://www.pantone.com

[2] Itten, Johannes *The Elements of Color: A Treatise on the Color System of Johannes Itten,* NY: John Wiley & Sons, 2001

[3] In reality, the selection of primary colors is arbitrary. The primary colors depend on the light source, the color of the background, and the biology of the color-sensing components of the eye. We choose red-yellow-blue when referencing painting or coloring on white background, like paper. We choose red-green-blue when referencing color placed on a black background, such as a TV or computer screen. We choose cyan-maroon-yellow-black when using overlapping inks to create color on a white background, and better reproduce true colors. We understand that the eye sees red-greenish yellow-blue-violet most clearly.

Color References Worth Checking Out

Rockport Publishers, **Color Harmony Workbook**, Gloucester, MA: Rockport Publishers, 1999.

Deeb, Margie. **The Beader's Guide to Jewelry Design**, NY: Lark Jewelry & Beading, 2014.

RULES OF COMPOSITION, CONSTRUCTION, AND MANIPULATION
5c. POINT, LINE, PLANE, SHAPE, FORM, THEME: Creating Something Out Of Nothing

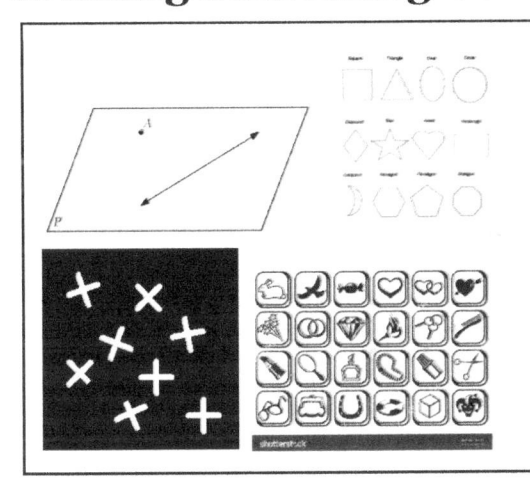

Guiding Questions:
(1) How does designer control relationship of mass to space?
(2) What does it mean to say that filling space with mass has risk?
(3) How do you differentiate points, lines, planes, shapes, forms, themes from each other?
(4) What is the Golden Ratio?

Key Words:	space	design thinking
point	mass	fluency
line	context	design elements
plane	composition	independent / dependent
shape	meaning / value	objects vs. structures
form	communication / dialectic	shared understandings
theme	risk	universal / subjective
emphasis / encompass	construction	parsimony
size / volume	manipulation	resonance
proportion	direction	focusing / attracting
placement	movement	positive / negative spaces
boundaries	dimensionality	
the golden ratio	surface	

Abstract

The artist creates something out of nothing. And the jewelry designer does the same, but also imposes this act on the person who wears the result, who in turn, decides whether to display or demonstrate its desirability and wearability, and all within a particular context or situation. So, we start with nothing into something. That something takes up space. That space might be filled with objects we call points, lines, planes, shapes, forms and themes. With whatever that space is filled, and however these objects are organized, the space and its composition convey meaning and value, communicated not merely to the designer, but as importantly, to the wearer and viewer, as well. As Design Elements, it is important to differentiate among the power of each of these objects to focus, anchor, direct, balance, move, expand, layer, synergize, coordinate, conform, bound, connect, and violate. The jewelry designer's ability to fill, manage and control space is a critical aspect of fluency in design.

POINT, LINE, PLANE, SHAPE, FORM, THEME:
Creating Something Out Of Nothing

The artist creates something out of nothing.
And the jewelry designer does the same, but also imposes this act on the person who wears the result, who in turn, decides whether to display or demonstrate its desirability and wearability, and all within a particular context or situation.

So, we start with nothing into something.

That something takes up space.

Space separates and connects us with things. It is these arrangements and contrasts of things positioned within a space which allows us to find meaning, feel connected, recognize implications.

That space might be filled with points, lines, planes, shapes, forms and themes. We might add color, texture and pattern.

With whatever that space is filled and organized, the space and its composition convey meaning and value, not merely for the jewelry designer, but as importantly, for the wearer and viewer, as well. Filling space with objects will always create a level of tension because any viewer will feel compelled to make sense of it all.

Making sense of it all is work. This work is risky – what if the wearer or viewer evaluates poorly? Or makes a mistake? Or shows bad judgement? Or is compelled to pretend to understand?

Filling space with a bunch of objects whose arrangement we want to label *jewelry* is just as full of risk. The arrangement must make sense. It must seem appealing. It must seem wearable. It must feel like something that will assist in making personal, social or cultural connections. It's always easier (and perhaps safer) for the person to turn and look away from any piece of jewelry. To reject the jewelry. Not wear it. Not buy it.

But jewelry designers do not want people to avoid their creations. So, it is important to also anticipate what happens when even more objects are added to this space and thus further expanding or delineating the composition. Further adding to and organizing and arranging these points, lines, planes, shapes, forms and themes into a design will continue to exacerbate things, increasing the risk, but also the reward, for the viewer to maintain their stance, keep looking at it, try it on, possess it, and keep trying to figure out what it all means, and what it all means for him or her.

Meaning and value emerge from some sort of dialectic-type interaction, first between designer and self, and then between designer and client, often reflected in the selection of materials and techniques as well as choices about arrangements. The meta-qualities and inspirations and aspirations underlying these decisions then transition into forms and themes.

This emergence of meaning and value is contextually bound by shared understandings and desires about whether the piece should be judged as finished and successful.

The choices are infinite.

Let's begin to decode points, lines, planes, shapes, forms and themes. The jewelry designer's ability to learn about, fill, manage and control space is perhaps the most critical set of fluency skills to develop.

[1]Points, lines, planes, and shapes are independent design elements, and forms and themes are their dependent cousins.

Independent design elements function a little like vowels in the alphabet, and can stand alone and be expressive. They can have expressive meanings independent of the context in which they are found. When viewed or experienced in context, however, that context can alter how they are perceived and received.

Dependent design elements function more like consonants, and typically require some combination with independent elements to have fully formed expressions. Dependent elements and their expression are very context-sensitive.

Whatever their independence or dependence, these design elements are progressively interrelated. As we move from point along the list to theme, we increase our power to express meaning, establish value, create tensions, resonate, and confirm or reject shared understandings about good design. As we use more than one of these elements – either more of the same element or combinations of different ones -- within the same composition, we also are increasing our artistic and design control, power, and ability to show intent, establish meaning, and achieve a successful result.

These design elements discussed here are considered *objects* to the extent that they are things to be positioned and manipulated. They are considered parts of *structures* to the extent that they are part of some shape, organization or arrangement. Both objects and structures express meaning and value, but structures moreso. Structures successfully earn the label *jewelry*, where their component parts do not.

Themes – the most complex of these design elements discussed here -- are explanatory meanings resulting from the interpretation of forms. They may be literal or abstract. They may be symbolic and layered. They may be culturally- or situationally-specific. *Themes connect stories to the individual, the culture, and the society.*

Forms, another design element, are especially coherent combinations and arrangements of points, lines, planes and shapes. They may be distinct or overlapping. They may be fully formed or partially formed. They reflect broader, deeper meanings and reflections – something considerably beyond the meanings of the component parts. *Forms give stories depth.*

Shapes are bounded lines and planes, delimiting spatial units which convey much more meaning than their individual component lines and planes could ever suggest on their own. Shapes function in 2- or 3-dimensions. Shapes are interpretable, whether they are immediately or easily recognized, or not. *Shapes give stories character.*

Planes are defined by the intersection of 2 lines, or the presence of 3 noncollinear (not on the same line) points, or 2 parallel lines, or a line and a point not on that line. Planes suggest the ideas of existence, thought, and development. Planes imply the possibilities for movement and dimension. *Planes are the stage upon which ideas unfold and stories may be told.*

Lines are defined as a series of points. *Lines imply the possibilities for boundaries, directions and movement.* They can be used to measure things. Lines channel ideas. They can demarcate that which is OK and sacred from that which is unacceptable or dangerous or profane. In jewelry, they can call your attention to one part of the body, and indicate that you should not move your gaze elsewhere.

Points change the nothingness of space into something-ness. They focus the attention. Points are the simplest geometric elements which imply the possibilities for imposing individual intent, meaning and value on the universe. *Points spark ideas.* The presence of two or more points can suggest relativity.

The jewelry designer cannot ignore any of this. As design elements, points, lines, planes, shapes, forms and themes are an integral part of the jewelry designer's tool box. As elements within compositions, they are to be constructed or manipulated into principled arrangements we call jewelry. They allow the designer to show his or her hand. They are some of the major building blocks the designer uses to convey meaning and connectedness, show intent and inspire others.

To some extent, as objects, these elements are universally shared and understood. When structured within various arrangements, sometimes these structures too can be universally shared and understood; oftentimes, however, the designer uses these structures to assert ideas or feelings or intents not necessarily recognized by everyone or satisfactory to everyone.

As Design Elements, it is important to differentiate among the power of each of these elements to...

(1) Focus the eye
(2) Anchor or establish some kind of predominance or hierarchy within a composition
(3) Direct the eye
(4) Establish balance, order, and a satisfying distribution of proportions and sizes, or their opposite
(5) Give a sense of movement and flow
(6) Give a sense of layering and dimension
(7) Synergize or marry the relationship between positive and negative space
(8) Establish a sense of coherence, coordination, sameness, unity, difference, and/or variety, or some grouping rules for elements
(9) Conform to the shape of the body
(10) Establish a silhouette or personal identity and culture
(11) Connect to a time frame, context, or situation
(12) Conform to or violate shared expectations or group norms about good design

As used with Principles of Composition, Construction and Manipulation, it is important to understand how each of these elements can enhance or impede the artist's ability to arrange objects and achieve a finished and successful piece of jewelry. Each can support or detract from a compelling arrangement.

The designer does not have to use all of these elements in any one piece of jewelry. But the designer does need to know what each can and cannot be used to do. The designer must develop that intuitive and fluent knowledge how each of these elements function. The goal of jewelry design is to communicate. Communicate the artist's inspirations and aspirations. Communicate the choices made to turn aspirations into concrete products. Communicate the self-identifying relevance of jewelry pieces to the wearers. Communicate the value and the associated risks for whether to touch, wear, buy or collect it. Communicate the socio-cultural or context-specific relevance of jewelry pieces both to wearers and to viewers.

Finally, each element should be used parsimoniously (that is, that Goldilocks point of *just right*), to attain a level of resonance. Our jewelry, at the minimum, should evoke an emotion, and more importantly, go a little beyond this and resonate.

POINTS

In math, the *point* exists but has no mass. However, for this and our other design elements discussed in this chapter, we use a looser definition in art and design. The *point* is the simplest geometrically based design element the can use to create something out of nothing and draw someone's attention to a piece. The *point* can be very small, or medium or large. It can be a simple circle, or a blob, or a square, or anything that might get interpreted as a *point*.

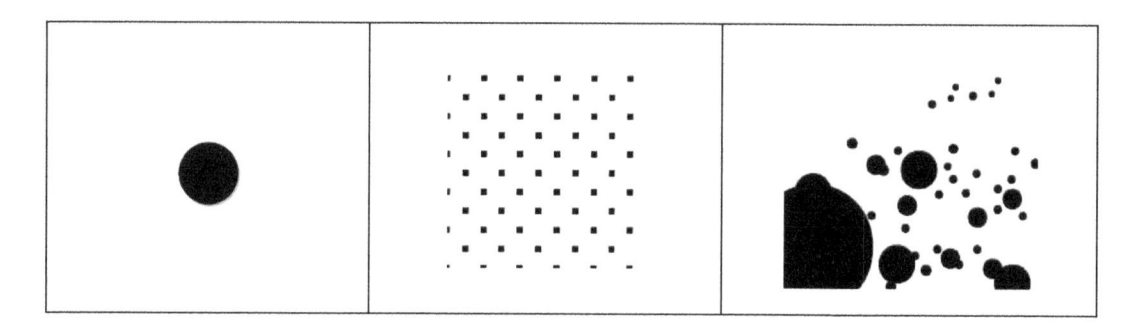

The point is the building block for everything else. Every mark we can make will be a combination of one or more points. Every line, plane, shape or form is essentially a point, regardless of its size.

Most importantly, the point calls one's attention to a place where no attention was called for or placed before. It creates a reference point. With 2 or more points, that reference point builds up much more meaning. It shows relativity in a relationship. It suggests distance and direction. It can suggest layering or dimension – think two over-lapping points.

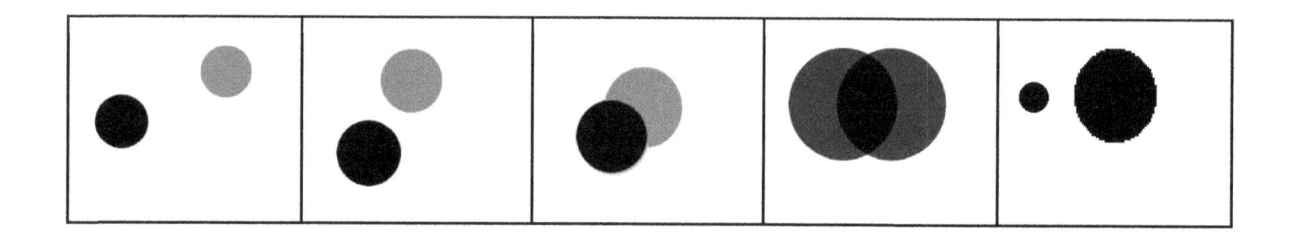

Relationships between and among points pose two especially important meanings. One, the relationship that emerges about *proportions* of the point(s) to the space around it. Two, the relationship that emerges about the *position* of the point(s) within the space around it. Proportions and positioning.

Jewelry Applications/Decoding Points

A continuous series of points	*Points directing your attention*	*Points which convey distance and relativity*	*A Point which steers your eye to the upper right, partly due to proportion and placement and color*

The jewelry designer usually starts with a collection of different kinds of points with some determination and a lot of experimentation to arrange them in some pleasing way. Some points might be various round beads. They might be beads of different shapes. They might be a clustering of beads into some shape or form. They might be a fully formed component or pendant.

The designer thinks about the distribution and balance of points. Sizes, relative sizes, shapes and variety of shapes are pondered over. Then points are placed, usually, with jewelry, in some kind of circle or silhouette. Their placement may establish a sense of balance, such as symmetry. Their placement might create a rhythm, either fast or slow.

The designer determines where any emphasis should go. Often the designer uses a pendant drop, some variation in proportion, or some color placement effect to call a viewer's attention to a certain part of the jewelry. These function as points.

The designer determines how emphasis, size, proportionate relationships and placement affect how the piece will be interpreted and decoded by others. In what way(s) does the point influence the space around it? Should attention be focused or directed? What kind of rhythm should be established? Should a feeling of closeness, apartness, integration or skew be created? Have the dots contributed to a sense of symmetry or asymmetry? Do the points lose their "point-ness" and suddenly get perceived as a lines or shapes, when they move closer together?

The designer decides the number of points to be used, and decides their parsimonious selection and placement. That is, the designer decides when enough points are enough. Using more than one point adds a level of tension to the piece. There is a competition for space and how position and proportion will affect interpretation of the designer's intent, whether the piece feels finished, and whether the piece is seen as successful.

Overlapping points create a *figure/ground* perspective. They change the nature of the space and the person's interaction with it. They add depth or layering. Overlapping points might get re-translated into a new point, or into a new shape.

LINES

Lines are defined by the connections between 2 or more points. Lines have length and width. They connect, they divide, they direct. The points along the line can attract or repel each other. They can emote strength, weakness, or harmony. They can excite, muddle or confuse. They can be actual or implied.

Whereas *points* are about *emphasis*, *lines* are mostly about *direction* and *movement*. A line is not attracting you to a point in space, but rather, it is directing you. Lines prevent the viewer from getting stuck staring at one point in your jewelry composition. They encourage the viewer to move around and take into account the whole piece.

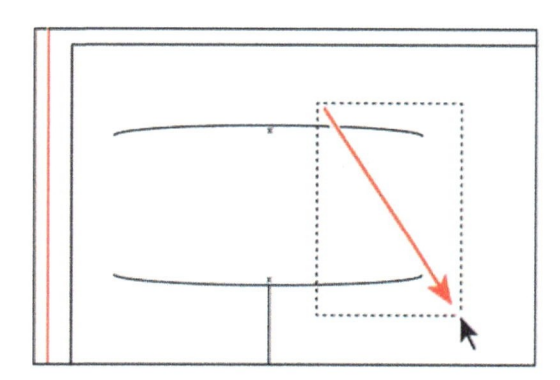

Lines both separate and join things. They establish a silhouette. They demarcate boundaries. They signal a beginning and an end, or travel in one or both directions all the way out to infinity, and perhaps beyond. Lines can violate boundaries, or establish walls around something.

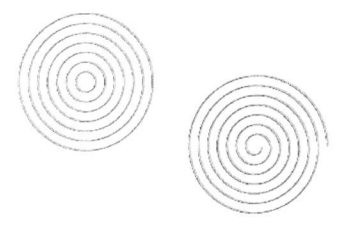

They can curve and curve around things. A line which curves around and connects its beginning to its end becomes a *circle*. If the line delineating the circle becomes too thick and fills all the negative space, it becomes a *point*. If the curving line does not meet itself, beginning to end, it becomes a *spiral*. A curved line usually conveys a different sense of beauty and romance than a straight line.

As lines become thicker, they begin to take on the characteristics of planes. To maintain their identity and integrity as lines, they must always be longer than they are wide. Changing the ratio of the length to the width has the greatest impact on how any line will be perceived and understood.

As lines become thinner, they more and more emphasize the quality of direction. As both endpoints of lines seem to extend towards infinity, they emphasize movement. If one endpoint is fixed, while the other endpoint is allowed to extend towards infinity, more tension is perceived as the space around the line is interpreted by the viewer.

Two or more lines together create a measure of things. People try to make sense of each line, sometimes in combination, but often as individual segments. The *interval space between the lines* becomes critical in this endeavor.

Eloquence, by Warren Feld, 2018, jasper, jade, Japanese seed beads

Here we have a 7-strand necklace. Look at the use of points, lines, planes and shapes. Look at the interval spaces between each strand.

How many points do you see?
How many lines?
Planes?
Shapes?
Forms?
Themes?

When two lines converge, they create an *angle* between them. This joint or connecting point becomes the nexus for things moving in two different or altering directions. The angle and juxtapositions of multiple angles can establish a rhythm. Angles smaller than 90 degrees generate perceptions of more rapid movement than angles larger than 90 degrees.

When two lines are separated, they often are perceived separately, each with its own identity. Think of the single vs. the multiple strand necklace or bracelet. The interval between the lines becomes a critical part of the story ascribed to each line separately, or lines in combination or sequencing. It is important how that interval's negative space is filled up or left empty. It is important how wide that interval is between each pair of lines. Pieces with narrower interval spaces have more tension resulting from how the lines are perceived and thought about.

The width of interval spaces between lines creates rhythm. The use of color can further enhance (or impede) this perception of rhythm within a piece of jewelry. Varying the intensity and values of the lines can create dimensionality, where some lines appear to advance and others appear to recede.

Thicker lines placed close together can change the gestalt, where the viewer's attention shifts from the original lines to the *negative interval spaces*, now seen as the *lines*.

Jewelry Applications/Decoding Lines

| Parallel lines | Curved lines | Directional lines | Perpendicular Lines |

Lines are design elements used to compose, construct and manipulate beads and other pieces into jewelry. They assist the designer in translating inspiration into aspiration, establishing intent, and securing shared understandings about whether the piece is finished and how successful that piece should be judged.

We've learned that the control over line includes choices about thinness or thickness, finite or infinite, continuous or sporadic, integrated or disjointed, connected or not, and spacing between intervals. The presence of more than one line, and the chosen attributes of each line, add more meaning, more complexity, and more opportunity for the jewelry designer to play with materials, techniques and designs.

The tensions underlying points get assessed and managed differently by the jewelry designer than those underlying lines. While the *point* is more about attracting your eye, the *line* is more about directing it. Points emphasize and focus and anchor. Lines add movement and flow. Points lead us to ideas about balance and predominance. Lines lead us to ideas about alignment, coordination, closeness, grouping. Lines add additional measures of meaning, such as those associated with violation, conformance, span of control, silhouette, dimensionality, boundaries and framing and walls.

PLANES

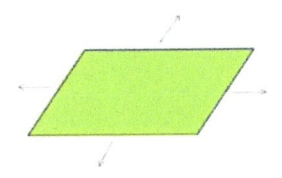

Planes are used to encompass a space. Planes suggest unity. Planes provide reference and boundaries and direction. They suggest dimension and movement. As such, the use of planes often makes it easier for the viewer to find and interpret meaning of all the other design elements found within or outside that plane. They create the stage for a story to be created and told.

Because of this, establishing planar relationships among design elements can also lead to a measured sense of history and time and timeliness. They can lead to more concrete understandings of context and situation within which the other design elements present themselves, and seek to affect.

Planes are created in different ways. These include,

(a) Two intersecting lines
(b) A line and a point not on that line
(c) Three points, one of which is not on the same linear path as the other two
(d) Two parallel lines

Planes are not restricted to a single point of view. They allow widespread placement and fragmentation.

Planes may overlap. They may be parallel. They may intersect. They may be flat or curved. Their boundaries may be linear or nonlinear. They may have clearly defined or diffuse boundaries. They may be warped and pulled in different directions.

Just as lines can be thought of as an accumulation of points, planes can be thought of as an accumulation of lines.

If not careful, planes can lose their identity and powers to establish expression and meaning. As a plane becomes larger, it sometimes takes on the characteristics of a point. It would then *emphasize* rather than *encompass*.

As it takes on the characteristics of a point, then its *contour* takes on a more critical importance, as it tries to retain and maintain its *plane*-ness, thus, diminishing the point-like characteristics. But then, as the contour gains greater significance, the plane increasingly reflects the attributes of a shape-like object. Again, the plane begins to lose its powers as a plane, and begins to orient rather than *encompass*.

For jewelry designers, planes can be seen to have *surfaces*. Textures and patterns may be added to these surfaces. *Textures* involve the placement of 2 or more design elements within the same space and which are seen to somehow relate to one another. Textures have visual impacts. When this structural relationship among textural objects seems to have some order or regularity to it, we refer to the texture as a *pattern*.

Textures and patterns may be 2- or 3-dimensional. They may be regular, predictable and statistical. Or they may seem random and non-statistical. They may be repeated or singular. They may be both visual and tactile. We may see textures and patterns which are layered or not, or smooth or rough.

Jewelry Applications/Decoding Planes

| *Simple planes* | *Multiple planes* | *Intersecting planes* | *Overlapping planes* |

For the jewelry designer, planes can become both a help and a hinderance. They can aid the designer in establishing a coherent point of view. But they can get away from the designer, and allow incoherence and irrelevance to slip into the composition.

The encompassing nature of planes has a big advantage for the jewelry designer. This allows the designer to build in a sense of context or situation. Each piece of jewelry will not work or is not wearable in each and every situation. It is very context-specific. Planes give the designer some control over context, which is very important.

SHAPES

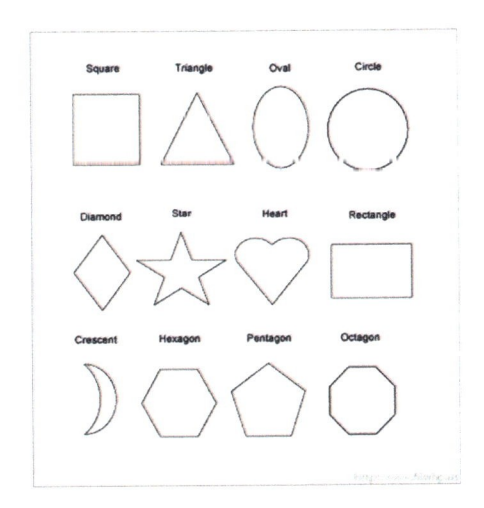

When we come to focus on the outer contours of a plane, we begin to recognize this design element as something we call a *shape*.

Shapes are areas in 2- or 3-dimensions which have defined or implied boundaries. They are somehow separated from the space surrounding them. Shapes may be delineated by lines. They may be filled or emptied. They may be formed by differences in color values and intensities. They may be formed by patterns and textures. They suggest both mass and volume.

Shapes may be organic or mechanical. They may relate to the background, foreground or middle ground. They may be geometrical (regular, predictable contours) or organic, distorted or overlapping, blended or distinct or abstract.

Shapes may be interrelated by angle, sometimes forcing a sense of movement and rotation.

More than one shape in a particular space may make one shape appear more active or more important or more prominent. This may change the perception of what that shape is about, particularly when shapes overlap. Secondary shapes may seem more point-like or line-like in relation to the primary shape.

When we recognize something as a *shape*, we begin to try to impose meaning on it. Shapes provide orientation. They are very powerful connectors between viewer and object. They may take on attribute qualities, such as masculine or feminine.

Shapes convey symbolic meanings. Triangles suggest action. They are dynamic. They are directional. They seem purposeful and strong. They have a power over the viewer, in that they can control the viewer's process of perception. Triangles can be made into pyramids, flags, arrows, beacons. They are often used as elements in religious symbols.

Square shapes denote honesty and stability. They are trusted, familiar, safe, comfortable. Most shapes we encounter are squares and rectangles. Squares could also symbolize rigidity and uniformity. *[An unexpected placement of squares within a piece, could evoke the opposite feelings and symbols.]*

Circle shapes suggest infinity. They are associated with protection (you're inside the circle or outside). They are associated with movement and freedom. They suggest completeness.

Shapes have meaning in and of themselves, and are not dependent on the human body for their expressive qualities and powers. When dependent on the human body, they become *forms*, rather than shapes.

Jewelry Applications/Decoding Shapes

Jewelry designers need to be able to relate the shape to the message they hope the shape will convey. The shape should reconfirm, rather than obscure, that message.

Repeated butterfly shapes with clear boundaries and no internal negative space.

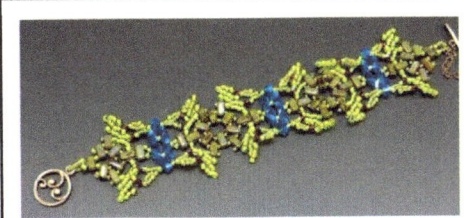

Implied butterfly shapes and no boundaries and considerable negative space.

Part of successfully working with shapes is controlling whether the boundaries are distinct, blurred or implied. Another important part is controlling how the interior space is depicted – such as, left empty and negative, shaded, colored, textured, either partially or fully, densely or not. A last important part is whether the shape represents a 2-dimensional or a 3-dimensional space.

THE GOLDEN RATIO

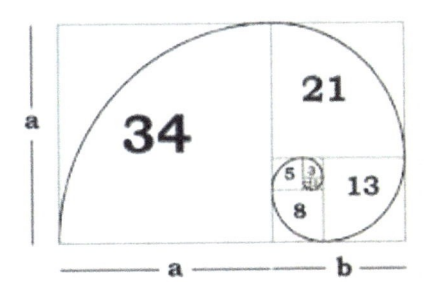

Golden Rectangle

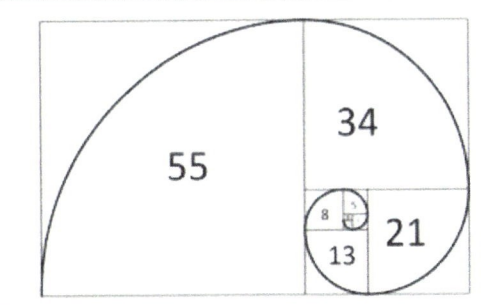

Fibonacci Curve
(connects all the golden ratio points within the plane, and creates a golden spiral)

There is a time-tested principle of good structure and design called the Golden Ratio. This is actually more of a tool, not a rule. Artists have used this ratio for hundreds of years, and there is no reason jewelry designers cannot attempt to use it as well. It is not a requirement, just an option to think about.

Supposedly, shapes with the proportions of the golden ratio (1:1.618) have the most appeal to human beings. Designs of buildings, painting compositions, body forms – and yes, even jewelry – which use the golden ratio to determine the placement of objects within a golden space typically yield structures with the most harmonious proportions and highest level of appeal.

In the Golden Rectangle, as pictured above, we first draw a line and divide it into two parts, one longer than the other.

In the picture, a = 34, and b = 21

We then draw a square using the longest length "a". So all 4 sides will equal "a".
We last close off our rectangle.

If a/b equals (a+b)/a, then we have the golden rectangle.

In the picture,

a/b would be 34/21 which equals 1.619

(a+b)/a would be (34+21)/34 or (55/34) which equals 1.617 *(close enough)*

We can keep dividing each rectangle into a square and a rectangle and establish golden rectangles within golden rectangles within golden rectangles. (Or we can keep doing this in reverse and keep getting larger and larger shapes.

As jewelry designers, we can use the golden rectangle and draw it over a person's body to establish the "plane" within which the piece of jewelry will function. If we know ahead of time that we want jewelry of a certain length, we can create the rest of the dimensions for our golden rectangle.

We can approach this in different ways. One way is to use the square of the golden rectangle to frame the face. We can set the length of "b" to be how far down below the chin we want the necklace to sit. Then the rectangle section of the golden rectangle shows the optimum space to work within. Another way would be to use the golden rectangle to define the full space we want our piece of jewelry to take up. This would reveal the ideal place to locate the centerpiece.

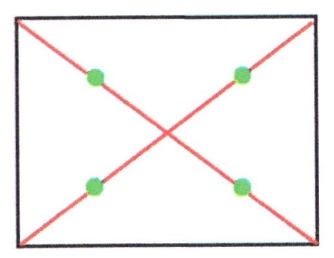

The eyes of the golden rectangle

Draw a straight line from each bottom corner to its opposite top corner on either side. They will cross in the exact center of the format. From the center to each corner, locate the midway point to each opposing corner.

The eyes of the golden rectangle supposedly are the most appealing points within this most appealing shape. Jewelry designers can use these points to place objects of interest, or to establish optimum points to change the pattern, texture or rhythm, or optimum points for interrelating pieces with multiple strands or which function on multiple planes.

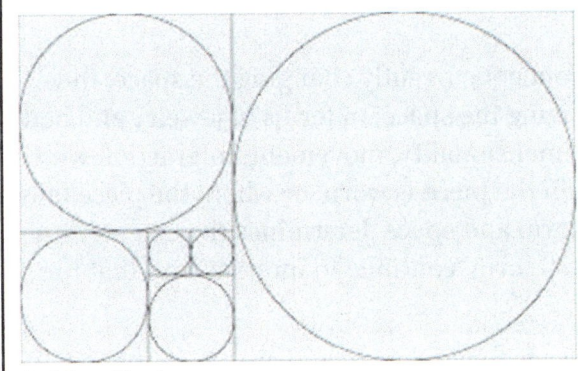

Golden Circle

A golden circle is one that fits perfectly within the square section of any golden rectangle.

Mathematicians have used the golden ratio to create many geometric shapes and forms.

FORMS

Form is any positive element in a composition. It may be related to points, lines, planes and shapes. Forms express meaning and are understood only at the boundary between jewelry and person. Forms add depth to meaning.

A form cannot be decoded and understood without referencing the space around it. For jewelry, this space is the wearer's body. A viewer must be able to understand and impose some meaning on the relationship between the form and the space (thus, the body) it occupies. A viewer must be able to differentiate the form or figure from the space (body) or ground (everything around the body).

The designer cannot change the form without concurrently changing the space, thus how things get interpreted and related to. Changing the space, in terms of jewelry and body, has a lot to do with such things as silhouette, dimensionality, movement, interaction with what the person is wearing, or the context within the piece is worn, or where the piece falls on the body. The tension established between form and space determines the extent, time, and motivation of the viewer to interact with that form, continue to interact with that form, and find it satisfying or not.

With jewelry, forms are primarily actualized as they relate to and are worn on the body. They convey and solidify the expressive relationships among design elements, person and context. Jewelry forms are not merely structures with wearability. They are expressive design elements which resonate their expressive purpose and power as they are juxtaposed and positioned against the curvilinearity the human body. Form is primarily a visual element, but its functionality – its impact on movement, drape, flow, durability and context – can affect its success, as well.

Form tends to be similar to shapes, but more 3D in reality or implied by illusion. Form can be delineated by light and shadow on it's surface, whether actual or illusory.

Jewelry Applications/Decoding Forms

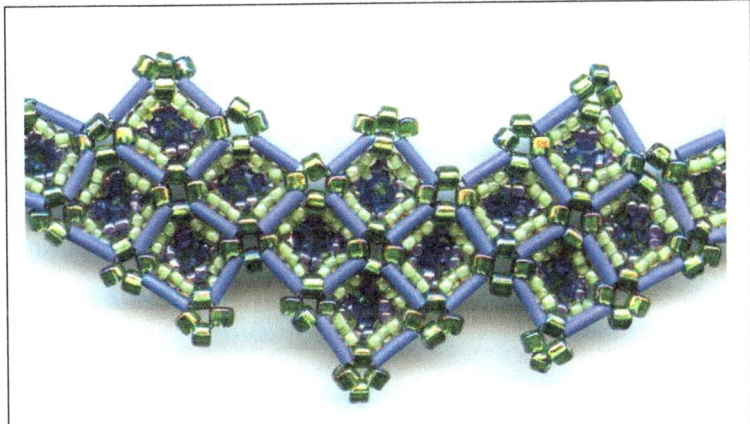

Forms supersede their constituent point, line and shape elements

For the jewelry designer, she or he must determine where the point, line, shape and plane end, and where the form begins. This means developing the decoding and fluency skills which can delineate and anticipate what happens to the expressive powers of the jewelry when the piece is worn.

The choice of form becomes a primary consideration in communicating the designer's message and intent.

The designer must manage the tensions between form and space, foreground (advancing) and background (receding), object (design element) and structure (arrangement). Good design becomes making strategic choices at the point jewelry meets the boundary of the body.

Forms can have magnetic powers, stickiness, and synergy. Forms can pull your eye in certain directions, or multiply, add, subtract or divide meaning and value, based on positioning, mass and volume. Forms can provide additional control over balance and movement felt within a piece.

THEMES

Themes are ideas which are conveyed by the visual, tactile and contextual experience with the piece of jewelry as worn. Most often themes are implied, rather than explicit. They relate the jewelry to the mind, and cannot be understood apart from the individual or group culture in which the jewelry is worn.

Themes are forms which reference, or can be interpreted to have reference, or inflect in some way some reference to individual, group, cultural, societal or universal norms, values and expectations.

Themes infuse or imply power, position, protection, or identification. They may be clear or abstract. They may be repeated or not. They may result from interpretations of individual forms, or whole compositions. They may be obvious or they may be symbolic.

Jewelry Applications/Decoding Themes

Thematic use of forms

Well-developed themes enhance excitement, interest and investigation. They add levels of meaning and create more depth of feeling and interpretation in jewelry. They increase the chances the designer's design will achieve a level of resonance. Themes can be representative or abstract, individual or repeated, easily accessible or not. They can be public or personal.

Themes decode expressive information which draws some of its meaning from the more general culture. They assist the maker, the wearer and the viewer in connecting with the pieces, interpreting them, and judging them. The very act of interpreting the themes present in jewelry is rewarding, as people make sense of things and reconfirm their understandings with the designer and other people around them. Involvement in a creative endeavor, like making sense of themes, engages the viewer in positive, gratifying ways.

Themes provide clues about motivation and intent and ways to judge this as good or bad, relevant or not. These motivations can have different purposes. They might be to assert power, to assert position, to protect, to identify, to connect, to communicate.

Themes more easily enable value judgments. Pieces are judged, not just as appealing or not, but also as right or wrong, and good or bad, and sacred or profane.

Themes can be in the form of symbols, patterns, or abstract forms. They reinforce a person's sense of connectedness to the larger group or social order around them.

IN SUMMARY

Points, Lines, Planes, Shapes, Forms, and Themes are objects used to turn nothingness into something.

That *something* holds meaning, asserts meaning and expresses meaning.

Points anchor.
Lines direct.
Planes encompass.
Shapes orient.
Forms provide ideas and referents.
Themes connect persons to culture.

Meaning is dialectic, in that how it is ultimately received and interpreted results, first, partly from the fluency of the jewelry designer to use these objects (and other design elements, as well) to translate inspiration into aspiration and aspiration into a finished result. And, second, partly from the various audiences of the designer and their shared understandings as they judge or negotiate about what it means for the piece of jewelry to be finished and what it means to be successful.

Arranging these objects into some organized composition provides a structure for them. Both the objects themselves, and the structures they are arranged and embedded in, convey expressive meanings. As these meanings get expressed within shapes, forms and themes, their complexity, tensions and implications become deeper and more resonant.

At some point in the design process, points, lines, planes and shapes take on the characteristics of forms and themes. That is, the jewelry is no longer decoded as a set of individual parts. Decoding jewelry becomes more contingent on how the jewelry relates to the body (forms) and how the jewelry relates to the individual or group culture within which it is worn (themes). The whole of the composition takes on meaning and value beyond that of the sum of its parts.

So, take a moment. Grab a pen and blank piece of paper. Draw a dot.

You are now an artist.

Draw a series of dots, lines, planes and shapes in the form of a necklace.

You are now an artist with an interest in jewelry.

Jot down some ideas how you would build upon your initial sketch and develop forms and themes. You might try to draw clear connections between sketch and inspiration. You might re-interpret what you drew as a series of components. You might select other design elements – particularly Color or Pattern or Texture – to better define the forms and establish them.

You are now a jewelry artist.

Think about how your developing piece of jewelry reflects your personal inspirations and intent. Anticipate how others will view your piece of jewelry and judge it as finished and successful. Try to reconstruct in your mind how the wearer will come to understand this piece of jewelry as somehow reconfirming a self-identity or social-identity. Think about clues you can look for to reconfirm to yourself that your jewelry has degree of resonance -- that others will not just appreciate it, but want to wear it.

You are now a jewelry designer.

	Now, take what you learned, and evaluate how points, lines, planes, shapes, forms and themes come together (or do not come together) in this piece done by one of my students. List the use of points. What is the artist trying to accomplish with the use of points? What is more satisfying? What is less satisfying? Now, ask yourself the same questions, next with the use of line, then with the use of plane, and so forth through shape, form and theme.

FOOTNOTES

[1]Bradley, *Steven, Points, Dots, And Lines: The Elements of Design Part II*, Web Design, 7/12/2010. This article incorporates many ideas from this article.
As referenced in: https://vanseodesign.com/web-design/points-dots-lines/

RULES OF COMPOSITION, CONSTRUCTION, AND MANIPULATION
5d. JEWELRY DESIGN PRINCIPLES: COMPOSING, CONSTRUCTING, MANIPULATING

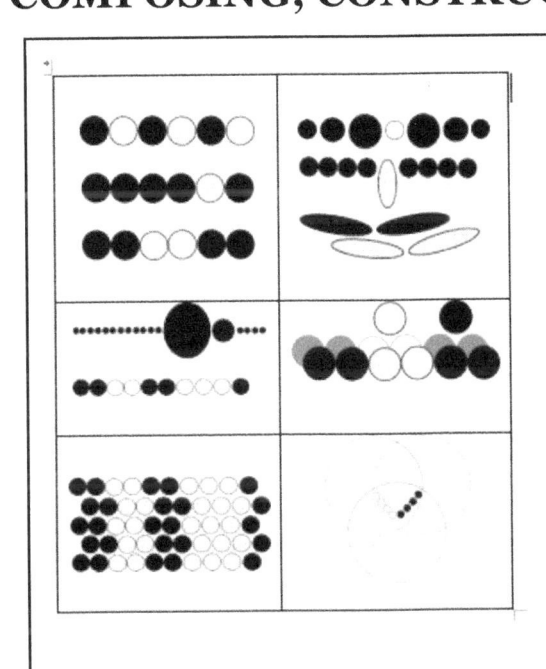

Guiding Questions:
(1) From the Art Tradition, the designer only has to master what are called Principles of Composition. What makes these insufficient?
(2) What are Principles of Composition, Construction and Manipulation?
(3) What can these Principles do for the designer? What does the designer want to achieve with these?
(4) To what extent are these Principles universally accepted and understood?
(5) How does the jewelry designer select and apply these?
(6) How do the art goals of unity and variety compare with the design goals of resonance and parsimony?

Key Words:		
design elements	disciplinary literacy	universal vs. subjective
principles	fluency	evoke emotion / resonance
composition	shared understandings	authentic performance
construction	good design	design thinking
manipulation	organizing / arranging	boundary between jewelry and body
rhythm	scheme	expressive
pointers	decode	attention
linear and planar relationships	unity and variety	engagement
interest	harmony	orientation
statistical distribution	movement	segmentation
balance	dimension	components
forms	symmetry	
temporal extension	scale	
physical extension	volume	
parsimony	placement	
	positioning	

Abstract:
It is not happenstance that some pieces of jewelry draw your attention, and others do not. It is the result of an artist fluent in design. That fluency begins with selecting Design Elements, but it comes to full fruition with the application, not only of the art world's Principles of Composition, but also the design world's Principles of Construction and Manipulation, as well. This is where the designer flourishes, shows a recognition of shared understandings and desires about good design, and makes that cluster of jewelry design choices resulting in a piece that is seen as both finished and successful. These Principles represent different organizing schemes the designer might resort to. Jewelry designers translate these Principles in a more synergistic and integrative manner than painters or sculptors. That is because jewelry presents different demands and expectations on the designer than paintings or sculptures. The better artist/designer achieves a level of disciplinary literacy – selecting Design Elements and applying Principles of Composition, Construction and Manipulation -- where fluency becomes automatic, accurate, and rapidly applied.

Some Pieces Of Jewelry Draw Your Attention. Others Do Not.

This is not a matter of happenstance. It is the result of an artist fluent in design. That fluency begins with the selection of Design Elements – the smallest meaningful units of design. It comes to full fruition, however, with the application, not only of the art world's Principles of Composition, but also the design world's Principles of Construction and Manipulation, as well. These principles, better thought of as *"organizing schemes"*, reflect what the individual designer wants to express, and how the individual designer anticipates how others will understand and respond to this expression.

Design Elements, which I have discussed in an earlier chapter [1], are like building blocks and function a bit like the *vowel and consonant letters of the alphabet*. They have form. They have meaning. They can be assembled into different arrangements which extend their meaning and usefulness in expression. Examples: color, shape, texture, point/line/plane, movement, dimensionality, and the like. Each Design Element has a set of expressive attributes. Color can be expressed as a color scheme, or as proportions, or as simultaneity effects. Shape can be geometric or dimensional or recognizable or symbolic. And so forth.

Design Elements function like a vocabulary. They represent universally accepted expressive content. Visualize the analogy between design elements and vocabulary. Picture a "*t*", perhaps combined with an "*h*", and then with an "*e*". Or, picture the difficulty in trying to combine a "*th*" with a "*z*". Or, still yet, picture how the "*c*" in "*cat*" is pronounced differently than the "*c*" in "*cents*", yet still recognized as a "*c*". In similar ways, the artist might decide to use the design elements of "*color*" and "*line,*" and combine them to yield another design element of "*movement.*" Literacy begins with the ability to decode, and this ability centers on the selection and use of Design Elements, and one or more of their expressive attributes.

Principles of Composition, Construction and Manipulation function more like a *grammar*. Given the Design Elements selected by the designer, Principles represent *organizing strategies* to which the designer resorts when attempting to achieve a piece that will be seen as both *"finished"* and *"successful"*, both by the designer, as well as that designer's audience(s). The designer might arrange several design elements and their expressive attributes to yield a higher level organizing principle. For example, the designer might combine *color(intensity) + line(direction) + shape(geometry) + placement(symmetry) + balance + material"* to yield a sense of *"rhythm."*

To continue our analogy with vocabulary, grammar and literacy, picture our "*t*", "*h*" and "*e*" put together to form a full word like "*thesaurus*", then expanded into an idea, like "*teachers like to use a thesaurus*", and further expressed, in anticipation of a response, to something like "*but students hate when the teacher asks them to use a thesaurus.*"

Literacy goes beyond decoding; it includes a fluency in how the Design Elements are organized, constructed and manipulated to evoke an emotional response. This involves an intuitive understanding of Principles of Composition, Construction and Manipulation, and how to apply them. While Design Elements are selected primarily based on shared, more universal understandings of what they express, often, Principles are applied in ways more reflective of designers's hand, and its subjective expression.

The successful jewelry designer has developed a ***fluency*** in the **_Disciplinary Literacy_** of jewelry design. Fluency is the ability of the designer to select and connect Design Elements smoothly, in visually and functionally and situationally appropriate ways with understanding. The idea of understanding is broadly defined, to include the designers's personal goals for expression, as well as the expectations and desires of all the audiences – the wearer, the viewer, the buyer, the seller, the collector, the student, the master. The better designer achieves a level of disciplinary literacy where fluency becomes automatic, accurate, and rapidly applied.

This Disciplinary Literacy in jewelry design has a structure all its own. There are four main components to it:

1) Vocabulary: Design Elements As The Basis Of Composition
2) Grammar: Principles of Composition, Construction and Manipulation
3) Strategy: Project Management[2]
4) Context/Culture: Shared Understandings and Desires[3]

This chapter focuses on the second component – *Principles*.

What Are Principles of Composition, Construction and Manipulation?

Jewelry Design is the strategic application of basic principles of organization and expression to achieve a piece which evokes emotion, resonates, and is appealing as it is worn. Traditionally the art and design worlds referred to these as "Principles of Composition." Often artists and designers get tripped up on the word *Principles*, and jewelry designers get a bit confused or frustrated with the word *Composition*.

The use of the word "*Principles*" in art and design can be somewhat confusing. These Principles do not represent a set of universal, dependable and repeatable standards to strive for, which we might assume, at first.

A different meaning about "*Principles*" applies here. A Principle is an *organizing scheme* as a way to combine design elements into a more pleasing whole composition. The design elements include things which are visual effects; but, for jewelry designers, they also include things which are functional, as well as things which are more social, psychological, cultural and situational. Principles inform designers in their expressive, authentic performances. Every designer is expected to apply these Principles, but only in ways the designer chooses. There might be better or worse ways to apply them, but no right or wrong ways.

Another aspect of confusion is the use of the word "*Composition*". I've expanded the phrase, though somewhat awkwardly, to "*Principles of Composition, Construction and Manipulation.*" The traditional art and design idea of "*composition*" covers two very different types of jewelry design literacy skills under a single label, namely decoding (*Design Elements*) and fluency (*Principles*). The better jewelry designer needs to learn and apply both aspects of disciplinary literacy, but each involves different ways of thinking. As a teacher, both require different sets of strategies for training and educating jewelry designers.

Jewelry designers, by the nature of jewelry, have to deal equally with functional aspects of design, not just artistic composition. Traditional Principles of Composition need to be re-oriented for the jewelry designers to be more sensitive to the more architectural aspects of design. The design choices are not only about selection and arrangement. They are about implementation and anticipation, as well. Design choices are also best understood at the boundary between the art of design and the body it adorns.

Limited to the idea of *composition*, jewelry might be judged successful as "art", as if it was displayed on a mannequin or easel. But jewelry, in reality, can only be judged as a *constructive, manipulated* result situated at the boundary between art and body and worn within a particular context. Jewelry can only be judged as "art as it is worn." As a result, the designer must anticipate the shared understandings and desires of the various audiences who might wear, view or buy their pieces.

In this chapter, I focus on **Principles of Composition, Construction and Manipulation**. The Principles, as organizing schemes, are intertwined, and, the use of one will often depend on another. Movement might be achieved by the placement of lines, which might also establish a rhythm. Such placement of lines might be symmetrically balanced, with line thinness and thickness statistically distributed evenly through the piece.

These organizing and arranging schemes might include:

- the Positioning and/or Ordering of *things* (*white/black/white/black vs. black/black/black/white*)
- the Volume or Area the piece takes up *(one row of beads vs. 3 rows of beads)*
- the Scale and Size of the pieces *(6mm 6mm 6mm vs. 10mm 10mm 10mm)*
- the Colors, Textures and Patterns of individual pieces, and/or sets or groupings of pieces *(matte/matte/shiny/matte/matte vs. shiny/shiny/matte/shiny/shiny)*
- the Forms *(identifiable sets of pieces, highly integrated)*
- the Materials
- the interplay of Light, Dark, Shadow, Reflection and Refraction *(dark/dark/transparent/dark/dark vs. transparent/transparent/dark/transparent/transparent)*
- the clasp assembly and other supporting systems

Some of these design Principles are applied in similar ways to all art forms, such as painting and sculpture, no matter what the medium.

For other Principles, jewelry creates its own challenges, because all jewelry places some different demands and expectations on the artist than painting or sculpture does.

After all, Jewelry...

- *Functions in a 3-dimensional space, particularly sensitive to position, volume and scale*
- *Must stand on its own as an object of art*
- *But must also exist as an object of art which interacts with the body, movement, personality, and quirks of the wearer*
- *Serves many purposes, some aesthetic, some functional, some social, cultural or situational*
- *Has a much more integrated and inter-dependent relationship of the center piece, strap, fringe, edge, bail and surface embellishment – an arrangement that traditional Art theory rejects. Art sees the center piece as the "art", and these other things as supporting, not artistic details, like a frame for a painting or a pedestal for a sculpture.*

Good jewelry should exude an energy. It should resonate. This energy results from how the designer applies these Principles to compose with, construct and manipulate light and shadow, and their characteristics of warmth and cold, receding and approaching, bright and dull, light and dark. The designer's piece is judged on whether the resulting piece feels coherent, organized, controlled, and *strategically* designed, again, as the jewelry is worn. Successful application of these Principles results in a piece which feels finished and successful.

The Principles include,

1. **Rhythm**
2. **Pointers**
3. **Linear and Planar Relationships**
4. **Interest**
5. **Statistical Distribution**
6. **Balance**
7. **Forms, Their Proportions, Distributions and Dimensionality**
8. **Temporal Extension: Time and Place**
9. **Physical Extension: Functionality**
10. **Parsimony** *(something similar to, but a little beyond harmony and unity)*

TABLE OF PRINCIPLES *(Organizing Schemes)*

Principles of Composition, Construction, and Manipulation	What the Principle is About	How Principle Might Get Expressed as Organizing Schema
1. *Rhythm*	*This is how the piece leads the viewer through sequences of steps. It is a measure of the degree the piece engages the viewer's eye.* *There is a continuance, a flow or a feeling of movement from one place of the piece to another.*	*Repetition* *Pattern* *Random* *Regular, Predictable* *Alternating* *Flowing, Wave-like, Sweeping* *Progressive* *Vertical, Horizontal, Diagonal, Overlapping, Piercing*

			Placement
Darting, Staccato, Steady, Inching, Measured
Edgy
Symphonic
	2. **Pointers**	Pointers are places of emphasis, dominance or focus. Certain elements assume more importance than others within the same composition.	Isolating
Directional
Contrast
Anomaly
Leading
Convergence
Size, Weight, Color Gradient
Framing
Focusing and Depth
Absence
Implied
	3. **Linear and Planar Relationships**	The degree the piece is not disorienting; obvious what is "up" and what is "down".

Orienting and Directional | Straight or Curved
2-D or 3D
Violating, Crossing or Intersecting, Interpenetrating
Parallel or Aligned
Perpendicular
Angular or Diagonal
Vector
Fixed, Directional, Infinite, or Disappearing
Continuous, Broken or Perforated
Radial
At Edges or Within; Framed or Bound
Thin or Thick
Textured or Smooth
Opaque or Transparent
Moving, Rotating, Spinning, Darting, Flashing
Silhouette |
| | 4. **Interest** | The degree the artist has made the ordinary…"noteworthy" | Add variety
Give person an experience
Vibrance, Intensity
Unexpected use or positioning
Surprise
Sense of strength or fragility
Symbolic meaning |

			Perspective *Inspirational* *Pattern* *Clash* *Juxtaposition* *Simultaneity effects*
	5. **Statistical Distribution**	*How satisfying the **numbers** and **sizes** and **measures** of objects within the piece are*	*Equality, Equity, Equal Weight, Mass, Volume, Visual Effect (or the opposite of equality)* *Randomness* *Color proportions* *Scale* *Measurements* *Numbers of*
	6. **Balance**	*How satisfying the **placement** of objects (and their attributes) is*	*Equilibrium in Weight, Mass, Volume, Visual Effect* *Symmetry or Asymmetry* *Pattern or No Pattern* *Regular or Irregular* *Equalizing visual forces* *Scale* *Permanent, Illusory, Contingent* *Placement, Alignment, Proximity, Repetition* *Radial* *Identical or Similar*
	7. **Forms, Their Proportions, Distributions, and Dimensionality**	*Jewelry often can be structured in terms of segments, components or forms. How the pieces get interconnected or amassed is of concern.*	*Unique, Singular, Parallel/Symmetrical, Repeated, Multiple* *Evolving* *Variety* *Segmentation* *2-D or 3-D* *Realistic or Abstract* *Geometric or Organic* *Complete or Incomplete* *Layering, Overlapping* *Fringing, Surface Embellishment* *Continuity* *Coordinating* *Clashing, Off-putting*

8. **Temporal Extension: Time and Place**	*Any piece of jewelry must be acceptable within a certain historical, social, cultural or situational context.*	*Visual Expectation* *Materials Expectation* *Techniques/Technology Expectation* *Referents, Inscriptions, Images* *Symbolism* *Themes* *Rule-bound or not* *Revival style or Contemporized Traditional style* *Appropriateness/Relevance to situation or context* *Coordination with situation or context*
9. **Physical Extension: Functionality**	*The degree the piece is designed so that it accommodates physical stresses when the piece is worn*	*Jointedness and Support (links, rivets, hinges, loops, unglued knots, and the like)* *Drape, Flow, Movement (built-in features allowing adjustment to body shape or body movement)* *Length, Fit* *Adjustability* *Choices of stringing material or assembly strategy* *Clasp Assembly (how piece attached to clasp)* *Strap, Bail, Pendant, Fringe, Embellishment* *Stiffness, Looseness, Bending, Conforming* *Inclusion of technology* *Structural Integrity* *Application of architectural principles of construction* *Physical mechanics* *Weight-bearing*

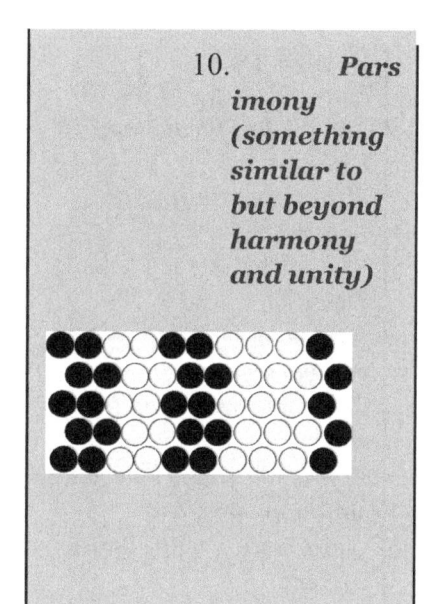

10. **Parsimony (something similar to but beyond harmony and unity)**	*There should be no nonessential elements; the addition or subtraction of one element or its attribute will make the piece less satisfying*	Length, Volume, Mass, Weight, Visual Effects Goodness of fit Sufficient balance between unity and variety to evoke an emotional response and resonance An economy in the use of resources A result which feels finished and successful, reflecting the artist's hand, as well as an anticipation of shared understandings among all audiences – viewer, wearer, buyer, seller, student, master

THE PRINCIPLES IN MORE DETAIL

1. Rhythm

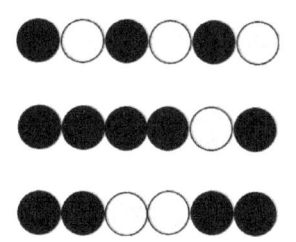

Movement is the path our eyes follow when we look at a work of art, and it is generally very important to keep a viewer's eyes engaged in the work. Without movement, artwork becomes stagnant. A few good strategies to evoke a sense of movement (among many others) are using diagonal lines, placing shapes so that they extend beyond the boundaries of the picture plane, and using changing values.

Rhythm is one Principle used to shape the viewer's experience with the piece. Rhythm is how the piece leads the viewer through sequences of steps. It is a measure of the degree the piece engages the viewer's eye.
There is a continuance, a flow or a feeling of movement from one place of the piece to another.

Repetition and pattern are key here. The artist might achieve a rhythm by varying or repeating colors, textures, sizes, forms. The rhythm might be slow, fast, predictable, random, staccato, measured, safe, edgy, and so forth. The intervals between repetitions and patterns can create a sense of rhythm in the viewer and a sense of movement. Repetitions and patterns can be random, regular, alternating, flowing, progressive – there are many directions the designer can go in establishing a rhythm. What is important is to anticipate what rhythm the person wearing the piece would desire.

When a piece has multiple and coordinated rhythms, we call this **Symphonic Rhythm**. For example, in a piece, there might be a clear rhythm set by the use of colors throughout the piece, as well as the positioning of definable forms, such as a series of beaded leaves or other shapes.

The Rhythm should assist the viewer in cognitively making a complete circle around the piece. You don't want the viewer to lose interest, get bored, or fall flat, before the eye and brain can make that complete circle.

Example:

Black-o-Black-o-Black-o-White-o-Black-o-Black-o-Black-o-White-o

Or,

Black-o-White-o-Black-o-White-o-Black-o-White-o-Black-o-White-o

The better designer can empower the design, if using Rhythm in the right way.

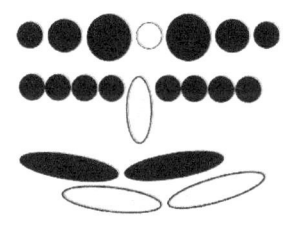

~~~~~~

2. Pointers

Pointers are places of emphasis, dominance or focus. Certain elements assume more importance than others within the same composition.

Pointers guide the viewer to a specific place, or focal point. Cognitively, you want to create the place for the eye/brain to come to rest.

Examples:

- *Something can be centered*
- *The color can be varied, say from dark to light, to serve as an "arrow" or "Pointer" to a section of the necklace*
- *The positioning of the clasp might serve as a pointer*
- *A dangling pendant might serve as a pointer*

- *The size of the beads can be varied, such as smallest to largest, to serve as an "arrow" or "Pointer"*
- *Coordinating the placement of Focal Point on jewelry with the pattern in the clothing upon which the piece will rest*
- *Something can be strategically off-centered.*

The better designer is able to capture the viewer's attention to more important parts of the piece.

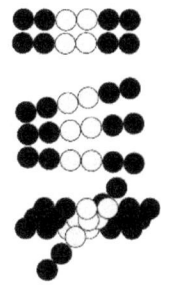

~~~~~~

3. Linear and Planar Relationships

This is the degree the piece is not disorienting to the viewer, or particularly confusing in terms of what is up and what is down.

People always need to orient themselves to their surroundings, so that they know what is up and what is down. They usually do this by recognizing the horizontal planes of the floor and the ceiling of a room (ground and sky outside), and the vertical planes of the walls of a room (buildings, trees and the like outside).

Jewelry must assist, or at least not get in the way, of this natural orienting process. It accomplishes this in how its "lines" are arranged and organized. If a piece is very 3-dimensional, then how its "planes" are arranged and organized becomes important, as well.

Design elements we might use to achieve a satisfactory planar relationship within our piece:

-- A strategic use of lines and planes
   -- shapes
   -- boundaries
   - -silhouettes
   -- contours
- Symmetry
- Or, more difficult to achieve, a satisfying asymmetry
- A planar pattern in how each section of the piece relates to the other

sections
- *How sections of the piece interlock*
- *How we "draw and interrelate" parallel lines/planes, perpendicular lines/planes and curved lines/planes within the piece*

Example:

How can a person truly pull off wearing only one earring? After all, visually, it pulls the person off to one side, thus violating the basic orienting planar relationships. What about the composition of the earring, allows this to work; what about the composition doesn't?

Example:
Wearing a necklace, where the clasp is worn on the side, instead of the back. Again, what about the composition of the necklace, allows this to work; what about the composition doesn't?

~~~~~~

4. Interest

●●●●●●●●

●·●·●·●·●

"*Interest*" means the degree to which the designer *makes the ordinary...noteworthy*.

Here the designer demonstrates how to balance off and control *variety* with *unity* and *harmony*. Without unity and harmony, the piece becomes chaotic. Without variety, the piece becomes boring, monotonous and uninteresting.

Arranging and organizing Design Elements might involve:

- *Selection of materials and mix of materials*
- *Selection of color combinations*
- *Varying the sizes of things*
- *Pushing the envelope on interrelating planar relationships among the sections of the jewelry*
- *Playing with the rhythm*
- *Clever use of a focal point*

When anticipating the expectations and desires of the wearer, viewer or buyer, the designer needs to make a connection for them between these things with what about the piece is of *Interest*. That connection might be a visual clue. It might be some ideas expressed in a marketing message.

~~~~~~

5. Statistical Distribution

The designer is always concerned with the number or size or scale or measurement of things. This principle focuses on these *statistics*. With this principle, we are *not* concerned with the placement or balance of things – just the numbers and measurements.

We ask: How pleasing and satisfying are ***the selection of*** the numbers, sizes, proportions, volumes/weights, and color/textures of objects the artist wants to use in the piece. The artist might, at this point, anticipate creating a pattern, or not.

Examples:

BIG-o-BIG-o-small-o-BIG-o-BIG-o-small-o-

PURPLE-o-PURPLE-o-PURPLE-o-YELLOW-o-PURPLE-o-YELLOW-o-

~~~~~~

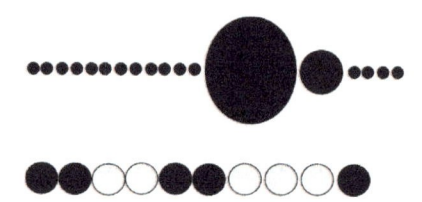

6. Balance

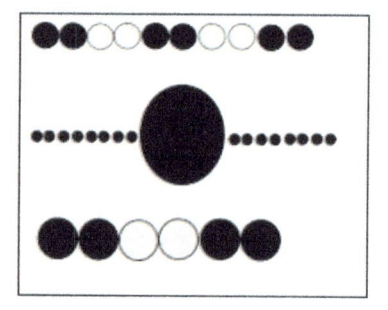

Balance has to do with placement. How pleasing or satisfying is ***the placement*** of objects (and their attributes) within a piece?

Usually, the designer is trying to achieve a feeling of equality in weight, attention or attraction of the various visual design elements. The design attributes would include such things as the positioning or relative positioning of the materials used, the colors, textures and patterns, the sizes and scales.

The designer might play with placement in terms of proximity, alignment or repetition.

There are different types of balance:

(1) *Symmetry*: the use of *identical* compositional units on either side of a vertical axis
(2) *Approximate symmetry*: the use of *similarly* balanced compositional units on either side of a vertical axis
(3) *Radial symmetry*: an even, radiating out from a central point to all four quadrants (directions) of the shape's plane (surface)
(4) *Asymmetry*: even though the compositional units are not identical on either side of a vertical axis, there is a "felt" equilibrium of the total piece. Often, with jewelry, this equilibrium depends on what clothes or other jewelry the person is wearing, or something about that person's body/body shape.

~~~~~~

7. Forms, Their Proportions, Distributions and Dimensionality

Jewelry often can be structured in terms of segments, components or forms. How are pieces interconnected or amassed? Is this achieved through optical effects or reality?

The designer is concerned with managing these structures in terms of proportions, distributions and/or dimensionality. The designer makes choices about how each part relates to the whole in terms of scale or relevance.

The designer might play with things like:

Layering	*Segmentation*
Surface embellishment	*Intervals between objects*
Fringing	*Intervals between patterns*
Curvature	*Repetition*
Overlapping planes	*Placement/Alignment of Symbols*
Balance	

The better designer creates pieces where the whole is greater than the sum of its parts.

Example:
Flat loomed bracelet and a button clasp, that sits so high on the bracelet, that it detracts from the 2-dimensional reason-for-being of the piece.

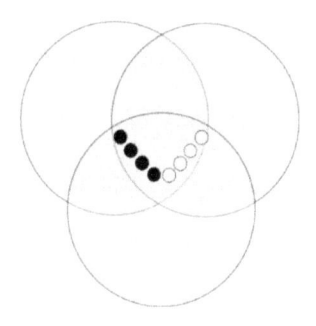

~~~~~~

8. Temporal Extension: Time and Place

Any piece of jewelry must be acceptable within a certain historical, social, cultural or situational context.

For example, is a piece appropriate for a wedding also appropriate for office wear? Is a great University of Tennessee Orange Necklace as successful when worn to a Vanderbilt football game?

Temporal Extension may narrowly refer to one specific wearer in particular, or more broadly to group, situational, social or societal expectations.

Other examples:

- *white pearls are associated with bridal jewelry*
- *using metalized plastic beads, where the plating chips off in a short period of time, should not be used in an heirloom*

> *bracelet*
> - *making a matching set of earrings and necklace for jewelry that typically should be worn as a matching set*
> - *gifting a carved jade pendant with a message-word carving inappropriate for the religion of the person receiving it*

~~~~~~

9. Physical Extension: Functionality

Any piece of jewelry must be functional when worn. Functionality has to do with such things as movement, drape, comfort, flow and durability. The piece of jewelry needs to feel comfortable when worn, always look good on the wearer no matter what the wearer is doing, and be durable. This involves a lot of building in understandings of physical mechanics and architectural principles of construction.

When there is (or should be) movement in a piece, there should be clear evidence that the designer anticipated where the parts came from, and where they are going to. Jewelry is worn by people who move, so the design should be a natural physical extension to such movements, and the stress they put on the piece.

For example, in a necklace, the clasp should remain on the neck, even as the beadwork moves with the person, without the necklace turning around on the neck, or breaking.

> *Example: The dangle earring which has the dangle stuck in a 90 degree angle.*
>
> *Example: The crimped bracelet which breaks at the crimp.*
> *Example: The bracelet too tight when the design is turned into a circle placed around the wrist*

10. Parsimony
(something similar to, but a little bit beyond harmony and unity)

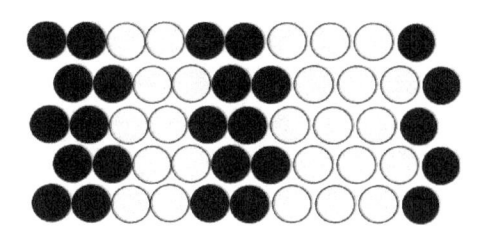

At the point where the piece is judged to be *finished* and *successful*, there should be no *nonessential elements*. When the piece is finished and successful, it should evoke emotions and resonate.

The designer should achieve the maximal effect with the least effort or excess.

There is a tendency of beaders and jewelry makers to over-do:

- *over-embellish the surface*
- *add too much fringe*
- *repeat themes and design elements too often*
- *use too many colors*

Parsimony vs. Unity

In art, the traditional measure of completion and success was a feeling or sense of "*Unity.*" Unity signified how everything felt all right. All the Design Elements used, and how they were coordinated and placed, were very coherent, clear, harmonious and satisfying. It was assumed that a sense of *Unity* would be universally recognized and understood.

I think the idea of *unity begins to* get at the place we want to end up. But this concept is not concrete enough for me. You can have unity, but the piece still seen as boring when there is no variety. This condition is unacceptable as a principled outcome of jewelry construction. Finished and successful jewelry should evoke emotions, but moreso, resonate. You can have unity, but the assessments rely too much on universal, objective perceptions of design elements and their attributes. The designer, the wearer, the viewer, the buyer and the situation are too easily left out of the equation.

Jewelry creation usually demands a series of judgment calls and tradeoffs between aesthetics and functionality, designer goals and audience understandings and expectations, a full palette of colors, shapes and textures and a very limited one. A measure of completeness and success needs to result from the forced choice decisions of the designer. It needs to account for the *significance* of the results, not just the *organization* of them. It needs to explain the *Why*, not just the *What*.

For me, the more appropriate concept here is *Parsimony*. Parsimony is sometimes referred to in art and design as *Economy*, but the idea of economy is reserved for the visual effects. For jewelry designers, we want that economy or parsimony to apply to functional and situational effects, as well. When the finished and successful piece is parsimonious, the relationship of all the Design Elements and their expressed attributes will be so strong, that to add or remove any one thing would diminish, not just the design, but rather the significance and desirability of the design.

Parsimony...
- Forces explanation; its forced-choice nature is most revealing about the artist's understandings and intentions
- Relies on evidence moreso than assumptions to get at criticality
- Focuses examination of the few elements that make a difference

~~~~~~

THINKING ROUTINE[4]:
LOOK – SCORE – EXPLAIN

LOOK:
CLASSICISM NECKLACE

Warren Feld, 2001.

Materials and Description:
Three strands, druk rondelles Czech glass, in matte amethyst, matte olivine, and matte topaz. Center, overlapping round agate stones (reddish with specks of purple, green and yellow).

At the center, each of the three strands pass through a 3-hole separator bar, and through one of three thin sterling silver tubes.

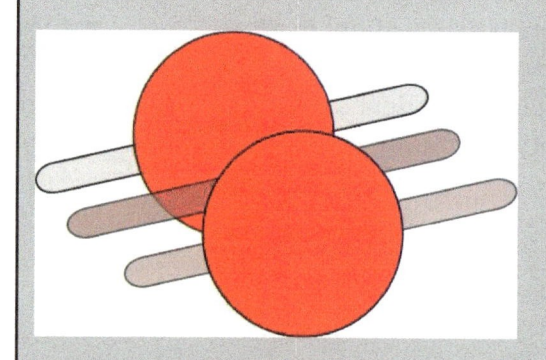

The centerpiece stones slide over the top and bottom tubes. The middle tube is sandwiched between the stones. These stones can spin around on the tubes, allowing them to adjust to body shape and movement, but the middle tube restricts the movement to maintain the general visual appearance as in the image.

S-clasp in back.

KEY DESIGN ELEMENTS: *(see key at bottom of table for list)*	KEY ATTRIBUTES OF DESIGN ELEMENTS:
1. COLOR	1a. Some Tonal quality and finish
	1b. Split Complementary color scheme
	1c. Gradation dark to light
2. BALANCE AND DISTRIBUTION	2a. Symmetry
3. SHAPE	3a. Same size druk rondelles
	3b. Round shape of centerpiece stones
4. POINT/LINE/PLANE	4a. Strong lines core design feature
5. MATERIALS	4b. Overlapping centerpiece stones establishes 2 planes; can move but restricted from violating planes
6. MOVEMENT	
7. DIMENSIONALITY	
8. TECHNIQUE/TECHNOLOGY	

	5a. Mixing glass, metal and gemstone
	6a. Center stones allowed to spin on tubes
	7a. Layering of center stones
	8a. Unexpected connection of strap to centerpiece

SCORE:

SCORE CARD ON PRINCIPLES:

DESIGN CRITERIA	Very Unsatisfying.......Very Satisfying
1. Rhythm	1 2 3 **4** 5
2. Pointers	1 2 3 4 **5**
3. Linear and Planar Relationships	1 2 3 **4** 5
4. Interest	1 2 **3** 4 5
5. Statistical Distribution	1 2 3 4 **5**
6. Balance	1 2 3 4 **5**
7. Forms	1 2 **3** 4 5
8. Temporal Extension: Time, Place	1 2 **3** 4 5
9. Physical Extension: Functionality	1 2 3 **4** 5
10. Parsimony	1 2 3 **4** 5

EXPLAIN:

RHYTHM:

How you see this playing out in this piece:

One smooth flow from clasp to centerpiece down straps.

Centerpiece stones a little discordant in shape and color, which can disrupt rhythm.

ESTABLISHED BY KEY DESIGN ELEMENTS:

BALANCE AND DISTRIBUTION
POINTERS

WHAT DESIGN CHOICES MIGHT WEAKEN OR STRENGTHEN THIS....
(examples: change length, shapes, lines, bead size, bead color, bead placement)

Weaken: Mixing different sizes; adding more colors within each strand; changing length

		WHAT IF CONTINGENCIES... *(examples: If cannot get some bead, color, size, finish, clasp, what could you resort to instead)* If cannot get any one of 3 colors or finishes or sizes, would have to change to 3 different split complementary colors and new stones for focal point
POINTERS: **How you see this playing out in this piece:** Overlapping stones in centerpiece	**ESTABLISHED BY KEY DESIGN ELEMENTS:** POINT/LINE/PLANE **WHAT DESIGN CHOICES MIGHT WEAKEN OR STRENGTHEN THIS....** *(examples: change length, shapes, lines, bead size, bead color, bead placement)* Strengthen: better color coordination between center piece and straps; select different shape than round for centerpiece stones Weaken: mix colors/sizes in strap; change rhythm in strap; add patterns **WHAT IF CONTINGENCIES...** *(examples: If cannot get some bead, color, size, finish, clasp, what could you resort to instead)* Would need to have alternative gemstones, similar sizing to original, color coordinated with strap colors	
LINEAR/PLANAR RELATIONSHIPS: **How you see this playing out in this piece:** Strong sense of line and downward direction	**ESTABLISHED BY KEY DESIGN ELEMENTS:** POINT/LINE/PLANE STRUCTURE/SUPPORT	

towards centerpiece, represented by 3 strand, strong implementation of 3-color scheme Overlapping planes in centerpiece, and where 3 strands converge on centerpiece.	**WHAT DESIGN CHOICES MIGHT WEAKEN OR STRENGTHEN THIS….** *(examples: change length, shapes, lines, bead size, bead color, bead placement)* Weaken: have less fluid structure support connecting one side through centerpiece to other side; have only one center stone rather than two which overlap **WHAT IF CONTINGENCIES…** *(examples: If cannot get some bead, color, size, finish, clasp, what could you resort to instead)* If hole in center stones not big enough to slide over sterling silver tube, would have to make holes larger, find thinner tubes or alternative stones
INTEREST: **How you see this playing out in this piece:** Overlapping stones in centerpiece, their color, size and shape Structure of tubes and stones in centerpiece, particularly in terms of allowing and restricting movement	**ESTABLISHED BY KEY DESIGN ELEMENTS:** POINT/LINE/PLANE MATERIAL MOVEMENT STRUCTURE/SUPPORT SHAPE **WHAT DESIGN CHOICES MIGHT WEAKEN OR STRENGTHEN THIS….** *(examples: change length, shapes, lines, bead size, bead color, bead placement)* Weaken: no overlap stones and no movement; put pattern or change bead sizes in strap Strengthen: other than round shape for centerpiece stones; better color coordination between center and strap **WHAT IF CONTINGENCIES…** *(examples: If cannot get some bead, color, size,*

	finish, clasp, what could you resort to instead) If could not create the structure creating the overlapping stone centerpiece, use a centerpiece with some dimension that supports the rhythm of the piece.
STATISTICAL DISTRIBUTION: **How you see this playing out in this piece:** One shape and size of bead in the 3 straps. Single color within each strand.	**ESTABLISHED BY KEY DESIGN ELEMENTS:** SHAPE COLOR **WHAT DESIGN CHOICES MIGHT WEAKEN OR STRENGTHEN THIS….** *(examples: change length, shapes, lines, bead size, bead color, bead placement)* Weaken: vary shape or add more colors **WHAT IF CONTINGENCIES…** *(examples: If cannot get some bead, color, size, finish, clasp, what could you resort to instead)* If could not get enough beads in specific size, shape, color for each strap, come up with different design.
BALANCE: **How you see this playing out in this piece:** Single color in each strand Symmetry Repeated same length in each strand	**ESTABLISHED BY KEY DESIGN ELEMENTS:** BALANCE/DISTRIBUTION POINT/LINE/PLANE FORM/SEGMENTS/COMPONENTS **WHAT DESIGN CHOICES MIGHT WEAKEN OR STRENGTHEN THIS….** *(examples: change length, shapes, lines, bead*

	size, bead color, bead placement) Weaken: Make piece unbalanced, or asymmetrical **WHAT IF CONTINGENCIES…** *(examples: If cannot get some bead, color, size, finish, clasp, what could you resort to instead)* If could not restrict the movement of the center stones, would lose visual balance; would have to come up with different strategy for restricting movement, or just use one, rather than two stones.
FORMS: **How you see this playing out in this piece:** Clear forms: - 3 strands, one of each color - clear sense of right side and left side and center - segmented centerpiece	**ESTABLISHED BY KEY DESIGN ELEMENTS:** FORM/SEGMENTS/COMPONENTS COLOR BALANCE/DISTRIBUTION POINTER SHAPE **WHAT DESIGN CHOICES MIGHT WEAKEN OR STRENGTHEN THIS….** *(examples: change length, shapes, lines, bead size, bead color, bead placement)* Weaken: create a size or color pattern in the straps, additional segmentation Strengthen: Different shape (and color) for centerpiece stones **WHAT IF CONTINGENCIES…** *(examples: If cannot get some bead, color, size, finish, clasp, what could you resort to instead)* If could not get enough beads in specific size, shape, color for each strap, come up with

	different design or color scheme.
TEMPORAL EXTENSION: **How you see this playing out in this piece:** Piece has a classical elegance to it. Can picture it worn in a more upscale social setting like a banquet or dinner party.	**ESTABLISHED BY KEY DESIGN ELEMENTS:** FORMS/SEGMENTS/COMPONENTS COLOR BALANCE/DISTRIBUTION BEAUTY/APPEAL CONTEXT/SITUATION/CULTURE **WHAT DESIGN CHOICES MIGHT WEAKEN THIS....** *(examples: change length, shapes, lines, bead size, bead color, bead placement)* Weaken: brighter or primary colors; glossy color finishes; shorter or longer length **WHAT IF CONTINGENCIES...** *(examples: If cannot get some bead, color, size, finish, clasp, what could you resort to instead)* If could not get enough beads in specific size, shape, color for each strap, come up with different design or color scheme.
PHYSICAL EXTENSION: **How you see this playing out in this piece:** The support structure for the centerpiece which both allows and restricts movement. The 3 strands on each side of the necklace can move independently and allow better movement, drape and flow.	**ESTABLISHED BY KEY DESIGN ELEMENTS:** STRUCTURE/SUPPORT TECHNIQUE/TECHNOLOGY **WHAT DESIGN CHOICES MIGHT WEAKEN OR STRENGTHEN THIS....** *(examples: change length, shapes, lines, bead size, bead color, bead placement)*

	Weaken: leave out middle tube which lays between top and bottom center stone; connect the 3 strands together at two or more places along their length. **WHAT IF CONTINGENCIES...** *(examples: If cannot get some bead, color, size, finish, clasp, what could you resort to instead)* If could not get support structure to work, come up with different design.
PARSIMONY: **How you see this playing out in this piece:** The choice of colors, materials, bead sizes, length of strands, symmetry	**ESTABLISHED BY KEY DESIGN ELEMENTS:** SHAPE COLOR POINT/LINE/PLANE MOVEMENT FORMS/SEGMENTS/COMPONENTS BALANCE/DISTRIBUTION MATERIAL **WHAT DESIGN CHOICES MIGHT WEAKEN OR STRENGTHEN THIS....** *(examples: change length, shapes, lines, bead size, bead color, bead placement)* Weaken: change any color, material, bead size, length, symmetry **WHAT IF CONTINGENCIES...** *(examples: If cannot get some bead, color, size, finish, clasp, what could you resort to instead)* If did not have sufficient access to these resources, would have to come up with a different design.

THINKING ROUTINE[4]:
LOOK – SCORE – EXPLAIN

LOOK: **THE BLUE WATERFALL NECKLACE** Warren Feld, 2001.	**Materials and Description:** Mix of glass, crystal, and sterling silver beads. Each segment of beads has a different number of bead, and different sizes/color/finish of beads within it. The colors are not part of a color scheme, and would be seen to clash if compared one to one outside of their use in the bracelet. Example: sapphire blues and montana blues; golds and silvers; matte and glossy. The segments nearer the clasp are shorter than those further from the clasp. The sterling silver tubes are all curved. There is no focal point per se. The clasp is an adjustable hook and eye choker clasp.
KEY DESIGN ELEMENTS: *(see key at bottom of table for list)* 1. COLOR 2. COLOR BLENDING 3. BALANCE AND DISTRIBUTION 4. POINT/LINE/PLANE 5. MOVEMENT 6. SHAPE 7. STRUCTURE / SUPPORT 8. FORM /SEGMENTS/ COMPONENTS	**KEY ATTRIBUTES OF DESIGN ELEMENTS:** 1a. No conformance to color scheme, though leans toward the monochromatic 2a. Simultaneity effects 3a. Feels balanced though there the distribution of sizes, numbers and segment lengths varies within each strand and between each strand 4a. Brings your eye down to a central place, but no specific focal point 4b. Curved lines distort the linearity 5a. Expresses feeling of moving water, but no moving parts 6a. Curved tubes key element 6b. Bead of different shapes

7a. Adjustable choker clasp allows wearer to adjust necklace to body, to achieve that optimum sense of balance and movement

8a. Consists of each length segments separating unequal length segments.
8b. Important that segments on both strands do not match up with each other, but feel staggered
8c. Important that no segment shows dominance or becomes a clear focal point.

SCORE:

SCORE CARD ON PRINCIPLES:

DESIGN CRITERIA	Very Unsatisfying.......Very Satisfying
1. Rhythm	1 2 3 4 **5**
2. Pointers	1 2 3 **4** 5
3. Linear and Planar Relationships	1 2 3 **4** 5
4. Interest	1 2 3 4 **5**
5. Statistical Distribution	1 2 **3** 4 5
6. Balance	1 2 3 **4** 5
7. Forms	1 2 3 4 **5**
8. Temporal Extension: Time, Place	1 2 3 **4** 5
9. Physical Extension: Functionality	1 2 3 4 **5**
10. Parsimony	1 2 3 4 **5**

EXPLAIN:

RHYTHM:

How you see this playing out in this piece:

The forms or segments alternate between clusters of beads and a curved sterling silver tube.

The length of each bead cluster varies, with longer clusters furthest from the clasp.

Staggered alignment of forms.

The perceived "weight" of the left side seems the same as the perceived "weight" of the right side.

ESTABLISHED BY KEY DESIGN ELEMENTS:

FORM, SEGMENTS, COMPONENTS
BALANCE, DISTRIBUTION

WHAT DESIGN CHOICES MIGHT WEAKEN OR STRENGTHEN THIS....
(examples: change length, shapes, lines, bead size, bead color, bead placement)

Weaken: making every bead cluster the same length and the same assortment of beads; having a clear focal point; using straight rather than curved tubes; having forms in both strands align more tightly.

WHAT IF CONTINGENCIES...
(examples: If cannot get some bead, color, size, finish, clasp, what could you resort to instead)

Can't get curved sterling silver tubes, will need to find alternative, either plated, or different sizes

---

POINTERS: **How you see this playing out in this piece:** There is no specific pointer per se, but piece feels as if it has a definite top and bottom, and brings your eye downward.	**ESTABLISHED BY KEY DESIGN ELEMENTS:** POINT, LINE, PLANE BALANCE, DISTRIBUTION **WHAT DESIGN CHOICES MIGHT WEAKEN OR STRENGTHEN THIS....** *(examples: change length, shapes, lines, bead size, bead color, bead placement)* Weaken: Adding too much color/size variation within each cluster of beads. **WHAT IF CONTINGENCIES...** *(examples: If cannot get some bead, color, size, finish, clasp, what could you resort to instead)* If desired effect of a waterfall was achieved, would have to rethink the piece.
LINEAR/PLANAR RELATIONSHIPS: **How you see this playing out in this piece:** Piece dependent on staggered clustering of points and connecting curved lines. The two strands and the forms suggest a greater dimensionality than 2-D.	**ESTABLISHED BY KEY DESIGN ELEMENTS:** POINT, LINE, PLANE FORMS, SEGMENTS, COMPONENTS **WHAT DESIGN CHOICES MIGHT WEAKEN OR STRENGTHEN THIS....** *(examples: change length, shapes, lines, bead size, bead color, bead placement)*

Weaken: making relationship of parts more consistent, including using straight lines rather than curves; lining up the two strands more symmetrically

WHAT IF CONTINGENCIES...
(examples: If cannot get some bead, color, size, finish, clasp, what could you resort to instead)

If piece felt too flat, work more with sizes and shapes of beads in each cluster.

INTEREST: **How you see this playing out in this piece:** Piece evokes feeling of a waterfall. Piece feels finished and successful.	**ESTABLISHED BY KEY DESIGN ELEMENTS:** COLOR BLENDING FORM, SEGMENTS, COMPONENTS SHAPE TEXTURE, PATTERN BALANCE, DISTRIBUTION LIGHT, SHADOW DIMENSIONALITY **WHAT DESIGN CHOICES MIGHT WEAKEN OR STRENGTHEN THIS....** *(examples: change length, shapes, lines, bead size, bead color, bead placement)* Weaken: making piece longer or shorter; making forms more consistent in size and design; giving piece clear focal point **WHAT IF CONTINGENCIES...** *(examples: If cannot get some bead, color, size, finish, clasp, what could you resort to instead)* The bead colors are carefully matched and coordinated through simultaneity effects. If cannot get same beads, near very close substitutes, or need to redesign cluster from start.

STATISTICAL DISTRIBUTION: **How you see this playing out in this piece:** Selection of colors, sizes and shapes within and across bead clusters. Numbers of clusters and numbers of sterling silver curved tubes.	**ESTABLISHED BY KEY DESIGN ELEMENTS:** POINT, LINE, PLANE BALANCE, DISTRIBUTION **WHAT DESIGN CHOICES MIGHT WEAKEN OR STRENGTHEN THIS....** *(examples: change length, shapes, lines, bead size, bead color, bead placement)* Weaken: more consistency in size, shape, color, form **WHAT IF CONTINGENCIES...** *(examples: If cannot get some bead, color, size, finish, clasp, what could you resort to instead)* The bead colors and sizes are carefully matched and coordinated through simultaneity effects. If cannot get same beads, near very close substitutes, or need to redesign cluster from start.
BALANCE: **How you see this playing out in this piece:** Piece feels balanced, although the forms do not line up, and in reality are made up of different colors/shapes/sizes of beads. Shorter clusters of beads near clasp; longer near bottom of necklace.	**ESTABLISHED BY KEY DESIGN ELEMENTS:** BALANCE, DISTRIBUTION FORM, SEGMENTS, COMPONENTS POINT, LINE, PLANE **WHAT DESIGN CHOICES MIGHT WEAKEN OR STRENGTHEN THIS....** *(examples: change length, shapes, lines, bead size, bead color, bead placement)* Weaken: more consistency in size, shape, color, form **WHAT IF CONTINGENCIES...** *(examples: If cannot get some bead, color, size, finish, clasp, what could you resort to instead)*

	If the placement of colors/shapes/sizes does not work, have to rethink the design.
FORMS: **How you see this playing out in this piece:** Two types of forms – bead clusters and single sterling silver curved tubes. Forms vary in length and makeup. Forms in both strands feel coordinated, but do not align or include the same or parallel colors/shapes/sizes.	**ESTABLISHED BY KEY DESIGN ELEMENTS:** POINT, LINE, PLANE FORM, SEGMENTS, COMPONENTS **WHAT DESIGN CHOICES MIGHT WEAKEN OR STRENGTHEN THIS….** *(examples: change length, shapes, lines, bead size, bead color, bead placement)* Weaken: More standardizing of lengths and bead colors, shapes, sizes; changing the patterning from alternating clusters and long curved tubes, to something else **WHAT IF CONTINGENCIES…** *(examples: If cannot get some bead, color, size, finish, clasp, what could you resort to instead)* Could not get curved tubes, have to rethink design.
TEMPORAL EXTENSION: **How you see this playing out in this piece:** We expect this piece can be worn both casually and formally. Piece has a very fluid feel to it, and we expect that this sense of fluidity will always be felt, no matter where the piece is worn.	**ESTABLISHED BY KEY DESIGN ELEMENTS:** REFERENTS POINT, LINE, PLANE FORM, SEGMENTS, COMPONENTS **WHAT DESIGN CHOICES MIGHT WEAKEN THIS….** *(examples: change length, shapes, lines, bead size, bead color, bead placement)* Weaken: More standardizing of lengths and bead colors, shapes, sizes; changing the patterning from alternating clusters and long curved tubes, to something else

WHAT IF CONTINGENCIES...
(examples: If cannot get some bead, color, size, finish, clasp, what could you resort to instead)

Could not get curved tubes, have to rethink design.

PHYSICAL EXTENSION: **How you see this playing out in this piece:** Adjustable necklace clasp allows wearer to adjust the piece, so that both strands lay so that they evoke this feeling of a waterfall. Otherwise, piece would not lay right on every body shape.	**ESTABLISHED BY KEY DESIGN ELEMENTS:** TECHNIQUE/TECHNOLOGY **WHAT DESIGN CHOICES MIGHT WEAKEN OR STRENGTHEN THIS....** *(examples: change length, shapes, lines, bead size, bead color, bead placement)* Weaken: use of fixed clasp **WHAT IF CONTINGENCIES...** *(examples: If cannot get some bead, color, size, finish, clasp, what could you resort to instead)* Could not get an adjustable choker clasp, would have to craft something to be adjustable
PARSIMONY: **How you see this playing out in this piece:** Piece is neither too short or too long. Forms in piece do not seem to need to be longer or shorter or more consistent or less consistent.	**ESTABLISHED BY KEY DESIGN ELEMENTS:** FORM, SEGMENT, COMPONENTS POINT, LINE, PLANE BALANCE, DISTRIBUTION COLOR BLENDING POINTER **WHAT DESIGN CHOICES MIGHT WEAKEN OR STRENGTHEN THIS....** *(examples: change length, shapes, lines, bead size, bead color, bead placement)* Weaken: More standardizing of lengths and

bead colors, shapes, sizes; changing the patterning from alternating clusters and long curved tubes, to something else; changing length or silhouette of necklace

WHAT IF CONTINGENCIES...
(examples: If cannot get some bead, color, size, finish, clasp, what could you resort to instead)

Could not achieve color blending, sense of balance, or an up-down orientation, then would need to rethink design.

FOOTNOTES

[1] Feld, Warren. "Jewelry Design Composition: Playing with Building Blocks Called Design Elements," 3/17/2018

[2] Feld, Warren. "Jewelry Design: A Managed Process," Klimt02, 2/2/18.
https://klimt02.net/forum/articles/jewelry-design-managed-process-warren-feld

[3] *Shared Understandings*. In another graduate education class, the major text reviewed the differences between understanding and knowledge. The question was how to teach understanding. Worth the read to gain many insights about how to structure teaching to get sufficient understanding to enrich learning. **_Understanding by Design_** by Grant Wiggins and Jay McTighe, 2nd Edition, Association for Supervision and Curriculum Development, 2005.

[4] *Thinking Routines*. I teach jewelry design. I find it useful to engage students with various ways of thinking out loud. They need to hear me think out loud about what choices I am making and what things I am considering when making those choices. They need to hear themselves think out loud so that they can develop strategies for getting more organized and strategic in dealing with information and making decisions. My inspiration here was based on the work done by **Visible Thinking by Project Zero** (http://www.visiblethinkingpz.org/VisibleThinking_html_files/pz.harvard.edu) **at Harvard Graduate School of Education** .

RULES OF COMPOSITION, CONSTRUCTION, AND MANIPULATION
5e. HOW TO DESIGN AN UGLY NECKLACE:
The Ultimate Designer's Challenge / You Be The Judge

	Guiding Questions: (1) What kinds of things make something Ugly? (2) What defines an Ugly Necklace? (3) Why is it more difficult to design an Ugly Necklace, than a Beautiful one? (4) What kinds of things make something less Ugly?

| *Key Words:*
ugly
beauty / appeal
cognition
approach / flee / anxiety response | rhythm
pointers
linear and planar relationships
interest
statistical distribution
balance
forms
temporal extension
physical extension
parsimony
wearable | *Principles of Composition, Construction, and Manipulation*
good design |

Abstract
It's not easy to do Ugly! Your mind and eye won't let you go there. We are prewired

with an anxiety response to help us avoid things that might harm us. So, it turns out, it is easier to design a beautiful piece of jewelry than an ugly one. Designing an ugly necklace, then, presents the designer with the ultimate challenge. To achieve a truly hideous result means making the hard design choices, putting ourselves in situations and forcing us to make the kinds of choices we're unfamiliar with, and taking us inside ourselves to places that we are somewhat scared about, and where we do not want to go. The International Ugly Necklace Contest (http://www.warrenfeldjewelry.com/wfjuglynecklace.htm) *(http://www.warrenfeldjewelry.com/wfjuglynecklace.htm), first announced in 2002, and held 10 times since then, was one of the programs we launched as a way to reaffirm our beliefs in a design-oriented, theory-based, professional jewelry design education curriculum. This chapter discusses the idea of "Ugly", and provides some clues to designers about achieving it.*

HOW TO DESIGN AN UGLY NECKLACE:
The Ultimate Designer's Challenge

Can you put together a well-designed and functional, yet UGLY, necklace? What kinds of things might you do if you were trying to design a necklace that is ugly, hideous, unsatisfying and what have you?

It's Not Easy To Do Ugly!

Your mind and eye won't let you go there. As research into color and design has shown, your eye and brain compensate for imbalances in color or in the positioning of pieces and objects – they try to correct and harmonize them.

You are pre-wired with an innate fear and anxiety response to subconsciously avoid anything that is disorienting, disturbing or distracting. You are genetically predisposed to avoid things that might hurt you or kill you, like snakes and spiders.

Moreover, necklaces are arranged in a circle. The circle shape itself errs on the side of beauty, and anything arranged, ordered or organized, such as the component parts of a necklace, will err on the side of beauty.

Because of all this, *beauty* is the norm. It is easier to design a *beautiful* necklace than an *ugly* one! How about that! Any jewelry designer who attempts to achieve "Ugly," has to have enough control and discipline to override, perhaps overcome, intuitive, internally integrated principles of good design.

To achieve a truly hideous result means making the hard design choices, putting ourselves in situations and forcing us to make the kinds of choices we're unfamiliar with, and taking us inside ourselves to places that we are somewhat scared about, and where we do not want to go.

These hard choices include things like:

- *Can I push myself to use more yellow than the purple warrants, and mix in some orange?*

- *Can I make the piece off-sided or disorienting, or not have a clear beginning, middle or end?*

- *Can I disrupt my pattern in a way that, rather than "jazz," results in "discord?"*

- *Can I work with colors and materials and patterns and textures and placements and proportions I don't like?*

- *Can I design something I do not personally like, and perhaps am unwilling, to wear around my neck?*

- *Can I create a piece of jewelry that represents some awful feeling, emotion or experience I'm uncomfortable with?*

- *Can I make something I know that others won't like, and may ridicule me for it?*

Because answering questions like these is not something people like to do, jewelry designers who attempt to achieve "Ugly," have to have a lot of control and discipline to override, perhaps overcome, intuitive, internally integrated principles of artistic beauty.

The best jewelry designers, therefore, will be those designers who can prove that they can design a truly Ugly Necklace. These are designers who can break the boundaries of form, material and technique.

What Is Ugly?

We often like to say that *beauty* (and by inference, *ugly*) is in the eye of the *beholder*. But once we utter that phrase, we deny the possibilities of design – and the perspective on beauty or ugly from the eye of the designer. If we take away too much power to create from the designer – something beautiful or something ugly – we begin to deny the need for the designer in the first place. We leave too much to the situation, and too little to our abilities as jewelry designers to translate inspiration into aspiration into finished designs which emotionally affect those around us. But the challenge of designing an Ugly Necklace shows us that without the designer, there can be no design, no resonant beauty, no parsimonious attention to appeal.

As designers, we like to think we are capable of designing something beautiful. As teachers, we like to believe we are capable of training someone to be a better designer – one who can more readily choose colors, patterns, textures, forms and arrangements – in universally pleasing ways. As a discipline, we like to think of good design as resulting from sets of learned information, insights and behaviors.

Different people interpret "Ugly" in different ways. Some might focus on the ugliness of each individual component. Some might use materials they feel convey a sense of ugly, such as llama droppings, or felted matted dog hair, or rusty nails, or cigarette butts, or a banana peel. Some might focus on mood and consciousness, and how certain configurations of pieces and colors evoke these moods or states of consciousness. Others might focus on combining colors which don't combine well. Still others might focus on how the wearer's own body would contribute to a sense of ugliness, when wearing the piece, such as the addition of a "Breast Pocket" which would lay just below the woman's breast, or peacock feathers that covered the wearer's mouth, or the irritating sounds of rusty cow bells, or the icky feeling of a rotting banana peel on the skin. Still others might view Ugly as a sense of psychological consciousness, such as being homeless, or an uncomfortable transition from adolescence to adulthood. For some Ugly might mean politically ugly, like Saddam Hussein of Iraq, or the trans-fats associated with fast foods.

It is not enough just to string a bunch of ugly beads on a wire. Ugly pieces, parts and components do not necessarily result in an ugly necklace. Actually, if you look at many ugly pieces or components, once they are arranged and organized, they no longer seem as ugly anymore. Organization and arrangement contribute their own qualities and sense of beauty which transcend the ugly parts.

Adding to the fun *(?difficulty?)*, designers want their ugly necklaces to also be functional and wearable. This goes to the heart of what jewelry is all about. Otherwise, they would merely be creating sculptures. The parts and techniques used to design an ugly necklace must also anticipate functional requirements. Otherwise, the piece of jewelry becomes a failure not only as a piece of jewelry, but of art, as well.

About The International Ugly Necklace Contest
(http://www.warrenfeldjewelry.com/wfjuglynecklace.htm)

The International Ugly Necklace Contest (http://www.warrenfeldjewelry.com/wfjuglynecklace.htm), first announced in 2002, and held 10 times since then, was one of the programs Land of Odds-Be Dazzled Beads (http://www.landofodds.com) (http://www.landofodds.com) launched as a way to reaffirm our beliefs in a design-oriented, theory-based, professional jewelry design education curriculum. The Contest was conceived as a fun way to break students out of the traditional craft mold, and get them to think, ponder, and translate their feelings and perceptions of what is UGLY into an organized and functional necklace design.

We made the contest international. We launched it on-line. Our goal was to politely influence the entire beading and jewelry making communities to think in different terms and to try to work outside the box. We also wanted very actively to stimulate discussion about whether there are universal and practical design theories which underlie beadwork and jewelry design, and which can be taught.

Can you really design UGLY, or is UGLY merely in the eye of the beholder?

Four conceptual precepts underlying the creation of the Contest itself included:
1. *The Necklace should be Ugly, yet still function as a piece of jewelry.*
2. *Better designers will demonstrate a degree of control over achieving these ends.*
3. *Better designers will show a sense of how both the larger context within which the jewelry is worn, as well as the overall effects of the wearer wearing the piece, will increase the piece's Ugliness.*
4. *Better designers will have an intuitive design sense; best designers will show some strategic control over the design process.*

Our judges evaluated each Ugly Necklace submission according to 10 jewelry design criteria *(See Below)*, and scored each criteria. Each criterion was weighted equally. The 10 necklaces with the highest average scores were selected as our 10 semi-finalists.

Ten Semi-Finalists were picked. They were asked to submit the actual necklaces to us, to be put on display at Be Dazzled Beads (https://landofodds.com/about-us/). We took images of each one – a full frontal image showing someone wearing the piece, a close-up, and a close-up of the clasp assembly. We posted these images, along with the poems, on-line (now on display here (http://www.warrenfeldjewelry.com/wfjuglynecklace.htm)) so that visitors to the site could vote for the winner and runner up. The winner got a $992.93 shopping spree on the Land of Odds web-site (http://www.landofodds.com); the runner-up got a $399.07 shopping spree on the web-site (http://www.landofodds.com).

NOW, You Be The JUDGE!

Below, I present three very different Ugly Necklace submissions. Each designer submitting their necklace must include the following in their packet:
1) *At least 4 images (front, back, someone wearing it, detail of clasp assembly)*
2) *A poem where they get to put into rhyme the kinds of things they were thinking when they made their various design decisions*
3) *A list of materials and techniques.*

Some of this material is provided below to assist you when scoring each piece.

And you might want to take some aspirin first. It's difficult to get your mind to evaluate things opposite to how you normally would do it.

The Judges Criteria

Each necklace is scored on 10 jewelry design criteria.

1. **Overall Hideousness** *(first impressions; piece has noteworthy elements which slant your impressions toward Ugliness)*
2. **Clever Use of Materials** *(something about the materials chosen contribute to a sense of Ugliness)*
3. **The Clasp Assembly** *(any creativity applied here?)*
4. **Color Principles** *(the more violations, the better)*

5. Balance or Arrangement *(the more violations, the better)*

6. Rhythm and Focus *(the more violations, the better)*

7. Orienting *(the more disorienting, the better)*

8. *Parsimony* *(adding or subtracting 1 more element would make the piece more appealing, satisfying, even beautiful rather than more ugly; artist achieved maximum ugly effect efficiently and economically)*

9. Wearability *(piece must be wearable; extra points if the wearing of the piece makes the piece even uglier)*

10. The Poem *(expresses artist's intent; artist shows power to translate intent into Ugly)*

The Criteria In More Detail

1. Overall Hideousness *(first impressions; piece has noteworthy elements which slant your impressions toward Ugliness)*

The idea of "Noteworthiness" is key here. Noteworthiness means the extent the artist took something ordinary and made it extraordinary.

The best examples were the unexpected use of familiar materials. For example, felted dog hair shaped into beads; llama droppings, colored and drilled to be used as beads; a toothbrush used as part of a clasp assembly; a banana peel used as a pendant drop.

In some cases, the artist tried to make the necklace into a political statement, such as the Saddam Hussein necklace with bullets and pink shoes; or the glutenous fast food necklace with the gummi hot dog and gummi bun as the clasp.

In many cases, found objects, insignificant on their own, were organized to call attention to special meanings, such as the grenade box found among shells at the beach; or the remaining parts of a cat along with the chicken bone that led to her demise; or plastic jewels that seemed electrifying to the designer as a young girl, and so not as an adult.

Other things the judges look at include the clasp assembly, the artist's anticipation of the effects of wearing the piece, the overall goals of the artist with the piece, and their first reaction to the piece.

2. Clever Use of Materials *(something about the materials chosen contribute to a sense of Ugliness)*

In too many cases, the jewelry artist chose ugly pieces and assumed that a necklace made of ugly pieces would itself be ugly as well. But as you can see from the images on this web-site (http://www.warrenfeldjewelry.com/wfjuglynecklace.htm) (http://www.warrenfeldjewelry.com/wfjuglynecklace.htm), this strategy does not work well.

The artist has to have a deeper understanding of why the materials are ugly. The artist also needs to stay focused and strategic enough in the design process, so that she or he maintains this sense of ugly as the necklace gets organized.

For example, one necklace used felted matted dog hair, and made beads out of this. This was a start at a clever use of materials. But once strung into a circle, the necklace looked like something someone might actually wear.

A necklace of cigarette butts, again once organized into a circle, doesn't look quite as ugly. In addition, the necklace over-used cigarette butts -- too many -- which started to make the necklace a bit boring. While "boring" might take us in the direction of "ugly", in this case, it diminished the power of the cigarette butts to make a statement about "ugly".

This criteria looks at the total picture. Not just the ugliness of each individual piece. But also the degree to which the assembly of pieces maintains this sense of ugliness. The concern here is "*design-cleverness* in the *USE* of materials".

3. The Clasp Assembly *(any creativity applied here?)*

A better clasp assembly is one that seems to be an integral part of the necklace, not just an after-thought or add-on. It should anticipate how it contributes to the ugliness of the piece, how it re-affirms the artist's concept and goals, and how it adds to the wearability of the piece.

Successful Clasp Assemblies:

A gummy hot dog closes into a candy gummy bun

There is an elaborate strap, zipper, and suspender toggles system as the clasp assembly. With different configurations of parts, the necklace may be worn as a choker, a back pack, a wrap, a fanny pack, a clutch, or a traditional over-the-shoulder and around the neck necklace.

A troll doll is the clasp. One end of necklace string is tied into a loop and wraps around the left hand of the troll doll. The other end of the necklace string is tied into a loop and wraps around the right hand of the troll doll. The two hands of the troll doll push apart to open up, and push closed to secure the necklace.

4. Color Principles *(the more violations, the better)*

The degree the piece violates good principles of color. This might include using colors in incorrect proportions; or which violate color schemes; or violate rules of dominance/submission; or disturbing arrangements - vertical vs. horizontal, shading and tinting, sharp vs. blurred boundaries, placements and balance, projecting forward vs. receding; or violating socio-cultural rules and expectations.

This is self-explanatory. For example, the appropriate proportions of yellow to purple should be 1:4, meaning in any grouping of 5 beads, 4 should be purple and 1 yellow. When you deviate from this, your piece gets uglier.

COLOR THEORY discusses the use of the color wheel to select colors that work together within a "scheme". There are many schemes, including Analogous, Complementary, and Split Complementary. An ugly necklace would select colors that violate this scheme. This might mean selecting colors that do not fit together within a scheme. It might mean using the wrong proportions of color within the scheme. It might also mean violating expectations about which colors should and should not predominate within the scheme.

See My Video Tutorial: [The Jewelry Designer's Approach To Color](https://so-you-want-to-be-a-jewelry-designer.teachable.com/p/the-jewelry-designer-s-approach-to-color) (https://so-you-want-to-be-a-jewelry-designer.teachable.com/p/the-jewelry-designer-s-approach-to-color) *(https://so-you-want-to-be-a-jewelry-designer.teachable.com/p/the-jewelry-designer-s-approach-to-color)*

5. Balance or Arrangement *(the more violations, the better)*

This is self-explanatory. Does the placement seem satisfying, such as a graduated necklace that starts with smaller sizes, works up to larger sizes in the center, then works back down to smaller sizes at the clasp? Or, not?

When looking at the piece, can you see alternative arrangements that might make the piece look even uglier?

Another aspect of bad balance and arrangement has to do with *dimensionality*. This is the degree, whether the piece is flat or 3-dimensional, that this is satisfying, or not. For example, a flat loomed piece with an extra large button clasp on the top of it, would probably be less satisfying than one with a smaller clasp on the end of the piece. Dimensionality can also be created through mixing beads or objects with different finishes, like mixing glossy and matte. An ugly mix somehow would feel dissatisfying.

6. Rhythm and Focus *(the more violations, the better)*

One of the goals of the jewelry artist is to motivate the viewer to take in, experience and appreciate the whole necklace. One of the major techniques is to create a rhythm with the patterning of the beads, and to create a focal point. This influences the viewer's brain/eye to want to see each part of the necklace from beginning to end, and then come to rest.

An ugly necklace, would either have no rhythm or a boring rhythm or a nauseating rhythm. It would fail to direct the viewer's eye. An ugly necklace would either have no focal point, or have a focal point that is in a very disorienting or disturbing place on the necklace, or be very disorienting or disturbing in and of itself. There would not be a natural place for the eye to come to rest.

7. Orienting *(the more disorienting, the better)*

Jewelry plays a critical psychological role for the viewer in a room or in a space. It orients them. It is one of the important things in any person's visual environment that lets the person know what is up and what is down, and what is right and what is left.

The natural state in life is to be dis-oriented. It takes walls and ceilings, trees and horizons, things with clear right angles, clear perpendicularity, obvious horizontal and vertical planes, to enable us to orient ourselves within any space. Otherwise people would have difficulty standing up, would fall down a lot, lose a sense of how to turn or position themselves, or feel paralyzed.

The wearing of jewelry plays a critical function here, in that it visually establishes for the viewer appropriate horizontal and vertical lines and planes. If you see someone with their earring dangle at a 90 degree angle, or their necklace turned around so that the clasp is showing when it shouldn't -- you know how uncomfortable this makes you feel, even wanting to cringe. And you know you want and need them to straighten things out. This jewelry is dis-orienting you, at a time when you subconsciously rely on it to be orienting.

If this wasn't important, things like the odd-angled dangle wouldn't bother you.... But we know that it does.

8. *Parsimony* *(adding or subtracting 1 more element would make the piece more appealing, satisfying, even beautiful rather than more ugly; artist achieved maximum ugly effect efficiently and economically)*

Once the designer has made their point, they don't need to keep making it. For example, one entry used plastic trolls to create a sense of Ugly. There were over 20 on the necklace, but in their particular design, 6 or 8 were probably sufficient to make the point. The additional trolls served no other purpose in this piece. Just throwing in a lot of ugly pieces together doesn't necessarily result in something that is uglier. The additional trolls could have been used to make additional design points, but they were not. Instead they added a sense of repetition and disinterest.

A necklace of felted dog hair beads was a very clever idea. It was over 36". No other design points were made, so an 18" necklace of felted dog hair beads would have been as good as 36". In a similar way, a very long necklace of cigarette butts would have been equally as good, or better if shorter, since no other design points were made.

9. *Wearability* *(piece must be wearable; extra points if the wearing of the piece makes the piece even uglier)*

From a design perspective, Jewelry is Art As It Is Worn.

In other words, you can only appreciate the artistic qualities and sensibilities of any piece of jewelry only when you see it worn -- as it moves with the body, as it conforms to the body, as it enhances the wearer's sense of self, and the viewer's sense of the situation and context.

In our contest, we set the rule that the piece has to be Wearable. This rule tends to make it more difficult to achieve "Ugly", but we've had some clever submissions that succeed here.

Some examples from our entries:

- Peacock feathers that would fill the wearer's mouth
- An over-the-shoulder necklace that struggles to stay on the shoulders
- A breast pocket strategically placed on the tip of the breast
- Bloody teeth or a rotting banana peel meant to be worn against the skin

To the judges, wearability means that there should be clear evidence that the designer anticipated where the parts came from, and where they are going to, when the piece is worn.

10. The Poem *(expresses artist's intent; artist shows power to translate intent into Ugly)*

The poem must relate to the piece. It should clearly explain the designer's goals and concept. It should detail the designer"s strategies for making the design choices she or he did.

The judges ask themselves, given what the artist wrote in the poem, to what degree have they successfully created an ugly piece of jewelry?

YOUR TURN TO JUDGE

Use the scoring sheets below to evaluate **UGLY NECKLACE #1** and **UGLY NECKLACE #2** and **UGLY NECKLACE #3**.

Or even try your own hand at designing an Ugly Necklace. Can you do it? **UGLY**

NECKLACE #1: *Brings Me To Tears*

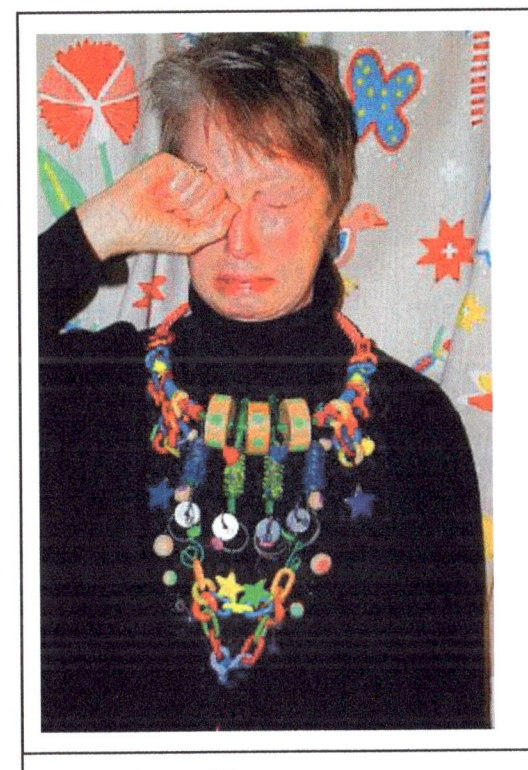

Materials:
Clasp Assembly: Button
  Toggle

Plastic chain, toy parts, yarn, clock parts, starts, paper tube rings

The Ugly Necklace

While sitting and thinking of something to do
A "masterpiece" that will create lots of Boo...
I discovered that ugly is a wonderful thing
That involves much more than some beads on a string.
One must think and design, construct and produce,
To achieve a piece that has a lot of "juice".
Something ugly but great, that's the thing that I made,
I sure hope that you'll like it or is it to Hate?!!!

SCORE SHEET UGLY NECKLACE #1: *Brings Me To Tears*	
	BEAUTIFUL .... HIDEOUS
1. Overall Hideousness (first impressions; piece has noteworthy elements)	1 2 3 4 5 6 7
2. Clever Use of Materials	1 2 3 4 5 6 7
3. The Clasp Assembly (any creativity applied here?)	1 2 3 4 5 6 7

4. Color Principles (the more violations, the better)	1 2 3 4 5 6 7
5. Balance or Arrangement (the more violations, the better)	1 2 3 4 5 6 7
6. Rhythm and Focus (the more violations, the better)	1 2 3 4 5 6 7
7. Orienting (the more disorienting, the better)	1 2 3 4 5 6 7
8. Parsimony (adding or subtracting 1 more element would make the piece worse; artist achieved maximum effect efficiently)	1 2 3 4 5 6 7
9. Wearability (piece must be wearable; extra points if the wearing of the piece makes the piece even uglier)	1 2 3 4 5 6 7
10. The Poem (expresses artist's intent; artist shows power to translate intent into Ugly)	1 2 3 4 5 6 7

UGLY NECKLACE #2: *Oooh! It Smells!*

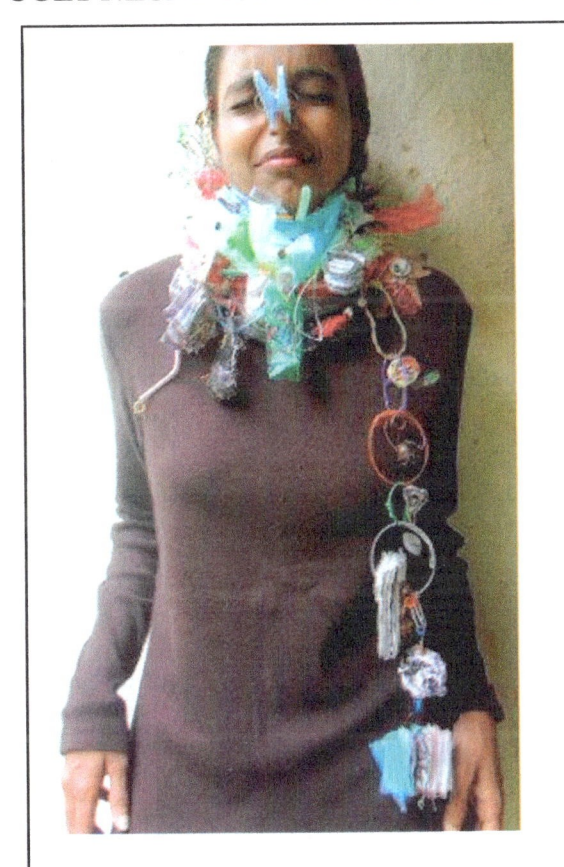

Materials:
Clasp Assembly: Toggle made from wires and straws

garbage bags+flyes+smell+garbage truck+cans+bottles+polythene layers+paper strips+paper rolls+air bags+paper blocks+bins+recycle logo+straw+birds+floating bags+crush paper+wire+drain water+cigars+newspaper+plastic lids+coloured water+bird dirt+urine+flating dirt on water

newspaper+match box+hand printed materials+leaflets+lotary tickets+tags+kitchen garbage+fish bone+coke cans+melted rubber+plastic+punch holes+apple wrap+bulb+paper beads+safety pin+paper strips+polythene strips+metal rings+melted candle+dead bodies of flys+wire

shopping bags + threads +balloons +air+copper wire+multi colour polymer beads+electrical wire+ buttons+ mesh+eyelets+paper strips+melting candles+coloured water+transparent tubes+copper tubes+oil+dead bodies of fish+mosquitoes+flys+staws+polymer rings+punch hole

Techniques: sawing+looping+olythene stringing+tie-ups+wire beading+coiling+bundling+drilling+layering+polything srining+polythene weaving

...recycle me...

I walk through the grimmy world
Gathering uglies from each dirty by-way
Every piece of ugly collected
A mirror of my life reflected
Can I recycle the world into something better
Do it now or wait for later
Can the stench out there be perfumed
Once the ugly pieces are all infused
Paper bundles, polethene, plastic, bags
All come together for the ugliest of rags
Around my neck like a becon of truth
of the ugly
    the dirty
        the reflection
            the collection
                of our world
                    poem...

UGLY NECKLACE #2: *Oooh! It Smells!*

	BEAUTIFUL .... HIDEOUS
1. Overall Hideousness (first impressions; piece has noteworthy elements)	1 2 3 4 5 6 7
2. Clever Use of Materials	1 2 3 4 5 6 7
3. The Clasp Assembly (any creativity applied here?)	1 2 3 4 5 6 7
4. Color Principles (the more violations, the better)	1 2 3 4 5 6 7
5. Balance or Arrangement (the more violations, the better)	1 2 3 4 5 6 7
6. Rhythm and Focus (the more violations, the better)	1 2 3 4 5 6 7
7. Orienting (the more disorienting, the better)	1 2 3 4 5 6 7
8. Parsimony (adding or subtracting 1 more element would make the piece worse; artist achieved maximum effect efficiently)	1 2 3 4 5 6 7
9. Wearability (piece must be wearable; extra points if the wearing of the piece makes the piece even uglier)	1 2 3 4 5 6 7
10. The Poem (expresses artist's intent; artist shows power to translate intent into Ugly)	1 2 3 4 5 6 7

UGLY NECKLACE #3: *Venerable Spirits*

Materials:
Clasp Assembly: Mother of Pearl Pendant as toggle bar, wire hook under claw as toggle ring

Red coral, red coral carved, hawk's claw, eagle's claw pearls, sterling silver heishi, turquoise heishi, antique silver beads, Tibetan turquoise, sterling and coral dragon, quartz crystal, base metal casting of Chinese foo dog, Moroccan cross, Mother of Pearl pendant converted into clasp.

Song of the Venerable Bede

"The New Age Market has decreed
there be more Spirit in their beads.
No more sufficient, ostentation;
they now require extrapolation
From world religions to their jewelry
which tempts designers to buffoonery.
This ugly necklace is evidence
of a bauble fraught with such mystical defense.

The Chinese foo dog guards the wearer on her Path as she pursues
enlightenment (the crystal quartz) and further arcane power through
Tibetan dragon and, of course, the inevitable, exotic, (this time Moroccan) yet
comfortingly familiar cross.

Carved Buddha sighs and on his breath the eagle feather rises
through several hundred turquoise beads (perpetually spiritual turquoise leads to
absolutely no surprises.)

The entire construct is entrusted to the grasping eagle claw
desperately snatching wisdom's pearl -- then more and more and ever more.

To underpin this dubious theme
and underscore the moral
the whole is strung on jagged pearls

> and allegedly branch coral.
> To string them neatly side by side implies
> that there might be
> some underlying sense or plan
> but close inspection indicates that evens view with odds
> while chaos helter-skelter reigns
> among the loose strung gods.
>
>
> And so, to close, the ancient pearl beyond all price is gained;
> through garish bead and highest price
> arcane wisdom has been obtained.
>
>
> And we another season rest
> whilst quoting van der Rohe
> that god is in the details or --
> wait -- could it be -- NO!
>
> Is that instead the devil there, lurking
> behind each carefully wired shank?
> God or devil; theologically impeccable and fair, we take both to the bank.

UGLY NECKLACE #3: *Venerable Spirits*	
	BEAUTIFUL .... HIDEOUS
1. Overall Hideousness (first impressions; piece has noteworthy elements)	1 2 3 4 5 6 7
2. Clever Use of Materials	1 2 3 4 5 6 7
3. The Clasp Assembly (any creativity applied here?)	1 2 3 4 5 6 7
4. Color Principles (the more violations, the better)	1 2 3 4 5 6 7
5. Balance or Arrangement (the more violations, the better)	1 2 3 4 5 6 7
6. Rhythm and Focus (the more violations, the better)	1 2 3 4 5 6 7
7. Orienting (the more disorienting, the better)	1 2 3 4 5 6 7
8. Parsimony (adding or subtracting 1 more element would make the piece worse; artist	1 2 3 4 5 6 7

achieved maximum effect efficiently)	
9. Wearability (piece must be wearable; extra points if the wearing of the piece makes the piece even uglier)	1 2 3 4 5 6 7
10. The Poem (expresses artist's intent; artist shows power to translate intent into Ugly)	1 2 3 4 5 6 7

FOOTNOTES

Deeb, Margie. The Beader's Guide To Jewelry Design: A Beautiful Exploration of Unity, Balance, Color & More. NY: Lark Jewelry & Beading, 2014.

The International Ugly Necklace Contest, sponsored by Warren Feld Jewelry (http://www.warrenfeldjewelry.com), Land of Odds (https://www.landofodds.com), Be Dazzled Beads (http://www.bedazzledbeads.com), LearnToBead.net. As referenced in: http://www.warrenfeldjewelry.com/wfjuglynecklace.htm

RULES OF COMPOSITION, CONSTRUCTION, AND MANIPULATION
5f. ARCHITECTURAL BASICS OF JEWELRY DESIGN: Building In The Necessary Support and Structure

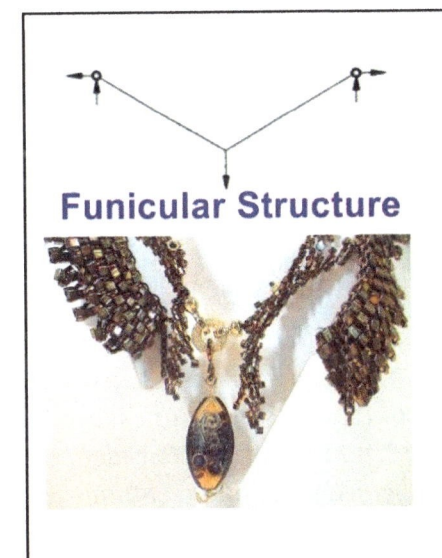

Funicular Structure

Guiding Questions:
(1) How do your choices in design positively or negatively affect how the piece moves and feels (support) and maintain its shape (structure) as the piece is worn?
(2) How do you redefine the steps in the techniques you use in architectural terms?
(3) How do you mitigate the points in your piece of least vulnerability?
(4) How do you optimize the 4 S's: strength, suppleness, stability and synergy?
(5) How will aging of materials used affect the integrity of the piece over time?
(6) What are the anatomical parts of a piece of jewelry?
(7) What are the behaviors of jewelry (and the various component parts) when subjected to mechanical forces?
(8) What are the separate architectural components of jewelry?
(9) What are the 5 types of architectural spaces in a piece of jewelry which must be managed?

Key Words:	*strap*	*design system*
architecture	*yoke*	*applied process*
materials	*break*	*equilibrium*
techniques	*clasp assembly*	*external / internal forces*
technologies	*break*	*jointedness*
support	*clasp assembly*	*mechanics*
structure	*frame*	*statics*
	focal point / centerpiece /pendant	*dynamics*
		force
hazards: shapes of either ***H, L, T,*** *or* ***U***	*bail*	*stress*
	canvas	*strain*
shape	*embellishment*	*horizontal structures*
movement, drape, flow	*types of spaces*	*vertical structures*

309

point of least vulnerability leveraging		rotational structures
		4 S's:
		    strength
		    suppleness
		    stability
		    synergy

Abstract:
I find that most jewelry designers do not learn their techniques with architectural principles in mind. They arrange a set of materials into a composition, and assume its success is solely based on the visual grammar they applied. But if the piece of jewelry doesn't wear well, feels uncomfortable, gets in a weird position making the wearer look clownish, or breaks or comes apart too easily, the jewelry designer has failed in their mission. So, whenever you create a piece of jewelry, it is important to try to anticipate how your choice of materials, techniques and technologies might positively or negatively affect how the piece moves and feels (called Support) and how its components maintain shape and integrity (called Structure) when worn. Towards this end, it is important to redefine your techniques and materials in architectural terms. Every jewelry making technique is an applied process (called a Design System) with the end goal of trying to reach some type of equilibrium. That is, steps taken to balance off all the external and internal forces impacting the piece. Achieving this balance means that the piece of jewelry is at its point of least vulnerability. This is where all the materials, techniques and technologies have been leveraged to optimize the four S's: Strength, Suppleness, Stability and Synergy.

ARCHITECTURAL BASICS OF JEWELRY DESIGN:
Building In The Necessary Support and Structure

Everything boils down to *support* and *structure*.

Support is anything about the materials, techniques or technologies used which allow the finished piece to best move, drape and flow while the piece is worn.
Structure is anything about the materials, techniques, or technologies used which allow the finished piece to maintain its shape and integrity while the piece is worn.

Constructing a bracelet or a necklace is really not much different than engineering and building a bridge. Bridges have purpose and functions. Jewelry has purpose and functions. These are very much the same. Bridges adjust to the environment. Jewelry adjusts to the body within a situation or context. The jewelry designer needs to anticipate how the piece will purpose and function and adapt within a context or situation or environment, as worn.

Designers have to worry about the bracelet or necklace maintaining its shape and not falling apart, in the face of many stresses which come from movement, adjustments, obstructions, twisting, body geography and contour, aging of materials, environmental conditions, and so forth. They need to anticipate how the piece will comfortably move, drape and flow while worn. They have to construct something that is appealing and friendly to the user. Designers have to be fluent in, and be able to apply, not just a visual grammar, but a functional grammar, as well.

This means that the jewelry artist needs to know a little bit about physical mechanics. A little bit about how to create, control and maintain shape. A little bit about how to build in support and jointedness. A lot about materials, how they go together and how they age together over time. A lot about how various jewelry making techniques enhance or impede support and structure over time. Some comfort about making tradeoffs and judgement calls between aesthetics and functionality. And their finished jewelry needs to reflect all this jewelry artist knowledge and fluency, so it maintains its appeal, its comfort and durability, but doesn't fall apart when worn.

We have all heard and seen the complaints.

- Clasp slips around neck to the front
- Necklace bezel settings turn around ending up facing backwards
- Earring dangle gets locked in a 90 degree angle
- Jump rings open up and bracelet pulls apart
- Necklace doesn't lay flat
- Earring dangles don't face the right way
- Stone pops out of its setting
- Stringing material breaks or pulls apart
- Finishes on beads and components flake off
- Necklace or bracelet breaks at the crimp
- Solder or glue doesn't hold
- Beads crack and string breaks in overly tight pieces
- Jewelry scratches on the neck or wrist

These kind of things which happen are not natural to jewelry. They are examples of bad jewelry design. They can be corrected by building in an architectural awareness of how materials and techniques function. They may need more support, such as loops, rings, and hinges, for example. They may need better structure, such as smarter selection of materials, or more strategic implementation of technique, or extra reinforcement at points of potential weakness.

This wire work bracelet pulls apart when worn. The jump rings open up. Upon closer inspection, we learn that the designer used dead soft wire to make the jump rings, and did nothing to harden the wire, either before or after shaping. Harding the wire, such as twisting it before shaping it, or starting with half hard wire may have solved this problem.

This necklace clasp has slipped to the front. This is not natural to jewelry; it is a design flaw. The clasp assembly has insufficient support or jointedness. This problem can more easily be prevented by building in more support. In this case, adding additional rings – at least one where the clasp is attached to the chain, and at least one to the ring on the other end of the chain – would probably suffice. Added support would absorb the stress movement places on the piece. Without it, the necklace will always turn around in the opposite direction to the force applied.

This earring dangle is stuck at a 90 degree angle. The problem is simple. There is insufficient support. This means that either the size of the loop where the dangle connects to the ear wire, is too small, or that the thickness of the wire making this loop is too thick for the opening on the ear wire.

SUPPORT SYSTEMS

Support systems are components or design elements we build into our pieces, which allow good movement, flow, and drape. This is known as *support* or jointedness. Sufficient support allows for the absorption or channeling of stress so that negative impacts on a piece of jewelry when worn are minimized.

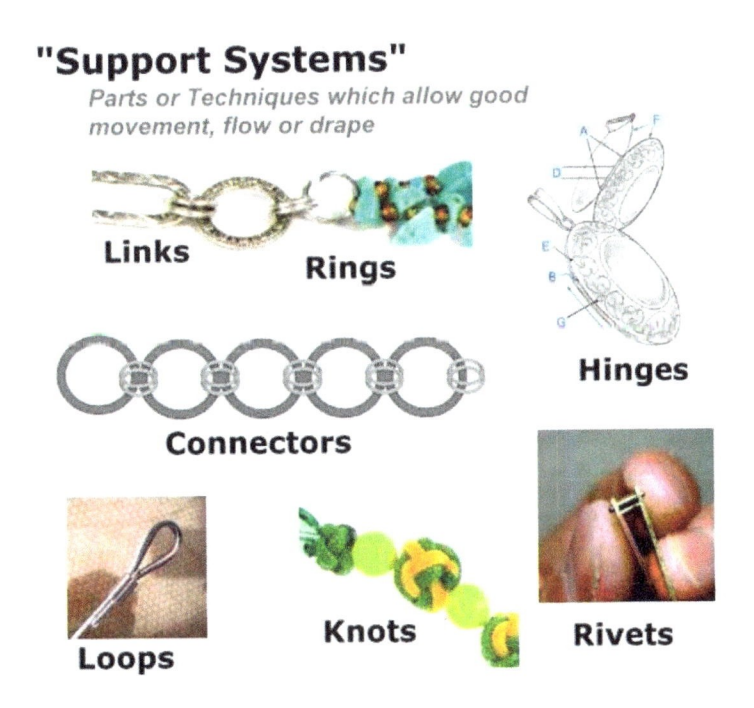

Support systems may be things like

- *Rings*
- *Loops*
- *Links*
- *Hinges*
- *Rivets*
- *Knots (unglued)*
- *Things which allow components to rotate around*

They may involve different kinds of chaining or connecting.

I include knots as support systems. Unglued knots provide a lot of support and jointedness. Glued knots do not. Glued knots are stiff, and increase the risk of breakage or support failure. Some knots are looser, like lark's head knots or weaver's knots or overhand knots. Looser knots provide a lot of support and jointedness. Other knots are tighter, like square knots and surgeon's knots, and provide less support and jointedness.

Without these kinds of support systems, pieces of jewelry become stiff. When jewelry is worn, movement puts a tremendous amount of force on all our parts. There is a lot of stress and strain on our beads, our stringing materials and other adornments. There is a lot of stress on the clasp assembly. There is a lot of stress on our larger components and forms. If everything is too stiff, movement would force these components to crumble, chip, crack or break.

The designer's choices about clasps, materials, string, technique, and design all affect the success or failure of the support systems integral to their pieces of jewelry.

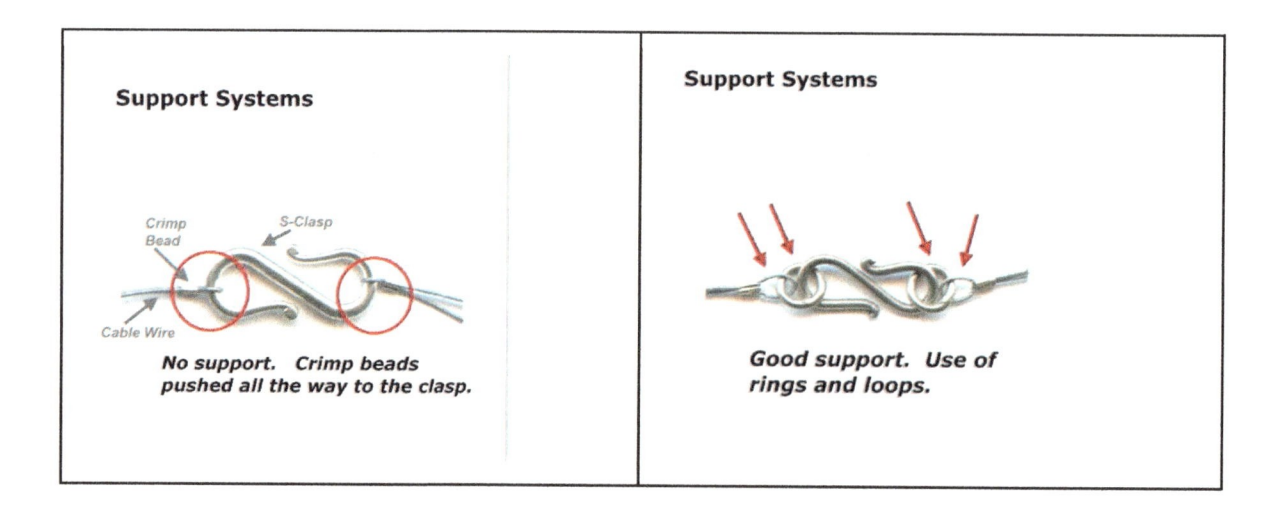

Support Systems

Crimp Bead — S-Clasp
Cable Wire

No support. Crimp beads pushed all the way to the clasp.

Support Systems

Good support. Use of rings and loops.

Often, when people string beads on cable wire, and crimp the ends of the wire to secure the clasp, they ignore concerns about support or jointedness. If the designer pushed the crimp all the way up to the clasp, the connection between crimped wire and clasp would be too stiff. It would not allow movement. It could not absorb any forces placed on the piece, such as from moving, pulling, tugging, getting caught on something, and the like.

When the connection between wire and clasp is too stiff, the metal pieces will bend back and forth, eventually breaking. In this case, the crimp bead is metal, the cable wire is metal and the clasp is metal. When someone wears a necklace or bracelet where no joint or support is created at the clasp, a couple of things might happen. The necklace or bracelet will start to pull on itself, and as the person moves, and necklace or bracelet moves, and the clasp slides up to the front. The turning around of the necklace or bracelet is that piece's response for alleviating the forces of stress. If, for some reason, the necklace or bracelet cannot turn around, then all these metal parts will bend back and forth and break.

The better designer, one more familiar with architectural considerations, will avoid these kinds of design flaws which result from leaving an inadequate amount of support or jointedness within the piece. Leaving an adequately sized loop on the cable, as it attaches to the clasp, thus *never* pushing the crimp all the way up to the clasp, allows for movement and support.

When there is sufficient support, in our necklace example, the clasp will always rest securely on the back of the neck, no matter if the wearer is sitting, dancing, or bending forward to pick something up. It will not turn around. It will not break.

Support Systems
Most jewelry findings will need an additional intervening ring

Eyelet on barrel clasp not strong enough to withstand forces of movement

Intervening Ring

Eyelet

without additional support provided by extra ring.

You will find that most clasps, and most jewelry findings, will need an extra intervening ring – either a jump ring, split ring or soldered ring, in order to have sufficient support and jointedness.

There are 4 key types of support systems:

Type of support	Type of movement allowed	Example
Loop	Allows multi-directional movement	Ring, Loop, Chain links, Netting
Pin	Allows uni-directional movement	Hinge, rivet
Roller	Allows rotational movement	Knot, Stringing material which can twist, Small spacer beads between larger beads
Rigid	Movement occurs through bending or absorbing additional stress and strain	Soldered joint, glued section, coil, spring

STRUCTURAL SYSTEMS

As designers, we always want to think about our piece of jewelry, its construction and execution in terms of what might happen when:

- **Pulling** left and right, or, up and down (*horizontal movement*)

- **Bearing weight** (*vertical movement*)

- **Balancing** (*from side to side or section to section*)

- **Twisting** (*rotational movement*)

These structures are described in reference to how external forces operate on them. The labels of *horizontal, vertical* and *rotational* do *not* refer to the placement or positioning of these structures, per se. They refer to the direction forces any structure must respond to. The structures we build into our jewelry help us manage shapes and their integrity as the piece of jewelry is worn. They help us achieve that sweet-spot among the four S's: strength, suppleness, stability and synergy.

Visualize these as if they were pieces of jewelry, like necklaces...

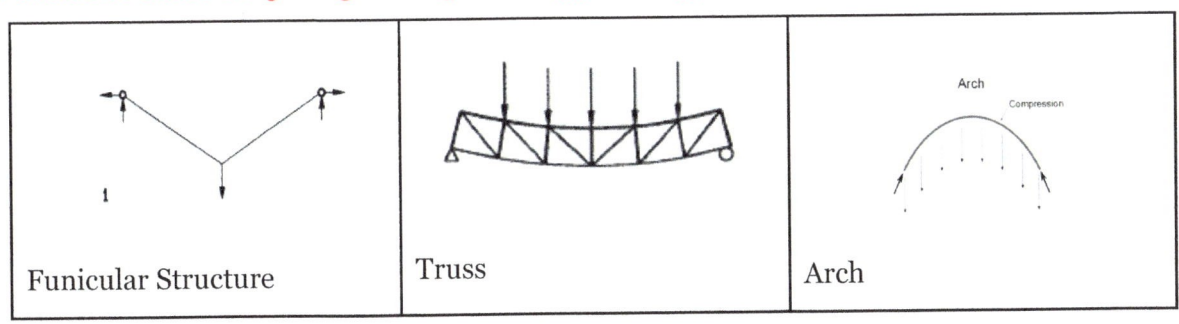

Funicular Structure	Truss	Arch

Horizontal structures assist us in managing the effects of horizontal movement, such as pulling, tugging, stretching. Horizontal structures are the most common ones we build into jewelry. Think of *spans*, and the things we hang off of spans, which, in turn, put stress on the places where each end of the span is attached. These include arches and trusses, funicular structures, and nets or webs. Horizontal structures can more easily deflect and deform their shapes in response to adverse forces pulling and tugging on them.

They may require adjustments in lengths to achieve better stability. Better stability might require inward sloping, thus shorter lines, as things get connected closer to the neck, and elongated outer boundaries. Well-designed Funicular and other horizontal structures will distribute the weight and channel the stresses placed on the piece in an equitable way. They will alleviate dead space, drooping, and unsatisfying drape and flow. Horizontal structures designed for strength will allow for more dimensionality, and allow the piece to include arches and puffed out components (vaults).

The success of horizontal systems is very dependent on the length of their **span**. Their ability to adapt to the adverse effects of mechanical forces may decrease (or increase) with their increasing length. As the length shortens, it becomes more important how well these structures can bend. As the length increases, it becomes more important how well these structures can deflect these forces.

Visualize these as if they were constructed components or foundational bases, such as out of metal or wire or beadwork

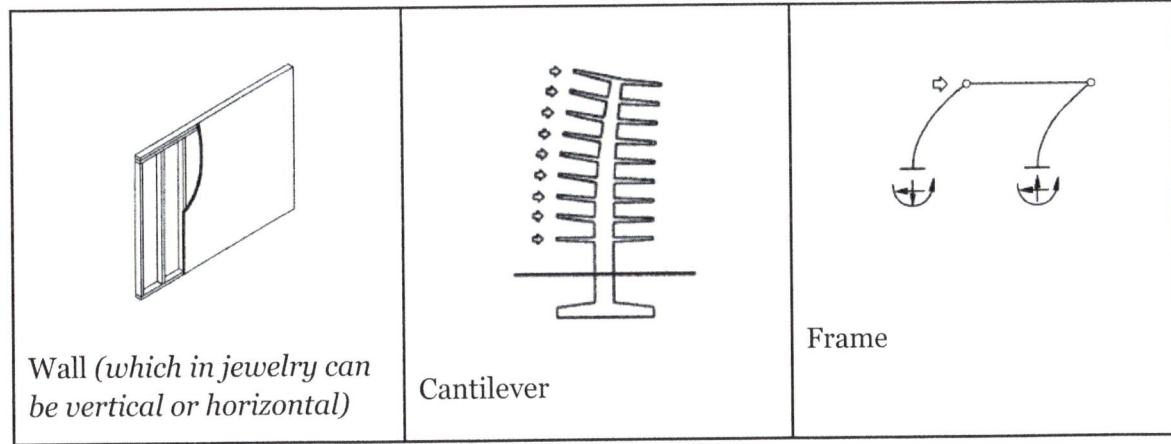

Wall (which in jewelry can be vertical or horizontal)	Cantilever	Frame

Vertical structures assist us in managing the effects of vertical movement, such as bearing weight or resisting bending. They hold things up and are used to build and secure shapes. These include things like walls, cantilevers and frames. They may be foundational bases for compositions. They may be a set of wires bounded together to secure them and leverage their properties in the finished piece. They may be bails or connectors for drops or charms. They may be columns. Most vertical structures are characterized by a certain amount of inflexibility, but will vary somewhat in flexibility by type or dimension (width, length, height). With vertical structures, we sometimes worry about shift or drift or bending out of shape.

Vertical structures, like **Walls**, are things which allow jewelry or jewelry components to find a satisfying point of stability between the effects of gravity and the effects of their own weight (loads).

Roma, a cubic right-angle weave necklace by Sabine Lippert (http://www.trytobead.com/en/Patterns-and-Kits/Necklaces/Roma-Pattern.html), *is composed of square-shaped vertical units of cubic right-angle weave*

This point of stability must hold when the jewelry is static (no movement when worn) as well as when it is dynamic (thus, movement when worn).

A ***Cantilever*** looks and functions like a tree with branches. This vertical structure allows for a lot of bending. You might visualize a necklace with a lot of charms or pendant drops cantilevered off a strap.

The Moment Frame is an additional type of vertical structure which allows for some temporary give and take. The Moment Frame might involve the addition of several support systems, like loops, rings or rivets, and may allow some bending and compression without deformity of the piece.

A Braced Frame involves the placement of some kind of diagonal element across a section of the piece, thus bracing two sides at that section. This functions similar to Trusses, and allows for bending and compression without deformity of the piece.

Last, ***Rotational structures*** assist us in managing the effects of rotational movement, such as twisting, rotating, slipping over or under, or curling. They enable these structures to deform without breaking. Rotational structures can be either horizontal or vertical. What is key is how they are attached. The Moment Frame is a good example. The points of connection are allowed to rotate, temporarily adjusting or bending in shape in response to outside forces, but then rotating back in place.

EVERY JEWELRY MAKING TECHNIQUE IS A TYPE OF *DESIGN SYSTEM*

Jewelry designers apply many different approaches to the creation of jewelry. They may string. They may bead weave. They may wire work. They may silversmith. They may work with fibers or glass or other unusual materials to create components and appealing arrangements for people to wear as jewelry.

Every technique has, at its heart, specifically, the ways it should be best implemented. That is the things which allow it to give jewelry **support**, and things which allow it to give jewelry **structure**.

Some techniques have a good balance between steps or strategies which support movement, drape and flow, with steps or strategies which structure shape and the maintenance of its integrity. I would label these more *advanced* or *evolved* techniques. Other techniques are sometimes stronger in one side of the equation, say support, and weaker on the other side, which would be structure, or vice versa. I would label these more *primitive* techniques.

Every technique or ***design system*** is an applied process with the end goal of trying to reach some type of ***equilibrium***. Each piece of jewelry is the designer's effort at figuring out, given the materials, techniques and technologies at hand, how to balance off all the external forces and internal stresses impacting the piece, all the while striving for the highest level of appeal that can be attained.

Achieving this balance means that the finished and successful piece of jewelry is at its ***point of least vulnerability***. This is where the materials, techniques and technologies have been leveraged to best concurrently optimize all of our four S's: **Strength, Suppleness, Stability** and **Synergy**.

Achieving this balance or equilibrium is partly a function of the materials chosen, and technologies applied, but mostly a function of how the designer selects techniques, makes choices about their implementation, and manages support and structure. Every technique will have some steps which require stronger, heavier, firmer, tighter, harder efforts, and some steps which require looser, lighter, weaker, softer efforts. Where the particular steps of the technique are supposed to lend more support, usually the designer will lighten up, and where the particular steps are supposed to lead to greater structural integrity, the designer will tighten up.

I find that most jewelry designers do not learn their techniques with architectural principles in mind. They arrange a set of materials into a composition, and assume its success is solely based on the visual grammar they applied. But if the piece of jewelry doesn't wear well, feels uncomfortable, gets in a weird position making the wearer look clownish, or breaks or comes apart too easily, the jewelry designer has failed in their mission.

I also find most jewelry designers apply their techniques with the same amount of strength, tightness, tension, sizing and proportion throughout, rather than learn to vary, manage and control these over the course of creating the piece. This suggests they are unaware of how the techniques they apply result in more or less support, and more or less structural integrity.

Let's explore some bead weaving examples. Bead weaving encapsulates and easily shows how all these support and structural issues come into play.

The Tuxedo Park Bangle Bracelet

Tuxedo Park Bangle Bracelet, Warren Feld 2014

The Tuxedo Park Bangle Bracelet is bead woven using a technique called *brick stitch*. The brick stitch is a very robust bead weaving stitch, in that it allows for a lot of support while at the same time allows for good structure. To phrase this another way, the brick stitch allows the piece to keep its shape and integrity, yet respond to all the forces and stress of movement. The thread pathway of this stitch allows each individual bead to self-adjust in response to stress, while concurrently influencing all the beads around it in how they individually adjust to this same stress.

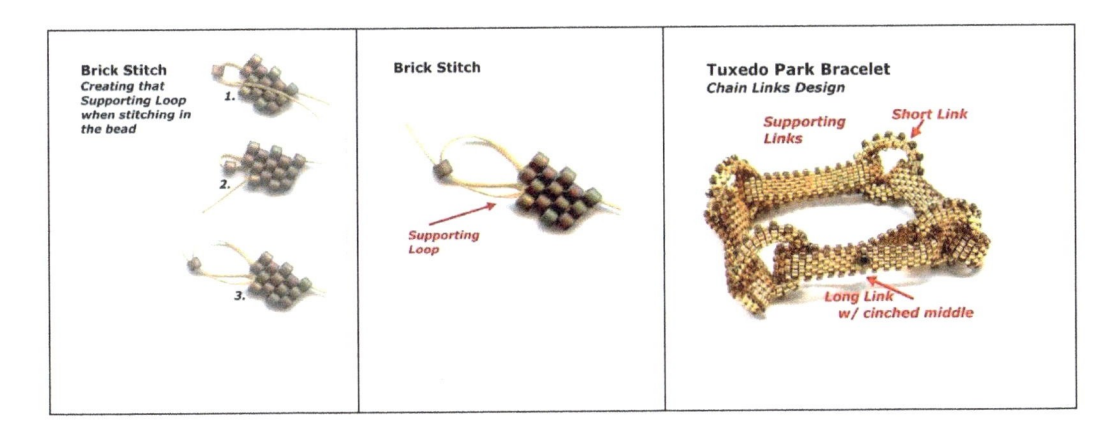

There are two major support systems in this bracelet.

The first support system is the thread path design system of the brick stitch itself. The brick stitch attaches the new bead to the previous row by snagging a thread loop between two beads. This looping not only ties all the beads together within our composition, but also, allows each bead and each row to bend in response to the forces of movement and then bend back into its original position. And, importantly, it allows this flexing all the while maintaining the solidity and shape of our component.

The thread-looping pattern of the stitch also allows us to manipulate the flat beadwork into a curve. It allows us to slide and stretch the bangle over our hand and also return to its original shape as it sits on the wrist.

It is important, while weaving the brick stitch, to maintain the integrity of the support systems, that is, of each thread-looping-over-thread intersection as best as can be. Anything done which disrupts this looping, will begin to stiffen the joints, so to speak. So, if our needle pierces an existing thread as we create the next loop-connection, this will begin to impede the support, or in a sense, those "swinging" properties of the looping. If we tie off the thread into a knot, such as when we end an old thread and begin a new one, this too will impede support. If we glue any knot, this will end all the support properties at that point in the piece.

The second major support system is in the design of the Tuxedo Park Bangle Bracelet itself. We are creating a chain of links. These links or "rings" provide support. That is, they allow the bangle to easily curve around the wrist and to freely move when worn.

In our long link, we have cinched and sewn down the middle of the link. This begins to disrupt that support in our chain-link. So, we have to be comfortable with the *size*, thus support, of our now bi-furcated two new ring openings on either side of this cinched long link. If these new openings are too small, one ring would lock into place with the preceding one, making the piece stiff, and thus, uncomfortable to wear, and perhaps putting too much pressure on the parts.

Russian Right Angle Weave Necklace

Russian Right Necklace
Right Angle Weave Technique

Russian Right Necklace, Warren Feld, 2008

It is important to understand each technique you use, whether a bead stringing technique, or wire working technique, or bead weaving stitch, or silversmithing technique, in terms of how it might enhance or impede support or structure. How might it allow movement. How might it absorb and direct the forces this movement places on our beads, stringing materials and other components within our piece. How it allows the piece to encompass a shape and maintain that shape as worn.

The Russian Right Angle Weave Necklace is an example of another bead weaving stitch which has great architectural properties allowing for both support and structure.

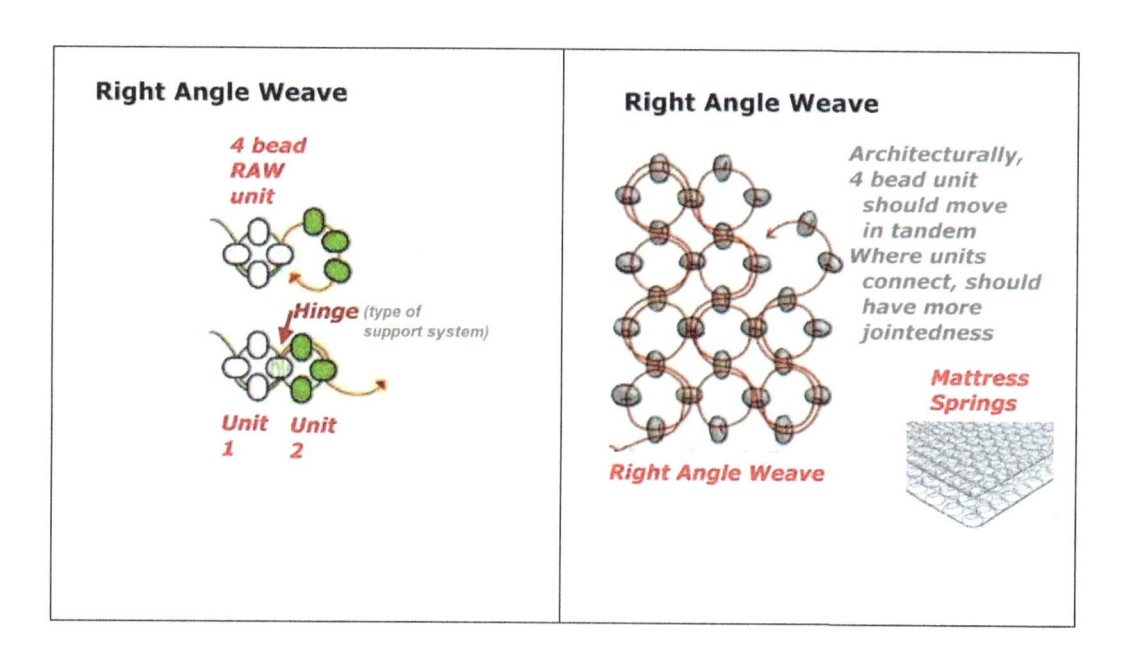

The basic right angle weave stitch begins with a circle of 4 beads. It then moves on to create a second circle of four beads. These two circles are linked with one shared bead, common to both circles, and which acts like a hinge. We want the beads within a RAW unit to be tightly stitched together. We want the connection through a shared bead between any two units to be more loosely connected.

Architecturally, we want each circle of 4 beads – what we call a *right angle weave unit*, to move in tandem, that is, all at the same time. In any piece, there will be many, many interconnected RAW units. We want for each right angle weave unit to be able to influence the movement of all other right angle weave units within the piece, but to also move somewhat independently of all other right angle weave units within our piece. Each unit should move as one. But, at the same time, each unit should be allowed to somewhat self-adjust to stress independently from the other units, but at the same time, affect the interdependency of all units within the piece.

The right angle woven piece should move like a coil spring mattress. Picture someone lying down on this mattress. Each coil adjusts somewhat independently to the pressure of the body part immediately above it. Yet each coil with the mattress also adjusts relative to the movement of the other coils as well. Nothing gets out of line. No matter what the person laying on the mattress does, or how they move around, all the coils adjust to the changes in weight very smoothly and coherently.

This is how right angle weave works, and maintains itself as a support system. To achieve the optimal performance with right angle weave, the designer would want their four beads within a unit to be as tightly connected as possible, so that they always move and respond to forces as a whole unit. The designer would want a looser tension at the place each right angle unit connects to another at the point of their shared bead.

Catenary Arches Bracelet

Bead woven catenary arches span the bracelet over a foundation base	*The foundation base is woven from alternating techniques – peyote for strength and right angle weave for suppleness. These alternating rows attach on either side to ladder stitched strips for stability.*

The catenary arches in the piece have to maintain their shape while worn. This means that they need to respond to vertical forces pushing down on them, as well as horizontal and rotation forces pulling, tugging and twisting them. After a lot of trial and error, I came up with this solution so that the arches would not squish, or flatten out into an S-

shape, or break, while the piece was worn.

The columns are built from seven 2-drop ladder-stitched segments. Each segment has 3 2-bead stacks (6 beads), woven in a triangle (stack 1 is attached to stack 2; stack 2 is attached to stack 3; stack 3 is attached to stack 1). The beads in each segment are stitched so that the 6 beads will always move as one.

The next segment is stitched to attach to the first, but with a looser attachment. This allows some independent movement and some interdependent movement.

The finished column is attached to supports (2-hole superduo beads) built into the two ladder-stitched strips on either side of the bracelet. This is a rigid support connection which responds well to rotational forces.

Then, a "keystone" bead is wedged between each segment across the column.

VULNERABILTY:
Areas of Potential Instability and Weakness

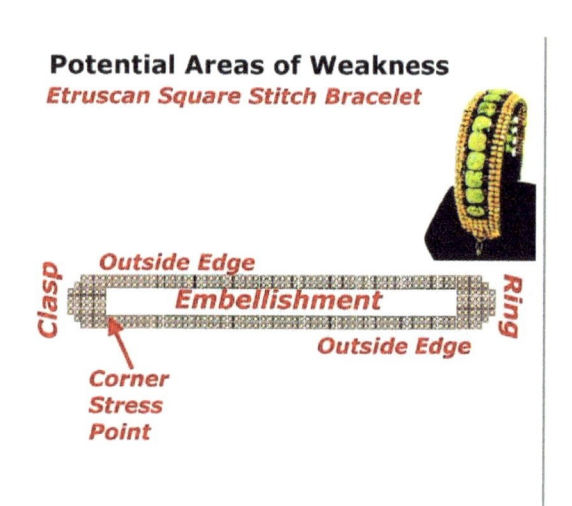

Whenever a project is begun, it is important to carefully anticipate and identify potential areas of instability and weakness. Where might your piece be vulnerable? Where might the forces of movement – horizontal, vertical or rotational, when the piece is worn, cause the stringing material or threads or beads or clasps to loosen up, pull apart, and perhaps break. Or the wire or metal to bend, distort or deform?

Most often, places of vulnerability occur where the structures or supports in place take on the shapes of either **H, L, T**, or **U**. Think of these shapes as **hazards**. These shapes tend to split when confronted with external or internal forces. They tend to split because each leg is often confronted with different levels or directions of force. The legs are not braced. These hazardous shapes cry out for additional reinforcements or support or structural systems.

Vulnerability and instability will also occur where the structures or supports are very thin or very soft or very brittle. They will occur at points where there is a slant or a wedge or an unusual angle.

Potential Areas of Weakness	Potential Areas of Weakness Things You Can Do To Strengthen Areas of Weakness
1. Where clasp attached 2. Outside edges 3. Stress points 4. Where a "shape" might get pulled out of shape or distorted 5. Where beads used have especially sharp holes 6. Any place which has been glued	1. Reinforcement 2. Choice of Stringing Material 3. Adding More Support By Choosing More Functional Clasps and Other Jewelry Findings 4. Building In Additional Architectural Structures

Pieces are vulnerable because the jewelry designer has made poor choices in selecting materials, techniques, or technologies, and in managing design from inspiration to execution. *REMEMBER:* A piece of jewelry results from a Design *System*. This system is a back and forth process of anticipating how others will judge the piece to be finished and successful, how choices are made and implemented regarding materials, techniques, arrangements and technologies in light of these shared understandings coupled with the designer's intent.

If the piece is vulnerable, then the designer has failed to reflect upon what things will make the piece endure. What will be expected of the piece when the person wearing it moves? As the piece moves from a static place, say from in a jewelry box, and then must transition to the body as a person begins to put it on, what are those transitional issues the piece must accommodate? What parts of the piece must always maintain their shape or position? What happens when the piece has to either shrink, elongate or expand? Does the piece need to bend or rotate for any reason? What happens to all the materials and pieces over time?

Reinforcements at points of potential instability and vulnerability can take many forms, such as:

- Anchoring
- Bracing
- Framing
- Attaching/Securing

- Connecting
- Blocking
- Adding in slack or elasticity
- Isolating the area

THE 4 S's:
Strength, Suppleness, Stability and Synergy

Jewelry must be designed, from an architectural standpoint, to find a special point of equilibrium. We call this the *point of least vulnerability*. This equilibrium point is a sweet efficient and effective spot among *Strength*, *Suppleness*, *Stability* and *Synergy*. As our choices force us to deviate from this optimized sweet-spot, our pieces of jewelry become more vulnerable when worn. They are more likely to distort and deform, pull apart, lose tension, and break.

To find this sweet-spot for any particular piece of jewelry, we first assess what shared understandings our various audiences will apply when determining if the piece is finished and successful. A big part of this is figuring out how a piece will be worn, how often a piece will be worn, and how long a duration this piece is expected to hold up. The designer assesses all this, then begins to incorporate personal artistic intent into the design process.

Strength involves choices we make about materials and techniques which prevent breaking. For example, a well-done soldering joint or correctly crimping to secure a clasp to cable wire, would increase the strength. A thicker cord might provide more strength than a thinner cord of the same material.

Suppleness involves choices we make about materials and techniques which maximize elasticity and flexibility. For example, the addition of intervening rings to various jewelry findings would increase suppleness. The use of stringing thread rather than a stringing wire, would increase suppleness.

Stability involves choices we make about materials and techniques which prevent deterioration, malformation or collapse. For example, we might reject coated beads for a project, or might use a multi-strand rather than a single-strand clasp for a multi-strand piece of jewelry. We might add extra reinforcement to the ends and the corners of pieces. We might wax our stringing materials to place a barrier between environmental and body chemicals which might affect them.

Synergy involves choices we make about materials, techniques, and technologies which not only reinforce our design, but also increase, enhance or extend the design's appeal and functionality. For example, a tight clustering of beads into an attractive pendant drop might be many times stronger, more supple, more stable and/or more appealing than any one bead alone.

**BEAD STRINGING:
THE FIRST AND PRIMARY
CONSIDERATION ABOUT
MINIMIZING STRESSES AND
STRAINS, and
ANTICIPATING ONE TYPE OF POINT
OF VULNERABILITY:** *THE
INTERPLAY OF THE SHARP HOLE
OF A BEAD AND THE CANVAS
(Stringing Material)*.

Dealing With Sharp Bead Holes
The hole of a bead is like a broken soda bottle. If I smashed a soda bottle on the side of a table, the hole of a bead would look very similar to the resulting jagged ring.
So, one of the first architecturally strategic things you need to do is to figure out ways to minimize the movement of the bead so that the jagged hole will not shred the stringing material, particularly if that material is thread, cable thread, or bead cord.
You need to anticipate two types of movement:
1) the movement *up and down* along the stringing material
2) the movement of the bead *rotating* around the stringing material
Some strategies:
  a. Minimize slack along the length of the project
  b. Take your stringing material through the holes of the beads more than once. You may want to fill the hole of the bead. Multiple strands through the hole will create their own tension and friction, minimizing rotation.
  c. Tie knots in your stringing material, and bring these tightly to the hole on either side of the bead.

Should I double my thread?
When you double your thread, it becomes difficult to maintain the thread tension on both legs. Often, one leg will not be as tight as the other, leaving slack through the length of your piece. Slack works against your architectural goals here.
To bring two cords through, I would bring one at a time. For some projects, this means going around the "circle" twice. For other projects, it means bringing one cord through, and pull tight, then following with the second cord through, pulling tight, going bead by bead, until you have worked your way all the way around.

PHYSICAL MECHANICS:
Statics and Dynamics

Mechanics represents the behaviors of the jewelry when subjected to the forces which arise when wearing a piece. These forces include movement. They include pulling, tugging, bending, stretching, realigning, readjusting, bearing weight, carrying weight, securing weight, brushing against, rubbing against, curving and taking the shape of the body, loose- to just-right- to tight-fit, positioning, repositioning, and the like.

Statics are descriptions of jewelry behaviors when that piece of jewelry is on the body, but at rest.

Dynamics are descriptions of jewelry behaviors when that piece of jewelry is on the body, and the body is in motion.

Forces are external to the piece of jewelry.

Stresses are internal to the piece of jewelry.

Strains result from the deformation of the jewelry, as it responds to either external forces or internal stresses.

As jewelry designers, we want to understand jewelry mechanical behaviors in terms of our 4 S's. We do not need to go into any of the math here. We primarily need to be aware of the kinds of things we need to think about, manage and control. Some of these things will be *forces* external to the materials and construction of our piece of jewelry. Other things will be internal *stresses* within our piece of jewelry. Our jewelry will *strain* to respond to either forces or stresses or both, until it can strain no more and it loses its shape, bends, dents, squishes, breaks or otherwise becomes unwearable.

We want to anticipate jewelry mechanical behaviors at the points of (a) maintaining shape *(strength)*, (b) maintaining comfort *(suppleness)*, (c) maintaining position or placement *(stability)*, and (d) right at that point where all the materials, techniques, and technologies are leveraged and optimized to their full effect *(synergy)*.

TYPES OF FORCES

FORCE TYPE	ACTION	RESULTS FROM
Tension	Elongates	Strain on parts
Compression	Shortens	Weight and Pressure
Shear	Sliding Force (things shift out of place, or finishes flake off)	Resistance to sliding of adjacent parts or defects in materials
Bending	Elongates one side, shortens the other	Unevenly applied weight and pressure
Torsion	Twists	A turning ofrce applied at some angle

Think about what the flow of forces through the piece of jewelry would be as worn in different situations. The wearer could be sitting, perhaps writing at a desk. The wearer might be walking, running, dancing, skipping, crouching, bending over, bending backwards. With mechanics, again, we want to think about our piece of jewelry, its construction and execution in terms of what might happen when:

- **Pulling** left and right, up or down (horizontal movement)
- **Bearing weight** (vertical movement)
- **Balancing** (from side to side or section to section), or
- **Twisting** (rotation)

What about our choices of materials, techniques or technology leads us to design jewelry which mechanically achieves these points of equilibrium of forces? What about the structures we use and the support systems we build in allows us (or prevents us) from achieving this point of force/stress equilibrium or least vulnerability?

DESIGNING IN ANTICIPATION OF THE EFFECTS OF PHYSICAL MECHANICAL FORCES

The fluent jewelry designer can think about art and about architecture and context. He or she can be able to anticipate the types of issues that arise, and the types of solutions that might be available. And he or she can evaluate and reflect upon the choices and successes or failures.

Jewelry takes quite a beating when worn. We want it to hold up. We don't want it to break. We don't want it to stretch out or distort or deform. We don't want the materials we use to fail, such as the finishes fading or rubbing off, the material cracking, or the material becoming too brittle or too soft relative to how it should function in the piece. We do not want the individual components to shift positions, or inadvertently glom on top of each other. We want the jewelry to make the person wearing look good, feel good, and get that sense of connectedness they seek when wearing a piece of jewelry.

> **WHAT IS HAPPENING TO YOUR BRACELET OR NECKLACE WHILE YOU ARE WEARING IT?**
>
> - The two ends, each attached to one side of the clasp, are moving and responding to stresses differently, with different countervailing forces. Picture grabbing one end of your piece with one hand, and the other end with the other hand, with both ends still attached to the clasp, and then pulling the two sides apart.
>
> - Some parts of your piece are more firmly secured in place than others on your stringing material or other canvas. The rub against clothing, perhaps a desk top. Each part is more or less vulnerable to pulling out or pushing in or coming off.
>
> - You have corner within your piece which approximates a right angle (an L-shape). The thread or wire securing this angle begins to pull apart or bend inappropriately.
>
> - Your stringing material stretches. What should have been hidden begins to peak out.
>
> - You have a pendant attached to the center of your necklace. It's bail isn't level and the pendant is especially heavy. Instead of a nice V-shape to the silhouette, the silhouette is off-balance and unflattering.
>
> - The pendant turns around and faces backwards
>
> - The beads are weighty, the stringing material is thin, and the beads clump up, distorting the natural circle of the piece
>
> - Hard wire components bend out of shape
>
> - The beads bounce up and down and chip, shatter and break
>
> - The jewelry gets wet and the color bleeds out of the beads and into the clothing fabric
>
> - The jewelry gets caught on something

The architecturally-sensitive designer will design for strength, suppleness, stability and synergy. The forces and stresses affecting these can be very complex. They might depend upon or vary based on physical dimensions (width, length, height and depth). They might depend upon or vary based on environmental considerations, such as cosmetics, perfumes, body oils, pollution in the air, or certain chemicals in someone's sweat. And of course they are dependent and may vary based on anything that causes movement or prevents movement, such as the movement of the wearer, the wind, getting something caught on something, brushing against something, twisting, bending, shaking, and the like.

Jewelry is both art and architecture, and must be thought about and implemented as such.

It is always important to remember to think about any technique applied as a *design system*.

This design system will include the characteristics of the materials used, the strategy for implementing the technique, the technology incorporated into the process, support and structure, and finding equilibrium – that point of least vulnerability -- among the 4 S's.

The design system is a process that is to be managed and controlled by the jewelry designer, in line with assessments about shared understandings and artist intent.

It is always important to visually and functionally specify how the design incorporates support.

It is always important to visually and functionally specify how the design incorporates structure.

And it is always important to remember we want to achieve a point of equilibrium -- that point of least vulnerability -- among the four S's: Strength, Suppleness, Stability and Synergy.

...if one is to be fluent and proficient in design!

ARCHITECTURAL ANALYSIS FOR JEWELRY DESIGN

When you are beginning your jewelry design process, and trying to visualize your piece from an architectural standpoint, you want to take into account five separate architectural components. Some aspects of these architectural components will be constant; others, variable. All, however, will need to be selected, arranged, managed and manipulated.

These five architectural components are,

 (1) *Shape*
 (2) *Size*
 (3) *Location within the piece*
 (4) *Orientation on the body*
 (5) *Treatment*

Shape. What are the various squares, tubes, rectangles, circles, ovals, ellipses, curves, cubes, spirals, triangles, solids that you want to use within your piece, or for your piece as a whole? Shapes are *design elements*, and follow rules for *selection* and *decoding*.

When we come to focus on the outer contours of a plane – something made up of lines, which in turn are made up of points -- we begin to recognize this design element as something we call a *shape*.

Shapes are areas in 2- or 3-dimensions which have defined or implied boundaries. They are somehow separated from the space surrounding them. Shapes may be delineated, bounded, framed, dissected, over-arched, tunneled-under by lines. They may be filled or emptied. They may be formed by differences in color, color values and intensities. They may be formed by patterns and textures. They suggest both mass and volume.

Shapes may be organic or mechanical. They may relate to the background, foreground or middle ground. They may be geometrical (regular, predictable contours) or organic, distorted or overlapping, blended or distinct or abstract.

Shapes may be interrelated by angle, sometimes forcing a sense of movement and rotation.

More than one shape in a particular space may make one shape appear more active or more important or more prominent. This may change the perception of what that shape is about, particularly when shapes overlap. Secondary shapes may seem more point-like or line-like in relation to the primary shape.

Size. What is the scale or relative sizes of our shapes?

When you are designing a piece of jewelry, size plays an important role in making a layout functional, attractive and organized.

Think about how the piece will ultimately be used, and whether size will affect its appeal, its functionality and how it is to be worn.

A second factor is appeal. You want the piece to attract the wearer or buyer. You also want the piece to attract others who view the piece as it is worn. Towards this end, you can contrast large and small elements or make something larger in an interesting way.

A third factor is using size to organize your piece. Again, you want to attract a viewer's attention. Typically we make the largest element the most important, and the smallest element the least important. Larger elements appear to be closer, and can be used to create some spatial/dimensional effects, as well.

Sizes are attributes of *design elements*.

Location. Shapes of various sizes must be placed and distributed within your piece to achieve concurrent and optimum appeal goals and functional requirements. Location has a lot to do with rules for *composition*.

They may be located at the edge, along the side, or at the center. They may be located on the surface or as part of a foundation or base. They may be hidden, supplemental or featured. They may be used to give a sense of receding or projecting forward.

Careful consideration is placed on the relation of the canvas to all the other components of the piece.

Remember the 4 S's: *Strength, Suppleness, Stability and Synergy*. Whatever materials you are using and techniques you are applying, always consider and evaluate where you are going to locate your structural elements and your support elements to maximize the 4 S's?

Orientation. What are the desired silhouette, directionality, movement, drape and flow of the piece? Where are the forces (internal and external) coming from which will be affecting the piece?

Orientation, too, has a lot to do with rules for *composition*.

Jewelry gives the wearer and viewer a sense of what is up and down, and right and left. It has direction. Sometimes it redirects.

Parts of the jewelry are exposed, and parts are not.

The silhouette forms a boundary on the body. Does the boundary have a clear purpose and effect? Does it emphasize the vertical or horizontal or diagonal. Is it symmetrical or asymmetrical? How much of the body is covered, and how much is exposed?

How do shape, size and location assist in orientation? Detract from it? Give the piece a sense of depth, length, width and height?

How much do you have to anticipate vertical and horizontal pressures pushing on the piece? How much do you have to anticipate up-and-down and left-and-right forces pulling on the piece? How should all this affect your choices about orientation?

Treatment. In what ways can you manipulate these sizes, shapes, locations and orientation(s)? Treatment involves rules for *manipulation*.

Treatment involves selection of materials and how their physical, sensorial and sensual properties are leveraged within your piece. This involves focusing on texture, pattern, color, opacity, reflectivity and the like.

Treatment also involves the selection, implementation and application of techniques to achieve optimum parsimony and resonance.

Treatment involves the management of relationships between space and mass, point / line / plane, and positive and negatives spaces.

Careful anticipation and attention are applied to the affects of natural and artificial lighting and shadows. This extends to relating lights to darks (contrasts), visual density, values, intensities, thinness or thickness.

Here, again, we pay careful attention to our 4 S's, with details and joints, structure and support. We clearly anticipate all issues and potential solutions resulting from the interplay of physical mechanics with our designs as the jewelry will be worn.

Five Types of Spaces To Manage

Each of the five architectural components may relate and be applied differently, given the particular space we are trying to fill with mass within our composition.

a. ***Major Space***: Any part of the piece of jewelry which portrays a sense of definite location or positioning within the piece. There might be a definable centerpiece or focal point. There might be distinct bail. There might be an area representing a larger size or a more powerful color.

b. ***Path Space***: Any part of the piece of jewelry which is directional.

c. ***Servant Space***: Any part of the piece of jewelry which acts primarily as a joint (any support element like a ring or loop or knot) or fastener (such as a clasp) or shape-maintainer (such as reinforcement).

d. ***Transition Space***: Any part of the piece of jewelry which serves as an articulation between or gradation into two dissimilar elements. This defines a separation, a join, a link, or a pause. Transition spaces from each segment of our piece to the next (*see Anatomy of a Necklace chapter*), such as Yoke to Break to Frame, must be critically examined. May involve elements of contrast or continuity.

e. ***Contingent Space***: Any part of the piece which anticipates either the curves and shapes of the body, or any contextual or situational requirements. Are there things which make the piece adjustable, such as a choker chain, or stringing on elastic, or a lengthy necklace which can be doubled-up to chain the silhouette? Does the piece look and feel like it would fit and be appropriate, given the context or situation in which it will be worn?

FOOTNOTES

G.G.Schierle, Architectural Structures, 1990-2006, As referenced in:
https://disegnodiezunibe.files.wordpress.com/2011/07/architectural-structures.pdf

Neiman, B. Architectural Analysis, College of Architecture, Texas Tech University, 9/2/2005.
As referenced in:
http://www.arch.ttu.edu/people/faculty/Neiman_B/reading05/2005_09_02_architectural_analysis.pdf

RULES OF COMPOSITION, CONSTRUCTION, AND MANIPULATION
5g. ARCHITECTURAL BASICS OF JEWELRY DESIGN: Anatomy of a Necklace

Guiding Questions:
(1) What are the structural parts of a necklace?
(2) To what extent are these parts a vital part of experiencing and appreciating the necklace as a whole?
(3) What are the design challenges each anatomic necklace parts present?

Key Words:	clasp assembly	embellishment
strap	frame	types of spaces
yoke	focal point / centerpiece	supplemental / integral
break	/pendant	
clasp assembly	bail	
break	canvas	

Abstract:
A necklace, or any type of jewelry, has a structure and an anatomy. Each part has its own set of purposes, functions and aesthetics. Understanding each type of structure or physical part is important to the designer.

ANATOMY OF A NECKLACE

BezelWorks Pendant, Bail, Strap, Warren Feld, 2012

A necklace, or any type of jewelry, has a structure and an anatomy. Each part has its own set of purposes, functions and aesthetics. Understanding each type of structure or physical part is important to the designer.

If we looked at these sections of a necklace from solely an *Art* standpoint, we might primarily focus on the centerpiece of the jewelry and consider The Strap (and most other parts) as supplemental and less important to the piece, in a similar relationship as the frame to a painting or the pedestal to a sculpture.

However, jewelry is a 3-dimensional object serving both aesthetic as well as functional purposes. As such, we need to be more sensitive to the entire jewelry-anatomy and both its Art *and* Architectural reason for being. Each part is integral to understanding jewelry as a singular design. This kind of thinking is at the core of what makes jewelry design, as a discipline, different than art.

Typical structural parts of a necklace might include,

The Strap: *The entire linear component of the piece, comprising Yoke, Clasp Assembly, and Frame*

The Yoke: *The part of The Strap behind the neck, typically 6-7" including clasp assembly*

The Clasp Assembly: *Part of The Yoke, and includes, not only the clasp itself, but rather all the pieces it takes to attach your Strap to the Clasp, including clasp, rings, loops or knots or crimps or chain at ends of stringing material*

The Frame: *The visually accessible part of The Strap, connecting to The Yoke at The Break point. On a 16" necklace, The Frame might be 9-10"*

The Break: *The point where The Yoke connects to The Frame, often at the collar bone on either side of the neck. Very often, this point is one of a critical change in vector – that means, the angle The Frame lays radically changes from the angle of The Yoke. Think of this as an inflection point.*

The Bail: *A separate part which drops the centerpiece or pendant drop below the line of the Frame*

The Focal Point, Centerpiece, or Pendant Drop: *A part which emphasizes or focuses the eye, usually dropped below the line of The Frame, but is sometimes a separate treatment of The Frame itself*

The Canvas: *Typically the stringing material or foundation of the piece*

The Embellishment: *Things added to the surface or edge of The Canvas, The Strap, or the Centerpiece which serve as decorative, rather than structural or supportive roles*

YOKE CLASP ASSEMBLY YOKE

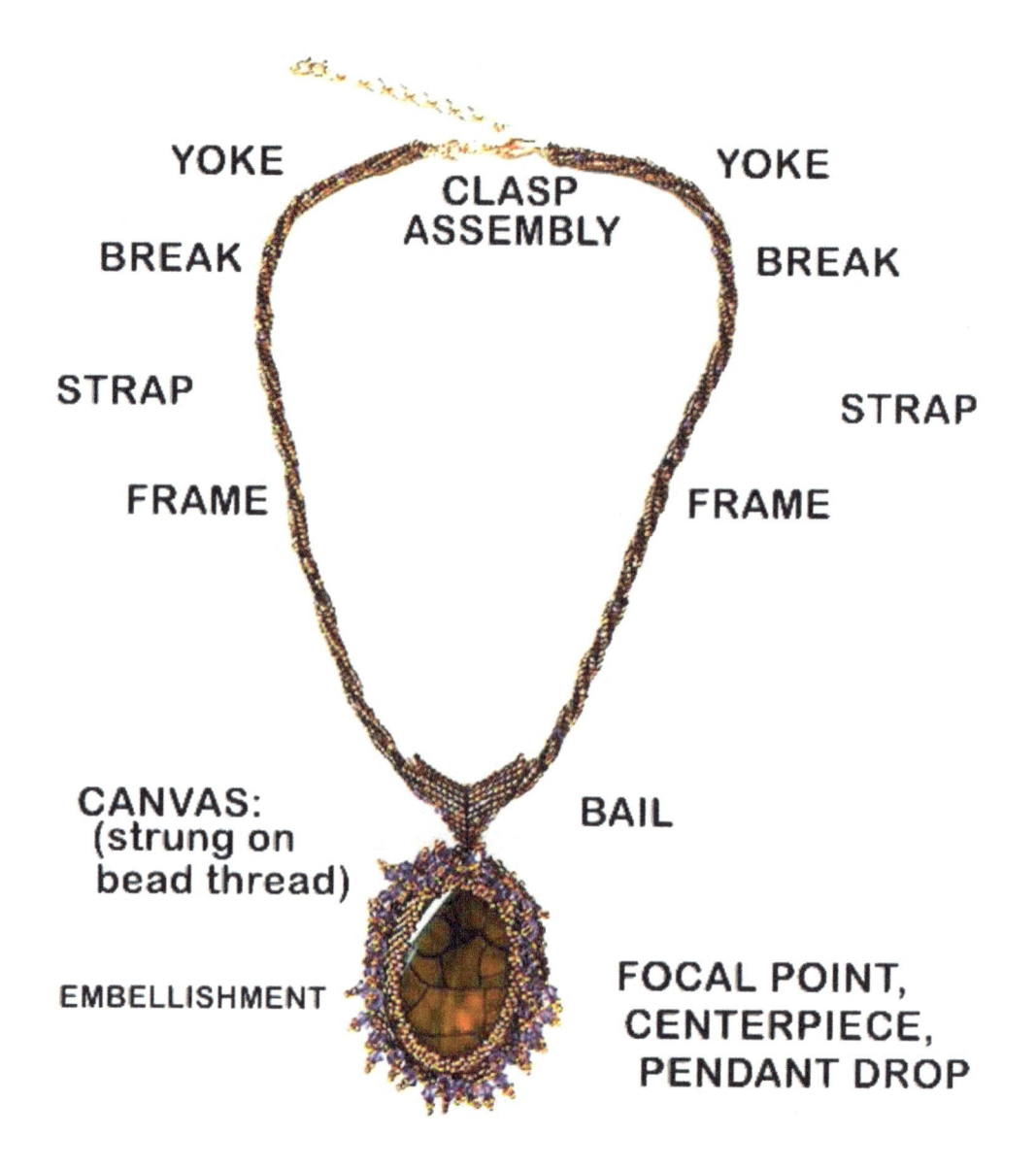

BREAK BREAK

STRAP STRAP

FRAME FRAME

CANVAS: (strung on bead thread) BAIL

EMBELLISHMENT FOCAL POINT, CENTERPIECE, PENDANT DROP

Each part of the body of a necklace poses its own special design challenges for the jewelry artist. These involve strategies for resolving such issues as:

- Making connections
- Determining angularity, curvature, and roundedness
- Transitioning color, pattern and texture
- Placing objects
- Extending lengths
- Adding extensions
- Creating balance and coherency

- Anticipating issues about compression, stretching, bending, load-bearing, and distortion
- Anticipating issues related to physical mechanics, both when the piece is static (not moving when worn) and dynamic (moving when worn)
- Keeping things organic, so nothing looks like an afterthought, or an outlier, or out of place, or something designed by a committee
- Determining which parts are critical to understanding the piece of jewelry as art as it is worn, and which parts are merely supplemental to the piece

The Strap

The Strap is that continuous line that extends from one end of the clasp to the other. The Strap may or may not consist of the exposed Canvas. The Strap typically delineates a silhouette or boundary. This usually sends the message to the viewer about where they may comfortably and appropriately place their gaze on the wearer's body.

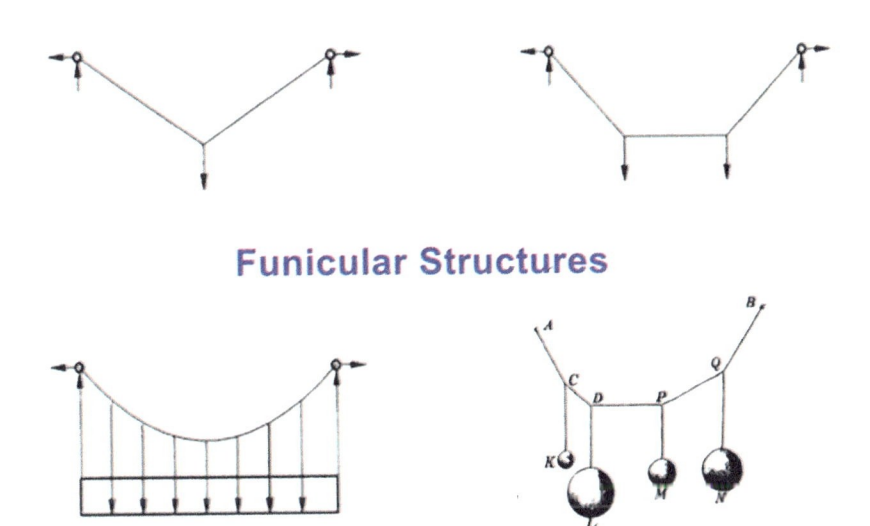

Funicular Structures

The Strap is a type of funicular structure. A funicular structure is one where something like a string or chain or cable is held up at two points, and one or more loads are placed on it. Loads increase tension. Loads lead to compression.

The placement can be centered or off-centered. If more than one object is placed on The Strap, each object can vary in mass, volume and weight. We do not want The Strap to break because of the weight or placement of any load or loads. We do want to control the resulting shape of the silhouette or curvature of The Strap which results from the weight or placement of any load or loads.

The span of The Strap is very sensitive to force and stress. A piece of jewelry may have more than one Strap. In this case, the span of each Strap, and their built in support and structural systems, must be tightly coordinated, if to respond optimally to forces and stresses.

The Yoke

The Yoke is one section of the *Strap* which is the part around the back of the neck, typically including *The Clasp Assembly*. The length of The Yoke, and whether the beginning and end parts of The Yoke should be exposed on the front of the body is something to be determined by the designer. The designer must also determine the proportional size of The Yoke relative to the remaining part of The Strap. The designer must determine what role the elements, such as beads, which comprise The Yoke, will play, and whether they should be an active part of the visual composition, and/or a critical part in the functional success of the piece, or merely supplemental. The Yoke balances the load requirements of the remaining Strap (The Frame), Bail and Pendant.

The Break

At the point The Yoke connects to the remaining Strap (called *The Break* leading to *The Frame*) on either side of the neck, this is a point of vulnerability, often assisted and reduced with the addition of support elements. Because it is at this point – The Break – where The Strap may alter its vector position in a dramatic way – that is, the angular positioning of the Strap at the point of The Break may vary a lot as The Strap continues around the front of the body – this is a major point of vulnerability.

There are always transitional issues at The Break. The designer needs to have strategies for managing these transitions. This might involve using visual cues and doing something with color or pattern/texture or rhythm or sizes. The designer might add support systems, such as rings, at this point. The designer must decide the degree The Frame should be visually distinct from The Yoke.

The Clasp Assembly

The Clasp Assembly is most often part of *The Yoke*. The Clasp Assembly includes, not just the clasp itself, but also all the other parts necessary to attach it to the Strap. There might be some additional soldered rings. There might be loops left at the ends of the stringing material. There might be crimp beads or knots or glue or solder. There might be some chain.

Whenever choosing a clasp, it is more important to think in terms of choosing a clasp assembly. You might want to use a very attractive clasp, but it may take so many parts and turns to attach it to your beadwork, that you end up with a visually ugly clasp assembly.

Occasionally, The Clasp Assembly is part of The Frame. This will present a different set of architectural issues and considerations.

The Frame

The Frame is that part of *The Strap* which connects to either side of *The Yoke* at *The Break*.

Too often, when the designer does not recognize the Yoke as distinct from The Frame – even if the transition is to be very subtle – less-than-satisfying things happen. Proportions may be off. The piece may not lay or sit as envisioned. The Strap may have too much embellishment going too high up The Strap. Sometimes the balance between Yoke and Frame is off – too much Yoke and not enough Frame. The change in vector angles between The Yoke and The Frame may pose many architectural issues for the designer.

Bi-Furcated Frame: A Frame visually split in half, usually at the center and in two equal parts, with a centerpiece focal bead or pendant drop in the middle. Here the designer needs to think whether the two lengths should move in a coordinated fashion, or not.

The Focal Point, Centerpiece or Pendant Drop

While not every necklace has a focal point, centerpiece or pendant drop, most do. The Focal Point gives the viewer's eye a place to rest or focus. Usually this is done with a Centerpiece or Pendant Drop.

Othertimes, The Focal Point is more integrated with The Strap. This might be created by graduating the sizes or beads or playing with color or playing with rhythm or playing with fringe.

A Centerpiece would be a part that extends beyond the line of The Frame, usually below it, around it, or in front of it. This forces transitional concerns between it and The Frame.

There should be a natural visual as well as functional transition from The Strap to The Focal Point, Centerpiece or Pendant Drop.

The Bail

The Bail is a part that drops the Centerpiece below the Frame, forcing additional transitional visual and functional concerns among Centerpiece, Bail and Frame. We are concerned about its impact on emphasis, harmony, balance, distribution of size and proportion, point, line, plane and shape. We are concerned about its ability to maintain stability, given the effects of gravity, the weight of the drop, and its relationship with and fit to The Frame of The Strap. Most Bails would be considered ***vertical structures***.

The Canvas

The Canvas typically refers to the stringing materials. However, in a layered piece, may refer to any created "background or foundation" off of which or around which the main composition is built. The Canvas might be either a horizontal structure (like an arch or truss) or a vertical structure (like a wall or frame). It might be exposed, partially covered, or fully covered. It might change materials or construction systems along its length, such as transitioning from a cable wire to a chain.

It is important to know what The Canvas is made of, and how its function and appeal might improve or weaken as its **Span** is lengthened or shortened, widened or narrowed, over time. The steepness of its slope or positioning might also affect its integrity.

Sometimes more than one Canvas are interconnected. You can picture a necklace with additional strands crossing the chest from one side of The Strap to the other. You might also have a necklace where strands radiate out at angles from the neck and across the chest.

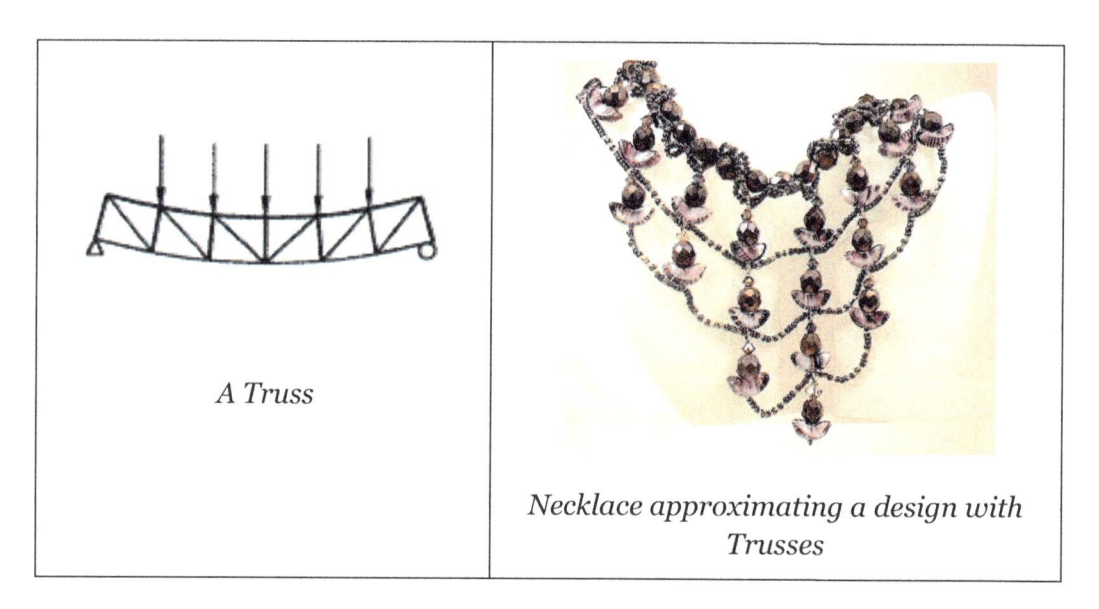

A Truss

Necklace approximating a design with Trusses

Architecturally, additional Canvases which span from one side to the other of a piece of jewelry operate like **Trusses, Arches or Support Beams.** These types of structures are referred to as **Horizontal Structures.**

The Embellishment

The Embellishment includes things like fringe, edging and surface decoration. Embellishments are decorative elements added for purposes of improving the visual appeal of a piece. Embellishments typically do not play any support or structural roles.

RULES OF COMPOSITION, CONSTRUCTION, AND MANIPULATION
5h. ARCHITECTURAL BASICS OF JEWELRY DESIGN: Sizing

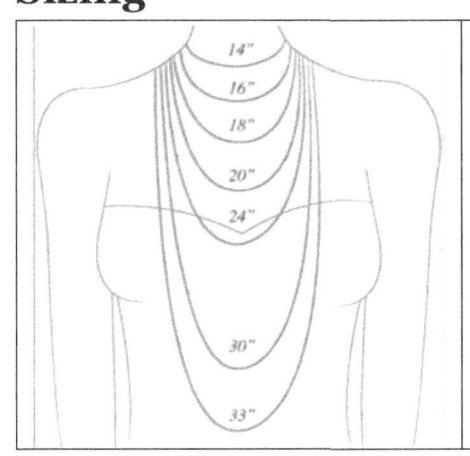

	Guiding Questions:
	(1) How do I determine the best size for the right fit and look?
	(2) How do I make the size adjustable for a piece?
	(3) How does face shape, body shape and contour, and other body features affect decisions about sizing?

Key Words:	*face*	*wardrobe*
sizing	*neck*	*skin tone*
standard sizing	*wrist*	*silhouette*
sizing customization	*finger*	*volume*
fit	*ankle*	*length*
look	*body type*	*adjustable*

Abstract:
To look great in a piece of jewelry -- whether a necklace, or chain, or pendant, or bracelet, or ring and the like – people should look to the face, the neck, the wrist, the finger, the ankle, the body type to get the right fit and look. There are often two main reasons why people do not wear their jewelry. First, it doesn't work with their wardrobe or skin tone. But second, it doesn't flatter them because of the silhouette, volume and length. Learning both about standard sizing and sizing customization measurement rules are critical for any jewelry designer.

SIZING

To look great in a piece of jewelry -- whether a necklace, or chain, or pendant, or bracelet, anklet or ring and the like – look to the face, the neck, the wrist, the finger, the ankle, the body type to get the right *fit* and *look*.

There are often two main reasons why people do not wear their jewelry. First, it doesn't work with their wardrobe or skin tone. But second, it doesn't flatter them because of the silhouette, volume and length.

343

When designing a piece of jewelry, it sometimes is helpful to make the size of the piece adjustable. This is usually accomplished with the design of the clasp assembly, such as adding a chain extension, or having 2 or 3 button loops.

Necklaces[1]

There are many standard length options for necklaces for women. If you have a narrower or wider neck than average, you may have to adjust these standards. If you have a longer or shorter neck, you might prefer a particular length over another.

When choosing a size, start with your neck. Narrow, thin necks might prefer shorter lengths. Thicker, fatter necks might prefer the medium size lengths.

Next, consider your upper torso. If the necklace length will place the necklace over your breast, be sure it flatters your appearance.

Third, consider your height. Short women are usually overwhelmed by longer lengths. Taller women sometimes look funny with short lengths.

Last, consider the shape of your face. Faces are usually described as oval, round, square and heart-shaped. Oval faces can wear any length. Round faces do better with longer lengths, and silhouettes that take the shape of a "V". Heart-shaped faces do better with shorter lengths, and silhouettes that are curved. Squarer, more rectangular faces do better with shorter lengths and rounded silhouettes.

LENGTH	COMMON NAME	PLACEMENT	UTILIZATION
14"	Collar	Tight around neck	Open-neck clothing
15 - 16"	Choker	Tight against base of throat	Almost everything
18"	Princess	On collarbone	Almost everything
20 to 24"	Matinee	Between collarbone and bust	Business or casual wear
28 to 36"	Opera	On the bust or an inch or two below	High necklines and evening wear
36 to 42"	Rope	Wrapped to sit on, or just below the center of the bust; belly button	Elegant business and evening wear; or bohemian casual

For men,

LENGTH	PLACEMENT
18"	Base of neck
20"	Collarbone; most common size
22"	A few inches below the collarbone; good for adding medallion
24"	Above the breast bone
30 to 36"	Above the belly button

Bracelets [1]

Usually, with bracelets, size is less an issue than with necklaces.

Measure the wrist at the wrist bone, using a piece of string or tape measure. If you use a string, it's best to use a bracelet sizing cone to determine the actual wrist measurement. If you like your bracelets to be somewhat loose, add ¾" or 1" to the measurement. With larger beads or adornments, the linear length against a ruler will have to be larger than the actual size of your wrist, since these larger components will pull the bracelet further out from your wrist as you wear the piece, thus increasing the circumference.

For women, most wear between a 6" and 7" length.

For men, most wear between a 7" and 8" length.

But obviously, there will be some deviation from the typical, because not everyone is a standard size.

Also, some people like to wear their bracelets tight to their wrist, while others like to wear them somewhat or very loose on their wrists.

For bangles, it becomes important to anticipate the width of the widest part of the hand for which the bangle has to slide over.

This bangle formula works in general, but, again, everyone's hand-width and wrist size will vary.

Formula for Bangle Width:
Inner Diameter * Pi = Wrist Size

Pi = 3.14

WRIST SIZE	ACTUAL LENGTH	INNER DIAMETER
6 1/2"	6 3/4"	2.1"
7"	7 1/2"	2.25"
7 1/2"	8 1/4"	2.4"
8"	9.00"	2.6"
8 1/2"	9 3/4"	2.75"

Anklets

Anklet sizes typically range from 8 – 9" for most women, but can be up to 10-11" for some women.

You measure the ankle around the widest part. It's a good idea to add another ¼" to 1" to the measurement so that the anklet will hang properly.

So, if the ankle measurement was 9", you would want to create a piece that would be 9 1.4 - 10" in length.

Rings[1]

Rings sizes are standardized and unisex, running in numbers (whole sizes and half sizes).

For women, standard size is 7, with the range from 5 to 9.

For men, standard size is 10, with the range from 8 to 12. Wider rings on men tend to run smaller in size when worn.

But again, as with necklaces and bracelets, people's finger sizes will often vary from the standards.

Also, fingers swell and contract in size, depending on the weather, heat and humidity, or how active a lifestyle some has, or with age. Some people prefer to order a ring size a half size larger to accommodate these kinds of things.

FOOTNOTES

[1] REEDS JEWELERS, Jewelry Wise, "Choosing the Right Necklace Length For You", As referenced in:
http://www.jewelrywise.com/just-for-you/article/choosing-the-right-necklace-length-for-you

Schwanke, Crystal. "Anklets" 6 Popular Types and Sizing Information," As referenced in:
https://jewelry.lovetoknow.com/Anklets

SECTION 6:

DESIGN MANAGEMENT

DESIGN MANAGEMENT
6a. THE PROFICIENT DESIGNER:
The Path To Resonance

"Vestment", Warren Feld, 2004, Miyuki cubes, seed beads and delicas, Austrian crystals, with 14KT, gold filled, sterling silver, and antiqued copper chain, clasps and other findings, lampwork bead by Lori Greenberg

Guiding Questions:
(1) How should the success of any piece of jewelry be measured?
(2) How does the designer achieve a level of resonance in their jewelry?
(3) To what extent must jewelry resonate with the wearer / viewer in order to be deemed successful?
(4) How does resonance differ from similar concepts in Art called unity, variety and emotional response?
(5) How do I self-assess the level of my proficiency in jewelry design?

Key Words:		
proficient	*communicating about design*	*composing*
resonance	*disciplinary literacy*	*constructing*
emotions	*fluency*	*manipulating*
expression	*rubric*	*design elements*
authentic performance	*self-assessment*	*principles*
creativity	*inspiration*	*materials*
intent	*aspiration*	*techniques*
risk	*shared understandings*	*metacognitive*
empathy	*contemplation*	*evidence*
universal vs subjective	*empowerment*	*context*
goals as standards of professional performance	*specification*	*backward-design*
unity and variety	*application*	*coherency*
	anticipation	*leverage*
		prototype

| *parsimony* | *thinking routine* | *iterative process* |

Abstract:

Jewelry Designers want to be successful. But things can get a little muddled when thinking about how to get there. Our teachers, our friends, our colleagues often disagree about what constitutes success in jewelry design. They offer a myriad of suggestions to measure success, which in reality, compete or conflict with one another. Because of this, we become unclear about what we should be doing and can often lose sight of what we want to end up with. The Design Perspective, however, makes things very clear. The Proficient Jewelry Designer has but one guiding star: To achieve Resonance. Everything else is secondary. We achieve Resonance by gaining a comfort in and proficiency with communicating about design. This comfort, or disciplinary fluency, translates into all our decoding, selecting, composing, constructing and manipulating choices. This is empowering. Our pieces resonate. We achieve success. A rubric for proficiency self-assessment follows at the end of the chapter.

THE PROFICIENT DESIGNER:
The Path To Resonance

Jewelry Designers want to be successful.

But things can get a little muddled when thinking about how to get there. Where should they start? What should they learn first? What materials should they accumulate? What techniques should they start with? Should they focus on the process of designing jewelry? Or moreso on making jewelry? Or still yet, on achieving certain target measures, such as numbers of pieces made, or numbers of sales, or numbers of venues in which their jewelry is sold? Are there qualitative things which are important to accumulate, such as self-satisfaction or customer-satisfaction? Desire? Value? Or style? Or recognition? Acceptance? Understanding?

Our teachers, our friends, our colleagues often disagree on how to get there, and tell us to look for, what turn out to be in effect, competing or conflicting measures of success. We can often lose sight of what we want to end up with. We get a lot of contradictory advice. How should we organize our creative work and our time? How should we select materials and techniques? How do we know when our piece is finished? How should we anticipate our client's desires? How should we showcase our jewelry? How do we place a value on our work? How should we be judged and evaluated? We need to perform, we want to perform authentically, but how – how should we perform as a jewelry designer? The search for answers can be very frustrating, confusing, even demoralizing.

But it shouldn't be. Every jewelry designer should have but one guiding star – *Resonance*. If our jewelry does not have some degree of *resonance*, we keep working on it. If the process of creative exploration and design does not lead us in the direction of *resonance*, we change it. If the results we achieve – numbers of pieces made and numbers of pieces sold – is not synced tightly with *resonance,* we cannot call ourselves designers.

The Proficient Jewelry Designer specifies those goals about performance which will lead to one primary outcome: *To achieve Resonance.* Everything else is secondary. Materials, techniques and technologies are selected with resonance in mind. Design elements are selected and applied with that idea of Resonance in mind. Principles of Composition, Construction and Manipulation are applied with that idea of Resonance in mind, with extra special attention paid to the *Principle of Parsimony* – knowing when enough is enough.

People may approach the performance tasks in varied ways. For some this means getting very detailed on pathways, activities, and objectives. For others, they let the process of design emerge and see where it takes them. Whatever approach they take in their creative process, – step-by-step or emergent process – for all designers, a focus on one outcome – *Resonance* – frees them up to think through design without encumbrance. It allows them to express meaning. It allows them to convey expressions in meaningful ways to others.

This singular focus on resonance becomes a framework within which to question everything and try to make sense of everything. Make sense of what the materials and techniques can allow them to do, and what they cannot. Make sense of what understandings and desires other people – clients, sellers, buyers, students, colleagues, teachers – will bring to the situation, when exploring and evaluating their work. Make sense of why some things inspire you, and other things do not. Make sense of why you are a jewelry designer designing jewelry. Make sense of the fluency of your artistic expression, what works, how it works, why it works.

We achieve Resonance by gaining a comfort and ease in communicating about design. This comfort and ease, or disciplinary fluency, has to do with how we translate our inspirations and aspirations into all our compositional, constructive and manipulative choices. It is empowering. Our pieces resonate. We achieve success.

Resonance, communication, success, fluency – these are all words that stand in place for an intimacy between the designer and the materials, the designer and the techniques, the designer and inspiration. They reflect the designer's aspirations. They reflect the shared understandings and desires of everyone the designer's jewelry is expected to touch. They reflect the designer's managerial prowess in bringing all these things together.

Resonance and disciplinary fluency result from a well-managed jewelry design process [3]. This process of creativity involves artist, audience and context. It is very interactional. Transactional. Integrative. Contingent.

For the artist, this process functions on several, coordinated levels, including…

1. Contemplation
2. Inspiration
3. Aspiration
4. Anticipation
5. Specification

6. Application
7. Fluency and Empowerment

1. CONTEMPLATION: An Intimacy with Materials and Techniques
Contemplation is a mystical theology.

Beads have a mystique to them. You stare at a bead and ask what it is. You put some thread on a needle, then the bead on the needle, and ask what to do. You stitch a few beads together, and wonder what will become of this. You create a necklace and ask how it will be worn. And you stare at each bead again, and, think where do all these feelings welling up within you come from – curiosity, beauty, peace and calm, reflection, satisfaction, magic, appeal, a sensuousness and sexuality. Your brain and eye enter into this fantastic dance, a fugue of focusing, refocusing, gauging and re-gauging light, color, shadow, a shadow's shadow, harmony, and discord.

You don't just bead and make jewelry. There's a lot involved here.

You have to buy (or fabricate) beads and findings and stringing materials, organize them, buy some extra parts, think about them, create with them, live with some failed creations, and go from there. If there wasn't something special about how our materials translate light into color, shade and shadow, then jewelry making would simply be work. But it's not.

You have to put one piece next to another…and then another. And when you put two beads next to each other, or one on top of the other, you're doing God's work. There's nothing as spectacular as painting and sculpting with light.

This bead before you -- why is it so enticing? Why do you beg it to let you be addicted? An object with a hole. How ridiculous its power. Some curving, some faceting, some coloration, some crevicing or texturing, some shadow, some bending of light. That's all it is. Yet you're drawn to it in a slap-silly sort of way.

When you arrange many beads, the excitement explodes exponentially within your being. Two beads together are so much more than one. Four beads so much more than two. A hundred beads so much more than twenty-five times four. The pleasure is uncontainable. You feel so powerful. Creative. You can make more of what you have than with what you started.

You need to select a method or strategy for arranging your beads. There are so many choices. Your organization should be appealing. It must enhance the power the bead has for you, then transcend as a power the bead has for others. It must be architecturally correct because this architecture determines the wear, drape and flow where the jewelry meets the person at the boundary between bead and body. And this architecture determines the structural integrity – how well the piece maintains shapes, forms and silhouettes.

And this assembling -- another gift. String through the hole, pull, tug, align, and string through the hole, pull, tug, align, and string through the hole, pull, tug, align, and string through the hole, pull, tug, align. So meditative. Calming. How could beads be so stress-relieving, other-worldly-visiting, and creative-exciting at the same time?

Contemplation. To contemplate the bead is to enter the deep reaches of your mind where emotion is one with geometry, and geometry is one with art, and art is one with physics, and beads are one with self.

Designing jewelry is an authentic performance task. This involves a profound intimacy with the materials (and techniques) the designer relies on. This intimacy means understanding how to select them, how to leverage their strengths and minimize their weaknesses, and how to manage their ability to enhance or impede resonance.

2. INSPIRATION: Becoming One with What Inspires You
Inspirations are sacred revelations you want to share through art and design.

The word inspiration comes from the Latin roots meaning "*to breathe into.*" But before you can breathe your inspiration into your jewelry, you need to become one with it.

There are these wonderfully exciting, sensually terrific, incredibly fulfilling things that you find as you try to imagine the jewelry you will create. They come from many sources: ideas, nature, images, people, behaviors. They might be realistic or abstract. They may be the particular color or pattern or texture or the way the light hits it and casts a shadow. They may be a need for order over chaos. They may be points of view. They may flow from some inner imagination.

For some reason, these inspirations take on a divine, sacred revelation for you – so meaningful that you want to incorporate them somehow into what you do. A fire in your soul. You want to translate these inspirations into colors, shapes, lines, patterns and textures. You want to impose an organization on them. You want to recapture their energy and power they have had over you. You feel compelled to bring these feelings into ideas, and these ideas into material objects.

There are many challenges to inspiration. That which we call *inspiring* can often be somewhat fuzzy. It might be a feeling. It might be a piece of an idea, or a small spot on an image. You might feel inspired but cannot put the *What* or the *Why* into words or images. On the surface, it may seem important to you, but unimportant to others. You the designer may not feel in control of the inspiration in that it seems like it is something which is evoked, not necessarily directed, by you.

When inspired, designers perceive new possibilities that transcend that which is ordinary around them. Too often, the designer feels passive in this process. This transcendence does not feel like a willfully generated idea. However, it needs to be. The successful designer – one who eventually can achieve a level of resonance – is one who is not only inspired *by*, but also inspired *to*. The object should, in its resonance, *inspire others to* recognize the designer's intent and to experience that which inspired him. This all requires a great deal of metacognitive self-awareness. The designer must be able to perceive the intrinsic value of the inspiring object, and how to extend this value in design, where the piece of jewelry becomes its expression.

Inspiration is motivating. Inspiration is not the source of creativity; creativity does not come from it. Inspiration, instead, should be viewed as a motivational response to creativity. It motivates the designer, through jewelry and its design, to connect this inspiration with others. It serves as a mediator between the self and the anticipated shared understandings and desires of others. The jewelry encapsulates the designer's ability to make this connection. When the connection is well-made, resonance follows.

But finding inspirations is not only personal, but more importantly, it is an effort to influence others. It is an act of translating the emotions which resonate in you into some object of art which, in turn, will inspire and resonate with others. How does the inspiration occur to you, and how do you anticipate how this inspiration might occur to others?

Too often we lose sight of the importance of inspiration to the authentic performance task of creating jewelry. We operate with the belief that anyone can be inspired by anything. There's nothing more to it. Moreover, inspiration gets downplayed when put next to the discussion of the effort of making jewelry itself. But it should not. Inspiration is not less important than perspiration. It plays an equal role in the creative process. The designer's clarity about why something is inspiring, and why this inspiration motivates the designer to respond, will be critical for achieving success, that is resonance.

3. ASPIRATION: Translating Creativity into A Technical Product Design
Aspiration motivates the designer to actualize inspiration.

Aspiration is where the designer translates inspiration into an expressive design concept. The designer begins to control and regulate what happens next. This involves selecting *Design Elements*[1] and clustering them to formulate meaningful expressions. The greater value the designer places on resonance, the stronger the aspiration will be to achieve it.

Aspiration is future-oriented. It requires a stick-to-it-ness. The designer must be sufficiently motivated to invest the time, energy and money into designing and making the jewelry that will not necessarily be finished, displayed or sold right away. It may require some additional learning and skills-development time. The designer may need to find a level of creativity within, and discover the kinds of skills, techniques and insights necessary for bringing this creativity to the aspired task at hand.

Aspiration requires the calculus: *Is it worth it?* It adds a level of risk to the project. It forces the designer to pay attention to the world around her or him. This world presents dynamic clues – what I discuss below as shared understandings – about opportunities, constraints, risks, contingencies, consequences, strategies and goals, and likely successes.

For some designers, motivation primarily is seen as *instinctual*. Think of *seat-of-the-pants*. Emergent, not controlled. A search for harmony, balance, rhythm, unity as something that feels right and looks right and seems right with the universe. Expressive, yes.

Imaginative, yes. But not necessarily resonant.

Achieving resonance, however, is, for the most part, more than instinctual. It has some deliberate quality to it. It is communicative. It requires a purposeful act on the part of the designer. It is a different type of motivation -- *intentional*. The designer might want to convey a specific emotion. Or advocate for some change. Or illustrate a point of view. The designer may want to entertain or teach. Heal. Attract mates. Propagandize. Where a jewelry's design is not reflective of an designer's intent, there can be no resonance.

4. ANTICIPATION: Shared Understandings And Desires[4]
Shared understandings and desires dictate opportunities, risks, contingencies and constraints.

The question of whether the audience correctly infers the presence of the designer's inspiration, and the sense of how the designer's hand comes into play within the design, remains. The answer revolves around a dynamic interaction between designer and audience, as they anticipate understandings they share and desire, and ones they do not.

Shared understandings should be enduring, transferable, big ideas at the heart of what we think of as *good jewelry design*. These shared understandings are things which spark meaningful connections between designer and materials, designer and techniques, and designer and client. We need, however, to recognize that the idea of *understanding* is very multidimensional and complicated.

Understanding is not one achievement, but more the result of several loosely organized choices. Understanding is revealed through performance and evidence. Jewelry designers must perform effectively with knowledge, insight, wisdom and skill to convince us – the world at large and the client in particular -- that they really understand what design is all about. This involves a big interpersonal component where the designer introduces their jewelry to a wider audience and subjects it to psychological, social, cultural, and economic assessment.

Understanding is more than knowledge. The designer may be able to articulate what needs to be done to achieve something labeled *good jewelry design*, but, may not know how to apply it.

Understanding is more than interpretation. The designer may be able to explain how a piece was constructed and conformed to ideas about *good jewelry design*, but this does not necessarily account for the significance of the results.

Understanding is more than applying principles of composition, construction and manipulation. It is more than simply organizing a set of design elements into an arrangement. The designer must match knowledge and interpretation about *good jewelry design* to the context. Application is a context-dependent skill.

Understanding is more than perspective. The designer works within a myriad of expectations and points of view about good jewelry design. The designer must dispassionately anticipate these various perspectives about design, and, bring some constructed point of view and knowledge of implications to bear within the design and design process.

We do not design in a vacuum. The designer must have the ability to empathize with individuals and grasp their individual and group cultures. If selling their jewelry, the designer must have the ability to empathize with small and larger markets, as well. Empathy is not sympathy. Empathy is where we can feel what others feel, and see what others see.

Last, understanding is self-knowledge, as well. The designer should have the self-knowledge, wisdom and insights to know how their own patterns of thought may inform, as well as prejudice, their understandings of good jewelry design.

How the jewelry designer begins the process of creating a piece of jewelry is very revealing about the potential for success, and ultimately achieving a level of resonance. The designer should always begin the process by articulating the essential shared understandings and desires against which their work will be evaluated and judged. For now, let's refer to this as *Backward Design*[5]. The designer starts with questions about assessment, and then allows this understanding to influence all other choices going forward.

Some *essential shared understandings* for good jewelry design, I would posit, might include the following:

1) Every designer has some creative ability, but may need to learn concepts and techniques and ways to apply them

2) Some understandings are universal and objective, particularly in reference to the selection, clustering and application of various Design Elements, such as color, shape, movement and dimension.

3) Other understandings are both objective and subjective. There is universal acceptance of what various organization and arrangement schemes -- Principles of Composition, Construction and Manipulation – might be applied by the designer. However, how they are actually applied, and how satisfying those are to various audiences, are very personal and subjective.

4) The strengths and limitations of various materials. techniques or technologies should be respected, maximizing the strengths and minimizing the limitations

5) Jewelry should communicate and reflect the designer's intent

6) Jewelry should affirm the wearer's purpose and identity in context

7) Jewelry can only be considered as art, as it is worn

8) We know the jewelry is finished and successful when the choices made and the tradeoffs among appeal, function, and context are implemented to the point we see *parsimony* and *resonance*.

5. SPECIFICATION: Goal-Orientation
It's not just what you do...It's how you get there.

At this phase, the designer applies Principles of Composition, Construction and Manipulation[2] for organizing and arranging things into a more complete whole with more elaborated expressions. Evidence of how these Principles are deliberately applied reflect the goal-orientation of the designer.

Jewelry designers are too quick to focus on the *outcome*, and too lax to focus on the *process*. It's always things like getting it done. Getting it to the client on deadline. Ending up with something concrete to show someone. Losing motivation over an extended period of time. Too much concentration on outcome can lead to taking shortcuts. Shortsightedness. Inflexibility. A misunderstanding, perhaps illusion about, whether the piece is finished and successful.

Designers more appropriately should focus on *goals*. Designers who are focused on goals tend to embrace process. It's about all the smart choices regarding composition, construction and manipulation you made at each increment along the way. By specifying goals, the designer is encouraged to find connections, and be connected to and aware of shared understandings and their impact on perceived success. When problems arise, a goal-oriented focus allows the designer to be flexible and problem solve. The designer is present from contemplation to inspiration and through to aspiration, anticipation, specification and application. The goal-orientation prevents the designer from becoming lost or paralyzed with inaction.

As process, the designer plays and experiments with ideas, design elements, arrangements, and thoughts about construction and manipulation. The designer might develop some components and test out ways to connect them. The designer might develop a prototype as a way to answer design questions. Has too much time been spent trying to make things look good? Are things working functionally? Are we uncovering some unknowns? Are there avenues of flexibility? How will my design choices play out and be judged? There is a lot of iteration – that is, back and forth – here.

You can see that the jewelry designer pursues several goals at once. The jewelry should be both appealing and functional. It should evoke emotion, elicit response, and resonate. The piece should show both unity and variety. The piece should create opinions, validate status, and reconfirm a situational, cultural or social identify. The piece should be reflective and communicative. It should be pleasurable to the maker, the wearer and the viewer alike. It should have value and be desirable.

When specifying goals, it is important to remember that not all goals are alike. The goals I am discussing here are the essential elements related to effective performance. The goals should be limited to the most critical things which need to happen. These more critical goals lead to an effective performance and result in a finished and successful piece of jewelry. This finished and successful piece of jewelry is reflective of the designer's hand and will resonate among a varied set of audiences.

The designer needs to set those goals which clarify what results need to be accomplished by the time any piece of jewelry is finished and showcased. Goals critical to the design process provide perspective. They are there to prevent the designer from achieving anything less than resonance. These goals relate to generating deep understandings and competence at performance. They are very integrated with Principles of Composition, Construction and Manipulation. They are not results-specific per se; they are moreso organizing and overarching. They serve as sign-posts to point to and highlight what jewelry designers need to engage with when thinking through and implementing expressions within design.

The jewelry designer specifies goals as standards of professional performance, such as...

- Leveraging the strengths and minimizing the weaknesses of desired materials and techniques
- Discussing and reflecting upon inspirations and motivations toward the expression of the creative self
- Defining aspirational intent, point of view, and what it means to connect to various audiences
- Delineating shared understandings and desires among self, wearer, viewer, student, teacher, collector, exhibitor, buyer and seller, in relationship to how the jewelry will be observed and assessed and worn within a context
- Elaborating on all artistic and architectural elements and principles which should come into play, and why
- Reflecting on personal learning throughout the process, particularly as it relates to developing and expanding on skills related to fluency in design
- Determining how skills, insights and lessons learned from the current project might be transferred to your next one

Within each generalized performance goal, the designer can further identify particular tasks, knowledges and skills required in order to accomplish them. Often, if the designer finds him- or her-self with too many choices about what to do, what to include, and how to proceed, then priorities and timeframes will need to be set, as well.

Resonance is more easily achieved when the designer approaches design as a process, an understanding of the myriad sets and levels of choices as made within a coherent system of creative thinking and activity, and with clear performance goals to guide the way. Well-defined goals and the smart application of Principles results in more authentic performance, thus showing the designer's intent and hand.

6. APPLICATION: Unity, Emotions, Resonance
Think like an assessor[6]...Find evidence related to desired results.

What is the evidence we need to know for determining when a piece is finished and successful? What clear and appropriate criteria specify what we should look at? What clues has the designer provided to let the various audiences become aware of the authenticity of the performance?

There are different opinions in craft, art and design about what are the most revealing and important aspects of the work, and which every authentic jewelry design performance must meet.

The traditional criteria used in the art world are that the designer should achieve *unity, variety* and *evoke emotions*. These, I feel, may work well when applied to paintings or sculpture, but they are insufficient measures of success when applied to jewelry. Jewelry involves the creation of objects where both artistic appeal as well as practical considerations of use are essential. The artistry of jewelry cannot be distinguished from that jewelry as it is worn, and the context within which it is worn. So, when referencing any jewelry's design, I prefer to use criteria of *parsimony* and *resonance*, instead. That is, we know when a piece is finished and successful only when the choices of the artist are deemed parsimonious, and the various audiences perceive the piece to resonate.

Parsimony vs. Unity/Variety

In art, the traditional measure of completion and success is a feeling or sense of "*Unity.*" Unity signifies how everything feels all right. All the Design Elements used, and how they were coordinated and placed, are very coherent, clear, balanced, harmonious and satisfying. I think the idea of *unity* begins to get at the place we want to end up. But this concept is not concrete enough for me as a jewelry designer.

What bothers me the most is that you can have unity, but the piece still be seen as boring when there is no *variety*. Criteria provided from the art perspective recognize this. But somehow tempering unity with variety starts to add some ambiguity to our measurements of finish and success. This ambiguity is unacceptable as a principled outcome of jewelry construction.

Another concern I have, is that you can have unity with variety, but, from the art perspective, these assessments rely too much on universal, objective perceptions of visual design elements and their attributes *(for example, the use of color schemes)*. Resonance is not about picking the correct color scheme. It is more about how that color scheme is used, manipulated, leveraged or violated within the piece. We must not leave the designer, the wearer, and the situation out of the equation. We must not minimize the designer's hand –

the artist's intent, thinking, strategizing, arranging, pushing the boundaries, even violating the universal, objective rules.

Jewelry creation usually demands a series of judgment calls and tradeoffs. Tradeoffs between aesthetics and functionality. Tradeoffs between designer goals and audience understandings, expectations and desires. Tradeoffs between a full palette of colors-shapes-textures and a very limited one. Any measure of completeness and success needs to result from the forced choice decisions of the designer. It needs to account for the *significance* of the results, not just the *organization* of them. It needs to explain the *Why*, not just the *What*.

For me, the more appropriate concept here is *Parsimony*. Parsimony is when you know enough is enough. When the finished and successful piece is parsimonious, the relationship of all the Design Elements – visual, functional as well as contextual -- and their expressed attributes will be so strong, that to add or remove any one thing would diminish, not just the design, but rather the significance of the design.

Parsimony is sometimes referred to in art as *Economy*, but the idea of economy is still reserved for the visual effects alone. The designer needs to be able to decide when enough is enough. For jewelry designers, we want that economy or parsimony to apply to functional and situational effects, as well.

> ***Parsimony...***
> *- forces explanation; its forced-choice nature is most revealing about the designer's understandings and intentions*
>
> *- relies on evidence moreso than assumptions to get at criticality*
>
> *- focuses examination of the few elements that make a difference*

Resonance vs. Evoking Emotions

Finished and successful jewelry should not only evoke emotions but should resonate.

Achieving Resonance is the guiding star for jewelry designers, at each step of the way.

Resonance is some level of felt energy that is a little more than an emotional response. The difference between saying that piece of jewelry is "*Beautiful*" vs. saying that piece of jewelry "*Makes me want to wear it*". Or that "*I want to touch it*". Or "*My friends need to see this.*" Or "*This is something I want to buy.*"

Resonance is something more than emotion. It is some kind of additional energy we see, feel and otherwise experience. Emotion is very reactive. *Resonance* is intuitive, involving, identifying. Emotion is very sympathetic. *Resonance* is more of an empathetic response where designer and audience realize a shared (or contradictory) understanding without losing sight of whose views and feelings belong to whom.

Resonance results from how the designer controls light, shadow, and their characteristics of warmth and cold, receding and approaching, bright and dull, light and dark. *Resonance* results from how the designer leverages the strengths of materials and techniques and minimizes their weaknesses. *Resonance* results from social, cultural and situational cues. *Resonance* results from how the designer takes us to the edge of universal, objective understandings, and pushes us ever so slightly, but not too, too far, beyond that edge.

Jewelry which resonates...

- is communicative and authentic	- lets the materials and techniques speak
- shows the artist's hand as intention, not instinct	- anticipates shared understandings of many different audiences about design elements and principles, and some obvious inclusion, exclusion or intentional violation of them
- evokes both an emotional as well as energetic response from wearer and viewer	
- shows both degrees of control, as well as moments of the unexpected	
- makes something noteworthy from something ordinary	- results from a design process that appears to have been more systemic (e.g., ingrained within an integrated process) than systematic (e.g., a step-by-step approach)
- finds the whole greater than the sum of the parts	
	- both appeals and functions at the boundary where jewelry meets person

Resonance functions on several levels during the design process.

Phase of Design Process	How Resonance Comes Into Play
1. **Contemplation** *Exhibiting an intimacy with the materials and techniques*	Shows understanding how to leverage the strengths and minimize the weaknesses in all materials and techniques used
2. **Inspiration** *Sharing sacred revelations through art and design*	Piece motivates someone to be as inspired as the designer was; the designer inspires *to*, not inspired *by*
3. **Aspiration** *Actualizing inspiration into a design*	The jewelry's concept and design clearly translates the designer's inspiration into that design

4. *Anticipation* *Shared understandings and desires dictate opportunities, risks, contingencies and constraints*	The Design Element choices provide evidence that the designer is aware of shared understandings and desires among various audiences which will be used to evaluate and judge the piece.
5. *Specification* *Clarifying what results need to be accomplished*	Evidence of how Principles of Composition, Construction and Manipulation are applied and the degree the piece feels like it resulted from a authentic performance by the designer.
6. *Application* *Strategically and parsimoniously applying Principles of Composition, Construction and Manipulation to establish evidence related to desired results*	Evidence why piece feels unified, parsimonious, and resonant, and why piece is worth the thought, time, and effort put into it
7. *Fluency and Empowerment* *Managing design process and demonstrating disciplinary literacy*	The designer has a comfort about communicating design thinking and intent, by relating choices of evidence to how finished the piece is, and how successful (resonant) it is.

7. FLUENCY[7] AND EMPOWERMENT:
Managing Choices In Expression

Empowerment is about successfully making choices. These are choices about expressing one's intent through art and design.

These choices could be as simple as whether to follow through on some inspiration. They might involve selection of elements of design, or principled arrangements of beads, forms and components. The designer will make choices about how to draw someone's attention to the piece, or, present the piece to a larger audience. The designer will make choices between aesthetics and functionality. She or he may decide to submit the piece to a magazine or contest. She or he may want to sell the piece and market it. The designer will make choices about how a piece might be worn, or who might wear it, or when it might be worn, in what context.

The fluent designer will be adept at making these choices. The better designer is able to bring a high level of coherence and consistency to the process of managing all this – intent, shared understandings, desires, knowledge and skills, evaluative review, and reflection and adjustment. This is called *"fluency in design"*.

Fluency is the ability of the designer to select and connect Design Elements smoothly, in visually and functionally and situationally appropriate ways with understanding. The idea of understanding is broadly defined, to include the designer's personal goals for expression, as well as the expectations and desires of all the audiences – the wearer, the viewer, the buyer, the seller, the student, the teacher, the collector, the exhibitor. The better designer achieves a level of disciplinary literacy where fluency becomes automatic, accurate, and rapidly applied.

The better, more fluent jewelry designer is able to anticipate how others will come to understand these mechanisms and the implications for applying them in one way or another. For example, the better and more fluent designer would be able to select and combine design elements to appropriately differentiate jewelry that would best be worn at work, and jewelry that would best be worn, say, when someone was going to a night club for dancing and socializing.

Lastly, fluency means that the designer has also been taught to look for, anticipate and incorporate context clues. Design does not occur in a vacuum. It has implications which become realized in a context. That context might be historical, personal, cultural or situational.

> *More proficient, fluent jewelry designers will be comfortable and somewhat intentional and fluid in their abilities to...*
>
> 1. *Leverage strengths and minimize weaknesses of materials and techniques.*
>
> 2. *Decode, select, cluster and apply Design Elements, and implement and apply various organizational arrangements related to Principles of Composition, Construction and Manipulation.*
>
> 3. *Work within shared understandings and desires about jewelry and its successful design.*
>
> 4. *Apply key knowledge and skills to achieve the desired result.*
>
> 5. *Anticipate how their work will be reviewed, judged and evaluated by criteria reflective of these same shared understandings.*
>
> 6. *Communicate their intent.*
>
> 7. *Step back, reflect, and validate all their thinking to reject any misunderstandings, and make adjustments accordingly.*

RUBRIC[8] AS THINKING ROUTINE

Designers need a simple map to all these ideas about literacy and fluency – something they can easily review and determine where their strengths and weaknesses are as they gain proficiency and fluency in design. One type of map is called a *rubric*.

A rubric is a table of criteria used to rate and rank *understanding* and *performance*. A rubric answers the question *by what criteria either understanding or performance should be judged*. The rubric provides insightful clues for the kinds of evidence we need to make such assessments. The rubric helps us distinguish degrees of performance, from the sophisticated to the naïve. The rubric encapsulates what an authentic jewelry design performance would look like.

Such a rubric is presented below for the designer to use as a *thinking routine*.[9] Here I have used one rubric to represent both (1) understanding and (2) performance, but, I could have easily created two separate rubrics toward this end. In this rubric table below, the rows represent contemplation, inspiration, aspiration, anticipation, specification, application, and fluency and empowerment. The columns represent the degrees of understanding and performance along a continuum, from *proficient* on one end to *not there yet* on the other. By way of example, I use the rubric to assess my performance with a piece I created called *Vestment* (Feld, 2004).

The Rubric...
RUBRIC: How Proficient Am I, As A Jewelry Designer, In Achieving Resonance?

UNDERSTANDING & PERFORMANCE	4- Proficient *Insightful, intuitive understanding, effectively established, with clear intent, and well supported by details*	3-Capable *Well-considered understanding, appropriately established and supported by details*	2-Shows Potential *Some plausible understanding, some consistency established and supported by details, but not always sustained*	1-Not There Yet *Superficial or no understanding, not consistent or sustained, perhaps vague or incomplete*
CONTEMPLATION *Exhibiting an intimacy with the materials, techniques, and technology*	Purposeful in selection of materials and techniques which synergistically work together Insightful understanding and clear ability to leverage strengths and minimize weaknesses of materials and techniques	Selects materials appropriate for technique used, and select technique appropriate for task at hand Some ability to leverage strengths and minimize weaknesses of materials and techniques	Selects materials and techniques which may have some fit with the task at hand, but could not articulate the reasons why Has limited understanding of the strengths and weaknesses materials and techniques bring to the task at hand	Does not understand the relationship between the selection of materials and techniques and the task at hand Has no understanding of the strengths and weaknesses materials and technique
INSPIRATION *Sharing sacred revelations through art and design*	Clearly recognizes intrinsic value between inspiration and the design of finished piece; invigorates inspiration Deliberately reflects on using	Some recognition of the connection between inspiration and the design of finished piece; applies inspiration Thinks how others might be inspired by and	Passively responds to inspiring objects while designing piece with some intent to evoke a personal emotion but limited intent to evoke that emotion in others; consumes inspiration	Either does not begin with an inspiration, or only a weak connection between an inspiring object and the design of a piece; somewhat unaware of inspiration

	inspiration and the design of the piece to motivate and energized others to so be inspired	emotionally connected to the piece as well	Does not think deeply about how the piece might inspire others	Does not think about how the piece might inspire others
ASPIRA-TION *Actualizing inspiration into a design*	Can clearly and intentionally translate a feeling or idea into a jewelry design or model; With considerable intention and control, select and arrange Design Elements, resulting in an inspiring design which resonates Can clearly determine risk-calculus comparing all costs associated with constructing piece relative to all benefits from how the finished piece will be received	Can, with some clarity, translate a feeling or idea into a jewelry design or model, and select Design Elements which come together well and evoke emotion Has an intuitive feel for the risk-calculus, comparing all costs associated with constructing piece relative to all benefits from how the finished piece will be received	Can translate a feeling or idea into a jewelry design or model, but mostly based on instinct rather than intent; can select Design Elements which result in a satisfying design Has not taken the time to think about the risk-calculus for implementing a design	A jewelry design emerges somehow, but there is little obvious connection to an inspiration or an designer's intention Does not know how to think about the risk-calculus for implementing a design
ANTICIPA-TION *Shared understandings and desires dictate opportunities, risks, contingencies and constraints*	Shows empathy; can anticipate others' points of view, and how to incorporate them with his/her own Can engage with others around this project Can specify shared	Can explain how a piece and its construction conforms to others' ideas of good jewelry design, and shows some evidence in applying this Anticipates some shared	Can explain, in an academic sense, how a piece fits broad understandings about good design, but is weak in applying this Is weak, in reality, at anticipating	Cannot explain or apply understandings of how a piece fits a definition of good design Does not anticipate others' shared understandings or desires about design, nor

	understandings and desires of various audiences, and how they may predetermine opportunities, risks, contingencies and constraints; is somewhat proactive about them

Can delineate and manage misunderstandings | understandings and desires, but is usually somewhat reactive to them, but sometimes, though often unintentionally, may be proactive about them.

Responds to misunderstandings | others' shared understandings and desires about design and is very reactive to them

Fumbles misunder-standings, sometimes even unintentionally creating them. | responds to them in any significant way

Ignores or is unaware of misunderstandings |
| **SPECIFICA-TION**

Clarifying what results need to be accomplished, and the performances involved | Can clearly define and articulate those performance goals necessary to achieve resonance, particularly those related to Principles of Composition, Construction and Manipulation

Can implement a coherent process and system of creative thinking and activity as a series of smart choices leading up to the finished product

Can make visible the consequences of his/her design process choices | Can define some performance goals necessary to achieve resonance, particularly those related to Principles of Composition, Construction and Manipulation

Can implement an organized process of creative production

Can identify some consequences related to his/her design process choices

Can identify misunder-standings and | Does not overtly define performance goals necessary to achieve resonance; however, may have an intuitive sense of some performance goals which need to occur, particularly those associated with Principles of Composition, Construction and Manipulation

Does not work within an organized process of creative production

Does not identify consequences related to his/her | Is not yet performance goal-oriented.

Does not understand how to define or work within an organized process of creative production

Cannot identify consequences related to his/her design process choices

Does not recognize, or incorporate shared understandings or misunderstandings into the creative process |

	Can identify what it will take to overcome misunderstandings, and flexibly problem solve, when necessary	determine some strategies in response, when necessary	design process choices Does not identify misunder-standings, nor develop strategies for overcoming these when they occur	
APPLICA-TION *Strategically and parsimoniously applying Principles of Composition, Construction and Manipulation to establish evidence related to desired results*	Provides in-depth, coherent, insightful, recognizable and credible reasons, based on evidence and both art and design theory, for all design choices, particularly tradeoffs among aesthetics, function and context Argues what is central to piece which makes it work; emphasizes application in context Leverages materials, techniques, design elements and principles in an especially novel way Determines confidently that piece is finished	Provides coherent, insightful reasons based on evidence in art theory for most design choices Weak or no tradeoffs among aesthetics, function and context. Uses materials, techniques, design elements and principles in novel way Judges based on personal and art theory assumptions when piece is finished and successful, that is unified with some variety, and evokes emotions Some explanation as to why finished piece is worth the thought, time,	Provides justifications for some design choices, but not grounded in art or design theory and perspective Does not make any accommodations among aesthetics, function and context Uses materials, techniques, design elements and principles in interesting or generally appealing way The piece is finished when the designer stops working on it; no judgements related to success No coherent explanation as to why finished piece is worth the thought, time,	Does not recognize the design process as a series of choices, or in any way rooted in art or design theory and perspective Does not understand that tradeoffs may need to get made among aesthetics, function and context Does not show significant understanding about materials, techniques, design elements, principles, and how to choose, cluster them Shows no confidence in determining whether piece is finished or successful. Assumes work

	and successful, that is parsimonious and resonant Justifies why finished piece is worth the thought, time, and effort put into it.	and effort put into it.	and effort put into it.	done is worth thought, time, and effort put into it.
EMPOWER-MENT *Managing design process and demonstrating disciplinary literacy*	Intuitive; metacognitive; can make choices based on intent, and anticipate implications of choices; can take a critical stance; can recognize personal and situational biases Effective and appearing almost effortless decoding Design Elements and applying Principles of Composition, Construction, and Manipulation; has complete and extensive knowledge about Elements and Principles and their application in context Can relate most, if not all, choices of evidence, both universal and	Somewhat intuitive; can articulate some of the intentional management choices and their implications made within design process; may not be fully aware of personal and situational biases Understands what is required for decoding Design Elements and applying Principles of Composition, Construction, and Manipulation, but does this with some effort and some varying degrees of effectiveness; has extensive knowledge of Elements and Principles Can point to many pieces of	Weak demonstration of process management; typically following step-by-step process outline or instructions where most choices have been made for the artist; unaware of implications of choices Doing some decoding of Design Elements and some applying of Principles, but with some difficulties or misconceptions; may have considerable but not full knowledge of Elements and Principles Can relate some of the choices and evidence,	No demonstration of process management; requires others to delineate the necessary design and implementation choices; unaware that there are implications for any choice Noticeable difficulties (or unable to do) decoding Design Elements and applying Principles; generally unfamiliar with full range of Elements and Principles Does not recognize the relationships among choice, evidence, and results

| | subjective, to how finished the piece is, and how successful (resonant) it is | evidence, both universally shared or subjective, to how finished the piece is, and how successful (resonant) it is | primarily universally shared, to how finished the piece is, and how successful (resonant) it is | |

RUBRIC:
How Proficient Am I In Achieving Resonance?
The piece...

"Vestment", by Warren Feld, 2008

I was contracted to do a series of workshops on Contemporizing Etruscan Jewelry. "Vestment" was one of the pieces I created as a contemporized version of a traditional Etruscan collar. *Contemporized* refers to drawing inspiration from a traditional piece, not reviving or imitating it per se.

With my contemporized version of this

If I were using the Rubric above to evaluate my conception, design and implementation of this piece – Vestment – I would be thinking about the following...

CONTEMPLATION
Score 4
Exhibiting an intimacy with the materials, techniques, and technology

The Ndebele stitch allows a fluidity and draping while still maintaining the basic shape. Using two small beads and a cube to make the Ndebele stitch, rather than the traditional four small beads to complete the stitch, adds resonance. Creating two overlapping layers of stitching creates unusual color/shadow effects while the piece is worn.

INSPIRATION
Score 4
Sharing sacred revelations through art and design

Etruscan Collar, I've used bead weaving techniques (Ndebele stitch and Petersburg chain stitch) to get a more dimensional effect, stronger color play, and a more contemporary sense of fashion and wearability.

The piece shown uses Miyuki cubes, seed beads and delicas, Austrian crystals, with 14KT, gold filled, sterling silver, and antiqued copper chain, clasps and other findings. With some pieces, I include artist-created handmade lampwork beads made by Lori Greenberg.

My Etruscan VESTMENT is worn like a scarf. It is meant to present a different jewelry profile than a typical necklace. It is at once formal and relaxed, complementing the body and fashion, rather than competing with it. The Vestment fastens in the front.

The main strips of the vestment are created using a double-layered, Ndebele stitch. These strips are attached to the clasp with an assemblage of pieces created using the Petersburg chain stitch.

Detail 1

This piece draws inspiration from form, cultural color preferences, yet results in a very contemporary piece with more fluidity, dimensionality, movement, and sensual appeal.

ASPIRATION
Score 4
Actualizing inspiration into a design

The design shows considerable intent and forethought in bringing together color, materials, techniques, forms, in a coherent arrangement.

ANTICIPATION
Score 3
Shared understandings and desires dictate opportunities, risks, contingencies and constraints

The piece is generally well-received, with some questions about how and when it is to be worn, and whether it is sufficiently contemporary in design.

SPECIFICATION
Score 3
Clarifying what results need to be accomplished, and the performances involved

At the time I created this design, my process was generally organized but with considerable

Detail 2	*trial and error. Tried to get result of appealing piece, had difficulty making tradeoffs between aesthetics and functionality. Did not have a clear understanding of resonance.*
Traditional Etruscan Collar	**APPLICATION** **Score 3** ***Strategically and parsimoniously applying Principles of Composition, Construction and Manipulation to establish evidence related to desired results*** *Was primarily driven by art theory, with more last minute choices about functionality. Otherwise, made strategic choices in selecting materials, construction techniques, and meeting most contemporary expectations.*
	EMPOWERMENT **Score 3** ***Managing design process and demonstrating disciplinary literacy*** *Was not fluent in design at this point in time. Most of my great strategic choices were more intuitive than intentional.*

FOOTNOTES

[1] Feld, Warren. "Jewelry Design Composition: Playing with Building Blocks Called Design Elements," 3/17/2018

[2] Feld, Warren. "Jewelry Design Principles: Composing, Constructing, Manipulating,"

4/25/2018

[3] Feld, Warren. "Jewelry Design: A Managed Process," Klimt02, 2/2/18.
https://klimt02.net/forum/articles/jewelry-design-managed-process-warren-feld

[4] *Shared Understandings*. In another graduate education class, the major text reviewed the differences between understanding and knowledge. The question was how to teach understanding. Worth the read to gain many insights about how to structure teaching to get sufficient understanding to enrich learning. **Understanding by Design** *by Grant Wiggins and Jay McTighe, 2nd Edition, Association for Supervision and Curriculum Development, 2005.*

[5] *Backward Design*. One of the big take-aways from **Understanding by Design** *(see footnote 3)* was the idea they introduced of "*backward design*". Their point is that you can better teach understanding if you anticipate the evidence others will use in their assessments of what you are trying to do. When coupled with ideas about teaching literacy and fluency *(see footnote 2)*, you can begin to introduce ideas about managing the design process in a coherent and alignable way.

[6] **Understanding by Design** *by Grant Wiggins and Jay McTighe, 2nd Edition, p. 146, Association for Supervision and Curriculum Development, 2005.*

[7] *Fluency*. I took two graduate education courses in Literacy. The primary text we used was **Literacy: Helping Students Construct Meaning** *by J. David Cooper, M. Robinson, J.A. Slansky and N. Kiger, 9th Edition, Cengage Learning, 2015.* Even though the text was not about jewelry designing per se, it provides an excellent framework for understanding what fluency is all about, and how fluency with language develops over a period of years. I have relied on many of the ideas in the text to develop my own ideas about a disciplinary literacy for jewelry design.

[8] *Rubrics*. **Understanding by Design** *by Grant Wiggins and Jay McTighe, 2nd Edition, p. 146, Association for Supervision and Curriculum Development, 2005.*

[9] *Thinking Routines*. I teach jewelry design. I find it useful to engage students with various ways of thinking out loud. They need to hear me think out loud about what choices I am making and what things I am considering when making those choices. They need to hear themselves think out loud so that they can develop strategies for getting more organized and strategic in dealing with information and making decisions. My inspiration here was based on the work done by **Visible Thinking by Project Zero** (http://www.visiblethinkingpz.org/VisibleThinking_html_files/pz.harvard.edu) ***at Harvard Graduate School of Education.***

DESIGN MANAGEMENT
6b. JEWELRY DESIGN: *A Managed Process*

Little Tapestries: Ghindia, 2012, by Warren Feld, brass beads, Japanese seed beads, Greek ceramic seed beads, Austrian crystal beads, chain, fireline cable thread. Photographed by Warren Feld

Guiding Questions:
(1) What does it mean to conceptualize jewelry design as a process?
(2) What does it mean to manage a process?
(3) What are the advantages for defining the jewelry design process as a system of managed choices?
(4) What kinds of things happen at the boundary between jewelry and person?
(5) How should the designer manage jewelry design choices at the boundary between jewelry and person?

Key Words: *jewelry design* *manage* *process* *design thinking*	*creative endeavor* *system* *choices* *boundary between jewelry and person*	*jewelry is only art as it is worn*

Abstract:
Jewelry designers rely on their creative skills to conceptualize, construct, and present their pieces. But it makes more sense, and leads to better success on all levels, when jewelry designers redefine jewelry design, not merely as a creative endeavor, but as a managed process, as well. First, this means understanding what they do as a system of integrated and interrelated choices. Second, this means understanding the implications for these choices at the boundary between jewelry and person. Third, this means recognizing the

tensions between creativity and production, and how to resolve these.

JEWELRY DESIGN
A Managed Process
"Jewelry is art, but only art as it is worn."

That's a powerful idea, -- *"as it is worn"* -- but, when making jewelry, we somewhat ignore it. We bury it somewhere in the back of our brains, so it doesn't get in the way of what we are trying to do. We relegate it to a phrase on the last page of a book we have promised ourselves to read sometime, so it doesn't put any road blocks in front of our process of creation.

We like to follow steps and are thrilled when a lot of the thinking has been done for us. We like to make beautiful things. But, we do not want to have to make a lot of choices. We don't want anything to disrupt our creative process.

We do not want to worry about and think about and agonize over jewelry *"as it is to be worn."* Let's not deal with those movement, architectural, engineering, context, interpersonal and behavioral stuff. We just want to make things.

To most artisans, making jewelry should never be work. It should always be fun.

Making jewelry should be putting a lot of things on a table in front of you, and, going for it.

Making jewelry just is. It is not something we want to worry about managing.

It is easy to make, copy or mimic jewelry someone else has designed, either through kits or through imitation.

Making jewelry is doing. Not thinking.

Creating. Not managing.

We prefer to make jewelry distinct from any context in which it might be worn or sold. We don't want someone looking over our shoulder, while we create. We don't want to adjust any design choice we make because the client won't like it, or, perhaps, it is out of fashion or color-shaded with colors not everyone likes. Perhaps our design choices at-the-moment do not fit with the necessities associated with how we need to market our wares to sell them. Our pieces might somehow be off-brand.

All too often, we avoid having to think about the difficult choices and tradeoffs we need to make, when searching for balance. That is balance among aesthetics, functionality, context, materials and technique. And balance between our needs as designers and the wearer's needs, as well. So, too, we shy aware from making any extra effort to please "others" or "them". Even though this hardly makes sense if we want these "others" or "them" to wear our jewelry or buy our jewelry or sell our jewelry or collect our jewelry creations.

Everything comes down to a series of difficult choices. We are resistant to making many of them. So we ignore them. We pretend they are choices better left to other people, though never fully sure who those other people are. We yearn to be artists and designers, but, resign ourselves to be craftspersons. We dabble with art, but avoid management, production and design.

We hate to make trade-offs between art and function; that is, allow something to be a little less beautiful so that it won't break or not drape and move well when worn. We hate to make things in colors or silhouettes we don't like. We hate to make the same design over and over again, even though it might be popular or sell well.

But make these kinds of choices we must! Your jewelry is a reflection of the sum of these choices. It is a reflection of you. You as an artist. You as a crafter. You as architect and engineer. You as social scientist. You as a business person. You as a designer.

So, the more we can anticipate what kinds of choices we need to make, and the more experience we have to successfully manage and maneuver within these choices, the more enjoyable and successful our jewelry designs become … and the more satisfying for the people for whom we make them.

JEWELRY DESIGN IS A MANAGEMENT PROCESS

Designers who are able to re-interpret the steps she or he goes through and see them in "*process*" terms, that is, *with organization and purpose,* have the advantage.

There are many different kinds of choices to be made, but they are interdependent and connected. Recognizing interdependency and connectedness makes it easier to learn about, visualize and execute these choices as part of an organized, deliberate and managed jewelry design process.

I am going to get on my soap box here. We tend to teach students to very mechanically follow a series of steps. We need, instead, to teach them "P*rocess*". Strategy. Insight. Connectedness. Contingency. Dependency. Construction. Context. Problem-Solving. Consequences.

Good jewelry design must answer questions and teach practitioners about <u>managing</u> the processes of anticipating the audience, selecting materials, implementing techniques, and constructing the piece from one end to the other. Again, this is not a mechanical process. Often, it is not a linear step-by-step pathway. There is a lot of iteration – that is, the next choice made will limit some things and make more relevant other things which are to happen next.

A "*process*" is something to be *managed,* from beginning to end, as the designer's knowledge, techniques and skills are put to the test. That test could be very small-scale and simple, such as creating a piece of jewelry to give to someone as a gift. Or creating a visual for a customer. Or when you need to know the costs. Or, that test could be very large-scale and more complex, such as convincing a sales agent to represent your jewelry in their showroom.

Better Jewelry Designers smartly manage their design processes at *the boundary between jewelry and person*. It is at this boundary where all the interdependencies of all the various types of choices we designers make are clearest and have the most consequence. It is at this point where the tensions between risks and rewards are most apparent. And it is at this point where the jewelry design process is best managed and controlled.

WELL-DESIGNED JEWELRY MUST BE MANAGED AT *THE BOUNDARY BETWEEN JEWELRY AND PERSON*

What exactly does it mean to "*manage design at the boundary between jewelry and person?*" What kinds of things happen at that boundary?

A person breathes. She moves. She sits at a desk, perhaps fidgeting with her jewelry. She might make sudden turns. She gracefully transitions from one space to another. She has shape, actually many shapes.

Her jewelry serves many purposes. It signifies her as someone or something. It expresses her feelings. Or status. Or future intentions. Or past history. It ties her to people and places, events and times. It suggests power, or lack thereof. It hides faults and amplifies strengths. It implies whether she fits with the situation.

Jewelry attracts. It attracts seekers of the wearer's attention. It wards off denigrators. It orients people to the world around them. It tells them a story with enough symbol, clue and information to allow people to decide whether to flee or approach, run away or walk toward, hide or shine.

Jewelry has a feel and sparkle to it. It reminds us that we are real. It empowers a sensuality and a sexuality. It elevates our esteem. Sometimes uncomfortable or scratchy. Sometimes not. Sometimes reflective of our moods. Othertimes not.

Jewelry is a shared experience. It helps similar people find one another. It signals what level of respect will be demanded. It entices. It repels. It offers themes both desirable and otherwise.

Jewelry has shape, form and mechanics. All the components must self-adjust to forces of movement, yet at the same time, not lose shape or form or maneuverability. If a piece is designed to visually display in a particular way, forces cannot be allowed to disrupt its presentation. Jewelry should take the shape of the body and move with the body. It should not make a mockery of the body, or, resist the body as it wants to express itself.

Jewelry defines a silhouette. It draws a line on the body, often demarcating what to look at and what to look away from. What to touch, and what to avoid. What is important, and what is less so.

Managing here at *the boundary between jewelry and person* means understanding what wearing jewelry involves and is all about. There is an especially high level of clarity at this boundary because it is here where the implications of any choice matters most.

The choice of stringing material anticipates durability, movement, drape. The choices of color and shape and silhouette anticipate aesthetics, tensions between light and shadow, context, the viewer's needs or personality or preferences at the moment. The choice of technique anticipates how best to coordinate choices about materials with purpose and objective. The choice of price determines marketability, and where it's out there, and whether it's out there.

You choose Fireline cable thread and this choice means your piece will be stiffer, might hold a shape better, might resist the abrasion of beads, but also might mean less comfort or adaptability.

You choose cable wire and this choice means that your piece might not lay right or comfortably. A necklace will be more likely to turn around on the neck. It might make the wearer look clownish. At the same time, it might make the stringing process go more quickly. Efficiency translates into less cost, thus less money charged, and perhaps more sales.

You choose to mix opaque glass with gemstone beads, mixing media which do not necessarily interact with the eye and brain in the same way. This may make interacting with the piece seem more like work or annoying.

The ends of your wirework will not keep from bending or unraveling, so you solder them. Visually this disrupts the dance you achieve with wire bending and cheapens it.

You choose gray-toned beads to intersperse among your brightly colored ones. The grays pick up the colors around them, adding vibrancy and resonance to your piece. The gaps of light between each bead more easily fade away as the brain is tricked into filling them in with color.

You mix metalized plastic beads in with your Austrian crystal beads. In a fortnight, the finish has chipped off all the plastic beads.

You construct a loom bracelet, flat, lacking depth or a sense of movement. Your piece may be seen as pretty, but out of step with contemporary ideas of fashion, style, and design.

If we pretend our management choices here do not matter, we fool ourselves into thinking we are greater artists and designers than we really are.

JEWELRY DESIGN MANAGEMENT:
BUILDING A STRUCTURE AND ORGANIZATION
FOR THINKING THROUGH DESIGN

Design management is multi-faceted. We intuitively know that *proper preparation prevents piss poor performance*. So let's properly prepare. *This means...*

1) **PROJECT**
Defining what I do as a *"Project To Be Managed"* -- My Project is seen as a *"system"*,

not merely a set of steps. The *"system"* encompasses everything it takes which enables creativity and leads it to success. These include things related to art, architecture, engineering, mechanics, technique, technology, management, behavioral and context analysis, problem-solving, and innovation. For some designers, these also include things related to business, marketing, branding, selling and cost-accounting.

2) INSPIRATION
Documenting, through image, writing or both, the kinds of things that are inspiring me and influencing my design

3) PURPOSE
Elaborating on the purpose or mission of my Project – why am I doing this Project as it applies to me, and as it applies to others?

4) SITUATION
Measuring the context and situation as these will/might/could impact my Project. Anticipating shared understandings and desires.

5) STRATEGY
Developing a strategy for designing my piece -- outlining everything that needs to come together to successfully work through my Project from beginning to end. Delineating Design Elements, which ones to use, and how I want to use them to express what I want to express. Prototyping, if need be.

6) SKILLS
Verifying, Learning or Re-Learning the necessary techniques and skills

7) SUPPLIES
Securing my supply chain to get all our materials, tools and supplies needed when I need them

8) CONSTRUCTION
Applying design principles of composition, construction and manipulation. Paying careful attention to building in architectural pre-requisites, particularly those involved with (a) support, jointedness, drape and movement, and (b) structure, shape and form.

9) SHOWCASE
Introducing my Jewelry Design to a wider audience. This might involve sharing, show-casing, or marketing and selling.

10) REPLICATION
Anticipating all that it will take to replicate the piece, if it is not a one-off, especially if I am developing kits or selling my pieces

11) REFLECTION
Evaluating whether I could repeat this or a similar Project with any greater efficiency or effectiveness – ***The better jewelry artist is one who is more reflective***

DESIGN THINKING

Designing jewelry demands that we both *do* and *think*. Create and manage. Experience and reflect.

The better Jewelry Designer sees any Project as a *system* of things, activities and outcomes. These are interconnected and mutually dependent. Things are sometimes linear, but most often iterative – a lot of back and forth and readjustments.

The better Jewelry Designer is very *reflective*. She or he thinks about every detail, plays mental exercises of what-if analyses, monitors and evaluates all throughout the Project's management. She or he thinks through the implications of each choice made. The Designer does not blindly follow a set of instructions without questioning them.

At the end of the day, your jewelry is the result of the decisions you made.

Something to think about.

HOW DO WE TEACH JEWELRY DESIGN THINKING AS A MANAGEMENT PROCESS

We should teach students to design jewelry, not craft it. Rather than have students merely follow a set of steps, we need to do what is called *"Guided Thinking"*.

For example, we might encourage students to construct and feel and touch similar pieces made with different materials, beads and techniques, and have them tell us what differences they perceive. We should guide them in thinking through the implications for these differences. When teaching a bead weaving stitch, I typically have students make samples using two different beads – say a cylinder bead and a seed bead, and try two different stringing materials, say Fireline and Nymo threads.

We also should guide them in thinking through all the management and control issues they were experiencing. Very often beginning students have difficulty finding a comfortable way to hold their pieces while working them. I let them work a little on a project, stop them, and then ask them to explain what was difficult and what was not. I suggest some alternative solutions – but do not impose a one-best-way – and have them try these solutions. Then we discuss them, fine-tuning our thinking.

I link our developing discussions to some goals. We want good thread tension management for a bead woven piece. We want the beads to lay correctly within the piece. We want the piece to feel fluid. We return to Guided Thinking. I summarize all the choices we have made in order to begin the project: type of bead, size of bead, shape of bead, type of thread, strategy for holding the piece while working it, strategy for bringing the new bead to the work in progress. I ask the students what ideas are emerging in their minds about how to bring all they have done so far together.

At this point, I usually would interject a *Mini-Lesson*, where I demonstrate, given the discussions, the smarter way to begin and execute the Project. In the Mini-Lesson, I *"Think Aloud"* so that my students can see and hear how I am approaching our Project.

And then I continue with Guided Thinking as we work through various sections of the Project towards completion. Whatever we do – select materials, select and apply techniques, set goals, anticipate how we want the Project to end up – is shown as resulting from a managed process of thinking through our design.

In "Guided Thinking", I would prompt my students to try to explain what is/is not going on, what is/is not working as desired, where the student hopes to end up, what seems to be enhancing/impeding getting there.

With guidance, demonstration and repetition, it is my hope that such thinking becomes a series of *Thinking Routines* my students resort to when starting a new project. As students develop and internalize more *Thinking Routines*, they develop greater *Fluency* with design.

And that should be our primary goal as teachers: *Developing our students' Fluency with design.*

First published,
JEWELERY DESIGN: A MANAGED PROCESS
Klimt02, 2/5/18
https://klimt02.net/forum/articles/jewelry-design-managed-process-warren-feld

LITTLE TAPESTRIES, Feld, 2012

Little Tapestries: Ghindia, 2012, Detail 1, At The Boundary Between Jewelry and Person Design Choice: This piece is constructed as a series of vertical columns where the beads in

the column move as "one". The columns are stitched together as if on hinges. This allows the piece to conform to the shape of the body, whether for different people who might wear the piece, or for a person who wants to wear the piece one day close to the neck, and another day further down on the bosom.

Little Tapestries: Ghindia, 2012, Detail 2, At The Boundary Between Jewelry and Person Design Choice: I used a chain and hook and eye clasp for the strap to allow for both the adjustment of the whole piece to accommodate the shape of the body, as well as to allow the wearer to wear the pendant component close to the neck, or further down on the bosom.

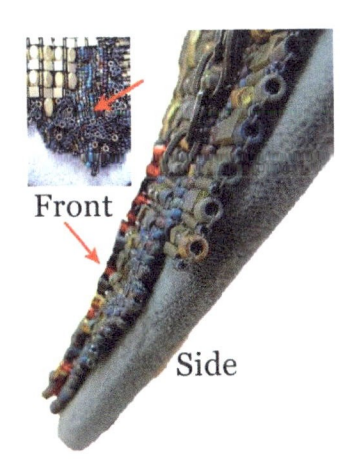

Little Tapestries: Ghindia, 2012, Detail 3, At The Boundary Between Jewelry and Person Design Choice: Not only was it important to capture the viewer's attention when directly

facing the piece. It was also important to capture that attention from other angles as well. Towards this end, I embedded very reflective red glass and crystal beads strategically along different parts of the side, but not noticeable in the front view.

DESIGN MANAGEMENT
6c. COMPONENT BASED DESIGN SYSTEMS:
Building Both Efficiency As Well As Effectiveness Into Your Jewelry Designs

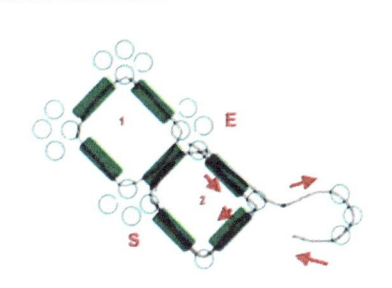

Blazing Barnacles, LYNAM, 2005

Guiding Questions:
(1) How does effectiveness differ from efficiency in jewelry design?
(2) Why is efficiency important to consider in the design process?
(3) What is a Component?
(4) What is a Component Based Design System?
(5) How does a Component Based Design System benefit me as a jewelry designer?
(6) What is DESIGN DEBT, and how do you control it?
(7) What is a Visual Audit and what documentation does it require?
(8) How do you develop standards, documentation, and scales for a Library of Components?
(9) How do you relate your components and component design system to the needs and wants of your clients?

Key Words:		
efficiency / effectiveness	*standards*	*branding*
components	*documentation*	*design debt*
reusability	*scale*	*visual audit*
repeatability	*modular*	*not context-specific*
design system	*replaceable*	*extensible*
voice and tone	*component inventory*	*encapsulated*
shared understandings	*usability*	*independent*
	patterns	*customer wants / needs*
	consistency	*contagion / word-of-mouth*

Abstract
Jewelry designers do not necessarily think of efficiencies when organizing and arranging

their designs. They primarily focus their thinking and energies on how to effectively and successfully go from one end to the other to achieve an object of beauty and appeal. But the next question becomes: Is this the most efficient, as well as most effective, way? Could the same piece be done just as well in less time? With less effort? With just as good of a result? Component Based Design is a process of building a piece of jewelry in pieces, sections or segments. A component is a something well-defined that feels like a whole unto itself. It can be a form. It can be a shape. It can be an object. It can be a set of steps or procedures. It has these kinds of characteristics: modularity, replaceability, portability and re-usability. Component Based Design unifies the design process and reduces variability in the numbers and types of choices we have to make as designers. It helps us tackle Design Debt. Design Debt refers to all the inefficiencies in the design process which add more time and effort to what you are trying to accomplish. This chapter finishes with discussion about how to create a Component Based Design System for jewelry designers.

Can Jewelry Designs Be Both *Effective* And *Efficient*?

Jewelry designers do not necessarily think of *efficiency* when organizing and arranging their designs. They ponder how to go from one end to the other, focusing their efforts on achieving an *effective* level of satisfaction and appeal. They think a lot about the use and placement of colors, textures and patterns. They figure out ways to attach a clasp. They jump from selecting design components to arranging them. And in this sense, visually, they tend to see their designs as a Gestalt – that is, they appreciate and evaluate their satisfaction with the piece as a whole. That piece as a whole should evoke a greater satisfaction, sense of finish and success moreso than the individual parts. And in general, that's the way it should be. Designers want to be effective as designers. This is what effectiveness is about.

But the next question becomes is this *efficient*, as well as *effective*? Could the same piece have been done just as well in less time? With less effort? With less thought about design elements and their arrangement? With less investment in all the beads and other pieces which eventually become finished pieces of jewelry? Is this a piece which could be created over and over again for multiple clients and larger productions? Could we be just as creative and just as effective by building in more efficiency into the process of design? Would adding an intervening step – that is, using design components to build components and then using components to build compositions – be smarter?

Re-thinking the design process in terms of components and component design systems provides one intriguing set of answers. Approaching design as a Component Based Design System is an especially good option for designers to incorporate, and for those designers who want to build their designing into a profitable business. Even if you are not headed in a business direction, thinking of design in terms of components and component systems offers a whole new way of creative thinking and design possibilities.

What Is A Component?

A component is a something well-defined that feels like a whole unto itself. It can be a form. It can be a shape. It can be an object. It can be a set of steps or procedures. It has these kinds of characteristics:

- Modularity
- Replaceability
- Portability
- Re-usability
- Functionality encapsulated within the component's design
- Is minimally dependent on the use or presence of other components
- Anticipates its implementation
- Intended to interface and interact with other components
- Not context specific
- Can be combined with other components to create new possibilities

If we think of a piece of jewelry as an architectural object, then it would be made up of a set of components which in some way conform to one another and interact with one another in a common, predictable way. The designer would create sets of components. Then any finished composition and design would be assembled from these components.

Components will range in complexity. In general, the more complex the component, the more limited its applications. The more re-usable your components are, the easier they are to design with. The more re-usable your components are, the easier it will be to scale your projects larger or smaller, longer or shorter, more volume or less volume. Components allow you to take something apart which isn't selling or no longer useful, and re-use all the parts.

What Is Component Based Design?

Component Based Design is a process of building a piece of jewelry in pieces, sections or segments.

These pieces are combinations of design elements.

These combinations of design elements become a set of smaller, manageable parts, which themselves are assembled into a piece of jewelry.

Systems of re-usable design components will allow any number of design possibilities. A component based design system provides a commonality within a visual language.

Instead of focusing on designing a particular product, the designer concentrates on creating a *design system*. The designer's principal responsibility in the formation of style is to create meaningful forms. These forms are more than shapes. These forms contain the essential elements which contribute to the jewelry's aesthetic and functional structure and composition. Some forms will be able to stand on their own; others, may be dependent on the presence and organization of others.

Component Based Design Systems enable the designer to build better products faster by making design re-usable. Re-usability allows designs to more easily be adapted to different body types, context-requirements, and/or scales.

Component Based Design Systems require clear documentation for each component, and a set of rules or standards for their use and assembly. Standards govern the purpose, style, and usage of these components. Documentation and standards help the designer avoid situations where you find yourself reinventing the wheel, so to speak. It helps the designer deal with such things as backlog, adapting different versions of a particular design, and concurrently managing both short-term and long-term goals and aspirations. It allows the designer to spend more time and focus on the trickier and more difficult part of coming up with designs specific or unique to each client.

How Is Component Design Helpful For Jewelry Designers?

Component Design allows for the designer to…
- *Design consistently*
- *Prototype faster*
- *Iterate more quickly*
- *Improve usability*

Design consistently. Standardized components used consistently and repetitively create a more predictable outcome. Standardized components also allow designers to spend less time focused on style, and more time developing a better user-experience and client outcome.

Prototype faster. Working within a coherent design system allows you to more quickly and easily organize your work flows. It allows you to experiment over and over again with the amount of prototypes and variants. Working with and within a design system should also provider greater and faster insights into design dilemmas and solutions.

Iterate more quickly. Design systems reduce the effort in design, from having to try out myriad colors, patterns, textures, scales and other design elements, to only having to try out a few components in the design system.

Improve usability. Should reduce inconsistent, unworkable or illogical combinations of things within any composition. In return, this should increase client satisfaction when wearing any piece of jewelry so created.

Design Systems Do Not Limit Creativity Or Design

Creating a design system does not limit or restrain the designer. In fact, it opens up more possibilities, more easily attainable. Design systems will also allow pieces to be easily customized and adapted to different situations. Design systems take away a lot of the worry about what to do next.

Design systems do not limit creativity. They offer a different way of allowing the designer to assert their creativity. The designer is still free to experiment, evolve, play, adapt. Design systems improve efficiency; they save time. Design systems do not constrain, restrain or otherwise limit the designer to work and think and speak and play as a designer.

Design systems can evolve and adapt to changes in styles and fashions. In fact, these systems trigger insights more easily apparent, as to how things need to change. After all, a change in one component will automatically define what changes need to be made in all other components it will interface and interact with.

Component based design systems are not one-shot, one-time deals. They are never complete. The work to create and maintain and improve

them is ongoing. These systems are living. But because a change in one component will trigger changes in others, the effort it takes to maintain and grow these system can be many times less than what happens when the designer does not rely on such a system.

Design Debt: Something Serious Which Needs To Be Managed

In more jargoned, but eye-opening, language, Component Based Design Systems reduce what is called *Design Debt*.

Design Debt refers to all the inefficiencies in your design process which adds more time and effort to what you are trying to accomplish, as you are designing any piece of jewelry. Design Debt continues to accumulate and increase as a project matures over time. Even after the designer has relinquished the project to the client, Design Debt will continue to accumulate if the designer fails to deal with it head on.

Design Debt includes things like…

- *Taking too much time to meet your goals*
- *Having to do too much research or experimentation when figuring out how to proceed*
- *Spending too much time thinking how to make a particular*

piece of jewelry unique or special for a certain client

Design Debt also includes all the good design concepts or solutions you skipped in order to complete your project on time. Design Debt includes all the additional time and effort you will have to make, should you have a backlog of projects which keep accumulating and accumulating as you are trying to finish the particular project you are now working on.

Some designers might approach the ever-accumulating Design Debt by cutting corners or relinquishing the project to the client prematurely. The designer might settle for a lower fee or less profitability. The designer might find that negative word-of-mouth is building too quickly with unsatisfied clients or demanding business stakeholders.

There are many sources of Design Debt, some very tangible, others less so. Examples of these sources of Design Debt include...

- The designer relies on an overabundance of non-reusable materials, or too much variation in inventory, or, inconsistent styles and conventions, all difficult to maintain

- The designer might start a project with assumptions, rather than research

- The designer might not have sufficient time or budget to implement each choice and step with care

- The designer might not have a full understanding of how each design element, form and component should best be arranged and interact within a particular composition

- The designer might be working with a partner or assistant, with incomplete information passing hands, as each works on the project

- The designer might not have a chance to test a design before its implementation or sale

- The designer might not get the opportunity to find out what happens with a particular piece after it has left the studio and the client wears it

- The designer might not have in place any formal or informal time and procedure for reflection and evaluation, in order to understand how various choices led to good or bad designs, or whether there is an improvement or degradation in the designer's brand due to good or bad performance

- The designer might rely on published patterns without the

wherewithal to adapt or customize them, or otherwise approach unfamiliar situations

Ultimately, Design Debt is measured in how satisfied our clients are with the products we design, and how that satisfaction affects what is referred to as *contagion* – the spread of word of mouth and its positive or negative impacts on our brand and reputation. Over time, Design Debt accumulates and becomes a great burden on any designer and design business.

Component Based Design Systems Help Us Tackle Design Debt

Anything which unifies the design process and reduces variability in the numbers and types of choices we make as designers will help us tackle Design Debt. That is what Component Based Design Systems are all about.

Component Based Design allows the designer to deal with a smaller number of pieces and variables at any one time.

Component Based Design leverages previous thinking and exploring, reducing the number of tasks which have to be done for each subsequent piece of jewelry.

And Component Based Design allows the designer to more easily and directly relate any kind of feedback to specific project design choices.

Creating A Component Based Design System

A Component Based Design System has...
- *Visual elements*
- *Modular elements*
- *Standards*
- *A voice and tone*
- *A relationship to client needs*

Your Component Based Design System can either be

(a) *Decoupled from any specific project*, which is effective for establishing a brand identity, or

(b) *Coupled to a specific project*, which is more effective for developing a line of jewelry made up of individual pieces.

Creating a Component Based Design System involves Six Key Task-Activities, which are…

> **(1) Conducting Visual Audit of Current Designs /** *Inventory*
>
> **(2) Determining Your Voice and Tone /** *Brand Identity*
>
> **(3) Designing A Component /** *Modular Elements*
>
> **(4) Creating Component Based Design System(s) /** *Library of Documentation and Standards*
>
> **(5) Defining Rules of Scale /** *Size, Volume, Distribution and Placement*
>
> **(6) Relating To Customer Needs /** *Shared Understandings and Desires*

(1) Visual Audit of Current Designs / *Inventory*

You will need to carefully review the visual elements you use in your current jewelry design practice.

You want to create a visual design language of discernable design elements, shapes, forms and components you are using now.

You will in effect be creating two inventories:

- First, a **Visual Inventory** of design elements which are visual features, and

- Second, a **Functional Inventory** of those beads, findings, shapes, forms and/or other component parts which are functional and interface with the wearer, such as clasp assemblies or things which allow a piece to move, drape and flow, or things which make a piece of jewelry adjustable, or things which allow a piece of jewelry to maintain a shape or position.

For each discernable set of design elements, *(such as, color, pattern, shape, form, movement, dimensionality)* or completely formed component, you would generate a description based on auditing the following *design elements*:

a. color, finish, pattern, texture
b. point, line, plane, shape, form, theme (typology)
c. sizing and spacing and scale (2-4 sets of standards of utilization; or by body type)

d. movement and dimensionality
e. canvas *(stringing materials; foundation)*
f. principles of composition, construction, manipulation; layouts
g. support systems *(allows movement, drape and flow)*, structural systems *(allows maintaining shapes or positions)* and other functional elements
h. plans, guidelines, icons

Your inventories can be a simple check-list, or more narrative descriptions.

By creating a 2-layer Inventory of Design – Visual and Functional – , you will be able to visualize the possible design components and patterns you might have at your disposal, as well as quantify what you are working with. Cataloging these details puts you in a better management/control position. This makes visible many of the consequences of your choices and selections in terms of managing Design Debt.

After you have finished creating your initial Inventory, review it. Identify where inconsistencies are. What things are must-haves? What things are superfluous?

Then look for things which go together or will be used together. Develop a simple system of categories to group things into. Keep the number of categories short. Examples of categories might include Patterns, Templates, Themes, User Interface, Foundations, Center Pieces, Color Palettes, Linkability.

(2) Determine Your Voice and Tone / *Brand Identity*

You want your parts, components and groupings of components, when used in the design of a piece of jewelry, to give the impression of you as a designer and/or your business's personality.

Look at your inventory and ask yourself: What are the more emotional, intangible qualities these seem to evoke? Do they evoke things, not only about my design sense today, but about what I aspire to be as a designer? How do I want my clients to respond to my pieces?

There should be a high level of coherence within your groupings of components. They should express a voice and tone, either of your entire brand, or of a particular line of jewelry you have created.

If there is not a high level of coherence, determine why not. What adjustments do you need to make in your inventory to achieve this?

(3) Design A Component / *Modular Elements*

Begin to take your visual inventory and re-imagine it as one or more collections or categories of components.

Types of components to think about:
- Re-usable
- Repeatable
- Build-upon / Connectible / Linkable
- Scale-able
- Evolvable over time
- Has necessary function
- Has necessary shape, form or theme
- Can easily interface with customer as the jewelry is worn

Some components will be ***modular and self-contained***, thus not dependent on the presence of other components. Some components will be ***compositional*** in that they fit or coordinate well with others. Some components will be ***generic***, thus usable in many different kinds of situations. And some components will be ***flexible*** because they can be tweaked and made to work in a variety of situations.

Now, actually begin to develop components. Towards this end, start with developing one component.

1st: List the key design elements, such as color, pattern, texture, shape, movement, dimensionality, and the like. These are the particular design elements you want associated with your core brand identity.

2nd: Define the smallest re-usable parts, such as beads, bead clusters, connectable links, stringing material and the like.

3rd: Scale up and define a complete component

4th: Scale up and define a composition consisting of several arranged components

5th: Fully layout the piece of jewelry, which will consist of one or more components and one or more compositions.

As you develop components, you will always need to keep in mind two things:

a) How you want the component to behave within your piece, and

b) How you want the component to interface with the client wearing the jewelry

CHAIN LINK COMPONENTS
A Simplified Example of Component Design

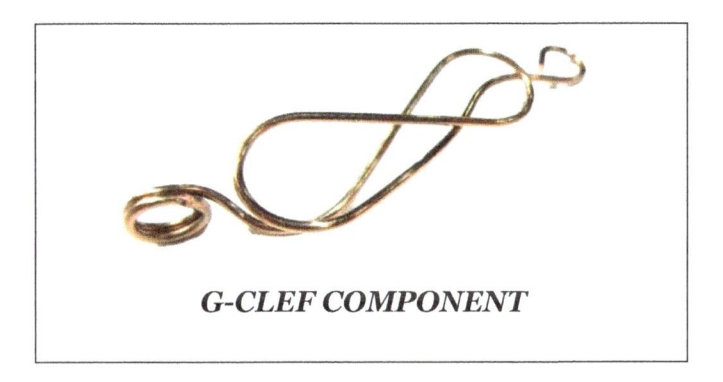

G-CLEF COMPONENT

I have a basic component I call a G-Clef Component. It is a simple chain link which is very connectable to other things. I use this as a simple example of a Component Based Design System.

I use this in several ways. I can use these as links in a standard chain. I can easily adapt two of these links to function as a hook and eye clasp. I can add beads between each link. I can use this as the basis for creating a pendant center piece. I can use this for earring dangles.

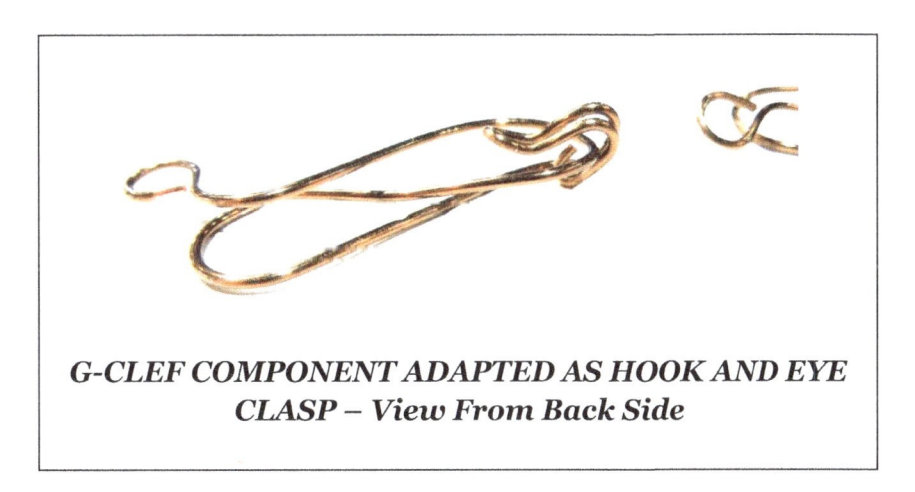

G-CLEF COMPONENT ADAPTED AS HOOK AND EYE CLASP – View From Back Side

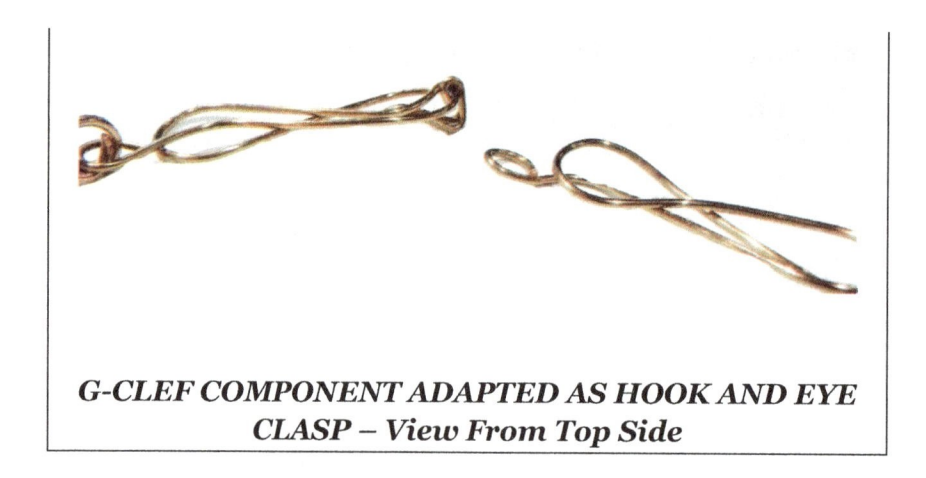

G-CLEF COMPONENT ADAPTED AS HOOK AND EYE CLASP – View From Top Side

The general infinity shape and reference to music (*I'm based in Nashville, Tennessee – "Music City USA"*) are easily incorporated into several lines of my jewelry, though there is one particular line of jewelry totally focused on this link component.

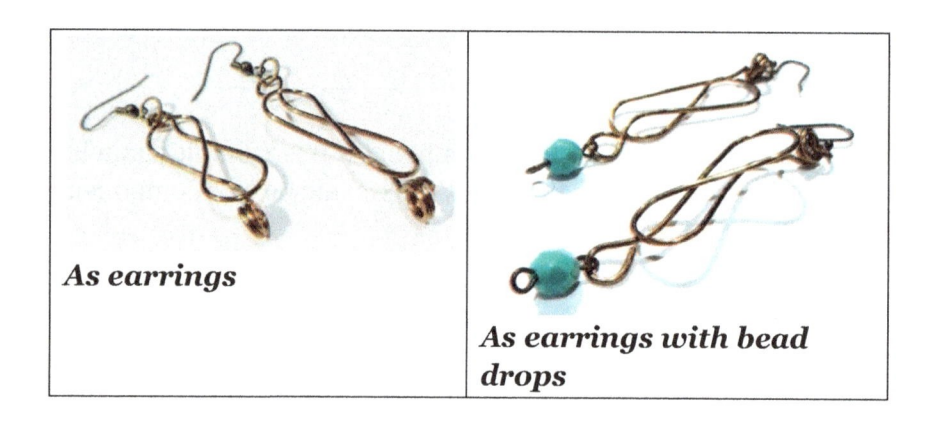

As earrings

As earrings with bead drops

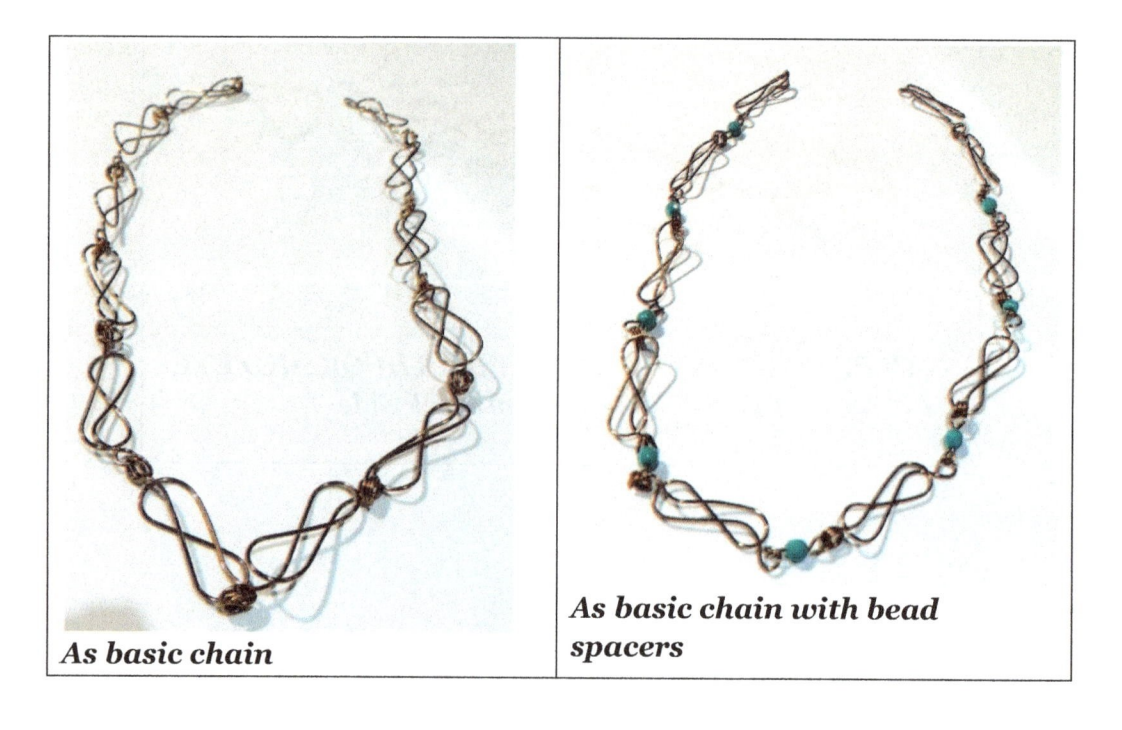

As basic chain

As basic chain with bead spacers

Chain with component adapted as pendant drop

My documentation for this component is as follows:

COMPONENT NAME: G-CLEF BASIC LINK
ID: CHAIN-GCLEF-001A
 	
Associated Jewelry Lines:
  - **CHAINS**
  - **G-CLEF**	

DESIGN ELEMENTS	NOTES
Color Family: Copper	*Branding*: use a lot of metal parts with antiqued finishes, especially added chains;
Finish: Metallic Antique Copper	
Texture: Smooth	can usually work in at least one of these components into every piece made
Pattern: Repeatable infinity shape music note reference	
Mass/Space: Line, curved	**Connectible link** is smallest component, but can add / embellish with beads, cabs, etc.
Sizing/Spacing: larger: 2" smaller: 1 ¼" 18 gauge wire, dead soft	Link can be adaptable to create many styles, types of jewelry, silhouettes, clasps
Movement: adequately sized loops allow for movement, drape	Easily embellish-able
Dimensionality: both ends of wire with loops should be pushed behind the "infinity" shape; gives nice layering effect	**Client experience:** easily recognize how to use piece, and how to combine pieces; recognizable shapes, style and profile; easily customizable
Canvas: 18ga wire	

COMPOSITION	NOTES
# components needed: 18" necklace – 11 18" necklace w/pendant – 12 18" necklace w/beads – 9 earrings – 2 earrings w/stones – 2	Hook single loop to triple loop **BE SURE THERE IS ADEQUATE JOINTEDNESS FROM COMPONENT TO COMPONENT**

CONSTRUCTION	NOTES
Support / Jointedness: sufficiently sized loops	
Structure / Shape: twist wire 20x to harden	
Connectivity/Adaptability: connect loop to loop	
Scale: - triple loop on one side and single loop on other side allows me to play with volumes and their placements - reduce length of piece - decrease or increase wire gauge thickness	
Start with 7 ½" of wire per component 18 ga wire, dead soft twist 20x to harden before shaping on wig jig	
Use Centaur Wig Jig to shape top peg: 4th arch down from top bottom peg: center hole	
3-coiled loop on top, vertically positioned (need 1 7/8" of wire) single coil loop on bottom, horizontally positioned (need ½" of wire)	
When adding parts using Eye pins (need 1 ½" to make these)	

SITUATIONAL / CONTINGENCY REQUIREMENTS	NOTES
None	

Two Other Examples Of Jewelry Designed Based On Components

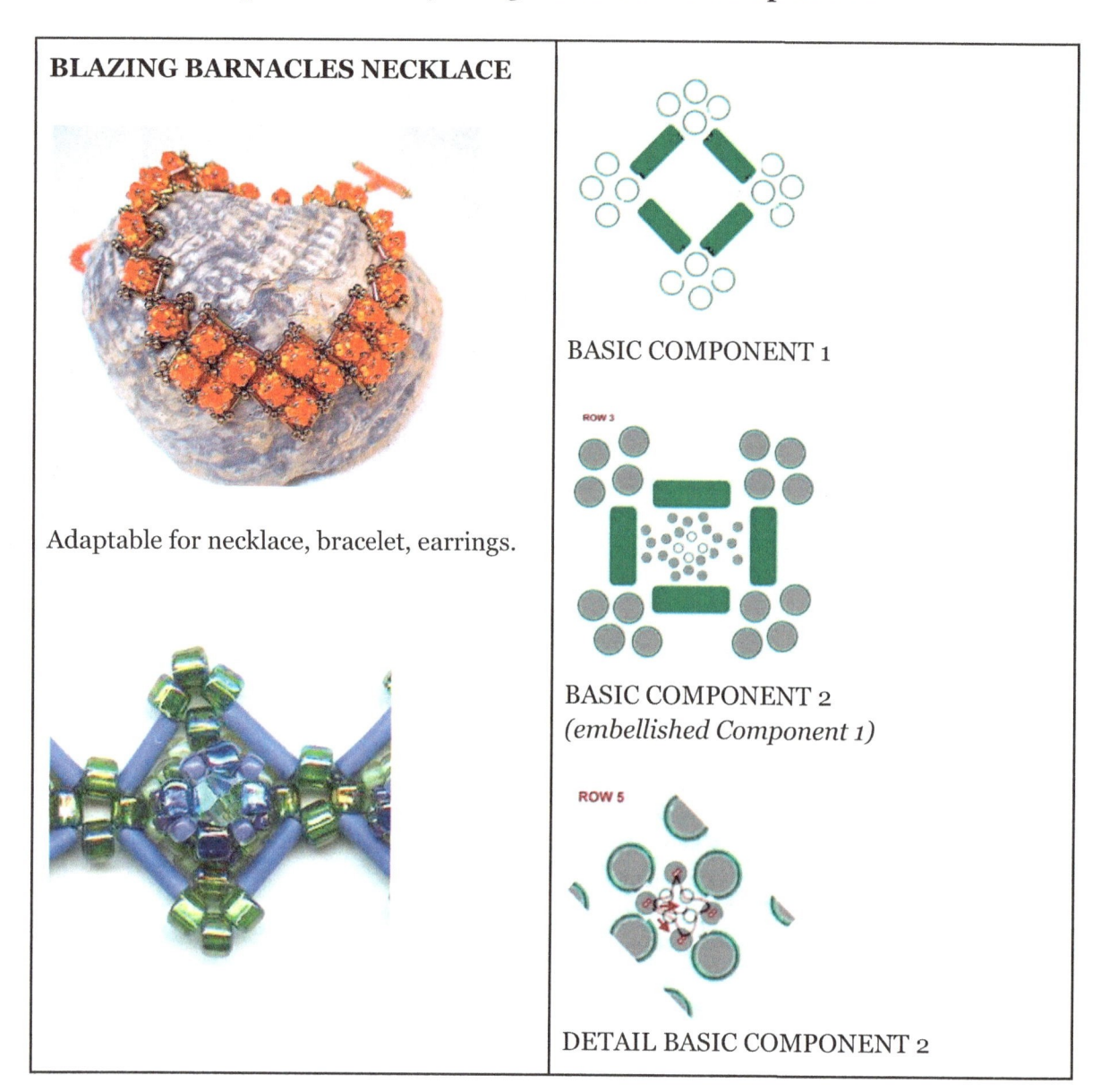

BLAZING BARNACLES NECKLACE

Adaptable for necklace, bracelet, earrings.

BASIC COMPONENT 1

BASIC COMPONENT 2
(embellished Component 1)

DETAIL BASIC COMPONENT 2

ColorBlock Bracelet

Adaptable for bracelet, necklace, earrings.

Can create different layer 2 patterns on top of layer 1.

Can easily adapt 1st and last component so as to create a clasp assembly.

COMPONENT 1a
(single layer foundation)

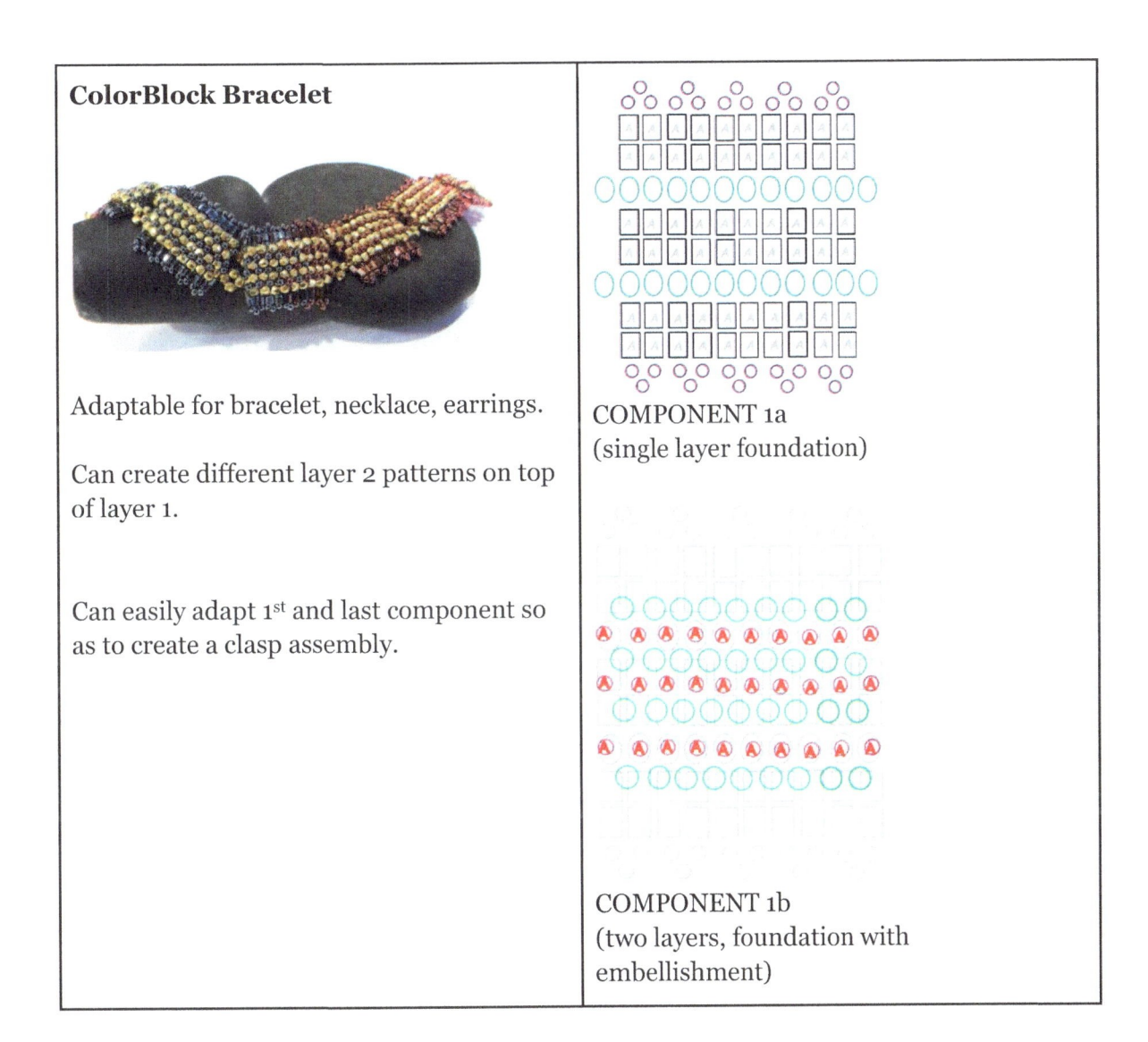

COMPONENT 1b
(two layers, foundation with embellishment)

(4) Component Based Design Systems / *Library of Documentation and Standards*

Your design system is much more than a pattern library. It is a collection of re-usable components which can be assembled together in any number of ways, and used to clearly signal and cement the identify of your brand as a whole, or of a particular line of jewelry you have developed.

As such, the system has *meaning*. It has *structure*. It embodies a *system of concepts* relevant to and representative of you as a designer and your design business or avocation. It is *resilient*.

Towards this end, to build in these meanings and intentions and expectations, you will develop a set of standards. Adhering to standards is how we manage and maintain consistency with how these meanings / intensions / expectations are expressed within any piece of jewelry we create. Following the standards is how we influence our clients to consistently come to share these understandings. Standards remove a lot of the arbitrariness in our design decisions. These standards should be put in writing, and be part of your documentation library.

Regardless of what materials, tools and techniques specific to your jewelry design practice, a successful design system will follow a core set of standards developed by you. These standards will inform you how components should be designed and how they should be organized within any composition.

These standards will focus on the following:

Brand touch points. What design elements or their arrangements evoke immediate associations with your jewelry designs?

Consistent client experience. What design elements, components or their arrangements result in a consistent client experience? When your client buys your jewelry and wears it, how does the client feel? How does the client want others to react, and does the client in fact get these reactions? When you client wears your jewelry, what needs, wants and desires does s/he want to be fulfilled, and how successful has your jewelry been towards this end? How do you maintain consistency in construction, functionality and durability of your pieces?

Coherent collection. To what extent do all the pieces in your collection similarly represent your brand and result in a similar, consistent client experience?

Naming conventions. What names should we give to our components, our pieces of jewelry, our lines of jewelry, our business and brand identity as a whole? How will these names resonate with our clients? Which names do you want to be universal, and which iconic?

Emphasis. What aspects of your jewelry do you want the client to focus on? Which aspects of your jewelry are most likely to trigger a conversation between you and the client, and between the client and that person's various audiences? Is that the conversation about your jewelry you want people to have?

Utility. What is each component, and how should you use it? What rules should you follow for building modular, composable, generic and flexible components? For linking and connecting them? How do you manage modifying any one component?

Potential. What determines if a component is to have a high potential value? Does the component have great commonality in use and/or re-use? Does the component have great business potential, whether or not it can be commonly used? Does the component have great potential in creating patterns or textures or shapes or forms or themes? Is the component technically feasible to create? Can this component be created within a certain timeframe, if there are time constraints? Does this component have the potential to excite others?

Codify, thus standardize, how components are described and detailed. Include information about basic design elements, such as color, pattern, texture, finishes. Give your component a name. Describe how you can adjust for scale – making something larger, smaller, with more volume, with less volume. Elaborate on any assembly considerations. Also anticipate in writing any situational or contingency requirements. Provide insights into how this component fits in with other components, or becomes the core component from which additional components might be fashioned. Write some notes about how the component is consistent with the standards for your brand / jewelry lines which you have developed. Last, take a picture of your component and include this image in your database.

(5) Scale / *Size, Volume, Distribution and Placement*

Scalability has to do with size and volume, and your strategies for adapting your component to different scales. You might think about a larger version for a necklace and a smaller version for a bracelet. You might think of modifying the component to increase its volume for use as a center piece pendant.

Scalability in jewelry will also refer to the ease of placing or distributing variations in size and/or volume.

Scalability begins with taking a modular approach to your jewelry design work. Additionally, your component must express some characteristics which are both generic as well as flexible. You want your components to be able to grow and shrink with the content of your pieces. I like to develop both a larger and a smaller version of each component, which I get very specific on and document. This usually gives me enough information should I still want to change size or volume.

(6) Relate To Customer Needs / *Shared Understandings and Desires*

For any design, it is a long journey from idea to implementation. This journey involves different people at different times along the way. The designer's ability to solve what is, in effect, a complex problem or puzzle becomes a performance of sorts, where the designer ferrets out in various ways – deliberate or otherwise – what the end users will perceive as making sense, having value and eliciting a desire powerful enough to motivate them to want to wear a piece of jewelry, buy it, utilize it, exhibit it or collect it. The designer, however, wants one more critical thing to result from this performance – recognition and validation of all the creative and managerial choices he or she made during the design process.

People will not use a design if their agendas and understandings do not converge in some way. They will interact with the designer to answer the question: *Do You Know What I Know?* If they get a sense, even figure out, that the answer is *Yes, they share understandings!* – they then become willing to collaborate (or at least become complicit) with the designer and the developing design.

A Component Based Design System forces the designer to incorporate these shared understandings into the development and organization of components. Component choices must be justified according to a set of standards. This set of standards relates design choices to how the client will perceive and respond to your brand identity or the identity you want any line of jewelry to reflect. A Component Design System creates tight guidance and boundaries, increasing not only the efficiency of your operation, but your effectiveness at developing jewelry which is consistent, coherent, user-friendly, user-desirable, and contagious.

Re-orienting your design practice towards a Component Based Design System may seem daunting, at first. But it gets easier and faster as the system grows and evolves. It is well worth the effort.

FOOTNOTES

Elliott, Gavin. "Design Debt: How to Identify Design Debt, Measure It and Overcome It." 5/7/20. As referenced in:
https://medium.com/@gavinelliott/design-debt-f8026795cc1c

Fanguy, Will. "A Comprehensive Guide To Design Systems." 6/24/19. As referenced in:
https://www.invisionapp.com/inside-design/guide-to-design-systems/

Feld, Warren. "Jewelry Design Composition: Playing With Building Blocks Called Design Elements," Medium.com, (2020).
As referenced in:
https://warren-29626.medium.com/jewelry-design-composition-playing-with-building-blocks-called-design-elements-d2df696551d8

Koschei, Jordan. "How To Tackle Design Debt." 4/19/17. As referenced in:
https://www.invisionapp.com/inside-design/tackle-design-debt/

Mazur, Michal. "What Is Design Debt and Why You Should Treat It Seriously." 8/12/18. As referenced in:
https://uxdesign.cc/what-is-design-debt-and-why-you-should-treat-it-seriously-4366d33d3c89#:~:text=In%20simple%20terms%2C%20design%20debt,the%20users%20will%20make%20do

Suarez, Marco, with Jina Anne, Katie Sylor-Miller, Diana Mounter, and Roy Stanfield. Design Systems Handbook. DesignBetter.Co by InVision.

SECTION 7:

INTRODUCING YOUR DESIGNS PUBLICLY

INTRODUCING YOUR DESIGNS PUBLICLY
7a. SHARED UNDERSTANDINGS AND DESIRES:
THE CONVERSATION CENTERED WITHIN A DESIGN

Part 1: What Are Shared Understandings and Desires?

Tibetan Tapestry Pendant, FELD, 2008

Guiding Questions:
(1) What are shared understandings and desires?
(2) How is the designer reflected back in their own work?
(3) Why do shared understandings and desires matter?
(4) What kinds of things does the designer need to know when eliciting and managing shared understandings and desires?
(5) Is there a formula for how the designer should proceed in his- or her role? Or is this on a case-by-case basis?
(6) How do assumptions, perceptions, expectations, values and desires come into play?
(7) How does the designer establish and manage shared understandings about assumptions, perceptions, expectations, values and desires?
(8) Are shared understandings and desires permanent or changing?
(9) What is effective risk communication?
(10) What happens to shared understandings when you relinquish your design to others?

Key Words:		
shared understandings	*progressive*	*risk and reward*
conversation	*authentic performance*	*paradigm*
assumptions	*evidence*	*craft*
expectations	*coherency*	*art*
perceptions	*resonance*	*design*
values	*contagion*	*universal*
desires	*dialog*	*subjective*
designer thinking	*dialectic*	*risk communication*
	flexibility / adaptability	*judgment*

| fluency
backward design | forced choices | rite of passage |

Abstract:

For any design, it is a long journey from idea to implementation. This journey involves different people at different times along the way. People will not wear / buy / reflect positively upon a design if their agendas, understandings and desires do not converge in some way with those of the designer. They will not buy a design or contract with the designer unless there are some shared understandings and desirability about what should happen and when, what will happen, and what the risks and rewards of the finished project will be. Shared understandings and desires are about recognizing intent and risk. Jewelry is both an outcome as well as an instrument for new shared understandings, new relationships, new behaviors, new reflections. As such, jewelry represents a commitment to a conversation – between designer and self and designer and client. The conversation allows for the management of shifting assumptions, expectations, perspectives, values and desires. Better designed jewelry shows the designer's conscious awareness of all the things affecting shared understandings and desires.

How You Are Reflected Back In Your Own Work

A piece of jewelry, so designed, is an object of beauty and functionality. But it is more than that. Jewelry is a unique form of artistic expression. It is not stationery as if hung like a painting in a museum. It has a different type of relationship with the wearer or viewer. It is meant to be worn on the body. It moves with the person. It adjusts positions as the person walks, sits, runs, turns, bends, maneuvers. It relates to clothing and hair styles and body shapes and sizes. It flows through many contexts and situations. Jewelry is expressive. Relational. Both an object and, more importantly, an intent.

Jewelry stands out because it has something to say about its context. Jewelry represents a commitment to a *conversation* – between designer and self, designer and client, and less directly but no less importantly, designer and all the various audiences of that client. Jewelry has something to say to the people who buy it and wear it. Without this conversation, people would not wear the jewelry. Or buy it. Or influence others to wear and buy it.

That conversation does not happen all at once. It does not start and stop at the beginning of the design process. It proceeds in fits and starts, sometimes in a clear direction, othertimes not. It does not fully resolve itself even after the piece is finished and then worn or bought or shared. That conversation continues as that piece is introduced to others and they react to it. It might get amplified. It might get simplified or made more complex and intricate. But it might get dampened, squashed, disrupted, distorted or discontinued, perhaps as readily.

The jewelry we design and make and wear speaks about ourselves as artists and our clients as persons. The conversations it triggers are somewhat unpredictable. The designer can be somewhat alone in converstaion, but maybe never alone when anticipating the reactions of others. In his or her head, but simultaneously complicit or perhaps collaborative with others, either in reality, or virtually and in the abstract. Design emerges from this dialogue, imaginative or otherwise. And design only emerges with some level of commitment to a conversation.

This commitment to a conversation, centered around any piece of jewelry, then is *progressive*. It is perspective shifting. It is reflective. It keeps going as everyone who interacts with the piece begins to formulate whether they like it or not. Whether it excites them or not. Whether they would wear it or buy it or utilize it or not. Whether it feels finished. Whether it seems successful. Whether it would suit some purpose, or fulfill some agenda. But the shifting perspectives and emerging collective, shared understandings and desires about the design always reflect back on the authentic performance of the designer. Endlessly reflective. In fact, there can never be an authentic performance by the designer without this commitment to a conversation.

Some designers are very aware of their thinking during their authentic performance in design; others are not. While the former is a more powerful position to be in, all designers – consciously or intuitively -- will need to figure out – before, during and after the design process – what criteria these various audiences will use to assess any piece of jewelry as meeting their needs, desires and requirements. How do they evaluate a piece of jewelry as coherent, relevant and resonant for them? How do they determine how much the designer's own design sense contributed to coherency, relevancy and resonance? How do they determine the risk to themselves for touching the jewelry, trying it on, buying it or showing others? How do they share these understandings and their desires with others as they wear the piece publicly? What makes these understandings sufficiently contagious so that others get excited about the piece, as well?

The better designer anticipates answers to these questions. The designer uses this information as *evidence* in formulating and judging the smartness of the choices to be made when designing and constructing a piece of jewelry. This evidence – good, bad or indifferent – forms the basis for *criticality*. It is a measurement. It states a position and measures the deviation. That criticality guides the designer all along the way from inspiration to aspiration to design to introducing the piece publicly. It encapsulates ideas about risks and rewards for the designer and for any one or more of that designer's audiences.

Evidence in this knowledge-building experience is assessed, managed and controlled. All designers want to get good at this. It is their way of inspiring their clients to recognize the designer's power in translating thoughts and feelings into design, that is, to reflect back the designer in their own design. We call this *coherency*. It is their way to excite their clients on an emotional level. We call this *resonance*. It is their way of influencing their clients to want to wear and buy their pieces. We call this *contagion*. As the clients wear their jewelry publicly, we also want to get their audiences to see and experience coherency, resonance and contagion.

Coherency. The degree that inspiration has been translated into aspiration and design with a clear recognition of the artist's hand.

Resonance. The degree that the designer's audience(s) demonstrate their level of assumptions, expectations, perceptions, values and desire as fulfilled by the jewelry.

Contagion. The degree to which the jewelry also appears coherent and resonant with the various client's audience(s).

Jewelry is both an outcome as well as an instrument for new shared understandings, new relationships, new behaviors, new reflections. It is a two-way mirror. It is a catalyst for exchange. It is a marker of validity. Jewelry is a product of creativity. Jewelry is a tool of engagement. Jewelry is a means toward criticality and legitimacy. Better designed jewelry shows the designer's conscious awareness of all these things and how they might play out in any situation. Authentic performances in anticipation of shared understandings and with no apologies. That's the goal, at least.

Why Shared Understanding and Desire Matters

For any design, it is a long journey from idea to implementation. This journey involves different people at different times along the way. The designer's ability to solve what is, in effect, a complex problem or puzzle becomes a performance of sorts, where the designer ferrets out in various ways – deliberate or otherwise – what the end users will perceive as making sense, having value and eliciting a desire powerful enough to motivate them to wear a piece of jewelry, buy it, utilize it, exhibit it or collect it. The designer, however, wants one more critical thing to result from this performance – recognition and validation of all the creative and managerial choices he or she made during the design process.

People will not use a design if their agendas, understandings and desires do not converge in some way. They will interact with the designer as long as they are uncovering answers to this question: *Do You Know What I Know?* If they get a sense, even figure out, that the answers are *Yes, they share understandings!* and, *Yes, the designer understands the basis for any or all of my desires!* – they then become willing to collaborate (or at least become complicit) with the designer and the developing design.

Sometimes this convergence of understandings and meanings and intents occurs in a happenstance sort of way. But more often, it won't happen without some degree of assertive leadership on the part of the designer. It is primarily up to the designer to establish these shared understandings. That is, the designer must take the lead to anticipate how they themselves should relate to their understanding of reality. The designer must invite the client to engage. So the designer, too, will ask the same question of the client that the client has asked of them:

Do You Know What I Know?

The answer to this simple question – *Do You Know What I Know?* -- is more than how the designer impresses the client and how the client impresses the designer. It is deeper than that. It is not surface meaning. It is not something descriptive. It is something critical. At its core are ideas about *intent* and *desire*. Its vocabulary gets very caught up in ideas about *risks* and *rewards*. The conversation to establish these shared understandings – we might call this a *dance* – proceeds on many levels, some assumptive, some perceptual, some through expectations, some through values and desires.

The designer, in effect, bridges the gap between how the designer sees the risks and rewards within any design process and outcome, and how the client might see these same risks and rewards. Both want to assess ahead of time whether the project will be satisfactory, feel finished, and meet their needs and desires. Both want to assess ahead of time whether there will be consequences, and what these consequences might be, should these communications and shared understandings about risk somehow fail or not meet expectations.

The designer wants to avoid any *miscommunication*. Any frustration. Any discomfort. So an in-depth, intuitive knowledge about shared understandings and desires, how to anticipate them, and how to incorporate them into the design process is necessary for the success of any design.

The designer should *not* assume there will be shared understandings. The designer should *not* assume that there will be a pleasant, conflict-free relationship with the client. The designer should *not* assume that any disagreement or miscommunication will be worked out at the beginning of the process and not have to be dealt with again. Nor, conversely, should the designer assume that any disagreement about elements of the design would negate shared understandings. The designer and client can agree to disagree as long as they share certain understandings, and as long as there is some level of agreement about the relationships the jewelry poses between risk and reward, thus desires.

Shared understandings and desires are about recognizing intent and risk. *They are about*

- Getting a sense of where the ideas for the design originate
- How the design process is to unfold
- What the design might be able to accomplish and what it might not
- What happens if conditions or intents and desires change over the course of the process
- How adaptable the designer is
- The chances the final design will feel finished and successful
- What criteria the final design needs to meet

If neither designer nor client understand intent and risk as each other sees it, there will be no shared understandings. The design will be ill-defined and poorly articulated. The role of desire will be misinterpreted or ignored. The designer's performance will be inauthentic. There will be no trust. No legitimacy. No satisfactory outcome.

While the need for establishing shared understanding in the design process might seem obvious, it does not often occur. Designers too often assume this will happen automatically. They present designs as *fait-accompli* – their success predetermined and prejudged as successful. They lose some level of management control when the client responds negatively. They fail to adapt or become too inflexible when the situation changes. The designs get implemented imperfectly. Worst of all, when the client takes possession of the design, the relationship ends.

SHARED UNDERSTANDINGS AND DESIRES:
THE CONVERSATION CENTERED WITHIN A DESIGN
Part 2: What Does The Designer Need To Know?

Gyrations, FELD, 2010

What Kinds Of Things Does The Designer Need To Know?
The designer needs to be able to assess and manage shared understandings and desires all through-out the design process.

The designer needs to be ...

(1)   Clear about the role designers should play, and how to relate to the client

Design is an occupation in the throws of becoming a profession. "Design" and the designer role are claimed by three very different perspectives – what are called *paradigms* -- about what the designer role should be about. These ways of looking at things come down to whether designers see their roles as *craft*, *art* or *design*. This can make it a little confusing about how the designer should go about assessing and managing shared understandings, and how the designer should relate to the client and his/her desires. To do so successfully, the designer may have to change their preferred paradigm, that is, how they think through what they should do.

(2) Aware of the primacy of subjective experiences

How people interact with designs is very subjective. The designer can predict some universal understandings about color, object and placement. But the designer also needs to be prepared to ferret out those subjective assumptions, perspectives, expectations, values and desires of the client (and the client's various audiences).

(3) Familiar with how designs have shared understandings influenced by desires, and why the development of these shared understandings is a social process

Conception, creation and implementation do not occur in a vacuum. They emerge as part of a social process. The recognition of a design – what it is, how useful it is, how enduring it is -- is not wholly determined by that design's objective characteristics. It is jointly determined. It involves a calculus of risks and rewards related to the consequences of making something, wearing something, buying something, sharing something, and critiquing something.

Designers Operate Within One Of Three Professional Paradigms

There are three different paradigms or approaches within which designers operate – *Craft, Art* or *Design*. Each paradigm is very coherent and rule- and expectation-bound. Each is a standard perspective and set of ideas.

Each approach seeks to provide the answers to the question: *Who Am I As A Designer?* Each approach steers the designer to play out their role differently. Each approach leads the designer to make different assumptions about the process, what skills and abilities need to come to bear, how to approach and interact with the client, and how to evaluate the success of the outcome. Each approach provides guidance about the outcome the designer should strive for.

Designing is about making choices. Each approach gives you different advice about the norms for acceptable conduct. It is important to be aware of all this, and if you are to develop the necessary skills and insights for assessing and managing shared understandings, you may have to change the paradigm-perspective you have been operating under.

THE CRAFT APPROACH

By far, the most typically-encountered approach is called the **Craft Approach**. The design process here is very mechanical. Tasks are reduced to step-by-step instructions, almost like paint-by-number. There is a clear beginning where you start your project, an organized middle, and a clear end when you finish it. Tasks are specified and carried out generically, that is, applied similarly over many design projects. The primary focus is on getting the job done with some attention to beauty and appeal. There is little concern about shared understandings, desires, perceptions and the like of any of the designer's client audiences, except, perhaps, for the designer him- or herself.

The Craft Approach assumes:
1. That the designer is either born with creative talents or not. Creativity is not something that you can learn.
2. The only thing that matters in design is to complete the task.
3. Designing is something anyone can do. It requires little to no specialized knowledge that must be garnered through a professional degree program.
4. In unfamiliar or new situations, there are no issues of adaptability. There is sort of a Have-Design-Will-Travel mentality.
5. Disciplinary literacy and fluency result from repetition and practice. The designer learns to be able to produce the same object over and over again.

Some consequences:
a. Since the singular goal is to get the job done, little thought or concern is placed on anticipating consequences and responding to them as they arise.
b. Appeal and beauty are primarily based on simply completing the project – no matter how it looks or feels or holds up with wear or use. It is assumed the project will be functional.
c. The designer is taught to start with a set of instructions or a pattern, and follow these mechanically. The instructions are assumed to be written correctly, need no further clarification, and should not be altered.
d. The better designer is one who has done more and more projects.
e. Easy to define an acceptable outcome – completing the project instructions from start to finish. It is assumed that there are few compositional issues, and that the project will be appreciated universally simply because it has been completed.

THE ART TRADITION

A second approach designers gravitate towards is the **Art Tradition**. The Art Tradition believes that the designer needs to learn a set of rules that can be used to apply to any situation where you are making jewelry. It is less important that you follow a set of steps. It's more important to know how to apply art theories – things like color, perspective, dimension, pattern, texture, balance, harmony, composition and the like -- to your project at each stage of the process, whatever that process is, and wherever that process takes you. In this paradigm, it becomes very important for the designer to anticipate shared understandings, in particular, about harmony and variety. It is assumed that the client audiences all desire that same perfect balance which harmony and variety bring to any piece of jewelry.

These art theories detail what defines successful (and unsuccessful) manipulation of design elements – universally and objectively -- within any piece of art or design. Design is seen as either a subset of painting or of sculpture. It is not seen as having its own discipline and medium, with its own special rules, theories, techniques and approaches, apart from those in art. Design is judged apart from the setting in which it is put into use.

What is nice about the Art Tradition, is that the goal is Beauty and there are issues of choice to be solved. The artist is not encumbered by having to follow specific steps or patterns. Nor is the artist encumbered by the structural and functional properties of all the pieces she or he uses -- only their beauty. The artist does not have to compromise Beauty for Functionality.

The Art Tradition assumes:
1. While different people have different creative abilities, everyone has some creative ability, and can be influenced in how to apply these creative talents.
2. What matters in design is how you approach the process. It is irrelevant whether the designer is deliberative or spontaneous. It does matter whether the designer applies the rules correctly at each increment of the way. The end result will be a very beautiful piece of jewelry.
3. Jewelry as art is really a form of sculpture or painting, and should be judged by the rules of sculpture or painting. The focus is on how you think through the process and make it intuitive.
4. The designer can achieve universally-accepted combinations and arrangements of design elements incorporated into any specific design piece or project.
5. Disciplinary literacy and fluency result from rehearsing theories and applying them over and over again until they become intuitive for any design choices you make.

Some consequences:
a. Little thought is given to issues of wearability or usability or durability.
b. The beauty of the design is as if it had been painted or sculpted. This is paramount.
c. The jewelry designer is taught that design is a matter of making choices, there are smarter choices to be made, and there are consequences when making any one choice. There is recognition that the artist may need to adapt to new or unfamiliar situations.
d. Design requires professional training and development over time.
e. Success results from universal understandings about how design elements should be combined and arranged so that they are harmonious, preferably with a bit of variety.

f. The full attention is on managing composition. Little attention or concern is placed on managing construction.

THE ART AND DESIGN PERSPECTIVE

A third approach to design is called the ***Art and Design Perspective***. This paradigm recognizes the importance of the Art Tradition, especially in understanding the design process as the culmination of a series of choices, each sensitive to the context within which they are made, and each with elements of risks, rewards and consequences. This approach adds, however, to the types of choices the designer is seen as making beyond those involving beauty and appeal. These include such things as functionality, usability, durability. There is attention to situation, value, desire, appropriateness. In this approach, both shared understandings as well as assessment of risk and reward as expressed by desire are fluid and negotiated, often re-negotiated, as the design process unfolds.

- Design creates its own challenges which the Art Tradition either ignores or cannot meet.

- Designs function in real (or virtual) 3-dimensional spaces, particularly sensitive to position, light/shadow, volume and scale.

- Design must stand on its own as an object of art, while simultaneously interacting with the people around it while they are using or utilizing it. Design alters people's relationships to it in the moment, across situations and settings, and over time.

- Design has to succeed where the responses to it are primarily subjective, even quirky. It serves many purposes for many wearers and viewers and users and responders. Some are aesthetic. Some functional. Some social, cultural and/or psychological.

In the Art and Design Perspective, designers learn their roles developmentally. That means, certain steps and rules should be learned before others, and that continual learning keeps building upon itself. While many designers initially learn their profession in a more shot-gun, less-than-organized way, it is necessary for them to, at some point, return to some basics and begin that developmental, hierarchical process.

There are many things to know and learn that present themselves in the design process – some art, architecture, engineering, behavioral science, social science, psychology, physics, mechanics, planning, marketing, administering, many techniques, many different materials, perhaps some computer coding and technology management, and the list goes on. The only way to become fluent in design is to gain an intuitive understanding how all these things are integrated, inter-related, and inter-dependent. That means developmentally learning how to become a design professional.

Designers work *backward*. That is, they first assess the shared understandings and desires of all their clients involved, and how they anticipate the design project will be understood as finished and successful. Then the designers begin to clarify what tasks they need to perform to get there. How deliberate they are in specifying and following through on the ordering of the tasks to be performed will vary, depending on their personality, experience and comfort level. They may not do everything a full scientific management approach might suggest if there is no cost-benefit in the use of this time and the materials; that is, if their assessment of shared understandings informs them that particular tasks are unnecessary to do.

The Art and Design Tradition assumes:
1. Everyone has creative abilities, but for most people, these need to be carefully groomed and attended to developmentally. Expressing creativity is not a matter of turning a switch on and off. It's a process that can be influenced by ideas and situations. The challenge is to teach people to become more intuitive in expressing their creative abilities and ideas.
2. What matters in design is that your project be judged as a work of art. In this case, the definition of *art* is specific to jewelry and its design, in anticipation of how it will be worn. Jewelry can only be understood as *art* as it is worn, and only as it is worn within a particular context or situation.
3. The end-user – the wearer or viewer, the buyer, the seller, the exhibitor, the collector, the student – responds to design mostly in a very subjective way.
4. Disciplinary literacy and fluency result from continual learning, rehearsing, and applying sets of integrated skills in different situations.

Some consequences:
a. This approach focuses on design issues. Beauty and appeal, along with functionality, wearability, durability, context, movement are all key considerations in selecting parts and interrelating these parts in a design. Very concerned with how you select parts and materials.
b. The beauty of the piece involves its construction, its lay-out, its consistency with rules of art theory, and how it holds up (physically and aesthetically) as it is worn in different situations. The focus is on how you organize your construction, piece by piece.
c. The jewelry designer is taught that design is a matter of making choices, there are smarter choices to be made, and there are consequences when making any one choice. Choices involve making strategic tradeoffs among appeal, functionality, and contextual relevance. There is recognition that the designer may need to adapt to new or unfamiliar situations.
d. Design requires continue professional training, development and re-training and re-development over time.

e. The full attention is on managing composition, manipulation and construction, and making hard choices where strategies conflict.

f. An acceptable outcome is one where the piece of jewelry or project design maintains a sense of itself as art, as the piece is worn or otherwise utilized. The piece or project should feel finished, parsimonious, usable and resonant to its intended client audience. The piece or project should reflect the designer's hand while at the same time reveal its intimacy with the client.

The Universal and the Subjective

In design, we play with design elements and objects, some of which are universally understood, like color schemes, and others in which clients respond to in very subjective ways.

For things universally shared and understood, we do not have to take the time to delineate and convey all the relevant information. Some of the relevant information is already understood. Designers do not have to spend a lot of time trying to anticipate and assess these universal, shared understandings.

These universals typically are predetermined. Sometimes by biology where our brains are prewired to either approach or flee. Universals are things which we approach. Other things we have to interpret and figure out, perhaps deciding to flee. Othertimes, by culture or society, where we learn automatically to recognize various symbols, objects and meanings, and play out certain roles. And, yet, still othertimes by psychology, where we make certain assumptions, interpretations and value judgments where we accept things as fact without needing further proof.

Most things we will encounter, however, are not universals. They are subjective. They get colored by assumptions, expectations, perceptions, values and desires. Our work, our interactions with clients, our marketing our products and services all revolve around interpretation. Interpretation is subjective and judgmental.

What designers do need to figure out, when working with any client, is how that person's assumptions, perceptions, expectations, values and desires will impact the design process and the resulting piece or project so designed.

SHARED UNDERSTANDINGS AND DESIRES:
THE CONVERSATION CENTERED WITHIN A DESIGN
Part 3: How Assumptions, Perceptions, Expectations, Values and Desires Come Into Play

A web-page from Land of Odds website, FELD designer, 2018

The Primacy of Subjectivity

The designer *needs / wants / demands* some level of acceptance by the client for the design. It is important to anticipate and assess how the client will form an opinion and make this kind of *judgment*.

For the client, some things will be accepted as true and right without proof. We call these things *assumptions*.

Other things for the client must be interpreted as to what they mean – a mental map or impression. We call these things *perceptions*.

The client will also have certain beliefs about what will happen or should have happened. We call these things *expectations*.

Last, the client will have certain preferences about what will or should happen which motivate the client to make certain judgments. Judgments are the result of assessments of risks relative to rewards, and what relationship of risks to rewards the client will put up with. We call these motivational preferences *values* or *desires*.

Clients Have Opinions and Judge

We all know this. When we first meet the client, they have opinions about us and judge us. As we are working on the project, they have opinions about us and judge us. When we hand over the project to them, they have opinions about us and judge us. This is OK. This is natural and to be expected.

- *Do they like it or not?*
- *Is it exciting to them or boring?*
- *Ugly or pretty?*
- *Useful or not?*
- *Worth it to them or not?*

As a designer who wants people to wear or use your designs, sell your designs, exhibit your designs, buy your designs, share your designs with others, then you need to understand how your clients form their opinions and make their judgments. You need to understand the implications, consequences, impacts, effects and affects this all brings to your designs and your design process. You need to begin to formulate how you will incorporate these understandings into your design process. And you need to figure out how you will influence their understandings so that they will recognize your skill and worth as a designer. All this is essential to the design process. It should be stating the obvious that things go awry whenever the interests and motivations of people are incompatible.

One cautionary note: Your clients will probably have a certain naivete. They may know little to nothing about design, construction, selection of materials and techniques, compositions and arrangements of design elements – everything you know a lot about.

Will they appreciate the difference between hand-made and machine made? Will they be accepting your choices about what to include and what not to include? Will they recognize good design and be able to differentiate it from bad? Will they demand of you a higher level of fluency in design and motivate you to meet higher expectations?

The better designer will look for ways to bring the client into the core of the design process. The designer will signal to the client that design requires some communication and conversation. The designer will take time to educate the client. The designer will guide the client through the process of eliciting assumptions, expectations, perceptions and values and desires. The designer will identify the emerging shared understandings and incorporate these into decisions about selecting materials and techniques, arrangements of objects within a design, and specifying tasks to be performed.

Assumptions

Our ideas and intents are supported by our *assumptions* about the world around us. Some assumptions are learned through our history and experiences. Some are taught to us. We take assumptions as givens and usually are unaware of them as we apply them. Except when our assumptions lead us on a path we do not want to travel.

Assumptions save us time and effort. As *truisms*, they allow us not to have to test and validate every little thing that comes our way. But they also can negatively affect our relationships, business or otherwise. We make assumptions about other people's behavior, other people's intentions, and our own behavior and intentions, and our assumptions can be off the mark. We may be laying a flawed foundation for our understanding of the relationship.

We need to identify and check our assumptions. We need to give our client the opportunity to identify and check their own assumptions. All this has to occur while developing a common, shared understanding of the design task at hand.

So, you can ask the client directly,

What do you want this piece or project to do for you?
What do you see me doing?
How familiar are you with the design tasks involved?

Assumptions are one of several things underlying client judgments. Let's talk about Perceptions.

Perceptions

Perceptions are ways of regarding, understanding or interpreting something. Perceptions are subjective, and each person has their own subtle differences, even when responding to the same design or event. In fact, different people may have very different perceptions about the same design or event. Their assumptions, expectations and values may further color their perceptions.

Each person filters their perceptions with each move, each conversation, and each situation. Such filters may contingently alter perceptions. Perceptions are not fixed. Any type of filter may result in *selectively* perceiving some things, but not others. In design work, our clients might selectively focus on brighter lights, louder sounds, stronger odors, sharper textures. Selective perception can add some more muddiness to the interaction and finding and developing the shared understandings necessary for success.

Adequately sharing understandings within a situation and among the people in it depends on the amount of information available to each person and how correctly they interpret it. Perception is one of the critical psychological abilities we have in order to survive in any environment.

The designer needs to be open to understanding how the client perceives the design tasks and proposed outcomes, and to adjust their own perceptions when the management of the relationship calls for this. **There is no formula here.** Each situation requires its own management strategy. Each designer is left with their own inventiveness, sensitivity, and introspective skills to deal with perceptions. But it comes down to asking the right questions and actively listening.

How does the client begin to understand your product or service?

Can the client describe what they think you will be doing and what the piece or product might look like when finished?
Can the client tell you how the finished piece or product will meet their needs and feelings?
Can the client tell you about different options?
How will they interpret what you want them to know?
What impressions do you want to leave with them?
Do they perceive a connection between you as a designer and your design work as proposed?
What levels of agreement and disagreement exist between your perceptions and theirs?
Can you get at any reasons which might explain their perceptions, and any agreement or difference?
Can you clear up any misperceptions?

Expectations

Expectations attach to perceptions. These are predispositions to perceive things in a certain way. They explain why people are more likely to prefer one interpretation or explanation over another.

Clients will have expectations about what the designer is like as a person. What the designer does. How the designer interacts with other people. How the designer sets a value and prices their work. What kind of ongoing information we will get. What are good and what are bad materials and techniques. What the finished product or project might look like. How useful that product or project might be.

When expectations are not met, there is a sense of frustration. Even paralysis. There might be feelings of disrespect or disregard. Why didn't the designer do what was expected? Use what was expected? Why am I unhappy with the finished product or project?

As with assumptions and perceptions, the designer needs to define a management role for him- or herself relative to client expectations.

Was the designer aware of the client's expectations?
Was the client asked about their expectations?
Was the designer skilled enough and insightful enough to meet those expectations?
Was it in the client's interest to steadfastly hold tight to their expectations, or to modify them?

Values and Desires

Values and desires are motivational. They signal a predisposition to act. They are a measure of the tradeoffs between the risks involved and the expected rewards. A social or economic calculation. A cognitive evaluation further affecting behavior. As such, they are a form of understanding.

Values and desires have a great impact on the assumptions people bring with them to the situation, and which ones they do not want to challenge. Values and desires have a great impact on the expectations people have, and which ones they want to prioritize. Values and desires have a great impact on the perceptions people have of the world, and which perceptions they want to act on.

Values and desires have two key components – the contributions of the designer and the motivations of the client. First, there is the value the designer places on the work, given the resources involved, the time spent, the skill applied, and meanings represented in the piece and importance to the designer. Second, there is the value the client places on the work, given their assumptions, perceptions, expectations, previous experience, and the socio-cultural-psychological context they find themselves in.

People project their feelings and thoughts and sensitivities onto the designed object, whether it be jewelry, an interior design, or a digitized representation online. These projections, however, can have many roots. Self-esteem. Self-expression. Social advantage. Tool of negotiation. Power.

Values and desires sometimes are expressed in monetary terms. Such and such a thing is priced at some dollar amount or assigned some worth also in monetary terms.

They more often are expressed with words. We hear words like *beautiful, satisfying, appealing*. And other words like *ugly, boring, scary*. Or phrases like *worth it, I want it, I want to buy it, I want to collect it*. Or more phrases like *the designer's pieces are in demand and rare*, or *the designer spent so much time making the piece*, or *the object contains several rare jewels*.

Sometimes the meanings associated with these words are relative, comparative or proportional. That is, they reveal more about values and desires. We hear phrases like *more satisfying, not as ugly as..., rarer than..., not as large as..., takes longer to make, about half as bright*, and so forth.

Values and desires, then, involve direction (*positive or negative*) and intensity (*a lot, somewhat, or a little*). Both designer and client, more often than not, have to filter their assumptions, perceptions and expectations a bit and sensitively trade-off various assumptions, perceptions and expectations each brings to the design situation. They do this by establishing value and desire. They establish value and desire by communicating about risks relative to rewards.

Communicating about risks and rewards takes the form of (a) identifying various design or design process options, (b) talking about their pros, cons and consequences, (c) attaching a sense of measurability (absolute or relative) to each option, and (d) selecting preferences for what should happen next.

SHARED UNDERSTANDINGS AND DESIRES:
THE CONVERSATION CENTERED WITHIN A DESIGN
Part 4: How Does The Designer Establish Shared Understandings?

Eloquence, FELD, 2018

How Does The Designer Construct Shared Understandings?

A key part of the designer's role is to interact with the various clients in such a way that construction of the relevant knowledge — assumptions, perceptions, expectations and values and desires — results in shared understandings. Not as difficult as all these big academic-type words sound.

The design process should be partly seen as creating a learning environment. The collective goal of this environment is to elicit shared understandings and feed back this information into all the choices involved with the design.

Design requires that *works* and *words* connect. As soon as we look at a design — even initially when that design is merely a fuzzy concept — we impose words on it. The words come from many sources. The designer. The critic. The teacher. The client. The buyer. The exhibitor. The seller. The collector. The user. The student. The public. The intents of imposing these words are myriad. *Design triggers words*. The designer needs to manage them.

Dialog has to happen between the designer and self, the designer and client(s), and the designer and all the audiences of the client(s) – either real or imagined.

Dialog involves…

- *Brainstorming*
- *Exploring points of view*
- *Challenging perceptions*
- *Delineating options*
- *Evaluating the risks and rewards associated with each option*
- *Anticipating consequences*
- *Expanding ideas and perspectives*
- *Sharing experiences and feelings of connection to the project*

The specific skills the designer applies include active listening, emotional reasoning, questioning, observing, probing, wondering, thinking out loud, synthesizing, connecting, creating, recognizing, interpreting, pushing and pulling.

The designer needs to know answers to these types of questions. When asking questions, if at all possible, the designer wants to frame them in such a way that they *force choices*. You do not want to elicit the easy Yes, No, or Ah-ha. You want to see how someone has to make a choice between one thing vs. another.

Examples of forced choices include things like,

- *either / or*
- *this or that*
- *prioritizing*
- *grouping*
- *categorizing*
- *if this, then what*
- *organizing and arranging*
- *timing*
- *specifying criteria for evaluation*
- *differentiating among what you think, what you know and what you want*

So, the designer might want to ask things like:

- *What to do and What not to do*
- *Why this is important and necessary, moreso than what other things*
- *Why the client needs the designer to do this but not that*
- *To what degree the piece or product will impact the client under a list of different circumstances*
- *How and why the client values the designer's work as well as the finished design above something else, like some other designer's work, or not having the design made at all*
- *What criteria the client will use to know that the finished design will have the intended value*
- *Why this material, and not some other*
- *Why this price/cost, and not something more or less expensive*
- *What alternative ways might the finished design will be valued*
- *If any task or process or design element can be different or better?*

A *dialectic* occurs to the extent that all parties actively listen to one another and think out loud. The design process needs to be welcoming. It should feel emotionally and cognitively comfortable. People should be free to express thoughts and free to disconnect from them when they change their minds. In a progressive and successful dialog, the participants will begin to shift their assumptions, expectations, perceptions, and values and desires, as necessary for the design project to proceed.

As the design process unfolds, then, all decisions, actions, words, focus and the like derive from these shared understandings and any associated desires. These shared understandings and desires encapsulate ideas about possibility, purpose, and project criteria. They lay out what the designer and client(s) want to do, where they want to go, and how they will do it to the satisfaction of all.

The finished design – jewelry in our case -- serves as a permanent record of meanings – those shared understandings --- negotiated and conveyed by the designer and all the collaborators (or at least people who have been complicit) along the way. As a permanent record, it implicitly documents action, purpose, value and desire. It represents a narrative measure of how risks have been traded off with rewards.

The finished design only serves as this permanent record to the extent that the design has been introduced publicly in a such a way that its shared understandings and associated desires are revealed. The permanency of this record may be ephemeral and only last for a short time. Although the design itself is fixed, interpretations of the shared understandings and associated desires underlying it may still change with the different contexts and situations or timeframes users of the design find themselves. The designer's job, even after completing the piece or project, may never be completely done.

Importantly, all this communicative interaction is how design significantly differs from art or craft. Design is a lived experience.

The designer should be able to

- *Distinguish the ideal from the real.*
- *Be aware of the interplay of the designer's reactions and those reactions of the various client audiences.*
- *Discern intent, value and desire, and the degree they are sufficient and enduring, as these evolve over the course of the design process.*
- *Specify tasks to be done which are truly supportive to the process of design management.*
- *Create a design process which, in effect, is a learning environment, conducive for the identification, negotiation, development and decision making which revolves around shared understandings and associated desires.*
- *Improve their accuracy in becoming aware of client assumptions, expectations, perceptions, and values and desires.*
- *Distinguish options regarding form, content, materials and approach, assign measures of risk and reward to each option, and prioritize them in line with developing shared understandings.*

Effective Risk Communication

One way to define the designer's role is to view it as *risk communication*. Effective risk communication involves understanding people and issues. This means an ability to elicit assumptions, expectations, perceptions and values and desires. This means an ability to clarify. An ability to either soften or intensify. An ability to organize and guide. An ability to prioritize, group, categorize, select among options. An ability to coordinate and resolve. An ability to maintain consistency over what could be a long period of time. An ability to share expertise and insights. An ability to restate things in measurable terms – exact numbers (*10 hours of work*) or relative concepts (*slightly longer than the last project*).

The client's opinions are influenced by trust in the credibility of available risk information. This could relate to little things like identifying why one color might be a better choice than another. This could relate to bigger things like identifying what location sales should occur which might be better than another. Or what situations or contexts wearing the jewelry might be most appropriate or rewarding. Or like what to perform better in-house, than not.

There are many such risks which must be assessed, measured, conveyed and agreed upon in the design process, including, among others, ...

- *Making tradeoffs between beauty and function*
- *Resolving conflicts between designer values and desires with those of the client*
- *Over-doing or under-doing the project*
- *Choosing the wrong materials and techniques*
- *Mismatching materials with techniques*
- *Determining a stopping point for the project*
- *Incorrectly anticipating the context within which the design is to function*
- *Managing the design process over a period of time, without losing motivation, commitment or focus*
- *Handling budgets, administration, product development, or marketing tasks*

How is this trust established? First off, the designer's competence and expertise should be on display. Next, the designer should be able to demonstrate empathy, honesty and commitment. The designer should be able to delineate options for each task or goal. The designer should be able to understand and accept the developing assessments of risk in the choices to be made. The designer should be able to explain why something would not be a concern. Finally, the designer should be organized and prepared, a good communicator, and show a willingness to coordinate or collaborate, if need be.

Designers, then, communicate the levels of risk involved with any choice. All choices have consequences. Making one choice usually negates the opportunity for making alternative choices. Subsumed within any choice are sensations about workability, implementability, worth, some measure of risk relative to some reward. The choices could be about selecting materials or techniques. They could be about which design elements to use, and which ones not. They could be about one compositional arrangement relative to another. They could be about which tasks to perform and when. They could be about criteria for determining whether a project should be judged finished and successful.

There are some keys to successful, adept messaging about risk. These include,

- *Having a clear purpose and educating others about the purpose (both designer's and client's), how these relate to assumptions, expectations, perceptions, values and desires, how to gain consensus*

- *Reducing all possible options to three or perhaps four major ones*
- *Supporting the pros and cons for each option with two to four facts*
- *Being up-front about uncertainty and possible consequences*
- *Detailing and explaining your preferences*
- *Explaining important conclusions about possible impacts with supporting reasons and details*
- *Tailoring the language to the client; working with the client to translate possible risks into language and measurements more familiar to that client*
- *Identifying things not yet known, such as having to learn techniques, or finding materials, or developing new forms or arrangements, or specifying a time frame for when you might be finished with the project*
- *Linking the project to past experiences or other things which the client might feel connected*
- *Asking the client to pre-test things and provide feedback and evaluation*
- *Keeping in regular touch with the client*
- *Being prepared for skepticism, controversy, misunderstanding, miscommunication or misdirection*
- *Being flexible, open to new ideas, and ready to suggest alternative solutions and ready to negotiate*
- *Not overlapping design projects; keeping things separate and compartmentalized*
- *If the overall project is especially large, breaking it up into a series of smaller projects; the project should be small enough so that risk and reward can be easily assessed, measured and made visible, and choices can be concise*
- *Having clear criteria for evaluating the project (and its continued value to and desirability for the client) at each increment of the way; allowing the criteria to grow, change and evolve, as necessary, without fostering disagreement*

Designer Thinking:
Literate, Fluent and Flexible in the Discipline of Design

When designers think like designers, they demonstrate a degree of leadership skills which goes a little beyond those of basic management. The fluent designer has the courage to have a vision and the wherewithal to stick with it until it is a finished product design. That designer has the courage to help others share understandings about the vision and how it will fit with their desires, as well. And that designer brings along that Designer Toolbox of strategies for adapting to unfamiliar or new situations.

Designers literate in design create learning environments within which communication and dialog flourish. These environments must allow for the free-flowing exchange of ideas, the expression of feelings and thoughts and values and desires, and the emergence of shared understandings.

The fluent designer attaches concepts to design elements. Meaning to compositional arrangements. Transforms assumptions, expectations, perceptions and values and desires. Comfortably adapts to new or unfamiliar situations. Anticipates the future, and strategically brings this knowledge to bear when defining current tasks and setting priorities. Is very aware of their own thought processes and is not afraid to share them, modify them or completely change them. Or, conversely, to respond to or re-shape those of others.

Designers literate in design are metacognitive. They are aware of their thinking and how their thoughts play out and impact any situation. They are aware of how their own thinking and their client's thinking is reflected back in the jewelry they have designed. If the designer does not provide a sense of the underlying intellect in the design of the jewelry, others cannot appreciate or anticipate what the designer was trying to accomplish.

Fluent designers are sensitive to what knowledges and skills they currently possess, which ones they do not, what ones they need to learn to complete the project at hand, and how to go about learning these.

They are critical in that they recognize the tradeoffs between risks and rewards of any choice – large or small – that they make vis-à-vis any project. They are able to articulate their critiques and raise questions about the project or process.

Relinquishing Your Jewelry Design To Others:
Saying *Good-bye!* A Rite Of Passage

One of the most emotionally difficult things designers do is saying *Good-bye!* to their designs as they hand them over to their client or otherwise expose their work publicly. The designer has contributed so much thinking and has spent so much time to the project that it is like ripping away an integral part of your being.

This is the moment where you want to maintain the conversation and engage with your audience, but look at this from a different perspective. Your relationship with your design is evolving and you need to evolve with it. Its innate intimacy is shifting away from you and getting taken over by someone else.

But you still have needs here. You want that client to ask you to design something else for them. You want the client to share your design with others, expanding your audience, your potential clients, your validation and legitimacy as a designer. And you want to prepare yourself emotionally to take on the next project.

Relinquishing control over your design is a rite of passage. At the heart of this rite of passage are shared understandings and how they must shift in content and perspective. Rites of passage are ceremonies of sorts. Marking the passage from one status to another.

There are three stages:

(1) Separation

You pass your design to others. You become an orphan. You have made a sacrifice and want something emotionally powerful and equal to happen to you in return. Things feel incomplete or missing. There is a void wanting to be fulfilled. You realize you are no longer sure about and confident in the shared understandings under which you had been operating .

(2) Transition (a betwixt and between)

There is a separation, a journey, a sacrifice. The designer is somewhat removed from the object or project, but not fully. The shared understandings constructed around the original project become fuzzy. Something to be questioned. Wondering whether to hold on to them or let go. Pondering what to do next. Playing out in your head different variations in or changes to these shared understandings. Attempting to assess the implications and consequences for any change.

These original shared understandings must undergo some type of symbolic ritual death if the designer is to move on. Leverage the experience. Start again. As simple as putting all the project papers in a box to be filed away. Or having a launch party. Or deleting files and images on a computer. Or accepting payment. Or getting a compliment. Or having a closure-meeting with the client to review the process after it has been completed.

(3) Reincorporation

The designer redefines him- or her-self vis-à-vis the designed object or project. The designer acquires new knowledge and new shared understandings. There is some reaffirmation. Triumph. This usually involves a new resolve, confidence and strategy for starting new projects, attracting new clients, and seeking wider acceptance of that designer's skills and fluency in design.

The designer has passed through the rite of passage. The jewelry or other designed object or project has been relinquished. The designer is ready to start again.

But as a designer, you will always be managing shared understandings. These most likely will have shifted or changed after the design is gone. And new ones will have to be constructed as you take on new assignments.

FOOTNOTES

Adamson, Glenn. **Thinking Through Craft**. 2007.

Baker, Jamie Feild. What is Shared Understanding? 6/24/2009. As referenced in: http://reverbconsulting.blogspot.com/2009/06/what-is-shared-understanding.html

Bittner, Eva Alice Christiane, and Leimeister, Jan Marco. **Why Shared Understanding Matters -- Engineering a Collaboration Process for Shared Understanding to Improve Collaboration Effectiveness in Heterogeneous Teams.** Year: 2013, Volume: 1, Pages: 106-114, DOI Bookmark:10.1109/HICSS.2013.608.

Canel, Melissa. The Role of Perceptions in Conflict. April 9, 2016. As referenced in: https://prezi.com/auvtd6yylkkf/the-role-of-perceptions-in-conflict/

Cheung, Chung Fai. **A Connected Critic: Can Michael Walzer Connect High-Mondernity with Tradition?** Understanding, 2006. As referenced in: http://www.emonastery.org/files/art/critic/2understanding.html

Clark, Garth. Shards. Ceramic Arts Foundation and Distributed Art Publications, 2003.

Cooper, J. David, Robinson, M, Slansky, J.A., and Kiger, N. **Literacy: Helping Students Construct**, 9th Edition, Cengage Learning, 2015.

Dunlop, Cole. You Are Not Worried Enough About Perceptions and Assumptions. May 7, 2014. As referenced in: https://www.authoritylabs.com/worried-enough-perceptions-assumptions/

Feld, Warren. Backward Design Is Forward Thinking. 2020. As referenced in: https://medium.com/@warren_29626/backward-design-is-forwards-thinking-design-in-practice-series-6f9a9f4f8cd9

Feld, Warren. Jewelry Design: A Managed Process. Klimt02, 2/2/2018. As referenced in: https://klimt02.net/forum/articles/jewelry-design-managed-process-warren-feld

Hector, Valerie. The Art of Beadwork. NY: Watson-Guptill Publications, 2005.

Kroeger, Andrew. Prevent Conflict By Knowing Your talent's Needs, Expectations, and

Assumptions. n.d. As referenced in: https://leadthroughstrengths.com/prevent-conflict-knowing-talents-needs-expectations-assumptions/

Mausolf, Judy Kay. How To Avoid 4 Communication Pitfalls: Assumptions, Perceptions, Comparison Expectations and Commitments. Spring, 2014. As referenced in:
https://www.practicesolutionsinc.net/assets/docs/communication_pitfalls.pdf
Progressive Dentist Magazine

Mazumdar, Pravu. All Art is a Critique of Reality. About Critique. Interview with Pravu Mazumdar. Klimt 02, 6/25/18. As referenced in:
https://klimt02.net/forum/interviews/all-art-is-critique-reality-about-critique-interview-pravu-mazumdar-carolin-denter?utm_source=phplist908&utm_medium=email&utm_content=HTML&utm_campaign=Criticism+is+not+the+application+of+a+norm+to+judge+a+work%2C+but+a+mode+of+cooperation+with+the+art.+All+Art+is+a+Critique+of+Reality%2C+the+new+klimt02+interview+about+critics%2C+with+Pravu+Mazumdar...+and+much+more.+Klimt02+Newsletter+423

Murray (https://artjewelryforum.org/authors/kevin-murray), Kevin. US VERSUS THEM IN THE CONTEMPORARY JEWELRY WORLD (https://artjewelryforum.org/us-versus-them-in-the-contemporary-jewelry-world), 06/18/2018. As referenced in:
https://artjewelryforum.org/us-versus-them-in-the-contemporary-jewelry-world

Norbeck, Edward. Rite of Passage. As referenced in:
https://www.britannica.com/topic/rite-of-passage

Ravick, Joseph. The Role Of Assumptions, Perceptions And Expectations In Conflict, n.d. As referenced in: https://adm.viu.ca/workplace-conflict/assumptions-perceptions-expectations

Saylor Academy. Understanding Culture, Chapter 2. 2012. As referenced in:
https://saylordotorg.github.io/text_leading-with-cultural-intelligence/s04-understanding-culture.html

Skinner, Damian. ALL THE WORLD OVER: THE GLOBAL AMBITIONS OF CONTEMPORARY JEWELRY. 6/15/12.

Schultz, Quentin. Servant Leadership Communication is Shared Understanding—Not Transmission, Influence, or Agreement. 9/25/17. As referenced in:
https://quentinschultze.com/communication-is-shared-understanding

Spool, Jared M. Attaining a Collaborative Shared Understanding. 7/3/18. As referenced in:
https://medium.com/@jmspool/attaining-a-collaborative-shared-understanding-dc70cf03f98f

ThoughtWorks Studios. "How do you develop a Shared Understanding on an Agile project? 2013. As referenced in:
http://info.thoughtworks.com/rs/thoughtworks2/images/twebook-developing-a-shared-understanding.pdf

Unumeri, Godwin Ogheneochuko. PERCEPTION AND CONFLICT. Lagos, Nigeria: National Open University of Nigeria, 2009. As referenced in:
https://nou.edu.ng/sites/default/files/2017-03/PCR%20276%20PERCEPTION%20%26%20CONFLICT_0.pdf

Verwijs, Christiaan. "Create shared understanding with 'What, So What, Now What' 8/4/2018. As referenced in:
https://medium.com/the-liberators/create-shared-understanding-with-what-so-what-now-what-6dda51d5bcf9

Vilajosana, Lluis Comin. Connotations and Contributions of the Maker: The Value of Jewels. 6/26/18.

Wiggins, Grant and Jay McTighe. *Understanding by Design, 2nd Edition*, Association for Supervision and Curriculum Development, 2005.

Yusuf, Bulama. Understanding Shared Understanding: 5 Ways to Improve Shared Understanding in Software Teams. 12/8/2019. As referenced in:
https://dev.to/bulsyusuf/5-ways-to-improve-shared-understanding-in-software-teams-1f62

INTRODUCING YOUR DESIGNS PUBLICLY
7b. "BACKWARD-DESIGN" IS FORWARDS THINKING

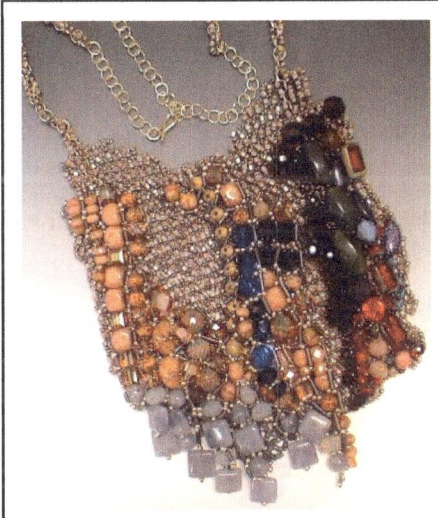

Little Tapestries / Ro Marie, FELD, 2013

Guiding Questions:
1. What is the most efficient and effective design process?
2. To what extent should the client's understandings and desires be taken into account?
3. What kinds of things happen when the client's understandings and desires are not taken into account?
4. What evidence should the design use when determining what the client's understandings and desires are?
5. What is backward-design? How does it differ from other approaches to the design process?
6. What is a Thinking Routine?

KEY WORDS:		
backward design	*proficiency*	*disciplinary literacy*
shared understandings	*design thinking*	*thinking routine*
assessor / assessment	*fluency*	*designer tool box*
evidence	*flexibility*	*finished / parsimonious*
desire	*comprehension*	*judgment*
		successful / satisfying
		contagious

Abstract:
How the jewelry designer begins the process of creating a design is very revealing about the potential for success. One of the things designers more literate in their discipline learn to do is called "Backward-Design." The designer starts with determining how their finished project will be assessed, "then works backward from there in specifying the tasks and methods to be employed." The designer begins the process by articulating the essential shared understandings and desires against which their work will be evaluated and judged. The designer starts with questions about assessment, and then allows this understanding to influence all other choices going forward. The designer anticipates what evidence others will use in their assessments of what the designer is trying to do. Jewelry design should not be seen as a set of steps per se. Rather, jewelry design is a way of thinking.

When The Designer Does Not Anticipate
The Understandings And Desires Of The Client

So often, jewelry designers struggle to figure out the reasons why their designs did not feel finished or as successful as they could be. After completing a project, they miss that feeling of proficiency and satisfaction. They get so caught up in the here and now of design that they forget to study what was, and fail to sufficiently anticipate what will happen when that design is introduced publicly – to the client, to the client's client and to the world.

Clients -- whether wearer, buyer, exhibitor, seller, collector, teacher, whatever -- sense this. When the jewelry designer does not share, or at least anticipate, the understandings and expectations of the client, the project could go awry. The designer could end up expending many unbillable hours trying to adjust, tweak, re-do, reconceive the project. And the whole process ends up not feeling good. Unfulfilling. A chore.

Often the core of the problem is the design approach to the project. Jewelry designers like to follow a linear process of design. This is an unfortunate remnant of the scientific management philosophy prevalent in the 1930's. A belief that everything can be reduced to a progressive series of steps, performed in an objective, almost-scientific way. Processed from a beginning, through a middle, and leading to an end. No iteration or back and forth. Little trial and error. Objectively gather information and data. Analyze it. Formulate a hypothesis. Test it. Draw conclusions. Set goals, objectives and activities accordingly. Organize resources. Arrange things in a pleasing manner and implement. Evaluate. Happy client, happy life.

But, as we all know, things aren't so linear. They aren't so clear-cut and pat. They are not so perfectly objective and universally understood. We have all felt these things:

- *Working with imperfect information.*
- *Often inarticulate clients.*
- *Or clients not understanding or appreciating or anticipating what you are trying to do.*
- *Some limits of access to resources we want and need.*
- *Not fully skilled in every single technique that might come to bear.*
- *Can often get caught up in our heads, sometimes over-thinking, othertimes not thinking enough.*
- *A fear of failing to know when enough is enough; not editing.*
- *A weak sense of what happens when we introduce our designs publicly.*
- *Never fully sure if we have achieved acceptable results.*

Jewelry design should not be seen as a set of steps per se. Rather, jewelry design is a way of *thinking*. That way of approaching the professional task with fluency, flexibility and comprehension. Here the jewelry designer must provide a sense of the underlying intellect in the design of the project, or else others cannot appreciate or anticipate what the designer was trying to accomplish. They need to sense the designer's thought process all along the way.

Towards this end, we want designers to get socialized into a disciplinary literacy as they pursue design as an occupation and profession. They need to learn how *design* differs from *art*. Achieving a harmony and some variety in design – the goal in an art project -- often falls short of client expectations. There's that "It's nice, but…" or "Where's the WOW factor I was looking for…" or "I like it, but I'm not sure how I'm going to wear it…" or "I like it but not enough to buy it…".

And professional, experienced jewelry designers need to learn how to tell *when enough is enough*. That is, they need to have this automatic, intuitive sense when if they added or subtracted one more thing from their design, it would not be as good. They need to edit.

One useful type of tool designers can resort to is called a *Thinking Routine*. The Thinking Routine is any structured way of asking yourself questions which help you organize your thoughts. You should have several Thinking Routines in your Designer Tool Box. These aid you in applying that disciplinary literacy you are forever developing and improving upon.

One Thinking Routing I want to introduce you to here is called "*Backward-Design*".

How the jewelry designer begins the process of creating a design is very revealing about the potential for success. One of the things designers more literate in their discipline learn to do is called "*Backward-Design*." The designer starts with determining how their finished project will be assessed, *then works backward from there in specifying the tasks and methods to be employed.*

The designer begins the process by articulating the essential shared understandings and desires against which their work will be evaluated and judged. The designer starts with questions about assessment, and then allows this understanding to influence all other choices going forward. The designer anticipates what *evidence* others will use in their assessments of what the designer is trying to do.

Given that the more successful designer "backward-designs," he or she would begin the process by anticipating those understandings about how their work will be assessed. The first assessment is how others, particularly the client, but including the client's audience(s) as well, will see the design as *finished*, complete, coherent, and parsimonious. The second assessment is how others will see the design as *successful*, satisfying, having the desired effect, contagious, and impactful.

The designer then is equipped to make three types of informed, purposeful choices:

1. Choices about composition
2. Choices about construction and manipulation

3. Choices about performance

These choices involve what to include and not include. How to organize and how not to organize. How to mesh things together and not mesh things together. How to introduce things publicly and not introduce things publicly.

Given what the client wants, your choices will be influenced by what *evidence* they will look for to know you have achieved it. These choices involve evidence about what tasks will be worthy to be accomplished, and the most efficient and effective ways to accomplish them. These choices signal that the designer really gets it and is ready to perform with understanding, knowledge and skill.

In backward-design, these choices emerge through dialect and communicative interaction. Choices about tasks are purposeful. Design is more seen and operated as an *action*, rather than an *object*.

When beginning the process of design, the designer thinks about assessment before beginning to think about what and how they will design. Designers do not wait until the end – what scientific management calls the *evaluation step* -- of the process. Thinking backward as a strategy for problem solving really isn't that difficult. While this may feel illogical or counter-intuitive, in the end it makes more sense.

Again, we can set up a backward-design process as a Thinking Routine. A Thinking Routine can help the designer internalize the backward-design process. It can help the designer sharpen their focus. The Routine becomes a way, used informally or formally based on your style, to structure the client intake process. It also becomes a way to force you to prioritize your tasks.

Here is a simple example useful for designers interested in backward-design, and which I call **DESIGN FRAMEWORK**.

DESIGN FRAMEWORK ROUTINE

1. DESIRED RESULTS

Desired Goals:
When the project is completed, what relevant, purposeful, desired goals will this design have addressed?
o
o
o

Understandings:
Clients will understand that…
o
o
o

Essential Questions:
Clients will have these key, critical questions about the project…
o
o
o

Knowledge:
When the project is finished, the Client will know that…
o
o
o

After Project Completed:
Client will be able to…
o
o
o

2. ASSESSMENT EVIDENCE

Performance Tasks:
Through what performance tasks will you the designer demonstrate what you have anticipated as the Client's desired understandings…
o
o
o

Evaluative Criteria:
By what evidence will Client recognize that you the designer heard and understood them…
o
o
o

By what evidence will Client recognize that the project is finished and successful?
o
o
o

3. YOUR PLAN OF ACTION

List Tasks (including opportunities for Client to rethink and revise their thinking)	Relationship of Task to Client Understanding and Desire	Evidence Client will use to judge completion of each task as finished and successful
1. 2. 3. 4.	1. 2. 3. 4.	1. 2. 3. 4.

How Do We Elicit This Information From The Client?

Critical here is the designer's ability to elicit a lot of information from the client. Information about expectations. Past experiences. Things they like and dislike. What they want to happen at the end. Assumptions, perceptions, expectations, values, desires, worth, risks, rewards. What the client's various audiences might expect and desire.

Understandings are often revealed through the exercises of comparing and contrasting or summarizing key ideas and images. We can provide pictures. We can take the client on an internet tour. We can ask the client to take us on an internet tour. During all this, we encourage the client to explain, interpret, apply, critique, prioritize, categorize, arrange, empathize or reveal prior knowledge about and experience with. This gives us a lot of information to start with.

We can then seek to find specific examples of what the client has worn in the past or has tried to buy recently. They can describe certain actions they have taken. They can share with you various pieces of jewelry they have designed or had designed for them, and their feelings about these. They can identify what types of jewelry they like to wear under which circumstances and situations. They can explain the "facts" as they present them. Or offer up "interpretations".

We then have to step back from our interactions with the client, and ask ourselves: Does the information we have collected provide enough evidence for us to determine a task plan? Can we see patterns and themes emerging? Hard and fast convictions? Things loosely connected? Are the client's understanding of the problem(s) to be solved consistent with those of the possible solution(s) which can be implemented?

Or is there still some ambiguity needing clarifying? Are any expectations unrealistic? If so, we return to interacting with the client to gather more evidence of their desires and understandings about what they want to be accomplished.

The Proficient and Successful Jewelry Designer

The proficient and successful jewelry designer is one who can generate designs which are engaging and effective, as judged by the client (and perhaps by extension, the client's various audiences).

The design process should allow the designer to identify and prioritize those tasks which are most relevant to or likely to achieve the end result. And in turn, reject or shorten tasks which do not.

The client should see the design as relevant, provoking, meaningful, self-affirming and energizing. The project should feel *finished*. It should meet the client's understandings about what constitutes *success*. You do not want the client to walk away thinking the design was merely the result of an academic exercise. You do not want the client to think or feel you have sold them a cookie-cutter solution.

The design process itself should impact not only the final product, but the client him- or herself. It should elevate the client's own sense of design and accomplishment. It should result in a client more competent when interacting with you and securing your services the next time.

FOOTNOTES

Backward-Design. I had taken two graduate education courses in Literacy and one in Planning that were very influential in my approach to disciplinary literacy. One of the big take-aways from **Understanding by Design** *by Grant Wiggins and Jay McTighe, 2nd Edition, Association for Supervision and Curriculum Development, 2005,* was the idea they introduced of "*backward-design*". Their point is that you can better teach understanding *[and my words, perform professionally]* if you anticipate the evidence others will use in their assessments of what you are trying to do. When coupled with ideas about teaching literacy and fluency *(see* **Literacy: Helping Students Construct Meaning** *by J. David Cooper, M. Robinson, J.A. Slansky and N. Kiger, 9th Edition, Cengage Learning, 2015),* you can begin to introduce ideas about managing the design process in a coherent and alignable way.
Understanding by Design by Grant Wiggins and Jay McTighe, 2nd Edition, Association for Supervision and Curriculum Development, 2005.
Literacy: Helping Students Construct Meaning by J. David Cooper, M. Robinson, J.A. Slansky and N. Kiger, 9th Edition, Cengage Learning, 2015

Thinking Routines. There are many different types of Thinking Routines. The Harvard Graduate School of Education has researched, evaluated and categorized these. These routines can be used in your own reflections with yourself, or as active tools when working with clients. They are used to help you understand and manipulate your world.
Project Zero's Thinking Routine Toolbox. (https://pz.harvard.edu/thinking-routines) Harvard Graduate School of Education.

SECTION 8:

DEVELOPING THOSE INTUITIVE SKILLS WITHIN

DEVELOPING THOSE INTUITIVE SKILLS WITHIN
8a. CREATIVITY ISN'T FOUND, IT'S DEVELOPED

Caterpillar Espiritu, FELD, (2014)

Guiding Questions:
(1) What is "creativity" and what is "creative thinking" in jewelry design?
(2) Why do you need to be creative?
(3) Why does creativity scare people?
(4) What does it take to become a creative person?
(5) Why are some people more creative than others?
(6) When does creativity happen?
(7) How do you know what to create?
(8) Is creativity something that can be taught?
(9) How do you overcome creativity blocks?

Key Words: creativity creative thinking creativity blocks	*developmental* *insight /inspiration* *establish value* *divergence* *convergence* *problem solving* *perception* *cognition* *differentiation*	*fluency* *flexibility* *elaboration* *originality* *complexity* *risk-taking* *imagination* *curiosity* *assessment* *implementation*

Abstract:
Creativity isn't found, it is developed. Creativity is a phenomenon where both something new and, at the same time, somehow valuable is created. While some people come to creativity naturally, in fact, everyone can develop their creative ability. Thinking creatively involves the integration and leveraging of three different kinds of ideas – insight and inspiration, establishing value, and implementing something. We work through creative thinking through divergence (that is, generating many possibilities), and convergence (that is, reducing the number of these possibilities). There are ten attributes associated with creative problem solving: fluency, flexibility, elaboration, originality, complexity, risk-taking, imagination, curiosity, assessment, and implementation. Last,

different strategies are discussed for enhancing creativity and overcoming creative blocks.

CREATIVITY ISN'T FOUND, IT'S DEVELOPED

Kierkegaard – and I apologize for getting a little show-off-y with my reference – once described *Creativity* as "a passionate sense of the potential." And I love this definition. *Passion* is very important. Passion and creativity can be summed up as some kind of intuitive sense made operational by bringing all your capabilities and wonderings and technical know-how to the fore. All your mechanical, imaginative and knowledge and skills grow over time, as do your abilities for creative thinking and applications. Creativity isn't inherently natural. It is something that is developed over time as you get more and more experience designing jewelry.

You sit down, and you ask, what should I create? For most people, especially those getting started, they look for patterns and instructions in bead magazines or how-to books or websites online. They let someone else make all the creative choices for them. The singular creative choice here is picking what you want to make. And, when you're starting, this is OK.

When you feel more comfortable with the materials and the techniques, you can begin to make additional choices. You can choose your own colors. You can make simple adaptations, such as changing out the bead, or changing the dimensions, or changing out a row, or adding a different clasp.

Eventually, however, you will want to confront the Creativity issue head on. You will want to decide that pursuing your innermost *jewelry designer*, no matter what pathway this takes you along, is the next thing, and right thing, to do. That means you want your jewelry and your beadwork to reflect your artistic hand. You want to develop a personal style. You want to come up with your own projects.

But applying yourself creatively is also work. It can be fun at times, but scary at others. There is an element of risk. You might not like what you end up doing. Your friends might not like it. Nor your family. Nor your client. You might not finish it. Or you might do it wrong. It always will seem easier to go with someone else's project, already proven to be liked and tested – because it's been published, and passed around, and done over and over again by many different people. Sometimes it seems insurmountable, after finishing one project, to decide what to do next. Exercising your creative abilities can sometimes be a bear.

But it's important to keep pushing on. Challenging yourself. Developing yourself. Turning yourself into a bead artist or jewelry designer. And pursuing opportunities to exercise your creative talents even more, as you enter the world of design.

What Is Creativity?

We create. Invent. Discover. Imagine. Suppose. Predict. Delve into unknown or unpredictable situations and figure out fix-it strategies for resolution and to move forward.

All of these are examples of *creativity*. We synthesize. Generate new or novel ideas. Find new arrangements of things. Seek out challenging tasks. Broaden our knowledge. Surround ourselves with interesting objects and interesting people. Again, these are examples of *creativity*.

Yet, creativity scares people. They are afraid they don't have it. Or not enough of it. Or not as much as those other people, whom they think are creative, have. They don't know how to bring it to the fore, or apply it.

But creativity shouldn't scare you. Everyone has some creative abilities within themselves. For most people, they need to develop it. Cultivate it. Nourish it. They need to learn various tools and skills and understandings for developing it, applying it and managing it. Creativity is a process. We think, we try, we explore, we fall down and pick ourselves up again. Creativity involves work and commitment. It requires a lot of self-awareness – what we call metacognition. It takes some knowledge, skill and understanding. It can overwhelm at times. It can be blocked at other times.

But it is nothing to be scared about. Creativity is something we want to embrace because it can bring so much self-fulfillment, as well as bring joy and fulfillment to others. Creativity is not some divine gift. It is actually the skilled application of knowledge in new and exciting ways to create something which is valued. Creativity can be acquired and honed at any age or any experience level.

For the jewelry designer, it's all about how to think creatively. Thinking creatively involves the integration and leveraging of three different kinds of ideas – *insight and inspiration*, *establishing value*, and *implementing something*.

> **(1) Seeing something out of nothing (insight, inspiration and perception).** Technically, we talk about this as controlling the relationship of *space* to *mass*. You begin with a negative space. Within this space, you add points, lines, planes and shapes. As you add and arrange more stuff, the mass takes on meaning and content. The designer has to apply creative thinking in finding inspiration, choosing design elements, arranging them, constructing them, and manipulating them.

> **(2) Valuing something (understanding and cognition).** Connections are made. Meaning and content, when experienced by people, result in a sense of appeal and value. We refer to this as *desire* and *expression*. Value can relate to the worth or cost of the materials, the intuitive application of ideas and techniques by the artist, the usefulness or functionality of the piece, or something rare about the piece. Value can center on the power to leverage the strengths of materials or techniques, and minimize their weaknesses. The designer has to apply creative thinking to anticipate how various audiences will judge the piece.

(3) Implementing something (synthesis and acceptance).

Jewelry design occurs within a particular interactive context and dialog. The designer translates inspirations into aspirations. Aspirations are then translated into design ideas. Design ideas are implemented, refined, changed, and implemented again until the finished product is introduced publicly. The design process has to be managed. When problems or road-blocks arise, fix-it strategies and solutions need to be accessed and applied. All this occurs in anticipation of how various audiences will respond to the jewelry, and convey their reactions to the artist, their friends, family and acquaintances, and make choices about wearing it and buying it and displaying it publicly. The designer has to apply creative thinking in determining why anyone would like the piece, want the piece, buy the piece, wear the piece, wear it publicly, and wear it again and again, or give it as a gift to someone else.

Types of Creativity

Creativity has two primary components:
(1) *Originality*, and
(2) *Functionality* or *Value*.

The idea of *originality* can be off-putting. It doesn't have to be. The jewelry, so creatively designed, does *not* have to be a totally and completely new and original design. The included design elements and arrangements do *not* have to be solely unique and never been done before.

Originality can be seen in making something stimulating, interesting or unusual. It can represent an incremental change which makes something better or more personal or a fresh perspective. It can be something that is a clever or unexpected rearrangement, or a great idea, insight, meaningful interpretation or emotion which shines through. It can include the design of new patterns and textures. It can accomplish connections among seemingly unrelated phenomena, and generate solutions. It can be a variation on a technique or how material gets used. It can be something that enhances the functionality or value of the piece.

Creativity in jewelry design marries that which is original to that which is *functional, valued, useful, worthwhile, desired*. These things are *co-dependent*, if any creative project is to be seen as successful. For jewelry designers, creativity is not the sketch or computer aided drawing. It is not the inspiration. It is not the piece which never sees the light of day, because then it would represent a mere object, not jewelry.

Creativity requires implementation. And for jewelry designers, implementation is a very public enterprise.

What Does It Take To Be Creative?

Creative people tend to possess a high level of energy, intuitiveness, and discipline. They are also comfortable spending a great deal of time quietly thinking and reflecting. They understand what it means to cultivate emotions, both within themselves, as well as relative to the various audiences they interact with. They are able to stay engaged with their piece for as long as it takes to bring it to completion. They fall in love with their work and their work process.

Creativity is not something that you can use up. To the contrary, the more you use your creativity, the more you have it. It is developmental, and for the better jewelry designer, development is a continual, life-long process of learning, playing, experimenting and doing.

To be creative, one must have the ability to identify new problems, rather than depending on others to define them. The designer must be good at transferring knowledge gained in one context to another in order to solve a problem or overcome something that is unknown. I call this developing a *Designer Tool Box* of *fix-it strategies* which the designer takes everywhere.

The designer is very goal-oriented and determined in his or her pursuit. But, at the same time, the jewelry designer also understands and expects that the design process is very incremental with a lot of non-linear, back-and-forth thinking and application. There is an underlying confidence and belief, however, that eventually all of this effort will lead to success.

How Do We Create?
It's not what we create, but how we create!

The creative process involves managing the interplay of two types of thinking – *Convergence* and *Divergence*. Both are necessary for thinking creatively.

Divergent thinking is defined as the ability to generate or expand upon options and alternatives, no matter the goal, situation or context.

Convergent thinking is the opposite. This is defined as the ability to narrow down all these options and alternatives.

The fluent jewelry designer is able to comfortably weave back and forth between *divergence* and *convergence*, and know when the final choices are parsimonious, finished, and will be judged as resonant and successful.

Brainstorming is a great example of how creative thinking is used. We ask ourselves *What If…? How about…? Could we try this or that idea…?* The primary exercise here is to think of all the possibilities, then whittle these down to a small set of solutions.

Creative Thinking

Creative thinking, first, involves cultivating divergent thinking skills and exposing ourselves to the new, the different, the unknown, the unexpected. It is, in part, a learning process. Then, next, through our set of convergent thinking skills, we criticize, and meld, and synthesize, and connect ideas, and blend, and analyze, and test practicality, as we steer our thinking towards a singular, realistic, do-able solution in design.

Partly, what we always need to remember, is that this process of creative thinking in jewelry design also assists us finding that potential audience or audiences – weaver, buyer, exhibitor, collector – for our creative work. Jewelry is one of those special art forms which require going beyond a set of ideas, to recognizing how these ideas will be used. Jewelry is art only when it is worn. Otherwise, it is a sculptural object.

There are 10 aspects to creative thought. Each should be considered as a separate set of skills, both for divergent as well as convergent thinking, which the jewelry designer wants to develop within him- or herself. Initially, the designer wants to learn, experiment with and apply these skills. Over time, the designer wants to develop a level of comprehension and fluency to the point that the application of each of these skills is somewhat automatic.

Fluency: Having a basic vocabulary in jewelry design, and the ability to see how these concepts and design elements are present (decoding) and arranged (composition, construction and manipulation).

Divergence: To generate as many possible design elements and combinations and fine-tunings to increase number of possible designs.

Flexibility: Ability to adapt selections and arrangements, given new, unfamiliar or unknown situations.

Divergence: To generate a range and variety of possible configurations leading to same solution.

Elaboration: Ability to add to, embellish or build upon ideas incorporated into any jewelry design.

Divergence: To generate the widest variety of attributes of design elements and combinations which have value-added qualities, given a particular design.

Originality: Ability to create something new or differentiated which has usefulness and value.

Divergence: To delineate many ideas and concepts which are both new or differentiated and have value.

Complexity: Ability to conceptualize difficult, multi-faceted, intricate, many-layered ideas and designs.

Divergence: To take a solution and break it down or reinterpret it into as many multiple facets or multiple layers as possible.

Risk-Taking: Willingness to try new things or think of new possibilities in order to show the artist's hand publicly and stand apart.

Divergence: To elaborate the widest possible scenarios for publicly introducing the piece, given various design options, as well as all the ways these potential audiences might interact, respond to and use the jewelry, and all the ways these audiences might influence others, as well.

Imagination: Ability to be inspired, and to translate that inspiration into an aspiration.

Divergence: To think of many ways an inspiration might be described, interpreted, or experienced physically, sensually and emotionally, and to identify the many different ways inspirations might be interpreted into a jewelry design.

Curiosity: Ability to probe, question, search, wanting to know more about something.

Divergence: To question the situation from many angles and perspectives.

Assessment: Ability to anticipate shared understandings, values and desires of various audiences for any piece of jewelry.

Divergence: To identify all the possible audiences a piece of jewelry might have, and all the different ways they might judge the piece as finished (*parsimonious*) and successful (*resonant*).

Implementation: Ability to translate aspirations into a finished jewelry design and design process.

Divergence: To delineate all the possibilities an aspiration might get translated into a design, evaluated against all the possibilities the design could be successfully, practically and realistically implemented.

Enhancing Creativity and Overcoming Creativity Block

So, what kinds of creative advice can I offer you about enhancing your creativity? How can you nurture your creative impulses? How can you overcome roadblocks that might impede you?

Here is some of my advice:

Success Stories. While you are fiddling with beads and wire and clasps and everything else, try to be as aware as you can of why your successes are successful. What are all the things you did to succeed? On what points does everyone agree the project succeeds? Share these observations about your successes with others.

Un-Block. Don't set up any roadblocks. Many people, rather than venture onto an unknown highway of creativity, put up walls to delay their path. If they just had the right beads. Or the right colors. Or sufficient time. Or had learned one more technique. Or had taken one more class. Or could find a better clasp. These are excuses. Excuses to avoid getting creative. Try to be conscious and aware of any roadblocks you might set up for yourself.

Adapt. Anticipate contingencies. It amazes me how many people come into my shop with a picture out of a magazine. We probably can find over half the components, but for the remaining components pictured which we don't have in stock, we suggest substitutes. But, NO, the customer has to have it exactly like the picture, or not at all. Not every store has every bead and component. Many beads and components are not made all the time. Many colors vary from batch to batch. Many established companies have components especially made up for them – and not available to the general public. The supplies of many beads and components are very limited – not unlimited. Always be prepared to make substitutions and adapt.

Play. Be a kid again. Let your imagination run wild. Try things. Try anything. If the world says your color combination is ugly, don't listen to them. Do it anyway. Ignore all restrictions. Forget about social and art conventions.

Be Curious. Play *What If...* games. What if a different color? What if a different technique? What if a different width or length? What if a different style of clasp? What if laid out horizontally instead of vertically? Re-arrange things. Tweak. Take out a bead board, and lay out beads and findings on the board, and re-order everything — Ask yourself: More or less satisfying?

Embrace the New / Challenge yourself. Don't do the same project over and over again, simply because you have proven to yourself that you can make it. While you might want to repeat a project, with some variations, to learn more things, too much doing of the same-ole, same-ole, can be very stifling.

Create An Imaginative Working Space / Manage Disruptions and Disruptors. You need comfortable seating, good lighting, smart organization of parts and tools and projects-in-process. Some people like music playing. If family or friends tend to interrupt you, explain to them you need some boundaries at certain times of the day or days of the week.

Evaluate / Be metacognitive. Learn from failures. You have invested time, money and effort into making these pieces. And not everything works out, or works out well. Figure out why, and turn these failed pieces into lessons and insights. Give yourself permission to be wrong. Build up your skills for self-awareness, self-management and self-assessment.

Take a break / Break your daily routine / Incubate it / Sleep on it. And if you suddenly find your productivity interrupted by Bead-Block and Artist-Block and Jeweler's-Block, put your project down. Take a break. Mull on things awhile. Put yourself in a different environment. Take a walk. Sleep. A period of interruption or rest from a problem may aid creative problem-solving in that it lets us let go of or forget some misleading cues, thoughts, feelings and ideas.

Network / Connect With Other Jewelry Designers and Artists / Collaborate on a Project. Here you want to tap into and absorb someone else's energy, knowledge and insights. Surround yourself with interesting and creative people. Learn different ways of knowing and doing. Get encouragement. Find a mentor. Take a workshop. Collaborate on a project. The fastest way to become creative is to hang around with creative people.

Do something out of the ordinary. Something unexpected. Or something just not done. This will shock your system to think in different ways. To see things in a new light. To recognize contradictions. Robert Alan Black gives great advice.
He shouts at the blocked: Break A Crayon.
He shouts again: Draw Outside The Lines.
And I would add and shout: Shock your system. Stick your hands into a bowl full of mud or jello.

These are all great advice.

Make creativity a habit. Make it routine in your daily life.
- Keep a journal. Write down your thoughts and experiences and insights.
- As you create a new piece, keep a running written log of all the choices you are making.
- Challenge yourself. Change colors, arrangements, sizes and shapes. Create forms and new components. Think of different silhouettes.
- Expand your knowledge base and skills. Look for connections with other disciplines.
- Surround yourself with interesting things and interesting people. Get together regularly. Collaborate. Take a field trip together.

What Should I Create?

The process of jewelry making begins with the question, *What Should I Create?*

You want to create something which results in an *emotional engagement*. That means, when you or someone else interacts with your piece, they should feel some kind of connection. That connection will have some value for them. They might see something as useful. It may have meaning. Or it may speak to a personal desire. It may increase a sense of self-esteem. It may persuade someone to buy it. It may feel especially powerful or beautiful or entertaining. They may want to share it with someone else.

You want to create something that you *care about*. It should not be about following trends. It should be about reflecting your inner artist and designer – what you like, how you see the world, what you want to do. Love what you are making. Otherwise, you run the risk of burning out.

It is easier to *create work with someone specific in mind*. This is called *backwards design*. You anticipate how someone else would like what you do, want to wear it, buy it, and then let this influence you in your selection about materials, techniques and composition. This might be a specific person, or a type of person, such as a potential class of buyers.

Keep things *simple and parsimonious*. Edit your ideas. You do not want to over-do or under-do your pieces. You do not have to include everything in one piece. You can do several pieces. Showing restraint allows for better communication with your audiences. Each piece you make should not look like you are frantically trying to prove yourself. They should look like you have given a lot of thought about how others should emotionally engage with your piece.

There is always a lot of pressure to brand yourself. That means sticking with certain themes, designs or materials. But this can be a little stifling, if you want to develop your creativity. *Take the time to explore new avenues of work.*

You want to *give yourself some time to find inspirations*. A walk in nature. A visit to a museum. Involvement with a social cause. Participation in a ritual or ceremony. Studying color samples at a paint store. A dream. A sense of spirituality or other feeling. A translation of something verbal into something visual. Inspirations are all around you.

Final Words of Wisdom

We don't learn to be creative We become creative. We develop a host of creative thinking skills. We reflect and make ourselves aware of all the various choices we make, the connections we see, the reactions we get, and the implications which result.

We need to be open to possibility.

We need to have a comfort level in taking the unknown or unexpected, and bridging the differences. That is, connecting what we know and feel and project to ideas for integrating all the pieces before us into a completed jewelry design. We need to become good translators, managing our choices from inspiration to aspiration to completed design.

We need to be able to hold on to the paradoxes between mass and space, form and freedom, thought and feeling, long enough so that we can complete each jewelry making project. We need to be comfortable while designing during what often become long periods of solitude.

We need to know jewelry and jewelry making materials and techniques inside and out. We need to know how to maximize their strengths and minimize their weaknesses. We need to be able to discover new ways of designing with them. It is critical that we put ourselves on a path towards greater fluency, flexibility and originality.

We must be willing to give and receive criticism.

We must be aware, not only of our desires, goals and understandings, but those of our various audiences, as well.

Be motivated by the design process itself, and not its possible and potential external rewards.

We must be very reflective and metacognitive of how we think, speak and work as jewelry designers.

We need to give ourselves permission to make mistakes.

We must design things we care about.

FOOTNOTES

Besemer, S.P. and D.J. Treffinger. Analysis of Creative Products: Review and Synthesis. Wiley Online Library, (1981).

Black, Robert Alan. Blog: http://www.cre8ng.com/blog/

Csikszentmihalyi, Mihaly. Creativity: Flow and the Psychology of Discovery and Invention. Harper Perennial; Reprint edition (August 6, 2013)

Guilford, J.P. Creativity. *American Psychologist, 5*, 444–454, 1950.

Koestler, Arthur. The Act of Creation. Last Century Media (April 1, 2014).

Lewis, Sarah. The Rise: Creativity, The Gift of Failure, and the Search for Mastery. NY: Simon & Schuster, 2014.

Lucy Lamp. "Inspiration in Visual Art Where Do Artists Get Their Ideas. As referenced in:
https://www.sophia.org/tutorials/inspiration-in-visual-art-where-do-artists-get-the

Maital, Shlomo. "How IBM's Executive School Fostered Creativity," Global Crisis Blog, April 7, 2014.
Summarizes Louis R. Mobley's writings on creativity, 1956.

March, Anna Craft. Creativity in Education. Report prepared for the Qualifications and Curriculum Authority, March, 2001.

Seltzer, Kimberly and Tom Bentley. The Creative Age: Knowledge and Skills for the New Economy. Demos, 1999.

Torrance, E. P. The Torrance Tests of Creative Thinking-Norms-Technical Manual Research Edition- Verbal Tests, Forms A and B-Figural Tests, Forms A and B. Princeton, NJ: Personnel Press, 1966.

Torrance, E. P. The Torrance Tests of Creative Thinking-Norms-Technical Manual Research Edition- Verbal Tests, Forms A and B- Figural Tests, Forms A and B. Princeton, NJ: Personnel Press, 1974.

Turak, August. "Can Creativity Be Taught," Forbes, May 22, 2011.

DEVELOPING THOSE INTUITIVE SKILLS WITHIN
8b. INSPIRATION AND ASPIRATION

The Inspiration

The Design
Canyon Sunrise, FELD, 2004

Guiding Questions:
1. What are the differences among Creativity, Inspiration and Aspiration?
2. What does it mean to "Inspire To...", and how does this differ from "Inspired By..."? How do you get others to share your inspiration?
3. Where do you find inspiration(s)?
4. Are inspirations the source of creativity?
5. How do you achieve Resonance through inspiration and aspiration?

Key Words: inspiration aspiration creativity inspire to finding inspiration(s)	resonance design actualization	motivation shared understandings

Abstract:
The words creativity, inspiration *and* aspiration *are often used interchangeably, and I think it's important that we draw a clearer distinction. Inspiration is not the source of creativity. Inspiration, instead, should be viewed as a motivational response to creativity. The successful designer – one who eventually can achieve a level of resonance – is one who is*

not only inspired by, but also inspired to. The core aspects of inspiration are evocation, transcendence, and approach motivation. Aspiration motivates the artist to actualize inspiration. Resonance results from how we translate inspirations and aspirations into a completed composition.

INSPIRATION AND ASPIRATION
"In the beginning, there was the idea."

The words *creativity*, *inspiration* and *aspiration* are often used interchangeably, and I think it's important that we draw a clearer distinction.

Creative people don't just sit around and wait for inspiration to strike. Inspiration is not the source of creativity. Rather, inspiration is the motivated response to the creative impulse. Aspiration, in turn, is the motivated response by the artist to actualize inspiration.

Creativity is **a phenomenon where both something new and, at the same time, somehow valuable is created**.

Inspiration is defined as, **the process of being mentally stimulated to do or feel something**.

Aspiration is, **a hope or ambition of achieving something**.

There are many dichotomies. Stimulation versus ambition. Excitement versus action. Idea versus value. And most significantly, external versus internal.

Inspiration is something we seek to ingest from outside. Aspiration is something we cultivate within ourselves.

I have been *inspired* by an extraordinary number of people over the course of my life. My mentors in college when I was struggling to decide between becoming an archaeologist or a psychologist. In my first job at New Brunswick Tomorrow where I guided a board of health care providers in creating a health plan for the city. In a subsequent job by government officials with a clear vision for health care in Tennessee. Finding inspirations has never been a challenge for me.

But I had never really *aspired* to be like anyone until I dropped out of the corporate race, and turned to jewelry designing. Corporate life in health care had never excited me or got my juices flowing before in the same way. But with jewelry design, I felt I could accomplish these wonderful designs, And, as my aspirations came into fruition, I began to feel that I could shape the field and profession of jewelry design and influence the way jewelry makers work in some way. I was filled with aspirations to be heard and to make a difference. The response to my aspirations, from students or people reacting to my written articles, inspired me. It filled me with aspirations, and I had to figure the details out. I had to be very self-directed to continue as a jewelry designer and begin to transform how it is understood as a professional endeavor all its own – apart from craft and apart from art.

INSPIRATION: Becoming One with What Inspires You
Inspirations are sacred revelations
you want to share through art and design.

The word inspiration comes from the Latin roots meaning *"to breathe into."* But before you can breathe your inspiration into your jewelry, you need to become one with it.

There are these wonderfully exciting, sensually terrific, incredibly fulfilling things that you find as you try to imagine the jewelry you will create. They come from many sources: ideas, nature, images, people, behaviors. They may be realistic or abstract. They may be the particular color or pattern or texture or the way the light hits it and casts a shadow. They may be a need for order over chaos. They may be points of view. They may flow from some inner imagination.

For some reason, these inspirations take on a divine, sacred revelation for you – so meaningful that you want to incorporate them somehow into what you do. A fire in your soul. You want to translate these inspirations into colors, shapes, lines, patterns and textures. You want to impose an organization on them. You want to recapture their energy and power they have had over you. You feel compelled to bring these feelings into ideas, and these ideas into material objects, and these material objects into organized arrangements.

There are many challenges to inspiration. That which we call *inspiring* can often be somewhat fuzzy. It might be a feeling. It might be a piece of an idea, or a small spot on an image. You might feel inspired, but, cannot put the What or the Why into words or images. On the surface, it may seem important to you, but unimportant to others. You the artist may not feel in control of the inspiration in that it seems like it is something that is evoked within, not necessarily directed by, you.

When inspired, artists perceive new possibilities that transcend that which is ordinary around them. Too often, the artist feels passive in this process. This transcendence does not feel like a willfully generated idea. However, it needs to be.

The successful designer – one who eventually can achieve a level of resonance – is one who is not only inspired *by*, but also inspired *to*. This all requires a great deal of metacognitive self-awareness. The designer must be able to perceive the intrinsic value of the inspiring object, and how to extend this value to others through design, where the piece of jewelry becomes its expression.

Inspiration is motivating. Inspiration is not the source of creativity; creativity does not come from it. Inspiration, instead, should be viewed as a motivational response to creativity. It motivates the artist, through jewelry and its design, to connect this inspiration with others. It serves as a mediator between the self and the anticipated shared understandings of others. The jewelry encapsulates the designer's ability to make this connection. When the connection is well-made, resonance follows.

But finding inspirations is not only personal, but more importantly, it is an effort to influence others. It is an act of translating the emotions which resonate in you into some object of art which, in turn, will inspire and resonate with others. How does the inspiration occur to you, and how do you anticipate how this inspiration might occur to others?

Too often we lose sight of the importance of inspiration to the authentic performance task of creating jewelry. We operate with the belief that anyone can be inspired by anything. There's nothing more to it. Moreover, inspiration gets downplayed when put next to the discussion of the effort of making jewelry itself.

But it should not. Inspiration awakens us to new possibilities. It allows us to transcend the ordinary, surface experiences. It propels us to design. It transforms how we perceive what we do and what we can do. Inspiration is not something that should be overlooked just because it is somewhat fuzzy and elusive.

Inspiration is not less important than perspiration. It plays an equal role in the creative process. The designer's clarity about why something is inspiring, and why this inspiration motivates the designer to respond, will be critical for achieving success, that is resonance.

The Core Aspects of Inspiration

In psychology, inspiration is seen to have three key qualities:
- *Evocation*
- *Transcendence, and*
- *Approach motivation*

Evocation. Inspiration is evoked. It feels spontaneous. Unintentional.

Transcendence: Inspiration transcends the ordinary to the noteworthy. It involves a moment of clarity, or at least a bit of clarity, which makes us aware of new possibilities. The moment itself may be vivid, very emotional, even passionate.

Approach motivation: The person strives to transmit, express or actualize their inspiration. The person, for whatever reason, wants to act on that inspiration.

Inspired people are more open to experience. They are not necessarily conscience about it. It just happens. It isn't willed. Inspired people appear to be more self-directed. They want to master their work. They do not consider inspiration a competitive sport, at least most don't. Inspired people focus on the subjective, intrinsic value of an object, not its external, objective worth.

Where Do You Find Inspirations?

Inspirations matter a lot. This may cause you to feel pressure to become inspired and find new topics and projects to work on, and feel helpless when you can't. But remember, inspirations cannot be willed. They are more spontaneous and transcendent. This does not mean, however, that inspiration is completely out of your control. If you put yourself in situations where you are more likely to find inspiration, you will find inspirations. You always need to be working towards finding it.

1. Look Around You

Notice something different. Focus on something and ask yourself why it exists, in the form that it is in, in the place your find it, in the uses you put to it. What if it wasn't there? What if it was different? When was the last time you used it? Could something else substitute for it?

Do you see patterns? Textures? Analogies where "A" is like"B"? Colors and color combinations? An interesting juxtaposition of lines or planes? Something unusual about the relationship of the background to the foreground?

In your workspace, surround yourself with inspiring images.

2. Go For A Walk

Try to find the things you don't often see or focus on. Try to declutter your mind, and fill it with new observations. Walk the same path at different times during the day, or when the weather changes. Find other pathways you think are similar or different and walk those, evaluating the similarities or differences.

3. Meet New People

Surround yourself with other inspiring and creative people. Go out of your way to meet them. Talk. Discuss. Dialog. Share an experience. Collaborate. Show genuine interest in what they do, how they do, why they do.

4. Get Lost

Take a wrong turn on the highway. Visit a place you have never been to before. Take it all in. What are your thoughts? Feelings? Emotions? Are you excited, scared, bored, in wonder?

5. Read or Watch Something New and Inspirational

The internet provides all kinds of resources to lose yourself in. Visit a museum. Change the channel on the TV. Check out a bookstore. But deviate from the same-ole, same-ole.

6. Change Your Routine

If you have a schedule, deviate from it. If you are a morning person, try being a night person for a few days. If you like to think and work in one setting, change the setting.

7. Learn Something New

Take a class. Do a tutorial. Try a different technique. Use different materials. Try something you are not good at.

How Does Inspiration Relate To Design?

Jewelry design is an extended process. Some of the process is planned, and some of it is spontaneous. At the beginning of the process we have Inspiration. We make choices, then question our choices, relating inspiration to aspirations to designs. We are critical, in a positive sense, and slowly maintain our attention and work through what is a more extended design process.

What is most important here is that you learn, not only to inspire others *by*, but how to inspire others *to*. That is, you want to learn how to translate an inspiration into a design in such a way that the wearer and the viewer are inspired to emotionally connect with the pieces as if they were following and identifying with your own thoughts and feelings.

They don't simply react emotionally by saying the piece is "*beautiful.*" The piece conveys more power than that. It resonates for them. They react by saying they *"want to touch it"* or *"want to wear it"* or *"want to buy it"* or *"want to make something like it"*. They come to feel and see and sense the artist's hand.

What Is Aspiration?

Aspiration is the motivational basis for wanting to translate your inspiration into a design. To aspire is to rise up to a great plan, an abundance of hope and desire. To aspire is to bring others into this plan, hope and desire. Aspiration is an inspired-related search for possibilities.

There are certain objective aspects to it. The artist is translating the inspiration into concrete concepts, such as color choice, material choice, and the choices of techniques and composition. The concepts are goal-oriented and have universally shared meanings. They are reasonable.

And there are certain subjective aspects to it. It is the designer who wants the thing, and finds pleasure in all this. It is the designer who wants others to experience the emotional content of the inspirations as the designer does. These subjective aspects are rational – they make sense for those people involved and affected.

ASPIRATION: Translating Creativity into A Technical Product Design
Aspiration motivates the designer to actualize inspiration.

Aspiration is where the designer translates inspiration into an expressive design concept. The designer begins to control and regulate what happens next. This involves selecting Design Elements[1] and clustering them to formulate meaningful expressions. The greater value the designer places on resonance, the stronger the aspiration will be to achieve it.

Aspiration is future-oriented. It requires a stick-to-it-ness. The designer must be sufficiently motivated to invest the time, energy and money into designing and making the jewelry that will not necessarily be finished, displayed or sold right away. It may require some additional learning and skills-development time. The designer may need to find a level of creativity within, and discover the kinds of skills, techniques and insights necessary for bringing this creativity to the aspired task at hand.

Aspiration requires the calculus: *Is it worth it?* It adds a level of risk to the project. A cost-benefit analysis. A wondering about the return on the investment of time, energy, and resources. Aspiration forces the designer to pay attention to the world around her or him. This world presents dynamic clues – what I discuss below as shared understandings – about opportunities, constraints, risks, contingencies, consequences, strategies and goals, and likely successes.

For some designers, motivation primarily is seen as *instinctual*. Think of *seat-of-the-pants*. Emergent, not controlled. A search for harmony, balance, rhythm, unity as something that feels right and looks right and seems right with the universe. Expressive, yes. Imaginative, yes. But not necessarily resonant.

Achieving resonance, however, is, for the most part, more than instinctual. It has some deliberate quality to it. It is communicative. It requires a purposeful act on the part of the designer. It is a different type of motivation -- *intentional*. The designer might want to convey a specific emotion. Or advocate for some change. Or illustrate a point of view. The designer may want to entertain or teach. Heal. Attract mates. Propagandize. Where a jewelry's design is not reflective of a designer's intent, there can be no resonance.

What Is The Relationship of Aspiration to Resonance?

We achieve Resonance by gaining a comfort and ease in communicating about design. This comfort and ease, or disciplinary fluency, has to do with how we translate our inspirations and aspirations into all our compositional, constructive and manipulative choices. It is empowering. Our pieces resonate. We achieve success.

Resonance, communication, success, fluency – these are all words that stand in place for an intimacy between the designer and the materials, the designer and the techniques, the designer and the inspiration. They reflect the designer's aspirations. They reflect the shared understandings of everyone the designer's jewelry is expected to touch. They reflect the designer's managerial prowess in bringing all these things together.

Anticipating Shared Understandings and Desires
Shared understandings and desires
dictate opportunities, contingencies and constraints.

The question of whether the audience correctly infers the presence of the designer's inspiration, and the sense of how the designer's hand comes into play within the design, remains. The answer revolves around a dynamic interaction between designer and audience, as they anticipate understandings they share, and ones they do not.

FOOTNOTES

CA Griffin Group. The Intersection of Inspiration and Aspiration. Jan 19, 2018.
As referenced in: https://medium.com/@craig_38900/the-intersection-of-aspiration-and-inspiration-23893e250bb3

Hess, Whitney. Inspiration and Aspiration. July 27, 2010.
As referenced in: https://whitneyhess.com/blog/2010/07/27/inspiration-and-aspiration/

Kaufman, Scott Barry. Why Inspiration Matters. Harvard Business Review, Nove 8, 2011.

Lamp, Lucy. Inspiration in Visual Art: Where Do Artists Get Their Ideas?
As referenced in: https://www.sophia.org/tutorials/inspiration-in-visual-art-where-do-artists-get-the

Metz, John. April 10, 2013.
As referenced in: https://www.thindifference.com/2013/04/do-you-have-to-aspire-to-inspire/

Sharma, Shashank. Comprehensive Guide To Finding Inspiration For Art: Everything you need to know about finding creative art inspiration, March 31, 2017.
As referenced in: https://blog.dextra.art/https-blog-dextra-xyz-comprehensive-guide-to-finding-inspiration-for-art-c9f2e764a5fc

DEVELOPING THOSE INTUITIVE SKILLS WITHIN
8c. YOUR PASSION FOR DESIGN:
Finding It, Developing It, and Embedding It In Your Designs

Image by FELD, 2020

Guiding Questions:
(1) What Is Passion?
(2) Can You Really Follow A Passion?
(3) Is It Necessary To Have A Passion?
(4) Where Does Passion Come From?
(5) Are Passion and Creativity The Same Thing?
(6) How Is Your Passion Developed?
(7) What If You Have A Passion For Something But Don't Do Anything About It?
(8) What Are The Characteristics Of A Passionate Person?
(9) How Does Being Passionate Make You A Better Designer?

Key Words: *passion* *design / designer* *creativity* *passionate person*	*motivation / determination* *self-affirmation* *satisfaction*	*passion must be developed* *curiosity* *passion to do or make* *passion for beauty* *passion for coherence*

Abstract:
While it is not necessary to have found your passion in order to be a good and successful designer, developing your passion for design can be very beneficial and worth the effort. With passion comes greater satisfaction, self-affirmation, creativity and motivation. With passion comes a greater ability to gain acceptance from clients about what your designs mean and can do for them. People are not born with passions. They find them, often in a round-about, circuitous way over a period of time. Once found, they need to be developed, cultivated and managed. And you don't want to get overwhelmed by your passions to the detriment of balance in your personal and work lives.

Can You Really Follow A Passion?

Is it necessary to have a passion?

Sometimes I get so sick and tired of this question. I get perplexed. What does it really mean? What are people really telling me when they say I should follow my passion?

What job or career or avocation should I pursue? Do I have an intense interest in anything? Does anything drive me? Motivate me? Capture my undivided attention? What do I wish I would have done? Or should have done? Or could have done? Is something to do with *design* the answer? Passion! That word is spoken so often.

Follow your passion! Follow your passion! Follow your passion!

You get told this over and over again so many times that you begin to question whether anyone has ever really been successful, or even been substantially motivated, to follow their passions. Especially those people who tell you to do so – surely, they have not actually found their passion. It seems so hard to find. A good goal, but let's get real. Insurmountable. There are lots of things I like and get very enthusiastic about, but I can't say I'm passionate about them. And you can't forget you have to earn a living, whether you are passionate about what you do or not.

You hear and read about finding your passion, so much so, that you feel if you haven't found yours, something must be wrong with you. And, certainly you think no one else has, either. The pressure, the pressure. Why is it so important to my family and friends and my inner still voice that I be passionate about something?

Their admonitions take different tones, from command, to pleading, to expressing concern and sorrow, to lowering their expectations for you. You see / feel/ know what they are really trying to say to you – sympathy, empathy, pity -- by those variations on the memes they throw at you.

You don't have to make a decision about a career until you find your passion!

Don't worry, you'll find something to be passionate about!

Not everyone finds their passion.

You begin to feel like a failure in life for not finding your passion. Or that so-and-so you went to school with found theirs… and you didn't.

The only way to stave all these folks off is to get a job that makes a lot of money. Pursuing money apparently is seen as a legitimate substitute for following your passion.

And that's what I did.

For almost 40 years.

I pursued money.

Until I found my passion.

My passion for design.

Specifically, jewelry design.

What Is Passion?

Passion, I have discovered over many years in the design world, is something key to a more fulfilling and successful career.

Passion makes sense for design.

Passion is an emotion.

Passion provides the fuel firing you to action.

Almost in spite of yourself.

Passion is often equated with determination, motivation, and conviction – all moving you in a particular direction. But these three concepts do not adequately capture what passion is all about. Passion challenges you. It is intriguing. It provides the principle around which you organize your life.

Passion is something more than a strong interest. Passion is a bit more energetic, directional. And when you want to change direction, emotionally, passion makes this very difficult. Passion is simultaneously a response somewhat divorced from any reason, but in the service of reason, as well. Once you have it, passion can be very sticky and hard to shake off.

Passion puts you to work. It helps you overcome those times when you get frustrated. Or bored. Or anxious.

Passion reveals what you are willing to sacrifice other pleasures for.

Passion is what helps you overcome those times when you get frustrated when something isn't working out exactly as you want, or when you are anxious about your ability to do something, or you get bored with what you are trying to do at the moment.

But passion is somewhat amorphous. Intangible. Not something solid enough or clear enough to grab and grip and get ahold of.

Is it Necessary To Have A Passion For Design?

In high school, I decided that my passion would be archaeology. I read books and articles about Middle East history and settlement patterns. I loved the idea of traveling. I loved history. I selected a college that had an excellent and extensive archaeology program.

That first fall semester, I took two archaeology classes. In one of these classes, week after week for 18 weeks, I sat through the examinations and resultant reports looking at the remains of a small grouping of houses in Iran. I saw the partial remains of some walls. An area the remains of which suggested it was a kitchen. And lots of dust and dirt and not much else.

The archaeological reports were each done by teams from different countries. From the scant evidence, the Russian report found the settlement to be communal and socialist. They based their conclusions on the positioning of the walls, the proximity of the kitchen area to the walls, and the remains mostly consisting of chicken bones. The German report found the settlement to be more democratic but still communal. Their evidence was based on the positioning of the walls, the proximity of the kitchen area to the walls, and the remains mostly consisting of chicken bones. And the American report found the settlement to be an early example of democracy and capitalism. Their evidence – can you guess? – was based on the positioning of the walls, the proximity of the kitchen area to the walls, and the remains mostly consisting of chicken bones.

I made a discovery in myself and about myself that first semester of college. Archaeology was not my passion. I changed majors. But still no passion.

I still yearned to be passionate about something, however. A goal. A Task. An activity. A career. Anything. My search took almost another 20 years.

Not having a passion did not affect my ability to work and do my job. But I felt some distance from it. Some disconnection. Something missing and less satisfying.

While it took me a long time to find my passion, for others it happens very quickly. You never know. In either case, passion is not something that falls down from the sky and hits you on the head. It is something that has to be pursued, developed and cultivated over time.

Pursuing your passion has many advantages. When you are passionate about something, you can more easily accomplish things which are difficult and hard. Your work and job and life feel more fulfilling. You feel you are impacting the world around you.

A passion for design enables you to become the best designer you can be. It builds within you a more stick-to-it-iveness, while you develop yourself as a designer over many years, and as you learn the intricacies of your trade and profession. Having a passion for design is a necessity if you are to come to an understanding of yourself as a professional practicing a discipline.

Passion gives us purpose. It attaches a feeling to our thoughts, intensifying our emotions. It is transformative. Empowering. Passion allows us to realize a vision within any context we find ourselves.

A *passion for design* allows us to navigate those tensions between the pursuit of beauty and the pursuit of functionality. It allows us to incorporate the opinions and desires of our clients into our own design work, without sacrificing our identities and integrities as designers. In a sense, it allows our design choices to reaffirm our ideas and concepts, tempering them with the needs, desires, and understandings of our client and the client's various audiences. It allows us, through our design decisions, to manage the vagaries in any situation and, ultimately, to get the professional recognition we seek. However, most of us – including and especially me – have not known how to pursue our passions. And we fail to do so.

Not only should we have to pursue a passion for meaningful work, but we must incorporate our passion into our everyday lives. Passion is not just about ourselves. Passion affects our friends and families and work mates. They suffer or benefit (*or both*) from our driven selves. Passion affects how we utilize our time. It affects how we see the world, define problems and anticipate solutions.

Passion can be a bitch, and it must be managed. Otherwise, without some ongoing management and a bit of reflection and skepticism, passion can have the opposite effect from what we desire in life. Poorly managed and integrated into our lives, passion can lead to less happiness, less satisfaction, less contentment and less personal growth. In spite of all this, having passion for what you do will result in many more positives than negatives in your design work.

Pursing our passion requires that we bring on our journey these four understandings:

(1) Passion is not innate to the individual. Passion must be developed.

(2) It is not easy to take this journey to find your passion, especially as it gets drawn out over a long period of time.

(3) Passion makes it easier to mediate and sustain our pathways through our interactions at work and through life.

(4) Passion can lead us astray, blinding us to its limits.

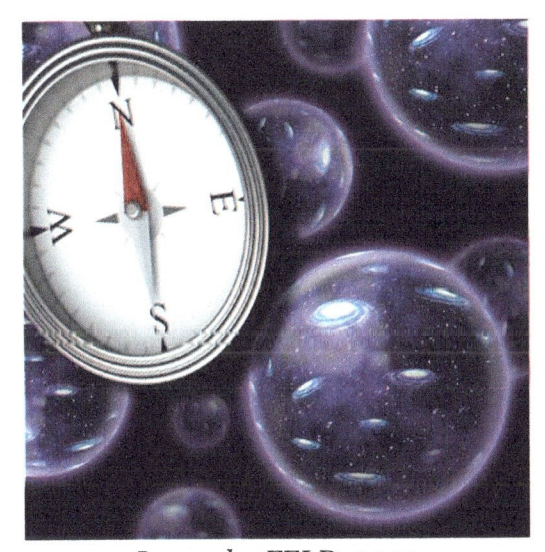

Image by FELD, 2020

Where Does Your Passion Come From?

It was always just a whispered aside. Something quiet. A glance in one direction, then back so no one would notice. A comment. And the only comment ever said out loud. But hushed. Always and only in that hushed voice. A voice conveying alarm. Embarrassment. Bravery. Humiliation. Horror. Survival. History. Culture.

"She has a number tattooed on her arm. Did you see it?"

And I had. It was difficult to hide. Everyone spoke with so many gestures and drama, whatever the subject, and the sleeves pulled up on their arms.

And not another word was said about it. It – the situation. The larger situation. I never knew their specific experiences. Nor their views. Nor their feelings. Nor their understandings.

They never shared their terror. Or spoke about their anxiety. Or explained what they thought had happened, or how they had managed to survive.

I could not see anything in their faces. Or their eyes. There was nothing different about their skin. Their height. Their weight. The way they walked. Or talked.

There were those in the room who escaped to America during or immediately after the war. There were those in the room who had escaped similar horrors, but many decades earlier, fleeing Poland and Russia and the Middle East. There were their children. And there were their children's children, I being one of them.

And while I was only 4 or 5 or 6 years old, I remember the collective feeling – even 60 years later-- of the hushed voice and the tattooed numbers. I was never privy to any person's history. I never heard about anyone's experience. It was inappropriate to talk about it. But that one memory conveyed it all. The full story. It sparked my curiosity. I had to make sense of things. I wrote the full story in my mind. And attached all the full emotions.

My curiosity grew and drove me to make sense of a lot of things as I grew up. Eventually, I found myself curious about jewelry, and began making jewelry. As many of my creations were less than satisfying and successful, I found myself more curious about design. And more emotionally attached to finding answers. My passion grew from there.

Passion Starts With Curiosity

It is the little things that come up every so often that imbues a curiosity in you. That makes you want to make sense of the world. Find understanding. Make sense of things where you do not know all the details. Or where things are headed. But you fill in the blanks anyway. And keep asking questions. To clarify. To intensify. To soften. To connect with other stories your curiosity has led you to.

Passion starts with *curiosity*. But not just curiosity. Passion is sparked by curiosity, but goes further. It creates this emotional energy within you to make meaning out of ambiguity. For passion to continually grow and develop, such derived meaning must be understood within a particular context, and all the people, actually or virtually present, who concurrently interact with that context, and your place in it.

Passion involves insights. Passion is about finding connections. Connections to insights and meanings. Connections to things which are pleasing to you. Connections to things which are contradictory. Connections to things which are unfamiliar or ambiguous. Connections to others around you. And finding them again. And reconnecting with them again. And again and again.

Passion requires reflection. It demands an awareness of why you make certain choices rather than others. Why particular designs draw your attention, and others do not. Why you are attracted to certain people (or activities), and others not.

Passion affects how you look at things and people. It is dynamic. It is communicative. It affects all your interactions.

Passion is not innate. You are not born with it. It is not set at birth waiting to be discovered. It is something to find and cultivate.

The elemental roots of my passion were present at a very early age. I was very curious. I tried to impose a sensibility on things. While I wanted people around me to *like* me, that wasn't really a part of my motivation. I wanted people to *understand* me as a thinking human being. And I was always that way.

In some respects, this situation when I was around 5 years old has been an example of the root of my passion. My jewelry designs resonate with that hushed, quiet voice. That voice conveys my intent through the subtle choices I make about color and proportion and arrangement and materials and techniques. I usually start each design activity by anticipating how others will come to understand what I hope to achieve. How they might recognize the intent in my designs. How my intent might coordinate with their desires.

My jewelry designs tell stories. They tell my stories. They tell my stories so that other people might be a little curious as well and connect with them. And understand my passion for design.

Are Passion and Creativity the Same Thing?

As designers, we bring our creative assets to every situation. But we must not confuse these with the passion within us. Passion and creativity are not the same thing. We do not need passion to be creative. Nor do we need passion to be motivated to create something.

Passion is the love of design. Creating is making an object or structuring a project.

Passion is the love of jewelry. Creating is making a necklace.

Passion is the love of color. Creating is using a color scheme within a project.

Passion is the love of fashion. Creating is making a dress.

After college, I had some great jobs. Lots of creativity. Not much passion.

I was a college administrator for a year. I was hired to organize the student orientation program. As new students arrived at the university in the fall, I created social activities, like dances and mixers and discussions. I arranged for greet and meets in each of the dorms. I worked with each club to generate their first meetings and some of the marketing materials. I set up religious orientations and services for Jewish, Christian and Islamic students. I set up orientations for women's affinity groups, black groups, latino groups, and many others. I wrote, photographed and published an orientation handbook and a new faces book. I even planned the food services menus for the first week. I did a lot. I loved it. It was very creative.

But not my passion.

I also had an opportunity to become the Assistant Editor of the American Anthropologist for a year. The regular Assistant wanted to go on a sabbatical. The Editor knew me and asked if I wanted to do her job for a year. I edited and saw to the publication of 2 ½ issues. I worked with anthropologists all over the world in helping them translate their work into publishable articles. I loved this job too. I did a lot. It was very creative.

But not my passion.

I decided to pursue a degree in City and Regional Planning. I was getting an inkling that I liked things associated with the word "design." I liked the idea of designing cities and neighborhoods and community developments. I was intrigued with transportation systems and building systems and urban development.

I was about to enter graduate training in City Planning, which meant moving from where I lived, but a family crisis came up. Physical planning – buildings, cities, roads, neighborhoods – had captured my interest. But I resigned myself, in order to accommodate family needs, to attend a graduate program close to home which emphasized social and health planning, instead.

I got a job as a city health planner, and worked for a private revitalization agency. I assisted in getting government approval for a rehabilitation center. I developed a local maternal-child health system. I guided a group of health care professionals in developing a health care plan for New Brunswick, New Jersey. I organized a health fair. I loved this job. I did a lot. It was very creative.

But not my passion.

As I have come to believe over many careers and many years, the better designer needs both passion and creativity. They reinforce each other. They accentuate. When both are appropriately harnessed, the joys and stresses of passion fuel creativity, innovation and design. Passion inspires. It is insightful. It motivates. Creativity translates that emotional imaging and feeling into a design. Creativity is opportunistic. It transforms things. It generates ideas. It translates inspirations into aspirations into finished projects.

The design process usually takes place over an extended period of time. There can be several humps and bumps. Passion gets us through this. It is that energizing, emotional, motivating resource for creative work. Passion is that strong desire and pressing need to get something done. Passion helps us, almost forces us, in fact, to build our professional identities around that activity we call design.

Passion reveals an insatiability for self discovery and self development. But this sense of self is always contingent upon the acceptance of others. Sounds a lot like the design process and working with clients. You don't need to be passionate to do design and do it well. You need passion to do design better and more coherently. You need passion to have more impact on yourself and others.

Image by FELD, 2020

How Is Your Passion For Design Developed?

I continued working in the health care field, teaching graduate school, doing consulting, government health policy planning, and, my last professional job, directing a nonprofit membership organization of primary health care centers.

Working in health care had become such a hollow experience for me, that I jumped off the corporate ladder when I was 36 years old. With a partner, we opened up a retail operation, in Nashville, Tennessee, where we sold finished jewelry, most of it custom made, as well as selling all the parts for other people interested in making jewelry themselves.

My partner was the creative one, and the design aspects of the business were organized around her work. I was the business person. I made some jewelry to sell, but my motivation was purely monetary. No passion yet.

During the first few years, it was painfully obvious that my jewelry construction techniques were poor, at best. The jewelry I made broke too easily. This bothered me. I was determined to figure out how to do it better.

This was pre-internet. There were no established jewelry making magazines at that time. In Nashville, there was a very small jewelry / beading craft community. No experience, no support. So I did a lot of trial-and-error. Lots of experimentation.

In these early years in our retail jewelry business, two critical things happened which started steering me in the direction of pursuing my jewelry design passion.

First, our store was located in a tourist area near the downtown convention center. Many people attending conventions lived in areas, especially California, where there were major jewelry making and beading communities. They shopped in our store, and from watching their shopping behaviors, seeing what they liked and did not like, and talking with them, I learned many insights about where to direct my energies.

Second, I began taking in jewelry repairs. It became almost like an apprenticeship. I got to see what design choices other jewelry makers made, and I looked for patterns. I got to see where things broke, and I looked for patterns. I spoke with the customers to get a sense of what happened when the jewelry broke, and I looked for patterns. I put into effect my developing insights about jewelry construction and materials selection when doing repairs, and I looked for patterns.

No passion yet, but I took one more big step. And passion was beginning to show itself on the horizon.

I was developing all this knowledge and experience about design theory and applications. Suddenly, I wanted to share this. I wanted to teach. But I wanted to have some high level of coherency underlying my curriculum. My budding passion for design saw design as a profession, not a hobby. I did not want to teach a step-by-step, paint-by-number class. I wanted to teach a way of thinking through design. I wanted my students to develop a literacy and fluency in design.

I inadvertently cultivated my passion for design over time. I did not really follow one. It was a journey. My passion for the idea of design did not necessarily match a particular job. I coordinated it with the job I had been doing. And over time, my job and my passion became more and more intertwined and coherent. For me, it was a long process. I honed my abilities. I leveraged them to create value – personal satisfaction and some monetary remuneration. My passion became my lifestyle. My lifestyle resonated with me.

Passion involves deep introspection. It requires you to be metacognitive – always aware of the things underlying your choices. It requires talking with people and testing out how different ideas or activities resonate with you. What do you care about? What changes in the world do you want to make? What is driving you? What if this or that? Are you willing to give up something else for this? Would people respect me if...?

During this journey, you will systematically test your assumptions about what you think your personal sense of purpose should be. For the most part, there may not be a single answer or one that will last forever. But you reach progressive levels of clarity which give you a sense of direction and fulfillment.

As a designer, it is more important to focus on personal connections represented in your passion, rather than on creating some material thing. You can steer your job to spend more time exploring the tasks you are passionate about and the people you like to share your passion with. Look for inspirations. Reflect on what you care about. It is a good idea to know yourself as a designer and why you are enthusiastic about it. Self-discipline and management go hand-in-hand with passion so that you maintain perspective and continue to create designs. You won't necessarily love everything you do, but your passion will keep you motivated to do it.

It's a cycle of self-discovery. But don't sit around waiting for the cycle to show up and start rotating. Keep trying new things. Exploring. Taking charge of your life. Revisiting things which interested you when you were younger. Thinking about things you never tire of doing. Thinking about things you do well. Recognizing things you like learning about.

What If You Have A Passion For Something, But You Don't Do Anything About It?

What if you have a passion for something, but you don't do anything about it? There could be several reasons for this:

- You have a good job, make good money, but are not passionate about it
- You have time constraints
- You are afraid of change or the unknown and unfamiliar
- Your family and social network are not supportive
- You tried something similar before, and were not successful
- You dislike the people you work with or play with
- The skills integral to your passion are not in demand or favor; they don't make you marketable, or sufficiently marketable to earn a living wage
- You cannot support yourself during the extended timeframe it would take to develop your skills

But, I think, one of the major reasons people do not cultivate their passion is that they do not understand it. It is not a pot of gold on the other side of the rainbow. It won't necessarily satisfy all your needs. It is a sensation without clear boundaries. It is best expressed among an audience that already is sensitive to and aware of your passion and how it fits with their own needs and desires. It is best expressed in a context in which it is respected.

Developing your passion takes work and commitment. Mastery of design does not spring from discovered passions. Instead, passion provides the motivation for you to learn and grow within the design profession. Initially, you might be pretty bad at professional tasks. They need to be learned and applied, then applied again. Eventually your mastery earns you some satisfaction, autonomy and respect.

What Are The Characteristics of a Passionate Designer?

A prominent country music star and her six-person entourage entered my store. They had heard about our jewelry design work, and were eager to see what we could make for the singer.

She had some specifics in mind. A necklace. It had to be all black. She wanted crosses all around it. Each cross had to be different. Each cross had to be black.

We accepted the challenge.

We began laying out some different ideas and options on the work table. The singer said No! to each idea. The entourage chimed in like a Greek chorus. (Admittedly a little weird and unnerving.) We weren't really getting anywhere, so we set another meeting date. We would put together more options, and get their opinions. Agreed.

The color of black was easily accomplished. We could string black beads or use black chain or black cord. It would be a challenge to find or design a lot of black crosses, but not impossible.

We put in a lot of hours gathering materials and developing some more prototype options.

The second meeting was no more fruitful than the first. The artist and her entourage could offer no additional insights about what they wanted. Our mock-ups were unacceptable.

We ended the meeting.

We were not, however, going to throw in the towel. Our passion would not let us.

In fact, we were intrigued by the puzzling puzzle put before us. Our passion energized us to continue the chase and find the solution.

We decided we needed more information about why this country music artist wanted this necklace, what outfit and styling she would wear it with, and why an assortment of differing black crosses was important to her.

We put on our anthropology, psychology and sociology hats and played Sherlock Holmes. We approached members of her entourage individually. Her entourage was made up of her stylists. We were able to fill in a lot of the blanks by talking with them. She was going to wear this piece on the road, performing in several concert venues. We got into some discussions about her religion, more specifically, how she practiced it. The best way to describe this was a pagan-influenced Christianity. We had enough information to go by. This was particularly important in picking out crosses, and arranging them around the necklace.

They loved our prototype, and we only had to do a little tweaking.

You know you are passionate when you...
1. Start your days early
2. Passions consume your thoughts all the time
3. Get more excited about things
4. Get more emotional, frustrated and even angry about things
5. Take more risks
6. Devote more of your time and other resources to your work – working harder, practicing more, spending more time developing your skills
7. Are eager to share what you are working on
8. Fight within yourself as well as with others (friends, family, clients) about managing the balance between work and everything else
9. Are optimistic about the future
10. Surround yourself with your work
11. More easily accept (and get past) failures and consequences
12. Do not easily give in to criticism or skepticism.
13. Have focus and plan things out more
14. Inspire others
15. Radiate your passions

Three Types Of Passions For Design

There are three types of passions designers might cultivate:

(1) The Passion To Do Or Make Something
(2) The Passion For Beauty and Appeal
(3) The Passion For Coherency

(1) The Passion To Do Or Make Something

The designer's passion is focused on an activity. They believe it is possible to make something out of nothing. Designers do, see, touch, compose, arrange, construct, manipulate. This passion is very hands-on and mechanical. Its drive is orderly, methodical, systematic, and directional.

(2) The Passion For Beauty and Appeal

The designer's passion is focused on beauty and appeal. They believe it is possible to do whatever it takes to create or develop something of beauty. Designers select, feel, sense, compose, arrange, construct, manipulate. This passion is very emotional and feeling. Its drive follows the senses, the intuitive, the inspiration with an eye always on the ultimate outcome – beauty and appeal.

(3) The Passion For Coherence

The designer's passion is focused on resolving tensions, typically between the need for beauty concurrently with the need for functionality. They believe it is possible to resolve these tensions. Designers think, analyze, reflect, organize, present, resolve, solve. This passion is very intellectual. Its drive is meaning, content, sense-making, conflict resolution and balance.

Whatever type of passion you see yourself as pursuing, it is passion nonetheless which motivates your creativity and sustains your attention long enough to get something done for someone else and fulfill their desires.

How Does Being Passionate Make You A Better Designer?

Not every professional designer is passionate about what they do. Nor do they have to be in order to do a good job and make money.

Passions do not solve your problems at work – the stresses, the difficult interpersonal relationships, the need to find people to pay you for what you do. They guide you to better resolve them.

Passions make the work extra special. The work becomes less a job, and more a process of continual growth and self-actualization. Passions help you more easily clarify the ambiguous and unfamiliar. They help you more readily overcome obstacles. They assist you in finding that sweet spot between fulfilling your needs and intents, and meeting those of others who work with you, pay you for what you do, critique, evaluate and recommend you.

Having a passion for something does not equate to having a professional career. Careers don't necessarily happen because you have a passion for them. But it is great to have your career and passion co-align. You have to build upon your passion, implement it, fine-tune it, and manage it over time.

The secret for successfully bringing all this together – your desires, the tasks you want to do and those you are required to do, the various audiences whose acceptance in some way is necessary for what you must accomplish -- is how you manage your passions.

Good passion management results in...
- More work getting done and more engagement with that work

- More work satisfaction and intrinsic rewards
- More self-actualization and development professionally
- Higher levels of creativity
- More trust in colleagues and clients
- More likely to feel purposeful and connected
- More capability in putting your imprint (*your artist's hand*) on your work to the point your work is meaningful and acceptable to others
- More fix-it strategies to store in your designer tool box, allowing you to be more adaptable to new or difficult situations

But just like with all good things, too much passion can be damaging.

Bad passion management could result in...

- Becoming a workaholic
- Having others exploit your willingness to work, do the hard stuff, take on unnecessary challenges and strive for success
- Losing a good balance between work life and personal life
- Suffering burn-out
- Becoming too over-confident, less likely to seek feedback, less likely to collaborate, less likely to seek clarification
- Becoming irritable, stressed, rigid, unwilling to compromise

Again, your passion must be managed. You want balance. You want to set aside times for self-reflection and self care.

Don't wait to follow your passion. Define and develop it within the context of your professional design career.

FOOTNOTES

Chen, Robert. "The Real Meaning of Passion," Embrace Possibility, March, 2015.
 As referenced in: https://www.embracepossibility.com/blog/real-meaning-passion/

Financial Mechanic. "Why 'Follow Your Passion' Is Bad Advice," Published: 05 July 2019 – Updated: 23 February 2020
 As referenced in: https://www.getrichslowly.org/follow-your-passion-is-bad-

advice/#:~:text=They%20found%20that%20people%20who,interest%20if%20it%20becomes%20difficult.

Fisher, Christian. "How To Define Your Passion In Life," Chron (Houston Chronicle), n.d.
 As referenced in: https://work.chron.com/define-passion-life-10132.html

Hill, Maria. "Are Passion and Creativity The Same Thing?" Sensitive Evolution, 11/11/2019.
 As referenced in: https://sensitiveevolution.com/passion-and-creativity/

Hudson, Paul. "10 Things That Truly Passionate People Do Differently," Elite Daily, April 9, 2014.
 As referenced in: https://www.elitedaily.com/money/entrepreneurship/10-things-that-truly-passionate-people-do-differently

Jachimowicz, Jon M. "3 Reasons It's So Hard To 'Follow Your Pasion'", Harvard Business Review, October 15, 2019
 As referenced in: https://hbr.org/2019/10/3-reasons-its-so-hard-to-follow-your-passion

Koloc, Nathanial. "Why 'Follow Your Passion' Is Pretty Bad Advice," Hot Jobs On The Muse
 As referenced in: https://www.themuse.com/advice/why-follow-your-passion-is-pretty-bad-advice

Millburn, Joshua Fields. "'Follow Your Passion' Is Crappy Advice," The Minimalists.
 As referenced in: https://www.theminimalists.com/cal/

Pringle, Zorana Ivcevic. "Creativity Runs On Passion," Psychology Today, 10/2019.
 As referenced: https://www.psychologytoday.com/us/blog/creativity-the-art-and-science/201910/creativity-runs-passion

Robbins, Kyle. "15 Things Truly Passionate People Do Differently," Lifehack, 2018.
 As referenced in: https://www.lifehack.org/articles/communication/15-things-truly-passionate-people-differently.html

Thompson, Braden. "What Is Passion and What It Means To Have Passion," Lifehack, 10/15/2019.
 As referenced in: https://www.lifehack.org/articles/lifestyle/what-means-have-passion.html

Unger, Roberto Mangabeira. Passion: An Essay On Personality. NY: The Free Press, 1984.
 Book downloadable: http://www.robertounger.com/en/wp-content/uploads/2017/10/passion-an-essay-on-personality.pdf

SECTION 9:

JEWELRY IN CONTEXT

JEWELRY IN CONTEXT
9a. CONTEMPORARY JEWELRY IS NOT A *"LOOK"* -- IT'S A WAY OF *"THINKING"*

"Canyon Sunrise", Warren Feld, designer, 2004, Austrian crystal, glass seed beads, 14KT gold chain and constructed clasp, fireline cable thread, photographer Warren Feld

Guiding Questions:
(1) What makes jewelry labeled "contemporary" different from other styles of jewelry?
(2) How should we apply this label?
(3) How is contemporary jewelry a way of thinking through design?
(4) Should contemporary jewelry restrict the types of materials or techniques to be considered legitimate?
(5) How are shared understandings and desires at the heart of contemporary jewelry?
(6) Are there rules for designing contemporary jewelry?
(7) What does it mean for the designer to substitute his or her value and perspectives for those of the general group, culture or society?

Key Words: contemporary modern style	intent rationality	authentic performance shared understandings rules / fixed frameworks

Abstract:

Contemporary Jewelry represents a specific approach for thinking through design. It is an approach where the designer substitutes their personal perspectives and values for those of the group, the culture or the society. The jewelry exemplifies, in essence, a design, the meaning of which is primarily based within the reasoned performance of the designer. Making jewelry is then, in essence, an authentic performance task. The jewelry artisan applies knowledge, skill and awareness in the anticipation of the influence and constraints of a set of shared understandings and desires. Shared understandings relate to composition, construction, manipulation and performance. These understandings are *enduring, transferable, big ideas at the heart of what we think of as "contemporary jewelry". They are things which spark meaningful connections between designer and materials, designer and techniques, and designer and client. Managing these connections is what we call "fluency in design".*

CONTEMPORARY JEWELRY IS NOT A "*LOOK*" -- IT'S A WAY OF "*THINKING*"

Jewelry Design is a professional discipline. Every legitimately defined profession has at its core a discipline-specific way of thinking. This includes core concepts, core rules, and core beliefs. And it includes professional routines and strategies for applying, manipulating and managing these. The good designer is fluent in how to think through design, and the good contemporary designer is fluent in how to think through design which earns the label *contemporary*.

But, the jewelry designer can only wonder at this with crossed eyes and bewilderment. As a profession, *jewelry design* balances a series of contradictions, most notably to what extent the practice is craft, art or design. This works against professional legitimacy.

Jewelry Design, as a *discipline*, is not always clear and consistent about its own *literacy* – that is, what it means to be fluent in design. Its core concepts, rules and beliefs are not well-defined, and often break down by medium (*think* beadwork, stringing, wirework, fiber arts, metal work, polymer and metal clay, lampwork-fused glass-blown glass, and others), by operational location – (*visualize* museum, gallery, studio, store, factory, workshop, class, home), and by the degree of involvement and commitment to the profession of the jewelry designer him- or herself. The diversity of materials, approaches, styles and the like make it difficult to delineate any unifying principles or professional image.

As designers, we see, feel and experience the evolving dynamics of an occupation in search of a profession. But our profession is still in search of a coherent identify. Perhaps we see this most often in debates over how we come to recognize what jewelry we think should be labeled *contemporary* and what jewelry should not.

On the one hand, the idea of *contemporary* can be very elucidating. On the other, however, we are not sure what *contemporary* involves, how the label should be applied, and what the label represents. Yet, our sense-making search for its meaning is at the forefront of the professionalization of jewelry design. Our persistent questioning about "*What is contemporary jewelry?*" opens up thinking and possibilities for every jewelry designer, working across many styles and with many materials, both experienced and novice alike.

The term *contemporary* is defined as *something occurring in our time*, and that can be very confusing for the jewelry designer. We get caught in a major *Identity Crisis* for lack of a clear, agreed-upon definition of *contemporary*. How we resolve this *Identity Crisis* around a common understanding of *contemporary jewelry* can go a long way, I believe, towards developing a coherent disciplinary literacy and professional identity for all jewelry designers.

Resolution can be very unifying.

Many conceptual questions about *contemporary jewelry* arise. We need to be very cognizant of how we think through our responses.

Does the label apply to every piece of jewelry made today? We see all kinds of styles, shapes, silhouettes, materials, techniques, fashions all around us. There appears to be no common denominator except that they all have been *created in our time*.

Should the label be applied to all this variation?

Could it?

Why would we want it to?

Does the label apply to a certain timeframe, with the expectation that it will be supplanted by another label sometime in the future?

What is *contemporary jewelry*?

Contemporary Is A Specific Approach For Thinking Through Design

I suggest that *contemporary jewelry* is not a specific thing. But rather it is a way of thinking through the design process. It is a type of *thinking routine*[1] which underlays the universal core of contemporary jewelry design.

Contemporary jewelry is not every piece of jewelry made in our time. It is, instead, jewelry designed and crafted with certain *shared understandings* in mind – understandings about *composition, construction, manipulation* and *performance*.

Contemporary jewelry is not associated with any particular color or pattern or texture. It is, instead, a strategy for selecting colors, patterns and textures.

Contemporary jewelry is not something that only a few people would make or wear, whether boring or outlandish. It is, instead, something most people recognize as wearable with some level of appeal.

Contemporary jewelry is not restricted to the use of unusual or unexpected materials or techniques. It is, instead, something which leverages the strengths or minimizes the weaknesses of any and all materials and/or techniques used in a project.

Contemporary jewelry is not a specific silhouette, or line, or shape, or form, or theme, but, instead, something which shows the artist's control over how these can be manipulated, used, played off of, and, even, violated.

Contemporary jewelry is an integral part of our culture. We wear jewelry to tell ourselves and to tell others we are OK. It is reflective of the sum of all our choices about how we think through our place among others, our relative value among others, our behaviors among others, our preferred ways to interact, challenge, conform, question, organize and arrange.

The contemporary jewelry designer is especially positioned to serve at the nexus of all this culture. The designer's ability to think through and define what *contemporary* means becomes instrumental for everyone wearing their jewelry to successfully negotiate the day-to-day cultural demands of the community they live in. Designers have a unique ability to dignify and make people feel valued, respected, honored and seen.

Think of all that power!

Each person stands at that precipice of acceptance or not, relevance or not. The jewelry designer has the power to push someone in one direction, or another.

If only we had the established profession and a disciplinary literacy to help us be smart about this.

FLUENCY[2] IN DESIGN:
Managing The Contemporary Design Process

Jewelry design is, in effect, an *authentic performance task*.

The jewelry designer demonstrates their knowledge, awareness and abilities to:

1. Work within our *shared understandings* about contemporary jewelry.

2. Apply key *knowledge and skills* to achieve the desired result – a contemporary piece of jewelry.

3. Anticipate how their work will be *reviewed, judged and evaluated* by criteria reflective of these same shared understandings.

4. Step back, *reflect*, and validate all their thinking to reject any misunderstandings, and *make adjustments* accordingly.

The better designer is able to bring a high level of coherence and consistency to the process of managing all this – shared understandings, knowledge and skills, evaluative review, and reflection and adjustment.

This is called *fluency in design*.

Shared Understandings[3]

Shared understandings should be enduring, transferable, big ideas at the heart of what we think of as *contemporary jewelry*. These shared understandings are things which spark meaningful connections between designer and materials, designer and techniques, and designer and client. We need, however, to recognize that the idea of *understanding* is very multidimensional and complicated.

Understanding is not one achievement, but more the result of several loosely organized choices. Understanding is revealed through performance and evidence. Jewelry designers must perform effectively with knowledge, insight, wisdom and skill to convince us – the world at large and the client in particular -- that they really understand what design, and with our case here, contemporary design, is all about. This involves a big interpersonal component where the artist introduces their jewelry to a wider audience and subjects it to psychological, social, cultural, and economic assessment.

Understanding is more than knowledge. The designer may be able to articulate what needs to be done to achieve something labeled *contemporary*, but may not know how to apply it.

Understanding is more than interpretation. The designer may be able to explain how a piece was constructed and conformed to ideas about *contemporary*, but this does not necessarily account for the significance of the results.

Understanding is more than applying principles of composition, construction and manipulation. It is more than simply organizing a set of design elements into an arrangement. The designer must match knowledge and interpretation about *contemporary* to the context. Application is a context-dependent skill.

Understanding is more than perspective. The designer works within a myriad of expectations and points of view about contemporary jewelry. The designer must dispassionately anticipate these various perspectives about contemporary design, and, bring some constructed point of view and knowledge of implications to bear within the design and design process.

We do not design in a vacuum. The designer must have the ability to empathize with individuals and grasp their individual and group cultures. If selling their jewelry, the designer must have the ability to empathize with small and larger markets, as well. Empathy is not sympathy. Empathy is where we can feel what others feel, and see what others see.

Last, understanding is self-knowledge, as well. The designer should have the self-knowledge, wisdom and insights to know how their own patterns of thought may inform, as well as prejudice, their understandings of contemporary design.

How the jewelry designer begins the process of creating a contemporary piece of jewelry is very revealing about the potential for success. The designer should always begin the process by articulating the essential shared understandings against which their work will be evaluated and judged. For now, let's refer to this as *Backwards Design*[4]. The designer starts with questions about assessment, and then allows this understanding to influence all other choices going forward.

When designing contemporary jewelry, the designer will push for shared understandings about what it means to be worthy of the label "*contemporary*." I propose the following five *shared understandings* as a place to start, and hopefully, to generate more discussion and debate.

These are,

1. ***Fixed Frameworks and Rules should not pre-determine what designers do.***

    Rules do exist, such as color schemes or rules for achieving balance or rhythm. But rules may be challenged or serve as guidelines for the designer. In fact, the designer may develop and implement rules of their own.

    Designers do not learn understanding if they are only able to answer a question if framed in one particular way. How he or she designs is of primary importance because it reveals design fluency and thinking. And this allows for a variety of approaches as well as an escape from any dominant definitions. Nothing is sacred.

2. ***Jewelry should extend, rework, and play with, or even push, the boundaries of materials, techniques and technologies.***

    Contemporary designers are meant to ask questions, evaluate different options and experiment widely. They do this in order to leverage the strengths and minimize the weaknesses of materials, techniques and technologies used. Their jewelry should reflect this.

3. ***Jewelry should evoke emotions and resonance.***

    The audience is an integral part of the success of contemporary jewelry. The viewer/wearer recognizes things in the piece and is allowed to, *(in fact, expected to)*, react and interpret. The designer's goal is to achieve a level of resonance.

4. ***Jewelry should connect people with culture.***

    Contemporary jewelry is not made for art's sake alone. Contemporary jewelry is made to connect to the world around us. It is meant to assist a person in recognizing how they want to live their lives, and how they want to introduce their view of themselves into the broader community or communities they live in.

5. ***Successful jewelry designs should only be judged as the jewelry is worn.***

    Jewelry is not designed in isolation from the human body. Its design should anticipate requirements for movement, drape and flow. Its design should anticipate the implications of the context in which the jewelry is worn. The implications for all jewelry design choices are most apparent at the boundary between jewelry and person.

Given that the designer "*backward-designs* [4]," he or she begins the process by anticipating those understandings about how their work will be assessed. The designer then is equipped to make three types of informed choices:

    A. Choices about *composition*

    B. Choices about *construction and manipulation*

    C. Choices about *performance*

The designer determines (a) what *design elements* to include in the piece, and then (b) applies *organizational schemes or principles for constructing and manipulating* them. The contemporary designer (c) measures these against our *shared understandings about contemporary design*. These measures are a continuum – degrees of contemporary, not either/or's or absolutes. In any given piece of jewelry, some design elements may be very contemporary, and others might not.

GOOD COMPOSITION:
Selecting and Articulating Upon Design Elements and Their Attributes

Jewelry making is a constructive process. It makes sense for the designer to begin with something like building blocks, which I call *design elements*. Design elements include things like color, movement, dimensionality, materials, use of space, and the like.

Each design element, in turn, encompasses a range of acceptable meanings, yet still reflective of that design element, and which are called *attributes*.

These design elements can be arranged in different configurations.

The combination of any two or more design elements can have synergistic effects.

Working with design elements is not much different than working with an alphabet. An alphabet is made up of different letters. Each letter has different attributes – how it is written, how it sounds, how it is used. Configurations of letters result in more sounds and more meanings and more ways to be used.

A person working with an alphabet has to be able to decode the letters, sounds and meanings, as letters are used individually as well as in combination. As the speaker becomes better at decoding, she or he begins to build in understanding of implications for how any letter is used, again, individually or in combination.

This is exactly what the jewelry designer does with design elements. The designer has to decode, that is, make sense of a series of elements and their attributes in light of our shared understandings about jewelry design. The contemporary designer decodes in light of our further shared understandings about contemporary jewelry design.

The designer might, for example, want to select from this list of *design elements* I have generated below. I have arranged these design elements into what is called a *thinking routine*[1]. The designer uses the routine to determine how each element might be incorporated into the piece, and how the desired attributes of each element relate to contemporary design. They might also use the routine to look for issues of true and false. They might use the routine to rate each element as to importance and uncertainty.

**THINKING ROUTINE: *YOU JUDGE:*
*MORE OR LESS CONTEMPORARY?***
Use this Routine to assess whether a piece of jewelry is more or less contemporary.

DESIGN ELEMENT	LESS CONTEMPORARY	MORE CONTEMPORARY
Dimensionality	Flat; Width/Length focus	Not Flat; Noticeable Width/Length/Height focus
Movement, Moving Elements	Little or no movement, either from the movement of actual components, or from how colors or patterns are used	Great sense of movement, either from the movement of components, or from how colors or patterns are used
Color, Color Blending	Follows color rules, resistant to violate them	Pushes color rules to the edge, or violates them
Light and Shadow	Little sense artist attempted to control light and shadow in a strategic sense	Great sense artist attempted to control light and shadow, strategically
Negative and Positive Spaces	Little sense artist attempted to control negative and positive spaces in a strategic sense	Great sense artist attempted to control negative and positive spaces strategically
Point, Line, Plane, Shape, Form	Conforms to expectations; comfortable working within basic parameters; unconnected to function	Violates expectations; challenges basic parameters; may be connected to function; may involve unexpected use of shape, point, line, plane, form
Theme, Symbols	If used, themes and symbols are simplistic and readily identified	If used, themes and symbols have a complex relationship to form and structure, and stimulate debate and discussion to fully make sense of them
Beauty and Appeal	Primary goal of piece is beauty	Synergistic relationship among

	and appeal	beauty, function, and context to achieve designer's ends
Structure, and Support	Little concern with movement, drape and flow; unwilling to sacrifice appeal for function or context	Considerable concern with movement, drape and flow, and a willingness to make tradeoffs between appeal, function, and context
Materials	Materials are selected for how they look	Materials are selected for how they function; designer leverages strengths and minimizes weaknesses
Craftsmanship	Disconnect from Artist as if Artist was anonymous	Shows Artist's Hand
Context, Situation, Culture	Pieces created for the sake of making something, or for the sake of beauty and appeal only	Pieces created in anticipation of shared understandings about contemporary jewelry
Balance, Distribution	Conforms to expectations; comfortable working within basic parameters	Violates expectations; challenges basic parameters
Technique(s)	Selected without questioning implications of how technique affects boundary between jewelry and person	Selected after questioning implications of how technique affects boundary between jewelry and person
Texture, Pattern	Conforms to expectations; comfortable working within basic parameters	Violates expectations; challenges basic parameters
Reference and Reinforce an Idea, Style	May or may not reference and/or reinforce symbolic meanings; if so, usually does so in a linear fashion, such as mimicking or repeating them	May or may not reference and/or reinforce symbolic meanings; if so, learns from them, and then, based on this learning, takes the references to another level
Source of Rationality	Society or culture provides the clues to make sense of things	The designer substitutes his or her own clues for making sense of things.

Example of some choices I made using the Routine when creating my piece *Canyon Sunrise* to determine whether it was more or less contemporary:

Canyon Sunrise, Warren Feld, 2004 **What are some things which make this piece more or less *Contemporary*?**	
Dimensionality	Two layers of beadwork. The top layer overlapping the bottom layer, where the first row of the bottom layer is attached to the 2nd row of the top layer, forcing a curvature along the top. The pendant sits on top of bottom layer and in line with top layer.
Moving Elements	The two layers are only connected at their tops. As the wearer moves, each layer can move somewhat independently of the other.
Color, Color Blending	The piece uses a 5-color scheme, but increases the natural proportions of one color relative to the others. There are many gaps of light between all the beads which calls for a color blending strategy(ies). The piece relies heavily on simultaneity effects, as well as the overlapping effects of transparent and translucent beads.
Technique(s)	The bead woven strips are allowed to fan out from the top, thus better accommodating the wearer's body.

GOOD CONSTRUCTION:
Applying Knowledge, Skills, Competencies
for Manipulating Design Elements

Design elements need to be selected, organized and implemented in some kind of satisfying design. Towards this end, the designer, consciously or not, anticipates our shared understandings in order to make these kinds of choices.

Selecting and arranging Design Elements are the most visible choices the designer makes. We can see the finished piece of jewelry. We interact with it. We question it. We get a sense of whether we want to emotionally respond to it. We either feel its resonance, or we don't.

Most designers manage intuitively, learning to make good choices as they receive feedback and assessment, and adjust their decisions accordingly. The better jewelry designers, however, show *"metacognitive awareness"* of all the things they have thought of, anticipated, structured, and accomplished during the design process as these relate to larger shared understandings about contemporary jewelry.

Let's return, for a minute, to the analogy with building blocks and the alphabet. The design elements are building blocks. I compared them to the letters of the alphabet. Building blocks have attributes, and letters have attributes. Attributes further define them and give them purpose.

The novice designer learns to decode these building blocks and their attributes. With more experience, the blocks, just like letters, get combined and constructed into words and phrases and larger, meaningful ideas and expressions.

In essence, the finished piece of jewelry is an exemplar of the jewelry artisan's *vocabulary and grammar of design*. The fluency in how the artist uses this vocabulary and grammar in designing their piece should be, I would think, especially correlated with the success and resonance of the piece.

Often, designerss implement their design element choices with attention and recognition to *Principles of Composition, Construction, and Manipulation*. These Principles are the rules or grammar for using design elements in a piece. They are organizational schemes. Given the designer's goals for beauty and function, the designer is free to apply the Principles in any way she or he sees fit. However, we expect to find this grammar underlaying all pieces of jewelry, whether the piece is contemporary or otherwise.

When we want to apply the label *contemporary*, however, we search for the choices and logic the designer has used for constructing design elements into a contemporary whole, and in anticipation of our shared understandings.

I suggest these 10 Principles of Composition, Construction, and Manipulation. All Principles need to be applied, yet each is different from and somewhat independent of the others. For example, the colors may be well chosen, but proportions or placement not right.

Principles of Composition, Construction, and Manipulation	What the Principle is About
Rhythm	*How the piece engages the viewer and directs their eye*
Pointers	*How the piece directs the viewer to a certain place or focal point*
Linear and Planar Relationships	*The degree the piece is not disorienting; obvious what is "up" and what is "down"*
Interest	*The degree the artist has made the ordinary…"noteworthy"*
Statistical Distribution	*How satisfying the numbers and sizes of objects within the piece are*
Balance	*How satisfying the placement of objects (and their attributes) is*
Forms, Their Proportions, Distributions, and Dimensionality	Jewelry often can be structured in terms of segments, components or forms. How the pieces interconnected or amassed is of concern. Piece should feel coherent.
Temporal Extension: Time and Place	Any piece of jewelry must be acceptable within a certain historical, cultural or situational context.
Physical Extension: Functionality	*The degree the piece is designed so that it accommodates physical stresses and strains when the piece is worn; points of vulnerability are attended to.*
Parsimony (something similar to but beyond harmony and unity)	*There should be no nonessential elements; the addition or subtraction of one element or its attribute will make the piece less satisfying*

GOOD PERFORMANCE:
Seeking Continual Feedback and Evaluation About Choices and Results

The jewelry designer brings *perspective*. The designer shows they can rise above the passions, inclinations and dominant opinions of the moment to do what their feelings, thoughts and reflections reveal to be best. And, at the same time, the designer shows that they can strive for a rapport, a sharing of values, an empathetic response, a type of respect deemed *contemporary*.

If we return to our alphabet analogy, it is necessary, but not sufficient, for the designer to assemble a palette of building blocks, thus, design elements, just like assembling letters of the alphabet into different expressions and basic sounds. It is necessary, but not sufficient, for the designer to apply a vocabulary and grammar for arranging these building blocks, thus for constructing a piece of jewelry, just like creating words, phrases and more complex expressions.

Most importantly, however, it is *both* necessary and sufficient for the designer to anticipate how the piece of jewelry, (like any word or expression), will be assessed prior to making any choice about design element or construction. The more coherent and aligned each aspect of this process is, the better managed. To the extent the designer can strategically manage this whole "*backwards*" design process, the more fluent in design that designer is. The more fluent in design, the more the finished piece reveals the designer's hand and resonates.

So, there is a very dynamic performance component to design. The contemporary jewelry designer needs to think about what criteria their client and the general culture and market will use as *acceptable evidence* of *contemporary* and *good contemporary design*, when the piece is introduced. The designer needs to think about things like *connection, emotion, resonance, integrity, market*.

The designer needs answers to several questions at this point:

What is the designer's process and routine for thinking about shared understandings and evidence of authentic performance?

How well have they anticipated these criteria of evaluation?

Has the designer created a continual feedback loop so that acceptable evidence is introduced throughout the full process of design?

To what extent will the eventual evaluation of the contemporary jewelry designer and their work be fair, valid, reliable, and a sufficient measure of their results?

FOOTNOTES

[1] *Thinking Routines*. I teach jewelry design. I find it useful to engage students with various ways of thinking out loud. They need to hear me think out loud about what choices I am making and what things I am considering when making those choices. They need to hear themselves think out loud so that they can develop strategies for getting more organized and strategic in dealing with information and making decisions. My inspiration here was based on the work done by **Visible Thinking by Project Zero** (http://www.visiblethinkingpz.org/VisibleThinking_html_files/pz.harvard.edu) ***at Harvard Graduate School of Education*** .

[2] *Fluency*. I took two graduate education courses in Literacy. The primary text we used was **Literacy: Helping Students Construct Meaning** by J. David Cooper, M. Robinson, J.A. Slansky and N. Kiger, 9th Edition, Cengage Learning, 2015. Even though the text was not about jewelry designing per se, it provides an excellent framework for understanding what fluency is all about, and how fluency with language develops over a period of years. I have relied on many of the ideas in the text to develop my own ideas about a disciplinary literacy for jewelry design.

[3] *Shared Understandings*. In another graduate education class, the major text reviewed the differences between understanding and knowledge. The question was how to teach understanding. Worth the read to gain many insights about how to structure teaching to get sufficient understanding to enrich learning. **Understanding by Design** by Grant Wiggins and Jay McTighe, 2nd Edition, Association for Supervision and Curriculum Development, 2005.

[4] *Backwards Design*. One of the big take-aways from **Understanding by Design** (*see footnote 3*) was the idea they introduced of "backwards design". Their point is that you can better teach understanding if you anticipate the evidence others will use in their assessments of what you are trying to do. When coupled with ideas about teaching literacy and fluency (*see footnote 2*), you can begin to introduce ideas about managing the design process in a coherent and alignable way.

JEWELRY IN CONTEXT
9b. CONTEMPORIZING TRADITIONAL JEWELRY:
Transitioning From Conformity To Individuality

Etruscan Collar and Inspired Contemporary Pieces

Guiding Questions
(1) How is contemporary jewelry different from traditional jewelry?
(2) To what degree should the contemporary piece reference the traditional piece which inspired it?
(3) Why do so many people draw inspiration from traditional pieces?
(4) To what degree should contemporary pieces conform to socio-cultural and historical norms?
(5) If the wearer does not feel a connection between the jewelry and society, culture or history, can the piece of jewelry still be successful?

Key Words: *contemporary* *traditional* *archeological / historicism /* *revival / deconstructive* *contemporized*	*connectedness* *styles* *essential and alive*	*conformity* *individuality*

Abstract
Many people, jewelry designers among them, draw inspirations from traditional jewelry styles. The common inspirational thread here is a feeling of connectedness, coupled with a desire to feel connected. But the core issue for jewelry designers today, striving to achieve jewelry which is more contemporary than merely a replay or reworking of traditional preferences and styles, is how to contemporize it. That is, how to construct ideas into objects, challenge history and culture, produce that which is in opposition to standardization and monotony. Contemporizing Traditional Jewelry has to do with how designers take these particular traditional forms and techniques, and both add in their personal style, as well as make them more relevant to today's sense of fashion, style and

individuality or personal expression. The challenge for the designer, when contemporizing traditional jewelry, is how to marry personal artistic intent with traditional ideas, keeping the jewelry design essential and alive for today's audience.

CONTEMPORIZING TRADITIONAL JEWELRY:
Transitioning From Conformity To Individuality

Many people, jewelry designers among them, draw inspirations from traditional jewelry styles. These styles could be ancient, like those of Egypt, Peru, Persia, India and China. These styles could be more recent, like those of Art Deco, Art Nouveau, and Modern. These styles could be primitive, like those of tribal cultures in the rain forests of Brazil or the savannas of Africa or the Native American traditions in North, Central and South America.

The common inspirational thread here is a feeling of connectedness, coupled with a desire to feel connected. These styles strongly reflect particular premises, cultures, moralities, characters, and perspectives. People not only identify and connect with these, but use these style traits – almost ideologies – to explain and position themselves within the larger social contexts in which they find themselves.

Traditions represent reasons. Reasons justify everyday life. These reasons are the conditions and shared understandings necessary to regulate ideas, to generate opportunities for success, and to minimize the risk that comes from making choices about what to do next. Traditions justify thought and action, and because many people share these traditional understandings, living life becomes safer, easier, clearer. Traditions help people to understand each other and predict their behaviors. Traditions are often expressed within the designs of jewelry.

Jewelry, then, often signifies certain traditions through imitation or reference, and when mirroring them, reaffirms the wearer's thoughts, actions, self-identity, and self-reflection. Jewelry design which recognizes tradition feels more understandable. It feels safer and less risky to say out loud that it is beautiful, knowing that others will think so, too. It is no wonder that many jewelers resort to traditional forms and themes of expression, traditional techniques, traditional materials, traditional uses of color, texture, pattern, point, line, plane and shape. It feels like a short-cut to success.

But the issue for jewelry designers today, striving to achieve jewelry which is more contemporary than merely a replay or reworking of traditional preferences and styles, is how to contemporize it. That is, how to construct ideas into objects, challenge history and culture, produce that which is in opposition to standardization and monotony. *Contemporizing Traditional Jewelry* makes sense because this mirrors how most people live their lives today. They adhere less rigidly to societal and cultural norms, and moreso create their own. Jewelry, and its identify-reconfirming role it plays for the wearer, should reflect this.

The contemporary jewelry designer who wants to incorporate traditional elements or styles in some way, must come to grips with...

1. How Traditional jewelry differs from Contemporary Jewelry
2. Why so many people draw inspirations and connectedness to traditional styles
3. How literal the designer should be when contemporizing a traditional piece

Contemporizing Traditional Jewelry

Contemporizing Traditional Jewelry has to do with how you take these particular traditional forms and techniques, and add both your personal style to the pieces, as well as make them more relevant to today's sense of fashion, style and individuality or personal expression. The challenge for the designer, when contemporizing traditional jewelry, is how to marry personal artistic intent with traditional ideas, keeping the jewelry design essential and alive for today's audience.

This may be trickier than it might first appear. To what degree should you reference the traditional design elements in your contemporary piece? Just the colors? The colors and the pattern? The materials? The stitching, stringing or other techniques? The structural components, as well? How do you break down the traditional piece, in order to better understand it? And how do you use this understanding to figure out how and what you should manipulate, as you design and construct your contemporary piece?

If you walked into a Museum of Contemporary Art, you would find some things that were abstract, but other things that were realistic or impressionistic or surrealistic. You would find a lot of individualized expression – works associated with a particular artist, rather than a particular culture. You would find a wide use of modern materials and techniques and technologies. You would find unusual or especially noteworthy assemblages of pieces or materials or colors or textures. You would find pieces that in some way reflect modern culture and sensibilities – fashions, styles, purposes, statements. The exhibits would change on a regular basis, and you would also find something new and different to experience and marvel at each time.

Traditional Art, on the other hand, suppressed individualized expression. Instead, whatever the art form, traditional art emphasized a restatement of its cultural narrative. That is, artists, working within that cultural tradition, would use similar materials, similar designs, and similar motifs. The artwork was a symbolic representation of that culture's values and self-image. The "doing of the artwork" was a reaffirmation of one's place within that culture. Simply, if you did the same kinds of things in the same kinds of ways as everyone else, this reaffirmed your membership within that group and culture. And if you visited a Museum of Traditional Art, there would be many displays of wonderful, sometimes elaborate, pieces, but the exhibits would never have to change.

Approaches To Contemporizing Traditional Jewelry

There are many approaches jewelry designers use to contemporize traditional jewelry. Some approaches rely on mimicking traditional visual styles, techniques and materials. Some approaches rely on modifications. Still others seek to reinterpret traditional elements or introduce new elements into traditional designs. And yet other approaches attempt to create a completely different aesthetic starting from some traditional core.

I want to develop a very narrow, legitimate lane for what should be called *Contemporized*. I want to differentiate the thinking and practice that underlies *Contemporizing*, from other things artists do when addressing traditional design in contemporary pieces.

The way these different approaches get defined in the literature can get very muddied, so I want to begin with some simple categorization before elaborating more on ideas about contemporizing traditional jewelry. It is important to know how *literal* the artist should be. It is equally as important to know how much of the *artist's hand* should be reflected in the new piece.

APPROACHES TO ADDRESSING TRADITIONAL DESIGN IN CONTEMPORARY PIECES

APPROACH	DESCRIPTION	DEGREE *NOW* FROM *THEN* IS DIFFERENTIATED	RISK FOR THE CONTEMPORARY DESIGNER
ARCHAEOLOGICAL	Preserving the style and techniques of historic artisans, characterized by attention to duplicating and mimicking period styles, craftsmanship, and materials.	All about what existed *then*, and what should be preserved.	No risk
HISTORICISM	Imitating or recreating the work of historic artisans, characterized by attention to accurate period detail and thinking. Very literal. If new elements are added, these do not compete with or overshadow the historic vernacular.	Primarily about what was relevant *then*, and what should be imitated or copied *now*.	Very little risk

***REVIVAL** (sometimes referred to as **CLASSICAL**)*	Begins with an existential or sentimental romanticism of feelings about lifestyles, beliefs, imagery, symbols, cultures strongly associated with a particular historic group, society or period. Characterized by use of traditional themes, materials and styles based on inspirations from the past. Mostly literal with opportunities for reinterpretation and expression.	Often emphasizes some contrast between antiquity and modernity, industrial and hand-crafted, power now vs. power then, *then* and *now*.	Some risk, but does not create a barrier or roadblock to design
DECONSTRUCTIVE	Here the designer begins with traditional pieces, components and materials, and breaks them up to form new pieces, components and materials. The new piece results from the parts of the old piece, but that is the only connection. Nothing is literal; everything is reinterpreted.	Emphasizes the *now*, not much of the *then*.	High risk
CONTEMPORIZED	The designer imbues the design with inspirations from a rich cultural past, but creates a piece that has the sense it belongs in contemporary time. Characterized by how tradition is leveraged to conceive new ideas and forms.	Emphasizes the *now*, sometimes with reference to the *then*, but not really a matter of differentiating *now* from *then*.	Considerable risk, where artist substitutes his/her ideas and values for those extending from various traditions.

Archaeological Approach

Zoe Davidson recreated this Pictish Necklace (circa 600 AD) using original techniques and materials

The *Archaeological Approach* seeks to replicate and preserve the original ways of making jewelry and the original materials used to make them. The goal is to bring to life how things were thought about and constructed back then for a new contemporary audience. New techniques, technologies and materials are not introduced. There is a purity of belief in the traditional craftsmanship, norms and values reflected in these pieces of jewelry.

Often the Archaeological Approach requires years of detective work. There is a sense of urgency to rescue the past before it decays or fades away.

There is an accompanying assumption that this is what people who make and wear jewelry want to see happen today. This assumption seems to bear out because so many people express some kind of connectedness to these pieces and how they were originally crafted. They draw a line from the past to the present, and the clearer and cleaner that line is, the more legitimate the present seems to be.

Historicism

Castellani Jewelry Company, Italian, circa 1927, reproduction of Roman piece to commemorate historic occasion

Historicism seeks to recreate or imitate the work of artisans in past periods of time, culture and society. There is great attention to accuracy of period detail. They might use new materials or modern equipment and technique, but these should never replace or overshadow the historic visual vernacular and grammar.

Historicism may draw parallels between the *then* and the *now*, but these are not sentimentalized or romanticized, as in Revival or Classicism approaches. In Historicism, the emphasis is on thoughts and reasons. History is presented as an analogy between then and now. It creates a logical linkage. Characteristics are specific and shared. *(This is in contrast to Revival or Classicism, where the emphasis is on feeling).* In Historicism, the past is presented as metaphor for now. As it was then, so it is now. It creates a meaningful, felt linkage. Characteristics are not necessarily literal, but are to be interpreted and experienced. Again, in contrast to Historicism, Revival styles *(discussed below)* more easily and powerfully evoke emotions, which is one of the primary goals of artists.

Revival or Classicism

Isadoras, Etruscan Earrings, 2015, created with the look and flourishes of gold, metal work, granulation, turquoise stones strongly associated with Etruscan style and culture, but befitting current earring styles, as well

    Revival or Classicism approaches reflect the influences of pivotal fashion eras. The goal in Revival or Classicism styles is to evoke a personal emotional experience, rather than something that is learned from afar or as part of an intellectual exercise. The romanticized experience is like a call to conversion or rebirth, with a radical change in one's sense of identity and existence. There is a sense of a revived spirit in relation to the standard, dull, repetitive and boring jewelry seen all over. Often revival jewelry evokes a reaction against modern technology, materials and ways. Sometimes there is a call or push to connect the present day to some glorious past.

    Revival approaches begin with inspirations from traditional themes and jewelry. The past is felt as a simpler and purer time, where the individual was much closer to the earth and the earth's spirit. Inspiration is coupled with the natural curiosity of peoples around the world, their events, and their pasts. The jewelry is not only an opportunity to express a personal identify and emotion, but a chance to explore something other than the everyday mundane and routine. There is always this underlying tension of comparison and contrast between the past and the present, the current situation and situations faced by others, the advantages and disadvantages of modern life and antiquity.

    The use of hand-craft, rather than machine-craft, is highlighted, even when the pieces are actually manufactured by machine. Jewelry is defined as art-centered and artist-centered, one-of-a-kind, again, in spite of the fact that it is often machine made and mass produced.

    Revival approaches often capitalize on the use of representative motifs and symbols. These are evocative elements. Often they are anti-Industrial. As often, they are used to either impose or ease restrictions upon the female form and expressions of sensuality.

Deconstructivism

Pieces by Walid, for CoutureLab, 2009

Deconstructivism tears apart old pieces, and repositions all the parts into a new design. It is a play on evoking those feelings of connectedness and recognizability in the wearer, but forcing that wearer to redefine or somehow rethink those feelings in terms meaningful for this individual and at the moment or within a context.

Deconstructivism anticipates the shared understandings of its various audiences about what contemporized jewelry should reflect, which include,

      a.   An appreciation for hand-craft

      b.   Equating things of wealth and value with elegance and status

      c.   Disengagement from, then a new re-engagement with ideas and values

      d.   Sense of eccentricity and individuality – uniqueness in a cookie-cutter era

      e.   Ephemeral – Here today, gone tomorrow

Contemporizing

Etruscan Collar and Inspired Contemporary Pieces (Feld, 2012)

Contemporizing traditional jewelry really has nothing to do with nostalgia for a bygone era. It might reinterpret tradition, but not preserve it. It may strategically utilize tradition and leverage something about it in the current context. While contemporized jewelry designs may be imbued with inspirations and symbolism from a rich cultural past, the design is kept contemporary. That means, the piece is seen as belonging in a contemporary time.

The contemporized traditional piece is conceived as a new idea with new forms emerging from the inspirations of an individual artist and with aspirations to be judged by various contemporary audiences as finished and successful. The jewelry designer, in effect, is bringing together modern aesthetics with traditional craftmanship, to give a fresh outlook on contemporary individual and/or group culture. The jewelry designer is using a visual grammar, partly rooted in tradition, to portray or reveal a different narrative.

The difficulty for the contemporizing artist is how to disconnect or divorce the wearer from the memories and traditions of the past, while still representing inspirations and influences of tradition within the piece. The past provides a visual alphabet and a strong and established sense of legitimacy of meanings that is difficult to compete with and overcome.

The jewelry designer must address and manage all the identify issues people have when viewing and experiencing traditional designs, or contemporary designs with traditional components. The ultimate goal is for the jewelry designer, through the design and implementation of the piece, to establish new ideas and meanings about identity, history, culture, the present, perspectives, challenges, moralities, values, and characterizations. This involves recognizing and managing the shared understandings among various client groups.

Contemporizing Etruscan Jewelry:
Process and Application

Etruscan Collar (circa 300 B.C.)

    I was contracted to do a series of workshops in Cortona, Italy regarding Contemporizing Etruscan Jewelry. I began with examining several pieces of Etruscan jewelry. For the Etruscans, jewelry was a display of wealth and a depository of someone's wealth maintained and preserved as jewelry. Jewelry tended to be worn for very special occasions and was buried with the individual upon her or his death. One piece, an Etruscan Collar, (*see above*), was one I immediately connected with.

    The challenge, here for me, was to create a sophisticated, wearable, and attractive piece that exemplified concepts about contemporizing traditional jewelry. I began to interpret and analyze it.

    I first broke it down in terms of its ***Traditional Components***.

    The use of Traditional Components serves many functions. When the whole group uses the same design elements -- materials, techniques, colors, patterns and the like -- this reinforces a sense of membership and community. Often Traditional choices are limited by what materials are available and the existing technologies for manipulating them. Traditional choices also reflect style and fashion preferences, as well as functional prerequisites.

    If you were contemporizing a traditional piece, the first thing you would need to do would be to re-interpret the piece – that is, *decode* it -- in terms of its characteristics and parts. These are the kinds of things you the designer can control: colors, materials, shapes, scale, positioning, balance, proportions, # of elements, use of line/plane/point, silhouette, etc.

    Traditional Components in our Traditional Etruscan Collar included:
- *Gold metal* plates, pendants and chain. The use of metal, especially precious metal was important to the Etruscans. They had a strong preference for gold.
- *Linearity*. In traditional work, there is often a regimented use of line and plane, with a greater comfort for simple straight lines and flat planes.

The Etruscans did not often use many variations of the line, such as a wavy-line or spiral.
- *Predictable, regular, symmetrical sequencing and placement* of rectangular metal objects, pendant drops, centered button clasp, and chain embellishment. Balance and symmetry are always key.
- *Flat*. The surface is flat, and there is little here that intentionally pushes any boundaries with dimensionality.
- *Rigidity* – seemed that, while it definitely makes a power statement, it would be uncomfortable to wear
- *Silhouette*. Brings attention to the wearer's face. Traditional silhouettes were often drawn to the face.
- *Focal Point*. Often resorted to clearly defined and centered focal point.
- *Wire and metal working* techniques. There were not many choices in stringing materials. Wire working, by creating links, rings, rivets, chains and connectors secured individual metal components. The metal plates were created using repousse.

The designer would also try to surmise who, why and when someone might wear the piece. A final assessment would be made about how finished and successful the Traditional piece would have been seen at the time it was made.

I researched what jewelry meant to the Etruscans, and how their jewelry compared to other societies around them.

There is considerable artistry and craftsmanship underlying Etruscan jewelry. They brought to their designs clever techniques of texturing, ornamentation, color, relief, filigree, granulation and geometric, floral and figurative patterning. While their techniques were borrowed from the Greeks and other Mediterranean cultures, the Etruscans perfected these to a level of sophistication not seen before, and not often even today.

While Roman law outlawed the wearing of more than one ring or more than ½ ounce of jewelry at any one time, the Romans loved their jewelry, and wore many pieces, in spite of this. Most Roman jewelry designs were rigid interpretations of Greek and Etruscan jewelry.

I reflected on what might it mean to contemporize these Etruscan and Roman pieces? In other words, how would we manipulate the design elements to end up with something that was contemporary, paid some kind of reference or homage to the traditional piece, and was also a satisfying work of art?

I designed each of these two contemporized pieces, each taking me in a slightly different direction in what it means to Contemporize Traditional Jewelry. The *Vestment* is definitely more literal, with a mix of Revival and Contemporized approaches. The *Collar* is more Contemporized.

Vestment, Feld, 2012

Materials: Japanese seed beads, cube beads, delicas, Swarovski 2mm rounds, 14KT findings, Lampwork glass bead, fireline cable thread

Two overlapping and staggered layers of Ndebele stitched strips

Etruscan Collar, Feld, 2012

Materials: Japanese seed beads, cube beads, delicas, Swarovski 2mm rounds, 14KT findings, fireline cable thread

Two overlapping and staggered layers of Ndebele stitched strips

Detail

Detail

To contemporize the traditional Etruscan Collar, I wanted to:

- *Simplify design.* Reference the overall sense of the design, but simplify the overall appearance a bit. Contemporary pieces find that point of parsimony -- not too many elements, not too few -- that best evokes the power of jewelry to resonate.
- *Use contemporary materials.* I wanted to use glass seed beads and cable

511

threads, with the addition of gold ornamentation and clasp.
- *Make it more feminine.* I wanted my piece to have a sexy-ness about it.
- *Give it a curvilinearity*, rather than a flatness and straightness. Dimensionality and curvilinearity are very characteristic of Contemporary design. Here two Ndebele bead woven strips are layered, overlapping and staggered to get a curved edge.
- *Coordinate color choices*, but not feel forced to match them.
- *Challenge strict linearity.* Keep the general symmetry, but with a lighter hand – for example, overlapping, staggered layers that don't conform as tightly to an outline boundary. I wanted less social conviction and more artistry and the representation of the artist's hand.
- *To break the sense of rigidity and predictability*, I used the Ndebele Stitch, which is very fluid with an unexpected herringbone patterning, and stitched two overlapped, staggered layers of beadwork together.
- *Use of simultaneity color effects.* The application of more involved color theories and tricks to create more of a sense of excitement, as well as more multi-dimensionality. There is a complex interplay of colors within either strip of Ndebele bead work, as well as between each strip, as one lays on top of the other.
- *Use of contemporary techniques.* The use of bead weaving techniques which result in a soft, malleable, piece that drapes well and moves well. The result with bead weaving is something much more cloth-like.

FOOTNOTES

Hector, Valerie. The Art of Beadwork. NY: Watson-Guptill Publications, 2005.

JEWELRY IN CONTEXT
9c. Fashion-Style-Taste-Art-Design: Coordinating Aesthetics With Pleasure

Guiding Questions:
1. To what degree does/should "fashion" influence our jewelry design decisions?
2. To what extent do you think "fashion" influences the choices women and men make when buying jewelry?
3. When we judge a piece as beautiful and appealing, is this primarily a matter of style or taste, or does it have more to do with art and design?
4. How does someone know whether the piece of jewelry they want to buy is right or wrong for them?
5. What does it mean to say that "we need to inhabit our jewelry"?
6. What does it mean to have Taste? What is "good" Taste? Is there such a thing as a universal sense of good taste?
7. What are the differences among Fashion, Style, Taste, Art and Design?
8. What purpose(s) does it serve for community or individual for Fashions and Styles and Tastes to change, and keep changing over time?

Key Words:	*design cues*	*Inhabit jewelry*
fashion	*right or wrong*	*change / changing*
style	*good or bad*	*applied fashion*
taste	*aesthetics*	*social function*
art	*consumption*	*influencer*
design	*expressive consumption modes*	*pleasure*

Abstract
How does the wearer or buyer of jewelry know they have made the right aesthetic choice? What are the cues and clues people use when making these consumer choices? How does

attention to fashion, taste, style, art and/or design help the wearer or the buyer lower the risk for making the wrong choice? This chapter discusses answers to these questions for the jewelry designer. That designer must be comfortable managing these things as they play out in a process of innovation, adoption, and diffusion. That designer must be sensitive to the fact that the rules underlying good aesthetics may or may not coordinate with those rules underlying a person's desire for pleasure.

How Can We Know We Have Made The *Right* Aesthetic Choices?

Wearers and buyers of jewelry often look for a socially acceptable way to confirm they've made the *right* aesthetic choices. They may have picked a blue necklace, but was it the *right* blue? They may have decided upon a 24" necklace, but was this the *right* length? They may have gone with gemstones, but were they the *right* gemstones?

What are these cues and clues people use when deciding to wear or purchase a piece of jewelry? They could listen to the jewelry designer, if that person is present at the point of a transaction. But more likely than not, the designer is not. They could look at how this designer's jewelry was displayed. Or the packaging. Or read the designer's description. Or look at images on a website. Or check out other people wearing this designer's jewelry. Yet, even if the designer were present, and all this other information were available, however, why should the wearer or buyer trust the designer? Isn't there still a high level of risk for making the less than or more than right or wrong choice?

Our wearer or buyer is a consumer of aesthetics, when selecting a piece of jewelry. They are probably not experts in jewelry design or jewelry making materials and techniques. They are looking for something appealing, but concurrently socially and psychologically acceptable. They may want to feel part of a larger group. Or, they may want confirmation about a sense of individual identity and a way to distinguish themselves from the larger group. They may want reassurance that they are living life the way life should be lived, at least according to social and cultural norms. And there is a perceived risk here, should they make the wrong choice. We want to experience aesthetic pleasures, but our insecurities often mean we look for validation from other people around us, when consuming those aesthetic pleasures.

The actual ways and the actual clues and cues we look for to legitimize our aesthetic choices will vary from person to person. But we can look at five different ways to define the consumption of aesthetic expression and pleasure to begin to get a kind of understanding for the dynamics of what is going on here. Each is associated with a set of socio-cultural rules and consequences when acquiring products like jewelry.

These five *expressive-consumption modes* are,

1. *Fashion*
2. *Taste*
3. *Style*

4. *Art*

5. *Design*

Let's settle on some initial ideas about each of these, and then elaborate further through the remainder of this chapter.

Fashion: Often considered the substitution of someone else's taste for your own, and is assumed to represent *Good Taste*. Fashion satisfies the needs of the person to feel connected to a group, to imitate a sense of good taste, and to adapt to changes around them. It considerably lowers the risk for any aesthetic choices.

Taste: A person's ability to recognize beauty in whatever form she or he finds it, in our case here, jewelry. *Good Taste* is associated with how well principles of beauty and art have been applied.

Style: Will vary with particular cultures or events or historical periods or individual identities. Style communicates an expectation about meaning and its expression and what form it should take within a composition as seen by the outlook of the jewelry wearer or buyer. It might be referenced by terms like classic, modern, religious, Gen-X, casual, and the like. The principal forces in the creation of style are tradition and the experience of other jewelry the person is familiar with. Style on one level is the way a person applies their taste when choosing an aesthetic. Styles change and evolve in response to the influence of contemporary life.

Art: Represents beauty regardless of context. Regardless of whether it is worn or sitting on an easel. There are no pragmatic considerations involved.

Design: Represents the recognition of the most parsimonious relationship between beauty and function within any one piece of jewelry as it is worn. Jewelry requires that the piece not only satisfies the aesthetic needs of the person, but also fulfills a practical need.

AESTHETICS

What is the *essence of beauty* – what we call *aesthetics*?

When someone wears or buys a piece of jewelry, the choice of any aesthetic, as represented by that piece of jewelry, can become very problematic. The idea of aesthetics must be thought through by the person as she or he decides to touch or wear or share or part with some money or to walk away from the jewelry item.

But one person's aesthetic sensibility is not necessarily the same as anyone else's. There are few universal aesthetic ideas. Most things are so subjective and so context- or situationally-specific. Rules defining personal pleasure and rules defining beauty and appeal may co-exist, but they are not necessarily the same or in harmony. We know this because, from person to person, tastes, styles and fashions differ.

One response, where such differences exist, is to rely on fashion and art to define for us how pleasure and appeal should co-exist at any one moment in time. If we cannot find universally-accepted, common rules of aesthetics, then perhaps, we should let the social group or the social majority define it for us. Beauty, then, becomes not a property of the object per se, but an aesthetic judgment based on a subjective feeling. Our sense of good taste or fashion or style or art or design is a constructed one; it is not inherent in any particular jewelry design.

This brings us back to the idea that people want to minimize their sense of risk when making the right choices about wearing or buying a piece of jewelry. There is this inner need for validation. Part of that need is met by constructing and communicating a feeling or thought about what a consensus about taste might look like. Such a consensus, in reality, does not exist. But an idea of it emerges from preferences, assumptions, expectations, values, and desires. An idea of it emerges from how well the jewelry designer has managed the design process. That is, how well the designer has anticipated shared understandings of the various client audiences the jewelry is meant for, and incorporated these into the content of the design.

CONSUMPTION

Fashion, Taste, Style, Art and Design are each closely linked to the idea of *consumption*. These represent different ways of identifying preferences for certain types of jewelry and which directly affect the wearer' or buyer's choices in the marketplace. These preferences do not, however, necessarily trigger the wearing or purchase of a piece of jewelry. The interaction of these preferences with consumption is more complex and more depending on social interaction or personal motivation and strategy. People tend to emulate others (or distinguish themselves from others) or seek to reconfirm certain ideas which create certain habits and preferences, which in turn influence consumption of one piece of jewelry over another.

Yes, people want agency. They want to be free to choose jewelry that gives them pleasure. But they want validation and acceptance, as well. Most of that results from the understandings about the content of the jewelry. That is, how the content relays meanings through the aesthetic and design choices of the jewelry designer. We want the people around us to know who we are and what we have become. Jewelry makes a big statement here.

FASHION

Fashion is the socially acceptable, culturally-endorsed and safe way to distinguish oneself from others, while at the same time, re-affirming membership in a group. The person is allowed to be both an individual as well as a member of a group. With fashion, the individual can have both a sense of taste of their own as well as expect others to share it. Jewelry, from a fashion perspective, is embedded with the same values as our own. It is assumed that the community of fashion is the real community of universal good taste. That assumption means that the rules of beauty and appeal are understood as directly linked to and in harmony with the rules of finding pleasure.

Fashion may be thought of encompassing two things:
(1) The jewelry object itself, and
(2) The process of gaining acceptance for that object.

That process moves from the designer to a client to that client's audiences and public acceptance. That process extends from inspiration to aspiration to implementation to early adoption by fashion influencers and the diffusion of the jewelry throughout a particular social network. Eventually, though, there is a decline of acceptance over time.

The fashion object – in this case jewelry – must have discernable characteristics. These must be perceivable. They must anticipate how others will understand them. They must be communicative. These characteristics must show value; that is, something about them must be measurable in either relative (*example, it's better than what I have now*) or objective terms (*example, it is worth twice as much as my other piece*).

Fashion denotes a broad social consensus about good taste. If a piece of jewelry is "not fashionable," it means that, at least in a particular moment, it would be judged as boring, monotonous, unsatisfying or even ugly.

TASTE

Taste is an individuals' personal aesthetic choices. Taste is how any individual judges what is beautiful, good and correct. These choices are influenced by social relations and dynamics.

Taste denotes preference. If a piece of jewelry is "not your taste," this means you don't like it.
Good Taste is something which is socially sanctioned.

STYLE

Style is about agency and choice. It is strongly influenced by broadly accepted social constructs, such as time period, geography, religion, class, cultural identify. Style suggests that anything can be acceptable as long as it makes you feel good and that you are showing your authentic self.

Style denotes the manner in which something is expressed. If a piece of jewelry is "not your style," this means it does not present your beliefs in the way you want them expressed. You won't wear it.

ART

Everyone wants a little art in their lives. They want beauty around them. It inspires them. It makes them feel good. They do not want to be encumbered with practical considerations in every moment of the day. Great color combinations and component arrangements are reassuring, pleasuring, uplifting. Jewelry communicates a sense of the designer's hands that have touched it, the imagination that created it, and the work that has gone into it.

Art denotes the way the design elements and composition reflect principles of harmony and variety embedded in art theories. If a piece of jewelry is "not art," this means it is not sufficiently harmonious. It lacks some appeal.

DESIGN

Jewelry, however, is not a framed painting hanging in a museum. It is something that is worn. It is something that must continue to look good, even as the person wearing it moves from room to room, one lighting situation to another, one context to another.

Design denotes the way tradeoffs are made between beauty and function in the most parsimonious way. If a piece of jewelry is *not yet judged designed*, this means that if you added (or subtracted) one more element to (or from) the piece, the piece could be judged as more finished and more successful. The piece is not done yet.

INFLUENCERS: Fashion Change Agents

Influencers are people positioned at the intersection of fashion, style and taste. They are fashion change agents. They are key to the dynamics of adoption and diffusion, coherence and contagion. They may play out these roles in an ephemeral, non-professional way, or, they may be prominent professionals in a community, a network or online. The jewelry designer is not necessarily positioned or skilled enough to adequately influence who wears or buys their jewelry. Today's jewelry designer needs to get a good sense of how influence and influencers operate within the creative marketplace for the pragmatic purposes of managing adoption and diffusion of the jewelry she or he has created.

Influencers are one of the backbones of internet culture. Their business model centers on ways to shape everything we do in our lives from how we shop to how we learn to how we dress. Influencers are part micro-celebrity and part entrepreneur. They are opinion leaders and have been able to garner a large audience. They have proven themselves to be able to exploit how people distribute their time and attention.

It is important to get a handle on the *change-agent role* of the influencer. Specifically,

a) The influencer is probably not one of the earliest adopters of a newly introduced piece or line of jewelry

b) The influencer communicates using both visual and verbal representations of the jewelry, and usually needs some assistance from the designer with content

c) Influencers as people are usually more interested about fashion-style-taste than the general public they are trying to influence; they may not be up-to-date on all the current fashions, but they have the inherent skills to communicate and legitimate and instigate any fashion choice

d) Influencers have the creative skill to aesthetically and artistically assemble stylish jewelry presentations; they can articulate what *good taste* means in the context the jewelry as presented; they are often creators of accepted standards of good jewelry design and dress behavior

The influencer plays multiple roles from innovator, information transmitter, opinion shaper, knowledge base, social legitimizer.

It is estimated that 50% of the female population and 25% of the male population monitor fashion information on a regular basis, from surfing websites, perusing magazines, shopping, and talking about fashion. But it the influencer who best locks in their attention to any particular fashion item.

APPLIED FASHION: Inhabiting Your Jewelry

The jewelry designer needs to be sensitive to how this all plays out from the wearer' or buyer's point of view.

My clients and my students repeatedly ask about what the current fashion colors are? Did I see what so-and-so was wearing on TV or at an awards show? But usually, at least in Nashville, TN, a sense of fashion plays a small part in the day-to-day decisions most people make about the jewelry they want to wear.

Buying a piece of jewelry for yourself – a necklace, a bracelet, earrings, a brooch, something else – isn't a task easily given to someone else. It's often not a spur of the moment thing either. You just don't rush off to the local boutique or the local Wal-Mart, grab whatever you see, and go home. I'm not talking about that impulse buy during your leisurely visit to the mall. I'm referring to purchasing those pieces of jewelry you know will have to do a lot of the hard work to accessorize your wardrobe and help you get the compliments and notice of your family, friends and co-workers you comport with and compete with each and every day.

No, buying a piece of jewelry for yourself is a multi-purposed moment, one which must be thought through carefully and one which must be savored. Lest you buy the wrong piece. That doesn't really go with what you intend to wear. Or is over-priced. Or poorly made. Or conveys the wrong impression about status. Or is out of fashion. Or something one of your friends already has.

The jewelry you buy has to conform to quite a long list of essential criteria before you could ever think of buying it. It is something you will wear more than once. As such, it is your companion. Your necklace is not merely lying around your neck. Or your bracelet around your wrist. Or your earrings dangling from your ears. Jewelry can cause you to lose face with others. It can irritate or scratch your skin, or get caught up in your hair. It might weigh you down or stretch or tear your ear lobes. Jewelry can break without warning in the most unexpected and embarrassing of places. It can get caught on things, sometimes hurting you in the process.

Jewelry conveys to the world something about who you really are, or think you are. As such, jewelry is very personal. Your private, innermost, most soul searching choices made very public for all to see. As you caress it, as you touch the smooth or faceted or crevice'd beads and metal parts or the clasp or the material the beads are strung on, when you twist and move the piece within your hand, you are confirming to yourself the extent to which your jewelry is doing its job.

When you buy new jewelry, the dilemmas multiply. How will the new compare to the old? Will it be able to handle all these responsibilities – looking good, representing you, fitting in with your wardrobe, meeting the expectations of others? Like divorcing, then remarrying, changing your jewelry can take some time for readjustment. And you do not want to be seen as noncommittal to your jewelry. This would sort of be like going to a hotel, but not unpacking your suitcase while staying in the room.

Conveying some sort of social or psychological distance from your jewelry can be very unsettling for others. So you need to *inhabit* it. You need to inhabit your jewelry, wear it with conviction, pride and satisfaction. Be one with it. Inhabiting jewelry often comes with a price. There becomes so much pressure to buy the *right* pieces, given all the roles we demand our jewelry to play, that we too often stick with the same brands, the same colors, the same styles, the same silhouettes.

We get stuck in this rut and are afraid to step out of it. Or we wear too many pieces of jewelry. The long earrings, plus the cuff bracelets on both arms, plus the head band, plus the hair ornament, plus the 7-strand necklace, plus the 5 rings. We are ever uncertain which piece or pieces will succeed at what, so hopefully, at least some combination or subset of what we wear will work out.

In a similar way, we wear over-embellished pieces – lots of charms, lots of dangles, lots of fringe, lots of strands. Something will surely be the right color, the right fit and proportion, the right fashion, the right power statement, the right reflection of me.

And our need to inhabit our jewelry comes with one more price. We are too willing to overpay for poorly made pieces in our desperation to have that right look. The $100.00 of beads strung on elastic string. The poorly dyed stones which fade in the light. The poorly crimped and overly stiff pieces with little ease for accommodating movement and frequent wear. It is OK to inhabit our jewelry. In fact, it is necessary, given all we want jewelry to do for us. But we need to be smart about it. We need to learn to recognize better designs and better designers.

This need not be expensive at all.

Just smarter.

FASHIONS CHANGE

Every jewelry designer should expect that many fashion preferences and desires will change over time, sometimes very quickly. Consumers can be fickle. They can get bored with the old. They search out new novelties all the time. They try to keep up with trends and fads. As the economy moves up and down, so too do consumer abilities to purchase at a particular price.

New materials come out on the market. So do new techniques and technologies. Clothing and hair styles change silhouettes. Seasons change. The climate is changing. Popular culture changes. Social media goes in a different direction. Something goes viral. Global trading opportunities change. Corporations come up with a catchy marketing campaign.

In contemporary culture, it also has become more okay for any individual to develop their own sense of style and fashion.

THE DANGER OF HOMOGENIZATION

If fashion, style and taste lead to everyone wearing and buying similar things, we begin to lose the need for the jewelry designer. The designer becomes more a technician. The task of design becomes more mechanical, step-by-step, ritualized. More likely the design process can be taken over by machines.

It is incumbent upon the designer to not lose sight of the essence underlying jewelry design. At its core, this is to create pieces which translate the designer's inspirations in ways which resonate with others to be similarly inspired. Jewelry design is a communicative collaboration of sorts between designer and client. This will always lead to a wealth of variety and variation never diminished by fashion, style or taste.

FOOTNOTES

Firat. Fuat A. 1991. The Consumer in Post-modernity. Advances in Consumer Research 18. 70–76.

Gronow, Jukka. "Taste and Fashion: The Social Function Of Fashion And Style," <u>Something Curated</u>, Helsinki, 8/16/2017.

Hebdige. D. 1983. Subculture. The Meaning of Style. London & New York: Methuen.

King, Charles W. "The Dynamics of Style and Taste Adoption and Diffusion: Contributions From Fashion Theory," Advances in Consumer Research Volume 07, eds. Jerry C. Olson, Ann Arbor, MI: 1980.

Noro, A. 1991. Muoto, moderniteetti ja 'kolmas'. Tutkielma Georg Simmelin sosiologiasta (Form, Modernity and the 'Third'. A Study of Georg Simmel's Sociology). Jyvaskyla: Tutkijaliitto.

Simmel. G. 1950. The Metropolis and Mental Life. In K. H. Wolf (ed.), The Sociology of Georg Simmel. Illinois: Free Press.

Simmel. G. 1991. The Problem of Style, Theory, Culture and Society 8. 63–71.

Wikipedia. "Aesthetics". As referenced in:
https://en.wikipedia.org/wiki/Aesthetics

Wikipedia. "Taste". As referenced in:
https://en.wikipedia.org/wiki/Taste

JEWELRY IN CONTEXT
9d. Designing With The Brain In Mind: Perception, Cognition, Sexuality

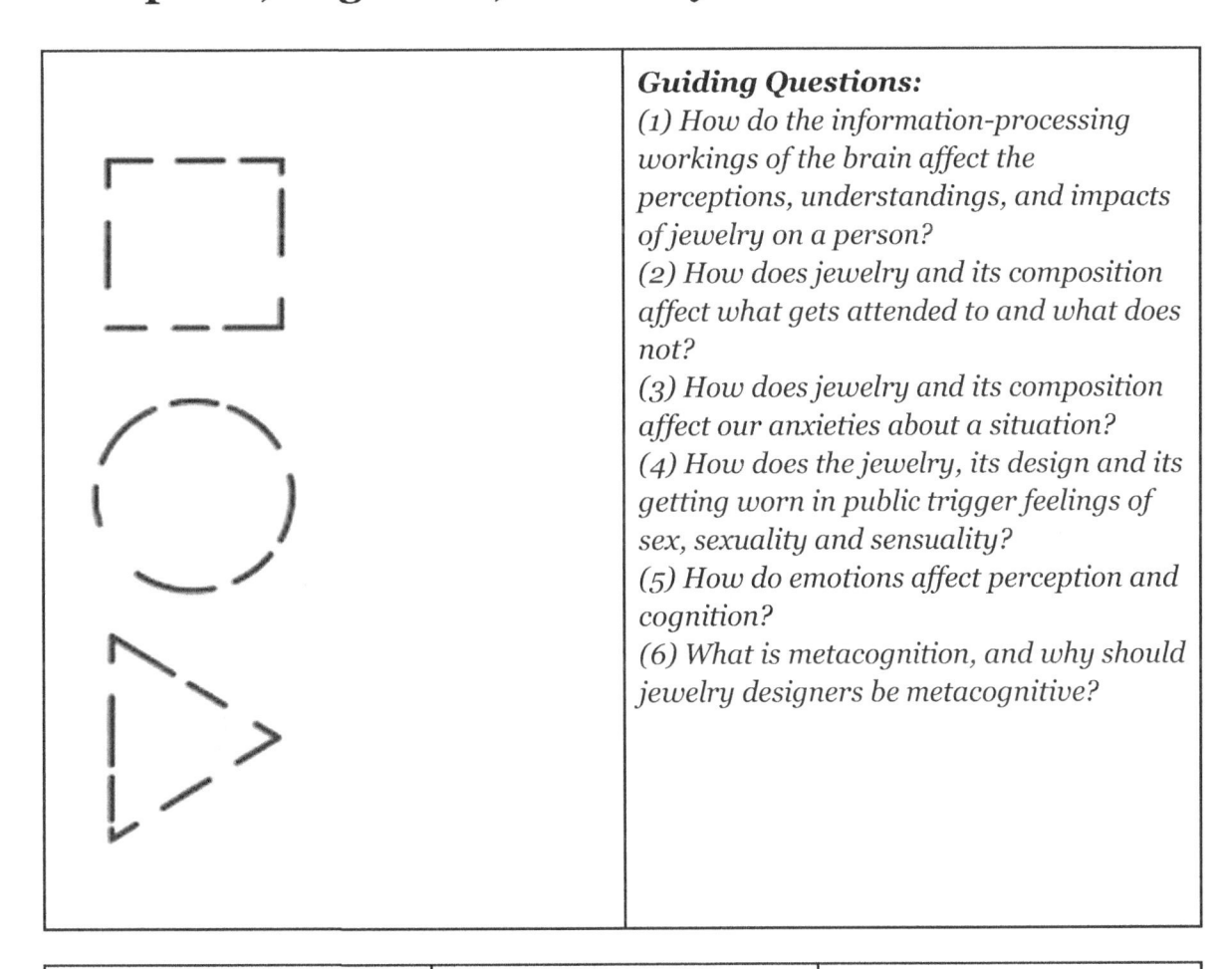

Guiding Questions:
(1) How do the information-processing workings of the brain affect the perceptions, understandings, and impacts of jewelry on a person?
(2) How does jewelry and its composition affect what gets attended to and what does not?
(3) How does jewelry and its composition affect our anxieties about a situation?
(4) How does the jewelry, its design and its getting worn in public trigger feelings of sex, sexuality and sensuality?
(5) How do emotions affect perception and cognition?
(6) What is metacognition, and why should jewelry designers be metacognitive?

Key Words:	*jewelry as object*	*understanding*
perception	*jewelry as intent*	*attention*
cognition	*senses / sensing*	*orienting*
sexuality / sex	*function*	*directing*
sensuality / gender	*anxiety / safety*	*filters / triggers*
parallel processing	*Gestalt*	*selective perception*
making a complete circle	*whole vs. parts*	*emotions*
finding a place to come to rest	*placing attention*	*metacognition*
	suggesting movement	

Abstract
Jewelry plays a lot of psychological functions for the wearer, the viewer, and the buyer, so it is important to understand some things about perception and cognition and how the

brain processes information. The jewelry designer plays with various design elements, let's call these parts. The designer arranges these parts into a composition, let's refer to this as the whole. The brain takes in information about, that is, attends to each part, and information about the whole, and assigns a meaning to these. The designer must anticipate all this, especially understanding Gestalt behavior. So the designer is not only dealing with aesthetic and functional considerations in their designs, but also the psycho-social-emotional triggers and filters which may result from how the brain processes all this. Some of these emotions may evoke a sense of sex, sexuality and sensuality. Last, jewelry designers must be very aware – metacognitive – of how they think through design, and be able to turn their experiences into thinking routines.

DESIGNING WITH THE BRAIN IN MIND

Jewelry plays a lot of psychological functions for the wearer, the viewer, and the buyer, so it is important to understand some things about perception and cognition and how the brain processes information. Jewelry is used to meet the individual's needs for self-esteem and self-actualization. A sense of oneness and uniqueness. Or conversely, a person might also rely on jewelry to create a sense of being a part of a larger group or community. Or a sense of survival and protection. A re-affirmation of values and perspectives. A connection to a higher power or spirituality. A sense of fantasy. An orientation to what is up and what is down and what is left and what is right.

The jewelry designer plays with various design elements, let's call these *parts*. The designer arranges these parts into a composition, let's refer to this as the *whole*. The brain takes in information about, that is, attends to each part, one by one, and then gathers information about the whole, and assigns a meaning to all these. Because of how the brain works, there may be several meanings that rise up to the surface, so the brain has to filter and prioritize these somehow. The resulting assigned meaning(s) results in some type of behavior. At its simplest level, the behavior is either one of *placing attention* or one of *suggesting movement*. The behavior, whatever it is, reaffirms for the observer that their goals are getting met or that there is some consistency and coherency with personal values and desires.

The designer must anticipate all this. So the designer is not only dealing with aesthetic and functional considerations in their designs, but also the psycho-social-emotional triggers and filters which may result from how the brain processes all this. Some of these emotions may evoke a sense of sex, sexuality and sensuality. Jewelry has sensual qualities. It has gender associations. It may symbolically represent what is safe and what is not safe to view or to touch.

PERCEPTION

Perceptions are ways of regarding, understanding or interpreting something. We perceive using our senses. We touch, we see, we feel, we hear, we smell, we sense positioning. Perceptions are subjective, and each person has their own subtle differences, even when responding to the same design or event. In fact, different people may have very different perceptions about the same design or event. Their assumptions, expectations and values may further color their perceptions.

Each person filters their perceptions with each move, each conversation, and each situation. Such filters may contingently alter perceptions. Perceptions are not fixed. They are very sensitive to the context and the situation. Any type of filter may result in *selectively* perceiving some things, but not others. In design work, our clients might selectively focus on brighter lights, louder sounds, stronger odors, sharper textures, silhouettes, proportions, placements and distributions, balance, harmony and variety. Selective perception can add some more muddiness to the interaction especially as designer and client try to find and develop the shared understandings about whether a piece of jewelry is to be judged as finished and successful.

Adequately sharing understandings within a situation and among the people in it depends on the amount of information available to each person and how correctly they interpret it. Perception is one of the critical psychological abilities we have in order to survive in any environment.

The designer needs to be open to understanding how the client perceives the design tasks and proposed outcomes, and to adjust their own perceptions when the management of the relationship calls for this. **There is no formula here.** Each situation requires its own management strategy. Each designer is left with their own inventiveness, sensitivity, and introspective skills to deal with perceptions. But it comes down to asking the right questions and actively listening.

For example,

How does the client begin to understand your product or service?
Can the client describe what they think you will be doing and what the piece or product might look like when finished?
Can the client tell you how the finished piece or product will meet their needs and feelings?
Can the client tell you about different options?
How will they interpret what you want them to know?
What impressions do you want to leave with them?
Do they perceive a connection between you as a designer and your design work as proposed?
What levels of agreement and disagreement exist between your perceptions and theirs?
Can you get at any reasons which might explain their perceptions, and any agreement or difference?
Can you clear up any misperceptions?

The jewelry designer needs to distinguish between how the jewelry is perceived when it is *not* worn from when it *is* worn. When not worn, jewelry is an *object* admired and perceived more in art or sculptural terms. When worn, jewelry is an *intent* where perceptions about the jewelry as object are intertwined, complicated, distorted, amplified, subjugated – you get the idea – with the needs and desires of the individual as that person presents the self and the jewelry as worn in context. Either set of perceptions may support one another, or they may be contradictory.

COGNITION

Cognition involves how the brain processes our perceptions, particularly when these perceptions are incomplete or contradictory or otherwise messy or unresolvable. Cognition focuses on how the brain takes in existing knowledge and creates new knowledge. Cognition is both conscious or unconscious, concrete or abstract, intuitive or conceptual. Cognition may influence or determine someone's emotions. Metacognition is your own awareness of your strategies and methods of thinking and problem-solving.

The brain takes in a lot of information all at once. The brain looks for clues. It compares clues to information stored in memory. Typically different parts of the brain will simultaneously process (*e.g., parallel processing*) either different clues or the same clues in different ways. Some information will have greater relevance or resonance than others. Some information will be rejected. Some information will be recategorized or reinterpreted.

You can think of all these mental processes going on in the brain as a huge, self-organizing undertaking, but happening within minute fractions of a second. What happens is very context- or situation-specific. The goal is the creation of some kind of understanding. This understanding will have some logic to it. It will be compatible with and reaffirm the individual's memories, assumptions, expectations, values and desires. This understanding will typically result in some kind of behavioral response. The response will most often be related to *attention* or *movement*. The understanding and the behavioral response will likely get stored in memory. *[When we talk about literacy and fluency in design, as in earlier chapters, with* attention, *we are developing our abilities to decode design elements. With* movement, *we are arranging design elements or constructing in anticipation of movement, drape and flow.]*

Attention

The cognitive process starts with *attention*. Attention has to do with how we focus on some perceptual information, and not on others. A key function of attention is how to identify irrelevant data and filter it out, enabling other more significant data to be distributed to other parts of the brain for further processing.

Picture a piece of jewelry. This jewelry will present many stimuli – color, placement, proportion, balance, volume, positioning, its relation to the human body, the context within which it is worn, perhaps how comfortable it feels, symmetry, and the list can go on and on.

Which perceptual clues are most important to the person who needs to decide whether to wear or buy it? Attention is the first cognitive step in determining how to answer this, though the observer does not always consciously grasp the specifics of what is going on.

There are two types of attention:
    (1) Orienting Attention, and
    (2) Directing Attention

Orienting Attention works more reflexively. For example, we are prewired in our brainstem with a fear or anxiety response. This helps us reflexively avoid snakes and spiders. This anxiety response has major implications for how people initially respond to jewelry as it is worn.

Say a stranger is in a room and wearing a necklace. You approach the entrance to this room. You see the stranger who is wearing the jewelry. Your brain has to instantaneously evaluate the situation and determine if it is safe for you to approach and continue to enter the room, or whether you need to be fearful and turn around and flee. Jewelry can play a key role here.

The jewelry signals the primary information the brain needs to make this judgment. Perceptions are filtered to the very basic and very elemental. First the viewer wants to be able to make a complete circle around the jewelry. Anything which impedes this – an ugly clasp assembly, poor rhythm, colors that don't work together, uncomfortable negative spaces – makes the brain edgy. If the brain gest edgy, the jewelry will start to get interpreted as boring, monotonous, unsatisfying, ugly, and we can go all the way to will cause death.

After the viewer makes that complete circle, a second perception kicks in and becomes key to whether the brain will signal it's either OK to approach or, instead, you better flee. This second perception is a search for a natural place for the eye/brain to come to rest. In jewelry we achieve this by such things as placing a pendant in the center or graduating the sizes of the beads or doing something with colors.

In slightly more technical terms, the jewelry draws the observer to a focal point at which they can sense an equilibrium in all directions. The viewer feels physically oriented. The jewelry composition presents a coordinated form which connects spaces and masses within something that feels / looks / seems like a unique harmony. The observer is made to feel, as she or he is attenuating to how mass relates to space within the composition, that not only is each element of the jewelry related to the ones preceding or following it, but that each element is contributing to the concept of the whole – the jewelry form as a whole is greater than the sum of its parts. There is continuity. There is coherence. Space and mass are interdependent. The distinction among parts is removed. The brain likes this. It searches for it. It makes it restful.

The full experience of the jewelry only gains its full meaning within its total expression. The significance of the total jewelry composition unfolds as the observer moves about its separate parts. This expression, in turn, as it relates to the attention processes of cognition, gets reduced to the confluence of the two clues of (a) *making a complete circle*, and (b) *finding a natural place to come to rest*. If the two clues are satisfied, the jewelry is viewed as finished and successful, and the immediate environment is seen as safe.

The jewelry designer controls the limits and the possibilities for attention. If jewelry design were merely a matter of organizing a certain number of parts, the process would be very mechanical and not at all creative. All jewelry design would be equally good (or more likely, bad). The purpose of good jewelry design is to express particular meanings and experiences for the wearer, viewer or buyer to attend to. Jewelry design is only successful to the extent these are fully communicated to the observer, and are fully sensitive to how perception and cognition play out in our brains. That is, how the jewelry, through its design, enhances or impedes perception and cognition.

Directing Attention, the other type of attention, signals to the observer the possibilities for or constraints on *movement*. It is more deliberate rather than reflexive. It can divide one's attention so that the person can pay attention to more than one thing at the same time. Using our example, there could be several strangers in the room, each wearing a different style and design of necklaces. As our observer walks into the room, attention can be shifted from one person / jewelry to another, or focused on one person / jewelry alone.

Directing Attention determines the potential for movement, so that the observer can anticipate the possibilities, or conceive the limits. With whatever piece of jewelry is worn, how freely or easily can the person shift positions, stand, run, dance, lay down? Will any type of movement change the appeal of the jewelry as worn? Is there anything about the design of the jewelry which anticipates different kinds of movements and positioning? Will the appeal of the jewelry remain should the wearer move to a different type of lighted situation or into a shadow? How much ease should be built into the construction of the piece? Or, in our short example, can the person move freely around the entire room?

The aesthetics of mass and space, such as the interplay of points, lines, planes and shapes, are rooted in a person's psychology in order to arouse predictable patterns of experience. There seems to be a constant human need to perceive and attend to spatial relationships which distinguish harmony from cacophony. This psychological response to form most likely is connected to a person's mechanisms for balance, movement and stature.

On the simplest level, observers use jewelry to assist them in knowing what is up and what is down, and what is left and what is right. Jewelry is used similarly in this directing sense as the floor, walls and ceiling are used towards this end in a room, or the horizon, landscape and trees are used outside. Without any clues about positioning, a human being would fall down and not be able to get up.

Picture, for example, how you might feel when the person standing next to you has one earring stuck in a 90 degree angle, or is only wearing one earring, or has a necklace mispositioned and slightly turned around the neck. You most likely feel a bit uncomfortable, perhaps uncomfortable enough to let the person know the jewelry needs to be adjusted in position, or that they seem to be missing an earring. Or perhaps not so comfortable to raise the issue publicly.

GESTALT: The Whole Vs. The Parts

One mechanism of cognition is called a *Gestalt*. At its root, Gestalt means that the whole composition is more meaningful than the meanings of its individual parts. There is a chicken and egg type of debate within the field about whether the person attends to the parts first with a stronger emergent whole, or whether the person needs to understand the whole first and use this understanding to interpret the parts. But for jewelry designers, we do not have to get into the debate here. Jewelry designers need to recognize that the resulting whole composition should always be more resonant, more finished-feeling and more successful than any of the individual design elements incorporated into the piece.

At its core, people are motivated to recognize entire patterns or configurations. If there are any gaps or flaws or mis-directions, the brain, cognitively, has a tendency to fill in the gaps or ignore the flaws or mis-directions. Where perceptual information does not exist or is somehow incomplete, the brain will fill in the blanks, so to speak, using perceptions about proximity, similarity, figure-ground, continuity, closure, and connection. This all involves work on the part of the brain. The brain may generate resistance towards this end, because it requires some effort within a somewhat unfamiliar situation, unless somehow coerced or tricked by aspects of the design choices themselves.

Jewelry will have a lot of gaps of light throughout. The individual beads and components do not fit together tightly like in a jig-saw puzzle. They do not blend into each other. They are distinct points of information. Instead, from the brain's point of view, these gaps are equivalent to cliffs and valleys between each one. The brain, in effect, is asked to jump from cliff to cliff. It may be resistant to do so. The brain wants harmony. The brain wants to connect the dots into a smooth line. Or, if the composition were separate lines, the brain wants to connect the lines into a smooth, coherent plane. Or, if there were several distinct lines and planes, the brain wants to integrate these into a recognizable shape or form. But again, all this is not automatic. The brain will resist to do any more work than necessary. The designer will need to make smart, influencing, persuading choices in the design. The Gestalt mechanism is a set of these kinds of choices.

The brain needs to be sufficiently motivated to make the effort to harmonize the pattern or configuration. Gestalt is one of the cognitive, motivating, innate forces the brain uses. In music, when the brain hears part of a melody, it not only hears the notes, but also something else, let's, for simplicity, call this a tune. This something else allows the brain to anticipate how the melody will continue. If the melody at this point changes key, the brain anticipates how the melody will play out in the new key as a similar tune but with different notes before it is played. How the brain interacts with a piece of jewelry has parallels.

One obvious example is the use of color simultaneity effects. Here the color of the next bead is affected by the color of the previous bead. Place a grey bead next to an orange bead, and the grey bead will take on some orange tones. Both beads get perceived as blended or bridged, even though, in reality, they are not. The observer generalizes the relationship between the two stimuli rather than the absolute properties of each. Take three beads, one emerald, one olivine and one grey. You would not normally find these two greens within the same composition. Place the grey bead between the two greens and, because of simultaneity effects, the two greens will harmonize as the grey forces a blending or bridging.

Jewelry designers need to learn the basic principles or laws of Gestalt. This allows them to predict the interpretation of sensation and explain the way someone will see their compositions. It allows them to anticipate how their jewelry will arouse predictable patterns of emotions and responses in others.

These laws can be used as guides for improving the design outcomes. They can be used to influence what design elements should be included. In what forms / volumes / placements / other attributes these design elements should take. How design elements should be arranged. How construction and function should best relate to aesthetics. How the jewelry should be worn. How the jewelry might coordinate with other clothes and accessories or contexts.

These principles are based on the following:

Principle of Proximity: *In an assortment of elements, some which are closer together are perceived as forming groups. Emphasizes which aspects of elements are associated.*

Principle of Similarity: *Elements within an assortment are grouped together if similar. This similarity could be by color or shape or other quality. If the assortment is comprised of many elements, some similar and some dissimilar, the brain will sort this out so that the similar ones, no matter where placed within the assortment, will be perceived and grouped together.*

Principle of Closure: *People tend to perceive objects as complete, even when incomplete, rather than focusing on any gaps or negative spaces. When parts of the whole are missing, people tend to fill in the missing parts. The brain is preset to attempt to increase the regularity of sensation or the equilibrium within an experience or event.*

Principle of Symmetry*: The mind perceives objects as being symmetrical and forming around a center or focal point. Similar symmetrical elements will be grouped as one. The brain will attempt to make something which is asymmetric be perceived as symmetric as best as it can. The brain equates symmetry to coherency. With asymmetrically design jewelry, the brain will seek to relate additional contextual variables, such as clothing style or hair style, to force that sensation of symmetry.*

Principle of Common Fate: *Elements are perceived as lines which move along the smoothest path. We perceive objects as having trends of motion. In jewelry design, think about something like rhythm. The beads are not moving in reality, but we perceive a direction and a quality of movement.*

Principle of Continuity: *Elements of objects tend to be grouped together, and therefore integrated into perceptual wholes, if they are aligned with an object. If two objects are next to each other or overlap, the brain tends to see each object distinctly as two separate wholes, if the elements within each object are aligned and continuous. Picture a 2-strand necklace. The brain will be primed to see these as 2 separate strands or wholes, rather than one whole necklace. Objects with abrupt and sharp directional changes will* *less likely be perceived as a whole.*

Principle of Past Experience: *Under some circumstances, visual stimuli are categorized according to past experience. Especially when faced with unknown or unfamiliar objects, the brain will resort to using past experience as a means for interpretation and whether to group elements within the objects as a whole.*

DESIGNS CREATE EMOTIONS

There is a growing body of knowledge of the mechanics of sensory processes in cognition. A good design creates positive emotions for the viewer, wearer and/or buyer. Jewelry designers need a deeper understanding of types of emotions and their psychological underpinnings.

People develop emotions with jewelry on three levels: (1) visceral (intrinsic), (2) behavioral (behavior), and reflective (reflection).

> *(1)* Visceral (wants to feel): attractiveness, first impressions, feelings
>
> *(2)* Behavioral (wants to do): usability, function, performance, effectiveness
>
> *(3)* Reflective (wants to be): meaning, impact, shared experience, psycho-socio-cultural fit

METACOGNITION

Metacognition is an awareness of your own thought and problem-solving processes. It involves a search for patterns and the meanings behind them. It involves a lot of reflection. It involves a sensitivity to the choices made when confronting any unfamiliar or unknown situation. It concerns an awareness of why some choices worked better than others, or not at all.

For jewelry designers, it is important to take metacognition one step further. It is important to turn your experiences into thinking routines. These routines are fix-it strategies you bring with you when overcoming difficult or unfamiliar situations. Better designers have a more complete and practiced set of fix-it strategies – what I refer to in earlier chapters as having a Designer Tool Box.

SEX, SEXUALITY, AND SENSUALITY

As a jewelry designer, you have to be very aware of the roles jewelry plays in sex, sexuality and sensuality. The act of sex. Everything leading up to it. Eroticism. Sensuality. Sex, however, differs from sensuality. Sensuality is how the jewelry brings out the sensual – the gratification of the appetite for visuals, sounds, tastes, smells and touch. Sensuality always makes jewelry desirable. But perhaps no two people experience the sensuality of a piece of jewelry in the same way.

These sex-sexuality-sensuality roles include,

(1)   *The Peacock Role*

(2)   *The Gender Role*

(3)   *The Safe Sex Role*

(1) The Peacock Role. One sexual role of jewelry is the *Peacock Role*. People wear personal adornment to attract the viewer's attention. This means that the jewelry not only needs to be flashy enough, or at least stylishly coherent, but also must contain culturally meaningful elements that the viewer will recognize and be sufficiently meaningful as to motivate the viewer to focus his or her attention on the jewelry and who is wearing it.

These culturally meaningful elements might include the use of color(s), talismans, shapes, forms. They clue the viewer to what is good, appealing, appropriate, and to what is not. But the jewelry must also provide clues to the individuality of the wearer – her (or his) personal style, social or cultural preferences, personal senses of the situation in which they find themselves.

(2) The Gender Role. Another of these sexuality roles – *The Gender Role* – is to define gender and gender-rooted culture. Certain jewelry, jewelry styles, and ways of wearing jewelry are associated with females, and others with males. Some are used to signal androgyny, others non-binary identity, polyamory or gender fluidity. You can easily label which jewelry looks more masculine, and which more feminine. Some jewelry is associated with heterosexuality, and others with homosexuality. I remember when men, in a big way, started wearing one earring stud, it was critical to remember whether to wear the stud in the left ear lobe (hetero) or the right one (gay). For engaged and married women, it is important to recognize which style of ring is more appropriate, and which hand and finger to wear these on.

(3) The Safe Sex Role. One of the most important sexuality roles, however -- *The Safe Sex Role* – concerns the placement of jewelry on the body. Such placement is suggestive of where it is safe, and where it is unsafe, to look at *(attention)* or to touch *(movement)* the person wearing it. The length of the necklace, relative to the neck, the breast, or below the breast. How long the earring extends below the lobe of the ear. Whether the person wears bracelets. The size of the belt buckle. If a person has body piercings, where these are – the navel, the eyebrow, the nose, the lip.

Jewelry calls attention to areas of the body the wearer feels are safe to view or touch. It's like taking a sharpie marker and drawing a boundary line across the body. Jewelry gives the viewer permission to look at these areas, say above the line, and not others below the line. Jewelry may give the viewer permission to touch these areas, as well. The wearer may want to call attention to the face, the neck, the hands, the ankle, but also to the breasts, the naval, the genital area.

We know that certain areas of the body are more sexually arousing than others. We know that different people are more or less comfortable with these areas on the body. But how does the wearer communicate that? How does the wearer communicate her (or his) personal views of what is sexually acceptable without having to physically and verbally interact with someone in order for that person to find out?

Jewelry. How jewelry is worn is one of the most critical and strategic ways for achieving this Safe-Sex goal. The linear form of the jewelry imposes a boundary line on the body. Do not cross it. And make no mistake, this boundary line separates the permissible from the impermissible, the non-erotic from the erotic, the safe from the unsafe. In a similar way the centerpiece focuses attention as if it were an arrow pointing the way. Jewelry is not just a style preference thing. It's a safe-sex preference thing, as well.

When news of the AIDS epidemic first burst on-stage in the 1980s, you witnessed a very dramatic change in jewelry and how it was worn. Right before the AIDS epidemic, large, long earrings were in style. Remember shoulder dusters. But as awareness of AIDS spread, most women stopped wearing earrings for awhile. Then gradually, they began wearing studs. Then very small hoops. It wasn't until around 2004 that some women wore the new chandelier earrings, and you saw longer earrings on actresses as they paraded down the red carpets of one award show after another.

Prior to AIDS, the necklace style was for longer necklaces – 24" to 36" long. The necklaces were full – multi-strand, lots of charms and dangles. Again, as awareness of AIDS spread, the necklace profile changed rapidly to no necklace at all, or to thin, short chains and chokers. You would typically find ONE charm, not many, on a necklace. Attention was pulled away from the genital area, the navel and the breasts, all the way back up to the face.

Prior to AIDS, necklaces and earrings were the best-sellers in my store. After AIDS, it became bracelets. Holding hands. Not necking. Not fondling. Not sexual intercourse. Holding hands was now the acceptable norm. This was safe.

Body piercings came into major vogue during the 1980s. And look what typically got pierced in this decade. Noses, belly buttons, eyebrows, lips. Think of this as a big Body Chart for safe sex.

As society became more understanding of AIDS and how it spread, the jewelry became larger. It extended to more areas of the body. People wore more of it. But in 2009, it was still restrained, when compared to what people wore before the 1980s.

In the sexual hunt between the sexes, jewelry plays an important boundary-defining role. Let's not forget about this. Jewelry, in some sense, is an embodiment of desire. Jewelry communicates to others how the wearer comes to define what desire might mean for the self. It communicates through placement, content, embellishment and elaboration.

Jewelry does not have to be visibly erotic, or include visual representations of sexual symbols, in order to play a role in sexuality and desire – a role that helps the hunter and the hunted define some acceptable rules for interacting without verbal communication.

FOOTNOTES

Canel, Melissa. The Role of Perceptions in Conflict. April 9, 2016. As referenced in:
https://prezi.com/auvtd6yylkkf/the-role-of-perceptions-in-conflict/

Dunlop, Cole. You Are Not Worried Enough About Perceptions and Assumptions. May 7, 2014. As referenced in:
https://www.authoritylabs.com/worried-enough-perceptions-assumptions/

Gangwani, Prachi. "Sexual or Sensual? Here's The Difference Between The Two," 9/30/2016. As referenced in:
https://www.idiva.com/relationships-love/sex/sexual-or-sensual-heres-the-difference-between-the-two/16093050

Mausolf, Judy Kay. How To Avoid 4 Communication Pitfalls: Assumptions, Perceptions, Comparison Expectations and Commitments. Spring, 2014. As referenced in:
https://www.practicesolutionsinc.net/assets/docs/communication_pitfalls.pdf
Progressive Dentist Magazine

Nguyen, Hoang. "10 Psychological Rules I Used To Make Users Love At First Sight," As referenced in:
https://blog.prototypr.io/10-psychological-rules-i-used-to-make-users-love-at-first-sight-55c71f99bfa1

Wellington, Kiki. "Sensual Vs. Sexual: Do you know the difference?", 11/7/20. As referenced in:
https://medium.com/sex-with-a-side-of-quirk/the-difference-between-sensuality-and-sexuality-3b1c4f4315f2

Wikipedia: Cognition. https://en.wikipedia.org/wiki/Cognition

Wikipedia: Gestalt Psychology. https://en.wikipedia.org/wiki/Gestalt_psychology

Wikipedia: Perception. https://en.wikipedia.org/wiki/Perception

9e. SELF-CARE

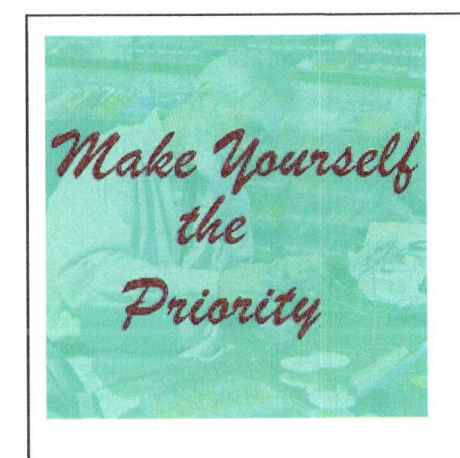

Make Yourself the Priority

Guiding Questions:
(1) How do you find your work-life balance? How do you set boundaries?
(2) How do you keep your business from running you?
(3) How do you handle mental and physical stress?
(4) How do you overcome doubt, self-doubt, and creativity blocks?
(5) How do you feed your soul?
(6) How do you overcome feelings of isolation?
(7) What kinds of things can you do to become a part of a jewelry design community?

Key Words:		
self care / yourself	*work-life balance*	*networking, relationships*
stress (mental, physical)	*doubt, self-doubt*	*isolation / connection*
	creativity, creativity blocks	

Abstract

Balancing work and life is a challenge for everyone, but particularly for creatives. Designing pieces of jewelry involves a complicated process of finding inspiration and translating often-fuzzy images and ideas into aspirations and then finished designs. The designer usually creates each piece of jewelry over an extended period of time, often in solitude and isolation. Moreover, the designer, by the very nature of jewelry, must introduce their pieces to the public, opening the designer to feedback and critique. Balancing work and life can be very stressful, both mentally and physically. If in the business of selling jewelry, then there can be additional financial stresses. Suggested are a series of things the jewelry designer can do to manage the balancing act. These things have to do with acting, organizing, thinking, nourishing, and relating.

Finding Work-Life Balance

There is always one more thing to do. One more piece to make. One more component to buy. One more social media post. One more supplier to talk to. One more client to get. One more family' or friend's demands to deal with. It's never-ending and can overwhelm you mentally, physically and financially. There is struggle. Slumps. Getting overwhelmed. Burn-out.

So the problems and resolutions depend on your ability to set boundaries. Limits on the use of your time. Allocations on the use your time. The places where you want to use any of your time. The people you want to interact with and share your time. Work-Life balance is never fully achieved; it's a continual give and take. More a *balancing*, than a balance.

This requires a high degree of honesty with yourself. Some facing of the realities of limited resources. Some confronting of your fears to get them out of the way. Some feeding of your soul – your creative self.

We call this self-care. Self-care is a management strategy for managing the ever-present tensions between work and life. Everyone needs a plan and program of self-care for themselves. This can be very formal or informal. It means recognizing when the balance has tilted too far in one or the other direction. It requires a self-care tool box of strategies to employ to correct any imbalances. But you need that balance and a plan and program for maintaining it. You want joy from jewelry creation. You want productivity. You want people to want to wear your jewelry, perhaps buying it. Below I discuss some ideas that you might incorporate into your own self-care routines.

Because creatives love what they do, they may be especially vulnerable to putting in too many work hours. They may isolate themselves too freely or for too long. Yes, you might get a lot of projects finished, but you are also shortchanging yourself. It is not a positive thing to be unbalanced. You need enrichment. You need time to reflect and relax. You need to feel connected to others.

Self-Care Can Be Hard

Self-Care might feel like a long list of to-do's. Eat. Take breaks. Phone calls, meetings and get-togethers. Time at the gym or salon. Adequate sleep. And so forth. This list might never get done to completion or satisfaction. It might feel burdensome. You might find yourself keep adding things to the list. This list, in and of itself, does not really resolve the tensions between work and life.

Knowing everything you need to do and should do is not the same as doing these. A more selective list where you can see the connections between your wellness and the activity will always make more sense.

Self-care takes work. It uses up time. It is one more thing to keep up with. Exerting effort can feel like a tall order – even when you know you will feel better after doing it. Again, a more realistic set of activities will be more manageable and effective.

For some people, taking time out for self-care generates a sense of guilt and shame. They feel they will be seen as avoiding work, instead of using self-care to enhance their work. Self-care should not be confused with an indulgence.

Handling Stress

One of the greatest challenges jewelry designers have is handling stress. There is the stress of finding inspiration. The stress of translating that inspiration into a concrete design. The stress of finding and selecting beads and other components, as well as colors, patterns and textures. The stress of placing mass within a negative space. The stress of construction. The stress of showing your jewelry to others. If you are selling your pieces, the added stresses of promotion, marketing, pricing and selling. You do not want all these stresses to add up to the point you become paralyzed – unable to start your project, finish your project or introduce it into the creative marketplace.

Stress can be both mental and physical. You need self-care for both.

Mental stress is often associated with doubt and self-doubt. Doubt holds you back from seizing your opportunities. It makes getting started or finishing things harder than they need to be. It adds uncertainty. It makes you question yourself. It blocks your excitement, perhaps diminishing it. You begin to question how to measure your progress and success, perhaps unfairly comparing yourself to other jewelry designers. You begin to fear criticism and rejection, whether real or imagined. While sometimes doubt and self-doubt can be useful in forcing you to think about and question your choices, it mostly holds you back.

Mental stress can be associated with pain. It begins to build and amplify when you think that mental and/or physical pain means you no longer will be able to make jewelry, at least the designs you prefer to make. Put a stop to these thoughts. With tools, physical aids and ergonomic solutions, and a good self-care plan of operation, you will be able to continue to design and make any jewelry you want.

The creative process can result in our feeling vulnerable. Not everything is clear at first. More fuzzy. More experimental. The creative process is messy. Nonlinear. A lot of back and forth iteration. Eventually creative ideas coalesce within a completed piece of jewelry. But this creative process may extend for long periods of time. Living with vulnerabilities is part of any jewelry designer's daily process. It is something to get used to. It makes having that good support system all that more important.

Physical stress is another concern. Making jewelry can take a physical toll on your body. Physical stresses begin as occasional pain, but eventually become major flare-ups. You might find yourself using your fingernails as tools, such as opening a split ring, or forcing a closure, or opening and closing a jump ring. After awhile, your fingernails start to split and crack and break. You might be do the same physical operation with your hands over and over again, slowly getting repetitive motion injuries, where your wrists hurt, the joints in your fingers hurt, your elbows hurt, your neck hurts. Your fingers may cramp up. You may be sitting in one position for a very long time, and over time, you begin to develop neck and back problems and knee problems and leg and foot problems. You may hate to wear your eyeglasses when you make jewelry. You forget the maxim: *If you need glasses to read, you need glasses to make jewelry.*

The immediate solution to physical stresses is to stop making jewelry. Give yourself a rest. Take time off. I know you want to be making jewelry, but you need to listen to your body. It is telling you it needs some time for healing.

The long term solution is to rely on tools and ergonomic furnishings. Tools are an extension of your hands (and other parts of your body). They reduce the stress on your hands (and other parts of your body). Ergonomic designs reduce the stresses and strains placed on your body and channel the negative energy elsewhere. There are ergonomic chairs, arm rests, arm rest and pulley systems, and the like. Also be sure seating is comfortable and lighting is good.

When returning to jewelry making, pace yourself. Take breaks. Do finger, arm and leg stretching exercises. Wear braces to support the wrist, thumb and elbow.

Solutions and Resolutions

How You Act
Work-life balance is really a balancing act.
- Look for places to pause your work.
- Train yourself to be able to put down your work before it is completed without the stress of leaving it unfinished or undone.
- Leave the house. Change locations. Take a walk or a drive. Take the day off.
- Take time off to relax and disconnect.

How You Organize
Good organization leads to more efficiency and effectiveness and better work-life balance.
- Designate one area of your house for your creative work, a different area for business work, and yet another area for thinking, meditating, reflecting and relaxing.
- Schedule sufficient times for creativity, times for business, and times for reflection.
- Keep your work area neat and generally organized, but not necessarily perfectly organized. Remember: Perfection is the enemy of the Good.
- Budget for things to go wrong. Don't put yourself on such a tight financial rope that any mistake or any supply issue or other business related issue creates panic.
- Plan for enough time in your schedule to acquire materials and supplies, learn a new technique if necessary, and communicate and work with clients, if this is part of your practice.
- Keep your website (and other promotional venues) up-to-date.

How You Think
Applying your creativity and finding work-life balance are actually sets of thinking

routines where you explore choices, narrow them down, and make selections.
- Remember that creativity involves more than staying seated in front of beads and other jewelry components in your work space. Creativity also involves looking for inspirations. It involves thinking through all the options for translating those inspirations into aspirations and then into specific design.
- Recognize that taking time away from work for self-care is a positive reflection on you. It is not something to hide or be ashamed of.
- It is not hard to set yourself up for failure. Set your expectations that are reasonable and realistic for you.
- Set attainable goals and objectives. Revisit these often as you work on any project.
- Remind yourself periodically why you like to create and make jewelry.
- Make sure you have something to get excited about – an activity or event, a book or movie, an exploration about jewelry design, exercising, yoga, whatever.

How You Nourish Mind and Body
A healthy mind and body will keep your creative juices flowing and make that work-life balance easier to maintain.
- Don't skip meals or avoid satisfying any hungry feelings when they occur.
- Hydrate often.
- It is difficult to make good jewelry design choices when you are tired. Be aware of times when you are overextended.
- Exercise. Take frequent breaks to move around a bit.
- Do some focused breathing exercises.
- Meditate.
- Go somewhere where you can let out your primal scream.
- Take a nap.
- Do something out of the ordinary for you. Make jewelry using your non-dominant hand. Stick your hands into a bowl of mud or jello.

How You Relate
Most jewelry is created in solitude. Feelings of isolation may build up. If not careful, this can negatively affect your work-life balance.
- Surround yourself with people who inspire you. Avoid people who are negative and toxic. Don't isolate yourself for too long a period.
- Spend time with real friends. Build up and maintain a supportive social network.
- Don't compare yourself and compete with others. Keep the focus on yourself.
- Talk things out. With others as sounding boards and informers, help

each other see what matters and what does not.
- Attach yourself to a group, say an online jewelry making group, or a local artist community group. But don't take up residence there.
- Moderation, moderation.
- Detach yourself from the online world for awhile, if you are spending too much time living there.
- Don't take criticisms personally.
- If in business, evaluate your pricing, selling and marketing strategies. Is the price you are getting for your jewelry reflective of your worth as a designer? Are your target markets in line with the styles and prices of your pieces?
- If in business, keep your clients aware of your progress.
- Turn some of your projects into collaborations.
- Attend classes and workshops.
- Enter juried exhibitions and competitions.
- Take part in group art critiques.

FOOTNOTES

Alexis, Renee. 7 Self-Care Tips For Artists and Creatives. Your Art Path, May 2021. As referenced in:
https://yourartpath.com/7-self-care-tips-for-artists-and-creatives

Artwork Archive. 7 Counterintuitive Self Care Habit For Artists. As referenced in:
https://www.artworkarchive.com/blog/7-counterintuitive-self-care-habits-for-artists

Branch, Allan and Steven Bristol. Chapter 16, Entrepreneur-Work Life Balance. Business Guide: Run Your Business, Don't Let Your Business Run You. LessEverything, 2018. As referenced in:
http://lesseverything.com/business-advice/entrepreneur-work-life-balance/

Clark, Alicia H., Psy.D. Why Does Self-Care Sometimes Feel So Hard? These 6 common pitfalls could be holding you back. 2/15/20. As referenced in:
https://www.psychologytoday.com/us/blog/hack-your-anxiety/202002/why-does-self-care-sometimes-feel-so-hard

Feld, Warren. Doubt / Self-Doubt: 8 Major Pitfalls For Designers…And What To Do About Them. (https://medium.com/design-warp/doubt-self-doubt-8-major-pitfalls-for-designers-and-what-to-do-about-them-fbbf1bec18de)9/5/2020. As referenced in:
https://medium.com/design-warp/doubt-self-doubt-8-major-pitfalls-for-designers-and-what-to-do-about-them-fbbf1bec18de

Hammond, Lee. Artists and Self-Esteem: 4 Tips To Overcome Insecurity. Artists Network, n.d. As referenced in:
https://www.artistsnetwork.com/art-inspiration/art-self-esteem/

Horejs, Jason. Working Alone | Breaking the Isolation that Can Surround the Pursuit of Art. Xanadu Gallery, 9/2/21. As referenced in:
https://reddotblog.com/working-alone-breaking-the-isolation-that-can-surround-the-pursuit-of-art-21/#comments

Mayher, Miguel, Director of Education, Professional Artist Institute. How To Handle Stress.

Mindful Art Studio. Overcoming Creativity Block. What Is Creative Self-Care? June, 2016. As referenced in:
https://mindfulartstudio.com/what-is-creative-self-care/

Tartakovski, Margarita, MS. 10 Ways to Overcome Creativity's No.1 Crusher. Psychcentral.com, 3/3/2013. As referenced in:
https://psychcentral.com/blog/10-ways-to-overcome-creativitys-no-1-crusher#1

SECTION 10:

TEACHING DISCIPLINARY LITERACY

10. TEACHING DISCIPLINARY LITERACY:
Strategic Learning in Jewelry Design

Guiding Questions:
(1) What is disciplinary literacy, and how should it be taught?
(2) What are the possibilities and limits for teaching jewelry design as its own discipline – apart from art and apart from craft?
(3) How might you teach jewelry design when defining jewelry as an "intent" rather than just an "object"?
(4) Why do we need more literature, fluent jewelry designers?

Key Words:		
disciplinary literacy	*automaticity / self-directed*	*marrying aesthetics to functionality*
basic literacy	*originality*	*curriculum*
intermediate literacy	*strategy / strategic thinking*	*design process*
fluency	*flexibility*	*decode / compose*
comprehension	*object vs. content vs. intent*	*Bloom's Taxonomy*
role(s) of jewelry	*resonance and parsimony*	*developmental approach*
guided thinking	*harmony and variety*	*rubric*
thinking routines	*think-alouds*	*multi-method*
questioning		*adjusting teaching styles*

Abstract:
Teaching literacy in jewelry design is a lot like teaching literacy in reading and writing. We want our students to comprehend. We want them to be able to be self-directed in organizing and implementing their basic tasks. We want them to be able to function in unfamiliar situations and respond when problems arise. We want them to make reasonable judgements on marrying aesthetics to functionality. We want them to develop an originality in their work. We want them to think like designers. And, we want a high level of automaticity in all this. The basic jewelry design curriculum does not accomplish this. There is an absence of strategy and strategic thinking. There is a weak commitment to jewelry design as a discipline, with its own vocabulary and ways of thinking through and doing and responding to different, often unfamiliar, situations as they arise. Without a commitment to embed the teaching of a disciplinary literacy within the standard curriculum, we will fail to impart that necessary learned awareness about fluency, flexibility, originality, and comprehension the designer needs to bring to the design process.

TEACHING DISCIPLINARY LITERACY
She said it wasn't her job!

This prominent jewelry instructor told me that it wasn't her job to teach anything beyond the basic steps for getting a project done. It was not her responsibility to share any insights, choices, compromises, fix-it solutions or design considerations she herself made when creating the original project – now taught as a class with a kit and a set of step-by-step instructions. If a student asked a specific question, she would gladly answer it. But otherwise, *it was not her job.*

This attitude is so prevalent in the standard jewelry making curriculum and education. Teachers stick very closely to the standard, basic curriculum. Facts, not ideas. Absolutes, not what-ifs. Step-by-steps, not creative thinking. Teachers rarely explain the implications for using one bead vs. another, or one stringing material vs. another, or one clasp vs. another, or one material vs. another, or one technique vs. another. They reluctantly dispense limited information, usually only when pressed, about how techniques might be varied. They rarely discuss the deeper meanings and potentialities underlying various problematic situations. They ignore the role and power of jewelry to influence human relations.

They have the student gloss over things as if, once seen and memorized, the student will automatically be able to make the right choices over and over, again and again. The teachers see themselves as easily transferring knowledge, skills and understandings to the student as if inoculating them as you would with a vaccine and a syringe. And the student becomes a star jewelry designer. Or not.

Teachers too often see jewelry making and design as a basic set of skills, easily adaptable and applicable to all kinds of jewelry making situations. They assume that the challenge of improving jewelry making skills would primarily be a function of making more and more jewelry.

This might be true for the novice student, but as the student moves from basic decoding to fluency, flexibility and originality in design, what was learned initially becomes less generally useful. For example, the student may learn about basic color schemes, but not how to adapt these in different situations, or leverage these to achieve an even more resonant result, or be more deliberate and intentional when choosing colors and determining how to use them.

There is an absence of strategy and strategic thinking. There is a weak commitment to jewelry design as its own discipline, with its own vocabulary and ways of thinking through and doing and responding to different, often unfamiliar, situations as they arise.

Jewelry, in the standard, traditional design education model and curriculum, is understood as an object. We can speak about and learn about it as an object. This object is distanced from the creative spark that created it. It is divorced from desire. Apart from the wearer or the viewer. Ignorant of context or situation. There are no deeper explanations, no pointing out implications, no experimenting with situational contingencies, no debating synergistic or other external effects. The student is run through color theories, materials composition, step-by-step jewelry construction as if learning a basic lexicon is sufficient and enough.

This whole traditional process of standard jewelry designer education ignores the required *disciplinary literacy*. It assumes the student is creative, or not. It approaches jewelry design as if it were a subset of some other discipline, usually art, or more specifically, painting or sculpture. It ignores architectural requirements allowing jewelry to move, drape and flow as it is worn. It assumes a high level of universal expectation and acceptance. It forgets that jewelry has personal, situational and social consequences. It pretends that jewelry design does not have any disciplinary requirements of its own. There are no specialized knowledges or ways of thinking unique to jewelry design alone.

It is weak at teaching the student, from a design perspective, how to decode design elements and how to combine them into compositions apart from basic art theory. It pretends there are no architectural issues underlying how jewelry functions. It recognizes most of the anatomy of a piece of jewelry – the strap, the bail, the yoke, the foundation base, the clasp assembly -- as supplemental to the *art* of the piece, as if these were to be understood, designed and crafted the same as a frame on a painting or a pedestal holding up a sculpture.

The standard curriculum assumes that the wearer and viewer have only a passive relationship to objects of jewelry. It ignores the fact that jewelry gains much of its appeal and power only as it is worn, and not as it sits on a mannequin or easel. It totally avoids confronting the fact that much of the power of jewelry results from how it instigates and sustains relationships – artist to self, designer to wearer, wearer to viewer, designer to seller, exhibitor to client, designer to collector, and so forth. And, it fails to impart that necessary learned awareness about fluency, flexibility, originality and comprehension the designer needs to bring to the design process.

It's not their job. It's not their job to assist the student's developing creative thinking or applying that creative spark towards better jewelry design.

It's not their job.

But, in fact, it is!

What Is Disciplinary Literacy?

Disciplinary Literacy[1] assumes there are real differences in the way professionals across fields participate and communicate. *Disciplinary literacy* encompasses those techniques and strategies used to teach designers to think like designers (or historians like historians or scientists like scientists, and so forth)[2]. Without this *disciplinary literacy*, students and professionals in a particular field would flounder and fail.

Disciplinary literacy refers to how the particular discipline creates, disseminates, and evaluates knowledge. Each discipline has its own way of looking at the world, defining things using a specific vocabulary, gathering information, specifying understandings, posing questions and problems, delineating solutions and using evidence to justify their ideas and conclusions.

An *artist* looking at jewelry, or a *craftsperson* looking at jewelry, for instance, would have different thought and interpretive processes than a *jewelry designer* looking at jewelry. Jewelry, after all, is different than a painting or sculpture or simple functional object. Jewelry is only art as it is worn. It must satisfy the requirements of both aesthetics and functionality. It exists in a 3-dimensional space. It is worn on the body. It establishes special relationships between designer and wearer, wearer and viewer, designer and seller, designer and collector. It encapsulates situational and socio-cultural meanings. To evaluate whether a piece of jewelry is finished and successful requires a different thought process than art or craft alone would provide.

There are key disciplinary differences in how a jewelry designer...

- *Chooses and evaluates evidence*
- *Relates evidence to a perspective*
- *Gains understanding*
- *Visualizes things*
- *Manipulates things*
- *Creates a truth and achieves an error-free solution*
- *Introduces things publicly*
- *Anticipates the shared understandings and desires of various audiences*
- *Reflects on experience*

Training in jewelry design should teach students the unique challenges they face within their discipline as they think through design and create jewelry. At each increment within the jewelry design process, they need to think like a designer. Not as an artist, nor like a craftsperson. As a designer. Finding evidence whether a piece is finished and successful. Linking causes to effects. Understanding how inspiration resulted in a finished design. Developing knowledge, understandings and skills to the level where they can transfer these to others. Generating a large number of ideas. Making inferences about the implications of any one choice. Producing things which are original. Responding to problematic or unanticipated situations. Finding new ways to adapt existing ideas to new conditions. Anticipating shared understandings about how their work will be evaluated, assessed and judged. Knowing when something is parsimonious and finished, and knowing when something resonates and is successful.

Types of Literacy

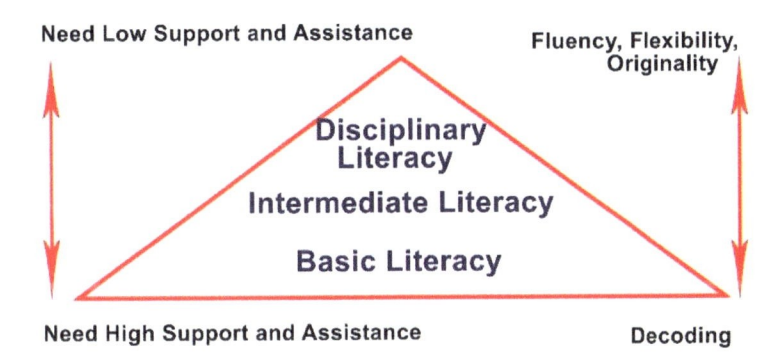

Diagram: A triangle with three tiers labeled (top to bottom) "Disciplinary Literacy", "Intermediate Literacy", and "Basic Literacy". Left side arrow: "Need Low Support and Assistance" (top) to "Need High Support and Assistance" (bottom). Right side arrow: "Fluency, Flexibility, Originality" (top) to "Decoding" (bottom).

There are three different types of literacy – *Basic*, *Intermediate*, and *Disciplinary*. The standard jewelry design curriculum typically focuses on Basic literacy, with some nod toward Intermediate. Both Basic, and to a large extent, Intermediate literacy are rooted in rationality, socially-sanctioned logic, and universal understandings.

Disciplinary literacy is usually ignored, but it should be incorporated and integrated within Basic and Intermediate literacy instruction. Disciplinary literacy adds a level of reason, where the individual artist can show his or her hand within the creation, and marry, or even replace, objective with subjective design choices and considerations. It dwells a lot on management and control issues underlying design. It anticipates dilemmas as these might arise from and further influence communication, interaction, and human relationships.

Basic Literacy

Basic literacy refers to the degree the student learns knowledge of high frequency concepts that underlie virtually all jewelry design and jewelry making tasks. These concepts are typically universally recognized and understood by artist and client alike. Here jewelry is understood as an *object*. An object has literal characteristics which the student can identify and list.

The student demonstrates this basic literacy by an ability to *decode*. The student can decode things like color use, rules of composition, materials selection, technique implementation and the like. The student picks up the basic words and definitions, links the vocabulary to relevant objects, and can identify their presence and use within any piece of jewelry. Each element and principle of design can be graphically represented, and the student begins to make connections between word and graphic. The student begins to recognize which design elements can stand alone, and which are dependent on the presence of other elements. The student can identify harmonious and balanced clusters of these design elements within compositions. The goal is an automaticity in *decoding*.

Intermediate Literacy

Here the student develops the knowledge to make more complex jewelry forms and designs. There is more comprehension. The student recognizes that the various design elements and principles have a range of variations in meaning and expression. In a similar way, the student begins to recognize that clusters of design elements and principles can also show variations in meaning and expression.

The student learns about different materials and what they can and cannot be used to achieve. Materials have names, places of origins, stories about how they get from one place to another, processes.

The student is introduced to variations in techniques and technologies. There is more than one way to accomplish things. There are more things that can be created using familiar techniques.

The student learns to problem-solve with various *Fix-It* procedures, like re-doing, changing tools, requesting help, looking things up, drawing analogies.

The student learns to process-plan. S/he begins to relate inspirations, aspirations and intentions to more critically evaluate their choices or the choices of others. Students are more able to stick with things and maintain attention to a more extended design process.

The student begins to learn how to design for an audience. This might be a client, or a purchaser, or an exhibitor, or a collector. This begins the developing understanding of how to meld personal held preferences with those of others.

Students monitor and reflect on their own comprehension. The goal is an automaticity in *fluency*.[4] Here jewelry is understood as *content*. As content, the jewelry as designed conveys meanings and expressions which the student can derive, and typically, are universally understood. The jewelry and its compositional design is still, however, mostly viewed objectively, as if sitting on an easel, not as it is worn.

Disciplinary Literacy

This involves a way of thinking and doing specific to the discipline. The student learns specialized literacy skills relevant to jewelry design as the jewelry is introduced and worn publicly. The student learns how *parsimony* and *resonance* as outcomes expressed in design differ from *harmony* and *variety* as expressed in art.

The student learns to anticipate *shared understandings*[5] and the role of *desire* among the many audiences the student works with, works in, and relates to. These include clients, sellers, exhibitors, collectors, wearers, viewers, and the artist him- or herself.

Much of the design process takes on the qualities of *backwards design*.[7] The designer begins the process by articulating the essential shared understandings and desires against which their work will be evaluated and judged. The designer starts with questions about assessment, and then allows this understanding to influence all other choices going forward."

The student has an ability to conceptualize and explain what jewelry means, how it is more an *action* than an *object*, and how this meaning emerges dialectically, as the jewelry is introduced publicly, worn, shared and displayed.

The student learns to recognize the dynamics of *coherency, decoherency, and contagion*. The artist's coherent choices about design become contagious, attracting someone to want to touch the piece, wear it, or buy it. To the extent others share the artist's ideas about coherence, the more likely the work will be judged finished and successful. Jewelry becomes more than an expression of meanings, but rather, it becomes an expression of meanings within context.

The process of coherence continues with the wearer, who introduces the piece into a larger context. There is more contagion. When efforts at design are less than successful, we begin to have decoherence. Decoherence may come in the forms of bad feedback, inappropriate feedback, less than satisfying feedback, or no feedback at all. The wearer may not get that sense of self s/he seeks. S/he may feel less motivated to wear the piece, or may store it, or give it away.

The student can comfortably and flexibly respond in unfamiliar situations or to new materials, techniques, technologies and requests, and take on larger challenges arising from higher levels of ambiguity, abstraction, subtlety, and contradiction. The student can find new ways to adapt existing ideas to new situations and requirements.

The student learns how to inspire *to*. That is, the student learns how to translate an inspiration into a design in such a way that the wearer and viewer are inspired *to*, not merely inspired *by*. They don't simply react emotionally by saying the piece is "*beautiful*." The piece resonates for them. They react by saying they "*want to wear*" it or "*want to buy it*" or "*want to make something like it*". They come to feel and see and sense the artist's hand.

The student learns how to manage a very involved, and often very long and time-consuming process of jewelry design, beginning with inspiration, then aspiration, then execution, and presenting the piece publicly for exhibit or sale. The student also picks up the skills and attitudes necessary to stick with what can be a very long process.

The goal is an automaticity in *design flexibility* and *originality*. Jewelry is understood as both *intent* and *dialectic communication*. Here the student can visualize, anticipate, and respond to all the things which might happen when the jewelry is introduced publicly where its value and worth is judged and determined.

Literacy in Jewelry Design

Teaching literacy in jewelry design is a lot like teaching literacy in reading and writing. We want our students to comprehend. We want them to be able to be self-directed in organizing and implementing their basic tasks. We want them to be able to function in unfamiliar situations and respond when problems arise. We want them to make reasonable judgements on marrying aesthetics to functionality. We want them to develop an originality in their work. We want them to think like designers. And, we want a high level of automaticity in all this.

Using literacy techniques, goals and concepts, we teach students to *read*, *write*, *express* and *express in context* when understanding jewelry and its design.

We teach the student to *read* jewelry. That means learning a basic vocabulary, as well as the various design elements, and how these design elements can either function on their own, or be arranged and clustered together within a design. They learn to describe the piece, including the name of the artist and the name of the piece, the style of the piece, when the piece was created, the materials used, the construction technique, and the use of design elements such as point, line, shape, form, space, texture, color, value and pattern.

We teach the student to *write* jewelry. The student constructs (*or anticipates how a particular designer has constructed*), then reflects, upon the choices made. That means learning various principles of composition, construction and manipulation. These affect arrangements as well as the juxtaposition and clustering of design elements, materials and techniques. They affect choices about maintaining shapes (structure). They affect choices about enhancing movement, drape and flow (support). Students learn how the placement and organization of elements, materials and techniques results in things like harmony, balance, contrast, variety, unity, emphasis, movement, depth, rhythm, focus, and proportions.

We further teach the student to be more "*expressive*" with jewelry. That means learning how jewelry signifies various meanings and evokes emotions. They learn to question and ponder through answers to questions like What did they think the designer was trying to say? Or What kind of reaction(s) would you expect to this piece of jewelry? What feelings does the jewelry convey? In what context would wearing the piece be especially relevant and appropriate? Are there things in the piece which might be symbolic or otherwise signify things which transcend the piece of jewelry itself?

Last, we teach the student to be "*expressive within a context*". That means understanding how jewelry functions communicatively, socially and psychologically within any context or situation. That means learning how various designers and various audiences use jewelry as a means of self-identity and self-esteem, and how the interaction of the designer with various audiences affects the success (or failure) of their continued relationship oriented around (and perhaps anchored to) the jewelry. It means delving into the how and why the jewelry would be valued or the worth determined or the evaluative judgements made, and, furthermore, how such judgements and determinations might be contingent in their expression. It also means understanding what jewelry is as it is worn, and the required artistic, functional and design choices and compromises which must be made, if the piece of jewelry is to be judged finished and successful.

Literacy in jewelry design includes such things as:

- Learning art and design vocabulary, including design elements, principles of composition, manipulation and construction, and basic vocabulary words
- Developing an understanding of a range of materials, how these

are selected, and the possibilities for their use, or mis-use, in any one project

- Developing a range of technical and technological knowledges and skills, how to vary them, and when to apply them and when not to apply them

- Translating inspirations into aspirations into specific designs and execution

- Choosing media, technique and strategy to convey concepts, forms and themes

- Organizing, managing and controlling a jewelry design process, from start to finish, especially over an extended period of time

- Deciphering the graphic representation of ideas

- Communicating these ideas through critique and analysis of jewelry genres, styles, media use, and artist/designer intent

- Reconciling tensions and conflicts between appeal and functionality, especially as the jewelry is worn

- Introducing their work to others, coordinating artist goals with marketing goals, and exhibiting or selling publicly

- Working with various client audiences, and translating, influencing or mitigating their understandings and desires about jewelry with those of the designer, whether a piece should be judged as finished and successful

- Figuring out *Fix-It* strategies where things do not turn out as desired, are uncertain, or things go wrong

- Reflecting on one's own thought processes and choices, increasing that metacognitive awareness of what things lead to better design

- Developing a personal style and originality and strategies for how these get reflected in the artist's finished compositions

Why Do We Need More Fluent Designers?

The standard curriculum and approach for teaching the making and designing of jewelry is commonly viewed as teaching *basic literacy*. This includes teaching a basic set of skills, widely adaptable and applicable to all kinds of jewelry making situations. These basic skills are highly generalizable and adaptable.

In the standard curriculum, it is assumed that the challenge of improving jewelry making skills is a function of making more and more jewelry. The designer, thus over time, would automatically evolve into a better designer with better, more satisfying, more appealing designs.

In some sense here, these ideas about teaching basic literacy are partly right. All students need a basic vocabulary. All jewelry designers need these basic perceptual and decoding skills which are very connected to their early progress in making jewelry. These skills are entailed in all jewelry designs and crafting tasks.

However, as the designer moves from basic decoding to fluency, flexibility and originality, the basics which were learned become less generally useful. For example, the designer may learn basic color schemes, but not learn how to adapt these in different situations, with components which do not easily match colors on the color wheel, and which present differently when used in combination, or under different lighting or contextual situations.

Our standard teaching curriculum, if that is all we teach, becomes less than useful. We rely on a bad assumption: *If we only provide adequate basic skills, so we assume, from that point forward, the student with adequate background knowledge will be able to design and make anything successfully.* When the emphasis is on giving out more information and instructions rather than on discussion and challenge, students have little chance to learn to think as a fluent jewelry designer.

But this also begs the question: *Why do we need more fluent designers?*

Isn't turning out basic technicians sufficient? Aren't there enough designers meeting everyone's jewelry needs? Even if there are not, will there be enough clients and customers who would want to see and purchase better, more insightful, jewelry designs?

My answer, obviously, is Yes! We need more fluent designers who have been taught and are fluent in a disciplinary literacy. That is because there are many things going on around us which increase the need for all this.

These include,

- The need to adapt to more global competition, better ride the ever-faster waves and changes of fashion and style trends, and more strategically confront and challenge global "sameness" in design
- The need to adapt, and adapt more quickly, to changes in technologies and materials
- Automaticity in how designers more easily and successfully meet their various client needs – self, wearer, viewer, seller, exhibiter, and collector
- Creating a clearer, publicly sanctioned professionalization of the jewelry design discipline
- Expanding the connectedness and networking of jewelry designers in today's world

- Increasing opportunities for more attention, visibility, communication, support, demand and income
- Encouraging individual student pursuits, diversity and experimentation

How Should Disciplinary Literacy Be Incorporated Into Jewelry Design Education?

Jewelry Design is rarely taught at this disciplinary level.

There is a need to identify what an advanced literacy curriculum in jewelry design might be, how it differs from that in art or craft, and how best to implement it.

We need to move away from the ideas of *"teacher of art"* or *"teacher of craft"*, and begin to understand the role of teacher as *"teacher of disciplinary literacy in jewelry design"*. How can we best prepare all jewelry design students for the thinking, the making, and the critically reflecting upon required by more intermediate and advanced work? How can we prepare students to be independent thinkers? Self-starters? What program of authentic learning more closely reflects what a jewelry designer does in the field?

A disciplinary literacy program should not, however, be understood as a separate curriculum. It is not something supplemental. Rather, disciplinary literacy should be a part of and embedded within all existing instruction, from basic to advanced. Disciplinary literacy should support the standard curriculum with literacy tools uniquely tailored to jewelry design.

Some ideas for integration...

1. Build more depth into what is already taught and increase student engagement
2. Leverage a wide range of resources – popular articles and images, academic articles, interviews, gallery exhibits and their presentation and marketing materials, online videos, bead and jewelry making magazines
3. Task students with communicating what they read, viewed, experienced and attempted to do, and elaborate more on their understandings
4. Ask questions which encourage students to think like jewelry designers
5. Model design strategies and fix-it strategies
6. Allow students to do more problem-solving and experimentation

Students should be encouraged to...		
Experiment **Perform** **Demonstrate** **Discuss findings** **Anticipate the understandings of others** **Monitor their thinking** **Deal with ambiguity**	**Problem solve** **Read** **Write** **Debate options** **Compare their work to others** **Challenge assumptions** **Go beyond the ordinary and obvious**	**Comment** **Communicate** **Ask questions** **Seek evidence to inform their work** **Gather information** **Detect bias** **Expose their ideas and works to others**

BLOOM'S TAXONOMY

If you are not already familiar with Bloom's Taxonomy (1956)[6], and its model's evolution and various adaptations in different disciplines, I urge you to do so. This is a particularly useful tool when teaching higher level thinking and creative problem solving. Are your lesson plans, assignments, projects, questioning strategies touching on each progressive level in Bloom's Taxonomy? The Taxonomy helps you evaluate the level of rigor in your instruction and the degree you are presenting your students and involving them in learning higher level thinking skills in a subject or discipline.

Bloom's Taxonomy

- **create**: Produce new or original work
  Design, assemble, construct, conjecture, develop, formulate, author, investigate
- **evaluate**: Justify a stand or decision
  appraise, argue, defend, judge, select, support, value, critique, weigh
- **analyze**: Draw connections among ideas
  differentiate, organize, relate, compare, contrast, distinguish, examine, experiment, question, test
- **apply**: Use information in new situations
  execute, implement, solve, use, demonstrate, interpret, operate, schedule, sketch
- **understand**: Explain ideas or concepts
  classify, describe, discuss, explain, identify, locate, recognize, report, select, translate
- **remember**: Recall facts and basic concepts
  define, duplicate, list, memorize, repeat, state

Vanderbilt University Center for Teaching

In jewelry design, we might adapt Bloom's Taxonomy like this...

Creating: designing, constructing, developing, producing, manipulating, translating inspiration into aspiration and aspiration into a design

Evaluating: judging, evaluating, appraising, defending, challenging, showing connections, linking design choices to emotional and resonant outcomes or sense that piece feels finished

Analyzing: comparing, contrasting, experimenting, testing, questioning, examining, what happens when analyses with different materials, techniques, technologies, and construction and composition strategies

> *Applying:* dramatizing, sketching, using, solving, illustrating, writing, demonstrating, instructing, diagramming, arranging, using different techniques and technologies in making jewelry
>
> *Understanding:* classifying, describing, discussing, explaining, paraphrasing, locating, translating, decoding
>
> *Remembering:* memorizing, listing, recalling, repeating, reproducing, copying, building up a specialized vocabulary
>
> *Source: Bloom's Taxonomy. Vanderbilt University. Center for Teaching. As reference at https://cft.vanderbilt.edu/guides-sub-pages/blooms-taxonomy/*

As teachers of jewelry design, we want to build up our students' design knowledge and skills through literacy – that is, disciplinary thinking. This means such things as,

1. Building prior knowledge – showing connections between what they are expected to do now with what they have done or experienced before

2. Building a specialized vocabulary and how to use this in context

3. Learning, applying, varying and experimenting with different materials, techniques and technologies

4. Practicing translating inspirations into aspirations

5. Learning to deconstruct complex visual representations of ideas which each piece of jewelry encapsulates

6. Using knowledge of artistic design elements and genres to identify main and subordinate ideas expressed within any piece

7. Articulating what the graphic representations mean and how they are used within a piece of jewelry, and how this supports the artist's intent

8. Posing disciplinary relevant questions

9. Critically comparing one piece of jewelry to others

10. Using reasoning with jewelry design, such as searching for alternatives, or selecting evidence to evaluate claims of finish and success

11. Enabling students to be metacognitive – that is, become aware of the ways in which they think, learn, create and problem-solve, and aware of how they overcome those times of creativity block

12. Anticipating shared understandings and desires about what it means for a piece to be judged as finished and successful

13. Bridging creative learning to the creative marketplace

What Are Some Specific Useful Techniques?

We should teach students to design jewelry, not draw it, not sculpt it, not craft it. And that should be our primary goal as teachers:

Developing our students' Fluency, Flexibility and Originality with design.

This involves:

> *(1)* a *Developmental Approach* and organization of knowledges, skills and understandings to be taught, usually taught as sets of interrelated, integrated skill sets, rather than one skill at a time

> *(2)* a *Multi-Method Teaching Plan and program* with a shared goal of teaching disciplinary literacy,

> *(3)* a *Rubric specifying degrees of accomplishment* and the criteria of evaluation – all shared with the student

> *(4)* a *willingness to Adjust Teaching Styles* because different students rely on different senses and strategies for learning

I am going to touch on each of these below, but you will find numerous articles in print and online which go into much more detail.

Developmental Approach

Think of jewelry design as a large matrix. The rows are the various knowledges, skills and understandings students need to master. The columns represent ordered stages of learning, indicating what needs to be learned first, second and third, etc.

In the example below, learning objectives were specified for an introductory bead stringing class. The learning objectives were characterized by skill level needed. These objectives were clustered together and taught as a set. The student could identify what things were learned at what level, and what things (and at what skill levels) still needed to be learned in another class. Emphasis was placed during the instruction to visibly point out to the student how each learning objective was interrelated to the others.

At the conclusion of the class, students were asked to self-evaluate what they learned about each learning objective, and what else they would like to know or learn about it. What were their take-aways, and what would they like to do next.

EXAMPLE MATRIX LEARNING OBJECTIVES	BEAD STRINGING Crimping		
	BEGINNER	**INTER-MEDIATE**	**ADVANCED**
TECHNICAL MECHANICS			
1. Holding Your Piece To Work It	BEGINNER		
2. Reading Simple Pattern, Figure and/or Graph; Diagramming	BEGINNER		
3. Selecting Stringing Materials	BEGINNER		
4. Selecting Clasps and other Jewelry Findings	BEGINNER		
5. Selecting Beads and other Components	BEGINNER		
6. Laying Out Your Piece	BEGINNER		
7. Identifying Areas of Potential Weakness, and Strategies for Dealing With These	BEGINNER		
8. Selecting and Using Adhesives			
9. Use of Tools and Equipment	BEGINNER		
10. Determining Measurements and Ease, including Width and Length of a Piece, Especially In Relationship To Bead Sizes	BEGINNER		
11. Finishing Off Threads, Cable Wires or Other Stringing Materials in Piece or Adding Threads/Cable Wires/Stringing Materials	BEGINNER		
UNDERSTANDING CRAFT BASIS OF STRINGING METHODS			
1. Starting the Piece	BEGINNER		
2. Implementing the Basic Method	BEGINNER		
3. Finishing Off Your Piece With A Clasp Assembly	BEGINNER		
4. Managing String/Cord/Thread/Wire Tension	BEGINNER		
5. Crimping	BEGINNER		
6. Making Simple and Coiled Loops Using Hard Wire			
7. Making and Using Connectors; Segmenting;			

Directional Control			
8. Adding Dangles and Embellishments			
9. Making Multi-Strands Piece			
10. Making Twist-Strands Piece			
UNDERSTANDING ART & DESIGN BASIS OF BEAD STRINGING			
1. Learning Implications When Choosing Different Sizes/Shapes of Beads, or Using Different Stringing Materials	BEGINNER		
2. Learning Implications When Choosing Different Kinds of Clasps, or Using Different Jewelry Findings and Components	BEGINNER		
3. Understanding Relationship of this Bead Stringing Method in Comparison to Other Types of Bead Stringing Methods	BEGINNER		
4. Creating Support Systems Within Your Piece In Anticipation of Effects of Movement, and other Architectural considerations	BEGINNER		
5. Understanding How Bead Asserts Its Need For Color When Stringing Beads			
6. Creating Your Own Design with This Bead Stringing Method, in Reference to Jewelry Design Principles of Composition			
7. Creating Shapes, Components and Forms To Use With This Bead Stringing Method, and Establishing Themes			
BECOMING BEAD STRINGING ARTIST & DESIGNER			
1. Developing A Personal Style			
2. Valuing or Pricing Your Work			
3. Teaching Others Bead Stringing Methods			
4. Promoting Yourself and Your Work			

When taking a developmental approach, you teach groups of integrated knowledges, skills and understandings. You teach technical mechanics concurrently with art and craft history, and concurrently with discipline-specific literacy. You introduce ideas of the things which come into play during the design process, and when the jewelry is introduced publicly. We want our students to be able to think strategically and critically, deal with unfamiliar or problematic situations, and be self directed.

In the Developmental Approach, you start with a cluster of a core set of skills. You show, demonstrate, and have the student apply, communicate about, and experiment with how these skills inter-relate in jewelry design.

You then introduce another cluster of knowledges, skills, and understandings. As with the core, you show, demonstrate, and have the student apply, communicate about, and experiment with how all these inter-relate. Then you repeat all this by teaching how this second cluster of things inter-relates to the core.

And again, you introduce a third cluster, and link to the second, then link to the core. And so forth.

Jewelry design covers a wide range of factors beyond the physical and structural aspects of jewelry. It incorporates aesthetics, structure, value systems, philosophies, sustainability, technologies, and their integrations. Thus the jewelry designer has to know some things about art, and some things about architecture, and about physical mechanics, and anthropology and psychology and sociology, and engineering, and be a bit of a party planner. Here, this developmental approach serves them well. It helps the student learn the inter-connectedness and inter-dependencies of them all, in a gradual, developmental, building-up-to-something sort of way.

Multi-Method Teaching Plan

Students need to come at jewelry design problems from different angles. Within each lesson, teachers need to gradually relinquish control over the learning process to the student. Using a single teaching method, such as having students keep rehearsing a series of steps, or relying on a single textbook won't cut it. We also need to infuse opportunities for reflection within virtually every activity.

Some of things I find especially useful include,

(a) Guided Thinking

(b) Thinking Routines

(c) Developing an effective questioning strategy

(d) Application, practice and experimentation

One approach is called *Guided Thinking*. Here, within each lesson, the teacher begins with controlling the information and how it is presented. This involves some lecture, some demonstration, some modelling. The teacher never insists that there is only one way to accomplish any task. Over the course of the lesson, the teacher gradually relinquishes more and more control to the student for directing the learning activity.

For example, we might encourage students to construct and feel and touch similar pieces made with different materials, beads or techniques, and have them tell us what differences they perceive. We should guide them in thinking through the implications for these differences. When teaching a stitch, I typically have students make samples using two different beads – say a cylinder bead and a seed bead, and try two different stringing materials, say Fireline and Nymo threads.

We also should guide them in thinking through all the management and control issues they were experiencing. Very often beginning students have difficulty finding a comfortable way to hold their pieces while working them. I let them work a little on a project, stop them, and then ask them to explain what was difficult and what was not. I suggest some alternative solutions – but do not impose a one-best-way – and have them try these solutions. Then we discuss them, fine-tuning our thinking.

After some trial-and-error and experimentation, I begin to introduce some goals. They had identified some management and control issues, and had some observations about what they were trying to do. I link these developing discussions to these goals. These are issues because…. And I let them fill in the blanks. What do they think needs to be happening here?

I begin to put words to feelings. I guide them in articulating some concrete goals. We want good thread tension management for a bead woven piece. We want the beads to lay correctly within the piece. We want the piece to feel fluid. We want an easier way to work the piece and hold it, so it doesn't feel so awkward.

We return to Guided Thinking. I summarize all the choices we have made in order to begin the project: type of bead, size of bead, shape of bead, type of thread, strategy for holding the piece while working it, strategy for bringing the new bead to the work in progress. I ask the students what ideas are emerging in their minds about how to bring all they have done so far together.

At this point, I usually would interject a *Mini-Lesson*, where I demonstrate, given the discussions, the smarter way to begin and execute the Project. In the Mini-Lesson, I *"Think Aloud"* so that my students can see and hear how I am approaching our Project.

And then I continue with Guided Thinking as we work through various sections of the Project towards completion. Whatever we do – select materials, select and apply techniques, set goals, anticipate how we want the Project to end up – is shown as resulting from a managed process of thinking through our design.

In "Guided Thinking", I would prompt my students to try to explain what is/is not going on, what is/is not working as desired, where the student hopes to end up, what seems to be enhancing/impeding getting there.

As the lesson proceeds, I reduce the amount of direction and information I provide. I relinquish this responsibility gradually to the student. The student is asked to try out a technique or strategy, then try an alternative. The student is asked to communicate the differences, their preferences, their explanations why, and what they might try to do next.

Experimentation with evaluation is encouraged. The student is asked to develop a more concrete jewelry project, and explain the various choices involved. What-if and what-next questions are posed. The student is allowed to follow a pathway that might be not as efficient, or even a dead-end. More discussion about what occurs begins. If the student asks me *what would happen if*, I tell them to try it and see, and then discuss their experience and observations.

Towards the end of the lesson, I prompt the student to communicate what they have done and what they have discovered. I ask them, in various ways, what take-aways they have from the class, or how they think they might apply what they learned in the future. I suggest the "what next." I identify different options and pathways they might pursue next. Metacognition and reflection are important skills for any jewelry designer to have.

And we're ready for the next lesson.

Another approach is called *Thinking Routines*. With guidance, demonstration and repetition, it is my hope that these experiences become a series of *Thinking Routines* my students resort to when starting a new project. As students develop and internalize more *Thinking Routines*, they develop greater *Fluency* with design.

Thinking Routines are different strategies for structuring a set of steps which lead a person's thinking. *"They are the patterns by which we operate and go about the job of learning and working together in a classroom environment. A routine can be thought of as any procedure, process, or pattern of action that is used repeatedly to manage and facilitate the accomplishment of specific goals or tasks. Classrooms have routines that serve to manage student behavior and interactions, to organizing the work of learning, and to establish rules for communication and discourse. Classrooms also have routines that structure the way students go about the process of learning. These learning routines can be simple structures, such as reading from a text and answering the questions at the end of the chapter, or they may be designed to promote students' thinking, such as asking students what they know, what they want to know, and what they have learned as part of a unit of study."*[3]

Some examples:

1. What Do You See.....What Do You Think.....What Do You Know
2. Think   Pair   Share
3. What Makes You Think That?
4. I used to think... Now I think...
5. Connect – Extend – Challenge
6. True for Who?
7. Look – Score -- Explain

We use Thinking Routines which mirror the kinds of thinking and analytic practices common to the discipline of jewelry design. We encourage students to reflect on what they were thinking. We ask how they were anticipating getting to the point where they would call their piece finished. We ask them whether there was some kind of order or routine to their process. We ask them what criteria they would use to know that they were successful. We ask them to anticipate what others would think, and whether others would agree that the piece was finished and successful.

These are some of the kinds of situations we want our students to develop thinking routines for:

    a. Exploration of experience for a purpose; translating inspiration into designs

    b. Selecting materials and techniques in recognition of how they might enhance or impede design goals.

    c. Search for meaning as conveyed by various design elements alone, clustered together, or arranged within a composition

    d. Formulating how to deal with unfamiliar tasks or roadblocks preventing the finishing of a task

    e. Completing well practiced technical tasks

    f. Varying well practiced technical tasks

    g. Contingent thinking and fix-it strategies

    h. Incorporating the shared understandings of others into the thinking about what constitutes a finished and successful design

    i. Introducing jewelry publicly, such as for exhibit or for sale

Another approach I want to point out is having an *Effective Questioning Strategy*. Students need to be engaged in thinking and talking about jewelry and its design and its powers when worn. The questions we ask them, and the way we phrase them, can have a big impact on this.

Questions should lead the student towards greater understanding. Ask questions which encourage students to think like jewelry designers and understand jewelry design as a series of problems to be solved. Questions should be structured based on these ideas:

- Decode piece of jewelry; measure jewelry's impact; relate to artist intent
- Correlation or causation when explaining and identifying design issues
- What q's weren't answered; ability to assess the information at hand relevant to the design problem
- Do the results solve the design problem and support the conclusions
- Other explanations for the results

- Given an artist intent, sketch a jewelry design
- Given a piece of jewelry to be sold, develop a sales pitch

Some pointers:

1. Avoid questions with Yes/No answers
2. Avoid questions which contain the answers, such as "don't you think the designer did a good job?"
3. Avoid questions which seem to have a particular answer in mind, such as "how did the designer use materials to represent the upper class?"
4. Do elicit questions with multiple answers.
5. Do elicit questions which incorporate each of our senses, not just the visual, such as "what sounds do you think this piece of jewelry would make?"
6. Do elicit questions of varying levels of difficulty and rigor.
7. Do elicit personal interpretations of ideas and feelings, coupled with questions about what evidence the student used to come to these conclusions.
8. Do elicit questions about how to value or judge worth, and how such values might differ among different audiences, and why.
9. Do elicit questions about contingent situations --- if such and such a variable or piece of information changed, how would our thoughts, feelings and understandings change?
10. Do elicit follow-up questions.
11. If no one responds immediately to a question, pause and wait about 5 seconds.
12. Encourage conversation among all participants in the room.
13. Encourage students to generate their own questions.

When looking at a piece of jewelry, students might be asked (*in reference to Bloom's Taxonomy*)[6] to:

DESCRIBE IT: What do you see? What else do you see? If you were describing this to another person who has not seen it, what would you say?

RELATE IT: What things do you recognize? In what ways do you feel connected to the piece? What about the piece would make you buy it? What about the piece would make you wear it? How does this piece of jewelry relate (to any other piece of jewelry)? What interests you the most in this piece? If you passed this piece of jewelry onto your children or grandchildren, do you think they would relate to it in the same way you did; explain? Would this jewelry be successful or appropriate in any culture or situation; explain with examples?

ANALYZE IT: What can you tell me about the design elements used in this piece of jewelry? About the arrangement and composition? About its construction? What type of person would wear this piece and why? What is the most critical part of this piece of jewelry which leads to its success (or failure)? What questions would you want to ask the designer? What internal or external forces will positively or negatively impact the piece? What about the piece creates good support, enabling it to move, drape and flow? What about the piece creates good structure, enable it to keep its shape and integrity when worn?

INTERPRET IT: What name would you give this piece of jewelry, and why did you pick this name? What sounds do you think this piece of jewelry would make? What role(s) would this piece of jewelry serve for the wearer, and why? Why do you think the designer made this piece of jewelry, and made it this way?

EVALUATE IT: Does this piece seem finished; explain? Would you see this piece as successful; explain? Would this piece evoke an emotion, and how? Does this piece resonate, and how? Does this piece feel parsimonious – that is, if you added (or subtracted) one more thing, would it make the piece seem less finished or successful; give some what-if examples to justify your conclusion? How has the artist selected and applied materials, techniques and technologies, and could better choices have been made and why? What do you think is worth remembering about this piece? What do you think other people would say about this piece? If you were selling this piece, what would be the selling points; explain? In what ways might this piece have value and worth for various audiences? Anticipating the artist's purpose and intent, to what degree was the artist successful? What would make the piece better, and what would make it worse?

RE-CREATE IT: If you were making a similar piece, what would you do similarly and what would you do differently; explain why? If you wanted to re-create something similar, but for a different audience or context than you thought it was originally made, what kinds of things might you do; explain? What would you change about the piece to make it more appealing to you? What would you change about the piece to change the "sound" it seems to make? How could we make the piece more Traditional? Or Avant Garde? How could you build in more or better support or structure? How might your own work be influenced (or not) by this piece? Have you learned something from this piece that would influence you to do something differently in your own work in the future; elaborate? If a particular color / material / finding had not been available, what could you substitute instead?

One last approach is encouraging lots of opportunities for *Application, Practice, and Experimentation*. Jewelry design students need time to create various understandings, correct or not, and to put these understandings to the test. They should be encouraged to imagine, experiment, play, practice and apply their emerging knowledges and skills. We need to ween them off the standard design-by-number curriculum. We should provide opportunities for students to develop the skills to work intuitively and practically in context.

Towards this end, we should

    a. Provide space/time for artistic creativity and discovery

    b. Provide opportunities to discuss, reflect and critique about the design, management and control issues which arose

    c. Have students actively anticipate, through discussion and/or writing, what kinds of reactions various audiences might have to various design and composition choices

    d. Ask students to compare and contrast various designs or design approaches, including what is appealing (or not) and wearable (or not) and representative of an artist's ideas and intent (or not)

    e. Students should be given various pieces to decode; that is, breaking them down into their essential design elements and compositional arrangements

    f. Students should be asked to reflect upon how the jewelry would hold up or be evaluated in different situations or cultures

    g. Students can be given different open-ended design tasks, such as creating a piece of jewelry that celebrates the student; or having students write "recipes" for the ingredients in a piece of jewelry and give these to other students to see what they come up with; or creating jewelry with social or political content; of develop a marketing and promotion strategy with a sales pitch for a particular piece of jewelry; or write a poem or short story about a piece of jewelry

A Rubric
RUBRIC[8] AS THINKING ROUTINE

Students who plan on becoming jewelry designers need a simple map to all these ideas about literacy and fluency – something they can easily review and determine where their strengths and weaknesses are, what kinds of courses they need to take, what kinds of learning goals they need to set in order to grow within the profession and gain proficiency and fluency in design over time. One type of map is a *rubric*.

A rubric is a table of criteria used to rate and rank *understanding* and/or *performance*. A rubric answers the question by what criteria *understanding* and/or *performance* should be judged. The rubric provides insightful clues for the kinds of evidence we need to make such assessments. The rubric helps us distinguish degrees of *understanding* and/or *performance*, from the sophisticated to the naïve. The rubric encapsulates what an authentic jewelry design education and performance would look like.

Here is one rubric we provide students to give them insight to the educational curriculum we offer in our program. We divide the program into Skill Levels, from *preparation* to *beginner, intermediate, advanced,* and *integrated*. We identify how jewelry is defined and conceptualized at each level. We specify the kinds of learning goals at each level – that is, what the students needs to have mastered before continuing on to the next level. We list the classes a student could take at each Skill Level.

BE DAZZLED BEADS: EDUCATIONAL RUBRIC:
Learning How To Think Like A Jewelry Designer

Learning Stage	Jewelry Defined As…	I know I've mastered this level when…	BEAD WEAVING CLASSES *Using needle and thread with seed beads to make things which approximate cloth*	BEAD STRINGING and HAND KNOTTING CLASSES *Putting beads on stringing material to make necklaces and bracelets*	WIRE WORKING and WIRE WEAVING CLASSES *Incorporating wires and sheet metal in jewelry by making shapes, structural supports, or patterns and textures*	BUSINESS OF CRAFT CLASSES *Bridging creative learning to the creative marketplace*	JEWELRY DESIGN CLASSES *Using creative skills to conceptualize, construct and present jewelry pieces*
PREPARATION		I have assembled basic supplies and tools, and set up a workspace	\multicolumn{5}{l	}{**ORIENTATION TO BEADS & JEWELRY FINDINGS CLASS** (**Required First Class*) *Here we teach you about the choices you will need to make when buying or using different kinds of beads, metals, findings, stringing materials, tools, and various jewelry making techniques. Focus on quality issues, contingencies and implications of making one choice over another*}

| BEGINNER (Decoding) | Object – defined apart from the maker, wearer and viewer, and apart from any inspiration or aspiration | I am familiar with the range of materials, beads, jewelry findings, components, stringing materials, tools and types of techniques used in jewelry making, and all associated quality issues and issues of choice.

I can identify and list the basic design elements present in any piece of jewelry.

I can explain which design elements are independent – that is, can function on their own, and which are dependent – that is, require the presence of other | * Bead Weaving Basics
* Basic Wrap Bracelet (laddering)

Clinics/Mini-Lessons:
- Flat Peyote
- Tubular Peyote
- Right Angle Weave
- Ndebele
- Petersburg Chain
- Brick Stitch
- Square Stitch
- Kumihimo
- Attaching End Caps | * Basics of Bead Stringing and Attaching Clasps
* Introduction to Pearl Knotting
* Mahjong Tile Bracelet
* Cozumel Necklace (micro-macrame)

Clinics/Mini-Lessons
- Crimping
- Elastic String
- Using Fireline
- Simple and Coiled Wire Loops
- Adjustable Slip Knots | * Wire Mix N Match Bracelet
* Viking Knit

*Wire Weave I: 2 base wires
*Wire Weave II: 3+ base wires

* Basic Soldering
* Intro to Silver Smithing

Clinics/Mini-Lessons:
- Simple and Coiled Wire Loops
- Let's Make Earrings on Head Pins
- Let's Make Earrings Off of Chain | * Getting Started In Business
* Pricing and Selling
* So You Want To Do Craft Shows
* Naming Your Business / Naming Your Jewelry

Clinics/Mini-Lessons:
- Pricing Formula | * Beads and Color |

| | | | design elements

I have mastered the mechanics of the major techniques in the interest area(s) I have chosen | | | | | |
|---|---|---|---|---|---|---|---|---|
| **INTERMEDIATE** *(Comprehending)* | *Content / Expression* – conveys and expresses meaning; reflects ideas about how inspiration is to be translated into a design; inspires someone to respond emotionally | I can select and arrange design elements into a pleasing composition.

I can anticipate both aesthetic and architectural requirements of my piece as it is to be worn.

I am comfortable self-directing my design process. I know 1 – 2 variations in techniques I use.
I am beginning to develop | * Various Workshops during year
* Aztec Wrap Bracelet

Clinics/Mini-Lessons:
- Peyote Cabochon Bezel | * Mala Necklace w/Tassel | * Wire Woven Cabochon Pendant
* Wire Woven Pagoda End Cap
* Cold Connections Bracelet
* Wire Wrap Bracelet w/Beads
* Wire Wrap Cabochon Pendant
* Wire Sparkle and Shine Necklace
* Wire Swirled Pendant w/Earrings
* Wire Contemporary Pendant

* Wire Woven Mayan Pendant | * Branding | * Jewelry Design I: Principles of Composition |

		"Fix-It" strategies when approaching new or difficult situations.			* Wire Woven Curvy Bracelet w/Beads		
ADVANCED *(Fluent, Flexible, Original)*	*Action / Intent / Communica-tive Interaction –* conveying content in context; design choices understood as emerging from interaction between artist and various client audiences; jewelry reflects artist's intent; recognize shared understandings about finish and success	I have well-developed tool box of "Fix-It" strategies for dealing with unknown situations, with a high degree of automaticity in their use.

I understand how parts of the mechanics of every technique I use allow the piece to maintain its shape (structure), and how other parts allow the piece to maintain good movement, drape and flow (support).

My jewelry reflects both parsimony | * Various Workshops during year | | | | *Jewelry Design II: Principles of Form, Function, Structure, Body, Mind, Movement
*Architectural Bases |

| | | in the choices of elements, and resonance in its expressive qualities for the wider audiences; I understand how this differs from traditional art concepts of "harmony" and 'variety'

I can anticipate shared understandings as these are used to judge my piece as finished and successful; I understand how wider audiences affect the coherence – decoherence-contagion impacts of my designs

I am very metacognitive of all the | | | | | |

		composition, construction, and manipulation choices I have made, and constantly reflective of the effects and implications of these choices	
INTER-RELATING AND INTEGRATING ALL LEVELS *(Disciplinary Literacy)*	How we begin to build and expand our definitions of jewelry and design	I am learning how all these things inter-relate, leading to better design and construction: - art - craft - design - architecture and engineering - physical mechanics anthropology, sociology, psychology - perception and cognition - management and control - systems theory - party	**JEWERLY DESIGN DISCUSSION SEMINARS** 1. Good Design 2. Contemporary Design 3. Composition 4. Manipulation 5. Resonance 6. Beads and Color 7. Points, Lines, Planes, Shapes, Forms, Themes 8. Architectural Basics 9. Contemporizing Traditional Jewelry 10. Mixed Media / Mixed Techniques 11. Designing An Ugly Necklace 12. Backwards Design 13. What Is Jewelry, Really? 14. Is Jewelry Making Teachable, or Merely Intuitive? 15. Can I Survive As A Jewelry Artist? 16. Creativity Isn't Found, It Is Developed 17. Jewelry Design Management 18. 5 Questions Every Jewelry Designer Should Have An Answer For 19. The Multiple Responsibilities of Being a Professional Jewelry Artist 20. Your Work Space 21. Design Theater 22. Overcoming Designer's Block 23. Fashion, Style, Taste or Art? 24. Threading the Business Needle

| | | planning
- creative
marketplace | |

Willingness To Adjust Styles To The Different Ways Students Think

Students learn in different ways. Some are more visual, some more oral, some more tactile, some more experiential. It is important that teachers vary their styles within each lesson.

For example, better instructions are presented not only with written steps, but also images illustrating each step, and diagrams or patterns explaining each step.

It is important to provide opportunities for students to reflect on what they did, and evaluate the thinking, management and control issues they confronted, and what they attempted to do to overcome these.

Last, it is just as important for the teacher to model (and think aloud) their own thought processes when attempting to design or construct a piece of jewelry.

Why Should The Teacher Be Motivated To Take A Disciplinary Approach?

The unwillingness of instructors to break out of that mold of standard craft or art content curriculum is rooted in many things.

For one, it is not very lucrative. Teaching disciplinary literacy on top of the standard content curriculum is more work. It requires more thought and integration. Initially, it requires more effort and planning. Yet the earned instructional fees would probably remain the same had the instructor not made the additional effort.

Teaching disciplinary literacy involves making very public and visible the teacher's design thinking and choices. The teacher is expected to model design behaviors. The teacher will introduce think-alouds, experimentation, thinking routines. The teacher, within each lesson, gradually relinquishes control of the teaching task to the student. The student takes over the design process, making more and more choices, whether good or bad, right or wrong. The student then evaluates, citing evidence, what appears to be working, what not working, some reasons why, and some possible consequences. These disciplinary literacy techniques might make the teacher feel very exposed, vulnerable and uneasy where such thinking and choices of the teacher might be questioned or challenged, or where the student begins to take over and assert control over learning about design.

Teachers must also expand their training and learning to go beyond art and craft. They must more clearly incorporate ideas about architecture and functionality into their teaching. They must make students aware of things related to physical mechanics, anthropology, sociology, psychology and situational analysis. They must train their students to be aware of how jewelry design is a process of communicative interaction. And they must make students aware of how the prospects and realities of introducing their work publicly also influence their design thinking.

Teacher reluctance to incorporate disciplinary learning into the standard curriculum might also be due to the fact that there is little professional recognition. The recognition that tends to exist gets very tied to criteria based on a standard content which understands jewelry as an object, not a dialectic between artist and relevant other. Jewelry design is an occupation becoming a profession, and it may feel safer for the teacher to remain in craft or art, rather than design, because the criteria for teacher evaluation is more well defined and agreed-upon.

And there is no student demand. Jewelry design is often viewed more as an avocation or occupation, rather than a professional pursuit. It's a way to exercise creative thoughts. A way to earn some extra money. A way to have fun. Jewelry design is not seen in professional terms with specialized knowledge and specific responsibilities.

Partly demand reflects low student expectations. There are assumptions that you cannot teach *creativity* – you have it or you don't. There are assumptions that anyone can make jewelry, and that once you learn some basic vocabulary and techniques, better design skills will naturally evolve over time. And these assumptions get affirmed because all students ever see and experience is good ole basic craft or art education.

Partly demand reflects some realities of the marketplace. Most people who buy jewelry have little understanding about quality issues, art and design considerations, who the artists are and what their reputations are. They don't know better so they don't demand better. Jewelry purchases skew heavily toward the upper classes. However, this does not mean that we should assume that better designed jewelry has to equate to more expensive jewelry.

It is my firm belief, however, that if instructors integrate disciplinary literacy – thinking routines for how designers think design – into the standard curriculum, both student and client demand will follow, as well as teacher pay and recognition.

As teachers of jewelry design, we should be motivated to create that demand for deeper, disciplinary learning. We need to support the professionalization of the field. We should want to make jewelry design even more fulfilling for our students.

Towards this end, we should teach jewelry design knowledge and skills development which lead to greater fluency, comprehension, self-direction, flexibility, originality and automaticity in design. This means developing our students as architects, as well as artists – in other words, as designers. It means helping our students develop those critical thinking skills so they can adapt to different design situations, and more easily problem-solve when things go awry. It means enabling our students to evaluate situations and contexts in ways which make clear how the shared understandings and desires of others impact the jewelry design process. It means giving our students a clear understanding of how creative thinking relates to the creative marketplace. It means teaching our students to be able to assert their worth – the worth of the pieces they create, their skills, their ideas, and their labor.

Only in these ways will we play an active part in enhancing the ability of our students to make a living from their artistry and design work. Only in these ways, moreover, will we elevate contemporary jewelry design so that it has a life outside the studio, and so that it doesn't get whipped by the whims of fashion or seen only as a design accessory.

How Should We Measure Successful Teaching?

In the standard design curriculum, it is relatively easy to measure our success as teachers. We can gauge how many students take our classes. We can refer to the number of concepts learned. We can count the number of successfully completed steps students have completed. We can get a sense of how many students are able to sell or exhibit their pieces.

What is more difficult to measure, from a disciplinary literacy standpoint, is how well our students are able to think, analyze, reflect, create and engage in jewelry design, given variation and variability in audience, client, context, situation, society and culture.

It is difficult, as well, to gauge the degree we have been able to elevate the importance of jewelry design as a profession. Something beyond craft. Something beyond occupation. Something even beyond art.

FOOTNOTES

[1] T. Shanahan, C. Shanahan. "Teaching disciplinary literacy to adolescents: Rethinking content-area literacy," *Harvard Educational Review*, 2008.

[2] Historians gathering evidence like letters, journals, newspaper articles, photographs, analyze them and compare then. They look for patterns and corroboration. From that they infer understanding and conclusions. The historian may take many paths and turns to discover information that may or may not be factual, but may be helpful.
Scientists set up controlled experiments, typically using information they consider facts, and interrelated these facts mathematically in order to establish understandings and conclusions. They go about things following the scientific method and approach, beginning with observations, formulating hypotheses, setting experiment and collecting data, and so forth.
Jewelry designers manage tensions between appeal and functionality. The successful managing of these tensions involves adequately anticipating the shared understandings of various client groups about whether a piece should be considered finished and successful. The designer is able to establish something in and about the piece which signals such

anticipation and understanding.

[3] *Thinking Routines*. I teach jewelry design. I find it useful to engage students with various ways of thinking out loud. They need to hear me think out loud about what choices I am making and what things I am considering when making those choices. They need to hear themselves think out loud so that they can develop strategies for getting more organized and strategic in dealing with information and making decisions. My inspiration here was based on the work done by **Visible Thinking by Project Zero** (http://www.visiblethinkingpz.org/VisibleThinking_html_files/pz.harvard.edu) *at* **Harvard Graduate School of Education** .
http://www.visiblethinkingpz.org/VisibleThinking_html_files/VisibleThinking1.html

[4] *Fluency*. I took two graduate education courses in Literacy. The primary text we used was **Literacy: Helping Students Construct Meaning** by J. David Cooper, M. Robinson, J.A. Slansky and N. Kiger, 9th Edition, Cengage Learning, 2015. Even though the text was not about jewelry designing per se, it provides an excellent framework for understanding what fluency is all about, and how fluency with language develops over a period of years. I have relied on many of the ideas in the text to develop my own ideas about a disciplinary literacy for jewelry design.

[5] *Shared Understandings*. In another graduate education class, the major text reviewed the differences between understanding and knowledge. The question was how to teach understanding. Worth the read to gain many insights about how to structure teaching to get sufficient understanding to enrich learning. **Understanding by Design** by Grant Wiggins and Jay McTighe, 2nd Edition, Association for Supervision and Curriculum Development, 2005.

[6] *Bloom's Taxonomy*.
Bloom, Benjamin S. 1956. *Taxonomy of educational objectives; the classification of educational goals*. New York: Longmans, Green.

Anderson, L. W., Krathwohl, D. R., & **Bloom**, B. S. (2001). A **taxonomy** for learning, teaching, and assessing: A **revision** of **Bloom's Taxonomy** of educational objectives (Complete ed.). New York: Longman.

Bloom's Taxonomy and the Arts. Incredible Art Department. As referenced in: https://www.incredibleart.org/files/blooms2.htm

Bloom's Taxonomy. Vanderbilt University. Center for Teaching. As referenced in: https://cft.vanderbilt.edu/guides-sub-pages/blooms-taxonomy/

[7] *Backwards Design*. I had taken two graduate education courses in Literacy and one in Planning that were very influential in my approach to disciplinary literacy. One of the big take-aways from **Understanding by Design** by Grant Wiggins and Jay McTighe, 2nd

Edition, Association for Supervision and Curriculum Development, 2005, was the idea they introduced of *"backwards design"*. Their point is that you can better teach understanding if you anticipate the evidence others will use in their assessments of what you are trying to do. When coupled with ideas about teaching literacy and fluency *(see* **Literacy: Helping Students Construct Meaning** *by J. David Cooper, M. Robinson, J.A. Slansky and N. Kiger, 9th Edition, Cengage Learning, 2015),* you can begin to introduce ideas about managing the design process in a coherent and alignable way.

SO YOU WANT TO BE A JEWELRY DESIGNER

Final Words of Advice

Final Words

Whether you are making jewelry as a hobby, an avocation or a business, it is important to fully understand what jewelry is, how it expresses the designer's inspirations and viewpoints, how it coordinates with the understandings and desires of the various client audiences who will wear, view, buy, exhibit or collect it.

You want your jewelry designs to be appealing. So knowing things about art theory is important. You want your pieces to be durable and functional, wear well, feel comfortable. So knowing things about architecture and physical mechanics becomes important. You want to make things that people want to wear and buy. So becoming aware and intuitive about how people understand what you are trying to do, perceive what you are trying to do, recognize how to value your pieces and what they might be worth and desirable to them becomes important. The qualities of finish and success in your jewelry and how it resonates with people can be very subjective, situational, cultural and/or psychological. So it is important to know things about culture and sociology and psychology and even some party planning.

Yes, there is a lot to know. Learning jewelry design is a continual, developmental process that never ends. But all of this taps into your excitement and passion or design.

I am confident,

That with a little practice,

You can become successful and accomplished as a jewelry designer.

For,
So You Want To Be A Jewelry Designer,

I'm Warren Feld

If you have any questions, you can always reach me through my website:
www.warrenfeldjewelry.com
warren@warrenfeldjewelry.com

So You Want To Be A Jewelry Designer (https://so-you-want-to-be-a-jewelry-designer.teachable.com/) – my online school – offers many in-depth video tutorials for you to learn, experience and grow as a jewelry designer.

Thank you again,

I'm Warren Feld.

SO YOU WANT TO BE A JEWELRY DESIGNER

Thank You and Request For Reviews

A Note from Warren Feld

Thank you so much for reading ***So You Want To Be A Jewelry Designer***.

If you enjoyed it, please take a moment to leave a review at your favorite online retailer such as Amazon USA or Amazon UK, or social media site.

I welcome contact from readers. At my website, you can contact me, sign up for my intermittent emails, purchase my jewelry and my kits, read my articles and blog and find me on social networking.

http://www.warrenfeldjewelry.com

-- Warren Feld

SO YOU WANT TO BE A JEWELRY DESIGNER

About Warren Feld, Jewelry Designer

*For **Warren Feld**, Jewelry Designer, (www.warrenfeldjewelry.com), beading and jewelry making have been wonderful adventures. These adventures have taken Warren from the basics of bead stringing and bead weaving, to pearl knotting, micro-macrame, wire working, wire weaving and silversmithing, and onward to more complex jewelry designs which build on the strengths of a full range of technical skills and experiences.*

What excites Warren is finding answers to such questions as:

- What does it mean to be fluent and literate in design?
- What are the implications for defining jewelry as an *object* versus as an *intent*?
- Why does some jewelry draw your attention, and others do not?
- How does jewelry design differ from art or craft?
- How do you judge a piece as finished and successful?

In 2000, Warren founded The Center for Beadwork & Jewelry Arts (CBJA) as the educational program for Be Dazzled Beads-Land of Odds in Nashville, Tennessee. The program approaches education from a Design Perspective. There is a strong focus on skills development. There is a major emphasis on teaching how to make better choices when selecting beads, other parts and stringing materials, and how to bring these altogether into a beautiful, yet functional, piece of jewelry. There are requirements for sequencing classes – that is, taking classes in a developmental order.

Theory is tightly wedded to applications throughout the program, from beginner to advanced classes. Since jewelry to be successful, unlike painting and sculpture, must interrelate aesthetics, function and context, much attention is paid to how such interrelationships should influence the designer.

Jewelry Design is seen as an authentic performance task. As such, the student explores ideas about artistic intent, shared understandings among all audiences, and developing evidence in design sufficient for determining whether a piece is finished and successful.

The design educational program is envisioned as preparing the student towards gaining a disciplinary literacy in design -- one that begins with how to decode the expressive attributes associated with Design Elements to a fluency in the management of Principles of Composition, Construction and Manipulation, as well as the systems management of the design process itself.

Warren leads a group of instructors at Be Dazzled Beads (www.bedazzledbeads.com). He teaches many of the bead-weaving, bead-stringing, pearl and hand knotting, wire weaving, jewelry design and business-oriented courses. He works with people just getting started with beading and jewelry making, as well as those with more experience.

His pieces have appeared in beading and jewelry magazines and books, including Perlen Posie ("Gwynian Ropes Bracelet", No. 21, 2014), Showcase 500 Beaded Jewelry ("Little Tapestries: Ghindia", Lark Publications, 2012). One piece ("Canyon Sunrise"), which won 4th place in Swarovski's *Naturally Inspired Competition* (2008), is in the Swarovski museum in Innsbruck, Austria. His work has been written up in *The Beader's Guide to Jewelry Design* (Margie Deeb, Lark Publications, 2014). He has been a faculty member at CraftArtEdu.com, developing video tutorials.

He has been selected as an instructor for the Bead & Button Show, June, 2019, teaching 3 pieces – Japanese Garden Bracelet, Etruscan Square Stitch Bracelet, and ColorBlock Bracelet. In March 2020, Warren led a travel-enrichment program on Celebrity Cruise Lines, centered on jewelry making, beginning with a cruise from Miami to Cozumel and Key West.

Personal style: multi-method, intricate color play, adaptive of traditions to contemporary design, experimental.

Warren is currently working on these books: SO YOU WANT TO BE A JEWELRY DESIGNER, and CONQUERING THE CREATIVE MARKETPLACE and PEARL KNOTTING…WARREN'S WAY.

Owner, Be Dazzled Beads in Nashville, and Land of Odds (https://www.landofodds.com) (https://www.landofodds.com).

He is probably best known for creating the international The Ugly Necklace Contest, where good jewelry designers attempt to overcome our pre-wired brains' fear response for resisting anything Ugly. He has also sponsored All Dolled Up: Beaded Art Doll Competition and The Illustrative Beader: Beaded Tapestry Competition.

Articles on Medium.com (https://warren-29626.medium.com/)

Jewelry Making Kits For Sale (http://www.warrenfeldjewelry.com/wfjkits.htm)

Artist Statement (http://www.warrenfeldjewelry.com/wfjartiststatement.html)

Teaching Statement (http://www.warrenfeldjewelry.com/pdf/TEACHING%20STATEMENT.pdf)

Portfolio (http://www.warrenfeldjewelry.com/pdf/PORTFOLIO.pdf)

Testimonials (http://www.warrenfeldjewelry.com/pdf/TESTIMONIALS.pdf)

Video Tutorials (https://so-you-want-to-be-a-jewelry-designer.teachable.com/)

Design Philosophy (http://www.warrenfeldjewelry.com/wfjdesignapproach.htm) (http://www.warrenfeldjewelry.com/wfjdesignapproach.htm)

warren@warrenfeldjewelry.com
www.warrenfeldjewelry.com

SO YOU WANT TO BE A JEWELRY DESIGNER

Other Articles and Tutorials

Thank you. I hope you found this book helpful.

Also, check out my website (http://www.warrenfeldjewelry.com/) (www.warrenfeldjewelry.com).

Enroll in my jewelry design and business of craft Video Tutorials (https://so-you-want-to-be-a-jewelry-designer.teachable.com) online.
- Orientation To Beads & Jewelry Findings
- Basics of Bead Stringing and Attaching Clasps
- Pearl Knotting… Warren's Way
- The Jewelry Designer's Approach To Color
- So You Want To Do Craft Shows…
- Naming Your Business
- Pricing And Selling Your Jewelry

Articles on Medium.com (https://warren-29626.medium.com/)

Articles on Art Jewelry Forum (https://artjewelryforum.org/library/author/warren-feld/)

Other Books by Warren Feld:

Conquering The Creative Marketplace (July 2022)

Pearl Knotting…Warren's Way
Order: https://www.amazon.com/dp/B09SBNJTFN

Made in the USA
Columbia, SC
21 July 2022